EXAMPLES OF CASE CITATIONS

- Miranda v. Arizona, 384 U.S. 436 (1966)—This case is found in volume 384 of *United States Reports,* starting on page 436 (and going on for however many pages); it was decided in 1966.

- Miranda v. Arizona, 86 S.Ct. 1602 (1966)—Miranda v. Arizona is also found in volume 86 of *Supreme Court Reporter,* starting on page 1602.

- Alabama v. White, 58 L.W. 4747 (1990)—This case is found in volume 58 of *United States Law Week,* starting on page 4747; it was decided in 1990.

- United States v. Bok, 188 F.2d 1019 (DC Cir. 1951)—This case is found in volume 188 of *Federal Reports,* Second Series, starting on page 1019; it was decided by the District of Columbia Federal Court of Appeals in 1951.

- United States v. Davis, 482 F.2d 893 (9th Cir. 1973)—This case is found in volume 482 of *Federal Reports,* Second Series, starting on page 893; it was decided by the Ninth Circuit Court of Appeals in 1973.

- Peterson v. City of Long Beach, 155 Cal Rptr 360 (1979)—This case is found in volume 155 of *California Reporter,* starting on page 360; it was decided by a state appeals court in California in 1979.

Criminal Procedure

Law and Practice

Fifth Edition

Rolando V. del Carmen
Sam Houston State University

Wadsworth
Thomson Learning™

Australia • Canada • Mexico • Singapore
Spain • United Kingdom • United States

Executive Editor, Criminal Justice: Sabra Horne
Development Editor: Barbara Yien
Assistant Editor: Ann Tsai
Editorial Assistant: Cortney Bruggink
Marketing Manager: Jennifer Somerville
Marketing Assistant: Ken Baird
Project Editor: Jennie Redwitz
Print Buyer: Karen Hunt
Permissions Editor: Bob Kauser
Production Service: Melanie Field, Strawberry
    Field Publishing

Text Designer: Andrew Ogus ■ Book Design
Photo Researcher: Melanie Field
Copy Editor: Tom Briggs
Cover Designer: Andrew Ogus ■ Book Design
Cover Images: Arrest—Doug Menuez; Police
    car—Izzy Schwartz; Broken glass—Bruce
    Heinemann. All photos © PhotoDisc.
Cover Printer: Phoenix Color Corporation
Compositor: TBH Typecast, Inc.
Printer: R. R. Donnelley, Crawfordsville

Photo credits:
page 1: © Joel W. Rogers/Corbis
page 57: © Mark Richards/PhotoEdit
page 111: © Spencer Grant/PhotoEdit
page 177: ©AFP/Corbis
page 285: © Joseph Sohm; ChromoSohm Inc./Corbis
page 365: © AFP/Corbis

For more information, contact
Wadsworth/Thomson Learning
10 Davis Drive
Belmont, CA 94002-3098
USA
http://www.wadsworth.com

International Headquarters
Thomson Learning
International Division
290 Harbor Drive, 2nd Floor
Stamford, CT 06902-7477
USA

UK/Europe/Middle East/South Africa
Thomson Learning
Berkshire House
168-173 High Holborn
London WC1V 7AA
United Kingdom

Asia
Thomson Learning
60 Albert Street, #15-01
Albert Complex
Singapore 189969

Canada
Nelson Thomson Learning
1120 Birchmount Road
Toronto, Ontario M1K 5G4
Canada

Library of Congress Cataloging-in-Publication Data

Del Carmen, Rolando V.
    Criminal procedure : law and practice / Rolando V.
        del Carmen—5th ed.
        p. cm.
    Includes bibliographical references and index.
    ISBN 0-534-51471-5
        1. Criminal procedure—United States.
    2. Criminal procedure—United States—Cases.   I. Title.

    KF9619.D45 2000
    345.73'05—dc21

    00-022269

Brief Contents

Contents

II. Levels of Proof and the Exclusionary Rule 57

3. Probable Cause and Reasonable Suspicion 58

4. The Exclusionary Rule 82

III. Searches and Seizures of Persons   111

5. "Stop and Frisk," Border Seizures, and Stationhouse Detentions   112

6. Arrests   138

IV. Searches and Seizures of Property   177

7. Searches and Seizures of Things   178

9. Plain View, Open Fields, Abandonment, and Electronic Surveillance   250

V. Identifications, Confessions, and Admissions   285

10. Lineups and Other Pretrial Identification Procedures   286

11. Confessions and Admissions: Miranda v. Arizona   317

VI. Constitutional Rights and the Consequences of Police Misconduct   365

12. Constitutional Rights of the Accused during Trial   366

Preface

Law enforcement is essentially what the term literally says—the enforcement of the law by duly authorized agents of the state—the police. As the term indicates, knowledge of the law is essential to law enforcement. Without it, an officer loses sight of the proper framework for "policing a free society"; with it, the officer becomes a trusted agent of the immense power of the state over people's lives and property. It is important that law enforcement officers know the law and adhere to it. Without knowledge of and adherence to law, public confidence wanes, and citizens feel betrayed by those sworn to protect them.

This text acquaints the reader with the various aspects of criminal procedure. Laws that govern policing are based primarily on the United States Constitution, United States Supreme Court decisions, and statutes passed by the United States Congress and state legislatures. This text focuses on these sources. Lower court decisions and agency policies are also given attention, particularly if they limit what officers can do.

This book covers basic topics relevant to law enforcement, from court systems to constitutional rights. The final chapter, Chapter 13, discusses a persistent concern in law enforcement—legal liabilities of police officers. Court decisions, in some cases leading to huge damage awards, have had an immediate impact on the daily workings of law enforcement agencies. Sensational incidents involving the police will continue to attract media attention and cause public concern. Legal liabilities must be studied and understood if they are to be minimized.

The study of law can be complex and tedious. It can also be confusing and frustrating, particularly when no authoritative guidelines are given by court decisions or statute. These realities must be recognized and accepted as an integral, albeit disturbing, part of criminal justice. The confusion and frustration are experienced not only by students and law enforcement personnel but also by judges, lawyers, and other professionals in the arena of criminal justice. The imperfections of the criminal justice system are pervasive and a matter of common knowledge. There is no perfect system in the search for ideal justice. One wonders whether justice itself is attainable to the satisfaction of all, particularly the victim and the accused.

Judges, prosecutors, defense lawyers, and court personnel have developed terms and concepts that are part of criminal justice process. Law enforcement officers must learn and understand them. Any law-oriented text written primarily for students and in-service personnel must present legal terms and concepts clearly and precisely without yielding to oversimplification. This text presents criminal procedure in a format and language designed to meet the needs and interests of nonlawyers and yet preserve the meaning and content of the law as interpreted by the courts.

The fifth edition of this book differs from the fourth edition as follows:

- Fourteen new U.S. Supreme Court cases have been added to the fifth edition, with March 15, 2000, being the cutoff date. These cases are:

  Campbell v. Louisiana (1998)
  City of West Covina v. Perkins (1999)
  Flippo v. West Virginia (1999)
  Florida v. White (1999)
  Knowles v. Iowa (1998)
  Maryland v. Dyson (1999)
  Minnesota v. Carter (1998)
  Pennsylvania Board of Probation and Parole v. Scott (1998)
  Richards v. Wisconsin (1997)
  Strickler v. Greene (1999)
  United States v. Balsys (1998)
  United States v. Ramirez (1998)
  Wilson v. Lane (1999)
  Wyoming v. Houghton (1999)

- Key Terms and Definitions remain at the end of each chapter, but a new Glossary has been added at the end of the book for composite reference.

- Some tables, charts, forms, and figures, as well as Highlight and At-a-Glance features, have been revised or replaced.

- Some Review Questions at the end of each chapter have been deleted and others added.

- Four Case Briefs at the end of chapters have been deleted and four new Case Briefs added. The deleted cases are Draper v. United States, Coolidge v. New Hampshire, Horton v. California, and South Dakota v. Neville. The new cases are Weeks v. United States, Alabama v. White, Chimel v. California, and Powell v. Alabama.

- Appendix A, which gives a case brief, has been changed from Miranda v. Arizona to the newer and shorter case of Minnesota v. Dickerson to coordinate with Appendix B.

- Appendix B now features the original of the case of Minnesota v. Dickerson, the case briefed in Appendix A. This sequence acquaints readers with what an original case looks like and how it is briefed.

- Appendix C, "Thirty Suggestions on How to Be an Effective Witness," was Appendix B in the fourth edition.

- Appendix D, "The Consitution of the United States," was Appendix C in the fourth edition.

These changes were made in response to suggestions from reviewers of the fourth edition and in the interest of better structure, sequence, and substance. It is hoped that these changes will enhance the quality of the book and make it a better learning source.

Organization of the Text

This text has several features that should help students understand the law and retain legal concepts:

- Frequent use of examples and illustrations

- Analysis and comparison of leading court cases

- A chapter outline at the beginning of each chapter

- Use of tables, figures, and highlights

- At-a-Glance summaries of key concepts

- Use of sample police forms

- Definitions of legal terms used in each chapter (at the end of the chapter)

- A list of cases discussed in the chapter and what the court held

- Case briefs of two or three leading cases at the end of each chapter

There are various paths to learning, none of which works equally well for everybody. Legal material, however, is perhaps best learned and retained through mastery of concepts reinforced by examples. As frequently as possible, this text defines a concept and then further clarifies it with an example. No two situations in law enforcement are exactly alike; hence, students must learn to apply legal principles to actual situations that sometimes involve great personal risk. If legal concepts are understood well, their application to actual field situations becomes easier. Memorizing a legal definition is much less important than understanding and applying it to real-life situations.

The topics in each chapter are arranged so they are easy to follow. The definitions of terms and the concise listing of principles of cases at the end of each chapter should reduce the need for note-taking and make it easier to review the chapter. The chapter summaries present the material in compact form; the discussion questions focus on important concepts in the book; and the in-text highlights call attention to statements or information deserving of special note.

Although the United States comprises fifty-two different court jurisdictions (the fifty states, the federal government, and the District of Columbia), criminal procedure rules apply nationwide and transcend state boundaries. The rules governing law enforcement have been "nationalized" and made applicable to all jurisdictions through U.S. Supreme Court decisions. Nonetheless, variations in procedures abound, particularly where such variations do not violate constitutional rights of the suspect or the accused. The legal doctrines and principles discussed in this text apply throughout the United States, except where state law, local ordinance, or agency policy declare otherwise and such variations are consistent with court decisions or the Constitution.

This text is written for a national audience and not for a particular state. It is also stressed that knowing the content of this text is no substitute for knowledge of specific state law or agency policy. That may be obtained from agency legal counsel or local lawyers.

Acknowledgments

Few texts are written without the help of colleagues and friends. The author would like to thank the following for contributions to this book: Jerry Dowling and Phillip Lyons of Sam Houston State University; John Scott Blonien, senior assistant attorney general of the state of Washington; Michael S. Vaughn of Georgia State University; Jeffery Walker of the University of Arkansas–Little Rock; David Carter of Michigan State University; Tom Hickey of Roger Williams University; Joseph Vaughn of Central Missouri State University; and Judge Emory Plitt of Hartford County, Maryland. My graduate and undergraduate students inspired the writing of this book. From them I learned a lot about the law and how student learning can be enhanced when reading legal material.

I owe special thanks to the reviewers of the fifth edition. As in the previous editions, the changes made in this edition are primarily in response to the perceptive and thoughtful comments of the reviewers. Chosen by the editors, they obviously knew whereof they wrote; they have all taught courses on criminal procedure and civil liberties for years. Their suggestions reflected a common concern that the book be made even more user-friendly and yet preserve accuracy. In alphabetical order, they are: Don Bradel, Bemidji State University; James Hague, Virginia Commonwealth University; Craig Hemmens, Boise State University; Martrice Hurrah, Shelby State Community College; W. Richard Janikowski, University of Memphis; Dave Kramer, Bergen Community College; and Robert Pagnani, Columbia-Greene Community College. Their reviews, suggestions, and comments have been invaluable. To them I express deepest appreciation for their contributions to this book.

I will continue to rely on colleagues, administrators, students, and reviewers for ideas and advice. Thank you for your help.

Rolando V. del Carmen
Distinguished Professor
of Criminal Justice (Law)
College of Criminal Justice
Sam Houston State University

I. Introduction

1.

The Court System and Sources of Rights

What You Will Learn in This Chapter

You will become familiar with the structures of the federal and state court systems, the effects and scope of their decisions, and the precedents they set for future cases. You will learn the distinction between jurisdiction and venue, the various sources of individual rights, and the way rights in the Federal Constitution have been made applicable to the states by the United State Supreme Court through the gradual process of incorporation.

Introduction

We focus on the structure of federal and state court systems in the United States. Criminal cases in the United States may be tried in federal and state courts if the act constitutes violation of the laws of both jurisdictions. However, most criminal cases are tried in state courts, since the maintenance of peace and order is primarily the responsibility of state and local governments. Important topics include the territorial effect of judicial decisions, the principle of stare decisis, the extent of federal and state jurisdiction, the principle of dual sovereignty, the legal concepts of jurisdiction and venue, and the various sources of individual rights. The chapter ends with a discussion of the incorporation controversy—how it developed and what role it plays in determining which constitutional rights now also extend to an accused in state prosecutions.

I. THE STRUCTURE OF THE COURT SYSTEM

The United States has a **dual court system,** meaning that *there is one system for federal cases and another for state cases.* (See Figure 1.1.) The term *dual court system* is, however, misleading. What the United States has is fifty-two separate judicial systems representing the court systems in the fifty states, the federal system, and the courts of Washington, DC. But because these systems have much in common, they justify a general grouping into two: federal and state.

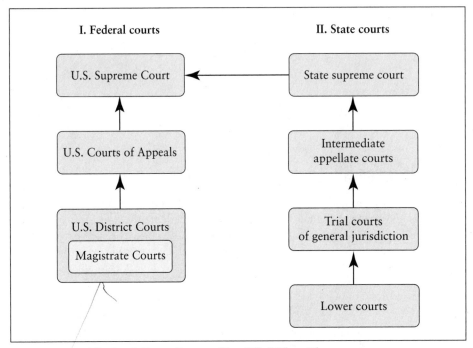

Figure 1.1 *The Dual Court System: Simplified Flow Chart*

A. The Federal Court System

Article III, Section 1 of the United States Constitution provides:

> The judicial Power of the United States shall be vested in one supreme Court, and in such inferior Courts as the Congress may from time to time ordain and establish. The Judges, both of the supreme and inferior Courts, shall hold their Offices during good Behavior, and shall, at stated Times, receive for their Services a Compensation, which shall not be diminished during their Continuance in Office.

The highest court in the federal court system is the U.S. Supreme Court. (*Note:* Whenever the word "Court" is used with a capital C in this text, the reference is to the U.S. Supreme Court. The word "court" with a lowercase *c* refers to all other courts on the federal or state levels.) It is composed of a chief justice and eight associate justices, all of whom are nominated and appointed by the president of the United States, with the "advice and consent" of the Senate. (See Table 1.1.)

Federal law, passed in 1869, fixed the number of U.S. Supreme Court justices at nine, but this number may be changed by law. Supreme Court justices enjoy life tenure and may be removed only by impeachment, which very rarely occurs. The Court is located in Washington, DC, and always decides cases **en banc** (*as one body*) and never in small groups or panels (*in division*). Six justices constitute a quorum, but the votes of five justices are needed to win a case. The Court meets to hear arguments and decide

TABLE 1.1 *Justices on the U.S. Supreme Court as of March 1997*

Justice	President Who Appointed	Law School	Confirmed
William Rehnquist*	Nixon	Stanford Law School	December 10, 1971
John Stevens	Ford	Northwestern University	December 17, 1985
Sandra Day O'Connor	Reagan	Stanford Law School	September 21, 1981
Antonin Scalia	Reagan	Harvard Law School	September 17, 1986
Anthony Kennedy	Reagan	Harvard Law School	February 3, 1988
David Souter	Bush	Harvard Law School	October 2, 1990
Clarence Thomas	Bush	Yale Law School	October 15, 1991
Ruth Bader Ginsburg	Clinton	Columbia Law School	August 3, 1993
Stephen Breyer	Clinton	Harvard Law School	July 29, 1994

Voting Record
Conservative: Rehnquist, Scalia, Thomas
Moderately conservative: Kennedy, O'Connor
Moderate: Breyer, Ginsburg, Souter, Stevens

* Chief justice
Source: Compiled by Michael S. Vaughn, Georgia State University.

cases beginning on the first Monday in October and continues sessions usually through the end of June of the following year. Court cases are argued and decisions are announced during this time, although the Court holds office throughout the year. Members of the U.S. Supreme Court are called justices. All others, from the Court of Appeals down to the lower courts, are called judges. (See Figure 1.2.)

By the **Rule of Four,** *at least four justices must agree for the Court to consider a case on its merits.* Thousands of cases reach the Supreme Court each year from various federal and state courts, but the Court considers only a limited number of cases (132 cases in 1988–89, 107 cases in 1992–93, and 75 cases in 1998–99, the lowest in almost four decades) on their merits. The rest are dismissed *per curiam,* meaning that the decision of the immediate lower court in which the case originated (whether it be a state supreme court, a federal court of appeals, or any other court) is left undisturbed. This action does not imply that the Supreme Court agrees with the decision of the lower court. It simply means that the case could not get the votes of at least four justices to give it further attention and consider it on its merits.

Next to the Supreme Court in the federal judicial hierarchy are the U.S. courts of appeals, officially referred to as the United States Court of Appeals for a particular circuit. As of 1999, these courts had a total of 179 judges and were located in thirteen judicial "circuits" (including the court of appeals for the federal circuit) in different regions of the country. Each circuit covers three or more states, except the District of Columbia, which has a whole circuit unto itself. (See Figure 1.3.) Each court has six or more judges, depending upon caseload for the circuit. The First Circuit has six judges, while the Ninth Circuit has twenty-eight.

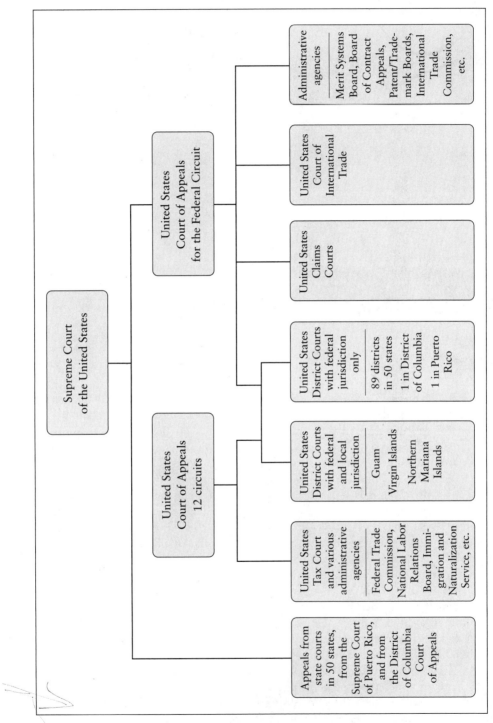

Figure 1.2 *The Federal Court System*

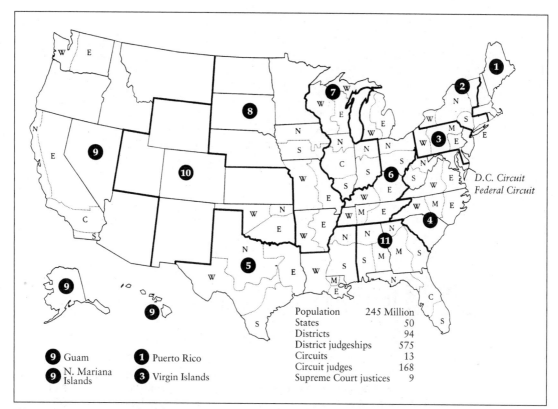

Figure 1.3 *Geographical Boundaries of U.S. Courts of Appeals and District Courts*

SOURCE: David W. Neubauer, *America's Courts and the Criminal Justice System,* 4th ed. (Pacific Grove, CA: Brooks/Cole, 1992), p. 44.

Judges of the courts of appeals are nominated and appointed by the president of the United States for life, with the advice and consent of the Senate, and can be removed only by impeachment. Unlike the Supreme Court, courts of appeals may hear cases as one body (en banc) or in groups (in divisions) of three or five judges.

Occupying the lowest level in the hierarchy of federal courts are the district courts, the trial courts for federal cases. The federal government has 646 federal judgeships located in ninety-four judicial districts in the United States, Guam, Puerto Rico, and the Virgin Islands. Each state has at least one judicial district, but some states have as many as four. Judges are nominated and appointed by the president of the United States for life, with the advice and consent of the Senate, and can be removed only by impeachment. In practice, a recommendation for appointment is made by the senior U.S. senator from that state if he or she belongs to the president's political party.

Also under the federal system are the U.S. magistrate courts, established primarily to relieve district court judges of heavy caseloads. They are presided over by U.S. magistrates (formerly called U.S. commissioners) and have limited authority, such as trying minor offenses and misdemeanor cases in which the possible penalty is incarceration of one year or less. They are also empowered to hold bail hearings, issue warrants, review habeas corpus petitions, and hold pretrial conferences in civil and criminal

TABLE 1.2 *1998 Salary Rates of Justices and Judges of the United States*

Office	Rate
Chief justice of the United States	$175,400
Associate justices of the Supreme Court of the United States	167,900
Judges, United States Courts of Appeals	145,000
Judges, United States District Courts	136,700
United States magistrate judges (full-time)	125,764

Source: The Internet: http://www.uscourts.gov.

cases. As of 1999, there were 345 full-time and 124 part-time magistrates in the United States. (See Table 1.2.)

B. The State Court System

The structure of the state court system varies from state to state. In general, however, state courts follow the federal pattern. This means that states have one state supreme court that makes final decisions on cases involving state laws and provisions of the state constitution. Texas and Oklahoma, however, have two highest courts—one for civil and the other for criminal cases. State courts decide nearly every type of case but are limited by the provisions of the U.S. Constitution and their own state constitution and by state law.

Below the state supreme court in the state judicial hierarchy are the intermediate appellate courts. Only thirty-five of the fifty states have intermediate appellate courts. Where they do not exist, cases appealed from the trial courts go directly to the state supreme court. Each state has trial courts with general jurisdiction, meaning that they try civil and criminal cases. They go by various names, such as circuit court, district court, or court of common pleas. New York's court of general jurisdiction is called the supreme court. Although these courts are of general jurisdiction, some states divide them according to specialty areas such as probate, juvenile, and domestic relations.

At the base of the state judicial hierarchy are lower courts such as county courts, justice of the peace courts, and municipal courts. They have limited jurisdiction in both civil and criminal cases and also deal with laws passed by county or city governments.

II. THE APPELLATE PROCESS

With rare exceptions, cases enter the federal and state judicial systems at the trial level. At that level, a jury or a judge (in the case of a bench trial) determines the facts of the case based on the evidence presented. By applying principles of law to the facts of the case, the jury or judge determines the outcome of the case; in criminal cases, this usually means conviction or acquittal.

By law, cases usually can be appealed at the next higher level of court. With convictions, the defendant may appeal the case to the next level; however, acquittals cannot be appealed by the government, except if the acquittal is based on a question of law, not of guilt or innocence. Courts of appeals do not hear further evidence and generally do not reevaluate the evidence presented in the trial court. Their function usually is to determine whether errors of law occurred during the trial or at sentencing. They afford a remedy for prejudicial errors but not for "harmless" ones that would not have affected the outcome.

The appeals court may either affirm, reverse, or reverse and remand the decision of the lower court. **Affirm** means that *the decision of the lower court where the case came from is upheld*. **Reverse** means that *the decision of the lower court where the case came from is overthrown, vacated, or set aside by the appellate court*. A **reverse-and-remand** decision is less final than an outright reversal of the lower court decision in that *the lower court's decision is reversed but the lower court has an opportunity to hear further arguments and to give another decision in the case*.[1]

If a defendant wins a reversal on an appeal, the case may be tried again without violating the constitutional prohibition against **double jeopardy**—*being punished more than once for the same offense*. This is because the right to protection against double jeopardy is considered to have been waived by the defendant if he or she appeals. In appealed convictions, the defendant is essentially saying, "Give me a new trial; there was something wrong with my conviction." This constitutes a waiver of the right to protection against double jeopardy.

III. THE TERRITORIAL EFFECT OF JUDICIAL DECISIONS

The jurisdiction of every U.S. court is limited in some way. One type of limitation is territorial or geographic. In a strict sense, each judicial decision is authoritative and has value as precedent for future cases only within the geographic limits of the area in which the deciding court has jurisdiction. Consequently, U.S. Supreme Court decisions on questions of federal law and the Constitution are binding on all U.S. courts, because the whole country is under its jurisdiction. Decisions of federal courts of appeals are the last word within circuits if there is no Supreme Court action. The First Circuit Court of Appeals, for example, settles federal issues for Maine, Massachusetts, New Hampshire, Rhode Island, and Puerto Rico, the areas within its jurisdiction. When a district court encompasses an entire state, as is the case in Maine, its decision on a federal law produces a uniform rule within the state. However, in a state such as Wisconsin, where there are multiple districts, there can be divergent and even conflicting decisions even on the district court level.

The same process operates in the state court systems, but in one regard, state supreme court decisions are recognized as extending beyond state borders. Since the

Constitution declares the sovereignty of the states within the area reserved for state control, the court of last resort in each state is the final arbiter of issues of purely state and local law. For example, the meaning that the California Supreme Court gives to a state statute or a municipal ordinance will be respected as authoritative even by the U.S. Supreme Court, unless it involves a constitutional question—in which case the U.S. Supreme Court becomes the final arbiter.

The existence of a dual court system and the limited jurisdictional reach of the vast majority of courts make it highly probable that courts will render conflicting decisions on a legal issue. An important function of the appellate process is to provide a forum for resolving these conflicts if the cases are appealed. If no appeal is made, the conflict remains. For example, a federal district court in the Southern District of Ohio may rule that jail detainees are entitled to contact visits, whereas another federal district court in the Northern District of that state, on a different case, may rule otherwise. The inconsistency will be resolved only if the federal appellate court for Ohio decides the issue in an appealed case.

Despite the territorial or geographic limitations of court decisions, there are important reasons decisions from other jurisdictions should not be ignored. First, there may be no settled law on an issue in a given area. When the issue has not previously been decided by a local court (known as a *case of first impression*), the local federal or state court will probably decide it on the basis of the dominant or "better" rule that is being applied elsewhere. The second reason is that law is evolving, not stagnant. Over a period of time, trends develop in the law. When a particular court senses that its prior decisions on a point are no longer in the mainstream, it may consider revising its holding, especially if the issue has not been settled by the U.S. Supreme Court. The decisions in other jurisdictions may enable lawyers to detect a trend and anticipate what local courts might do in the future.

IV. THE PRINCIPLE OF STARE DECISIS (JUDICIAL PRECEDENT)

"**Stare decisis**" is a Latin term that literally means *to abide by, or adhere to, decided cases.* Courts generally adhere to stare decisis: When a court has laid down a principle of law as applicable to a certain set of facts, it will adhere to that principle and apply it to all future cases with similar facts and circumstances. Stare decisis is also known as the principle of **judicial precedent,** meaning that *decisions of courts have value as precedent for future cases similarly circumstanced.* However, it is precedent only for those cases that come within that court's jurisdiction. For example, the decisions of the Fifth Circuit Court of Appeals are valued as precedent only in the states (Texas, Louisiana, and Mississippi) within the territorial jurisdiction of the court. By the same token, the decisions of the Florida Supreme Court are precedent only in cases decided by Florida courts. U.S. Supreme Court decisions are precedent for cases anywhere in the United States. For example, the case of Miranda v. Arizona is precedent for cases involving custodial interrogation, so all cases decided in the United States on that issue must be decided according to *Miranda*. Variations do occur, however, since the facts of cases differ. Therefore, the Court can refine, modify, or expand the *Miranda* doctrine. Moreover, the doctrine of stare decisis or judicial precedent can be discarded at any time by the court that decided it. *Miranda* has been modified and refined by the Court a number of times in subsequent cases (see chapter 11, "Confessions and Admissions"). Although it is unlikely, the Court could also abandon the *Miranda* doctrine at any time or prescribe a different rule, based on what the Court determines is required by the Constitution. All that is needed to overturn a judicial precedent are the votes of at least five justices of the Court.

V. FEDERAL VERSUS STATE JURISDICTION

The basic rule that determines whether a criminal case should be filed and tried in federal or state court is this: Generally, if an act is a violation of federal law, the trial will be held in a federal court; if the act is a violation of state law, the trial will be held in a state court. A crime that violates both federal and state laws (such as kidnapping, transportation of narcotics, counterfeiting, or robbery of a federally insured bank) may be tried in both federal and state courts if the prosecutors so desire. For example, if X robs the Miami National Bank, X can be prosecuted for the crime of robbery under Florida law and for robbery of a federally insured bank under federal law. The prosecutions are for the same act but involve two different laws. There is no double jeopardy because of the concept of **dual sovereignty:** *Federal and state governments are considered sovereign each in their own right.*

The double jeopardy prohibition (the rule that no person may be punished for the same offense more than once) applies only to successive prosecutions for the same offense by the same sovereign jurisdiction. By dual sovereignty, federal and state governments constitute two separate sovereignties, so double jeopardy does not apply. The prosecution of the police officers in the Rodney King beating case in Los Angeles illustrates this concept. The first prosecution took place in 1991 in Simi Valley, California, under the California Penal Code. All four officers were acquitted. About a year later, they were tried again by federal prosecutors in Los Angeles for essentially the same act, but under federal law. Two of the officers were convicted. But no double jeopardy was involved, because although the officers were prosecuted twice for essentially the same offense, the prosecutions were authorized by two separate sovereignties—state and federal.

As the preceding example suggests, the sovereignty that first obtains custody of the suspect is usually allowed to try him or her first. In most cases, this will be the state. Although the federal government can try X for the same offense, it will probably refrain from doing so if X has been convicted and sufficiently punished under state law. The state would do likewise if the sequence were reversed, although some states have laws against state prosecution for a criminal act that has been prosecuted by the federal government. In sum, although successive prosecutions by separate sovereignties are constitutional, they may be prohibited by state law or administrative policy. Moreover, a prosecutor may not want to file the case, even if he or she can, because of the expense involved or if "justice has been served," perhaps because the defendant has been sufficiently punished.

VI. JURISDICTION VERSUS VENUE

The terms *jurisdiction* and *venue* can be confusing. Sometimes used interchangeably, they nevertheless represent very different concepts. **Jurisdiction** refers to *the power of a court to try a case*. A court's jurisdiction is defined by the totality of the law that creates the court and limits its powers; the parties to litigation cannot vest the court with jurisdiction it does not possess. Defects in the subject matter jurisdiction of a court (for example, when a civil case is tried in a criminal court, which does not have the authority to try it) cannot be waived by the parties and can be raised at any stage of the litigation, including on appeal. In order to render a valid judgment against a person, a court must also have jurisdiction over that person. The fact that a defendant has been brought to court against his or her wishes and by questionable methods does not invalidate the jurisdiction of the court. In Frisbie v. Collins, 342 U.S. 519 (1952), the Court ruled that an invalid arrest is not a defense against being convicted of the offense charged. In that case, the accused, while living in Illinois, was forcibly seized, handcuffed, blackjacked, and then taken back to Michigan by law enforcement officers. The Court ruled that the power of a court to try a person for a crime is not impaired by the fact that the person has been brought within the court's jurisdiction through forcible abduction. The Court said, "It matters not how a defendant is brought before the court; what matters is that the defendant is before the court and can therefore be tried."

A more recent case involves former Panamanian dictator General Manuel Noriega. In December 1989, the U.S. government sent troops to Panama, arrested Noriega, and then flew him to Florida to face narcotics trafficking charges. Noriega protested, claiming that U.S. courts had no jurisdiction over him because the Panama invasion, which led to his arrest, violated international law. The U.S. courts ruled, however, that the method of arrest did not deprive the courts of jurisdiction. Noriega was tried in the United States, convicted, and sentenced to forty years in prison.[2]

The concept of **venue** is place oriented. It flows from the policy of the law that *cases must be tried in the place where the crime was committed, where a party resides, or where another consideration justifies a trial in that place*. Legislation establishes mandatory venue for some types of cases and preferred venue for others. In criminal cases, the trial is usually held in the place where the crime was committed. But the venue may be changed and the trial held in another place for causes specified by law. This change is made to assure the accused of a fair and impartial trial in cases that have had such massive pretrial publicity or strong community prejudice as to make it difficult to select an impartial jury. The motion for a change of venue is usually filed by the defendant. The decision of a trial judge to grant or deny the motion is seldom reversed on appeal.

VII. SOURCES OF RIGHTS

The rules governing criminal proceedings in the United States come from four basic sources: constitutions (federal and state), statutes, case law, and court rules.

A. Constitutions

1. The Federal Constitution

Constitutions are the first and most authoritative sources of rights. The U.S. Constitution contains the most important rights available to an accused in a criminal prosecution. These safeguards are enumerated in the **Bill of Rights,** which are *the first ten amendments to the U.S. Constitution.* The constitutional rights in the Bill of Rights are the minimum rights given to individuals facing criminal prosecution. They can be expanded and an accused can be given more rights by state constitutions and by federal and state law. The constitutions of the various states also contain provisions designed to protect the rights of individuals in state criminal proceedings. These rights are basically similar to those enumerated in the Bill of Rights but apply only to a particular state. For example, most state constitutions guarantee the right to counsel and cross-examination and prohibit self-incrimination.

The following list contains the federal constitutional provisions most often used in law enforcement cases and the rights they guarantee.

- **Amendment I:** "Congress shall make no law respecting an establishment of religion, or prohibiting the free exercise thereof; or abridging the freedom of speech, or of the press; or the right of the people peaceably to assemble, and to petition the Government for a redress of grievances."
  - Freedom of religion
  - Freedom of speech
  - Freedom of the press
  - Freedom of assembly
  - Freedom to petition the government for redress of grievances

- **Amendment II:** "A well regulated Militia, being necessary to the security of a free State, the right of the people to keep and bear Arms, shall not be infringed."
  - Right to keep and bear arms

- **Amendment IV:** "The right of the people to be secure in their persons, houses, papers, and effects, against unreasonable searches and seizures, shall not be violated, and no Warrants shall issue, but upon probable cause, supported by Oath or affirmation, and particularly describing the place to be searched, and the persons or things to be seized."
  - Protection against unreasonable search and seizure (including arrest)

- **Amendment V:** "No person shall be held to answer for a capital, or otherwise infamous crime, unless on a presentment or indictment of a Grand Jury, except in cases arising in the land or naval forces, or in the Militia, where in actual service in time of War or public danger, nor shall any person be subject for the same offense to be twice put in jeopardy of life or limb, nor shall be compelled in any criminal case to be a witness against himself, nor be deprived of life, liberty, or property, without due process of law; nor shall private property be taken for public use, without just compensation."

- Right to a grand jury indictment for capital or other serious crime
- Protection against double jeopardy
- Protection against self-incrimination
- Prohibition against the taking of life, liberty, or property without due process of law

- **Amendment VI:** "In all criminal prosecutions, the accused shall enjoy the right to a speedy and public trial, by an impartial jury of the State and district wherein the crime shall have been committed, which district shall have been previously ascertained by law, and to be informed of the nature and cause of the accusation; to be confronted with the witnesses against him; to have the compulsory process for obtaining witnesses in his favor, and to have the Assistance of Counsel for his defence."

  - Right to a speedy and public trial
  - Right to an impartial jury
  - Right to be informed of the nature and cause of the accusation
  - Right to confront witnesses
  - Right to summon witnesses
  - Right to have assistance of counsel

- **Amendment VIII:** "Excessive bail shall not be required, nor excessive fines imposed, nor cruel and unusual punishments inflicted."

  - Protection against excessive bail
  - Protection against cruel and unusual punishment

- **Amendment XIV:** "All persons born or naturalized in the United States and subject to the jurisdiction thereof, are citizens of the United States and of the State wherein they reside. No State shall make or enforce any law which shall abridge the privileges or immunities of citizens of the United States; nor shall any State deprive any person of life, liberty, or property, without due process of law; nor deny to any person within its jurisdiction the equal protection of the laws."

  - Right to due process
  - Right to equal protection

2. State Constitutions

In addition to the Federal Constitution, all fifty states have their own constitutions. Many state constitutions have their own bills of rights and guarantees of protection against deprivation of rights by state government. The provisions of these constitutions must be consistent with the provisions of the Federal Constitution, or else they may be declared unconstitutional if challenged in court. The provisions of state constitutions or state law sometimes give defendants more protection than those allowed under the Federal Constitution. The general rule is that, if state constitution or state law gives a defendant *less* protection than the U.S. Constitution provides, such limitation is unconstitutional and the U.S. Constitution prevails. But if provisions of the state constitution or state law give a defendant *more* protection than the U.S. Constitution provides, such grant of protection by the state prevails. For example, assume that a state constitution, for some unlikely reason, requires a defendant to testify even when the result is self-incrimination. Such provision will be declared unconstitutional because it contravenes the provisions of the Fifth Amendment. By contrast, the U.S. Supreme Court has ruled that trustworthy statements obtained in violation of the Miranda rule may be used to impeach (challenge) the credibility of a defendant who takes the witness stand (Harris v. New York, 401 U.S. 222 [1971]). However, if a state's constitution (as interpreted by state courts) or state law prohibits the use of such statements to impeach the credibility of a witness, they cannot be used in that state.

B. Statutes

Federal and state statutes frequently cover the same rights mentioned in the U.S. Constitution but in more detail. For example, an accused's right to counsel during trial is guaranteed by the U.S. Constitution, but it may also be given by federal or state law and is just as binding in court proceedings. Moreover, the right to counsel given by law in a state may exceed that guaranteed in the Federal Constitution. The right to a lawyer during probation revocation, for instance, is not constitutionally required, but many state laws give probationers the right to counsel during probation revocation hearings. The right to jury trial is not constitutionally required in juvenile cases, but it may be given by state law.

C. Case Law

Case law is *the law as enunciated in cases decided by the courts*. The courts, when deciding cases, gradually develop legal principles that become law. This law is called *unwritten* or *judge-made* law, as distinguished from laws passed by legislative bodies. Written laws often represent the codification of case law that has become accepted and is practiced in a particular state.

Case law is sometimes confused with *common law*. The two are similar in that neither kind of law is a product of legislative enactment but has evolved primarily through judicial decisions. They differ in that common law *originated from the ancient and unwritten laws of England*. Although later applied in the United States, common law is generally derived from ancient usages and customs or from the judgments and decrees of the courts recognizing, affirming, and enforcing those usages and customs. Although common law and case law both result from court decisions, common law usually does not have value as precedent in a state, particularly in criminal cases. By contrast, case law has value as precedent within the territorial jurisdiction of the court that issued the opinion.

D. Court Rules

Various rules have developed as a result of the courts' supervisory power over the administration of criminal justice. Federal courts have supervisory power over federal criminal cases, and state courts have similar power over state criminal cases. The rules promulgated by supervisory agencies (such as some states' supreme courts) have the force and effect of law and therefore must be followed. For example, the highest court of some states may promulgate regulations that supplement the provisions of those states' laws on pleading and procedure. They cover details that may not be included in the states' codes of criminal procedure.

VIII. THE INCORPORATION CONTROVERSY: DOES THE BILL OF RIGHTS APPLY TO THE STATES?

Over the years, one issue affecting individual rights has been litigated in federal courts. That issue is the **incorporation controversy,** or *whether the Bill of Rights in the U.S. Constitution (referring to Amendments I–X) protects against violations of rights by the federal government only or whether it also limits what state and local government officials can do.* For example, the Fourth Amendment states, in part, "The right of the people to be secure in their persons, houses, papers, and effects, against unreasonable searches and seizures, shall not be violated." Does this limitation apply only to federal officials (such as FBI agents, who are thereby prohibited from making unreasonable searches or seizures), or does it also apply to the conduct of state and local officials (such as police officers)?

A. Background

The most important safeguards available to an accused in the United States are found in the Bill of Rights. These ten amendments were ratified as a group and made part of the U.S. Constitution in 1791, two years after the Constitution itself was ratified by the original thirteen states. Initially, the Bill of Rights was viewed as limiting only the acts of federal officers, because the Constitution itself limited only the powers of the federal government, not the states. State and local officers were originally limited only by provisions of their own state constitutions, state laws, or local ordinances.

In 1868, the Fourteenth Amendment was passed. Section 1 of that amendment states, in part, "No State shall make or enforce any law which shall abridge the privileges or immunities of citizens of the United States; nor shall any State deprive any person of life, liberty, or property, without due process of law; nor deny to any person within its jurisdiction the equal protection of the laws." This provision clearly applies to the states ("No State shall make or enforce . . .") and has two main clauses: the due process clause and the equal protection clause. The **Due Process Clause** of the Fourteenth Amendment has been interpreted over the years by the U.S. Supreme Court as *"incorporating" most of the provisions of the Bill of Rights,* giving rise to the incorporation controversy. Therefore, although the fundamental rights granted by the Bill of Rights were originally meant to cover only violations by federal officers, the wording of the Fourteenth Amendment (specifically, the Due Process Clause) has been interpreted by the Court, in various cases over the years, to prohibit violations of rights by either federal or state officers. In other words, those rights that are incorporated under the Fourteenth Amendment apply to state as well as federal criminal proceedings.

B. Approaches to Incorporation

The question of what constitutional rights are to be incorporated into the due process clause of the Fourteenth Amendment (and therefore held applicable to the states) and what are not is an issue decided by the U.S. Supreme Court. Over the years, various justices have taken differing approaches to the incorporation controversy. These approaches may be classified into four "positions": selective incorporation, total incorporation, total incorporation plus, and the case-by-case approach. (For a leading case on how the Supreme Court incorporates a right, read the Duncan v. Louisiana case brief at the end of this chapter.)

Most U.S. Supreme Court justices since the mid-1920s have taken the **selective incorporation** approach. This selectiveness in the choice of rights to be incorporated has led to another name for this approach—the "honor roll" position. This approach asserts that *only those rights considered "fundamental" should be incorporated under the due process clause of the Fourteenth Amendment so as to apply to state criminal proceedings.* Other criteria used by the Court in deciding whether to incorporate a right are (1) whether a right is among those "fundamental principles of liberty and justice which lie at the base of our civil and political institutions," (2) whether it is "basic in our system of jurisprudence," and (3) whether it is a "fundamental right essential to a fair trial." Regardless of the phrase used, selective incorporationists claim that the due process clause of the Fourteenth Amendment requires only fundamental fairness in state proceedings, not the automatic "lock, stock, and barrel" application of all provisions of the Bill of Rights. Selective incorporation has been the predominant approach since the Court began hearing incorporation cases. (For the leading case on selective incorporation, read the Palko v. Connecticut case brief at the end of this chapter.)

Justices who have taken the second approach—**total incorporation**—argue that *the Fourteenth Amendment's due process clause should be interpreted as incorporating all the rights given in the first ten amendments to the U.S. Constitution.* This position was enunciated by Justice Hugo Black, who wrote in a concurring opinion in 1968, "I believe as strongly as ever that the Fourteenth Amendment was intended to make the Bill of Rights applicable to the states" (Duncan v. Louisiana, 391 U.S. 145 [1968]). His is a blanket and uncomplicated approach: It proposes to incorporate, "lock, stock, and barrel," all the provisions in the Bill of Rights.

The third approach—**total incorporation plus**—is an extension of total incorporation. It proposes that, *in addition to extending all the provisions of the Bill of Rights to the states, other rights ought to be added, such as the right to clean air, clean water, and a clean environment.* Justice William O. Douglas, an activist jurist, was the main advocate of this approach, but over the years it has failed to gain converts in the Court.

The fourth approach—**case-by-case incorporation**—advocates *an examination of the facts of a specific case to determine whether there is an injustice so serious as to justify extending the provisions of the Bill of Rights to that particular case.* It is otherwise known as the "fair trial" approach, because the standard used is whether the accused obtained a fair trial. It differs from the selective incorporation approach in that selective incorporation focuses on whether a specific right (such as the right to counsel) is to be made applicable to the states. By contrast, the case-by-case approach more narrowly focuses on the facts of a specific case to decide whether *that particular case,* given its peculiar facts, should come under the due process clause. The problem with the case-by-case approach is that the application of the Bill of Rights becomes unpredictable and totally dependent on the facts, so a particular case has little or no value as precedent.

C. The Definition of Fundamental Rights

As the *Palko* case shows, the Court has defined *fundamental rights* as those "of the very essence of a scheme of ordered liberty" and "principles of justice so rooted in the traditions and conscience of our people as to be ranked as fundamental." These rather vague, though lofty, phrases really mean that the Court will determine on a case-by-case basis whether a particular right should be incorporated.

D. Rights Held to Be Fundamental and Incorporated

In specific cases, the court (using the selective incorporation approach) has held that the following provisions of the Bill of Rights apply in both federal and state proceedings:

- First Amendment provisions for freedom of religion, speech, assembly, and petition for redress of grievances (Fiske v. Kansas, 274 U.S. 380 [1927])

- Fourth Amendment protections against unreasonable arrest, search, and seizure (Wolf v. Colorado, 338 U.S. 25 [1949])

- Fifth Amendment protection against self-incrimination (Malloy v. Hogan, 378 U.S. 1 [1964])

- Fifth Amendment prohibition against double jeopardy (Benton v. Maryland, 395 U.S. 784 [1969])

- Sixth Amendment right to counsel (Gideon v. Wainwright, 372 U.S. 335 [1963])

- Sixth Amendment right to a speedy trial (Klopfer v. North Carolina, 386 U.S. 213 [1967])

- Sixth Amendment right to a public trial (In re Oliver, 333 U.S. 257 [1948])

- Sixth Amendment right to confrontation of opposing witnesses (Pointer v. Texas, 380 U.S. 400 [1965])

- Sixth Amendment right to an impartial jury (Duncan v. Louisiana, 391 U.S. 145 [1968])

- Sixth Amendment right to a compulsory process for obtaining witnesses (Washington v. Texas, 388 U.S. 14 [1967])

- Eighth Amendment prohibition against cruel and unusual punishment (Robinson v. California, 370 U.S. 660 [1962])

In incorporating a right, the Supreme Court expressly states that a fundamental right in the Bill of Rights is made applicable to the states through the due process clause of the Fourteenth Amendment. For example, in Duncan v. Louisiana, 391 U.S. 145 (1968), the Supreme Court ruled that the right to trial by jury, guaranteed to defendants in federal trials under the Sixth Amendment, must also be given to defendants in state courts because of the due process clause of the Fourteenth Amendment. Hence, that right is deemed guaranteed.

E. Rights Not Incorporated

Although the following rights are required in federal proceedings, the states do not have to grant an accused these rights unless they are required by the state constitution or state law:

- Fifth Amendment guarantee of grand jury indictment

- Eighth Amendment prohibition against excessive bail and fines

F. Nationalization of the Bill of Rights

Through a process of selective incorporation using the Fourteenth Amendment's Due Process Clause, persons facing federal or state criminal charges now enjoy the same rights, except the rights to grand jury indictment and to protection against excessive bail and fines. In effect, the Bill of Rights is now applicable throughout the United States; it has become "nationalized." It makes no difference whether an accused is tried in New York, Illinois, California, or any other state or by the federal government—the accused's basic rights are now the same because of incorporation. As a result, in no other field of

AT A GLANCE

The Court System and Sources of Rights

DUAL COURT SYSTEM: Federal and state.

APPEAL: Process by which an appellate court may affirm, reverse, or reverse and remand.

EFFECT OF DECISIONS: Binding only within the territory of that court. Decisions of higher courts are binding on lower courts in that jurisdiction.

JURISDICTION: Power of a court to try a case.

VENUE: Place where the case is tried.

WHO HAS JURISDICTION: If an act is a violation of federal law, federal court; if an act is a violation of state law, state court.

SOURCES OF RIGHTS: Constitution, statutes, case law, and court rules.

INCORPORATION CONTROVERSY: Whether the Bill of Rights protects against violations of rights by the federal government only or does it also limit actions of state and local government officials.

APPROACHES TO INCORPORATION: Selective incorporation, total incorporation, total incorporation plus, and case by case. Selective incorporation is the approach most used by the court.

RIGHTS INCORPORATED: All rights in the Bill of Rights, except the rights to grand jury indictment and the prohibition against excessive bail and fines.

law are the rights of individuals in the United States as similar as they are in the processing of an accused.

Summary

The United States has a dual court system: It has one system of courts on the federal level and another on the state level. In general, a court decision is binding only within the limits of that court's jurisdiction. Only the decisions of the U.S. Supreme Court are applicable nationwide. Sometimes this system leads to inconsistent lower court decisions; such inconsistency remains until resolved by an appellate court.

If an act violates a federal law, it is tried in a federal court; if it violates state law, it is tried in a state court. Some acts are punishable by both federal and state law. In such cases, the offender may be prosecuted and convicted twice, if the prosecutors so desire, without violating the constitutional prohibition against double jeopardy. Some states have laws prohibiting state prosecution for the same offense if the accused already has been tried in a federal court.

Originally, the Bill of Rights of the Constitution was applied only to federal criminal prosecutions. Its guarantees, except for the right to grand jury indictment and the prohibition against excessive bail, are now extended to state criminal cases. Selective incorporation is the process by which those rights considered fundamental have been incorporated into state criminal proceedings through the Due Process Clause of the Fourteenth Amendment. Because of incorporation, the provisions of the Bill of Rights have, in effect, been held applicable throughout the country.

Review Questions

1. "The United States has a dual court system." Discuss what that statement means.

2. What is the Rule of Four?

3. "A court decision is effective only within a limited jurisdiction." What does that mean?

4. A criminal act is usually prosecuted under state law. May the same act also be prosecuted under federal law? Give an example.

5. Distinguish between jurisdiction and venue.

6. What did the U.S. Supreme Court say in Duncan v. Louisiana?

7. What is the incorporation controversy? How did it originate?

8. Distinguish between "total incorporation" and "selective incorporation."

9. Name five rights that have been made applicable to the states by means of the Due Process Clause of the Fourteenth Amendment.

10. Name two rights that have not been incorporated.

Key Terms and Definitions

affirm (a decision): The situation in which a decision of the lower court where the case came from is upheld by the appellate court.

Bill of Rights: The first ten amendments to the U.S. Constitution.

case-by-case incorporation: An approach that looks at the facts of a specific case to determine whether there is an injustice so serious as to justify extending the provisions of the Bill of Rights to that state case.

case law: The law as enunciated in cases decided by the courts.

common law: Law that originated from the ancient and unwritten laws of England.

double jeopardy: Being punished more than once for the same offense.

dual court system: The two court systems of the United States, one for federal cases and the other for state cases.

dual sovereignty: The concept that federal and state governments are sovereign each in their own right.

Due Process Clause: A provision in the Fourteenth Amendment of the Constitution stating that no state shall deprive any person of life, liberty, or property without due process of law.

en banc decision: A decision made by an appellate court as one body, not in divisions.

incorporation controversy: The issue of whether the Bill of Rights of the U.S. Constitution protects against violations of rights by the federal government only or also limits what state government officials can do.

judicial precedent: The concept that decisions of courts have value as precedent for future cases similarly circumstanced.

jurisdiction: The power of a court to try a case.

reverse (a decision): The situation in which a decision of the lower court where the case came from is overthrown, vacated, or set aside by the appellate court.

reverse and remand (a decision): The situation in which a decision by the lower court is reversed but the lower court has an opportunity to hear further arguments and give another decision in the case.

Rule of Four: A rule providing that the Supreme Court needs the votes of at least four justices to consider a case on its merits.

selective incorporation: An approach holding that the Fourteenth Amendment's due process clause should be interpreted to incorporate only those rights granted in Amendments I–X of the Constitution that are considered fundamental; this is the position advocated by most Supreme Court justices.

stare decisis: Literally, "to abide by, or adhere to, decided cases."

total incorporation: An approach holding that the Fourteenth Amendment's due process clause should be interpreted to incorporate all the rights granted in Amendments I–VIII of the Constitution; this position is advocated by some Supreme Court justices.

total incorporation plus: An approach proposing that, in addition to extending all the provisions of the Bill of Rights to the states, other rights ought to be added, such as the right to clean air, clean water, and a clean environment.

venue: The place or territory in which a case is tried.

Principles of Cases

Duncan v. Louisiana, 391 U.S. 145 (1968) A crime punishable by two years in prison, although classified under Louisiana law as a misdemeanor, is a serious crime. Therefore, the defendant is entitled to a jury trial.

Frisbie v. Collins, 342 U.S. 519 (1952) An invalid arrest is not a defense to being convicted of the offense charged.

Harris v. New York, 401 U.S. 222 (1971) Trustworthy statements obtained in violation of the Miranda rule may be used to impeach the credibility of a defendant who takes the witness stand.

Palko v. Connecticut, 302 U.S. 319 (1937) The due process clause of the Fourteenth Amendment applies to the states and therefore incorporates those provisions of the Bill of Rights that are "of the very essence of a scheme of ordered liberty." The provisions to be incorporated are those that involve "principles of justice so rooted in the traditions and conscience of our people as to be ranked as fundamental." The double jeopardy provision of the Fifth Amendment does not come under this category and therefore does not apply to the states. (The double jeopardy provision of the Fifth Amendment has since been incorporated and held applicable to the states, so this part of the *Palko* decision is no longer valid.)

Case Briefs

The Leading Case on Selective Incorporation

Palko v. Connecticut, 302 U.S. 319 (1937)

Facts: Palko was charged with first-degree murder in the state of Connecticut. He was found guilty of murder in the second degree and sentenced to life imprisonment. The prosecution appealed the verdict, and the Connecticut Supreme Court ordered a new trial on the grounds that an error of law in the lower court had prejudiced the state. At the second trial, additional evidence was admitted and additional instruc-

tions were given to the jury. A conviction for first-degree murder was returned, and Palko was sentenced to death. He questioned the legality of the second conviction, claiming double jeopardy under the constitutional right guaranteed by the Fifth Amendment as made applicable to the states by the Due Process Clause of the Fourteenth Amendment.

Issue: *Is the double jeopardy provision of the Fifth Amendment applicable in state criminal prosecutions by way of the Due Process Clause of the Fourteenth Amendment? No.*

Supreme Court Decision: The Due Process Clause of the Fourteenth Amendment applies to the states and therefore incorporates those provisions of the Bill of Rights that are "of the very essence of a scheme of ordered liberty." The provisions deemed incorporated are those that involve "principles of justice so rooted in the traditions and conscience of our people as to be ranked as fundamental." The double jeopardy provision of the Fifth Amendment does not come under this category and therefore does not apply to the states. The second conviction was upheld.

Case Significance: The *Palko* case illustrates the standards used by the Court, under the selective incorporation approach, to determine whether a constitutional right should be held to be applicable to the states under the Due Process Clause of the Fourteenth Amendment. The standards used were "of the very essence of a scheme of ordered liberty" and "principles of justice so rooted in the traditions and conscience of our people as to be ranked as fundamental." By 1937, when the *Palko* case was decided, only the First Amendment and the right to counsel had been found to fit the above tests. Since then, most provisions of the Constitution have been incorporated by the Fourteenth Amendment, including the prohibition against double jeopardy. If the *Palko* case were decided today, the decision would be different.

Excerpts from the Decision: "We have said that in appellant's view the Fourteenth Amendment is to be taken as embodying the prohibitions of the Fifth. His thesis is even broader. Whatever would be a violation of the original Bill of Rights (Amendments 1 to 8) if done by the federal government is now equally unlawful by force of the Fourteenth Amendment if done by a state. There is no such general rule.

"The Fifth Amendment provides, among other things, that no person shall be held to answer for a capital or otherwise infamous crime unless on presentment or indictment of a grand jury. This court has held that, in prosecutions by a state, presentment or indictment by a grand jury may give way to informations at the instance of a public officer. . . . The Fifth Amendment provides also that no person shall be compelled in any criminal case to be a witness against himself. This court has said that, in prosecutions by a state, the exemption will fail if the state elects to end it. The Sixth Amendment calls for a jury trial in criminal cases and the Seventh for a jury trial in civil cases at common law where the value in controversy shall exceed twenty dollars. This court has ruled that consistently

with those amendments trial by jury may be modified by a state or abolished altogether. . . .

"The Due Process Clause of the Fourteenth Amendment may make it unlawful for a state to abridge by its statutes the freedom of speech which the First Amendment safeguards against encroachment by the Congress . . . or the like freedom of the press . . . or the free exercise of religion . . . or the right of peaceable assembly, without which speech would be unduly trammeled . . . or the right of one accused of crime to the benefit of counsel. . . . In these and other situations immunities that are valid as against the federal government by force of the specific pledges of particular amendments have been found to be implicit in the concept of ordered liberty, and thus, through the Fourteenth Amendment, become valid as against the states.

"The line of division may seem to be wavering and broken if there is a hasty catalogue of the cases on the one side and the other. Reflection and analysis will induce a different view. There emerges the perception of a rationalizing principle which gives to discrete instances a proper order and coherence. The right to trial by jury and the immunity from prosecution except as the result of an indictment may have value and importance. Even so, they are not of the very essence of a scheme of ordered liberty. To abolish them is not to violate a 'principle of justice so rooted in the traditions and conscience of our people as to be ranked as fundamental.' Few would be so narrow or provincial as to maintain that a fair and enlightened system of justice would be impossible without them. What is true of jury trials and indictments is true also, as the cases show, of the immunity from compulsory self-incrimination. This too might be lost, and justice still be done. Indeed, today as in the past there are students of our penal system who look upon the immunity as a mischief rather than a benefit, and who would limit its scope, or destroy it altogether. No doubt there would remain the need to give protection against torture, physical or mental. . . . Justice, however, would not perish if the accused were subject to a duty to respond to orderly inquiry. The exclusion of these immunities and privileges from the privileges and immunities protected against the action of the states has not been arbitrary or casual. It has been dictated by a study and appreciation of the meaning, the essential implications of liberty itself."

The Leading Case on How the Supreme Court Incorporates a Right

Duncan v. Louisiana, 391 U.S. 145 (1968)

Facts: Duncan was convicted in a Louisiana court of

simple battery (a misdemeanor punishable under Louisiana law by a maximum sentence of two years in prison and a $300 fine). Duncan requested a jury trial, but the request was denied because, under Louisiana law, jury trials were allowed only when hard labor or capital punishment could be imposed. Duncan was convicted and given sixty days in jail and fined $150. He appealed to the U.S. Supreme Court, claiming that the state's refusal to give him a jury trial for a crime punishable by two or more years of imprisonment violated his constitutional right.

Issue: *Was the state's refusal to give the defendant a jury trial for a crime that carried a two-year imprisonment as maximum sentence a violation of the constitutional right to a jury trial in the Sixth Amendment as incorporated through the Due Process Clause of the Fourteenth? Yes.*

Supreme Court Decision: A crime punishable by two years in prison, although classified under Louisiana law as a misdemeanor, is a serious crime, and therefore the defendant is entitled to a jury trial.

Case Significance: The *Duncan* case made the right to trial by jury applicable to the states in cases in which the maximum penalty is two years' imprisonment, regardless of how state law classifies the offense. Although *Duncan* did not clearly state the minimum, a subsequent case (Baldwin v. New York, 399 U.S. 66 [1972]) later held that any offense that carries a potential sentence of more than six months is a serious offense, so a jury trial must be afforded on demand. This requirement applies even if the sentence actually imposed is less than six months.

Excerpts from the Decision: "The Fourteenth Amendment denies the States the power to 'deprive any person of life, liberty, or property, without due process of law.' In resolving conflicting claims concerning the meaning of this spacious language, the Court has looked increasingly to the Bill of Rights for guidance; many of the rights guaranteed by the first eight Amendments to the Constitution have been held to be protected against state action by the Due

Process Clause of the Fourteenth Amendment. That clause now protects the right to compensation for property taken by the State; the rights of speech, press, and religion covered by the First Amendment; the Fourth Amendment rights to be free from unreasonable searches and seizures and to have excluded from criminal trials any evidence illegally seized; the right guaranteed by the Fifth Amendment to be free of compelled self-incrimination; and the Sixth Amendment rights to counsel, to a speedy and public trial, to confrontation of opposing witnesses, and the compulsory process for obtaining witnesses.

"The test for determining whether a right extended by the Fifth and Sixth Amendments with respect to federal criminal proceedings is also protected against state action by the Fourteenth Amendment has been phrased in a variety of ways in the opinions of this Court. The question has been asked whether a right is among those 'fundamental principles of liberty and justice which lie at the base of all our civil and political institutions,' Powell v. Alabama, 287 U.S. 45, 67 (1932); whether it is 'basic in our system of jurisprudence,' In re Oliver, 333 U.S. 257, 273 (1948); and whether it is 'a fundamental right, essential to a fair trial,' Gideon v. Wainwright, 372 U.S. 335, 343–344 (1963); Malloy v. Hogan, 378 U.S. 1, 6 (1964); Pointer v. Texas, 380 U.S. 400, 403 (1965). The claim before us is that the right to trial by jury guaranteed by the Sixth Amendment meets these tests. The position of Louisiana, on the other hand, is that the Constitution imposes upon the States no duty to give a jury trial in any criminal case, regardless of the seriousness of the crime or the size of the punishment which may be imposed. Because we believe that trial by jury in criminal cases is fundamental to the American scheme of justice, we hold that the Fourteenth Amendment guarantees a right of jury trial in all criminal cases which —were they to be tried in a federal court—would come within the Sixth Amendment's guarantee. Since we consider the appeal before us to be such a case, we hold that the Constitution was violated when appellant's demand for jury trial was refused."

 # Notes

1. H. J. Spaeth, *An Introduction to Supreme Court Decision Making* (San Francisco: Chandler, 1972), p. 71.

2. *Time Magazine*, December 14, 1998, p. 44.

2.

Overview of the Criminal Justice Process

Chapter Outline

What You Will Learn in This Chapter

You will learn about the procedures used in sequence by the criminal justice system before trial, during trial, and after trial. These procedures start with the filing of a complaint or an arrest by the police and end with the appeal of a sentence after a defendant is convicted. You will also read some words of caution about the variations in procedures in different states, or even within a state, and the differences that sometimes arise between the procedures prescribed by law and the Constitution and those actually used by the system.

Introduction

We now present an overview of the criminal justice process from a legal perspective. (See Figure 2.1.) The procedure is divided into three time frames: before trial, during trial, and after trial. In the great majority of cases, an arrest triggers criminal justice procedures against the accused. In some cases, however, the procedure is initiated through the filing of a complaint that leads to the issuance of a warrant. Procedure during trial starts with the selection of jurors and ends with a court or jury verdict. If the accused is found guilty, the sentencing phase follows, after which the defendant may appeal the conviction and sentence. (See Figure 2.2.) The chapter concludes with some words of caution concerning the difference between theory and practice in criminal justice procedures. (See Table 2.1.)

I. THE PROCEDURE BEFORE TRIAL

A. The Filing of a Complaint

A **complaint** is *a charge made before a proper officer alleging the commission of a criminal offense.* It may be filed by the offended party or by a police officer who has obtained information about or witnessed the criminal act. The complaint serves as a basis for issuing an arrest warrant. If the accused has been arrested without a warrant, the

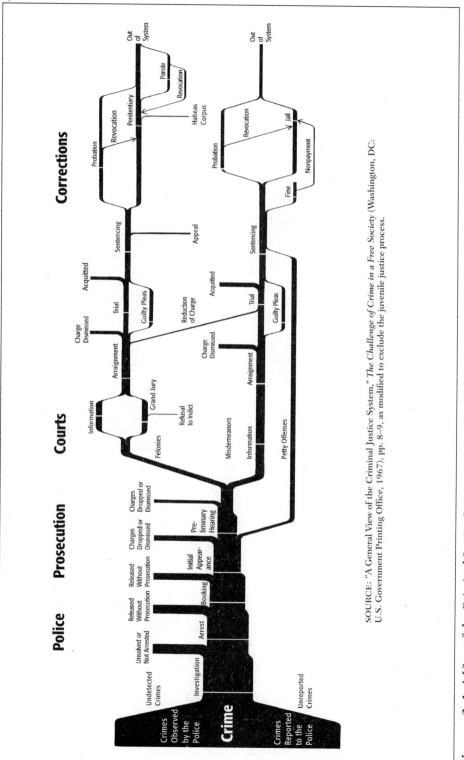

Police Prosecution Courts Corrections

SOURCE: "A General View of the Criminal Justice System," *The Challenge of Crime in a Free Society* (Washington, DC: U.S. Government Printing Office, 1967), pp. 8–9, as modified to exclude the juvenile justice process.

Figure 2.1 *A View of the Criminal Justice Process*

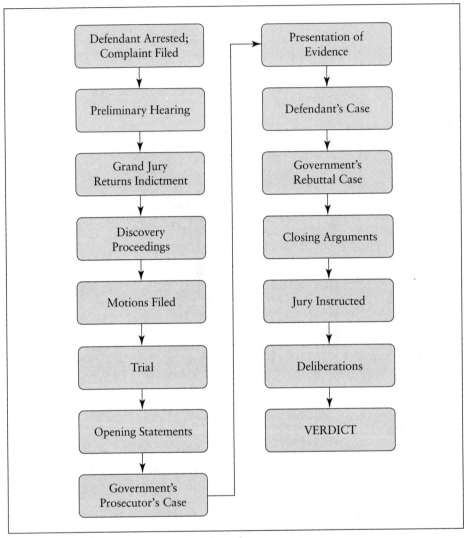

Figure 2.2 *A Summary of Criminal Trial Progressions*

SOURCE: Internet: http://www.uscourts.gov.

complaint is prepared and filed at the defendant's initial appearance before the magistrate, usually by the arresting officer. (See Form 2.1.)

B. The Arrest

There are two kinds of arrest: arrest with a warrant and arrest without a warrant. In *arrest with a warrant,* a complaint has been filed and presented to a magistrate, who has

TABLE 2.1 *Criminal and Civil Cases Compared*

	Criminal	**Civil**
1. Who files	Government	Usually a private person or entities
2. Purpose	Seek punishment for the crime committed	Seek monetary damage and/or an injunction for violation of a duty or obligation
3. What must be proved	a. A crime has been committed, and b. The defendant commited the crime	a. Existence of a legal contractual duty or obligation, and b. A breach of that duty or obligation resulting in harm
4. Proof required to win	Guilt beyond a reasonable doubt (about 95% certainty of guilt)	Preponderance of evidence (more than 50% certainty)
5. Bill of Rights	Limits conduct of government officials	Does not apply to conduct of private persons
6. Lawyers	Prosecutor for the government; private lawyers, government-supplied lawyers, or public defender for defendant	Own lawyer(s) for each side
7. If trial by jury	Usually a unanimous jury vote for conviction or acquittal	Usually a nonunanimous jury vote
8. Defendant's presence in court	Required, with exceptions	Not required
9. Testimony	Accused cannot be forced to testify in court	Defendant can be forced to testify in court
10. Appeal	Defendant can appeal a conviction; government cannot appeal an acquittal, except on questions of law, if allowed	Either side can appeal

read it and found probable cause to justify the issuance of an arrest warrant. In contrast, *arrest without a warrant* usually happens when a crime is committed in the presence of a police officer or, in some jurisdictions, by virtue of a citizen's arrest for specified offenses. As many as 95 percent of all arrests are made without a warrant. This rate is significant because it implies that the officer must be convinced of the presence of probable cause before making the arrest. Such belief is later established in a sworn complaint or testimony. (See Form 2.2.)

Statutes in many states authorize the use of a citation or summons rather than an arrest for less serious offenses. A **citation** is *an order issued by a court or law enforcement officer commanding the person to whom the citation is issued to appear in court at a specified date to answer certain charges.* A **summons** is *a writ directed to the sheriff or other proper officer requiring that officer to notify the person named that he or she must appear in court on a day named and answer the complaint stated in the summons.* In either case, if the person fails or refuses to appear in court as scheduled, an arrest warrant is issued. Citations and summonses have the advantage of keeping a person out of jail

```
STATE OF MISSOURI    )
                     ) ss.
COUNTY OF CLINTON    )

        IN THE ASSOCIATE CIRCUIT COURT OF CLINTON COUNTY, MISSOURI

STATE OF MISSOURI,                      )
                  Plaintiff            )
                                       )
    -vs-                               )      Case No.
                                       )
                                       )
                  Defendant            )
```

C O M P L A I N T

_____, being duly sworn, deposes and states that in

the County of Clinton, State of Missouri, heretofore, to-wit: on or about

_____, one _____, in violation

of Section 570.120, RSMo, committed the Class A misdemeanor of passing bad checks

punishable upon conviction under Sections 558.011.1(5) and 560.016, RSMo, in that the

defendant, with purpose to defraud, issued a check in the amount of $_____,

drawn upon the _____, dated _____,

payable to _____, knowing that such check would not

be paid.

   Affiant further states that he has actual personal knowledge of the facts, matters and
things above set out and is a competent witness thereto.

                                        _____
                                        Plaintiff

Subscribed and sworn to before me this ____ day of _____, 19 ____.

                                        _____
                                        Clerk of the Associate Circuit Court

Form 2.1 _Complaint_

pending the hearing. They also save the police officer the time and paperwork that go
with arrest and booking.

C. Booking at the Police Station

Booking consists of _making an entry in the police blotter or arrest book indicating the suspect's name, the time of arrest, and the offense involved._ Prior to this, the arrestee is

STATE OF
RHODE ISLAND
AND
PROVIDENCE
PLANTATIONS

AFFIDAVIT AND ARREST WARRANT

AFFIDAVIT

AFFIANT		AGENT OF					
DEFENDANT		ADDRESS	NO.	STREET	CITY/TOWN		STATE

AFFIDAVIT

Your affiant upon oath states that he has reason to believe and does believe that grounds for issuance of an arrest warrant exists and states the following facts on which such belief is founded:

IF SPACE IS NOT SUFFICIENT,
CHECK (X) HERE AND
☐ ATTACH ADDITIONAL
INFORMATION

AFFIANT

X

SUBSCRIBED AND SWORN TO BEFORE ME AT (CITY/TOWN)		DATE	JUDGE OR DISTRICT COURT, JUSTICE OF SUPERIOR COURT OR ANY OTHER AUTHORIZED OFFICER
			X

ARREST WARRANT

STATE, EX REL	CITY/TOWN	COUNTY	DATE OF BIRTH	DIVISION	WARRANT DATE
				RHODE ISLAND DISTRICT COURT	
VS. DEFENDANT		ADDRESS	NO.	STREET	CITY/TOWN	STATE

TO ANY AUTHORIZED OFFICER: Affidavit (and complaint) having been made to me under oath, and as I am satisfied that there is probable cause for the belief therein set forth that grounds for issuing an arrest warrant exists, you are hereby commanded to arrest the defendant forthwith and to bring him before a judge of this court without unnecessary delay.

BAIL	SURETY	DATE SIGNED	JUDGE OR DISTRICT COURT, JUSTICE SUPERIOR COURT OR ANY AUTHORIZED OFFICER
$	☐ with ☐ without		X

RETURN OF SERVICE

I have apprehended the within named defendant and have presented him/her before the court as herein commanded.

SERVICE	MILEAGE	DATE OF RETURN	AUTHORIZED OFFICER
$	$		X

POLICE COPY

Form 2.2 *Affidavit and Arrest Warrant*

searched for weapons or any evidence that might be related to a crime, and his or her belongings are inventoried. If the offense is serious, the suspect may also be photographed and fingerprinted. Before or after booking, the suspect is usually placed in a "lockup," which is a place of detention run by the police department (usually in major cities), or in jail in smaller cities or communities where no lockups are necessary. In most jurisdictions, the arrestee is allowed a telephone call, usually to a lawyer or a family member with whom he or she might want to be in touch. In some jurisdictions, the arrestee is allowed to post a predetermined amount of bail for minor offenses, on promise that he or she will appear in court at a particular time. If bail is not posted or is denied, the person is kept under detention until such time as he or she can be brought before a magistrate. (See Form 2.3.)

HOUSTON POLICE DEPARTMENT
Prisoners Booking Information Blotter

S.S. NO. _____   D.O.B. _____   D.L. NO. _____   STATE _____

LAST NAME	FIRST	MIDDLE	ALIAS	DATE

RACE SEX AGE	OCCUPATION	ADDRESS	PHONE NO.

ARRESTED BY   EMP. NOS.   UNIT No.   ☐ HPD   ☐ OTHER   TIME of ARREST
1
2
TRANSPORTED BY   LOCATION
1
2   INCIDENT# _____
PHYSICAL CONDITION   INDICATE APPROPRIATE CHARGE(S)
                                   MUNICIPAL _____   DETAIN (Hold) DIV. _____
                                              CHARGE(S)

DETAILS:
CLOTHING DESCRIPTION   SUPERVISORS AUTHORIZATION (when needed)

VEHICLE YEAR	Make	Model	Color	License No.	Towed By	Location Stored

Form NO. HPD-00035

Form 2.3 *Booking Information Blotter*

D. Appearance before a Magistrate after the Arrest

In some states, this step is known as *the initial appearance, presentment,* or *arraignment on the warrant.* Most states require that an arrested person be brought before a judge, magistrate, or commissioner "without unnecessary delay." What that means varies from state to state, depending on state law or court decisions. In federal and most state proceedings, a delay of more than six hours in bringing the suspect before the magistrate is one factor to be considered in determining whether any incriminating statements made by the accused were in fact voluntary. Other jurisdictions do not specify the number of hours but look at the surrounding circumstances and decide on a case-by-case basis whether the delay was unnecessary.

Once before a magistrate, the arrestee is made aware of his or her rights. This procedure usually includes giving the **Miranda warnings,** which have five components:

1. You have a right to remain silent.

2. Anything you say can be used against you in a court of law.

3. You have a right to the presence of an attorney.

4. If you cannot afford an attorney, one will be appointed for you prior to questioning.

5. You have the right to terminate this interview at any time.

The suspect is also informed of such other rights as may be given by statute. These vary from state to state and may include the right to a preliminary hearing, confrontation, and a speedy trial; the right not to incriminate oneself; and *the exclusion in court of illegally obtained evidence*—the **exclusionary rule.**

Many jurisdictions require magistrates to give the Miranda warnings when the suspect is brought in, but the warnings must also be given by the arresting officer if he or she questions the suspect prior to the appearance before a magistrate. Failure to issue the warnings makes the suspect's statements inadmissible in court. Conversely, if the officer does not need to ask the suspect any questions (as would usually be the case in arrests with a warrant), the Miranda warnings need not be given. The officer arrests the person named in the warrant and brings him or her before a magistrate or judge.

If the charge is a misdemeanor, the arrestee may be arraigned while before the magistrate and required to plead to the pending charge. Many misdemeanor cases are disposed of at this stage, through either a guilty plea or some other procedure. If the charge is a felony, the arrestee ordinarily is not required to plead to the charge at this time. Rather, he or she is held for preliminary examination on the felony charge.

E. The Setting of Bail

Bail is defined as *the security required by the court and given by the accused to ensure that the accused appears before the proper court at a scheduled time and place to answer the charges brought against him or her.* In theory, the only function of bail is to ensure the appearance of the defendant at the time set for trial. In practice, bail has also been used as a form of **preventive detention** *to prevent the release of an accused who might otherwise be dangerous to society* or whom the judge might not want to release. The Court has upheld as constitutional a provision of the Federal Bail Reform Act of 1984 that permits federal judges to deny pretrial release to persons charged with certain serious felonies, based on a finding that no combination of release conditions can reasonably assure the community of safety from such individuals (United States v. Salerno, 481 U.S. 739 [1987]).

By statute in a number of states, the magistrate or judge before whom the proceedings are pending may free the accused through **release on recognizance (ROR)** (without monetary bail). This usually happens when the accused has strong ties in the community and seems quite likely to appear for trial. If he or she fails to do so, an arrest warrant may be issued.

F. The Preliminary Examination

An accused charged with a felony is usually entitled to a **preliminary examination** (called a *preliminary hearing* or *examining trial* in some states), to be held before a magistrate within a reasonably short time after arrest. Preliminary examinations closely resemble trials, except that their purpose is more limited and the hearing magistrate is generally not the judge who will preside over the actual trial in the case. Representation by counsel and cross-examination of witnesses are allowed.

Preliminary examinations are usually held for three main purposes:

1. **Determination of probable cause.** The primary purpose of the preliminary hearing is to ascertain whether there is probable cause to support the charges against the accused. If not, the charges are dismissed. This process keeps unsupported charges of grave offenses from coming to trial and thereby protects people from harassment, needless expenditure, and damage to their reputation. What is the maximum time an arrested person can be detained without a probable cause determination? A 1991 Supreme Court decision is instructive, because it sets a tentative limit. The Court held that detention of a suspect for forty-eight hours without any probable cause hearing is presumptively reasonable. If the time to hearing is longer than that, the burden of proof shifts to the police to prove reasonableness. But if the time to hearing is shorter, the burden of proof to establish unreasonable delay shifts to the detainee (County of Riverside v. McLaughlin, 111 S.Ct. 1661 [1991]). A subsequent case held McLaughlin applicable to all cases that had not been decided at the time of the McLaughlin decision (Powell v. Nevada, 54 CrL 2238 [1992]).

2. **Discovery.** This is *a procedure used by either party in a case to obtain information that is in the hands of the other party and is necessary or helpful in developing the case.* The scope of discovery in a criminal case is usually limited to materials or evidence specified by law to be discoverable. Discovery procedures in criminal cases are usually one-sided in favor of the defense, because the accused can often invoke the guarantee against self-incrimination and refuse to turn over relevant evidence to the prosecution.

3. **Decision on "binding over."** Some states use the preliminary examination to determine if the accused will be "bound over" for a grand jury hearing. In these states, there must be a finding of cause at the preliminary examination before a grand jury hearing will be held. Other states use the preliminary examination to determine whether the accused should be bound over for trial, bypassing grand jury proceedings altogether.

In some cases, a preliminary examination is not required:

- **When an indictment has been handed down prior to preliminary examination.** If the grand jury has previously returned an indictment (usually because the case was referred to it before arrest), a preliminary examination is not required. The grand jury proceedings constitute a determination that there is probable cause and thus that the accused should stand trial.

- **When a misdemeanor is involved.** In most jurisdictions, preliminary examinations are not required in misdemeanor cases, because only lesser penalties are involved. The accused goes directly to trial on the complaint or information filed by the district attorney.

- **When there is a waiver of preliminary examination.** The accused may voluntarily give up the right to a preliminary examination. For example, a plea of guilty to the charge generally operates as a waiver of the preliminary examination. The accused is thereupon bound over for sentencing to the court having jurisdiction over the crime involved.

After the preliminary hearing, the magistrate may do any of the following:

1. **"Hold defendant to answer."** If the magistrate finds probable cause, naming facts that would lead a person of ordinary caution or prudence to entertain a strong suspicion of the guilt of the accused, the accused is "held to answer" and bound over for trial in a court having jurisdiction over the offense charged.

2. **Discharge the defendant.** If the magistrate does not find probable cause, the defendant is discharged.

3. **Reduce the charge.** Most states allow the magistrate to reduce a felony charge to a misdemeanor on the basis of the results of the preliminary hearing. This enables grand juries and higher courts to avoid being swamped with cases that really belong in the lower courts.

G. The Decision by the Prosecutor to Charge

There is discretion in all areas of criminal justice, but particularly in policing and prosecution. After a suspect is taken into custody, or even before that, the police usually have discretion to charge or not to charge him or her with an offense. As the seriousness of the offense goes up, the discretion of the police diminishes. For example, the police have almost no discretion to charge or not to charge the suspect with an offense in homicide cases. Minor traffic offenses, however, may be disposed of by the police "on the spot."

The prosecutor also exercises immense discretion. In most states, the prosecutor is not under the control of any superior other than the electorate. This discretion is most evident in the prosecutor's decision to charge or not to charge. In the words of former attorney general and U.S. Supreme Court justice Robert Jackson, "[T]he prosecutor has more control over life, liberty and reputation than any person in America." In most cases, the prosecutor has the final say on whether a suspect should be prosecuted. Should the prosecutor decide to charge even if the evidence is weak, a suspect can do little else but go to trial and hope for an acquittal. Conversely, if the evidence is strong but the prosecutor still declines to charge, there is little anyone can do legally to persuade the prosecutor to charge. Even after a suspect has been charged, the prosecutor may file a **nolle prosequi** motion, *which seeks a dismissal of the charges.* Such a motion is almost always granted by the court.

H. A Grand Jury Indictment versus an Information

A criminal prosecution is initiated by the filing of an accusatory pleading in the court having jurisdiction. Prior to the filing, the accused will have appeared before a magistrate to be informed of his or her rights and to post bail. The accused also will have had

TABLE 2.2 *Grand Juries and Trial (Petit) Juries Compared*

Grand Jury	Trial Jury
1. Usually composed of sixteen to twenty-three members with twelve votes required for an indictment	1. Usually consists of twelve members, with a unanimous vote required for conviction
2. Choice usually determined by state law, with "jury of peers" not a consideration	2. Usually chosen from voter registration list and driver's license rolls, with "jury of peers" a consideration
3. Does not determine guilt or innocence; function is to return indictments or conduct investigations of reported criminality	3. Decides guilt or innocence and, in some states, determines punishment
4. Retains the same membership for a month, six months, or one year; may return several indictments during that period	4. Different jury for every case
5. Hands down indictments based on probable cause	5. Convicts on the basis of evidence of guilt beyond a reasonable doubt
6. May initiate investigations of misconduct	6. Cannot initiate investigations of misconduct

a preliminary examination to determine whether there is probable cause for him or her to be bound over for trial. However, the prosecution formally commences when the government files an indictment or information. An **indictment** is *a written accusation of a crime filed by the grand jury* and signed by the grand jury foreman, whereas an information is filed directly by the prosecutor. In states using the grand jury system, an indictment is usually required in felony offenses, but an information is sufficient in misdemeanors. (See Table 2.2.)

A **grand jury hearing,** *in which a decision is made whether to charge a suspect with an offense,* is not a right guaranteed under the U.S. Constitution in all criminal prosecutions. However, most states today use it, some on an optional basis. It is required in all federal felony prosecutions. It is a peculiar institution in that "it belongs to no branch of the institutional government" (the executive, the legislative, or the judiciary) and is intended to "serve as a buffer or referee between the government and the people who are charged with crimes" (United States v. Williams, 112 S.Ct. 1735 [1992]).

The grand jury proceedings start when a **bill of indictment,** defined as *a written accusation of a crime,* is submitted to the grand jury by the prosecutor. Hearings are then held before the grand jury, and evidence is presented by the prosecutor to prove the accusation. Traditionally, the hearings are secret, since the charges may not be proved and hence it would be unfair to allow their publication. For the same reason, unauthorized persons are excluded, and disclosure of the proceedings is generally prohibited. The accused has no right to present evidence in a grand jury proceeding. However, the accused may be given an opportunity to do so at the discretion of the grand jury. A person appearing before the grand jury does not have a right to counsel, even if he or she is also the suspect. The reason is that the grand jury proceeding is merely an investigation, not a trial. Sworn grand jury testimony can be used at trial to impeach witnesses should they testify differently.

If the required number of grand jurors (usually twelve) believes that the evidence warrants conviction for the crime charged, the bill of indictment is endorsed as a "true bill" and filed with the court having jurisdiction. The bill itself constitutes the formal accusation. If the jury does not find probable cause, the bill of indictment is ignored and a "no bill" results.

An **information** is *a written accusation of a crime prepared by the prosecuting attorney in the name of the state.* The information is not presented to a grand jury. To safeguard against possible abuse, most states provide that a prosecution by information may be commenced only after a preliminary examination and commitment by a magistrate or after a waiver thereof by the accused. The "probable cause" needed in every grand jury indictment is thus assured by the reviewing magistrate.

The information filed by the prosecutor must reasonably inform the accused of the charges against him or her, giving the accused an opportunity to prepare and present a defense. The essential nature of the offense must be stated, although the charges may follow the language of the penal code that defines the offense.

I. The Arraignment

At a scheduled time and after prior notice, the accused is called into court for an **arraignment,** *in which he or she is informed of the charges against him or her and asked how he or she pleads.* The accused's presence during arraignment is generally required, except in minor offenses. If the accused has not been arrested, or if he or she is free on bail and does not appear, a bench warrant or **capias**—*a warrant issued by the court for an officer to take a named defendant into custody*—will be issued to compel his or her appearance. An exception in many states provides that an accused charged with a misdemeanor may appear through a lawyer at the arraignment.

J. The Plea by the Defendant

A **plea** is *an accused's response in court to the indictment or information that is read to the accused in court.* There are generally three kinds of pleas in modern criminal justice practice: nolo contendere, not guilty, and guilty. Some states add a fourth plea: not guilty by reason of insanity.

1. A Nolo Contendere Plea

A **nolo contendere plea** literally means *"no contest."* In essence, the defendant accepts the penalty without admitting guilt. The effect of this plea is the same as that of a guilty plea, but the defendant may benefit in that the plea cannot be used as an admission in any subsequent civil proceeding arising out of the same offense. For example, suppose X pleads nolo contendere to a criminal charge of driving while intoxicated. This plea cannot be used as an admission of guilt in a subsequent civil case brought against X by the injured party to recover damages. The injured party must independently prove the liability of X and not simply rely on the nolo contendere plea. By contrast, had X pleaded guilty to the charge of driving while intoxicated, the plea could have been used by the injured party in a civil case. The guilty plea automatically establishes X's civil liability, relieving the plaintiff of the burden of having to prove it.

Nolo contendere pleas are permitted in federal courts and in the courts of about half the states, usually for nonserious offenses and at the discretion of the judge. Even where such pleas are permitted, however, the accused generally does not have an absolute right to make the plea. It can be made only with the consent of the prosecution or with the approval of the court. It is also generally used only for misdemeanor offenses, although some states allow its use even for felonies.

2. A Plea of Not Guilty

If the defendant pleads not guilty, the trial is usually scheduled to take place within two or three weeks. The delay is designed to give both the prosecution and the defense time to prepare their cases. When the defendant refuses to plead, or when the court is not sure of the defendant's plea, the court will enter a not guilty plea.

Between the filing of the not guilty plea and the start of the trial, the defense lawyer often files a number of written motions with the court. One of the most common is a *motion to suppress* evidence that allegedly was illegally seized. The motion requires a hearing at which the police officer who made the search testifies to the facts surrounding the seizure of the evidence and the court determines whether the evidence was, in fact, illegally obtained. Another common motion is a *motion for a change of venue,* which is often made when there has been prejudicial pretrial publicity against the accused.

3. A Plea of Guilty

When a defendant pleads guilty, the record must affirmatively show that the plea was voluntary and that the accused had a full understanding of its consequences. Otherwise, the plea is invalid (Boykin v. Alabama, 395 U.S. 238 [1969]). By pleading guilty, the defendant waives several important constitutional rights (such as the right to trial by jury, the right to confront witnesses, and protection against self-incrimination). Therefore, it is necessary to make sure that the accused knew exactly what he or she was doing and was not coerced into making the plea.

A plea of guilty that represents an intelligent and informed choice among alternatives available to the defendant is valid even if it is entered in the hope of avoiding the death penalty (Brady v. United States, 397 U.S. 742 [1970]). Likewise, a plea of guilty is valid even if the defendant does not admit guilt or continues to assert his or her innocence, provided that there is some basis in the record for the plea. All that is required for a valid guilty plea is a knowing waiver of the rights involved, not an admission of guilt (North Carolina v. Alford, 400 U.S. 25 [1970]). In the same case, the Supreme Court ruled that it is constitutional for a judge to refuse to accept a guilty plea from a defendant if that defendant continues to maintain his or her innocence.

a. Plea Bargaining Frequently, with *plea bargaining, a defendant is induced to plead guilty to a lesser charge in order to save time and expense and avoid the uncertainty of a trial.* In these cases, the plea must be voluntary, and the accused must have a full understanding of its consequences.

Not all guilty pleas are the result of plea bargaining. Many people plead guilty for other reasons, without bargaining with the prosecutor. Conversely, not all plea bargains result in a guilty plea; the terms may be unacceptable to either side or to the judge. Some forms of "inducement" may be inherently unfair or coercive; a plea obtained by such means is involuntary and therefore invalid. For example, a threat to prosecute the accused's spouse as a codefendant (despite lack of evidence) would invalidate the plea because of improper pressure.

b. Enforcement of the Prosecutor's Promise If a plea is based to any significant degree upon the prosecutor's promise, that promise must be fulfilled. If not, either the agreement or promise is specifically enforced or the plea may be withdrawn (Santobello v. New York, 404 U.S. 257 [1971]). In this case, the state of New York indicted Santobello on two felony counts. After negotiations, the prosecutor in charge of the case agreed to permit Santobello to plead guilty to a lesser offense and agreed not to make any recommendation as to the sentence to be imposed. Santobello then pleaded guilty, but during sentencing a few months later, a new prosecutor asked for the maximum sentence to be imposed. The judge imposed the maximum, but he later maintained that the request was not the reason the maximum sentence was imposed and that he was not influenced by it. The defendant moved to withdraw his guilty plea, but the request was denied by the judge. On appeal, the Supreme Court ruled that, once the trial court accepts a guilty plea entered in accordance with a plea bargain, the defendant has a right to have the bargain enforced. Therefore, the judge must decide either to enforce the agreement or to allow the defendant to withdraw the guilty plea. (Read the Santobello v. New York case brief at the end of this chapter.)

To avoid the awkward result of the *Santobello* case, most prosecutors tell the accused what they will recommend or not recommend for a possible sentence in exchange for a guilty plea, but they stipulate that the judge is not legally obligated to honor that recommendation. In many states, the judge is required to ask the parties in open court about the terms of the plea bargain. If the terms are unacceptable, the judge enters a not guilty plea for the defendant and then tries the case. One study found that, about 30 percent of the time, judges asked the defendant if promises other than the plea-bargaining agreement had been made. The same study showed that, in 65 percent of the cases, judges asked defendants if any threats or pressures had caused them to plead guilty. Judges rejected only 2 percent of the guilty pleas encountered in the study.[1]

Since an involuntary plea violates a defendant's constitutional rights, it may be withdrawn at any time. However, what constitutes an involuntary plea is a difficult issue and must be determined by the court on a case-by-case basis. Federal procedure permits a voluntary guilty plea to be withdrawn only before sentence is imposed—except that the court may permit a withdrawal after sentencing "to correct manifest injustice." Some states follow the federal procedure, and others simply do not allow the withdrawal of voluntary pleas.

Plea bargaining is controversial; nonetheless, only a few jurisdictions have abolished it. Among them are Alaska and some counties in Louisiana, Texas, Iowa, Arizona, Michigan, and Oregon. Plea bargains may be prohibited by state law or by agency policy prescribed by chief prosecutors or judges. The predominant view is that, because they reduce the number of cases that come to trial, plea bargains are an essential and necessary part of the criminal justice process.

II. THE PROCEDURE DURING TRIAL
A. The Selection of Jurors

A panel of jurors is assembled according to procedures established by state law. Twenty-three of the fifty states use the voter registration list as the sole source of names for jury duty. Ten states and the District of Columbia use a merged list of voters and holders of driver's licenses.[2] The jury commissioner then sends letters of notification to the prospective jurors with instructions to report at a specific time and place for possible jury duty. Most states have various statutory exemptions for jury duty, the most common of which are undue hardship, bad health, and status as an officer of the court. Many states by law also exempt people in specific occupations, such as doctors, dentists, members of the clergy, elected officials, police officers, fire fighters, teachers, and sole proprietors of businesses.[3]

Prospective jurors may be questioned to determine whether there are grounds for challenge. This process is known as **voir dire,** meaning *"to tell the truth."* In federal courts, the trial judge usually asks the questions, although the judge may permit counsel to conduct the examination or submit questions for the judge to ask the jury. In most state courts, lawyers themselves ask the questions.

The types of jurors chosen by lawyers for trials has, in itself, become an issue. Ideally, jurors in any trial must be impartial, meaning they are not prone to either convict or acquit. In reality, however, neither side wants impartial jurors. Both the prosecutor and the defense want jurors who are sympathetic to their side. The use of consultants by both sides has become common in high-profile criminal cases. For example, both the defense and the prosecution used consultants to choose jurors in the celebrated O. J. Simpson trial and the Menendez brothers trials. There is nothing unconstitutional about this practice, and, unless prohibited by state law, "loading up the jury" will continue—at least in cases where either or both sides can afford to hire jury consultants.

There are two types of challenges to prospective jury members: challenge for cause and peremptory challenge.

1. Challenge for Cause

A **challenge for cause** is a *dismissal of a juror for causes specified by law.* Although the causes vary from state to state, typical causes are that the person is not a qualified voter in the state or county, the person is under indictment for or has been convicted of a felony, the person is insane, the person is a prospective witness for either party in the case, the person served in the grand jury that handed down the indictment, the person has already formed an opinion on the case, or the person is biased for or against the defendant.

2. Peremptory Challenge

A **peremptory challenge** is *a dismissal of a juror for which no reason need be stated.* Thus, such challenges are made entirely at the discretion of each party. The number of peremptory challenges allowed varies from one state to another and may also depend upon the seriousness of the offense. The more serious the offense, the more peremptory challenges may be allowed. For example, the prosecution and the defense may be allowed six peremptory challenges each in misdemeanor cases and twelve in felony cases. For capital offenses, the number may go as high as sixteen or twenty. Peremptory challenges have been identified as a reason minorities are underrepresented in trial juries. Recent Supreme Court decisions hold that peremptory challenges based on race or gender are unconstitutional, if such challenges are, in fact, admitted by the lawyer (which is unlikely) or proved by the opposing party.

B. Opening Statements

1. By the Prosecution

The prosecutor's opening statement acquaints the jury with the nature of the charge against the accused and describes the evidence that will be offered to sustain the charge. Opinions, conclusions, references to the character of the accused, argumentative statements, and references to matters on which evidence will not be offered are out of place, and the defense may object to them.

2. By the Defense

There is a difference of opinion as to the tactical value of an opening statement by the defense. Some argue that the defense should not risk assuming the burden of proving something in the minds of the jury, as would be the case if such a statement were made. Others note that failure to make a statement may imply a weak or nonexistent defense. It is generally considered best for the defense to make its opening statement after the prosecution has presented its entire case; in some jurisdictions, it can be made only at that time.

C. The Presentation of the Case for the Prosecution

After opening the case, the prosecutor offers evidence in support of the charge. Although physical evidence may be introduced, most evidence takes the form of testimony of witnesses. Witnesses are examined in the following order:

1. Direct examination (by the prosecutor)

2. Cross-examination (by the defense lawyer)

3. Redirect examination (by the prosecutor)

4. Recross-examination (by the defense lawyer)

Theoretically, this cycle can continue on and on, but the judge usually puts a stop to the examination of witnesses at this stage. After presenting all its evidence, the prosecution rests its case.

D. The Presentation of the Case for the Defense

When the prosecution has rested, the defendant or the defendant's lawyer opens the defense and offers supporting evidence. Witnesses are examined in the order noted on page 41, with the defense lawyer conducting the direct examination and the prosecutor cross-examining the witness. After presenting all the evidence, the defense rests its case.

1. Motions Prior to the Verdict

Defendants can avail themselves of various motions prior to jury deliberations and a verdict. The most common are motions for acquittal, for a directed verdict of acquittal, and for a mistrial.

a. A Motion for Acquittal In most cases, the defense moves for a judgment of acquittal at the close of the prosecution's case on grounds of failure to establish a **prima facie case**—a *case established by sufficient evidence*; it can be overthrown by evidence presented by the other side. This motion alleges that the prosecution failed to introduce sufficient evidence on a necessary element of the offense charged, such as intent in a homicide. If the motion is denied by the judge (as it usually is), the defendant may renew the motion to acquit at the close of the case.

b. A Motion for a Directed Verdict of Acquittal At the close of the presentation of evidence in a jury trial, the defendant may make a **motion for a directed verdict of acquittal**—again on the grounds that *the prosecution failed to introduce sufficient evidence concerning the offense charged*. A few states do not permit a motion for a directed verdict, on the theory that the right to a jury trial belongs to the prosecution as well as to the accused, so the judge cannot take the case away from the jury. However, most states allow the judge to direct a verdict of acquittal as part of the court's inherent power to prevent a miscarriage of justice through conviction on insufficient evidence. Motions for acquittal or for a directed verdict of acquittal are based on the legal tenet that in a criminal case all elements of the offense—and not just the issue of guilt or innocence—must be proved by the prosecution beyond a reasonable doubt. If the prosecution fails to do this (for example, failing to establish beyond a reasonable doubt that the defendant was present at the scene of the crime), the defense does not have to present its own evidence in order to win an acquittal.

c. A Motion for a Mistrial Improper conduct at trial constitutes grounds for a mistrial (in which the trial is declared invalid). A **motion for a mistrial** may be made prior to jury deliberations. Grounds for a mistrial include such errors as the introduction of inflammatory evidence and prejudicial remarks by the judge or prosecution.

E. Rebuttal Evidence

After both sides have presented their main case, each has an opportunity to present **rebuttal evidence.** This means that the prosecution may present *evidence to destroy the credibility of witnesses or any evidence relied on by the defense, and vice versa.* Cross-examination seeks to destroy the credibility of witnesses, but direct contrary evidence is often more effective. It is particularly so when the defense is an alibi, meaning that the accused maintains that he or she was not at the scene of the crime at the time it was committed.

F. Closing Arguments

In most jurisdictions, the prosecution presents its closing argument first; the defense replies; and the prosecution then offers a final argument to rebut the defense. The prosecution is given two presentations because it bears the heavy burden of proving guilt "beyond a reasonable doubt."

1. The Prosecution's Argument

The prosecution summarizes the evidence and presents theories on how the evidence should be considered to establish the defendant's guilt. The prosecutor's summation may sometimes include improper remarks, to which the defense may object and which (if serious enough) may even lead to a mistrial, new trial, or reversal on appeal.

2. The Defense's Argument

The closing argument by the defense is an important matter of tactics and strategy. Generally, the defense emphasizes the heavy burden of proof placed on the prosecution —namely, proof of the defendant's guilt beyond a reasonable doubt on all elements of the crime charged. The defense then stresses that that obligation has not been met, so the defendant must be acquitted. Neither prosecutor nor defense counsel is permitted to express a personal opinion about the defendant's innocence or guilt. It is improper, for example, for a defense lawyer to tell the jury, "I am personally convinced that my client did not commit the crime." The facts as presented must speak for themselves without the lawyer's interjecting his or her own beliefs.

G. The Judge's Instructions to the Jury

The trial judge must instruct the jury properly on all general principles of law relevant to the charge and the issues raised by the evidence. In some states, judges do this after the closing arguments; other states give judges the option of doing so before or after the closing arguments. For example, in the O. J. Simpson trial, Judge Lance Ito gave his jury instructions before the closing arguments.

Included in these instructions are the elements of the particular offense and the requirement that each element and the defendant's guilt be proved beyond a reasonable doubt. Most states empower the trial judge to comment on the evidence, but some states forbid such comment—leaving the assessment of the nature and credibility of the evidence to the jury. In most criminal cases, the parties—especially defense counsel —will ask the court that certain instructions be used. The court must decide whether to give, refuse, or modify the instructions proposed by the parties; decide which additional instructions it will give; and advise counsel of its decision. Often an informal conference on instructions is held among the judge, prosecutor, and defense counsel, but the decision on what instructions to give rests with the judge. Any errors in the instructions can be challenged on appeal.

H. Jury Deliberation

The foreperson of the jury is usually elected by the jury members immediately after the jury has been instructed by the judge and has retired from the courtroom to start its deliberations. The foreperson presides over the deliberations and gives the verdict to the court once a decision has been reached.

Jury deliberations are conducted in secret, and jurors are not subject to subsequent legal inquiry, regardless of their decision. However, nothing prevents a juror from later voluntarily discussing the details of the deliberation. Jurisdictions differ as to whether members of a jury—during the trial and/or during deliberations—should be kept together (sequestered) or allowed to return to their respective homes at night or during weekends. **Sequestration** is most often imposed in sensational cases. Most states permit the trial judge to order sequestration at his or her discretion. How long a jury should be kept in deliberation in case of jury indecision is up to the judge.

Concerns about possible jury nullification have arisen primarily as a result of the much-debated verdicts in certain high-profile cases, including the O. J. Simpson trial and the first Menendez brothers trial. **Jury nullification** refers to instances *when the jury decides a case contrary to the weight of the evidence presented during trial.* Jury nullification, a term used extensively by the media and the public, is difficult to prove or disprove and does not have much legal significance for purposes of an appeal. If a jury decides to acquit a defendant, charges based on the same offense cannot be brought again, regardless of the weight of the evidence presented during the trial.

I. The Verdict—Guilty or Not Guilty

A jury or judge's **verdict** is *the pronouncement of guilt or innocence*—"guilty" or "not guilty." In some states, a third verdict is "not guilty by reason of insanity"—in which case a civil proceeding follows to have the defendant committed to a mental institution. In federal and most state trials, the jury vote for conviction or acquittal must be unanimous. Failure to reach a unanimous vote either way results in a hung jury and a mistrial. The length of time a jury must deliberate before a hung jury is declared is determined by the judge. If the jury is dismissed by the judge because it cannot agree on the result, the case may be tried again before another jury. There is no double jeopardy, because the first jury did not agree on a verdict.

The U.S. Supreme Court has held that state laws providing for a less-than-unanimous vote for conviction are constitutional and will be upheld—at least in the case of a required 10-to-2 vote (Apodaca v. Oregon, 406 U.S. 404 [1972]). A law providing for a 9-to-3 jury vote for conviction is also constitutional (Johnson v. Louisiana, 406 U.S. 356 [1972]). (Read the Apodaca v. Oregon case brief at the end of this chapter.)

The U.S. Supreme Court has decided that a state law providing for a six-member jury in all criminal cases, except those involving the death penalty, is valid. Most states, however, provide for twelve-member juries in felony trials (Williams v. Florida, 399 U.S. 78 [1970]). Unlike those of twelve-member juries, the verdicts of six-member juries must be unanimous (Burch v. Louisiana, 441 U.S. 130 [1979]). But the Court has also decided that five-person juries are unconstitutional because they would not permit effective group discussion; would diminish the chances of drawing from a fair, representative cross-section of the community; and might impair the accuracy of fact finding (Ballew v. Georgia, 435 U.S. 223 [1978]).

After the jury has announced its verdict, the defendant has a right to have the jury polled. The jury must then express its vote in open court, either as a group or individually.

III. THE PROCEDURE AFTER TRIAL

A. Sentencing

Sentencing is *the formal pronouncement of judgment by the court or judge on the defendant after conviction in a criminal prosecution, imposing the punishment to be inflicted.*[4] In most states, sentences are imposed by the judge only; but in a few states, the defendant may choose to be sentenced by the judge or the jury after a jury trial. In capital cases, states generally require that no death sentence be imposed unless by the jury of twelve members after a jury trial. Some states and the federal government follow sentencing guidelines, curtailing the judicial discretion inherent in indeterminate sentencing; other jurisdictions do not have sentencing guidelines and leave a lot more discretion to judges.

The imposition of sentence usually does not immediately follow a guilty verdict, particularly for serious offenses. This is because many states require that a presentence investigation report (PSIR) be prepared to help determine the proper sentence. The

PSIR is either required by law or ordered by the judge; it is usually prepared by a probation officer or the probation department. The last part of a PSIR often contains a recommendation by the probation officer as to what sentence might properly be imposed in view of all the circumstances surrounding the case and the defendant.

In plea-bargained cases, the sentence is imposed by the judge, but most judges merely follow the sentence agreed on by the prosecutor and the defense lawyer or the accused. Although the sentencing power is associated with and assigned to the judge, the actual sentence imposed is the result of several influences. First, there is the legislature, which determines the fixed or maximum and minimum penalty to be imposed. The prosecutor and defense lawyer usually determine the sentence to be given in plea-bargained cases. For serious offenses, the probation officer is ordered by law or the judge to conduct a PSIR, which usually contains a recommended sentence. Whatever prison term is set by the judge is subject to the provisions of the parole law in states that use determinate sentencing. Parole boards thus have a say as to how long an inmate stays in prison. Finally, in practically all states, the governor can issue a pardon or a commutation of the sentence.

In states where juries may impose the sentence at the option of the accused, juries usually determine guilt or innocence and, for a verdict of guilty, decide on the sentence at the same time. Some states, however, have a **bifurcated procedure,** in which *the guilt-innocence stage and the sentencing stage are separate.* In those states, after a defendant is found guilty, the jury receives evidence from the prosecution and the defense concerning the penalty to be imposed. The rules of evidence are relaxed at this stage, so evidence not heard during the trial (such as the previous record of the accused and his or her inclination to violence) may be brought out. The jury deliberates a second time to determine the penalty.

Most states give the sentencing power to the judge, even when the case is tried before a jury. After receiving a guilty verdict from the jury, the judge usually postpones sentencing for a couple of weeks. The delay enables him or her to hear posttrial motions (such as a motion for a new trial or a directed verdict) and to order a probation officer to conduct a presentence investigation. The judge has the option of using the presentence investigation report in any manner, meaning that he or she may accept any recommendation made by the probation officer or disregard it completely. Despite controversy, most states now allow the defense lawyer or the accused to see the PSIR, thus affording an opportunity to rebut any false or unfair information contained in the PSIR.

B. Appeal

After the sentence is imposed, there is usually a period of time (such as thirty days) during which the defendant may appeal the conviction and sentence to a higher court. There is no constitutional right to appeal, but all states grant defendants that right by law or court procedure. In some states, death penalty cases go straight from the trial court to the state supreme court, bypassing state courts of appeals.

Theoretically, any criminal case may go as high as the U.S. Supreme Court on appeal, as long as either federal law or constitutional issues are involved. In reality, however, the right is curtailed by the Rule of Four—the practice of the Court of deciding an appealed case on its merits only if four out of the nine Court members favor doing so. Out of the thousands of cases brought to the Court each year, comparatively few are actually heard on their merits. If the Court refuses to hear a case, the decision of the immediate lower court (be that a state supreme court or a federal court of appeals) holds. In cases that do not involve any federal issue—as when an appeal is based solely on a state constitutional provision or a state law, with no reference to any federal law or constitutional right—decisions by state supreme courts are final and unappealable. If an appeal succeeds and the conviction is reversed, the defendant can be tried again for the same offense, because by appealing a conviction a defendant is deemed to have waived his or her right to protection against double jeopardy. The decision whether to prosecute again is made by the prosecutor. However, if the conviction is reversed on appeal because there was not enough evidence to support a conviction, there cannot be a new trial.

C. Habeas Corpus

While a person is in prison for however long a time (for example, a prisoner has served fifteen years of a twenty-year sentence), and the appellate process has been exhausted, he or she can file a writ of habeas corpus alleging that the incarceration is unconstitutional and invalid. **Habeas corpus** (a Latin term that literally means "you have the body") is *a writ directed to any person detaining another, commanding that person (usually a sheriff or a prison warden) to produce the body of the prisoner in court and to explain why detention is justified and should be continued.* It is a remedy against any type of illegal restraint by the government and is frequently called the Great Writ of Liberty. Habeas corpus is always available to anyone deprived of freedom, although successful filings are rare.

A writ of habeas corpus is distinguished from an appeal primarily in that a writ is usually filed to secure a person's release from prison after appeals on the conviction have been exhausted and after the defendant has started serving time. It is a separate proceeding from the criminal case that led to the conviction. (See Table 2.3.) The main difference between an appeal and a habeas corpus case may be illustrated as follows: Suppose X is charged with, tried, and convicted of murder in California. The murder case is titled "State of California v. X." Right after conviction, X may appeal her conviction through the California courts and up to the U.S. Supreme Court (if a federal or constitutional question is involved). Suppose X has exhausted her appeals and her conviction has been upheld by the appellate courts. X must now serve time in a California prison. While serving time, X obtains or discovers evidence that the jury in her trial was tampered with by the prosecution. X can no longer file an appeal because that process has long been exhausted. But she can file a writ of habeas corpus seeking her release. The title of the case will be "X v. Y," Y being the director of the California prison that is detaining her. Even if X wins her release, however, she may be tried again for the same offense. Her filing a habeas case constitutes a waiver of her right to protection against

TABLE 2.3 *Appeal and Habeas Corpus Compared*

Appeal	Writ of Habeus Corpus
1. A direct attack upon the conviction	1. A collateral attack, meaning a separate case from the criminal conviction
2. Part of the criminal proceeding	2. A civil proceeding
3. Purpose is to reverse conviction	3. Purpose is to secure release from prison
4. Filed only after conviction	4. May be filed any time a person is deprived of freedom illegally by a public officer, before or after conviction
5. Accused has been convicted but may be free on bail	5. Person is serving time or is detained illegally; cannot be filed if person is free
6. Based on any type of error made during the trial	6. Based on a violation of a constitutional right, usually during the trial
7. Must be undertaken within a certain period of time after conviction; otherwise, the right of action lapses	7. Right of action does not lapse; may be filed even while person is serving time in prison
8. All issues must be raised from the trial record	8. New testimony may be presented

double jeopardy since she is, in essence, saying, "Give me a new trial; the first one was unconstitutional or invalid."

IV. CAUTION: THE PROCEDURE MAY NOT BE WHAT THIS BOOK SAYS IT IS

A. Application to Felony Cases

The procedure just outlined applies mainly to felony cases. Misdemeanors and petty offenses are usually processed in a simpler and more expeditious way. Whether a crime is a felony or a misdemeanor depends on the law of the state and so can vary from one state to another. Generally, a **felony** is a *crime punishable by death or imprisonment in a state prison* (as opposed to imprisonment in a local jail), or is a crime for which the punishment is imprisonment for more than one year. All other criminal offenses are considered **misdemeanors.**

B. Variation among States

The procedure just discussed applies in federal court and in most state courts. However, there are differences from state to state, and the terms used may vary. For example, some states use the grand jury for charging a person with a serious crime, while others do not use a grand jury at all. Some states allow jury trial for all offenses, while others impose restrictions. As long as a particular procedure is not required by the U.S. Constitution, states do not have to use it. Although criminal procedure has largely been "nationalized," discretion still abounds, particularly when the exercise of such discretion is not considered a violation of fundamental rights.

C. Variation within a State

Likewise, there may be variations in procedure among different courts in a given state even though all are governed by a single state code of criminal procedure. Thus, the procedures used in, say, the courts of San Francisco to process felony or misdemeanor offenses may not be exactly the same as those in Los Angeles. Differences exist because of the idiosyncrasies and preferences of judicial personnel or long-standing practices peculiar to a jurisdiction. For example, some jurisdictions hold preliminary hearings in all cases, while others hardly ever hold preliminary hearings. Some jurisdictions refer misdemeanor cases to a grand jury; others do not. Certain cities may hold a suspect for a maximum of forty-eight hours without a hearing; other cities hold night court to ensure that detainees are given a hearing almost immediately. Variations in procedure are tolerated by the courts as long as they are not violations of the law or basic constitutional rights.

D. Theory versus Reality

The procedures just outlined, as well as those found in codes and textbooks, are the prescribed procedures. But there may be differences between the ideal (prescribed) procedure and reality (the procedures actually used by local criminal justice agencies). Many agencies have their own "convenient" and "traditional" ways of doing things, which may be at odds with procedures prescribed by law or court decisions. Nevertheless, these procedures continue to be used, either because of ignorance or because they have not been challenged. In some cases, courts tolerate certain practices as long as they do not grossly compromise the constitutional and statutory rights of the accused.

Summary

Our criminal justice process involves proceedings before trial, during trial, and after trial. Procedure before trial covers the time from the filing of the complaint to the time of the defendant's plea. Procedure during trial begins with the selection of jurors and ends with a verdict of conviction or acquittal (or a mistrial). Procedure after trial involves sentencing and appeal. Even after the appeals process has been exhausted, habeas corpus is always available to a prisoner who can establish that he or she is in prison unconstitutionally or without a valid justification.

Overview of the Criminal Justice Process

I. PROCEDURE BEFORE TRIAL

A. Filing of complaint: By offended party or a police officer.

B. Arrest: With or without a warrant. Sometimes a citation or summons is used instead of an arrest.

C. Booking: Recording the suspect's name, time of arrest, and offense involved; inventorying his or her belongings; photographing and finger-printing him or her; and so on.

D. Appearance before magistrate: Without unnecessary delay. The arrestee is made aware of his or her rights.

E. Bail: Set by the magistrate; or the defendant is released on his or her own recognizance.

F. Preliminary examination: Usually held for determination of probable cause, for discovery purposes, or for determination to bind over. Not required when there is a prior indictment, when a misdemeanor is involved, or when waived.

G. Decision to charge: The prosecutor has the discretion to charge or not to charge. The decision is usually not reviewable or appealable.

H. Indictment or information: An indictment is a charge made by the grand jury; an information is a charge filed by the prosecutor. An indictment is required in most states for serious offenses.

I. Arraignment: The accused appears before a judge, is informed of the charges, and is asked how he or she pleads.

J. Plea: Nolo contendere, not guilty, or guilty.

II. PROCEDURE DURING TRIAL

A. Selection of jurors: Use of voir dire. Types of challenges include for cause and peremptory.

B. Opening statements: By prosecution and defense, each summarizing the evidence to be presented and their version of the case.

C. Presentation by prosecution: The offer of evidence supporting the charge.

D. Presentation by defense: The offer of evidence for the accused. Before the defense starts or after it rests, a motion may be filed for acquittal, a directed verdict of acquittal, or a mistrial. Motions are usually rejected by the court.

E. Rebuttal evidence: Evidence presented by either side to destroy the credibility of witnesses or evidence presented by the other side.

F. Closing arguments: By the prosecution and then by the defense.

Overview of the Criminal Justice Process (continued)

    G. Judge's instructions to jury: Includes the elements of the offense charged and the caution that each element must be proved beyond a reasonable doubt.

    H. Jury deliberation: Jurors may be sequestered, at the option of the judge. How long a jury is to deliberate, in case of indecision, is up to the judge.

    I. Verdict: Pronouncement of guilt or innocence. If guilty, sentencing follows, but not necessarily immediately.

III. PROCEDURE AFTER TRIAL

    A. Sentencing: Punishment handed down by judge or jury, depending on state law.

    B. Appeal: Allowed within a certain period of time. There is no constitutional right to appeal, but it is allowed in all states by law. Theoretically, an appeal may go to the U.S. Supreme Court; in reality, few appeals are accepted by the Court, so the decision of the court where the case came from holds.

    C. Habeas corpus: May be filed any time during incarceration; the petitioner seeks release from incarceration, alleging that the incarceration is illegal or unconstitutional.

    The federal courts and practically all states follow a code of criminal procedure that details the procedure to be used in processing offenders in their respective jurisdictions. It is important for a law enforcement officer to know exactly what is prescribed by law for his or her jurisdiction, because the officer will be held accountable for that procedure as prescribed by the legislature and interpreted by the courts of the state.

Review Questions

1. What are the two kinds of arrests? Discuss how each is initiated.

2. Distinguish between a grand jury and a trial jury.

3. What is the advantage of a nolo contendere plea over a guilty plea, from the defendant's point of view?

4. Distinguish between challenge for cause and peremptory challenge in jury trials.

5. What is a motion to suppress evidence?

6. Suppose a state passed a law saying that a nonunanimous jury vote can result in conviction. Would the law be constitutional? Discuss.

7. Define sentencing.

8. What is meant by a bifurcated trial procedure?

9. Give four distinctions between a criminal case and a civil case.

10. What is the main distinction between an appeal and a writ of habeas corpus?

Key Terms and Definitions

arraignment: A procedure by which, at a scheduled time and after prior notice, the accused is called into court, informed of the charges against him or her, and asked how he or she pleads.

bail: The security required by the court and given by the accused to ensure that the accused appears before the proper court at the scheduled time and place to answer the charges brought against him or her.

bifurcated procedure: A trial in which the determination of guilt or innocence and sentencing are separate.

bill of indictment: A document submitted to the grand jury by the prosecutor, accusing a person of a crime.

booking: The making of an entry in the police blotter or arrest book, indicating the suspect's name, the time of arrest, and the offense involved. If the crime is serious, the suspect may also be photographed or fingerprinted.

capias: A warrant issued by a judge, requiring an officer to take a named defendant into custody.

challenge for cause: A challenge to the fitness of a person for jury membership on the basis of causes specified by law.

citation: An order issued by a court or law enforcement offi-cer commanding the person to whom the citation is issued to appear in court at a specified time to answer certain charges.

complaint: A charge made before a proper officer, alleging the commission of a criminal offense.

discovery: A procedure used by either party in a case to obtain information that is in the hands of the other party and is neces-sary or helpful in developing the case.

exclusionary rule: The exclu-sion in court of evidence ille-gally obtained.

felony: A criminal offense pun-ishable by death or imprison-ment of more than one year.

grand jury: A jury, usually composed of from twelve to twenty-three members, that determines whether a suspect should be charged with an offense. A grand jury indict-ment is required in some states only for serious offenses.

habeas corpus: Literally, "you have the body"; it is a remedy used if a person seeks release from an allegedly illegal or unconstitutional confinement.

indictment: A written accusa-tion filed against the defendant by a grand jury, usually signed by the jury foreperson.

information: A written accusa-tion of a crime, prepared by the prosecuting attorney without referring the case to a grand jury.

jury nullification: The situation in which a jury decides a case contrary to the weight of the evidence.

Miranda warnings: Warnings informing suspects of their right to remain silent, the fact that anything they say can be used against them in a court of law, their right to counsel, and the fact that, if they are indi-gent, counsel will be provided by the state.

misdemeanor: A crime punish-able by a fine or imprisonment for less than one year; not as serious as a felony.

motion for a directed verdict of acquittal: A motion by the defendant at the close of the presentation of evidence in a jury trial, asking the court for an acquittal on the grounds that the prosecution failed to introduce sufficient evidence concerning the offense charged.

motion for a mistrial: A motion filed by the defense seeking dis-missal of the charges because of improper conduct on the part of the prosecution, judge, jury, or witnesses during the trial.

nolle proseque: A motion filed by the prosecutor that seeks dismissal of the charges.

nolo contendere plea: Literally, "no contest"; a plea made when the defendant does not contest the charges. The effect is the same as that of a guilty plea, except that the plea cannot be used against the defendant as an admission in any subsequent civil proceeding arising out of the same offense.

peremptory challenge: A challenge to a prospective juror without stating a reason; the challenge is made entirely at the discretion of the challenging party. This is the opposite of "challenge for cause," in which a reason for the challenge, usually specified by law, must be stated.

plea: An accused's response in court to the indictment or information that is read to the accused in court.

plea bargaining: A process whereby a defendant is induced to plead guilty, to save the time, expense, and uncertainty of a trial, usually in exchange for a lighter sentence.

preliminary examination (or hearing): A hearing held before a magistrate to determine whether there is probable cause to support the charges against the accused. This takes place before the grand jury hearing.

preventive detention: The detention of an accused person, not for purposes of ensuring his or her appearance in court, but to prevent possible harm to society by dangerous individuals.

prima facie case: A case established by sufficient evidence; it can be overthrown by contrary evidence presented by the other side.

rebuttal evidence: Evidence introduced by one party in the case to discredit the evidence given by the other side.

release on recognizance (ROR): An arrangement whereby the court, on the basis of the defendant's promise to appear in court as required, releases the defendant without requiring him or her to post money or securities.

sentencing: The formal pronouncement of judgment by the court or judge on the defendant after conviction in a criminal prosecution, imposing the punishment to be inflicted.

sequestration: The practice of keeping members of the jury together and in isolation during a jury trial, to prevent their decision from being influenced by outside factors.

summons: A writ directed to the sheriff or other proper officer, requiring the officer to notify the person named that he or she is required to appear in court on a day named and answer the complaint stated in the summons.

verdict: A jury or judge's pronouncement of guilt or innocence.

voir dire: Literally, "to tell the truth"; a process whereby prospective jurors may be questioned by the judge or lawyers to determine whether there are grounds for challenge.

 ## Principles of Cases

Apodaca v. Oregon, 406 U.S. 404 (1972) State laws providing for a less-than-unanimous vote for conviction are constitutional, at least in the case of a required 10-to-2 vote.

Ballew v. Georgia, 435 U.S. 223 (1978) Five-person juries are unconstitutional, because they would not provide effective group discussion; would diminish the chances of drawing from a fair, representative cross-section of the community; and might impair the accuracy of fact finding.

Boykin v. Alabama, 395 U.S. 238 (1969) When a defendant pleads guilty, the record must affirmatively show that the plea was voluntary and that the accused had a full understanding of its consequences. Otherwise, the plea is invalid.

Brady v. United States, 397 U.S. 742 (1970) A plea of guilty that represents an intelligent choice among alternatives available to the defendant—especially when represented by competent counsel—is not involuntary simply because it is entered in the hope of avoiding the death penalty. If otherwise voluntary and informed, the plea is valid.

Burch v. Louisiana, 441 U.S. 130 (1979) Unlike those of twelve-member juries, the verdicts of six-member juries must be unanimous.

County of Riverside v. McLaughlin, 111 S.Ct. 1661 (1991) Detention of a suspect for forty-eight hours without any probable cause hearing is presumptively reasonable. If the time to hearing is longer than that, the burden of proof shifts to the police to prove reasonableness. But if the time to hearing is shorter, the burden of proof to establish unreasonable delay rests on the person detained.

Johnson v. Louisiana, 406 U.S. 356 (1972) A law providing for a 9-to-3 jury vote for conviction is constitutional.

North Carolina v. Alford, 400 U.S. 25 (1979) A guilty plea is not invalid simply because the defendant does not admit guilt, or even continues to assert innocence, provided that there is some basis in the record for the plea. All that is required for a valid guilty plea

is a knowing waiver of the rights involved, not an admission of guilt.

Santobello v. New York, 404 U.S. 257 (1971) Once the court has accepted a guilty plea entered in accordance with a plea bargain, the defendant has a right to have the bargain enforced. If the prosecution does not keep the bargain, the court should decide whether the circumstances require enforcement of the plea bargain or whether the defendant should be granted an opportunity to withdraw the guilty plea.

United States v. Williams, 112 S.Ct. 1735 (1992) The grand jury belongs to no branch of the institutional government; it is an independent body, intended to serve as a buffer between the government and people who are charged with crimes.

Williams v. Florida, 399 U.S. 78 (1970) A state law providing for a six-member jury in all criminal cases, except those involving the death penalty, is valid.

 # Case Briefs

The Leading Case on Plea Bargaining

Santobello v. New York, 404 U.S. 257 (1971)

Facts: The state of New York indicted Santobello on two felony counts. After negotiations, the assistant district attorney in charge of the case agreed to permit Santobello to plead guilty to a lesser offense and agreed not to make any recommendation as to the sentence. Santobello then pleaded guilty, but during sentencing a few months later, a new assistant district attorney asked for the maximum sentence to be imposed. The judge imposed the maximum but later maintained that the request was not the reason the maximum was imposed and that he was not influenced by it. The defendant moved to withdraw his guilty plea, but the request was denied.

Issue: May a plea be withdrawn if the prosecution fails to fulfill all its promises, even if the result would have been the same had the prosecution kept its promise? Yes.

Supreme Court Decision: Once the court has accepted a guilty plea entered in accordance with a plea bargain, the defendant has a right to have the bargain enforced. If the prosecution does not keep the bargain, a court should decide whether the circum-

stances require enforcement of the plea bargain or whether the defendant should be granted an opportunity to withdraw the guilty plea. In this case, the broken promise (although not maliciously broken) by the prosecutor to make no sentencing recommendation pursuant to a guilty plea is sufficient to vacate the judgment and remand the case back to the trial court.

Case Significance: Santobello gives reliability to the bargaining process, in that the defendant can now rely on the promise of the prosecutor. If the defendant relied on that promise as an incentive for pleading guilty and the promise is not kept, the guilty plea can be withdrawn.

Excerpts from the Decision: "The plea must, of course, be voluntary and knowing and if it was induced by promises, the essence of those promises must in some way be made known. There is, of course, no absolute right to have a guilty plea accepted. A court may reject a plea in exercise of sound judicial discretion.

"This phase of the process of criminal justice, and the adjudicative element inherent in accepting a plea of guilty, must be attended by safeguards to ensure the defendant what is reasonably due in the circumstances. Those circumstances will vary, but a constant factor is that when a plea rests in any significant degree on a promise or agreement of the prosecutor, so that it can be said to be part of the inducement or consideration, such promise must be fulfilled.

"On this record, petitioner 'bargained' and negotiated for a particular plea in order to secure dismissal of more serious charges, but also on condition that no sentence recommendation would be made by the prosecutor. It is now conceded that the promise to abstain from a recommendation was made, and at this stage the prosecution is not in a good position to argue that its inadvertent breach of agreement is immaterial. The staff lawyers in a prosecutor's office have the burden of 'letting the left hand know what the right hand is doing' or has done. That the breach of agreement was inadvertent does not lessen its impact.

"We need not reach the question whether the sentencing judge would or would not have been influenced had he known all the details of the negotiations for the plea. He stated that the prosecutor's recommendation did not influence him and we have no reason to doubt that. Nevertheless, we conclude that the interests of justice and appropriate recognition of the duties of the prosecution in relation to promises made in the negotiation of pleas of guilty will be best served by remanding the case to the state courts for further consideration. The ultimate relief for which petitioner is entitled we leave to the discretion of the state court, which is in a better position to decide whether the circumstances of this case require only that there be specific performance of the agreement on the plea, in which case petitioner should be resentenced by a different judge, or whether, in the view of the state court, the circumstances require granting the relief sought by petitioner, i.e., the opportunity to withdraw his plea of guilty. We emphasize that this is in no sense to question the fairness of the sentencing judge; the fault here rests on the prosecutor, not on the sentencing judge.

"Vacated and remanded."

The Leading Case on Nonunanimous Juries

Apodaca v. Oregon, 406 U.S. 404 (1972)

Facts: Apodaca, Cooper, and Madden were convicted respectively of assault with a deadly weapon, burglary on a dwelling, and general larceny before separate Oregon juries. None of the convictions was unanimous. The vote in the cases of Apodaca and Madden was 11 to 1, and the vote in Cooper's case was 10 to 2. Oregon law provided that a defendant could be con-

victed even if the vote was 10 to 2 for conviction. All three defendants appealed, alleging that a less-than-unanimous jury violates the right to trial by jury in criminal cases specified by the Sixth and the Fourteenth Amendments.

Issue: *Does a state law that provides for conviction on a less-than-unanimous vote violate the Sixth Amendment provision on the right to jury trial? No.*

Supreme Court Decision: Although the right to a jury trial has been incorporated and held applicable to the states through the Fourteenth Amendment, the unanimous-verdict aspect of this right is not so fundamental as to be required by due process. Therefore, although the states must give the defendant a jury trial, they do not have to provide for a unanimous verdict.

Case Significance: This decision held, by a 5-to-4 vote, that there is nothing in the Constitution that requires states to convict defendants only by unanimous vote of the jury. The Court rejected the argument that a unanimous jury is required to give substance to the "reasonable doubt" standard of the Due Process Clause, saying that the "reasonable doubt" standard developed separately from both the jury trial and the unanimous verdict. Note that the nonunanimous decision in Oregon was allowable by virtue of statute. Although not many states have passed nonunanimous jury statutes, the message in *Apodaca* is clear—that the Constitution does not require unanimous juries. In the case of Oregon, the law provided for a minimum vote of 10 to 2 for conviction. Whether a 9-to-3, 8-to-4, or 7-to-5 vote would also be constitutional was not decided by the Court. The result of the decision is that defendants may receive lesser jury protection in state than in federal courts, if the state legislature so wishes.

Excerpts from the Decision: "Our inquiry must focus upon the function served by the jury in contemporary society. As we said in *Duncan*, the purpose of trial by jury is to prevent oppression by the Government by providing a 'safeguard against the corrupt or overzealous prosecutor and against the compliant, biased, or eccentric judge.' Duncan v. Louisiana, 391 U.S., at 156. 'Given this purpose, the essential feature of a jury obviously lies in the interposition between the accused and his accuser of the commonsense judgment of a group of laymen. . . .' Williams v. Florida, supra, at 100. A requirement of unanimity, however, does not materially contribute to the exercise of this commonsense judgment. As we said in *Williams,* a jury will come to such a judgment as long as it consists of a group of laymen representative of a cross section of the community who have the duty and the opportunity to deliberate, free from outside attempts at intimidation, on the question of a defendant's guilt. In terms of this function we perceive no difference between juries required to act unanimously and those permitted to convict or acquit by votes of 10 to two or 11 to one. Requiring unanimity would obviously produce hung juries in some situations where nonunanimous juries will convict or acquit. But in either case, the interest of the defendant in having the judgment of his peers interposed between himself and the officers of the State who prosecute and judge him is equally well served.

"Petitioners nevertheless argue that unanimity serves other purposes constitutionally essential to the continued operation of the jury system. Their principal contention is that a Sixth Amendment 'jury trial' made mandatory on the States by virtue of the Due Process Clause of the Fourteenth Amendment, Duncan v. Louisiana, supra, should be held to require a unanimous jury verdict in order to give substance to the reasonable doubt standard otherwise mandated by the Due Process Clause.

"We are quite sure, however, that the Sixth Amendment itself has never been held to require proof beyond a reasonable doubt in criminal cases. The reasonable doubt standard developed separately from both the jury trial and the unanimous verdict. As the Court noted in the *Winship* case, the rule requiring proof of crime beyond a reasonable doubt did not crystallize in this country until after the Constitution was adopted. And in that case, which held such a burden of proof to be constitutionally required, the Court purported to draw no support from the Sixth Amendment."

Notes

1. Bureau of Justice Statistics, *Report to the Nation on Crime and Justice* (Washington, DC: U.S. Government Printing Office, 1983), p. 65.

2. Ibid., p. 67.

3. Ibid.

4. *Black's Law Dictionary* (St. Paul, MN: West, 1968), p. 1528.

II. Levels of Proof and the Exclusionary Rule

3.

Probable Cause
and Reasonable Suspicion

What You Will Learn in This Chapter

You will become familiar with both the theoretical and the practical meaning of probable cause. Probable cause is arguably the most important concept in policing, because it must be present for many police actions to be valid. You will learn the three general ways whereby probable cause is established and how it compares with other levels of proof required in various aspects of police work. You will also learn about reasonable suspicion and how it compares to probable cause. Finally, you will discover who has the final say as to whether probable cause or reasonable suspicion exists—the trial court or the appellate court.

Introduction

If there is one legal term with which police officers must be thoroughly familiar, it is probable cause. That term is used extensively in police work and often determines whether the police acted lawfully. If the police acted lawfully, the arrest is valid and the evidence obtained is admissible in court. Without probable cause, the evidence will be thrown out of court. In one case, the Supreme Court stated, "The general rule is that every arrest, and every seizure having the essential attributes of a formal arrest, is unreasonable unless it is supported by probable cause" (Michigan v. Summers, 452 U.S. 692 [1981]). The "probable cause" requirement in police work is based on the Fourth Amendment of the U.S. Constitution, which states, "The right of the people to be secure in their persons, houses, papers, and effects, against unreasonable searches and seizures, shall not be violated, and no Warrants shall issue, but upon probable cause. . . ."

Another legal term often used in policing is reasonable suspicion. With reasonable suspicion, police can stop and frisk, but it cannot be the basis for a valid arrest. While we know that reasonable suspicion has a lower degree of certainty than probable cause, the two terms are sometimes difficult to distinguish because they can be subjective. Determinations of probable cause and reasonable suspicion during trial are made by the trial court, but such determination can be reviewed by appellate courts if the case is appealed.

I. WHAT CONSTITUTES PROBABLE CAUSE?

A. Probable Cause Defined

Probable cause has been defined by the Supreme Court as *more than bare suspicion; it exists when "the facts and circumstances within the officers' knowledge and of which they had reasonably trustworthy information are sufficient in themselves to warrant a man of reasonable caution in the belief that an offense has been or is being committed."* The Court added, "The substance of all the definitions of probable cause is a reasonable ground for belief of guilt . . ." (Brinegar v. United States, 338 U.S. 160 [1949]). In the words of one observer:

> The Court measures probable cause by the test of *reasonableness,* a necessarily subjective standard that falls between mere suspicion and certainty. Facts and circumstances leading to an arrest or seizure must be sufficient to persuade a reasonable person that an illegal act has been or is being committed. Always the test involves the consideration of a particular suspicion and a specific set of facts. Hunches or generalized suspicions are not reasonable grounds for concluding that probable cause exists.[1]

B. "Man of Reasonable Caution"

The term **"man of reasonable caution"** (some courts use the term "reasonable man" or "ordinarily prudent and cautious man") does not refer to a person with training in the law, such as a magistrate or lawyer. Instead, it refers to *the average "man on the street"* (for instance, a mechanic, butcher, baker, or teacher) who, under the same circumstances, would believe that the person being arrested had committed the offense or that items to be seized would be found in a particular place. Despite this, however, the experience of the police officer must be considered in determining whether probable cause existed in a specific situation. In United States v. Ortiz, 422 U.S. 891 (1975), the Court ruled that "officers are entitled to draw reasonable inferences from these facts in light of their knowledge of the area and their prior experience with aliens and smugglers." Given their work experience, training, and background, police officers are better qualified than the average person in the street to evaluate certain facts and circumstances. Thus, what may not amount to probable cause to an untrained person may be sufficient for probable cause in the estimation of a police officer because of his or her training and experience. This is particularly true in property or drug cases, in which what may look like an innocent activity to an untrained person may indicate to a police officer that a criminal act is taking place.

AT A GLANCE

The Legal versus the Practical Definition of Probable Cause

LEGAL DEFINITION: Probable cause exists when "the facts and circumstances within the officers' knowledge and of which they had reasonably trustworthy information are sufficient in themselves to warrant a man of reasonable caution in the belief that an offense has been or is being committed."

PRACTICAL DEFINITION: Probable cause exists when it is more likely than not (more than 50 percent certainty) that the suspect committed an offense or that the items sought can be found in a certain place.

C. A Practical Definition— More Than 50 Percent Certainty

For practical purposes, probable cause exists when an officer has trustworthy evidence sufficient to make "a reasonable person" think it more likely than not that the proposed arrest or search is justified. In mathematical terms, this means that the officer (in cases of arrest or search without a warrant) or the magistrate (in cases of arrest or search with a warrant) is more than 50 percent certain that the suspect has committed the offense or that the items can be found in a certain place. It is important to note, however, that the "more than 50 percent" certainty standard is a very safe estimate of the degree of certainty for probable cause. Most courts would probably be satisfied with something less than a 50 percent certainty. For instance, in Illinois v. Gates, 462 U.S. 213 (1983), the Court ruled:

> Probable cause is a fluid concept—turning on the assessment of probabilities in particular factual contexts—not readily, or even usefully, reduced to a neat set of legal rules. . . . While an effort to fix some general, numerically precise degree of certainty corresponding to "probable cause" may not be helpful, it is clear that "only the probability, and not a prima facie showing, of criminal activity is the standard of probable cause."

D. Who Determines Probable Cause?

In searches and seizures without a warrant, probable cause is determined by the officer initially. In searches and seizures with a warrant, the initial determination is made by the magistrate who issued the warrant. Both determinations are reviewable by the trial court or by an appellate court if the case is later appealed.

Since probable cause, if later challenged in court, must be established by police testimony in warrantless arrests or searches, it is important that the police officer observe keenly and take careful notes of the facts and circumstances establishing that probable cause existed at the time he or she acted. For example, if an officer arrests a person seen coming out of a building at midnight, the officer must be able to articulate (if asked to do so later in court) what factors led him or her to make the arrest—such as the furtive behavior of the suspect, nervousness when being questioned, possession of what appear to be stolen items, and prior criminal record.

E.   When Are Arrests and Searches Illegal?

If no probable cause existed at the time the officer took action, the fact that probable cause is later established does not make the act legal; the evidence obtained cannot be used in court. For example, suppose an officer arrests a suspicious-looking person, and a body search reveals that the person had several vials of cocaine in her pocket. The evidence obtained cannot be used in court because there was no probable cause to make the arrest.

When officers seek to obtain a warrant from a magistrate, it is important that the affidavit itself establishes probable cause. This is because what is not included in the affidavit cannot be used to determine probable cause even if the officer knew about that information at the time the affidavit was submitted. For example, suppose Officer P states in the affidavit that her information came from an informant. If this is insufficient to establish probable cause, the fact that Officer P in fact had a second informant who added information to that given by the first informant cannot save the warrant from being invalid if that fact is not included in the affidavit (Whiteley v. Warden, 401 U.S. 560 [1971]). In short, what is not in the affidavit does not count toward establishing probable cause.

Probable cause is never established by what turns up after the initial illegal act. Suspicion alone is never sufficient grounds for an arrest. However, what starts off as mere suspicion can develop into probable cause sufficient to make an arrest. For example, suppose a police officer asks questions of a motorist who failed to stop at a stop sign. The officer suspects that the driver may be drunk. If the initial inquiries show that the driver is, in fact, drunk, then the officer may make a valid arrest. Also, any evidence obtained as a result of the arrest is admissible in court.

An officer may have probable cause to arrest without having personally observed the commission of the crime. For example, suppose that, while out on patrol, an officer is told by a motorist that a robbery is taking place in a store down the block. The officer proceeds to the store and sees a man running toward a car with goods in his hands. The man sees the police car, drops the items, gets into the car, and tries to drive away. In this case, probable cause is present, and so an arrest would be valid.

The Supreme Court recognizes that affidavits or complaints are often prepared hastily in the midst of a criminal investigation. Therefore, the policy is to interpret the allegations in a commonsense rather than an overly technical manner and to consider the affidavit sufficient in close cases (United States v. Ventresca, 380 U.S. 102 [1965]).

F. What Can Be Used to Establish Probable Cause?

In establishing probable cause, the officer may use any trustworthy information even if the rules of evidence prohibit its admission during the trial. For example, hearsay information and prior criminal record (both inadmissible in a trial) may be taken into consideration when determining probable cause. In cases of hearsay information, trustworthiness depends on the reliability of the source and the information given. Reliance on prior criminal record requires other types of evidence. The key point is that, in determining whether probable cause exists, the magistrate may consider any evidence, regardless of source.

Because probable cause is based on a variety and totality of circumstances, police officers must report accurately and exhaustively the facts that led them to believe that probable cause existed. As one publication notes:

> Probable cause can be obtained from police radio bulletins, tips from "good citizen" informers who have happened by chance to see criminal activity, reports from victims, anonymous tips, and tips from "habitual" informers who mingle with people in the underworld and who themselves may be criminals. Probable cause can be based on various combinations of these sources.[2]

In case of doubt, it is better to include too much rather than too little information, provided such information is true.

II. WHEN IS PROBABLE CAUSE REQUIRED?

Probable cause is required in four important areas of police work: (1) arrests with warrant, (2) arrests without warrant, (3) searches and seizures of property with warrant, and (4) searches and seizures of property without warrant. An arrest is, of course, a form of seizure—but a seizure of a person, not of property. Although the definition of probable cause is the same in all four situations, important differences exist as well.

A. Arrest of Persons versus Search and Seizure of Property

In cases of *arrest,* the probable cause concerns involve whether an offense has been committed and whether the suspect did, in fact, commit the offense. In contrast, in cases of *search and seizure of property,* the concerns are whether the items to be seized are connected with criminal activity and whether they can be found in the place to be searched. It follows, therefore, that what constitutes probable cause for arrest may not constitute probable cause for search and seizure—not because of different definitions but because the officer is looking at different aspects. For example, suppose a suspect is being arrested in her apartment for robbery, but the police have reason to believe that the stolen goods are in her getaway car, which is parked in the driveway. In this case, there is probable cause for arrest but not for a search of the apartment, except for a search that is incidental to the arrest.

B.   With a Warrant versus without a Warrant

In arrests and seizures with a warrant, the determination of probable cause is made by the magistrate to whom the complaint or affidavit is presented by the police or victim. In this case, the officer does not have to worry about establishing probable cause. However, such a finding of probable cause by the magistrate is not final. It may be reviewed during the trial, and if probable cause did not, in fact, exist, the evidence obtained is not admissible in court. In some jurisdictions, the absence of probable cause in a warrant must be established by the defendant through clear and convincing evidence—a difficult level of evidence for the defendant to establish, and certainly higher than probable cause.

By contrast, in arrests and searches and seizures without warrant, the police officer makes the determination of probable cause, usually on the spot and with little hesitation. This determination is subject to review by the court if challenged at a later time, usually in a *motion to suppress* evidence before or during the trial. Moreover, a trial court's determination of probable cause can be reviewed by an appellate court if the case is appealed.

Two consequences arise from the absence of probable cause in search and seizure cases. First, the evidence obtained cannot be admitted in court during the trial, hence possibly weakening the case for the prosecution. Second, the police officer may be sued in a civil case for damages or, in extreme cases, subjected to criminal prosecution.

The Supreme Court has expressed a strong preference for the use of a warrant in police work. Because the affidavit has been reviewed by a neutral and detached magistrate, the issuance of a warrant assures a more orderly procedure and is a better guarantee that probable cause is, in fact, present. In reality, however, most arrests and searches are made without a warrant under the numerous exceptions to the warrant requirement.

III.   WHAT ARE THE ADVANTAGES IN OBTAINING A WARRANT?

Police officers are advised to obtain a warrant whenever possible for two basic reasons. First, there is a presumption of probable cause, because the affidavit or complaint has been reviewed by the magistrate who found probable cause to justify issuing a warrant. The arrest or search and seizure is therefore presumed valid unless the accused proves otherwise in court through clear and convincing evidence. But it is difficult for the accused to overcome the presumption that the warrant is valid. If the finding of probable cause is reviewed during the trial, the court's remaining task is simply to determine if there was a substantial basis for the issuing magistrate's finding of probable cause, not to look at specific factual allegations (Illinois v. Gates, 462 U.S. 213 [1983]).

A second advantage is that having a warrant is a strong defense in civil cases for damages brought against the police officer for alleged violation of a defendant's constitutional rights. The only exception to a warrant being a valid defense in civil cases for damages is the serving of a warrant that is clearly invalid due to obvious mistakes that the officer should have discovered, such as the absence of a signature or failure to specify the place or person subject to the warrant. For example, suppose a police officer is sued for damages by a person who alleges that she was arrested without probable cause. If the arrest was made by virtue of a warrant, the officer will likely not be held liable (with the exception mentioned above) even if it is later determined in the trial or on appeal that the magistrate erred in thinking that probable cause existed.

IV. HOW IS PROBABLE CAUSE ESTABLISHED?

Probable cause may be established in three general ways: (1) the officer's own knowledge of particular facts and circumstances, (2) information given by a reliable third person (informant), and (3) information plus corroboration. In all these cases, the officer must be able to establish probable cause, although in different ways.

If the officer seeks the issuance of an arrest or a search and seizure warrant, probable cause is established through an affidavit (although some states allow what is in writing to be supplemented by oral testimony). If the officer acts without a warrant, probable cause is established by oral testimony in court during the trial. It is therefore important for the officer to be able to state clearly, whether in an affidavit or in court later, why he or she felt that probable cause was present.

In some cases, in addition to the evidence contained in the affidavit, the police officer presents oral evidence to the judge. Courts are divided on whether such oral evidence should be considered in determining probable cause; some courts consider it while others do not.

In one case, the Court ruled that a suspect's reputation for criminal activity may be considered by the magistrate issuing the warrant when determining probable cause (United States v. Harris, 403 U.S. 573 [1971]). In that case, the officer's affidavit submitted to the magistrate to support a request for a search warrant stated that the suspect "had a reputation with me for over four years as being a trafficker of nontaxpaid distilled spirits, and over this period I have received numerous information from all types of persons as to his activities." The affidavit further stated that another officer had located illicit whiskey in an abandoned house under the suspect's control and that an informant had purchased illegal whiskey from the suspect. While implying that a suspect's reputation for criminal activity can never by itself be sufficient to establish probable cause, reputation combined with factual statements about the suspect's activity may be considered by the magistrate issuing the warrant.

A. An Officer's Own Knowledge of Facts and Circumstances

The officer's own knowledge means that the information is obtained personally by the officer, using any of his or her five senses. These are the sense of sight (Officer P sees X stab Y), hearing (Officer P hears a shotgun blast), smell (Officer P smells marijuana while in an apartment), touch (Officer P frisks a suspect and touches something she knows is a gun), and taste (Officer P tastes something alcoholic). All these are in contrast to knowledge supplied by another person. Factors that a police officer may take into account in establishing belief that probable cause exists include, but are not limited to, the following:

- The prior criminal record of the suspect
- The suspect's flight from the scene of the crime when approached by the officer
- Highly suspicious conduct on the part of the suspect
- Admissions by the suspect
- The presence of incriminating evidence
- The unusual hour
- The resemblance of the suspect to the description of the perpetrator
- Failure to answer questions satisfactorily
- Physical clues, such as footprints or fingerprints, linked to a particular person
- The suspect's presence in a high-crime area
- The suspect's reputation of criminal activity

It is hard to say to what extent some or any of the preceding factors contribute to establishing probable cause. That would depend on the type of event, the strength of the relationship, and the intensity of the suspicion. One factor may be sufficient to establish probable cause in some instances; in others, several factors may be required. The preceding list is not exhaustive, and courts have also taken other factors into account.

B. Information Given by an Informant

1. An Informant Engaged in Criminal Activity: Aguilar v. Texas

In Aguilar v. Texas, 378 U.S. 108 (1964), the Court established a two-pronged test for determining probable cause on the basis of information obtained from an informant engaged in criminal activity (who therefore has low credibility with the court):

AT A GLANCE

Probable Cause

LEGAL DEFINITION: Probable cause exists when "the facts and circumstances within the officers' knowledge and of which they had reasonably trustworthy information are sufficient in themselves to warrant a man of reasonable caution in the belief that an offense has been or is being committed."

PRACTICAL DEFINITION: More likely than not (more than 50 percent certainty).

TEST USED: "Man of reasonable caution."

OFFICER'S EXPERIENCE: Must be considered.

WHO DETERMINES: Magistrate (in warrant cases) or officer (in no-warrant cases), but findings are subject to review during trial and appeal.

WHEN REQUIRED: During arrests (with or without a warrant) and searches (with or without a warrant).

EFFECT OF ABSENCE: The act is illegal, and evidence obtained must be excluded by the court.

HOW ESTABLISHED: Officer's own knowledge, information given by an informant, or information plus corroboration.

ADVANTAGES WHEN OBTAINED: Probable cause is presumed present and is a good defense in civil cases for damages.

WHAT CAN BE USED: Any trustworthy information, even that not admissible during trial.

COMPARED TO OTHER LEVELS OF PROOF: Lower than clear and convincing evidence; higher than reasonable suspicion; the same as preponderance of the evidence.

- **Prong 1: reliability of informant.** The affidavit must describe the underlying circumstances from which a neutral and detached magistrate may find that the informant is reliable—for example, "Affiant [a person who makes or subscribes to an affidavit] received information this morning from a trustworthy informant who has supplied information to the police during the past five years and whose information has proved reliable, resulting in numerous drug convictions."

- **Prong 2: reliability of informant's information.** The affidavit must describe the underlying circumstances from which the magistrate can find that the informant's information is itself reliable and not the result of mere rumor or suspicion—for example, "My informant told me that he personally saw Henry Banks, a former convict, sell heroin worth $500 to a buyer named Skippy Smith, at ten o'clock last night in Banks's apartment located at 1300 Shady Lane, Apt. 10, and that Banks has been selling and continues to sell drugs from this location."

The *Aguilar* test was reiterated five years later in Spinelli v. United States, 393 U.S. 410 (1969). In *Spinelli,* the defendant was convicted in federal court of interstate travel in aid of racketeering. The evidence used against Spinelli was obtained by use of a search warrant issued by a magistrate authorizing the search of Spinelli's apartment. The warrant was issued based on an affidavit from an FBI agent that stated four things:

1. That the FBI had kept track of Spinelli's movements on five days during the month of August 1965. On four of those five occasions, Spinelli was seen crossing one of two bridges leading from Illinois into St. Louis, Missouri, between 11 A.M. and 12:25 P.M.

2. That an FBI check with the telephone company revealed that an apartment house near a parking lot that Spinelli frequented had two telephones listed under the name of Grace P. Hagen.

3. That Spinelli was known by federal law enforcement agents and local police "as a bookmaker, an associate of bookmakers, a gambler, and an associate of gamblers."

4. That the FBI "has been informed by a confidential informant that William Spinelli is operating a handbook and accepting wagers and disseminating wagering information by means of the telephones" listed under the name of Grace P. Hagen.

Upon conviction, Spinelli appealed, saying that the information in the above affidavit did not establish probable cause sufficient for the issuance of a search warrant. The Court agreed and reversed the conviction, on the following grounds: Allegations 1 and 2 in the affidavit reflect only innocent-seeming activity and data: "Spinelli's travels to and from the apartment building and his entry into a particular apartment on one occasion could hardly be taken as bespeaking gambling activity; and there is nothing unusual about an apartment containing two separate telephones." Allegation 3 is "but a bald and unilluminating assertion of suspicion that is entitled to no weight in appraising the magistrate's decision." Allegation 4 must be measured against the two-pronged *Aguilar* test. The Court then concluded that the reliability of the informant was not established; neither did the affidavit prove the reliability of the informant's information.

The *Spinelli* case illustrates the types of allegations that are not sufficient to establish probable cause. It also restates the two-pronged *Aguilar* test and concludes that neither prong was satisfied by the affidavit. However, the *Aguilar* and *Spinelli* decisions have now been modified by Illinois v. Gates, discussed below. (Read the Spinelli v. United States case brief at the end of this chapter.)

a. The Old Interpretation of Aguilar Court decisions interpreted the two prongs in *Aguilar* as separate and independent of each other. This meant that the reliability of each—informant and information—had to stand on its own and be established separately before probable cause could be established. For example, the fact that an informant is absolutely reliable (prong 1) cannot make up for the lack of a description of how the informant obtained his or her information (prong 2).

b. The New Interpretation of Aguilar: *Illinois v.* Gates The "separate and independent" interpretation of the two prongs in *Aguilar* was overruled by the Supreme Court in Illinois v. Gates, 462 U.S. 213 (1983). (Read the case brief of Illinois v. Gates at the end of this chapter.)

In *Gates,* the Court abandoned the requirement of two independent tests as being too rigid, holding instead that the two prongs should be treated merely as relevant considerations in the totality of circumstances. Therefore, **"totality of circumstances"** has replaced "separate and independent" as the standard for probable cause in the *Aguilar* test. Said the Court:

> [W]e conclude that it is wiser to abandon the "two-pronged test" established by our decisions in *Aguilar* and *Spinelli.* In its place we reaffirm the totality of the circumstances analysis that traditionally has informed probable cause determinations. The task of the issuing magistrate is simply to make a practical, common-sense decision whether, given all the circumstances set forth in the affidavit before him, including the "veracity" and "basis of knowledge" of persons supplying hearsay information, there is a fair probability that contraband or evidence of a crime will be found in a particular place. And the duty of a reviewing court is simply to ensure that the magistrate had a "substantial basis for . . . concluding" that probable cause existed.

The new test, therefore, is this: *If a neutral and detached magistrate determines that, based on an informant's information and all other available facts, there is probable cause to believe that an arrest or a search is justified, then the warrant may be issued.*

Under the *Gates* ruling, if an informer has been very reliable in the past, his or her tip may say little about how he or she obtained the information. Conversely, if the informant gives a lot of detail and says that he or she personally observed the event, then doubts about the informant's reliability may be overlooked. Corroboration by the police of the informant's story and/or all other available facts may be taken into account in determining probable cause based on the "totality of circumstances."

c. The Identity of the Informant The Constitution does not require an officer to reveal the identity of an informant either to the magistrate when seeking the issuance of a warrant or during the trial. As long as the magistrate is convinced that the police officer is truthfully describing what the informant told him or her, the informant need not be produced, nor his or her identity revealed. For example, based on an informant's tip, police arrested a suspect without a warrant and searched him in conjunction with the arrest. Heroin was found on his person. During the trial, the police officer refused to reveal the name of the informant, claiming that the informant was reliable because the information he had given in the past had led to arrests. After being convicted, the defendant appealed. The Court held that a warrantless arrest, search, and seizure may be valid even if the police officer does not reveal the identity of the informant, because other evidence at the trial proved that the officer did rely on credible information supplied by a reliable informant. The Court added that the issue in this case was whether probable cause existed, not the defendant's guilt or innocence (McCray v. Illinois, 386 U.S. 300 [1967]).

An exception to the preceding rule is that, when the informant's identity is material to the issue of guilt or innocence, his or her identity must be revealed. If the state refuses to reveal the identity of the informant, such a case must be dismissed. Under what circumstances the informant's identity is material to the issue of guilt or innocence is a matter to be determined by the judge. In *McCray,* the Court said that the determination of whether the informant's name should be revealed "rests entirely with the judge who hears the motion to suppress to decide whether he needs such disclosure as to the informant in order to decide whether the officer is a believable witness." If the judge decides that the informant's name should be disclosed because such disclosure is material (although nobody knows what that really means) to the issue of guilt or innocence, then the police must either drop the case in order to preserve the anonymity of the informant or disclose the name and thereby blow his or her cover. An alternative to disclosing the informant's name in court is to hold an *in camera* (private) hearing, producing the informant before the judge only so that the informant may be interviewed by the judge in private.

2. An Informant Not Engaged in Criminal Activity

The preceding discussion focused on informants who are themselves engaged in criminal activity and who therefore suffer from low credibility. If the information comes from noncriminal sources, the courts tend to look more favorably on the informant's reliability.

a. Information Given by an Ordinary Citizen Most courts have ruled that the ordinary citizen who is either a victim of a crime or an eyewitness to a crime is a reliable informant, even though his or her reliability has not been established by previous incidents. For example, suppose a woman tells an officer that she has personally witnessed a particular individual selling narcotics in the adjoining apartment, gives a detailed description of the alleged seller, and describes the way sales are made. There is probable cause to obtain a warrant or (in exigent circumstances) to make a warrantless arrest.

b. Information Given by Another Police Officer Information given by a police officer is considered reliable by the courts. In one case, the Court noted, "Observations of fellow officers of the government engaged in a common investigation are plainly a reliable basis for a warrant applied for by one of their number" (United States. v. Ventresca, 380 U.S. 102 [1965]).

Sometimes the police officer makes an affidavit in response to statements made by other police officers, as in cases of inside information from a detective or orders from a superior. The court has implied that under these circumstances the arrest or search is valid only if the officer who passed on the information acted with probable cause.

c. "Stale" Information In search and seizure cases, problems may arise concerning whether the information provided has become "stale" after a period of time. The problem is peculiar to search and seizure cases, because in these cases the issue is always whether evidence of a crime may be found at that time in a certain place. In one case, the Court held that there was no probable cause to search for illegal sale of alcohol in a hotel where the affidavit alleged that a purchase of beer had occurred more than three weeks earlier (Sgro v. United States, 287 U.S. 206 [1932]). A more recent case involved an informant's claim that he had witnessed a drug sale at the suspect's residence approximately five months earlier and had observed a shoe box containing a large amount of cash that belonged to the suspect. The Court said that this was stale information that could not be used to establish probable cause (United States v. Leon, 468

U.S. 897 [1984]). However, the Court has not specified how much time may elapse between the informant's observation and the issuing of warrant, stating instead that the issue "must be determined by the circumstances of each case."

C. Information plus Corroboration

If probable cause cannot be established by using information provided by the informant alone (despite the now more liberal *Gates* test for determining probable cause), the police officer can remedy the deficiency by conducting his or her own corroborative investigation. Together, the two may establish probable cause even if the informant's information or the corroborative findings alone would not have been sufficient. For example, suppose an informant tells a police officer that she heard that X is selling drugs and that the sales usually are made at night in the apartment of X's girlfriend. That information alone would not establish probable cause. However, if the officer, acting on the information, places the apartment under surveillance, sees people going in and out, and is actually told by a buyer that he has just purchased drugs from X inside the apartment, there is strong basis for probable cause either to arrest X without a warrant (if exigent circumstances exist) or to obtain a warrant from a magistrate.

A leading case on information plus corroboration is Draper v. United States, 358 U.S. 307 (1959). In that case, a narcotics agent received information from an informant that the petitioner had gone to Chicago to bring three ounces of heroin back to Denver by train. The informant also gave a detailed description of Draper. Given this information, police officers set up surveillance of trains coming from Chicago on the mornings of September 8 and 9, the dates the informant had indicated. On seeing a man who fit the informant's description, the police moved in and made the arrest. Heroin and a syringe were seized in a search incident to the arrest. During trial, Draper sought exclusion of the evidence, claiming that the information given to the police failed to establish probable cause. Ultimately, the Supreme Court disagreed, saying that information received from an informant that is corroborated by an officer may be sufficient to provide probable cause for an arrest, even though such information was hearsay and would not otherwise have been admissible in a criminal trial.

V. PROBABLE CAUSE COMPARED WITH OTHER LEVELS OF PROOF

Probable cause is only one **level of proof**—defined as *the proof required for an act or happening to be legal*—under the rules of evidence. (See Table 3.1.) Despite quantification, with regard to the level of proof needed for police work, it's important to recognize that all the legal concepts discussed here, including probable cause, are ultimately subjective, meaning that what may be probable cause to one judge or jury may not be to

TABLE 3.1 *Levels of Proof*

Level of Proof	Degree of Certainty	Type of Proceeding
Absolute certainty	100%	Not required in any legal proceeding
Guilt beyond a reasonable doubt	95%	Convict an accused; prove every element of a criminal act
Clear and convincing evidence	80%	Denial of bail in some states and insanity defense in some states
Probable cause*	More than 50%	Issuance of warrant; search, seizure, and arrest without warrant; filing of an indictment
Preponderance of the evidence*	More than 50%	Winning a civil case; affirmative criminal defense
Reasonable suspicion	30%	Stop and frisk by police
Suspicion	10%	Start a police or grand jury investigation
Reasonable doubt	5%	Acquit an accused.
Hunch	0%	Not sufficient in any legal proceeding.
No information	0%	Not sufficient in any legal proceeding.

* Probable cause and preponderance of the evidence have the same level of certainty—more than 50%. This means that anything above 50% will suffice. The difference is that "probable cause" is used in criminal proceedings, whereas "preponderance of the evidence" is usually used in civil proceedings, although aspects of a criminal proceeding use this term as well.

another. The levels and percentages in Table 3.1 should, however, afford the officer a good working awareness of the meaning of the legal terms often used by courts. Although the quantification of level of proof is subjective in that what represents 50.01 percent certainty to one judge may be less than that to another, the levels of proof are not interchangeable. For example, reasonable suspicion always ranks lower in degree of certainty than probable cause but higher than mere suspicion.

VI. REASONABLE SUSPICION VERSUS PROBABLE CAUSE

Another important term in law enforcement is *reasonable suspicion,* a level of proof required by the courts in stop and frisk cases. As Table 3.1 indicates, it ranks below probable cause but above suspicion in degree of certainty. Reasonable suspicion has not been defined with precision by the Court. In one case, however, the Court said:

Reasonable suspicion is a less demanding standard than probable cause not only in the sense that reasonable suspicion can be established with information that is

HIGHLIGHT

Reasonable Suspicion Not Clearly Defined

Reasonable suspicion has not been defined with precision by the Supreme Court. In one case, however, the Court stated: "Reasonable suspicion is a less demanding standard than probable cause not only in the sense that reasonable suspicion can be established with information that is different in quantity or content than that required to establish probable cause, but also in the sense that reasonable suspicion can arise from information that is less reliable than that required to show probable cause."

Alabama v. White, 496 U.S. 325 (1990).

different in quantity or content than that required to establish probable cause, but also in the sense that reasonable suspicion can arise from information that is less reliable than that required to show probable cause. (Alabama v. White, 496 U.S. 325 [1990]).

Black's Law Dictionary defines **reasonable suspicion** as that *"quantum of knowledge sufficient to induce an ordinarily prudent and cautious man under circumstances to believe criminal activity is at hand. It must be based on specific and articulable facts, which, taken together with rational inferences from those facts, reasonably warrant intrusion."*[3]

Despite quantification of the levels of proof, the Supreme Court has noted that articulating precisely what reasonable suspicion and probable cause mean is simply not possible: "They are commonsense, non-technical conceptions that deal with 'the factual and practical considerations of everyday life on which reasonable and prudent men, not legal technicians, act. . . . They are instead fluid concepts that take their substantive content from the particular contexts in which the standards being assessed is . . . correlative to what must be proved" (Ornelas et al. v. United States, 59 CrL 2100 [1996]). The Court added that "this Court has a long-established recognition that standards of reasonableness under the Fourth Amendment are not susceptible of Procustean application," that "each case is to be decided on its own facts and circumstances," and that the limitations by the Fourth Amendment "will have to be developed in the concrete factual circumstances of individual cases."

Clearly, probable cause and reasonable suspicion are "fluid" concepts that cannot be defined with precision. Quantifying terms, as is done in Table 3.1, is simply a way to establish rankings and to clarify concepts. The degrees of certainty attached to each concept cannot be precise. It is, however, important to remember the following: (1) Probable cause requires a higher degree of certainty than reasonable suspicion; (2) both terms are subjective, so that what is probable cause or reasonable suspicion to one officer, judge, or juror may not be to another; (3) if information, such as a tip, has a low degree of reliability (quality), more information (quantity) will be required to establish probable cause or reasonable suspicion than if the information were more reliable; (4) both terms are additive, meaning that the more facts an officer can articulate, the greater is the likelihood that probable cause or reasonable suspicion will be established;

AT A GLANCE

Reasonable Suspicion

DEFINITION: Quantum of knowledge sufficient to induce an ordinarily prudent and cautious person under the same circumstances to believe criminal activity is at hand. Must be based on specific and articulable facts.

DEGREE OF CERTAINTY: Around 30 percent.

WHEN REQUIRED: During stop and frisk cases.

WHO DETERMINES: Initially the officer, but reviewable by a magistrate, trial judge, and appellate court judge.

COMPARED TO OTHER LEVELS OF PROOF: Lower than probable cause, but higher than suspicion.

and (5) totality of circumstances must be considered when evaluating whether reasonable suspicion or probable cause exists.

VII. APPEALING A FINDING OF PROBABLE CAUSE OR REASONABLE SUSPICION

As noted previously, the finding of probable cause is initially made by a police officer (in arrests or property searches without warrant) and by a judge or magistrate in arrests or searches with warrant. Reasonable suspicion is always initially determined by the officer in stop and frisk cases. However, these determinations are not binding; they can always be, and often are, challenged during trial. Should the challenge be made, usually in a defendant's motion to suppress the evidence obtained, the trial court then makes a determination whether probable cause or reasonable suspicion did, in fact, exist.

A trial court's determination of probable cause or reasonable suspicion is not final and can be reviewed on appeal. In one case, the defendants had pleaded guilty to possession of cocaine with intent to distribute, but they reserved the right to appeal the federal district court's denial of their motion to suppress the evidence of cocaine found in their car. The court had ruled that the officer had reasonable suspicion to stop and question the petitioners as they entered their car, as well as probable cause to remove one of the car's panels, which concealed two kilos of cocaine. The issue raised on appeal was whether a trial court's findings of reasonable suspicion and probable cause are final or whether they can be reviewed by an appellate court on appeal.

In Ornelas et al. v. United States, 59 CrL 2100 (1996), the Supreme Court held that the ultimate questions of reasonable suspicion to stop and presence of probable cause to make a warrantless arrest "should be reviewed *de novo*" (meaning anew, afresh, or a second time) on appeal. The Court stressed that "we have never, when reviewing a probable-cause or reasonable-suspicion determination ourselves, expressly deferred to the trial court's determination." It added that "independent review is therefore necessary if appellate courts are to maintain control of, and to clarify the legal principles." The Court cautioned, however, that "a reviewing court should take care both to review findings of historical fact only for clear error and to give due weight to inferences drawn from those facts by resident judges and local law enforcement officers."

In sum, while trial court findings of probable cause and reasonable suspicion are reviewable on appeal, such review must be based on clear error and give due weight to whatever inferences and conclusions may have been drawn by the trial judge and law enforcement officers.

Summary

The term *probable cause* comes from the Fourth Amendment to the Constitution; it applies to arrests, searches, and seizures. Probable cause exists when the facts and circumstances within the police officer's knowledge and of which he or she has trustworthy information are sufficient in themselves to justify to a "man of reasonable caution" the belief that an offense has been or is being committed or that property subject to seizure can be found in a particular place or on a particular person. For practical purposes, probable cause exists when the police have trustworthy evidence sufficient to make a reasonable person think it more likely than not that the proposed arrest or search is justified. Mathematically speaking, this means that the officer must be more than 50 percent certain of the person's guilt or of the presence of the item sought.

Probable cause is required in all arrests and searches, with or without a warrant. Although the definition of probable cause is the same in all situations, the person making the determination and the aspects to be considered may differ. A police officer is advised to obtain a warrant from a magistrate whenever possible, since this provides a strong protection against civil liability and creates a presumption of the legality of the arrest or search. Probable cause may be established through personal knowledge of the facts by the police officer, through information given by other persons, or by a combination of both sources.

Reasonable suspicion is defined as that "quantum of knowledge sufficient to induce an ordinarily prudent and cautious man under similar circumstances to believe criminal activity is at hand." It is the level of proof needed in stop and frisk cases. Probable cause and reasonable suspicion are subjective terms whose meanings can vary from one person to another.

Probable cause and reasonable suspicion determinations by trial judges are reviewable on appeal, but such reviews must be based on clear error and give due weight to conclusions drawn by the trial court judge and law enforcement officers.

Review Questions

1. What is the U.S. Supreme Court's definition of probable cause? For practical purposes, when does probable cause exist?

2. What are the advantages of obtaining a warrant, whenever possible, in arrest and in search and seizure cases?

3. What are the three general ways whereby probable cause may be established? Discuss each.

4. How has the case of Illinois v. Gates changed the interpretation of the two-pronged test established earlier in Aguilar v. Texas?

5. What did the U.S. Supreme Court say in Spinelli v. United States?

6. What are the various levels of proof in evidence and the degree of certainty of each?

7. Define reasonable suspicion. For what purpose may it be used in law enforcement?

8. May a trial court's finding of probable cause or reasonable suspicion be reviewed by an appellate court on appeal? Explain.

Key Terms and Definitions

level of proof: The degree of certainty required by law for an act or happening to be legal.

"man of reasonable caution": Not a person with training in the law, but rather an average "man on the street" who, under the same circumstances, would believe that the person being arrested had committed the offense or that items to be seized would be found in a particular place.

probable cause: More than mere suspicion; it exists when "the facts and circumstances within the officers' knowledge and of which they have reasonably trustworthy information are sufficient in themselves to warrant a man of reasonable caution in the belief that an offense has been or is being committed."

reasonable suspicion: That "quantum of knowledge sufficient to induce an ordinarily prudent and cautious man under similar circumstances to believe criminal activity is at hand. It must be based on specific and articulable facts, which, taken together with rational inferences from those facts, reasonably warrant intrusion."

"totality of circumstances" test (on information given by an informant): The test that, if a neutral and detached magistrate determines that, based on an informant's information and all other available facts, there is probable cause to believe that an arrest or a search is justified, then the warrant may be issued. This replaces the "separate and independent" two-pronged test of the *Aguilar* decision.

Principles of Cases

Aguilar v. Texas, 378 U.S. 108 (1964) The Supreme Court established a two-pronged test for determining probable cause on the basis of information obtained from an informant: (1) reliability of the informant and (2) reliability of the informant's information. Both conditions of the test must be satisfied before probable cause can be established on informa-

tion obtained from an informant. (*Note:* The independent, two-pronged *Aguilar* test was replaced in 1983 by the "totality of circumstances" test in the Illinois v. Gates decision.)

Alabama v. White, 496 U.S. 325 (1990) Reasonable suspicion is a less demanding standard than probable cause. It can be established with information different in quantity or content from that required to establish probable cause. It may also be established with the help of an anonymous telephone tip.

Brinegar v. United States, 338 U.S. 160 (1949)
Probable cause is more than bare suspicion; it exists when the facts and circumstances within the officers' knowledge and of which they had reasonably trustworthy information are sufficient in themselves to justify "a man of reasonable caution" in the belief that an offense has been or is being committed. The substance of all the definitions of probable cause is a reasonable ground for belief of guilt. This amounts to less evidence than would justify condemnation or conviction.

Draper v. United States, 358 U.S. 307 (1959)
Information received from an informant that is corroborated by an officer may be sufficient to provide probable cause for an arrest even though such information was hearsay and would not otherwise have been admissible in a criminal trial.

Illinois v. Gates, 462 U.S. 213 (1983) A warrant may be issued on the basis of affidavits that are entirely hearsay (such as when a police officer swears to facts reported to him or her by the crime victim, witnesses, or police informants). However, the affidavit must show by a *totality of the circumstances* that there is a fair probability that contraband or evidence of a crime will be found in a particular place. Among the considerations are whether the affidavit shows that (1) the informant is reliable and (2) the informant's information is reliable. (*Note:* The *Gates* decision preserves the two-pronged test established under *Aguilar,* but it does not treat the two aspects separately and independently. Instead, the "totality of circumstances" approach is used, meaning that whatever deficiencies there may be in one can be supplemented or overcome by the other.)

McCray v. Illinois, 386 U.S. 300 (1967) A warrantless arrest, search, and seizure may be valid even when the police officer does not reveal the identity of the informant, if other evidence at the trial proves that the officer did rely on credible information supplied by a reliable informant. The issue in this case was whether probable cause existed, not the defendant's guilt or innocence.

Michigan v. Summers, 452 U.S. 692 (1981) The general rule is that every arrest, as well as every seizure

having the essential attribute of a formal arrest, is unreasonable unless supported by probable cause.

Ornelas et al. v. United States, 59 CrL 2100 (1996) An appellate court that reviews the legality of police conduct that is taken without a warrant should conduct a *de novo* (new or fresh) review of the trial's ultimate questions of reasonable suspicion and probable cause and not simply accept the trial court's decision that reasonable suspicion or probable cause did exist.

Sgro v. United States, 287 U.S. 206 (1932) There was no probable cause to search for illegal alcohol sales in a hotel where the affidavit alleged that a purchase of beer had taken place more than three weeks earlier. The grounds for probable cause had become "stale."

Spinelli v. United States, 393 U.S. 410 (1969) "Innocent-seeming activity and data" and a "bald and unilluminating assertion of suspicion" in an affidavit are not to be given weight in a magistrate's determination of probable cause. An officer may use credible hearsay to establish probable cause, but an affidavit based on an informant's tip must satisfy the two-pronged *Aguilar test.*

United States v. Harris, 403 U.S. 573 (1971) A suspect's reputation for criminal activity may be considered by the magistrate issuing the warrant when establishing probable cause.

United States v. Leon, 468 U.S. 897 (1984) Five-month-old information from an informant is "stale" and cannot be used to establish probable cause. In this case, an informant supplied information that he had witnessed a sale of drugs at suspect's residence approximately five months earlier and had at that time observed a shoe box containing a large amount of cash that belonged to the suspect.

United States v. Ortiz, 422 U.S. 891 (1975) In determining probable cause, "officers are entitled to draw reasonable inferences from . . . facts in light of their knowledge of the area and their prior experience with aliens and smugglers."

United States v. Ventresca, 380 U.S. 102 (1965) The Supreme Court recognizes that affidavits or complaints are often prepared hastily in the midst of a criminal investigation. Therefore, the policy is to interpret the allegations in a commonsense rather than in an overly technical manner and to uphold the sufficiency of the affidavit in close cases.

Case Briefs

The Leading Case on the Sufficiency of Allegations for Probable Cause

Spinelli v. United States, 393 U.S. 410 (1969)

Facts: Spinelli was convicted by a federal court of interstate travel in aid of racketeering. The evidence used against Spinelli was obtained by use of a search warrant issued by a magistrate, authorizing the search of his apartment. The warrant was issued on the basis of an affidavit from an FBI agent that stated the following:

1. That the FBI had kept track of Spinelli's movements on five days during the month of August 1965. On four of those five occasions, Spinelli was seen crossing one of two bridges leading from Illinois into St. Louis, Missouri, between 11 A.M. and 12:15 P.M.

2. That an FBI check with the telephone company revealed that an apartment house near a parking lot that Spinelli frequented had two telephones listed under the name of Grace P. Hagen.

3. That Spinelli was known to the affiant and to federal law enforcement agents and local police "as a bookmaker, an associate of bookmakers, a gambler, and an associate of gamblers."

4. That the FBI "has been informed by a confidential reliable informant that William Spinelli is operating a handbook and accepting wagers and disseminating wagering information by means of the telephones" listed under the name of Grace P. Hagen.

Issue: *Did the above affidavit contain probable cause sufficient for the issuance of a search warrant?* No.

Supreme Court Decision: Allegations 1 and 2 in the affidavit reflect only innocent-seeming activity and data: "Spinelli's travels to and from the apartment building and his entry into a particular apartment on one occasion could hardly be taken as bespeaking gambling activity; and there is nothing unusual about an apartment containing two separate telephones." Allegation 3 is "but a bald and unilluminating assertion of suspicion that is entitled to no weight in appraising the magistrate's decision." Allegation 4 must be measured against the two-pronged *Aguilar* test. Here, the reliability of the informant was not established; neither did the affidavit prove the reliability of the informant's information. The affidavit therefore failed to establish probable cause, so the conviction was reversed and remanded.

Case Significance: The *Spinelli* case illustrates the types of allegations that are insufficient to establish probable cause. It restates the two-pronged *Aguilar* test for probable cause if the information comes from an informant. However, note that the *Aguilar* test, though still valid, has been modified by Illinois v. Gates.

Excerpts from the Decision: "Applying these principles to the present we first consider the weight to be given the informer's tip when it is considered apart from the rest of the affidavit. It is clear that a Commissioner could not credit it without abdicating his constitutional function. Though the affiant swore that his confidant was 'reliable,' he offered the magistrate no reason in support of this conclusion. Perhaps even more important is the fact that *Aguilar*'s other test has not been satisfied. The tip does not contain a sufficient statement of the underlying circumstances from which the informer concluded that Spinelli was running a bookmaking operation. We are not told how the FBI's source received his information—it is not alleged that the informant personally observed Spinelli at work or that he had ever placed a bet with him. Moreover, if the informant came by the information indirectly, he did not explain why his sources were reliable. . . . In the absence of a statement detailing the manner in which the information was gathered, it is especially important that the tip describe the accused's criminal activity in sufficient detail that the magistrate may know that he is relying on something more substantial than a casual rumor circulating in the underworld or an accusation based merely on an individual's general reputation.

"We conclude, then, that in the present case the informant's tip—even when corroborated to the extent indicated—was not sufficient to provide the basis for a finding of probable cause. This is not to say that the tip was so insubstantial that it could not properly have counted in the magistrate's determination. Rather, it needed some further support. When we look to the other parts of the application, however, we find nothing alleged which would permit the suspicions engendered by the informant's report to ripen into a judgment that a crime was probably being committed. As we have already seen, the allegations detailing the FBI's surveillance of Spinelli and its investigation of the telephone company records contain no suggestion of criminal conduct when taken by themselves—and they are now endowed with an aura of suspicion by virtue of the informer's tip. Nor do we find that the FBI's reports take on a sinister color when read in light of common knowledge that bookmaking is often carried on over the telephone and from premises ostensibly used by others for perfectly normal purposes. Such an argument would carry weight in a situation in which the premises contain an unusual number of telephones or abnormal activity is observed . . . but it does not fit this case where neither of these factors is present. All that remains to be considered is the flat statement that Spinelli was 'known' to the FBI and others as a gambler. But just as a simple assertion of police suspicion is not itself a sufficient basis for a magistrate's finding of probable cause, we do not believe it may be used to give additional weight to allegations that would otherwise be insufficient."

The Leading Case on Probable Cause Based on an Informant's Information

Illinois v. Gates, 462 U.S. 213 (1983)

Facts: On May 3, 1978, the police department of Bloomingdale, Illinois, received an anonymous letter that included statements that the Gateses were engaged in selling drugs; that the wife would drive their car to Florida on May 3 to be loaded with drugs, and the husband would fly down a few days later to drive the car back; that the car's trunk would be loaded with drugs; and that the Gateses then had more than $100,000 worth of drugs in their basement. Acting on the tip, a police officer determined the Gateses' address and learned that the husband had made a reservation on a May 5 flight to Florida. Arrangements for surveillance of the flight were made with an agent of the Drug Enforcement Administration (DEA), and the surveillance disclosed that Gates took the flight, stayed overnight in a motel room registered in his wife's name, and left the following morning with a woman in a car bearing an Illinois license plate, heading north. A search warrant for the Gateses' residence and automobile was then obtained from an Illinois state court judge on the basis of the Bloomingdale police officer's affidavit setting forth the foregoing facts and a copy of the anonymous letter. When the

Gateses arrived at their home, the police were waiting. In a search of the house and car, the police discovered marijuana and other contraband.

Issue: Did the affidavit and the anonymous letter provide sufficient facts to establish probable cause for the issuance of the warrant? Yes.

Supreme Court Decision: Yes, probable cause was established. The rigid two-pronged test under *Aguilar* and *Spinelli* for determining whether an informant's tip establishes probable cause for issuance of a warrant is abandoned, and the "totality of circumstances" approach is substituted in its place. The task of an issuing magistrate is simply to make a practical, commonsense decision whether, given all the circumstances set forth in the affidavit, there is a fair probability that contraband or evidence of a crime will be found in a particular place. Here, the judge issuing the warrant had a substantial basis for concluding that probable cause to search the Gateses' home and car existed. Under the "totality of circumstances" test, corroboration of details of an informant's tip by independent police work is of significant value. Even standing alone, the facts obtained through the independent investigation of the Bloomingdale police officer and the DEA at least suggested that the Gateses were involved in drug trafficking. In addition, the judge could rely on the anonymous letter, which had been corroborated in major part by the police officer's efforts. The conviction was affirmed.

Case Significance: The two-pronged independent test for establishing probable cause under *Aguilar,* in cases in which information is given by an informant, is now replaced by the "totality of circumstances" test, making it easier for police officers to establish probable cause for issuing a warrant.

Excerpts from the Decision: "This totality-of-the-circumstances approach is far more consistent with our prior treatment of probable cause than is any rigid demand that specific 'tests' be satisfied by every informant's tip. Perhaps the central teaching of our decisions bearing on the probable cause standard is that it is a 'practical, nontechnical conception.' Brinegar v. United States, 338 U.S. 160, 176 (1949). 'In dealing with probable cause, . . . as the very name implies, we deal with probabilities. These are not technical; they are the factual and practical considerations of everyday life on which reasonable and prudent men, not legal technicians, act.' Id., at 175. Our observation in United States v. Cortez, 449 U.S. 411, 418 (1981), regarding 'particularized suspicion,' is also applicable to the probable cause standard: 'The process does not deal with hard certainties, but with probabilities. Long before the law of probabilities was articulated as such, practical people formulated certain common-sense conclusions about human behavior; jurors as factfinders are permitted to do the same—and so are law enforcement officers. Finally, the evidence thus collected must be seen and weighed not in terms of library analysis by scholars, but as understood by those versed in the field of law enforcement.'

"As these comments illustrate, probable cause is a fluid concept—turning on the assessment of probabilities in particular factual contexts—not readily, or even usefully, reduced to a neat set of legal rules. Informants' tips doubtless come in many shapes and sizes from many different types of persons. As we said in Adams v. Williams, 407 U.S. 143, 147 (1972): 'Informants' tips, like all other clues and evidence coming to a policeman on the scene, may vary greatly in their value and reliability.' Rigid legal rules are ill-suited to an area of such diversity. 'One simple rule will not cover every situation.'

"Moreover, the 'two-pronged test' directs analysis into two largely independent channels—the informant's 'veracity' or 'reliability' and his 'basis of knowledge.' . . . There are persuasive arguments against according these two elements such independent status. Instead, they are better understood as relevant considerations in the totality-of-the-circumstances analysis that traditionally has guided probable cause determinations: a deficiency in one may be compensated for, in determining the overall reliability of a tip, by a strong showing as to the other, or by some other indicia of reliability. . . .

"If, for example, a particular informant is known for the unusual reliability of his predictions of certain types of criminal activities in a locality, his failure, in a particular case, to thoroughly set forth the basis of his knowledge surely should not serve as an absolute bar to a finding of probable cause based on his tip. . . . Likewise, if an unquestionably honest citizen comes forward with a report of criminal activity—which if fabricated would subject him to criminal liability—we have found rigorous scrutiny of the basis of his knowledge unnecessary. . . . Conversely, even if we entertain some doubt as to an informant's motives, his explicit and detailed description of alleged wrongdoing, along with a statement that the event was observed first-hand, entitles his tip to greater weight than might otherwise be the case. Unlike a totality-of-the-circum-

stances analysis, which permits a balanced assessment of the relative weights of all the various indicia of reliability (and unreliability) attending an informant's tip, the 'two-pronged test' has encouraged an excessively technical dissection of informants' tips, with undue attention being focused on isolated issues that cannot sensibly be divorced from the other facts presented to the magistrate."

The Leading Case on Reasonable Suspicion

Alabama v. White, 496 U.S. 325 (1990)

Facts: Police responded to an anonymous telephone call that conveyed the following information: that White would be leaving her apartment at a particular time in a brown Plymouth station wagon with the right taillight lens broken, that she was in the process of going to Dobey's motel, and that she would be in possession of about an ounce of cocaine hidden inside a brown attache case. The police saw White leave her apartment without an attache case, but she got in a car matching the description given in the telephone call. When the car reached the area where the motel was located, a patrol unit stopped the car and told White she was suspected of carrying cocaine. After obtaining her permission to search the car, the police found the brown attache case. Upon request, White provided the combination to the lock; the officers found marijuana and arrested her. At the station, the officers also found cocaine in her purse. White was charged with and convicted of possession of marijuana and cocaine. She appealed her conviction, saying that the police did not have reasonable suspicion required under Terry v. Ohio, 392 U.S. 1 (1968), to make a valid stop and that the evidence obtained therefore should be suppressed.

Issue: *Did the anonymous tip, corroborated by independent police work, constitute reasonable suspicion to justify a stop? Yes.*

Supreme Court Decision: The stop made by the police was based on reasonable suspicion, and so the evidence obtained was admissible in court. Reasonable suspicion is a less demanding standard than probable cause. It can be established with information different in quantity or quality from that required to establish probable cause. It may be also be established with the help of an anonymous telephone tip.

Case Significance: This case categorically states that reasonable suspicion is not as demanding a standard as probable cause and that it can be established with information that is different in quality and quantity from that required for probable cause. The information here from the anonymous telephone call would likely not, in and of itself, have established reasonable suspicion. The Court said that "although it is a close question, the totality of the circumstances demonstrates that significant aspects of the informant's story were sufficiently corroborated by the police to furnish reasonable suspicion." What established reasonable suspicion in this case was therefore a combination of an anonymous telephone tip and corroboration by the police.

Excerpts from the Decision: "When . . . an informant is shown to be right about some things, he is probably right about other facts that he has alleged,

including the claim that the object of the tip is engaged in criminal activity. It is, thus, not unreasonable in this case to conclude . . . that the independent corroboration by the police of significant aspects of the informer's predictions imparted some degree of reliability to the other allegations made by the caller. . . . What is important was the caller's ability to predict [White's] future behavior, because it demonstrated inside information. . . . When significant aspects of the caller's predictions were verified, there was reason to believe not only that the caller was honest, but also that he was well informed, at least well enough to justify the stop. Under the totality of circumstances, the anonymous tip, as corroborated, showed sufficient grounds of reliability to justify the investigatory stop of White's car."

 # Notes

1. Kermit L. Hall (ed.), *The Oxford Companion to the Supreme Court of the United States* (New York: Oxford University Press, 1992), pp. 681–682.

2. John G. Miles, Jr., David B. Richardson, and Anthony E. Scudellari, *The Law Officer's Pocket Manual* (Washington, DC: Bureau of National Affairs, 1988–89), 6:4.

3. *Black's Law Dictionary*, 6th ed., abridged (St. Paul, MN: West, 1991), p. 875.

4. The Exclusionary Rule

What You Will Learn in This Chapter

You will become familiar with the exclusionary rule—an important rule designed by the courts to control police misconduct. You will learn its definition, source, and background, and will gain insight into how the rule has been applied to federal and state criminal proceedings. You will also learn what types of evidence are admissible or not admissible in a court of law and what the current exceptions to the rule are. Finally, you will become familiar with possible alternatives to and the future of the exclusionary rule.

Introduction

The exclusionary rule is a controversial rule in criminal evidence that has generated debate among criminal justice professionals at all levels. No other rule of evidence has had as much impact on criminal cases. The rule is applied by the courts and has a direct effect on day-to-day law enforcement. The rule continues to undergo modification and refinement in Supreme Court decisions, but the extent of future changes is impossible to predict. Regardless of future direction, every law enforcement officer should be thoroughly familiar with the exclusionary rule because the success or failure of criminal prosecutions sometimes depends on it.

I. GENERAL CONSIDERATIONS

A. The Exclusionary Rule Defined

The **exclusionary rule** provides that *any evidence obtained by the government in violation of the Fourth Amendment guarantee against unreasonable search and seizure is not admissible in a criminal prosecution to prove guilt.* U.S. Supreme Court decisions strongly suggest that the exclusionary rule applies only to Fourth Amendment search and seizure cases. But what happens if the constitutional right violated is a Fifth, Sixth,

HIGHLIGHT

Court's Justification for the Exclusionary Rule

"The effect of the Fourth Amendment is to put the courts of the United States and Federal officials, in the exercise of their power and authority, under limitations and restraints as to the exercise of such power and authority, and to forever secure the people, their persons, houses, papers, and effects, against unreasonable searches and seizures under the guise of law. This protection reaches all alike. . . . The tendency of those who execute the criminal laws of the country to obtain conviction by means of unlawful seizures and enforced confessions, the latter obtained after subjecting accused persons to unwarranted practices destructive of rights secured by the Federal Constitution, should find no sanction in the judgments of the courts, which are charged at all times with the support of the Constitution, and to which people of all conditions have a right to appeal for maintenance of such fundamental rights."

Weeks v. United States, 232 U.S. 383 (1914).

or Fourteenth Amendment right? For example, suppose X is charged with an offense and retains a lawyer to represent her. Nonetheless, the police interrogate X in the absence of her lawyer—a violation of her Sixth Amendment right to counsel. Or suppose X is interrogated by the police while in custody without having been given the Miranda warnings—a violation of her Fifth Amendment right to protection against self-incrimination. In both instances, the evidence obtained is inadmissible, but will it be suppressed under the exclusionary rule?

The Court has repeatedly stated that only suppression based on a violation of the Fourth Amendment guarantee of protection against unreasonable search and seizure, including any evidence obtained from such a violation, comes under the exclusionary rule. In United States v. Leon, 468 U.S. 897 (1984), the Court said that the exclusionary rule is a "judicially created remedy" designed to safeguard Fourth Amendment rights." Therefore, not every violation of a constitutional right comes under the exclusionary rule. Evidence obtained in violation of any of the other constitutional rights is also excludable in a criminal trial—but not under the exclusionary rule. For example, suppose a confession is obtained without giving the suspect his or her Miranda warnings. Miranda is primarily a Fifth Amendment right to protection against self-incrimination, so what is violated in this example is the suspect's Fifth Amendment rights. The evidence is excludable anyway (usually as a due process violation under the Fifth or Fourteenth Amendments), but not under the exclusionary rule, which applies only to Fourth Amendment violations.

The exclusionary rule does not apply, however, if the violation is merely administrative regulation rather than constitutional (United States v. Caceres, 440 U.S. 741 [1979]). For example, suppose police departmental policy prohibits home searches without written consent. If an officer obtains evidence in the course of a home search without written consent, the exclusionary rule does not apply because written consent is not required under the Constitution for the search to be valid. The evidence is admissible unless it is excludable under state statute or court decisions.

B. The Purpose of the Rule

The Court has stated in a number of cases that the primary purpose of the exclusionary rule is to deter *police misconduct,* adding in one case that where "the exclusionary rule does not result in appreciable deterrence, then, clearly, its use . . . is unwarranted" (United States v. Janis, 428 U.S. 433 [1976]). The assumption is that, if the evidence obtained illegally is not admitted in court, police misconduct in search and seizure cases will cease or be minimized. The rule now applies to federal and state cases. This means that evidence illegally seized by state or federal officers cannot be used in any state or federal prosecution. In the words of one writer:

> The exclusionary rule is the primary means by which the Constitution's prohibition of unreasonable searches and seizures is currently enforced; thus it is seen by some as the primary protection of personal privacy and security against police arbitrariness and brutality. It is also the basis for judges' decisions to exclude reliable incriminating evidence from the trials of persons accused of crime, and it is thus considered by others to be little more than a misguided loophole through which criminals are allowed to escape justice.[1]

C. A Judge-Made Rule

Is the exclusionary rule a constitutional or a judge-made rule? If the rule is mandated by the Constitution, then the Supreme Court cannot eliminate it, and neither may it be changed by Congress. If it is judge-made, however, the Court may eliminate it at any time, or, arguably, it can be modified by Congress. Some writers maintain that this rule of evidence is judge-made—that it cannot be found in the Constitution. Its proponents disagree, claiming that the rule is of constitutional origin and therefore beyond the reach of Congress, even if Congress should want to limit it. The proponents point to a statement of the Court, in Mapp v. Ohio, 367 U.S. 643 (1961), that "the exclusionary rule is an essential part of both the Fourth and Fourteenth Amendments." However, the Court has more recently ruled in favor of the concept that the exclusionary rule is a judge-made rule of evidence. In Arizona v. Evans, 56 CrL 2175 (1995), the Court stated, "The exclusionary rule operates as a judicially created remedy designed to safeguard against future violations of Fourth Amendment rights through the rule's general deterrent effect."

D. Historical Development

1. Federal Courts

The exclusionary rule is of U.S. origin. In the words of one observer, "The exclusionary rule is the creation of the Supreme Court of the United States. It was unknown to the

HIGHLIGHT

The Origin of the Exclusionary Rule

"Under the exclusionary rule, evidence obtained in violation of the Fourth Amendment cannot be used in a criminal trial against the victim of the illegal search and seizure. The Constitution does not require this remedy; it is a doctrine of judicial design. Excluded evidence is often-times quite reliable and the 'most probative information bearing on the guilt or inno-cence of the defendant.' Nevertheless, the rule's prohi-bition applies to such direct evidence, as well as to the 'fruit of the poisonous tree'—secondary evidence derived from the illegally seized evidence itself."

United States v. Houltin, 566 F.2d 1027 (5th Cir. 1978).

English law our ancestors brought with them to America and unknown to the generations that adopted the Fourth Amendment as part of the Constitution."[2]

The first exclusionary rule case was decided by the Court in 1886 when it held that the forced disclosure of papers amounting to evidence of a crime violated the constitutional right of the suspect to protection against unreasonable search and seizure, so such items were inadmissible in court proceedings (Boyd v. United States, 116 U.S. 616 [1886]). It was not until 1914, however, that evidence illegally obtained by federal officers was held to be excluded in all federal criminal prosecutions (Weeks v. United States, 232 U.S. 383 [1914]). In the *Weeks* case, the Court stated:

> The efforts of the courts and their officials to bring the guilty to punishment, praiseworthy as they are, are not to be aided by the sacrifice of those great principles established by years of endeavor and suffering which have resulted in their embodiment in the fundamental law of the land. . . . To sanction such proceedings would be to affirm by judicial decision a manifest neglect, if not an open defiance, of the prohibitions of the Constitution, intended for the protection of the people against such unauthorized action.

From 1914 to 1960, federal courts admitted evidence of a federal crime if the evidence had been illegally obtained by state officers, as long as it had not been obtained by or in connivance with federal officers. This dubious practice was known as the **silver platter doctrine,** *a procedure that permitted federal courts to admit evidence illegally seized by state law enforcement officers and handed over to federal officers for use in federal cases.* Under this doctrine, such evidence was admissible because the illegal act was not committed by federal officers. In 1960, the Court put an end to this questionable practice by holding that the Fourth Amendment prohibited the use of illegally obtained evidence in federal prosecutions, whether obtained by federal or by state officers, thereby laying to rest the silver platter doctrine (Elkins v. United States, 364 U.S. 206 [1960]).

2. State Courts

In 1949, the Court held that state courts were not constitutionally required to exclude illegally obtained evidence, so the exclusionary rule did not apply to state prosecutions (Wolf v. Colorado, 338 U.S. 25 [1949]). In 1952, the Court modified that position somewhat by ruling that, although the exclusionary rule did not apply to the states, some searches were so "shocking" as to require exclusion of the evidence seized under the due process clause. However, these were limited to cases involving coercion, violence, or brutality (Rochin v. California, 342 U.S. 165 [1952]). Finally, in Mapp v. Ohio, the Court overruled the *Wolf* decision and held that the Fourth Amendment required state courts to exclude evidence obtained by unlawful searches and seizures.

II. THE EXCLUSIONARY RULE AS APPLIED TO THE STATES: MAPP V. OHIO

In Mapp v. Ohio, 467 U.S. 643 (1961), the defendant was convicted of knowingly possessing certain lewd and lascivious books, pictures, and photographs, in violation of Ohio law. Three Cleveland police officers went to Mapp's residence, knocked on the door, and demanded entrance. However, after telephoning her attorney, Mapp refused to admit them without a search warrant. The officers again sought entrance three hours later when at least four additional officers had arrived on the scene. When Mapp did not come to the door immediately, the police forced their way in. Meanwhile, Mapp's attorney arrived, but the officers would not permit him to see his client or to enter the house. Mapp demanded to see the search warrant, which the officers by then claimed to have.

A paper, claimed to be a warrant, was held up by one of the officers. Mapp grabbed the "warrant" and placed it in her bosom. A struggle ensued in which the officers handcuffed Mapp because, they claimed, she was belligerent. In handcuffs, Mapp was forced into her bedroom, where the officers searched a dresser, a chest of drawers, a closet, and some suitcases. They also looked into a photo album and through personal papers belonging to Mapp. The search spread to include a child's bedroom, the living room, the kitchen, a dinette, and the basement of the building and a trunk found in it. The obscene materials, for possession of which Mapp was ultimately convicted, were discovered in the course of that widespread search. At the trial, no search warrant was produced by the prosecution, nor was the absence of a warrant explained. The seized materials were admitted into evidence by the trial court, and the defendant was convicted. On appeal, the Court excluded the evidence, holding that the exclusionary rule prohibiting the use of evidence in federal courts if illegally obtained is now applicable to state criminal proceedings.

Mapp is significant because since 1961 the exclusionary rule has been applied to federal and state criminal prosecutions. Before *Mapp,* the use of the exclusionary rule was left to the discretion of the states; some used it while others did not. It is perhaps the second most important law enforcement case ever to be decided by the Court, the first being Miranda v. Arizona, discussed in chapter 11. (Read the Mapp v. Ohio case brief at the end of this chapter.)

What caused the Court to change its mind on the exclusionary rule, which, twelve years earlier in Wolf v. Colorado, 338 U.S. 25 (1949), it had ruled was not applicable in state prosecutions? In *Mapp,* the Court said that the *Wolf* case was decided on factual grounds, implying that factual circumstances rather than philosophical considerations guided the Court's decision. The Court then noted that, when *Wolf* was decided, almost two-thirds of the states were opposed to the exclusionary rule; but since then more than half of those states, either by legislation or judicial decision, had adopted the Weeks rule excluding illegally obtained evidence in their own criminal prosecutions. The Court further noted that *Wolf* was partially based on the assumption that "other means of protection" against officer misconduct made the exclusionary rule unnecessary. The Court considered that to be a mistake, finding instead that the experience of California and other states had established that "such other remedies have been worthless and futile" and had therefore decided to abandon what the Court deemed the "obvious futility of relegating the Fourth Amendment to the protection of other remedies." Clearly, the Court realized the need to apply the exclusionary rule to all criminal prosecutions so as to protect Fourth Amendment rights.

III. PROCEDURES FOR INVOKING THE EXCLUSIONARY RULE

In both federal and state courts, the basic procedure for excluding evidence on a claim of illegal search and seizure is a *pretrial motion to suppress* the evidence. If the accused loses at this pretrial hearing, the issue can be raised again at the time the material is offered into evidence during trial. If the accused loses at trial, the issue can be raised on appeal. Failing that, the same issue can be raised in a postconviction proceeding, such as in a habeas corpus case (a proceeding in which a prisoner seeks freedom based on alleged violations of constitutional rights during trial). Indeed, opportunities to invoke the exclusionary rule in a criminal case are virtually unending. The burden of proof in a motion to suppress the evidence depends on whether the search or seizure in question was made with or without a warrant. If the search or seizure was pursuant to a warrant, there is a presumption of validity. The burden is therefore on the accused to show that the warrant was issued without probable cause. This is a heavy burden for the accused to bear, because it usually takes clear and convincing evidence (a higher degree of certainty than probable cause) to prove that probable cause did not, in fact, exist. In contrast, if the search was made without a warrant, the prosecution has the burden of establishing probable cause or, in its absence, of proving that the search was an exception to the warrant requirement. To establish probable cause, the police officer usually must testify during the hearing on defendant's motion to suppress.

If the evidence is admitted by the trial judge, the trial proceeds, and the prosecution uses the evidence. Should the accused be convicted, the defense may appeal to the appellate court the allegedly erroneous decision to admit the evidence. If the trial judge decides to exclude the evidence, most jurisdictions allow the prosecution to appeal that decision immediately; otherwise, the effect of the allegedly wrongful decision might be the acquittal of the defendant. If the defendant is acquitted, there can be no appeal at all, which would thus deprive the prosecution of any opportunity to challenge the judge's decision to suppress.

If a motion to exclude was made in a timely manner, it is an error for the court to receive evidence obtained by illegal search or seizure. On appeal, such mistakes automatically lead to the reversal of any conviction, unless the admission of the evidence is found by the appellate court to be a harmless error. To prove **harmless error,** the *prosecution must show beyond a reasonable doubt that the evidence erroneously admitted did not contribute to the conviction.* To establish harmless error, it is not enough for the prosecution to show that there was other evidence sufficient to support the verdict. Rather, it must show that there is no reasonable possibility that a different result would have been reached without the tainted evidence (Chapman v. California, 386 U.S. 18 [1967]).

The exclusionary rule may be invoked only by the person whose Fourth Amendment rights have been violated, meaning the person whose reasonable expectation of privacy was breached by law enforcement personnel. The Court has held that an overnight guest, while the owner of the residence was away, has legal grounds to cite the exclusionary rule (Minnesota v. Olson, 495 U.S. 91 [1990]) because that guest has a reasonable expectation of privacy. In a somewhat related and more recent case, however, the Court decided that defendants who were on a short-term visit and who, together with the lessee, "used the apartment for a business purpose—to package drugs," had no legitimate expectation of privacy in the apartment. Therefore, the action by a police officer in looking in an apartment window through a gap in the closed blinds and observing the defendants and the apartment's lessee bagging cocaine did not violate defendants' legitimate expectation of privacy. (Minnesota v. Carter, 64 CrL 158 [1998]). Note, however, that the issue raised in *Carter* was not one of **standing**—meaning *whether defendants could properly raise the issue*—but instead whether defendants' Fourth Amendment rights were violated.

IV. WHAT IS NOT ADMISSIBLE?

A. Illegally Seized Evidence

Illegally seized evidence includes contraband, fruits of the crime (for example, stolen goods), instruments of the crime (such as burglar tools), or "mere evidence" (shoes, shirt, or the like connecting a person to the crime), which, if seized illegally, may not be admitted at a trial to show the defendant's guilt.

B. "Fruit of the Poisonous Tree"

The **"fruit of the poisonous tree" doctrine** states that *once the primary evidence (the "tree") is shown to have been unlawfully obtained, any secondary or derivative evidence (the*

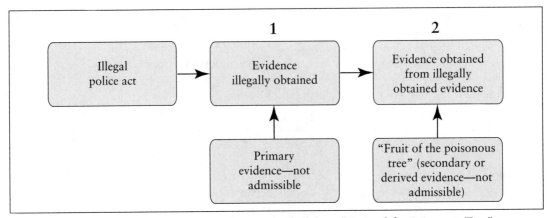

Figure 4.1 *Evidence Illegally Obtained Distinguished from "Fruit of the Poisonous Tree"*

"fruit") derived from it is also inadmissible (Silverthorne Lumber Co. v. United States, 251 U.S. 385 [1920]). (See Figure 4.1.) This rule is based on the principle that evidence illegally obtained should not be used to gain other evidence, because the original illegally obtained evidence "taints" all evidence subsequently obtained. The tainted secondary evidence (some courts prefer to call it "derivative evidence" or "secondary evidence") can take various forms.

- **Example 1:** The police conduct an illegal search of a house and find a map that shows the location of the stolen goods. Using the map, the police recover the goods in an abandoned warehouse. Both the map and the goods are inadmissible as evidence, but for different reasons. The map is not admissible because it is illegally seized evidence; the goods (physical evidence) are not admissible either because they are fruit of the poisonous tree.

- **Example 2:** Police officers make an illegal search of D's house and find heroin. They confront D with the evidence, and she confesses to possession of an illicit drug. D's confession is the fruit of the illegal search (verbal evidence) and must be excluded.

- **Example 3:** The police obtain a confession from X without giving him the Miranda warnings. X tells the police the location of the murder weapon, which the police subsequently recover. X's confession is inadmissible because it is illegally obtained evidence; the murder weapon is inadmissible because it is fruit of the poisonous tree.

In sum, these two types of inadmissible evidence may be distinguished as follows: Illegally seized evidence is obtained as a direct result of the illegal act (the search), whereas the fruit of the poisonous tree is the indirect result of the same illegal act. The fruit of the poisonous tree is thus at least once removed from the illegally seized evidence, but it is equally inadmissible.

V. EXCEPTIONS TO THE EXCLUSIONARY RULE

Court decisions have identified situations in which the evidence obtained is admissible in court although something may have been wrong initially with either the conduct of the police or the court that issued the warrant. These exceptions fall into four categories: good faith, inevitable discovery, purged taint, and independent source.

A. The "Good Faith" Exceptions

Over the years, the Court has carved out several **"good faith" exceptions** to the exclusionary rule, whereby *evidence obtained by the police is admissible in court even if there was an error or mistake as long as such error or mistake was not committed by the police or, if committed by the police, the error or mistake was honest and reasonable.* These exceptions, as articulated in decided cases, are as follows: (1) when the error was committed by the judge or magistrate, (2) when the error was committed by a court employee, (3) when the police erroneously, but reasonably and honestly, believed that the information they gave to the magistrate when obtaining the warrant was accurate, (4) when the police reasonably believed the person who gave authority to enter the premises had authority to give consent, and (5) when the police action was based on a law that was later declared to be unconstitutional. Under the good faith exceptions, it is not enough that the officer claim that he or she did not know that the act was illegal. What is needed is an honest and "objectively reasonable belief" (as later determined by a judge or jury, if the issue arises) on the part of the officer that the act was valid.

1. When the Error Was Committed by the Judge or Magistrate, Not by the Police: The Sheppard and Leon Cases

The first significant good faith exception to the exclusionary rule applies when the error was committed by the judge or magistrate and not by the police. The Court held in Massachusetts v. Sheppard, 468 U.S. 981 (1984), that evidence obtained by the police acting in good faith on a search warrant that was issued by a neutral and detached magistrate, but that is ultimately found to be invalid, may be admitted and used at the trial.

In the *Sheppard* case, a police detective executed an affidavit for an arrest and search warrant authorizing the search of Sheppard's residence. The affidavit stated that the police wished to search for certain described items, including clothing of the victim and a blunt instrument that might have been used on the victim. The affidavit was reviewed and approved by the district attorney. Because it was a Sunday, the local court was closed, and the police had a difficult time finding a warrant application form. The detective finally found a warrant form previously used in another district in the Boston area to search for controlled substances. After making some changes in the form, the detective presented it and the affidavit to the judge at his residence, informing him that the warrant form might need further revisions. The judge concluded that the affidavit established probable cause to search the residence and told the detective that the necessary changes in the warrant form would be made. The judge made some changes, but he did not change the substantive portion, which continued to authorize a search for controlled substances, nor did he alter the form so as to incorporate the affidavit. The judge then signed the warrant and returned it and the affidavit to the detective, informing him that the warrant was of sufficient authority in form and content to authorize the search. The ensuing search of Sheppard's residence was limited to the items listed in the affidavit, and several incriminating pieces of evidence were discovered. The defendant was convicted of first-degree murder in a trial at which the evidence obtained under the warrant was used. On appeal, the Court ruled that the evidence obtained was admissible in court because the officer conducting the search had acted in good faith, relying on a search warrant that had been issued by a magistrate but that was subsequently declared to be invalid.

In a companion case decided that same day, United States v. Leon, 468 U.S. 897 (1984), the Court made the same decision on a different set of facts. Acting on information from a confidential informant, officers of the Burbank, California, police department had initiated a drug-trafficking investigation that involved surveillance of Leon's activities. On the basis of an affidavit summarizing the officer's observations, the police prepared an application for a warrant to search three residences and Leon's automobiles for an extensive list of items. The application was reviewed by several deputy district attorneys, and a state court judge issued a warrant that was apparently valid. When Leon was later indicted for federal drug offenses, he filed motions to suppress the evidence seized. The trial court excluded the evidence on the grounds that no probable cause had existed for the issuance of the warrant, because the reliability of the informant had not been established and the information obtained from the informant was stale. This decision was affirmed by the court of appeals. The government then took the case to the Supreme Court solely on the issue of whether a good faith exception to the exclusionary rule should be recognized. The Court ruled that the Fourth Amendment's exclusionary rule should not be applied to bar the use in the prosecution's case of evidence that has been obtained by officers acting in reasonable reliance on a search warrant issued by a detached and neutral magistrate but ultimately found to be invalid because probable cause was lacking.

The *Sheppard* and *Leon* cases are arguably the most important cases decided on the exclusionary rule since Mapp v. Ohio. They represent a significant, although narrow, exception to the exclusionary rule and thus a breakthrough that police proponents have long been advocating. In these cases, the Court said that there were objectively reasonable grounds for the police's mistaken belief that the warrants authorized the searches. The officers took every step that could reasonably have been taken to ensure that the warrants were valid. The difference between these two cases is that in *Sheppard* the issue was the improper use of a form (a technical error) by the judge, whereas in *Leon* it was the use of a questionable informant and stale information by the judge to determine probable cause. The cases are similar, however, in that the mistakes were made by the judges, not the police. When the warrants were given to the officers, anyone would have concluded that each authorized a valid search. In the *Sheppard* case, the Court noted:

> An error of constitutional dimension may have been committed with respect to the issuance of the warrant in this case, but it was the judge, not the police officer, who made the crucial mistake. Suppressing evidence because the judge failed to make all the necessary clerical corrections despite his assurance that such

changes would be made will not serve the deterrent function that the exclusionary rule was designed to achieve.

And in the *Leon* case, the Court concluded:

> The exclusionary rule is designed to deter police misconduct rather than to punish the errors of judges and magistrates. Admitting evidence obtained pursuant to a warrant while at the same time declaring that the warrant was somehow defective will not reduce judicial officers' professional incentives to comply with the Fourth Amendment, encourage them to repeat their mistakes, or lead to the granting of all colorable warrant requests.

In sum, the Court reasoned that the evidence was admissible because the judge, and not the police, erred; therefore, the exclusionary rule did not apply, because it is designed to control the conduct of the police, not of judges. However, at least one state supreme court (Pennsylvania) has ruled that evidence seized with a deficient search warrant cannot be used in state court based on the provisions of the state constitution, even if the police acted in good faith when obtaining the warrant. Therefore, what the exclusionary rule allows as an exception may be negated by state case law or provisions of the state constitution.

2. When the Error Was Committed by a Court Employee: Arizona v. Evans

The most recent good faith exception to the exclusionary rule was decided by a divided Court in *Arizona v. Evans*, 56 CrL 2175 (1995). In that case, Evans was arrested by the Phoenix, Arizona, police during a routine traffic stop when a patrol car computer indicated that there was an outstanding misdemeanor warrant for his arrest. A subsequent search of Evans's car revealed a bag of marijuana. He was charged with possession of marijuana. Evans moved to suppress the evidence under the exclusionary rule, saying that the misdemeanor warrant was dismissed seventeen days before the arrest but was not entered in the computer due to court employee error. This claim was, in fact, true. Evans was convicted and appealed, claiming that the evidence obtained should have been held inadmissible under the exclusionary rule. The Court rejected Evans's claim and admitted the evidence, arguing as follows:

> The exclusionary rule does not require suppression of evidence seized in violation of the Fourth Amendment where the erroneous information resulted from clerical errors of court employees. The exclusionary rule is a judicially created remedy designed to safeguard against future violations of Fourth Amendment rights through its deterrent effect. . . . The exclusionary rule was historically designed as a means of deterring police misconduct, not mistakes by court employees.

In admitting the evidence, the Court stressed the following: (1) The exclusionary rule historically has been designed to deter police misconduct, not to deter mistakes committed by court employees; (2) Evans in this case offered no evidence that court employees are inclined to ignore or subvert the Fourth Amendment or that lawlessness by court employees required the extreme Court action of exclusion of the evidence; and (3) there was no basis to believe that the application of the exclusionary rule would have a significant effect on the behavior of court employees responsible for informing the

HIGHLIGHT

A Dissenting View on the Applicability of the Exclusionary Rule

In his dissent in Arizona v. Evans (56 CrL 2175 [1995]), Justice John Paul Stevens wrote that the Fourth Amendment "is a constraint on the power of the sovereign, not merely on some of its agents," adding that the "deterrent purpose extends to law enforcement as a whole, not merely to the arresting officer." This is an interesting interpretation because the Bill of Rights has long been interpreted as applying to acts of government officials, and not just to acts of the police. Thus far, however, the Court has consistently held that only acts of law enforcement officers come under the exclusionary rule.

police that the warrant had been dismissed. (Read the Arizona v. Evans case brief at the end of this chapter.)

3. When the Policed Erred but Honestly and Reasonably Believed That the Information They Gave to the Magistrate When Obtaining the Warrant Was Accurate: Maryland v. Garrison

In Maryland v. Garrison, 480 U.S. 79 (1987), police officers obtained a warrant to search "the premises known as 2036 Park Avenue, third-floor apartment" for drugs and drug paraphernalia that allegedly belonged to a person named McWebb. The police honestly believed that there was only one apartment at the location. In fact, however, there were two apartments on the third floor, one belonging to McWebb and the other one belonging to Garrison. Before the officers became aware that they were in Garrison's apartment instead of McWebb's, they discovered contraband that led to Garrison's conviction for violating provisions of Maryland's Controlled Substance Act. Garrison appealed his conviction, claiming that the evidence obtained by police was inadmissible based on the exclusionary rule. The Court disagreed, stating that "the validity of a warrant must be judged in light of the information available to officers when the warrant is sought." The Court added:

> Plainly, if the officers had known, or even if they should have known, that there were two separate dwelling units on the third floor . . . they would have been obligated to exclude respondent's apartment from the scope of the requested warrant. But we must judge the constitutionality of their conduct in light of the information available to them at the time they acted. . . . The validity of the warrant must be assessed on the basis of the information that the officers disclosed, or had a duty to discover and to disclose, to the issuing magistrate.

4. When the Police Reasonably Believe That the Person Who Gave Authority to Enter the Premises Had Authority to Give Consent: Illinois v. Rodriguez

A good faith exception has been fashioned by the Court under the "apparent authority" principle. In Illinois v. Rodriguez, 497 U.S. 117 (1990), suspect Rodriguez was arrested in his apartment and charged with possession of illegal drugs that the police said were in plain view when they entered his apartment. The police gained entry into Rodriguez's apartment with the assistance of a certain Fischer, who told police that the apartment was "ours" and that she had clothes and furniture there. She unlocked the door with her key and gave the officers permission to enter. In reality, Fischer had moved out of the apartment and therefore no longer had any common authority over it. The Court held that the consent given by Fischer was valid because the police reasonably and honestly believed, given the circumstances, that she had authority to give consent, thus resorting to the apparent authority principle as one of the exceptions to the exclusionary rule.

5. When the Police Action Was Based on a Law That Was Later Declared Unconstitutional: Illinois v. Krull

In Illinois v. Krull, 480 U.S. 340 (1987), police officers entered the wrecking yard belonging to Krull without a warrant and found evidence of stolen vehicles. Such warrantless entry was authorized by state statute. The next day, however, a federal court declared the statute unconstitutional, saying that it permitted police officers too much discretion and therefore violated the Fourth Amendment. On appeal, the Court did not dispute the constitutionality of the statute, saying instead that the evidence obtained was admissible under the good faith exception to the exclusionary rule. The Court concluded that suppression is inappropriate when the fault is not with the police, but—as in this case—with the legislature.

Some legal scholars believe that the good faith exceptions to the exclusionary rule, as enunciated in the preceding cases, "will hasten the ultimate demise of the exclusionary rule and weaken its application." Others believe that these decisions should be interpreted and applied very narrowly—only to cases in which the police are not at fault or, if the mistake is by the police, such mistake is honest and the officer's belief in the legality of the act is reasonable. Despite all these rulings, there has been no indiscriminate application of the good faith exception to the exclusionary rule. The more reasonable view appears to be that the good faith exception has been and will continue to be applied cautiously by the Court. The belief by some law enforcement officers that courts will automatically admit evidence obtained illegally as long as the officer believes in good faith that what he or she did was legal is unsupported by case law.

B. The "Inevitable Discovery" Exception

The **"inevitable discovery" exception** relates to the fruit of the poisonous tree doctrine; it is usually limited to instances in which the evidence obtained is a weapon or a body. In a number of cases, the Supreme Court has ruled that *evidence is admissible if the police can prove that they would inevitably have discovered the evidence anyway by lawful means, regardless of their illegal action.* For example, while the police were taking a suspect back to Des Moines from Davenport, Iowa, where he surrendered, they induced him to tell them the location of the body of the girl they believed he had murdered by appealing to the suspect (whom the police addressed as "Reverend"), saying that it would be nice to give the deceased a Christian burial. The police did not directly question the suspect but instead asked him to "think it over." Before the departure from Davenport, the suspect's lawyer had repeatedly requested that no questioning take place during that drive. The suspect led the police to the body of the murdered girl. While conceding that the police violated the defendant's right to counsel by encouraging him to discuss the location of the body, the Court nevertheless admitted the evidence on the grounds that the police would have discovered it anyway. At the time that the police were being led by the suspect to the body, the searchers were approaching the actual location, so the body would inevitably have been found (Nix v. Williams, 467 U.S. 431 [1984]).

An article in the *FBI Law Enforcement Bulletin* issues the following caution about the inevitable discovery exception: "Under the inevitable discovery doctrine, it is not sufficient to allege that the evidence *could* have been found in a lawful fashion if some hypothetical events had occurred. It must be shown that the evidence inevitably *would* have been discovered." The writer adds that "the inevitable discovery exception ensures that the exclusionary rule does not go beyond that limited goal of deterring illegal police conduct by allowing into evidence those items that the police would have discovered legally anyway."[3]

C. The "Purged Taint" Exception

The **"purged taint" exception** also relates to the fruit of the poisonous tree doctrine. It applies when *the defendant's subsequent voluntary act dissipates the taint of the initial illegality.* A defendant's intervening act of free will is sufficient to break the causal chain between the tainted evidence and the illegal police conduct, so the evidence becomes admissible. For example, in one case, the police broke into a suspect's house illegally and obtained a confession from him, but the suspect refused to sign it. The suspect was released on his own recognizance. A few days later, he went back to the police station and signed the confession. The Court said that the suspect's act manifested free will and therefore cleaned the tainted evidence of illegality (Wong Sun v. United States, 371 U.S. 471 [1963]). Note, however, that to break the causal connection between an illegal arrest and a confession that is the fruit of the illegal arrest, the intervening event must be meaningful. For example, in another case, after an unlawful arrest, a suspect confessed to the commission of a robbery. Even though the suspect received three sets of Miranda warnings and met briefly at the police station with friends prior to the confession, the Court said that these events were not meaningful and that the evidence obtained was therefore not admissible during the trial (Taylor v. Alabama, 457 U.S. 687 [1982]).

D. The "Independent Source" Exception

The **"independent source" exception** holds that *evidence obtained is admissible if the police can prove that it was obtained from an independent source not connected with the illegal search or seizure* (United States v. Crews, 445 U.S. 463 [1980]). In the *Crews* case, the Court said that the initial illegality (illegal detention of the suspect) could not deprive the prosecutors of the opportunity to prove the defendant's guilt through the introduction of evidence wholly untainted by police misconduct. For example, in another case, a fourteen-year-old girl was found in the defendant's apartment during an illegal search. The girl's testimony that the defendant had had carnal knowledge of her was admissible because she was an independent source that predated the search of the apartment. Prior to the search, the girl's parents had reported her missing, and a police informant had already located her in the defendant's apartment (State v. O'Bremski, 423 P.2d 530 [1967]).

There are differences between the independent source and the purged taint exceptions. Under the independent source exception, the evidence was obtained from a source not connected with the illegal search or seizure. Thus, although the evidence might be viewed as suspect, it is admissible, because no illegality was involved (as when evidence was legally obtained before the police committed an illegal act). By contrast, under the purged taint exception, the evidence was obtained as a result of an illegal act, but the defendant's subsequent voluntary act removes the taint of the initial illegal act (as in the *Wong Sun* case, in which the suspect went back to the police station and voluntarily signed the confession). The subsequent voluntary act, in effect, purges the evidence of its initial illegality.

VI. PROCEEDINGS TO WHICH THE RULE DOES NOT APPLY

A. Private Searches

Since the Fourth Amendment's prohibition against unreasonable searches and seizures applies only to the actions of governmental officials, prosecutors may use evidence illegally obtained by private individuals (by methods such as illegal wiretap or trespass) as long as the police did not encourage or participate in the illegal private search. In one case, the Court said that the Fourth Amendment's "origin and history clearly show that it was intended as a restraint upon the activities of sovereign authority, and was not intended to be a limitation upon other than governmental agencies" (Burdeau v. McDowell, 256 U.S. 465 [1921]).

B. Grand Jury Investigations

A person being questioned by the grand jury cannot refuse to answer questions on the grounds that the questions are based on illegally obtained evidence (such as information from an illegal wiretap). The reason is that the application of the exclusionary rule in such proceedings would unduly interfere with the grand jury's investigative function (United States v. Calandra, 414 U.S. 338 [1974]).

C. Sentencing

Some lower courts have likewise permitted the trial judge to consider illegally obtained evidence in fixing sentence after conviction, even when the same evidence had been excluded during the trial because it was illegally obtained. During sentencing, they reason, a trial judge should consider any reliable evidence. The fact that it was obtained illegally does not necessarily affect its reliability. The evidence is not admissible, however, if state law prohibits its admission.

D. Violations of Agency Rules Only

The evidence is admissible if the search violates only an agency rule, but not the Constitution. Such violation does not offend fundamental fairness under the Constitution. For example, suppose police department rules provide that a person suspected of driving while intoxicated who refuses to take a blood-alcohol test must be informed that the refusal may be used as evidence against him or her in court. Failure by the police to give this warning does not exclude the evidence (South Dakota v. Neville, 459 U.S. 553 [1983]). An exception is made if state law provides that such evidence is not admissible.

E. Noncriminal Proceedings

The exclusionary rule applies only to criminal proceedings, not to proceedings such as civil or administrative hearings. Illegally obtained evidence may be admissible against another party in a civil tax proceeding or in a deportation hearing. It may also be admissible in administrative proceedings, as when an employee is being disciplined. For example, illegally obtained evidence may be admissible in cases in which a police officer is being investigated by the internal affairs division for violation of departmental rules. However, court decisions have established that even in administrative cases there are instances when illegally obtained evidence may not be admitted. One is if state law or agency policy prohibits the admission of such evidence. Another is if such evidence was obtained in bad faith, as when evidence against a police officer under investigation is obtained illegally and for the purpose of establishing grounds for disciplinary action.

F. Parole Revocation Hearings

In a recent case, the Court held that the exclusionary rule does not apply in state parole revocation proceedings (Pennsylvania Board of Probation and Parole v. Scott, 63 CrL 393 [1998]). In Scott, parole officers conducted what was later considered an

The Exclusionary Rule Basics

PURPOSE: To deter police misconduct.

APPLIED TO: Evidence obtained in violation of the Fourth Amendment.

SOURCE: Judge-made rule based on the Fourth Amendment.

WHEN INVOKED: Before trial, during trial, on appeal, or on habeas corpus.

WHAT IS EXCLUDED: Illegally seized evidence and "fruit of the poisonous tree."

LEADING CASES:

Weeks v. U.S. (1914)—Applied the exclusionary rule to federal criminal cases.

Mapp v. Ohio (1961)—Applied the exclusionary rule to state criminal cases.

WHAT IF TRIAL JUDGE ADMITS EXCLUDABLE EVIDENCE? No reversal if the trial court error is harmless. If harmful, conviction is reversed.

EXCEPTIONS: Some good faith exceptions, inevitable discovery, purged taint, and independent source.

RULE DOES NOT APPLY TO: Private searches, grand jury investigations, postconviction sentencing, agency rule violations, noncriminal proceedings.

THE FUTURE: May undergo refinements but is here to stay.

---

invalid search because of the absence of reasonable suspicion to believe that a parole violation had, in fact, occurred. The Court held that the exclusionary rule does not apply to parole revocation proceedings primarily because the rule does not apply "to proceedings other than criminal trials" and because application of the rule "would both hinder the functioning of state parole systems and alter the traditionally flexible, administrative nature of parole revocation proceedings." Although *Scott* involved parole revocation, there is good reason to believe that the exclusionary rule does not apply to probation revocation proceedings either, given the similar goals and functions of parole and probation.

VII. ARGUMENTS IN SUPPORT OF THE EXCLUSIONARY RULE

Among the arguments in support of the exclusionary rule[4] by its proponents are the following:

1. It deters violations of constitutional rights by police and prosecutors. A number of studies and testimonies by police officers support this contention.

2. It manifests society's refusal to convict lawbreakers by relying on official lawlessness—a clear demonstration of our commitment to the rule of law that states that no person, not even a law enforcement official, is above the law.

3. It results in the freeing of the guilty in a relatively small proportion of cases. A 1978 study by the General Accounting Office found that, of 2,804 cases in which defendants were likely to file a motion to suppress evidence, exclusion succeeded in only 1.3 percent. Moreover, the same study reported that, of the cases presented to federal prosecutors for prosecution, only 0.4 percent were declined by the prosecutors because of Fourth Amendment search and seizure problems.[5] Another study in 1983 found that "only between 0.6 and 2.35 percent of all felony arrests are 'lost' at any stage in the arrest disposition process (including trials and appeals) because of the operation of the exclusionary rule."[6]

4. It has led to more professionalism among the police and increased attention to training programs. Fear that evidence will be excluded has forced the police to develop greater expertise in their work.

5. It preserves the integrity of the judicial system, because the admission of illegally seized evidence would make the court a party to violations of constitutional rights.

6. It prevents the government, whose agents have violated the Constitution, from profiting from its wrongdoing. Somebody has to pay for the mistake—better it be the government than the suspect who has already been wronged.

7. It protects the constitutional right to privacy.

VIII. ARGUMENTS AGAINST THE EXCLUSIONARY RULE

Opponents, including justices in the Supreme Court, have argued strongly in opposition to the exclusionary rule. Among their arguments are the following:

1. In the words of Justice Benjamin Cardozo, "The criminal goes free because the constable has blundered." It is wrong to make society pay for an officer's mistake—punish the officer, not society.

2. It excludes the most credible, probative kinds of evidence—fingerprints, guns, narcotics, dead bodies—and thereby impedes the truth-finding function of the courts.[7]

3. It discourages internal disciplinary efforts by law enforcement agencies. If police are disciplined when the evidence will be excluded anyway, they suffer a double setback.

4. It encourages police to perjure themselves in an effort to get the evidence admitted. Particularly in major cases, the police might feel that the end justifies the means: It is better to lie than to let a presumably guilty person go free.

5. It diminishes respect for the judicial process and generates disrespect for the law and the administration of justice.[8]

6. There is no proof that the exclusionary rule deters police misconduct. In the words of Chief Justice Warren Burger, "There is no empirical evidence to support the claim that the rule actually deters illegal conduct of law enforcement officials."

7. Only the United States uses the exclusionary rule; other countries do not.

8. It has no effect on those large areas of police activity that do not result in criminal prosecutions. If the police make an arrest or search without any thought of subsequent prosecution (such as when they simply want to remove a person from the streets overnight or when they confiscate contraband so as to eliminate the supply), they do not have to worry about the exclusionary rule, because it takes effect only if the case goes to trial and the evidence is used.

9. The rule is not based on the Constitution; it is only an invention of the Court.[9]

10. It does not punish the individual police officer whose illegal conduct led to the exclusion of the evidence.

IX. ALTERNATIVES TO THE EXCLUSIONARY RULE

The continuing debate on the exclusionary rule has produced several proposals to admit the evidence obtained and then to deal with the wrongdoing of the police. Among the proposals are the following:

■ **An independent review board in the executive branch.** This proposal envisions a review board composed of nonpolice personnel to review allegations of violations of constitutional rights by the police. The problem with this alternative is that police oppose it, because it singles them out among public officials for differential treatment. Moreover, outsiders are viewed by the police as unlikely to be able to understand the difficulties and dangers inherent in police work.

- **A civil tort action against the government.** This would mean filing an action seeking damages from the government for acts of its officers. It poses real difficulty for the plaintiff, who would have to shoulder the financial cost of the litigation. Most defendants do not have the resources to finance a civil case, particularly after a criminal trial. Low damages awards against police officers usually discourage the filing of civil tort actions, except in egregious cases.

- **A hearing separate from the main criminal trial but before the same judge or jury.** The purpose of the hearing is to determine if, in fact, the officer behaved illegally in obtaining the evidence used during the trial and, if so, to impose the necessary sanctions on the officer. Although this is the least expensive and most expedient alternative, its effectiveness is questionable. If the violation is slight, the judge or jury will not look with favor on what may be considered an unnecessary extension of the original trial. Furthermore, if the criminal trial ends in a conviction, the chances of the officer being punished for what he or she did become remote.

- **Adoption of an expanded good faith exception.** The final report of the Attorney General's Task Force on Violent Crime in the late 1980s proposed a good faith exception different from and broader than that allowed by the Court in the *Sheppard* and *Leon* cases. The proposed good faith exception covers all cases in which the police would claim and can prove that they acted in good faith (not just when the magistrate issues an invalid warrant). It is based on two conditions: (1) The officer must allege that he or she had probable cause for the action in question, and (2) the officer's apparent belief that he or she was acting legally must be a reasonable one. These are questions of fact that will be determined by the judge or jury. Opponents fear that this proposal would lead to more violations of rights, using good faith as a convenient excuse. Good faith is a vague concept that is best determined on a case-by-case basis; it may therefore vary from one judge or jury to another. It is also maintained that this exception discourages training and rewards lack of knowledge. (The theory is that the more untrained and uninformed the police officer, the greater the claim to good faith his or her ignorance would permit.)

- **Adoption of the British system.** Under the British system, the illegally obtained evidence is admitted in court, but the erring officer is subject to internal departmental sanctions. The objection is that this system is not effective even in England, where the police system is highly centralized and generally has attained a higher level of professionalization. Internal discipline by peers has been and is a problem in U.S. policing; the public will most likely view this as an ineffective means of control.

Perspective on the Exclusionary Rule

The fate of the exclusionary rule over the long run is difficult to predict. It has endured for seventy turbulent years. Do the *Leon* and *Sheppard* decisions portend further modifications and exceptions to the rule by our highest Court? To two of the dissenters in those cases, "it now appears that the Court's victory over the Fourth Amendment is complete." Undoubtedly, to several of the justices in the majority, the decisions were a blow struck for criminal justice and against a rule that Chief Justice Burger has called "conceptually sterile and practically ineffective."

Source: Bradford P. Wilson, "Exclusionary Rule," *Crime File Study Guide* (Rockville, MD: National Institute of Justice, n.d.), p. 3.

X. THE FUTURE OF THE EXCLUSIONARY RULE

The debate on the exclusionary rule continues in some quarters, although the intensity has receded in recent years. Proponents and opponents of the exclusionary rule range across a continuum, from the purists to the accommodationists. Some proponents want the rule to remain intact and to be applied strictly, the way it was applied in the two decades after Mapp v. Ohio. Any concession is interpreted as widening the door that eventually leads to the doctrine's demise. Others are not so unbending, agreeing instead to "logical" and "reasonable" exceptions. Some opponents are not satisfied with such victories as the *Sheppard, Leon,* and other cases involving the good faith exception. They want to scrap the rule completely and admit the evidence without reservation or subsequent sanctions. Still others feel that the exclusionary rule should be modified, but there is no consensus as to what that modification should be.

What, then, of the future? The controversy surrounding the exclusionary rule has abated, but the debate will not completely fade away. In view of the several exceptions carved out in Court decisions (as discussed in this chapter), the exclusionary rule is no longer as controversial as it once was, nor is it as much a controlling force in law enforcement as when it first emerged. In the words of one observer:

> The exclusionary rule today is a shadow of that envisioned in *Weeks*. Ironically, the "deterrence rationale" has been invoked to permit so many uses of unconstitutionally seized evidence that the rule's efficacy as a deterrent may well be diminished. Certainly, unconstitutionally seized evidence can often be used to the government's advantage.[10]

During his time on the Supreme Court, Chief Justice Burger called for the rule's abolition, calling it "conceptually sterile and practically ineffective." Other justices have publicly expressed dissatisfaction with the rule and want it to be abolished or modified. They have made some inroads, but chances of complete abolition appear remote. To paraphrase Mark Twain, reports concerning the demise of the exclusionary rule are greatly exaggerated.

Summary

The exclusionary rule states that evidence obtained by the government in violation of the Fourth Amendment guarantee against unreasonable searches and seizures is not admissible in a criminal prosecution to prove guilt. Its main purpose is to deter police misconduct—the assumption being that if the evidence obtained illegally is not admitted in court, police misconduct in search and seizure cases would abate.

Since 1914, the exclusionary rule has been applied to federal criminal prosecutions, but it was not until 1961 that the rule was extended to state prosecutions. Illegally seized evidence is excluded under the rule; so are fruits of the poisonous tree, meaning evidence obtained as an indirect result of police misconduct. There are several exceptions to the exclusionary rule, the most notable being the good faith exceptions. In these cases, the evidence obtained is admissible if the officer acted in good faith, whether that faith be based on a warrant issued by a magistrate or a law passed by the legislature that is later declared invalid or unconstitutional. Court decisions have reaffirmed the principle that the exclusionary rule does not apply if the error or misconduct is committed by persons other than the police.

There are arguments for and against the rule. The debate used to be brisk and intense. Of several proposed alternatives to the exclusionary rule, none has gained general endorsement by those who bemoan the rule and would like to see it abandoned. Although the rule has undergone modification and erosion, it is premature to consider it seriously weakened or damaged. Chances are it is here to stay.

Review Questions

1. What is the exclusionary rule? Does it apply only to violations of Fourth Amendment rights or to violations of any constitutional right?

2. Is the exclusionary rule a constitutional or a judge-made rule? May it be modified by the U.S. Congress through legislation?

3. What did the Court hold in Mapp v. Ohio? Why is that case significant?

4. Distinguish between illegally seized evidence and the "fruit of the poisonous tree."

5. What is the good faith exception to the exclusionary rule? Give Court decisions in which the good faith exception applies.

6. Name at least four types of proceedings to which the exclusionary rule does not apply. Discuss each.

7. Give four arguments in support of the exclusionary rule, and discuss each.

8. Give four arguments against the exclusionary rule, and discuss each.

9. Give four alternatives to the exclusionary rule, and discuss each.

10. Discuss the future of the exclusionary rule.

Key Terms and Definitions

exclusionary rule: The rule of evidence providing that any evidence obtained by the government in violation of the Fourth Amendment's guarantee against unreasonable search and seizure is not admissible in a criminal prosecution to establish the defendant's guilt.

"fruit of the poisonous tree" doctrine: The doctrine holding that, once the primary evidence (the "tree") is shown to have been unlawfully obtained, any secondary evidence (the "fruit") derived from it is also inadmissible.

"good faith" exceptions: Exceptions to the exclusionary rule holding that evidence obtained by the police is admissible in court even if there was an error or mistake as long as such error or mistake was not committed by the police or, if committed by the police, was honest and reasonable.

harmless error doctrine: The doctrine holding that, if a motion to exclude illegally seized evidence is made on time, it is an error for the court to receive the evidence. This mistake requires a reversal on appeal of any conviction, unless admission of the evidence is found to be a harmless error.

"independent source" exception: An exception to the exclusionary rule holding that evidence obtained is admissible, despite its initial illegality, if the police can prove that it was obtained from an independent source that is not connected to the illegal search or seizure.

"inevitable discovery" exception: An exception to the fruit of the poisonous tree doctrine holding that the evidence is admissible, despite its initial illegality, if the police can prove that they would inevitably have discovered the evidence by lawful means, regardless of their illegal action.

"purged taint" exception: An exception to the fruit of the poisonous tree doctrine, applicable when the defendant's subsequent voluntary act dissipates the taint of the initial illegality. A defendant's intervening act of free will is sufficient to break the causal chain between the tainted evidence and the illegal police conduct, so that the evidence becomes admissible.

silver platter doctrine: A doctrine applied in federal courts from 1914 to 1960, under which evidence of a federal crime that had been illegally obtained by state officers was admissible in federal courts, although it would not have been admissible if it had been obtained by federal officers.

standing: The issue of whether a party in a case is the proper party to raise a legal issue.

Principles of Cases

Arizona v. Evans, 56 CrL 2175 (1995) The exclusionary rule does not require suppression of evidence seized in violation of the Fourth Amendment where the erroneous information resulted from clerical errors of court employees.

Boyd v. United States, 116 U.S. 616 (1886) The forced disclosure of papers amounting to evidence of a crime violated the constitutional right of the suspect to protection against unreasonable search and seizure, so the papers were inadmissible in court proceedings.

Burdeau v. McDowell, 256 U.S. 465 (1921) The Fourth Amendment's origin and history clearly show that it was intended as a restraint upon the activities of sovereign authority, not a limitation upon other, nongovernmental agencies.

Chapman v. California, 386 U.S. 18 (1967) In attempting to demonstrate mere "harmless error," it is not enough for the prosecution simply to show that there was other evidence sufficient to support the verdict. Rather, it must show that there was no reasonable possibility that a different result would have been reached without the tainted evidence.

Elkins v. United States, 364 U.S. 206 (1960) The Fourth Amendment prohibits the use of illegally obtained evidence in federal prosecutions, whether the evidence be obtained by federal or state officers. This case did away with the silver platter doctrine.

Illinois v. Krull, 480 U.S. 340 (1987) Evidence obtained by the police in accordance with a state law that is later declared unconstitutional is admissible in court as part of the good faith exception to the exclusionary rule.

Illinois v. Rodriguez, 497 U.S. 117 (1990) Consent given by somebody whom the police reasonably and honestly believed had authority to give consent is valid.

Mapp v. Ohio, 367 U.S. 643 (1961) The exclusionary rule, which prohibits the use of evidence obtained as a result of unreasonable search and seizure, is applicable to state criminal proceedings.

Massachusetts v. Sheppard, 468 U.S. 981 (1984) Evidence obtained by search is admissible in court when the officer conducting the search acted in objectively reasonable reliance on a search warrant that is subsequently declared to be invalid.

Minnesota v. Carter, 64 CrL 158 (1998) Defendants who were on a short-term visit and who, together with the lessee, used the apartment for a business purpose—to package drugs—had no legitimate expectation of privacy in the apartment. Therefore, the action of a police officer in looking in the apartment window through a gap in the closed blind and observing the defendants and the apartment's lessee bagging cocaine did not violate defendants' Fourth Amendment rights.

Minnesota v. Olson, 495 U.S. 91 (1990) An overnight guest, while the owner of the residence was away, has standing to raise the exclusionary rule.

Nix v. Williams, 467 U.S. 431 (1984) Evidence discovered because of a violation of the Sixth Amendment is admissible if the evidence would have been discovered anyway by lawful means. The prosecution must show "inevitable discovery" by a preponderance of evidence and need not prove absence of bad faith by the law enforcement officer responsible for the violation of the Sixth Amendment.

Rochin v. California, 342 U.S. 165 (1952) Even before the exclusionary rule was applied to the states, the Court held that some searches were so "shocking" as to require exclusion of the evidence seized. These cases were limited to acts of coercion, violence, or brutality.

Silverthorne Lumber Co. v. United States, 251 U.S. 385 (1920) Once the primary evidence (the "tree") is shown to have been unlawfully obtained, any secondary evidence (the "fruit") derived from it is also inadmissible. This case enunciated the fruit of the poisonous tree doctrine.

South Dakota v. Neville, 459 U.S. 553 (1983) Evidence obtained is admissible if the search does not violate the Constitution but only violates an agency rule.

State v. O'Bremski, 423 p.2d 530 (1968) Evidence obtained in an illegal search is admissible when testimony from an independent source predates the search.

Taylor v. Alabama, 457 U.S. 687 (1982) To break the causal connection between an illegal arrest and a confession that is the fruit of the illegal arrest, and therefore make the evidence admissible, the intervening event must be meaningful.

United States v. Caceres, 440 U.S. 741 (1979) The exclusionary rule does not apply if the violation involves administrative policy, and not a constitutional right.

United States v. Calandra, 414 U.S. 338 (1974) A person being questioned by the grand jury cannot refuse to answer questions on the grounds that the questions are based on illegally obtained evidence.

United States v. Crews, 445 U.S. 463 (1980) Illegally obtained evidence is admissible if the police can prove that it was obtained from an independent source not connected to the illegal search or seizure.

United States v. Houltin, 566 F.2d 1027 (5th Cir. 1978) Under the exclusionary rule, evidence obtained in violation of the Fourth Amendment cannot be used in a criminal trial against the victim of the illegal search or seizure. The Constitution does not require this remedy; it is a doctrine of judicial design.

United States v. Leon, 468 U.S. 897 (1984) The Fourth Amendment's exclusionary rule should not be applied to bar the prosecution from using evidence that has been obtained by officers acting in reasonable reliance on a search warrant that is issued by a detached and neutral magistrate but that is ultimately found to be invalid because it lacked probable cause.

United States v. Paroutian, 299 F.2d 486 (2nd Cir. 1962) An unlawful search taints all evidence obtained at the search or through leads uncovered by the search. However, the rule extends only to facts that were actually discovered by a procedure initiated by the unlawful act. If information that could have

emerged from an unlawful search in fact stems from an independent source, the evidence is admissible.

Weeks v. United States, 232 U.S. 383 (1914) Evidence illegally obtained by federal officers is inadmissible in federal criminal prosecutions.

Wolf v. Colorado, 338 U.S. 25 (1949) State courts were not constitutionally required to exclude illegally obtained evidence, so the exclusionary rule did not apply to the states. This decision was overturned in 1961 in Mapp v. Ohio.

Wong Sun v. United States, 371 U.S. 471 (1963) A defendant's intervening act of free will is sufficient to break the causal chain between tainted evidence and illegal police conduct; thus, the evidence otherwise illegally obtained becomes admissible.

Case Briefs

The Leading Case on the Application of the Exclusionary Rule to Federal Prosecutions

Weeks v. United States, 232 U.S. 383 (1914)

Facts: Weeks was arrested for using the postal service to transport tickets for a lottery. Other officers searched Weeks's home without a warrant and seized various articles and papers that were then turned over to the United States Marshall Service. Later that same day, police officers returned with a marshal and again searched Weeks's home without a warrant and seized letters and other articles. Weeks was charged with and convicted of unlawful use of the postal service.

Issue: Is evidence illegally obtained by federal law enforcement officers admissible in court? No.

Supreme Court Decision: Evidence illegally obtained by federal law enforcement officers is not admissible in federal criminal prosecutions.

Case Significance: This decision was a landmark in that, for the first time, the Court applied the exclusionary rule systemically, meaning to all criminal prosecutions in federal courts. Prior to this, exclusion of evidence was decided on a case-by-case basis and not based on a category of prosecutions. As significant as this decision was, the Court, for decades, declined to apply the Weeks rule to state criminal prosecutions.

That led to a dubious practice known as the silver platter doctrine, whereby federal courts admitted evidence of a federal crime if it was obtained illegally by state law enforcement officers, as long as there was no connivance with federal officers. That changed in 1961 in the case of Mapp v. Ohio, 367 U.S. 643 (1961), in which the Court ruled that illegally obtained evidence is not admissible in federal or state criminal prosecutions.

Excerpts from the Decision: "The effect of the Fourth Amendment is to put the courts of the United States and Federal officials, in the exercise of their power and authority, under limitations and restraints as to the exercise of such power and authority, and to forever secure the people, their persons, houses, papers, and effects, against all unreasonable searches and seizures under the guise of law. This protection reaches all alike, whether accused of crime or not, and the duty of giving to it force and effect is obligatory upon all intrusted under our Federal system with the enforcement of the laws. The tendency of those who execute the criminal laws of the country to obtain conviction by means of unlawful seizures and enforced confessions, the latter often obtained after subjecting accused persons to unwarranted practices destructive of rights secured by the Federal Constitution, should find no sanction in the judgments of the courts, which are charged at all times with the support of the Constitution, and to which people of all conditions have a right to appeal for the maintenance of such fundamental rights."

The Leading Case on the Extension of the Exclusionary Rule to the States

Mapp v. Ohio, 367 U.S. 643 (1961)

Facts: Mapp was convicted of possession of lewd and lascivious books, pictures, and photographs in violation of Ohio law. Three Cleveland police officers went to Mapp's residence pursuant to information that a person who was wanted in connection with a recent bombing was hiding out in her home. The officers knocked on the door and demanded entrance, but Mapp, telephoning her attorney, refused to admit them without a warrant. The officers again sought entrance three hours later, after the arrival of more police officers. When Mapp did not respond, the officers broke the door open. Mapp's attorney arrived but was denied access to his client. Mapp demanded to see the search warrant the police claimed they had. When a paper supposed to be the warrant was held up by one of the officers, Mapp grabbed the paper and placed it in her bosom. A struggle ensued, and the paper was recovered after Mapp was handcuffed for being belligerent. A search of the house turned up a trunk that contained obscene materials. The materials were admitted into evidence at trial, and Mapp was convicted of possession of obscene materials.

Issue: *Is evidence obtained in violation of the Fourth Amendment guarantee against unreasonable search and seizure admissible in state court? No.*

Supreme Court Decision: The exclusionary rule that prohibits the use of evidence obtained as a result of unreasonable search and seizure is applicable to state criminal proceedings.

Case Significance: The *Mapp* case is significant because the Court held that the exclusionary rule was thenceforth to be applied nationally, thus forbidding both state and federal courts from admitting evidence obtained illegally in violation of constitutional protection against unreasonable search and seizure. The facts in the *Mapp* case are given above, as detailed in the Court decision, to show why it was relatively "easy" for the Court to decide to exclude the evidence. In the minds of the Court justices, the facts in *Mapp* illustrate what can happen if police conduct is not restricted. *Mapp* was therefore an ideal case for the Court to use in settling an issue that had to be addressed: whether the exclusionary rule should now be applicable to state criminal proceedings. The facts in *Mapp* made it easier for the Court to answer that question in the affirmative.

Excerpts from the Decision: "Since the Fourth Amendment's right of privacy has been declared enforceable against the States through the Due Process Clause of the Fourteenth, it is enforceable against them by the same sanction of exclusion as is used against the Federal Government. Were it otherwise, then just as without the *Weeks* rule the assurance against unreasonable federal searches and seizures would be 'a form of words,' valueless and undeserving of mention in a perpetual charter of inestimable human liberties, so too, without that rule the freedom from state invasions of privacy would be so ephemeral and so neatly severed from its conceptual nexus with the freedom from all brutish means of coercing evidence as not to merit this Court's high regard as a freedom 'implicit in the concept of ordered liberty.'"

The Leading Case on the Good Faith Exception to the Exclusionary Rule

Arizona v. Evans, 56 CrL 2175 (1995)

Facts: Officers saw Evans going the wrong way on a one-way street in front of the police station. Evans was stopped, and officers determined that his driver's license had been suspended. When Evans's name was entered into a computer data terminal, it indicated that there was an outstanding misdemeanor warrant for Evans's arrest. While being handcuffed, Evans dropped a hand-rolled cigarette that turned out to be marijuana. A search of Evans's car revealed more marijuana under the passenger's seat. At trial, Evans moved to suppress the evidence as the fruit of an unlawful arrest because the arrest warrant for the misdemeanor had been quashed seventeen days prior to his arrest but had not been entered in the computer due to clerical error of a court employee. This was, in fact, true. The motion was denied, and Evans was convicted.

Issue: *Does the exclusionary rule require suppression of the evidence of marijuana obtained from Evans? No.*

Supreme Court Decision: The exclusionary rule does not require suppression of evidence seized in violation of the Fourth Amendment where the erroneous information resulted from clerical errors of court employees.

Case Significance: This case adds another exception to the exclusionary rule: when the error is committed by court employees instead of by the police. The exclusionary rule was fashioned to deter police misconduct, so the Court has refused to apply it to cases where the misconduct was not by the police. Previous cases have held that if the error is committed by the magistrate (as in Massachusetts v. Sheppard and United States v. Leon) or by the legislature (as in Illinois v. Krull), the exclusionary rule does not apply. The theme in these cases is that, if the error is not committed by the police, then the exclusionary rule should not apply because it was meant to control the behavior of the police. *Evans* is therefore consistent with the Court's holding in previous cases, and the ruling came as no surprise. The unanswered question is whether other errors by any public officer other than the police would be an exception to the exclusionary rule and therefore make the evidence admissible. The dissent in *Evans* argued that the Fourth Amendment prohibition against unreasonable searches and seizures applies to the conduct of all government officers, not just that of the police. The majority in *Evans* disagreed, preferring to focus on the original purpose of the exclusionary rule—which is to control police conduct.

Excerpts from the Decision: "The exclusionary rule operates as a judicially created remedy designed to safeguard against future violations [by police officers] of Fourth Amendment rights through the rule's deterrent effect. [The application of the exclusionary rule was to police officers rather than court employees (see United States v. Leon, 468 U.S. 897 [1974]). The Court found] no sound reason to apply the exclusionary rule as a means of deterring misconduct on the part of judicial officers [because application of the exclusionary rule to court personnel could not be expected to alter the behavior of the arresting officer. Furthermore] there [was] no indication that the arresting officer was not acting objectively reasonably when he relied upon the police computer record. Application of the *Leon* framework supports a categorical exception to the exclusionary rule for clerical errors of court employees."

Notes

1. Bradford P. Wilson, "Exclusionary Rule," *Crime File Study Guide* (Rockville, MD: National Institute of Justice, n.d.), p. 1.

2. Ibid.

3. *FBI Law Enforcement Bulletin,* September 1997, pp. 29, 32.

4. For an excellent discussion of the arguments for and against the exclusionary rule, see Yale Kamisar, Stephen H. Sach, Malcolm R. Wilkey, and Frank G. Carrington, "Symposium on the Exclusionary Rule," *Criminal Justice Ethics* 1, 1982, pp. 4ff. Some arguments for and against the exclusionary rule in these lists are taken from that source.

5. *Houston Chronicle,* July 8, 1979, sec. 4, p. 2.

6. A study by Thomas Davies, as cited in *The Oxford Companion to the Supreme Court of the United States,* ed. Kermit L. Hall (New York: Oxford University Press, 1992) p. 266.

7. Supra note 4, p. 118.

8. Steven Schlesinger, "Criminal Procedure in the Courtroom," in *Crime and Public Policy,* ed. James Q. Wilson (San Francisco: ICS Press, 1983), p. 195.

9. Supra note 1, p. 1.

10. Supra note 6, p. 266.

III. Searches and Seizures of Persons

5.

"Stop and Frisk," Border Seizures, and Stationhouse Detentions

Chapter Outline

Case Briefs

Terry v. Ohio

What You Will Learn in This Chapter

You will become familiar with the concept of "stop and frisk," a police practice given approval by the Court in Terry v. Ohio. You will learn that stop and frisk, although often used as one term, is actually separable into two concepts, each having its own meaning and purpose. You will also learn the limits of a frisk, as delineated in the case of Minnesota v. Dickerson, and how the stop and frisk rule applies in immigration and border situations. Finally, you will find out about the need for probable cause for fingerprinting and interrogation.

Introduction

We now deal with stop and frisk and other forms of intrusion into a person's freedom. In these cases, no arrest can be made, because probable cause has not been established. However, what starts off as a form of stop and frisk can quickly turn into an arrest if subsequent developments lead the police to conclude that probable cause has been established. The forms of intrusion discussed here are stop and frisk, immigration and border seizures, and stationhouse detention.

I. STOP AND FRISK—IN GENERAL

A. Issue and Origin

A legal issue in policing is whether a police officer may stop a person in a public place (or in an automobile), question the person about his or her identity and activities at the time, and frisk the person for dangerous (and perhaps illegally possessed) weapons. A "stop" and a "frisk" are forms of searches and seizures and therefore come under the Fourth Amendment. But because they are less intrusive than an arrest, they may be carried out based on *reasonable suspicion* rather than on *probable cause*.

Several states have passed **stop and frisk laws** that *allow an officer, based on reasonable suspicion rather than on probable cause, to stop a person in a public place and ask questions to determine if the person has committed or is about to commit an offense and to* *frisk the person for weapons if the officer has reasonable concern for his or her personal safety.* Other states, and some federal courts, have upheld such practices in judicial decisions even without statutory authorization. Underlying both statutory and judicial approval of stop and frisk is the notion that this practice does not constitute an arrest (although it comes under the Fourth Amendment) and therefore can be justified on less than probable cause.

B. The Leading Case in Stop and Frisk: Terry v. Ohio

One of the most important cases in law enforcement, and the landmark case that declared stop and frisk constitutional, is Terry v. Ohio, 392 U.S. 1 (1968). On October 31, 1963, a police detective observed two men on a street in downtown Cleveland at about 2:30 P.M. It appeared to the detective that the two men were "casing" a store: Each walked up and down, peering into the store window, and then both returned to the corner to confer. At one point, a third person joined them but left quickly. The detective observed the two men rejoin the third man a couple of blocks away. The detective then approached them, told them who he was, and asked for some identification. Receiving a mumbled response, the detective frisked the three men. Terry and one of the other men were both carrying handguns. They were tried and convicted of carrying concealed weapons.

On appeal, the Supreme Court held that the police have the authority to detain a person briefly for questioning even without probable cause to believe that the person has committed a crime. Such an investigatory stop does not constitute an arrest and is permissible when prompted by both the observation of unusual conduct that would lead to a reasonable suspicion that criminal activity is about to take place and the ability to point to specific and articulable facts to justify that suspicion. After the stop, an officer may frisk the person if the officer reasonably suspects personal danger to him- or herself or to other persons. The last paragraph of the majority opinion in Terry v. Ohio sets the foundation and rules for stop and frisk:

> We . . . hold today that where a police officer observes unusual conduct which leads him reasonably to conclude in light of his experience that criminal activity may be afoot and that the person with whom he is dealing may be armed and presently dangerous, where in the course of investigating this behavior he identifies himself as a policeman and makes reasonable inquiries, and where nothing in the initial stages of the encounter serves to dispel his reasonable fear for his own or others' safety, he is entitled for the protection of himself and others in the area to conduct a carefully limited search of the outer clothing of such persons in an attempt to discover weapons which might be used to assault him. Such a search is a reasonable search under the Fourth Amendment, and any weapons seized may properly be introduced in evidence against the person from whom they are taken.

(Read the Terry v. Ohio case brief at the end of this chapter.)

C. The Guidelines

Terry v. Ohio set the following guidelines, in sequence, to determine whether a stop and frisk is valid.

1. The Stop

a. Circumstances The police officer must observe unusual conduct that leads him or her reasonably to conclude, in the light of his or her experience, that (1) criminal activity is about to take place or that criminal activity has just taken place and (2) the person with whom he or she is dealing may be armed and presently dangerous.

b. Initial Police Action In the course of investigating such behavior, the officer must (1) identify himself or herself as a police officer and (2) make reasonable inquiries.

2. The Frisk

If the two requirements listed previously are satisfied, the officer, for his or her own protection, and that of others in the area, may conduct a carefully limited search (patdown) of the outer clothing of the person in an attempt to discover weapons that might be used to assault him or her. The guidelines given in Terry v. Ohio are usually translated into instructions in police manuals as the steps officers are to follow in stop and frisk cases. These are:

1. Observe.

2. Approach and identify.

3. Ask questions.

If the answers do not dispel the officers' concern for safety, they then follow this procedure:

1. Conduct a pat-down of the outer clothing.

2. If a weapon is felt, confiscate it and arrest the suspect (optional).

3. Conduct a full body search after the arrest (optional).

If, in the course of a frisk under these circumstances, the officer finds a dangerous weapon, he or she may seize it, and the weapon may be introduced in evidence against the party from whom it was taken. An example, taken from the *Law Officer's Pocket Manual,* goes like this: An officer observes two men loitering outside a bank in broad daylight. The men confer several times in front of the bank, looking through the bank's windows. Each wears a topcoat although it is a warm day. One of the suspects goes to a car parked directly across from the bank and sits behind the wheel. As the bank guard leaves the bank, the second suspect starts to head into the bank. The officer can then stop the suspect, identify him- or herself, ask for an explanation of the suspect's conduct, and then frisk the suspect if the answers do not alleviate the officer's suspicions. There is reason, based on the officer's experience, to believe that criminal activity is about to take place, that the suspects are likely to be armed, and that they pose a threat to public safety.[1]

HIGHLIGHT

The Reasonable Suspicion Requirement

In order to stop and detain someone under the Fourth Amendment, the U.S. Constitution requires that a law enforcement officer justify the stop on something more than a mere suspicion or hunch. The stop must be based on an articulable and reasonable suspicion that criminal activity is afoot. In developing and articulating reasonable suspicion, a profile [such as a drug courier profile] can be a useful tool in categorizing and attaching particular significance to otherwise innocent behavior. However, each decision to detain an individual must be judged on the individual facts available to an officer at the time of the stop, viewed in light of the officer's training and experience.

Source: William U. McCormack, "Detaining Suspected Drug Couriers," *FBI Law Enforcement Bulletin*, June 1991, pp. 31–32.

3. Reasonable Suspicion

To be valid there must be reasonable suspicion to stop and reasonable suspicion to frisk. The term **reasonable suspicion** has not been defined with precision by the Court. In one case, however, the Court said, "Reasonable suspicion is a less demanding standard than probable cause not only in the sense that reasonable suspicion can be established with information that is different in quantity or content than that required to establish probable cause, but also in the sense that reasonable suspicion can arise from information that is less reliable than that required to show probable cause" (Alabama v. White, 496 U.S. 325 [1990]). To justify a stop, *reasonable suspicion must be anchored in specific objective facts and logical conclusions based on the officer's experience.* Such general considerations as the high-crime nature of the area are no substitute for specific facts about the suspect or the suspect's conduct.[2] Reasonable suspicion cannot be based on a mere hunch (which has zero percent certainty) or even a general suspicion (which may have 10 percent certainty). Specific objective facts are needed.

On a scale of certainty, reasonable suspicion ranks lower than probable cause but higher than suspicion. In one case, the Court held that an appellate court that is asked, on appeal, to review the legality of police actions taken without a warrant should conduct a de novo (new) review of the trial court's finding on the ultimate issues of reasonable suspicion and probable cause, and not simply rely on the trial court's findings (Ornelas et al. v. United States, 59 CrL 2100 [1996]).

II.   STOP AND FRISK—TWO SEPARATE ACTS

Although the term *stop and frisk* is often used as though one continuous act were involved, they are actually two separate acts, each having its own requirements for legality. They are best understood if discussed separately.

HIGHLIGHT

Reasonable Suspicion as a Standard in Policing

"Reasonable suspicion is a less demanding standard than probable cause not only in the sense that reasonable suspicion can be established with information that is different in quantity or content than that required to establish probable cause, but also in the sense that reasonable suspicion can arise from information that is less reliable than that required to show probable cause. . . . Reasonable suspicion, like probable cause, is dependent upon both the content of information possessed by police and its degree of reliability. Both factors—quantity and quality—are considered in the 'totality of the circumstances—the whole picture.'"

Alabama v. White, 496 U.S. 325 (1990).

A. The Stop

A **stop** *is justified only if the police officer has reasonable suspicion, in light of his or her experience, that criminal activity is about to take place or has taken place.* A stop for anything else (such as to search for evidence) is illegal. For example, one officer stopped a suspect on the grounds that (1) he was walking in an area that had a high incidence of drug traffic, (2) he "looked suspicious," and (3) he had not been seen in that area previously by the officer. The Court held that these circumstances, although amounting to vague suspicion, did not meet the "reasonable suspicion based on objective facts" test, so the stop was unconstitutional (Brown v. Texas, 443 U.S. 47 [1979]). In November 1999, the Court agreed to decide whether a person's unprovoked flight when seeing an approaching police officer is so inherently suspicious a behavior as to justify a stop and frisk (Illinois v. Wardlow, No. 98-1036 [2000]). This issue was resolved on January 12, 2000. See Highlight box on page 123 for details.

Note, however, that what starts as a stop may turn into a valid arrest if probable cause is suddenly established. For example, suppose while on patrol late one night in a neighborhood notorious for burglary, Officer P sees a person emerge from an alley carrying something bulky. Officer P asks him to stop, whereupon he drops the object and takes off running. Officer P would have probable cause to arrest that person because of the combination of circumstances.

1. When Is a Stop a Seizure under the Fourth Amendment?
United States v. Mendenhall

The Fourth Amendment forbids unreasonable searches and seizures. Not all contacts with the police, however, constitute a seizure. The question is, When is contact with the police a "stop" that constitutes a seizure under Fourth Amendment protection, and therefore requiring reasonable suspicion, and when is it a "stop" that does not constitute a seizure under the Fourth Amendment?

The Court has answered this question, stating, "We conclude that a person has been 'seized' within the meaning of the Fourth Amendment only if, in view of all of the circumstances surrounding the incident, a reasonable person would have believed that he was not free to leave" (United States v. Mendenhall, 446 U.S. 544 [1980]). Here, three phrases stand out: (1) "in view of all of the circumstances," (2) "a reasonable person," and (3) "free to leave." In *Mendenhall*, federal officers approached a suspect as she was walking through an airport concourse. They identified themselves and asked to see her identification and airline ticket, which she produced and the officers inspected. She later alleged that what the officers did amounted to a seizure (a stop) that was illegal unless supported by reasonable suspicion. On appeal, the Court disagreed, saying that what happened in this case did not constitute a seizure. It cited such circumstances in this case as these: (1) The incident took place in a public concourse; (2) the agents wore no uniforms and displayed no weapons; (3) they did not summon the suspect to their presence, but instead approached her and identified themselves as federal agents; and (4) they requested, but did not demand to see, her ticket. Merely approaching the suspect, asking her if she would show them her ticket, and then asking a few questions did not constitute a seizure under the Fourth Amendment. In the same case, the Court gave examples of circumstances that might indicate a seizure, even if the person did not attempt to leave. These include the display of a weapon, some physical touching by the officer, or the use of language or tone of voice indicating that compliance with the officer's request might be compelled. The Court then noted, "In the absence of some such evidence, other inoffensive contact between a member of the public and the police cannot, as a matter of law, amount to a seizure of that person." In sum, cicumstances determine whether contact with the police constitutes a seizure.

2. Are Stops Based on Hearsay Information Valid?

An investigative stop based on second-hand or hearsay information is valid. For example, in one case, a police officer on patrol in a high-crime area received a tip from a person known to the officer that a suspect was carrying narcotics and had a gun. The officer approached the suspect's parked automobile and ordered him to step out. When the suspect responded by rolling down his window, the officer reached into the car and removed a loaded pistol from the suspect's waistband. The suspect was then arrested, and a subsequent search of the car led to the recovery of additional weapons and a substantial quantity of heroin. The Court rejected the defense's contention that a stop and frisk cannot be based on second-hand information, saying that the information from the known informant "carried enough indicia of reliability to justify" the forcible stop of the suspect (Adams v. Williams, 407 U.S. 143 [1972]).

3. Is a Stop Based on an Anonymous Tip Valid?

The preceding case involved information obtained by the police from a known informant. But what if the tip is anonymous? The Court has ruled that an anonymous tip, corroborated by independent police work, may provide reasonable suspicion to make an investigatory stop if it carries a sufficient indicia of reliability (Alabama v. White, 496 U.S. 325 [1990]). In this case, the police received an anonymous telephone tip that a certain White would leave a certain apartment at 3:00 P.M. in a brown Plymouth station wagon with a broken taillight, that she would be going to Dobey's Motel, and that she would have cocaine in a brown attaché case. The police immediately proceeded to the apartment building, where they saw a vehicle matching the anonymous caller's description. They then observed White leaving the building and driving the vehicle. The police followed her to Dobey's Motel, where she consented to a search of her vehicle, which revealed marijuana. White was then arrested; a subsequent search found cocaine in her purse. She was tried and convicted. On appeal, she sought suppression of the evidence, alleging that the search was illegal because the stop was not based on reasonable suspicion. The Court disagreed, saying that "standing alone, the tip here is completely lacking in the necessary indicia of reliability, since it provides virtually nothing from which one might conclude that the caller is honest or his information reliable and gave no indication of the basis for his predictions regarding White's criminal activities." However, "although it is a close question, the totality of the circumstances demonstrates that significant aspects of the informant's story were sufficiently corroborated by the police to furnish reasonable suspicion."

In a closely related issue, in November 1999, the Court agreed to rule on whether police officers may stop and frisk someone based solely on an anonymous, uncorroborated tip that the person is carrying a gun (Pennsylvania v. Allen, No. 98-1910). This case is different from Alabama v. White, in that in *White* the tip was corroborated by independent police work. In the case that is to be decided by the Court, there was no police corroboration; instead, the police argued that "the presence of a concealed weapon is inherently so alarming as to tip the constitutional balance in favor of a brief investigatory detention." This is important because, "ordinarily, an anonymous tip that describes seemingly innocent behavior (such as standing on a particular corner) and that has not been verified by further police work gives the police an insufficient basis on which to detain someone, even briefly."[3] This issue should be resolved soon.

4. Is Information Based on a Flyer from Another Jurisdiction Sufficient for a Stop?

The Court has decided that the police may stop a suspect on the basis of reasonable suspicion that the person is wanted for investigation in another jurisdiction (United States v. Hensley, 469 U.S. 221 [1985]). In this case, Hensley was wanted for questioning in connection with an armed robbery in St. Bernard, Ohio. The police circulated a "wanted" flyer to neighboring police departments. The police in nearby Covington, Kentucky, saw Hensley's car a week later and, knowing that he was wanted for questioning, stopped him and discovered firearms in the car. He was later convicted in federal court of illegal possession of firearms. He appealed the conviction, claiming that the stop was illegal because there was no probable cause, so the evidence obtained should have been excluded. In a unanimous opinion, the Court held that the police may act without a warrant to stop and briefly detain a person they know is wanted for investigation by a police department in another city. If the police have a reasonable suspicion, grounded in specific and articulable facts, that a person they encounter was involved in or is wanted for questioning in connection with a completed felony, then a "Terry-type" stop is permissible. Any evidence legally obtained as a result of that stop is admissible in court. In the *Hensley* case, the Court publicly recognized the need among law enforcement agencies for rapid communication and cooperation, saying:

In an era when criminal suspects are increasingly mobile and increasingly likely to flee across jurisdictional boundaries, this rule is a matter of common sense: it minimizes the volume of information concerning suspects that must be transmitted to other jurisdictions and enables police in one jurisdiction to act promptly in reliance on information from another jurisdiction.

5. Are Stops Based on "Drug Courier Profile" Alone Valid?

May a person who fits a **"drug courier profile"**—referring to *identifiers developed by law enforcement agencies indicating the types of individuals who are likely to transport drugs*—be stopped by the police? The Court has said that profiles are helpful in identifying people who are likely to commit crimes, but a drug courier profile alone does not justify a Terry-type stop. What is needed is that the facts, taken in totality, amount to a reasonable suspicion (United States v. Sokolow, 490 U.S. 1 [1989]). The emphasis is on *totality of circumstances.* In this case, Sokolow purchased two round-trip tickets for a flight from Honolulu to Miami. The facts surrounding that purchase, known to Drug Enforcement Administration (DEA) agents, were as follows: (1) Sokolow paid $2,100 for two round-trip tickets from a roll of $20 bills; (2) he traveled under an assumed name that did not match his listed telephone number; (3) his original destination was Miami, a place known for illicit drugs; (4) he stayed in Miami for only forty-eight hours, although the flight from Honolulu to Miami and back took twenty hours; (5) he appeared nervous during his trip; and (6) he had luggage, but none was checked. Because of these facts, which fit a drug courier profile developed by the DEA, Sokolow and his companion were stopped and taken to the DEA office at the airport, where their luggage was sniffed by a trained dog. Cocaine was found, and Sokolow was convicted of possession with intent to distribute. On appeal, the Supreme Court said that there was nothing wrong with the use of a drug courier profile in this case, because the facts, taken together, amounted to reasonable suspicion that criminal conduct was taking place. The Court noted that whether the facts in this case fit a profile was less significant than the fact that, taken together, they established a reasonable suspicion that justified a stop; therefore, the stop was valid.

Sokolow indicates that, although a drug courier profile is helpful, the totality of circumstances is more important in establishing reasonable suspicion. The Court noted that the activities of Sokolow, taken in isolation and individually, were consistent with innocent travel, but taken together they amounted to reasonable suspicion. In sum, there is nothing wrong with using drug courier profiles for a stop if the facts in a particular case, taken together, amount to reasonable suspicion. But the practice of using drug courier profiles alone to stop people, whether they be in airports or motor vehicles, is unconstitutional, according to the Court.

6. Are Stops Based on Racial Profile Alone Valid?

Stops based on racial profile alone have generated a lot of controversy. A lawsuit brought by black and Latino men is currently pending against the New York City Police Department challenging its stop and frisk policy.[4] A 1999 report by the state attorney general in New York notes that "blacks and Hispanics are much more likely than whites to be stopped and frisked by New York City Police Officers, often without legal reason." The same report states that "blacks were stopped six times more often than whites, while Hispanics were stopped four times more often."[5] The Court has not directly addressed this issue, but it is safe to say that stopping a motorist based on race alone is unconstitutional as a violation of the Equal Protection Clause. The more difficult question is whether race can be taken as one factor in the "totality of circumstances" when determining reasonable suspicion for a stop. Again, the issue has not been addressed by the Court, but the United States Court of Appeals for the Second Circuit has held that "police officers in Oneonta, New York, did not violate the Constitution when they tried to stop every black man in town in 1992 after a woman said she had been robbed in her home by a young black man." The court "questioned the police's tactics but ruled that they did not constitute discriminatory racial profiling because the officers were trying to find a suspect in a specific crime based on a description."[6] This issue will likely reach the U.S. Supreme Court in the near future.

7. Can Suspects Be Forced to Answer Questions?

A suspect who is stopped cannot be forced by the officer to reply to questions, but such refusal may give the officer sufficient justification to frisk because such refusal may fail to dispel suspicions of danger. Such refusal may also be taken to help establish probable cause, provided other circumstances are present.

8. What Is a Reasonable Scope and Duration of a Stop?

An investigatory stop must be temporary and not last any longer than necessary under the circumstances to achieve its purpose. Officers cannot detain a person for as much time as is convenient. This has been decided by the Court in a number of cases.

In one case, the Court held that a ninety-minute detention of an air traveler's luggage was excessive. In that case, the suspect's luggage was detained long enough to enable a trained dog to sniff for marijuana. The Court decided that the initial seizure was justified under Terry v. Ohio but added that the ninety-minute delay exceeded the permissible limits of an investigative stop: "Although we decline to adopt any outside time limitation for a permissible Terry stop, we have never approved a seizure of the person for the prolonged ninety-minute period involved here and cannot do so on the facts presented by this case" (United States v. Place, 462 U.S. 696 [1983]).

In another case, the Court held that the removal of a detainee without his consent from the public area in an airport to the police room in the airport converted the stop to an arrest. In this case, airport narcotics police stopped the suspect because he fit the drug courier profile used to identify people who are likely to be drug couriers. When the agents asked for and examined his ticket and driver's license, they discovered that he was traveling under an assumed name. They then identified themselves as narcotics agents and told the suspect that he was suspected of being a drug courier. Without his consent, they took him to a separate police room about forty feet away from the main concourse. One officer sat with the suspect in the room while another officer retrieved the suspect's luggage from the airline and brought it back to the room. The agents then asked the suspect if he would consent to a search of the suitcases. The suspect took out a key and unlocked one of the bags, which contained drugs. The Court concluded that, although the initial stop and questioning was valid, the subsequent conduct of the officers was "more intrusive than necessary" to carry out the limited investigation permitted under stop and frisk; therefore, it constituted an arrest. Since the police were interested mainly in gaining consent to search the suspect's luggage, there was no need to isolate him to gain that consent (Florida v. Royer, 460 U.S. 491 [1983]).

In a third case, a certain Luckett was stopped for jaywalking. He was detained for longer than was necessary to write out a ticket because the police wanted to radio head-quarters on an unsubstantiated hunch that there was a warrant for Luckett's arrest. The court of appeals held that the duration of the stop was unreasonable and that it turned the stop into an arrest. Since there was no basis at that time for an arrest, the detention was therefore unlawful (United States v. Luckett, 484 F.2d 89 [1973]).

In a fourth case, United States v. Sharpe, 470 U.S. 675 (1985), the Court found it reasonable for the police to detain a truck driver for twenty minutes. The driver was sus-pected of carrying marijuana in a truck camper. The length of the stop was due in part to the fact that the driver attempted to evade the stop, causing the two officers pursuing him to become separated. The officer who performed the stop therefore had to wait fif-teen minutes for his more experienced partner to arrive before making the search. Mar-ijuana was found in the camper, and the driver was arrested. The Supreme Court held that, to determine whether a detention is reasonable in length, the court must look at the purpose to be served by the stop and the time reasonably needed to carry it out. It added that courts should refrain from second-guessing police officers' choices, espe-cially when the police are acting in a swiftly developing situation, as in this case. This case indicates that the reasonableness of a stop must take into account not just the length of time involved but the needs of law enforcement as well.

In sum, it is difficult to state categorically how much time is sufficient for a valid stop. What we do know is that the Court uses this test: whether the stop is longer than necessary under the circumstances to achieve its purpose. If it is, the contact ceases to be a stop and becomes an arrest, which is invalid unless based on probable cause. This is determined by courts on a case-by-case basis, taking into account the circumstances surrounding the case.

9. What Degree of Intrusiveness Is Permissible?

The investigative method used must be that which is least intrusive and reasonably available to verify or dispel the officer's suspicion. Anything more intrusive makes the act invalid. Therefore, the greater the degree of police control over a detainee, the greater the likelihood that reviewing courts will impose the higher standard of probable cause. In the absence of some justification, the display of weapons by the police when making an investigative stop might turn a stop into an arrest. But the display of weapons in itself does not automatically convert a stop into an arrest. Lower courts tend to look at the display of weapons on a case-by-case basis to determine if the stop has been con-verted into an arrest because of such a display of force. The Supreme Court has not clarified what amount of force, if any, can be used by the police in stop and frisk cases.

B. The Frisk

1. Does a Frisk Automatically Follow a Stop?

A **frisk** *should follow only if there is nothing in the initial stages of the encounter that would dispel fears about the safety of the police officer or of others, based on reasonable sus-picion.* There is only one purpose of a frisk: protection of the officer or of others. In *Terry,* the Court said:

The Police May Stop and Frisk a Person Who Runs

The latest U.S. Supreme Court case on stop and frisk is Illinois v. Wardlow (No. 98-1036 [2000]), decided on January 12, 2000. In that case, Chicago police were patrolling an area known for narcotics traffic. Upon seeing the officers, Wardlow ran and was chased by the police. He was caught, the police patted him down, and they found a loaded Colt .38 pistol and arrested him. Tried and convicted, Wardlow appealed saying that the stop and frisk were illegal because the officers had no right to suspect him of a crime simply because he ran away. The Court disagreed, saying that Wardlow's presence in a high crime area in itself did not support reasonable suspicion of criminal activity, but added that "a location's characteristics are relevant in determining whether the circumstances are sufficiently suspicious to warrant further investigation." The Court then said that "it was Wardlow's unprovoked flight that aroused the officers' suspicion" and that "nervous, evasive behavior is another pertinent factor in determining reasonable suspicion, and headlong flight is the consummate act of evasion." All these factors justified the stop and frisk because, taken together, they amounted to reasonable suspicion.

When an officer is justified in believing that the individual whose suspicious behavior he is investigating at close range is armed and presently dangerous to the officer or to others, it would appear to be clearly unreasonable to deny the officer the power to take necessary measures to determine whether the person is in fact carrying a weapon and to neutralize the threat of physical harm.

A frisk after a stop should take place only if justified by concerns of safety for the officer and for others, not as an automatic consequence of a valid stop. For example, suppose X is stopped by a police officer late one night in a dimly lighted street on reasonable suspicion that X is about to commit an offense. The officer asks X questions to which X gives evasive answers, appearing uneasy and nervous. The officer may go ahead and frisk, because nothing in the initial encounter has dispelled reasonable concern for the safety of the officer or of others. By contrast, suppose that after the stop and initial questioning, the officer becomes convinced that X in fact resides in one of the nearby apartments and that he is returning home from a trip to a nearby store to buy cigarettes. The officer has no justification to go ahead and frisk.

The Court has stated that the *totality of circumstances,* meaning the whole picture, must be taken into account when determining the legality of a frisk. The detaining officers must have a specific, objective basis for suspecting the stopped person of criminal activity (United States v. Cortez, 449 U.S. 411 [1981]).

2. How Extensive May the Frisk Be?

A frisk must be limited initially to a pat-down of a person's outer clothing, and only an object that feels like a weapon may properly be seized. The object may turn out not to be a weapon, but if it feels like one, the frisk is justified. Conversely, if the object does not feel like a weapon, it cannot be seized. For example, suppose that, after a valid stop based on reasonable suspicion, a police officer has reasonable fear that the suspect

The Limits of a Frisk

"Although the officer was lawfully in a position to feel the lump in respondent's pocket, because *Terry* entitled him to place his hands upon respondent's jacket, the court below determined that the incriminating character of the object was not immediately apparent to him. Rather, the officer determined that the item was contraband only after conducting a further search, one not authorized by *Terry* or by any other exceptions to the warrant requirement. Because this further search of respondent's pocket was constitutionally invalid, the seizure of the cocaine that followed is likewise unconstitutional."

Minnesota v. Dickerson, 53 CrL 2186 (1993).

may be armed. She then frisks the suspect and in the process feels something soft that cannot possibly be considered a weapon. She cannot legitimately seize the object in question.

Possible confusion has arisen over the extent of the frisk after a stop because of the decision in United States v. Robinson, 414 U.S. 218 (1973). In the *Robinson* case, the Supreme Court held that a body search after an authorized arrest for driving without a permit is valid even when the officer admits that there was no possible danger to him or her and therefore no reason to look for a weapon. However, *Robinson* involved an arrest, not a stop and frisk, so arrest laws applied. Once the stop and frisk turns into an arrest based on probable cause, then the *Robinson* decision applies, and a body search may now be conducted. However, a frisk alone does not justify a body search, because its limited purpose is officer protection.

Use of force beyond a pat-down for weapons is likely to convert the contact into an arrest instead of a frisk. In one case, the Court of Appeals for the Sixth Circuit, in United States v. Robinson, 949 F.2d 851 (6th Cir. 1991), said: "When actions by the police exceed the bounds permitted by reasonable suspicion, the seizure becomes an arrest and must be supported by probable cause."

3. What Precisely May an Officer Do During a Frisk?

Minnesota v. Dickerson, 53 CrL 2186 (1993), clarified the limits of what the police can or cannot do in the course of a frisk. Police officers in Minnesota, noticing a suspect's evasive actions when approached, coupled with the fact that the suspect had just left a building known for cocaine traffic, decided to investigate further. They ordered the suspect to submit to a frisk. The frisk revealed no weapons, but the officer conducting it testified later that he "felt a small lump in suspect's jacket pocket." Upon examining the lump with his fingers, the officer concluded it was crack cocaine. He then reached into the suspect's pocket and retrieved what indeed turned out to be a small bag of cocaine. The suspect was convicted of possession of a controlled substance. On appeal, Dickerson contended that the evidence should have been suppressed, because its seizure was illegal in that it went beyond a pat-down search.

The Supreme Court held that objects that police detect in the course of a valid protective frisk under Terry v. Ohio may be seized without a warrant, but only if the officer's sense of touch ("plain feel") makes it *immediately apparent* that the object, although nonthreatening, is contraband, so that probable cause is present. In this case, however, the officer went beyond the lawful scope of *Terry* when, having concluded that the object he felt inside the suspect's jacket was not a dangerous weapon, he proceeded to "squeeze, slide, and manipulate it" in an effort to determine if it was contraband. Given the circumstances under which the evidence was obtained, the Court considered the evidence inadmissible.

Dickerson is significant because it clarifies what an officer may validly confiscate in the course of a frisk and under what circumstances. The Court held that what the officer did in this case was illegal, because even though he felt no danger to his person during the frisk, he went ahead anyway and conducted a further search, saying, "I examined it with my fingers and it slid and it felt to be a lump of crack cocaine in cellophane," which he then confiscated. Officers during a frisk have only one justification for confiscating anything: when they feel something that might reasonably be considered to be a weapon.

It is important to understand, however, that a valid frisk can turn in an instant into a valid search if the officer, in the course of the frisk, has probable cause to think that the object is seizable. For example, suppose Officer F frisks a suspect because she has reasonable grounds to believe that the suspect is carrying a weapon. While frisking, she feels something under the suspect's clothing, and although it does not feel like a weapon, the reasonable conclusion is that it is contraband—based on her experience as an officer in that area. Officer F may seize the item based on probable cause. In this case, the seizable nature of the object must be "immediately apparent" to the officer for the seizure to be valid. Said the Court in *Dickerson*:

> Although the officer was lawfully in a position to feel the lump in respondent's pocket, because *Terry* entitled him to place his hands upon respondent's jacket, the court below determined that the incriminating character of the object was not immediately apparent to him. Rather, the officer determined that the item was contraband only after conducting a further search, one not authorized by *Terry* or by any other exception to the warrant requirement.

4. What Constitutes "Plain Touch"?

Minnesota v. Dickerson is considered in many quarters as officially recognizing the use of the "plain touch" (also known as "plain feel") doctrine in law enforcement. For a long time, the Supreme Court has recognized the more popular "plain view" doctrine (discussed in chapter 9), which holds that items in plain view are subject to seizure by officers because they are not protected by the Fourth Amendment. Although using the sense of touch has long been accepted by the courts as a way of establishing probable cause, the *Dickerson* case reiterated the Supreme Court's recognition of this "variant" of the plain view doctrine. The **plain touch doctrine** states that *"if the officer, while staying within the narrow limits of a frisk for weapons, feels what he has probable cause to believe is a weapon, contraband or evidence, the officer may expand the search or seize the*

HIGHLIGHT

The Plain Touch Doctrine

Although using the sense of touch has long been accepted by the courts as a way of establishing probable cause, the *Dickerson* case reiterated the Supreme Court's recognition of this variant of the plain view doctrine. The plain touch doctrine states that "if the officer, while staying within the narrow limits of a frisk for weapons, feels what he has probable cause to believe is a weapon, contraband or evidence, the office may expand the search or seize the object." It differs from plain view in that what is used to determine probable cause is the sense of touch.

object."[7] In Minnesota v. Dickerson, the search would likely have been considered valid had the officer testified that, although what he touched did not feel like a weapon, it was immediately apparent to him, given his experience and the totality of circumstances, that the object was contraband.

5. Are "Fishing Expeditions" Allowed?

The frisk cannot be used for a **fishing expedition** *to see if some type of usable evidence can be found on the suspect.* Its only purpose is to protect the police officer and others in the area from possible harm. A frisk for any other reason is illegal and leads to the exclusion of any evidence obtained, regardless of how incriminating the evidence may be. Since the sole purpose of a frisk is police protection, anything felt in the course of the frisk that does not feel like a weapon cannot legally be seized. For example, suppose Officer X frisks a person because she suspects, after a valid stop, that the person is dangerous. In the course of the pat-down, Officer X feels a soft object in the person's pocket that she thinks might be cocaine. If confiscated based on that suspicion alone, the evidence is not admissible in court, because Officer X did not think that what she felt was a weapon, nor did she have probable cause to conduct a search. Suppose, however, that in the course of that frisk Officer X also comes across something that feels like a weapon. That weapon can be confiscated and the suspect arrested and then searched. If the cocaine is found in his pocket in the course of that search, such evidence is admissible because the frisk, which led to the arrest and subsequent search, is valid.

6. Is Consent to Frisk Based on Submission to Police Authority?

Consent to frisk based on submission to police authority is not voluntary and intelligent and is therefore invalid. As in all search and seizure cases, consent must be obtained without coercion or intimidation. For example, suppose Officer P, after a valid stop but without fearing for his life, tells a suspect in an authoritative tone that he would like to conduct a frisk—to which the suspect accedes. Such a frisk is not valid because consent, if at all given, was likely an act of submission to police authority and therefore not voluntary or intelligent. Validity would depend on how that alleged consent was obtained.

7. Can an Officer Frisk after a Stop without Asking Questions?

In Terry v. Ohio, the Court stated:

> Where in the course of investigating this behavior he identifies himself as a policeman and makes *reasonable inquiries,* and where nothing in the initial stages of the encounter serves to dispel his reasonable fear for his own or others' safety, he is entitled for the protection of himself and others in the area to conduct a carefully limited search of the outer clothing of such persons in an attempt to discover weapons which might be used to assault him [emphasis added].

This can be interpreted to mean that *reasonable inquiries* are required before a frisk. There may be instances, however, when a frisk is justified without the officer having to ask questions right after the stop. This is likely to occur in cases where the officer has reasonable suspicion that the person stopped, even before questions are asked, poses a danger to him or her or to others. The Court in *Terry* said that a frisk is justified if a "reasonably prudent man in the circumstances would be warranted in the belief that his safety or that of others was in danger." The only possible exception is if state law requires the officer to make reasonable inquiries before conducting a frisk.

III. DISTINCTIONS BETWEEN STOP AND FRISK AND ARREST

The concepts of stop and frisk and arrest can be confusing. Both involve a restriction of an individual's freedom by the police, and both can lead to a similar result—the individual's being charged with a crime. The confusion can be avoided if the distinctions between these two concepts are clearly understood. These distinctions are as follows:

	Stop and Frisk	Arrest
1. Degree of certainty needed	Reasonable suspicion	Probable cause
2. Extent of intrusion	Pat-down for weapons	Full body search
3. Purpose	Stop—to prevent criminal activity or to determine if a crime has taken place	To take the person into custody
	Frisk—to ensure the safety of officers and others	
4. Warrant	Not needed	Required, unless arrest falls under one of the exceptions
5. Duration	No longer than necessary to achieve the purpose	In custody until legally released
6. Force allowed	Stop—none	Reasonable force
	Frisk—pat-down	

Stop and Frisk of Motorists

"Motorists are subject to stop and frisk under the same circumstances as pedestrians. Moreover, a police officer may order the driver to step out of the car after a routine stop for issuance of a traffic ticket, even if the officer has no reasonable suspicion that the driver poses a threat to officer safety."

Pennsylvania v. Mimms, 434 U.S. 106 (1977).

IV. OTHER APPLICATIONS OF STOP AND FRISK

A. Motor Vehicles

Motorists are subject to stop and frisk under the same circumstances as pedestrians. Moreover, a police officer may order the driver to step out of the car after a routine stop for issuance of a traffic ticket, even if the officer has no reasonable suspicion that the driver poses a threat to the officer's safety (Pennsylvania v. Mimms, 434 U.S. 106 [1977]). In the *Mimms* case, two police officers, while on routine patrol, observed Mimms driving an automobile with an expired license plate. The officers stopped the vehicle for the purpose of issuing a traffic summons. One of the officers approached and asked Mimms to step out of the car and produce his owner's card and operator license. Mimms alighted, whereupon the officers noticed a large bulge under his sports jacket. Fearing that it might be a weapon, one officer frisked Mimms and discovered in his waistband a .38-caliber revolver loaded with five rounds of ammunition. Mimms sought to exclude the evidence during trial, claiming that it was obtained illegally. On appeal, the Court rejected Mimms's contention, saying that, once a police officer has lawfully stopped a vehicle for a traffic violation, he or she may order the driver to get out even without suspecting any other criminal activity or threat to the officer's safety. After the driver has stepped out, if the officer then reasonably believes that he or she may be armed and dangerous, the officer may conduct a frisk. Note, however, that while the authority of an officer to ask a driver to step out of the car is automatic after a valid stop, a frisk should be undertaken only if there is reasonable suspicion of a threat to officer safety.

B. Weapons in a Car

The police may also conduct a brief search of the vehicle after a stop, if the officer has reasonable suspicion that the motorist is dangerous and that there might be a weapon in the vehicle to which the motorist may have quick access.[8] If an officer has reasonable suspicion that a motorist who has been stopped is dangerous and may be able to gain control of a weapon in the vehicle, the officer may conduct a brief search of the passenger compartment even if the motorist is no longer inside the car. Such a search should be limited, however, to areas in the passenger compartment where a weapon might be found or hidden.

V. STOP AND FRISK APPLIED TO IMMIGRATION AND BORDER SEARCHES

A. Forced Temporary Detention

The rule is that Fourth Amendment standards govern the detention, interrogation, and arrest of suspected illegal aliens. The Court has said that, for the purpose of questioning, an immigration officer may detain against his or her will an individual reasonably believed to be an alien. The Court added:

> We hold that immigration officers, in accordance with the Congressional grant of authority found in Section 287(a)(1) of the Immigration and Naturalization Act, may make forcible detentions of a temporary nature for the purposes of interrogation under circumstances created by reasonable suspicion, not arising to the level of probable cause to arrest, that the individual so detained is illegally in this country. (Au Yi Lau v. United States Immigration and Naturalization Service, 445 F.2d 217, 223 [9th Cir.], cert. denied, 404 U.S. 864 [1971])

The person searched need not be entering the country. Anyone found in a "border area" is subject to search on the basis of reasonable suspicion, including visitors, employees, and transportation workers. Moreover, the area in which a border search may be conducted is not limited to the actual point of territorial entry. It may also be conducted at any place that is the "functional equivalent" of the border, such as an established station or intersection near the border or the place where an airplane first lands. For example, O'Hare Airport in Illinois is the functional equivalent of a border for international flights landing there.

B. Vehicles Stopped at Fixed Checkpoints

It is permissible for border officials to stop vehicles at reasonably located, fixed checkpoints (such as those set up in the interior) to question occupants of vehicles, even without reasonable suspicion that the vehicles contain illegal aliens. Moreover, no warrant is needed before setting up a checkpoint for immigration purposes (United States v. Martinez-Fuerte, 428 U.S. 543 [1976]).

AT A GLANCE
Stop and Frisk

BASIS: The Fourth Amendment prohibition against unreasonable searches and seizures.

HOW AUTHORIZED: By law or court decision.

PURPOSE:

Stop—to prevent criminal activity or to respond if criminal activity has just taken place.

Frisk—to protect officer and others.

CERTAINTY NEEDED:

Stop—reasonable suspicion.

Frisk—reasonable suspicion.

WHAT IS REASONABLE SUSPICION: Less than probable cause but more than mere suspicion. It must be based on specific, objective facts.

WHAT OFFICER IS ALLOWED TO DO:

Stop—ask questions.

Frisk—conduct a pat-down for weapons.

LIMITATIONS:

Stop—(1) must be temporary and no longer than necessary to achieve its purpose; (2) must be the least intrusive.

Frisk—(1) cannot squeeze, slide, or manipulate during a pat-down; (2) cannot be used as a "fishing expedition" for evidence.

C. Detention for Questioning Based on Reasonable Suspicion

Border patrol agents must have reasonable suspicion in order to detain and question the occupants of a car. However, a roving patrol cannot detain persons for questioning in an area near the border solely because the occupants of the vehicle "looked Mexican" (United States v. Brignoni-Ponce, 422 U.S. 873 [1975]). That fact alone does not constitute reasonable suspicion.

D. Factory Surveys of Aliens

Immigration officials sometimes conduct **"factory surveys,"** in which they *pay surprise visits to factories and ask employees questions to determine if they are illegal aliens*: "What is your nationality?" "Where were you born?" and so on. The Court has declared that this type of brief questioning does not constitute a Fourth Amendment "seizure," so no "particularized and objective basis" for suspecting the worker of being an illegal alien need be shown before conducting the survey (Immigration and Naturalization Service v. Delgado, 466 U.S. 210 [1984]).

 ## E. Detention of Alimentary Canal Smugglers

In a case involving the alimentary canal smuggling of narcotics across the nation's borders, the Court held that reasonable suspicion (instead of probable cause) is sufficient to permit customs agents at the border to detain a traveler suspected of engaging in this offense. The Court also concluded that agents were justified in detaining a traveler (who was suspected of having swallowed balloons containing drugs) for twenty-seven hours before they found drugs in her rectum and arrested her. The Court emphasized that such detention was necessary because of "the hard-to-detect nature of alimentary canal smuggling and the fact that the detention occurred at the international border." The Court took into account the needs of law enforcement under those circumstances and concluded that what the customs agents did was reasonable. Had this not been an immigration and border seizure case, the Court would not have considered the length of time involved to be reasonable.

VI. STATIONHOUSE DETENTION

Stationhouse detention is *less than arrest but is a greater limitation of freedom than the on-the-street detention in a stop and frisk. It is used in many jurisdictions for obtaining fingerprints or photographs, ordering police lineups, administering polygraph examinations, or securing other identification or nontestimonial evidence.*

 ## A. For Fingerprinting

In a rape case involving twenty-five youths who were detained for questioning and fingerprinting when the only leads were a general description and a set of fingerprints, the Supreme Court excluded the evidence obtained from fingerprints. But the Court also implied that detention for fingerprinting might be permissible even without probable cause to arrest. However, the Court made it clear that "narrowly circumscribed procedures" were required, including at least some objective basis for suspecting the person of a crime, a legitimate investigatory purpose for the detention (such as fingerprinting), detention at a time not inconvenient for the subject, and a court order stating that adequate evidence existed to justify the detention (Davis v. Mississippi, 394 U.S. 721 [1969]).

In a more recent case, however, the Court held that mere reasonable suspicion alone does not permit the police to detain a suspect at the police station to obtain fingerprints. Therefore, when the police transported a suspect to the stationhouse for fingerprinting without his consent, probable cause, or prior judicial authorization, the detention violated the Fourth Amendment. Said the Court:

> Our view continues to be that the line is crossed when the police, without probable cause or a warrant, forcibly remove a person from his home or other place in which he is entitled to be and transport him to the police station, where he is detained, although briefly, for investigative purposes. We adhere to the view that such seizures, at least where not under judicial supervision, are sufficiently like arrests to invoke the traditional rule that arrests may constitutionally be made only on probable cause. (Hayes v. Florida, 470 U.S. 811 [1985])

It must be noted, however, that in the *Hayes* case the suspect was transported to a stationhouse for fingerprinting without his consent. In cases, therefore, where such consent is obtained, probable cause should not be necessary. The problem is that courts consider the confines of a stationhouse as generally coercive; therefore, voluntary and intelligent consent may later be a problem if the absence of probable cause is challenged. Should the officer rely on consent, it is best to make it clear to the suspect that he or she is not under arrest, that he or she can leave at any time, and that the fingerprinting is purely voluntary. Moreover, the suspect's signature on a waiver form, duly witnessed, strengthens the officer's claim of voluntary and intelligent consent.

In the same case, however, the Court said that field detention (as opposed to stationhouse detention) for purposes of fingerprinting a suspect does not require probable cause as long as (1) there is reasonable suspicion that the suspect has committed a criminal act, (2) there is reasonable belief that the fingerprinting will either negate or establish the suspect's guilt, and (3) the procedure is promptly effectuated.

B. For Interrogation

The Court has held that probable cause is necessary for a stationhouse detention accompanied by interrogation (as opposed to just fingerprinting), even if no expressed arrest is made. In one case, the defendant was asked to come to police headquarters, where he received his Miranda warnings, was questioned, and ultimately confessed. There was no probable cause to arrest him, but there was some reason for the police to suspect him in connection with the crime being investigated. The Court held that the defendant was, in fact, arrested, and not simply stopped on the street, so probable cause was required to take him to the police station. Since that was absent, the confession obtained could not be admissible in court (Dunaway v. New York, 442 U.S. 200 [1979]). The Court added that the detention of Dunaway in this case was indistinguishable from a traditional arrest, because he was not questioned briefly where he was found but instead was transported to a police station and would have been physically restrained if he had refused to accompany the officers or had tried to escape from their custody.

Summary

Police have access to forms of limitation of a person's freedom other than an arrest. "Stop and frisk" is a police practice whereby a person is stopped in public and questioned. If the officer senses that the person may be dangerous, then a frisk follows for the purpose of removing any weapon. Although stop and frisk is often used as a single term, it actually represents two separate acts—a stop and a frisk. A stop is justified only if the officer has reasonable suspicion that criminal activity is about to take place or has taken place. A subsequent frisk is justified only if there is nothing in the initial stages of the encounter that would dispel reasonable fear for the safety of the officer or of others. The purpose of a frisk is officer safety; any act that goes beyond a pat-down for weapons (such as sliding, squeezing, or manipulating what the officer feels in the course of a pat-down) is illegal. What happens during the stop and frisk can, however, instantly lead to an arrest if the officer subsequently finds that there is probable cause to believe that the suspect has committed a crime.

Stationhouse detention is less than an arrest but constitutes a greater limitation of freedom than on-the-street detention in a stop and frisk. The Court has decided that reasonable suspicion alone does not permit the police to detain a suspect at the police station to obtain fingerprints; there must be probable cause or prior judicial authorization. Stationhouse detention accompanied by interrogation also requires probable cause, even if no formal arrest is made.

Review Questions

1. Although often used as one phrase, "stop" and "frisk" constitute two separate acts. When may an officer stop and when may an officer frisk?

2. What did the Court say in the case of Terry v. Ohio? The *Terry* decision used the phrase "reasonable suspicion" to justify stop and frisk. What does that phrase mean?

3. Is there any definite length of time after which a stop becomes an arrest? Explain. Are stops based on drug courier profiles alone valid?

4. Distinguish between stop and frisk and arrest.

5. What does Minnesota v. Dickerson say about the scope and extent of what an officer can do during

a frisk? Was the evidence obtained by the officer in that case admissible in court? Explain your answer.

6. What are stationhouse detentions? Are they valid if based on reasonable suspicion? Discuss.

7. May border officials, on the basis of suspicion, stop vehicles at checkpoints to ask if they contain illegal aliens? May they conduct a search?

8. Distinguish between stop and frisk and stationhouse detention.

9. "Stop and frisk applies to motor vehicles." What does this statement mean?

10. What are "factory surveys"? Are they valid?

Key Terms and Definitions

drug courier profile: Identifiers developed by law enforcement agencies indicating the types of individuals who are likely to transport drugs.

factory survey: A practice whereby immigration officials pay surprise visits to factories and ask employees questions to determine if they are illegal aliens.

fishing expedition: A search conducted by law enforcement officers with no definite seizable contraband or items in mind, in hopes of finding some usable evidence.

frisk: The pat-down of a person's outer clothing after a stop to see if he or she has a weapon or something that feels like a weapon, which can be seized by the officer; frisk is performed for the protection of the officer and of others.

plain touch doctrine: The doctrine that, "if the officer, while staying within the narrow limits of a frisk for weapons, feels what he has probable cause to believe is a weapon, contraband or evidence, the officer may expand the search or seize the object."

reasonable suspicion: A degree of proof that is less than probable cause, but more than suspicion. It is sufficient to enable a police officer to conduct a stop and frisk. Reasonable suspicion must be anchored in specific objective facts and logical conclusions based on officer's experience. It represents a degree of certainty (around 20 percent) that a crime has been or will be committed and that the suspect is involved in it.

stationhouse detention: A form of detention, usually in a police facility, that is short of arrest but greater than the on-the-street detention of stop and frisk. It is used in many jurisdictions for obtaining fingerprints or photographs, ordering police lineups, administering polygraph examinations, or securing other identification or nontestimonial evidence.

stop: The brief detention of a person when the police officer has reasonable suspicion, in light of his or her experience, that criminal activity is about to take place.

stop and frisk: A police practice that allows an officer, based on reasonable suspicion rather than on probable cause, to stop a person in a public place and ask questions to determine if that person has committed or is about to commit an offense and to frisk the person for weapons if the officer has reasonable concern for his or her personal safety.

Principles of Cases

Adams v. Williams, 407 U.S. 143 (1972) The Fourth Amendment does not require a police officer who lacks the precise level of information necessary for probable cause to arrest simply to shrug his or her shoulders and allow a crime to occur or a criminal to escape. A brief stop of a suspicious individual, in order to determine his or her identity or to maintain the status quo momentarily while obtaining more information, may be most reasonable in light of the facts known to the officer at the time. The basis for stop and frisk need not be the officer's personal observa-

tions; the information may be given by a reliable informant.

Alabama v. White, 496 U.S. 325 (1990) Reasonable suspicion is a less demanding standard than probable cause, not only because it can be established with information different in quantity or content from that required to establish probable cause, but also because reasonable suspicion can arise from information that is less reliable than that required to show probable cause.

Au Yi Lau v. United States Immigration and Naturalization Service, 445 F.2d 217 (9th Cir.), cert. denied, 404 U.S. 864 (1971) An immigration officer may, for purposes of questioning, detain against his or her will an individual reasonably believed to be an alien. Detention may be based on reasonable suspicion that the individual so detained is illegally in this country; probable cause is not required.

Davis v. Mississippi, 394 U.S. 721 (1969) By implication, a suspect may be fingerprinted even without probable cause to arrest. For it to be valid, however, narrowly circumscribed procedures are required —including at least some objective basis for suspecting the person of a crime, a legitimate investigatory purpose for the detention, scheduling of the detention at a time not inconvenient for the subject, and a court order that adequate evidence existed to justify the detention.

Dunaway v. New York, 442 U.S. 200 (1979) Probable cause is necessary for stationhouse detention of a suspect when accompanied by interrogation (as opposed to just fingerprinting), even if no formal arrest is made.

Florida v. Royer, 460 U.S. 491 (1983) Although the initial stopping and questioning of a suspect who fell within the drug courier profile was valid, the subsequent conduct of the police was more intrusive than necessary to carry out the limited investigation permitted under stop and frisk.

Hayes v. Florida, 470 U.S. 811 (1985) Mere reasonable suspicion alone does not permit the police to detain a suspect at the police station to obtain fingerprints. Therefore, when the police transported a suspect to the stationhouse for fingerprinting without his consent, probable cause, or prior judicial authorization, the detention violated the Fourth Amendment. However, reasonable suspicion is sufficient for field detention for fingerprinting.

Immigration and Naturalization Service (INS) v. Delgado, 466 U.S. 210 (1984) Factory surveys in which INS officials pay surprise visits to factories and ask employees questions to determine if they are in this country legally do not constitute a Fourth Amendment seizure, so no specific, objective basis for suspecting the worker of being an illegal alien need be shown.

Michigan v. Long, 463 U.S. 1032 (1983) If an officer has reasonable suspicion that a motorist who has been stopped is dangerous and may be able to gain control of a weapon in the car, the officer may conduct a brief search of the passenger compartment even if the motorist is no longer inside the car. Such search should be limited to areas in the passenger compartment where a weapon might be found or hidden.

Minnesota v. Dickerson, 53 CrL 2186 (1993) A frisk that goes beyond that allowed in Terry v. Ohio in stop and frisk cases is not valid. In this case, the search went beyond the pat-down search allowed by *Terry* because the officer "squeezed, slid, and otherwise manipulated the packet's content" before knowing it was cocaine.

Ornelas et al. v. United States, 59 CrL 2100 (1996) An appellate court that is asked, on appeal, to review the legality of police conduct that was made without a warrant should conduct a de novo (new) review of the trial court's finding on the ultimate issues of reasonable suspicion and probable cause and not simply rely on the trial court's findings.

Pennsylvania v. Mimms, 434 U.S. 106 (1977) A police officer may order the driver of a vehicle to step out of the vehicle after a routine stop for issuance of a traffic ticket, even if the officer has no reasonable suspicion that the driver poses a threat to his or her safety.

Terry v. Ohio, 392 U.S. 1 (1968) The police have the authority to detain a person briefly for questioning even without probable cause to believe that the person has committed a crime. Such an investigatory stop does not constitute an arrest. It is permissible when prompted by the observation of unusual conduct leading to a reasonable suspicion that criminal activity may be afoot and when the officer can point to specific and articulable facts to justify that suspicion. Subsequently, an officer may frisk a person if the officer reasonably suspects that he or she is in danger.

United States v. Brignoni-Ponce, 422 U.S. 873 (1975) The foreign-looking appearance of passengers in a car is not by itself sufficient grounds for even a brief stop for questioning. Reasonable suspicion must be present.

United States v. Hensley, 469 U.S. 221 (1985) The police may act without a warrant to stop and briefly detain a person they know is wanted for investigation by a police department in another jurisdiction. If the police have a reasonable suspicion, grounded in specific and articulable facts, that a person they encounter was involved in or is wanted for questioning in connection with a completed felony, then a "Terry-type" stop may be made to investigate that suspicion. Any evidence legally obtained as a result of that stop is admissible in court.

United States v. Luckett, 484 F.2d 89 (1973)

Detaining a person (who was stopped for jaywalking) for longer than was necessary to write out a ticket—because the police wanted to radio headquarters on a completely unsubstantiated hunch that there was a warrant for his arrest—constitutes detention of unreasonable length. The detention had therefore turned into an arrest.

United States v. Mendenhall, 446 U.S. 544 (1980)

"A person has been seized within the meaning of the Fourth Amendment only if, in view of all the circumstances surrounding the incident, a reasonable person would have believed that he was not free to leave."

United States v. Montoya de Hernandez, 473 U.S. 531 (1985)

Detention for twenty-seven hours of a suspect for alimentary canal drug smuggling was reasonable because of the hard-to-detect nature of that type of smuggling and the fact that the detention occurred at the international border, where the Fourth Amendment balance of interests weighs heavily in favor of the government.

United States v. Place, 462 U.S. 696 (1983)

The detention of an air traveler's luggage for ninety minutes so a trained dog could sniff it for marijuana constituted an excessive investigative stop.

United States v. Robinson, 414 U.S. 218 (1973)

A body search, after an authorized arrest for driving without a permit, is valid even when the officer admits that there was no possible danger to him or her and therefore no reason to search for a weapon.

United States v. Robinson, 949 F.2d 851 (6th Cir. 1991)

"When actions by the police exceed the bounds permitted by reasonable suspicion, the seizure becomes an arrest and must be supported by probable cause."

United States v. Sharpe, 470 U.S. 675 (1985)

The twenty-minute detention of a truck driver, who was suspected of carrying marijuana in a truck camper, was reasonable because the truck driver had attempted to evade the stop, causing the two officers pursuing him to become separated. The Court said that courts should refrain from second-guessing police officers' choices in a stop, especially when the police are acting in a swiftly developing situation.

United States v. Sokolow, 490 U.S. 1 (1989)

Taken together, the circumstances in this case (which included the use of a drug courier profile) established a reasonable suspicion that the suspect was transporting illegal drugs, so the investigative stop without a warrant was valid under the Fourth Amendment. Although the use of a drug courier profile was helpful, the totality of the circumstances was more important in establishing reasonable suspicion.

Case Briefs

The Leading Case on Stop and Frisk

Terry v. Ohio, 392 U.S. 1 (1968)

Facts: Police detective McFadden observed two men on a street in downtown Cleveland at approximately 2:30 P.M. on October 31, 1963. It appeared to McFadden that the two men (one of whom was petitioner Terry) were "casing" a store: Each walked up and down, peering into the store window, and then both returned to the corner to confer. At one point, a third man joined them but left quickly. After McFadden observed the two rejoining the same third man a couple of blocks away, he approached them, told them who he was, and asked them for identification. Receiv-

ing a mumbled response, the officer frisked all three men. Terry and one of the other men were carrying handguns. Both were tried and convicted of carrying concealed weapons. They appealed.

Issue: Is stop and frisk valid under the Fourth Amendment? Yes.

Supreme Court Decision: The police have the authority to detain a person briefly for questioning even without probable cause to believe that the person has committed a crime. Such an investigatory stop does not constitute an arrest and is permissible when prompted by both the observation of unusual conduct leading to a reasonable suspicion that criminal activity may be afoot and the ability to point to specific and articulable facts to justify that suspicion. Subsequently, an officer may frisk a person if the officer reasonably suspects that he or she is in danger.

Case Significance: The *Terry* case made clear that the practice of stop and frisk is valid. Prior to *Terry,* police departments regularly used stop and frisk either by law or by judicial authorization. But its validity was doubtful because the practice is based on reasonable suspicion instead of probable cause, which is necessary in arrest and search cases. The Court held that stop and frisk is constitutionally permissible despite the lack of probable cause for either full arrest or full search, and despite the fact that a brief detention not amounting to full arrest is a seizure, requiring some degree of protection under the Fourth Amendment.

Excerpts from the Decision: "The Fourth Amendment provides that 'the right of the people to be secure in their persons, houses, papers, and effects, against unreasonable searches and seizures, shall not be vio-

lated.' This inestimable right of personal security belongs as much to the citizen on the streets of our cities as to the homeowner closeted in his study to dispose of his secret affairs. . . . We have recently held that 'the Fourth Amendment protects people, not places,' Katz v. United States, 389 U.S. 347, 351 (1967), and wherever an individual may harbor a reasonable 'expectation of privacy,' id., at 361 (Mr. Justice Harlan, concurring), he is entitled to be free from unreasonable governmental intrusion. Of course, the specific content and incidents of this right must be shaped by the context in which it is asserted. For 'what the Constitution forbids is not all searches and seizures, but unreasonable searches and seizures.' Elkins v. United States, 364 U.S. 206, 222 (1960). Unquestionably petitioner was entitled to the protection of the Fourth Amendment as he walked down the street in Cleveland. . . . The question is whether in all the circumstances of this on-the-street encounter, his right to personal security was violated by an unreasonable search and seizure."

Notes

1. John G. Miles, Jr., David B. Richardson, and Anthony E. Scudellari, *The Law Officer's Pocket Manual* (Washington, DC: Bureau of National Affairs, 1988–89), 4:1–4:2.

2. Ibid.

3. Linda Greenhouse, "Does a Tip about a Gun Justify a Stop and Frisk?" *New York Times,* November 2, 1999, p. 1. Internet: http://www.nytimes.com/library/politics/scotus/articles/110299gun-carry.html.

4. Mark Hamblett, "Racial Profiling Suit against NYPD Survives," *New York Law Journal,* October 21, 1999, p. 1.

5. "Report: NYC Cops Search Blacks More," *New York Times,* December 1, 1999, p. 1. Internet: http://nytimes.com/aponline/a/AP-NYC-Police-Searches.html.

6. "Extensive Search of Black Men Is Upheld as Nondiscriminatory," *New York Times,* October 27, 1999, p. 2.

7. Steven L. Emanuel and Steven Knowles, *Emanuel Law Outlines: Criminal Procedure* (Larchmont, NY: Emanuel, 1998), p. 129.

8. Supra note 1, 4:3.

6.

Arrests

What You Will Learn in This Chapter

You will be introduced to the "top ten" list of searches and seizures involving persons. You will learn the definition and elements of an arrest, the types of authorized arrests, and the procedures used after an arrest. You will also gain insight into what the police can and cannot do during and after an arrest. Finally, you will know what can be done after an arrest and what the consequences of an illegal arrest are.

Introduction

The Fourth Amendment to the U.S. Constitution provides that "the right of the people to be secure in their persons . . . against unreasonable . . . seizures, shall not be violated." Arrest constitutes a "seizure" of a person, so the restrictions of the Fourth Amendment apply. Police officers must be well informed about the law of arrest, because successful prosecution usually depends upon the legality of the arrest. If the arrest is legal, then searches of the arrestee and the area within his or her control are also legal; conversely, if the arrest is illegal, any evidence obtained thereafter is not admissible in court.

The validity of an arrest is determined primarily by federal constitutional standards, particularly the requirement of probable cause. An arrest, with or without a warrant, cannot be valid unless there is probable cause—as determined by federal constitutional standards. In arrest cases (as distinguished from searches and seizures), probable cause "exists if the facts and circumstances known to the officer warrant a prudent man in believing that the offense has been committed." State provisions that are inconsistent with federal standards are invalid and unconstitutional, but state statutes may give more rights to a suspect than are required by the Fourth Amendment.

I. SEIZURES OF PERSONS—IN GENERAL

A. Seizure and the Fourth Amendment

In analyzing seizure cases under the Fourth Amendment, the first question is whether, given the circumstances, a seizure under the Fourth Amendment has occurred. If no

There Is No "Bright-Line" Rule When a Person Has Been "Seized"

No bright-line rule applicable to all investigatory pursuits can be fashioned. Rather, the appropriate test is whether a reasonable man, viewing the particular police conduct as a whole and within the setting of all the surrounding circumstances, would have concluded that the police had in some way restrained his liberty so that he was not free to leave. As the court states: "The test is necessarily imprecise because it is designed to assess the coercive effect of police conduct, taken as a whole, rather than to focus on particular details of that conduct in isolation. Moreover, what constitutes a restraint on liberty prompting a person to conclude that he is not free to 'leave' will vary, not only with the particular police conduct at issue, but also with the setting in which the conduct occurs."

Michigan v. Chesternut, 486 U.S. 567 (1988).

such seizure has occurred, then the provisions of the Fourth Amendment do not apply since those provisions apply only against "unreasonable searches and seizures." If a seizure did, in fact, occur, the question becomes, What kind of seizure was it? and What kind of protection is given by the courts in that kind of seizure?

B. Arrest As But One Form of Seizure

Seizures of persons are usually associated with arrest, but arrest is only one form of seizure—although certainly one of the most intrusive. There are other intrusions into a person's freedom that do not constitute arrest but nonetheless come under the protection of the Fourth Amendment. For example, stop and frisk, border searches, and roadblocks all come under the Fourth Amendment, but the constitutional requirements for these types of police actions are different from those for an arrest because they are lesser forms of intrusion. The term *seizure* under the Fourth Amendment is therefore broader than the term *arrest*. *Every arrest is a seizure, but not every seizure is an arrest.*

C. The "Top Ten" List of Searches and Seizures Involving Persons

Based on Court decisions, the intrusiveness of searches and seizures of persons under the Fourth Amendment may be ranked as follows (with number 10 being the most intrusive and number 1 the least intrusive):

10. Surgery to remove a bullet from a suspect's chest (Winston v. Lee, 470 U.S. 753 [1985])

9. Anal and cavity searches (Kennedy v. Los Angeles Police Department, 887 F.2d 920 [9th Cir. 1989])

8. Arrest (United States v. Santana, 427 U.S. 38 [1975])

7. Removal of blood in a hospital (Schmerber v. California 384 U.S. 457 [1966])

6. Stationhouse detention (Hayes v. Florida, 470 U.S. 811 [1985])

5. Stop and frisk (Terry v. Ohio, 392 U.S. 1 [1968])

4. Immigration and border searches (Au Yi Lau v. United States Immigration and Naturalization Service, 445 F.2d 217 [9th Cir. 1971])

3. Vehicle stops in general (Carroll v. United States, 267 U.S. 132 [1925])

2. Sobriety checkpoints (Michigan Department of State Police v. Sitz, 496 U.S. 444 [1990])

1. Roadblocks to control the flow of illegal aliens (United States v. Martinez-Fuerte, 428 U.S. 543 [1976])

Some contacts with the police are not protected at all by the Fourth Amendment because the degree of intrusiveness is considered by the courts to be minimal or nonexistent. Illustrative examples include asking a driver to get out of a car after having been stopped (Pennsylvania v. Mimms, 434 U.S. 106 [1977]), boarding a bus and asking questions that a person is free to refuse to answer (Florida v. Bostick, 111 S.Ct. 2382 [1991]), riding alongside a person "to see where he was going," (Michigan v. Chesternut, 486 U.S. 657 [1988]), and asking questions of witnesses to a crime. In November 1999, the Supreme Court agreed to decide the issue of whether manipulation by a police officer of a bus passenger's carry-on luggage is a form of search that is illegal absent suspicion about that particular passenger (Bond v. United States, No. 98-9349). This issue will soon be decided.

The "top ten" list is merely illustrative and admittedly subjective; individual perceptions may differ on which is more intrusive. Its significance, however, lies in that it shows how, over the years, Court decisions have, in essence, established a sliding scale of intrusion, as well as a sliding scale of constitutional protection. *The more severe the intrusion, the greater is the protection afforded by the courts.* Not all seizures of persons are protected equally by the courts just because they come under the Fourth Amendment. For example, the Court has held that a surgery, under general anesthetic, to remove a bullet from a suspect's chest for use as evidence cannot be undertaken *even with probable cause and a judicial order* (the highest possible form of protection in Fourth Amendment cases) unless there are compelling reasons for it because such a procedure is highly intrusive and violates the Fourth Amendment (Winston v. Lee, 470 U.S. 753 [1985]). By contrast, stopping drivers at roadblocks for brief questioning, routinely conducted at permanent checkpoints, does not need much protection because this is not highly intrusive (United States v. Martinez-Fuerte, 428 U.S. 543 [1976]).

HIGHLIGHT

A Home Is a Person's Castle

"The poorest man may in his cottage bid defiance to all the forces of the Crown. It may be frail—its roof may shake —the wind may blow through it—the storm may enter—the rain may enter— but the King of England can- not enter—all his force dares not cross the threshold of the ruined tenement."

Statement by Lord Chatham to the House of Commons in 1763, as quoted in John C. Hall, "Entering Premises to Arrest: The Threshold Question," *FBI Law Enforcement Bulletin,* September 1994, p. 27.

D.   Whose Perception Prevails in Seizures?

Whose perception determines whether a person has been seized? This question is important because the perception of the police may be different from that of a suspect. For example, arrest may not be in an officer's mind when detaining a suspect, but the suspect may feel he or she is under arrest. Whose perception determines whether a person has been seized—that of the police or of the person detained?

The answer is, neither. In a leading case, the Supreme Court held that the appropriate test to determine if a seizure has occurred is whether a *reasonable person,* viewing the particular police conduct as a whole and within the setting of all the surrounding circumstances, would have concluded that the police had in some way restrained a person's liberty so that he or she was not free to leave (Michigan v. Chesternut, 486 U.S. 567 [1988]). The Court in *Chesternut* said that there can be no single clear, hard-and-fast rule applicable to all investigatory pursuits. In that case, after observing the approach of a police car, Chesternut began to run. Officers followed him "to see where he was going." As the officers drove alongside Chesternut, they observed him pull a number of packets from his pocket and throw them down. The officers stopped and seized the packets, concluding that they might be contraband. Chesternut was arrested, and a subsequent search revealed more narcotics. Chesternut was charged with felony narcotics possession and convicted. On appeal, he sought exclusion of the evidence, alleging that the officers' investigatory pursuit "to see where he was going" constituted a seizure under the Fourth Amendment. The Supreme Court rejected this contention, noting that Chesternut was not seized before he discarded the drug packets and that the activity of the officers in following him to see where he was going did not violate the Fourth Amendment. Therefore, the evidence was admissible.

Another case using the same test is Florida v. Bostick (111 S.Ct. 2382 [1991]). In that case, without any suspicion and with the intention of catching drug smugglers, two uniformed law enforcement officers boarded a bus in Fort Lauderdale, Florida, that was en route from Miami to Atlanta. The officers approached Bostick and asked to see some identification and his bus ticket. The officers also asked Bostick for consent to search his bag and told him he could refuse consent. Bostick consented to the search of his bag, and cocaine was found. In court, he sought to suppress the evidence, alleging it was improperly seized. On appeal, the Supreme Court held that the evidence was admissible. The Florida Supreme Court had adopted an inflexible rule stating that the officers' practice of "working the buses" was per se unconstitutional. The U.S. Supreme Court rejected the Florida rule, holding that the result of such a rule was that the police in Florida (as elsewhere) could approach persons at random in most places, ask them questions, and seek consent to search, but they could not engage in the same behavior on a bus. Rather, the Court said, "[T]he appropriate test is whether taking into account all of the circumstances surrounding the encounter a reasonable passenger would feel free to decline the officers' requests or otherwise terminate the encounter."

Who or what is a "reasonable person" under this standard? That is ultimately for a judge or a jury to decide.

II. ARREST DEFINED

An **arrest** is defined as *the taking of a person into custody against his or her will for the purpose of criminal prosecution or interrogation* (Dunaway v. New York, 442 U.S. 200 [1979]). It occurs "only when there is governmental termination of freedom of movement through means intentionally applied" (Brower v. County of Inyo, 486 U.S. 593 [1989]).

An arrest deprives a person of liberty by legal authority. But mere words alone do not normally constitute an arrest; there must be some kind of restraint. A person's liberty must be restricted by law enforcement officers to the extent that the person is not free to leave on his or her own volition. It does not matter whether the act is termed an "arrest" or a mere "stop" or "detention" under state law. When a person has been taken into custody against his or her will for purposes of criminal prosecution or interrogation, it is an arrest under the Fourth Amendment, regardless of what state law says. For example, suppose state law provides that a police officer may "detain" a suspect for four hours in the police station for questioning without having "arrested" that person. If the suspect is, in fact, detained in the police station against his or her will, that person has been "arrested" under the Constitution and is therefore entitled to any rights given to suspects who have been arrested. Conversely, no arrest or seizure occurs when an officer simply approaches a person in a public place and asks if he or she is willing to answer questions—as long as the person is not involuntarily detained. A voluntary encounter between the police and a member of the public is not an arrest or a seizure. For example, there is no seizure if an officer approaches a person who is not suspected of anything and, without show of force or intimidation, asks questions of the person—who may or may not respond voluntarily.

An important question is, How long can the suspect be detained and how intrusive must the investigation be before the stop becomes an arrest requiring probable cause? The answer depends upon the reasonableness of the detention and of the intrusion. The detention must not be longer than that required by the circumstances, and it must take place by the "least intrusive means," meaning that it must not be more than that needed to verify or dispel the officer's suspicions. In the words of the Court: "In assessing whether a detention is too long to be justified as an investigative stop, we consider it appropriate to examine whether the police diligently pursued a means of investigation that was likely to confirm or dispel their suspicions quickly, during which time it was necessary to detain the defendant" (United States v. Sharpe, 470 U.S. 675 [1985]). Detention for a longer period of time than is necessary converts a stop into an arrest.

In sum, a person has been arrested if, under the totality of circumstances, a reasonable person would not have felt free to leave. This is the same rule that applies in seizures of persons in general, such as in stop and frisk, and not just in arrest cases. Who or what is a reasonable person is ultimately a question for a judge or jury to decide. In one case, the Court took the circumstances into consideration: "the threatening presence of several officers, the display of a weapon by an officer, some physical touching of the person or the citizen, or the use of language or tone of voice indicating that compliance with the officer's request might be compelled" (United States v. Mendenhall, 446 U.S. 544 [1980]).

III. ELEMENTS OF AN ARREST

Four essential elements must be present for an arrest to take place: seizure and detention, intention to arrest, arrest authority, and the understanding of the individual that he or she is being arrested.

A. Seizure and Detention

Restraint of the person may be either actual or constructive. **Actual seizure** is accomplished *by taking the person into custody with the use of hands or firearms* (denoting use of force without touching the individual) *or by merely touching the individual without the use of force.* **Constructive seizure** is accomplished *without any physical touching, grabbing, holding, or use of force.* It occurs when the individual peacefully submits to the officer's will and control.

Mere words alone do not constitute an arrest. The fact that a police officer tells a person, "You are under arrest," is not sufficient. The required restraint must be accompanied by actual seizure or peaceful submission to the officer's will and control. Furthermore, mere authority to arrest alone does not constitute an arrest. There must be either an actual or a constructive seizure. When none of that takes place, no arrest has taken place.

The case of California v. Hodari, 111 S.Ct. 1547 (1991), illustrates the element of seizure and detention in an arrest situation. In that case, two police officers were patrolling a high-crime area of Oakland, California, late one night. They saw four or five youths huddled around a small red car parked at the curb. When the youths saw the police car approaching, they fled. Officer Pertoso, who was wearing a jacket with the word "POLICE" embossed on its front, left the car to give chase. Pertoso did not follow one of the youths, who turned out to be Hodari, directly; instead, he took another route that brought them face to face on a parallel street. Hodari was looking behind himself as he ran and did not turn to see Officer Pertoso until they were right in front of each other —whereupon Hodari tossed away a small rock. The officer tackled Hodari and recovered the rock, which turned out to be crack cocaine. The issue brought to the Supreme Court on appeal was whether Hodari had been seized within the parameters of the Fourth Amendment, thus necessitating a warrant, when he dropped the crack cocaine. The Court said no and admitted the evidence, saying:

> To constitute a seizure of the person . . . there must be either the application of physical force, however slight, or where that is absent, submission to the officer's "show of authority" to restrain the subject's liberty. No physical force was applied in this case, since Hodari was untouched by [Officer] Pertoso before he dropped the drugs. Moreover, assuming that Pertoso's pursuit constituted a "show of authority" enjoining Hodari to halt, Hodari did not comply with that injunction and therefore was not seized until he was tackled. Thus, the cocaine abandoned while he was running was not the fruit of a seizure . . . and his motion to exclude evidence of it was properly denied.

In sum, there was no actual seizure because no physical force had been applied prior to the suspect's tossing away of the crack cocaine, nor had the suspect voluntarily submitted to the authority of the officer (constructive seizure).

B. Intention to Arrest

In the words of one police manual, "You have made an arrest as soon as you indicate by words or action your intention to take the person to the police station or before a judicial officer, or otherwise to take him into custody."[1] In this case, the intention to arrest is clear because it is either expressed or clearly implied in the officer's action. Without the requisite intent, there is no arrest even if a person is temporarily stopped or inconvenienced. For example, no arrest is occurring when an officer pulls over a motorist to issue a ticket, asks a motorist to step out of his or her car, stops a motorist to check his or her driver's license, or stops a person to warn of possible danger. In these cases, there may be a temporary deprivation of liberty or a certain amount of inconvenience, but there is no intent on the part of the police officer to take the person into custody; therefore, there is no arrest.

The requirement of intention to arrest is hard to prove because it exists in the mind of the police officer. There are cases, however, in which actions clearly indicated that the officer intended to take the person into custody, even though intent to arrest was later denied by the officer. For example, when an officer places handcuffs on a suspect, the intent to arrest likely exists even if the officer denies such intent.

When it is not clear from the officer's act whether there was intent to arrest, the Supreme Court has said that "a policeman's unarticulated plan has no bearing on the question whether a suspect was 'in custody' at a particular time" (Berkemer v. McCarty, 468 U.S. 420 [1984]). The test is the interpretation of a reasonable person, regardless of what the officer had or did not have in mind.

C. Arrest Authority

Authority to restrain distinguishes arrest from deprivations of liberty (such as kidnapping or illegal detention) committed by private individuals. When there is proper authorization, the arrest is valid; conversely, when proper authorization is lacking, the arrest is invalid. Invalid arrest can arise in the following cases: (1) when the police officer mistakenly thinks he or she has authority to arrest and (2) when the officer knows that he or she is not authorized to make the arrest but does so anyway.

Whether a police officer has arrest authority when off duty varies from state to state. Some states authorize police officers (by law, court decision, or agency policy) to make an arrest any time they witness a criminal act. In these states, the officer is, in effect, on duty twenty-four hours a day, seven days a week, for purposes of making an arrest, whether in uniform or not. Other states limit the grant of arrest power to when the officer is on duty.

D. Understanding by the Arrestee

The understanding that he or she is being arrested may be conveyed to the arrestee through words or actions. In most cases, the police officer says, "You are under arrest," thereby conveying intention through words. Similarly, some actions strongly imply that a person is being taken into custody, even though the police officer makes no statement. Examples of actions that strongly imply arrest include when a suspected burglar is subdued by police and taken to a squad car and when a person is being handcuffed to be taken to the police station even though no words are spoken. The element of understanding is not required for an arrest in the following instances: (1) if the suspect is drunk or under the influence of drugs and does not understand what is going on, (2) if the suspect is insane, and (3) if the suspect is unconscious.

IV. TYPES OF AUTHORIZED ARREST

There are generally two types of authorized arrest: *arrest with a warrant* and *arrest without a warrant*. The Supreme Court has repeatedly expressed preference for arrests with warrants. In one case, the Court said: "Law enforcement officers may find it wise to seek arrest warrants where practicable to do so, and their judgments about probable cause may be more readily accepted where backed by a warrant issued by a magistrate" (United States v. Watson, 423 U.S. 411 [1976]). Most arrests, however, are made without a warrant, so case law on arrests with a warrant has not been extensive. Nonetheless, an important body of case law has emerged from the Court over the years.

A. Arrest with a Warrant

Black's Law Dictionary defines an **arrest warrant** as *"a writ or precept issued by a magistrate, justice, or other competent authority, addressed to a sheriff, constable, or other officer, requiring him to arrest the body of a person therein named, and bring him before the magistrate or court to answer, or to be examined, concerning some offense which he is charged with having committed."*[2] (See Form 6.1.)

1. Issuance of a Warrant

To secure the issuance of a warrant, a complaint (by the offended party or by the police officer) must be filed before a magistrate, showing probable cause for arrest of the accused. It must set forth facts showing that an offense has been committed and that the accused is responsible for it. If it appears to the magistrate from the complaint and accompanying documents or testimony that probable cause exists for the charges made against the accused, the magistrate issues an arrest warrant.

In most states, the issuance of arrest warrants is strictly a judicial function and must therefore be performed by a judge or judicial officer. The issuing party must also be "neutral and detached." However, some states hold that, since the requirement of probable cause is designed to be applied by laypeople (as when a police officer arrests a suspect without a warrant upon probable cause), a nonjudicial officer such as a court clerk may properly issue warrants if empowered to do so by statute and if otherwise "neutral and detached." For example, the Court has decided that a municipal court clerk can issue an arrest warrant for municipal ordinance violations as long as such issuance is authorized by state law (Shadwick v. City of Tampa, 407 U.S. 345 [1972]).

The term **neutral and detached** means that the issuing officer is *not unalterably aligned with the police or prosecutor's position in the case.* Several cases illustrate its meaning.

- **Example 1:** A magistrate who receives a fee when issuing a warrant but not when denying one is not neutral and detached (Connally v. Georgia, 429 U.S. 245 [1977]).

- **Example 2:** A magistrate who participates in the search to determine its scope lacks the requisite neutrality and detachment (Lo-Ji Sales, Inc., v. New York, 442 U.S. 319 [1979]).

- **Example 3:** A state's chief investigator and prosecutor (state attorney general) is not neutral and detached, so any warrant issued by him or her is invalid (Coolidge v. New Hampshire, 403 U.S. 443 [1971]).

Supreme Court Form No. 21

WARRANT FOR ARREST

(FOR USE IN ANY COURT IN EITHER MISDEMEANOR OR FELONY CASES)

STATE OF MISSOURI,

County of   } ss.

IN THE   COURT WITHIN AND FOR SAID COUNTY

THE STATE OF MISSOURI TO ANY PEACE OFFICER IN THE STATE OF MISSOURI:

You are hereby commanded to arrest
who is charged with

alleged to have been committed within the jurisdiction of this court and in violation of the laws of the State of Missouri, and to bring him forthwith before this court to be here dealt with in accordance with law; and you, the officer serving this warrant, shall forthwith make return hereof to this court.

WITNESS THE HONORABLE   , Judge of

the said court and the seal thereof, issued in the county and state aforesaid on this   **day of**   , 19

Judge/Clerk of said Court

RETURN:

Served the within warrant in my County of
and in the State of Missouri on this   **day of**   , 19
by arresting the within named   and producing him before the said court on the
day of   , 19

Form 6.1 *Warrant*

The warrant requirement assumes that the complaint or affidavit has been reviewed by a magistrate before it is issued. Therefore, presigned warrants, which are used in some jurisdictions, are of doubtful validity. Nonetheless, they continue to be used, primarily because their use has not been challenged in court.

2. Contents of a Warrant

The warrant must describe the offense charged and contain the name of the accused or, if that is unknown, some description by which he or she can be identified with reasonable certainty. Thus, a **"John Doe" warrant**—one *in which only the name "John Doe"* *appears because the real name of the suspect is not known to the police*—is valid only if it contains a description of the accused by which he or she can be identified with reasonable certainty. A John Doe warrant without such a description is invalid, since it could be used by the police to arrest almost anyone and therefore lends itself to abuse.

3. Service of a Warrant

An arrest warrant is directed to, and may be executed by, any peace officer in the jurisdiction. In some states, a properly designated private citizen can also serve a warrant.

   a. Service within a State Inside the state of issuance, a warrant issued in one county or judicial district may be served by peace officers of any other county or district in which the accused is found. Some states, such as Texas and California, have statutes giving local peace officers statewide power of arrest—thereby allowing the peace officers of the county or district where the warrant was issued to make the arrest anywhere in the state. Even if statewide power of arrest is given, it is better, whenever possible, to inform local police agencies of activity within their jurisdiction, as a matter of courtesy and avoidance of jurisdictional misunderstanding.

   b. Service outside a State A warrant generally does not carry any authority beyond the territorial limits of the state in which it is issued. For example, an arrest cannot be made in Illinois on the basis of a warrant issued in Wisconsin. There are exceptions, perhaps the most important of which is **"hot pursuit"** (or fresh pursuit). Most states have adopted a uniform act *authorizing peace officers from one state who enter another in hot pursuit to arrest the suspect for a felony committed in the first state.* Another exception is when an in-state officer makes an arrest based on a "hit," referring to a finding that a warrant has been issued for a person in another state and known by the in-state officer through a national computer search.

   c. Time of Arrest In general, felony arrests may be made at any time, day or night, but misdemeanor arrests are usually made during daylight hours. In some states, an arrest for any crime—felony or misdemeanor—can be made at any hour of the day or night.

   d. Possession and Expiration of Warrant The arresting officer need not have the arrest warrant in his or her possession at the time of the arrest as long as it is shown to the accused after the arrest, if so requested. An arrest warrant should be executed without unreasonable delay. But unlike a search warrant, which must be served within a limited period of time, an arrest warrant does not expire until it is executed or withdrawn.

   e. Announcement of Police Presence Federal and many state statutes require that an officer making an arrest or executing a search warrant announce his or her purpose and authority before breaking into a dwelling. The idea is to enable voluntary compliance and avoid violence. Breaking into the premises without first complying with the announcement requirement may or may not invalidate the entry and any resulting search, depending on the law or court decisions in the state. Some states invalidate the entry and resulting search; others do not.

Is "Knock and Announce" Required?

"Given the long-standing common-law endorsement of the practice of announcement, we have little doubt that the Framers of the Fourth Amendment thought that the method of an officer's entry into a dwelling was among the factors to be considered in assessing the reasonableness of a search or seizure."

This is not to say, of course, that every entry must be preceded by an announcement. The Fourth Amendment's flexible requirement of reasonableness should not be read to mandate a rigid rule of announcement that ignores countervailing law enforcement interests. . . . the common-law principle of announcement was never stated as an inflexible rule requiring announcement under all circumstances."

Wilson v. Arkansas, 57 CrL 2122 (1995), at 2124.

The Court has addressed the issue of whether the knock-and-announce rule is required by the Constitution. The Court said that it is, but not in all cases. In Wilson v. Arkansas, 115 S.Ct. 1914 (1995), police officers obtained an arrest warrant for the suspect and a search warrant for her home. At Wilson's residence, the officers identified themselves as they entered the home through an unlocked door and stated that they had a warrant. They did not, however, knock and announce since there is no such requirement under Arkansas law. The police seized various drugs, a gun, and some ammunition. Tried and convicted of violating state drug laws, Wilson moved to suppress the evidence, saying that knock and announce was required by the Fourth Amendment in all cases. In a unanimous opinion, the Court ruled that the "knock and announce common law principle is part of the Fourth Amendment's requirement that searches and seizures be reasonable." It quickly added, however, that this did not mean that every entry should be preceded by an announcement, recognizing that "the common law principle of announcement was never stated as an inflexible rule requiring announcement under all circumstances." More significantly, the Court said that "[t]he Fourth Amendment's flexible requirement of reasonableness should not be read to mandate a rigid rule of announcement that ignores countervailing law enforcement interests." In essence, the Court held that, although knock and announce is part of the requirement of reasonableness in searches and seizures, it not a rigid rule and is subject to exceptions based on law enforcement interests. Such "reasonableness" need only be based on reasonable suspicion, not on probable cause.

The Court in *Wilson* did not enumerate the legally acceptable exceptions to the knock-and-announce rule. Instead, the Court stated:

For now, we leave to the lower courts the task of determining the circumstances under which an unannounced entry is reasonable under the Fourth Amendment. We simply hold that although a search or seizure of a dwelling might be constitutionally defective if police officers enter without prior announcement, law enforcement interests may also establish the reasonableness of an announced entry.

There are cases in which, because of **exigent circumstances,** an announcement is not required or necessary. The usual instances are these:

- When announcing presents a strong threat of violence or danger to the officers —for example, when the police are serving a warrant on a fugitive who is armed and dangerous.

- When there is danger that contraband or other property sought might be destroyed. Some states permit a magistrate to issue so-called no-knock searches, particularly in drug cases. They authorize entry without announcement, because otherwise the evidence might be destroyed. The constitutionality of such statutes has not been fully tested, although they have been upheld by lower courts.

- When officers reasonably believe that persons within the premises are in imminent peril of bodily harm.

- When people within are reasonably believed to be engaged in the process of destroying evidence or escaping because they are aware of the presence of the police.

- When the person to be arrested is in the process of committing the crime.

Exceptions to the announcement requirement are governed by law, court decisions, and agency regulations and so vary from state to state. The Court has ruled, however, that blanket exceptions are not allowed in drug-dealing cases even by judicial authorization (Richards v. Wisconsin, 61 CrL 2057 [1997]). In this case, a judge in Wisconsin created a rule that dispensed with the knock-and-announce requirement in all warrants to search for evidence involving drug deals. The justification for the rule was that drug-dealing cases frequently involved threats of physical violence or possible destruction of evidence anyway, so there was no need to knock and announce. The Supreme Court disagreed, saying that the Fourth Amendment does not allow a bright-line exception to the knock-and-announce requirement in cases involving felony drug dealing, and adding that even in these cases exceptions to the requirement must be made case by case, based on the reasonableness requirement. The Court did not say whether any type of blanket exception would be allowed at all. It is safe to say, however, that if the Court is disinclined to allow a blanket exception in drug-dealing cases, it is hard to imagine what types of cases might justify a blanket exception.

In a 1998 case, the Court held that the knock-and-announce rule does not set a higher standard for unannounced entries even if they involve property damage (United States v. Ramirez, 62 CrL 2108 [1998]). In this case, federal agents had a warrant authorizing unannounced entry to search the defendant's home for a fugitive, a certain Shelby, an escaped prisoner who had a prior record of violence and who, according to an informant, was in Ramirez's home. The agents set up a portable loudspeaker system and announced that they had a search warrant. Simultaneously, they broke a single window in the garage to discourage occupants from rushing to the garage where, the informant said, weapons were kept. Ramirez later admitted that he had fired a weapon because he thought his house was being burglarized, that he had a gun, and that he was a convicted

A Summary of the Knock-and-Announce Rule

The general rule is that the Constitution requires officers to knock and announce their presence when making arrests or conducting searches, with or without a warrant. Exceptions to this rule are determined by the states, either by law or court order. A blanket exception, such as that given by a judge in drug-dealing cases, is unconstitutional. Exceptions must therefore be determined by judges on a case-by-case basis and cannot be based on the nature of the case, serious though the case may be.

felon, but not the person sought by the agents. Indicted on charges of being a felon in possession of firearms, he sought to exclude the evidence, claiming that there were insufficient exigent circumstances to justify the agents' destruction of his property when executing the warrant. The Court disagreed, saying that the Fourth Amendment does not hold law enforcement officers to a higher standard when the no-knock entry results in property destruction. That standard, set in Wilson v. Arkansas, 514 U.S. 927 (1995), is that a no-knock entry is justifiable if officers have reasonable suspicion that obeying the rule would be dangerous or futile or would hamper effective investigation. That standard was met in this case.

4. Search Warrants and Third-Party Residences

In the absence of exigent circumstances, police officers executing an arrest warrant may not search for the person named in the warrant in the home of a third party without first obtaining a separate search warrant to enter the home. For example, in one case, federal agents learned from an informant that a federal fugitive could probably be found at a certain address. They procured a warrant for his arrest, but the warrant did not mention the address. Armed with the arrest warrant, the agents went to the address, which was the residence of a third party. The Court held that the arrest warrant could not be used as a legal authority to enter the home of a person other than the person named in the warrant; a search warrant had to be obtained (Steagald v. United States, 451 U.S. 204 [1981]). Note that the *Steagald* case involved the residence of a third party; this restriction does not apply when the place to be entered is the fugitive's residence.

In a subsequent case, the Court said that a warrantless, nonconsensual entry of a residence to arrest an overnight guest was not justified by exigent circumstances and therefore violated the Fourth Amendment (Minnesota v. Olson, 495 U.S. 91 [1990]). In that case, the police suspected a certain Olson of being the driver of a getaway car used in a robbery and murder. The police arrested the suspected murderer and recovered the murder weapon. They then surrounded the home of two women with whom they believed Olson had been staying. Without seeking permission and with weapons drawn, they entered the home and found Olson hiding in a closet. They arrested him, and he implicated himself in the crime. On appeal, Olson sought to exclude his statement, saying that there were no exigent circumstances to justify the warrantless entry. The Court agreed, saying that Olson's status as an overnight guest was in itself sufficient to show that he had an expectation of privacy in the home, which society was prepared to recognize as reasonable. The Court further said that there were no exigent circumstances justifying the warrantless entry, so the statement could not be admitted in court.

5. Legal Authorizations Other Than an Arrest Warrant

a. Citation A **citation** is *a writ from a court ordering a person to appear in court at a specified time.* Statutes in many states authorize the use of a citation for less serious offenses, such as traffic violations. A citation means the offender does not have to be taken into custody for that offense at that time. In the event of failure to appear at the time and date indicated, however, a warrant of arrest may be issued.

b. Bench Warrant A **bench warrant** is *a writ "from the bench," used to arrest and bring nonappearing defendants before the court.*

c. Capias **Capias,** literally meaning "you take," is the general name for several types of writ that *require an officer, for various causes, to take a defendant into custody.*[3] A capias is more generic than a bench warrant in that it is used to bring a person before the court for a variety of reasons, some of which are not necessarily related to a criminal case (as in case of protecting a witness or hearing judgment). It may also be issued when a defendant skips bail or is indicted by a grand jury, if the defendant is not already in custody. In contrast, a bench warrant is more specific; it is usually issued to effect an arrest when a person has been found in contempt, when an indictment has been handed down, or when a witness disobeys a subpoena.

B. Arrest without a Warrant

Although arrest warrants are preferred by the courts and desirable for purposes of protecting police from liability lawsuits, they are, in fact, seldom used in police work and are not constitutionally required, except in home arrests. About 95 percent of all arrests are made without a warrant. Police officers have a general power to arrest without a warrant. Laws vary from state to state, but the following provisions on warrantless arrests are typical.

1. Arrests for Felonies

a. Crimes Committed in the Presence of Officers This authority is based on common law principles, which have since been enacted into state statutes. For example, suppose, while on patrol, an officer sees a robbery being committed. She can make the arrest without a warrant. The term *in the presence* of a police officer refers to knowledge gained firsthand by the officer as a result of using any of his or her five senses—sight, hearing, smell, touch, or taste. Therefore, the police may make a warrantless arrest if probable cause is established by such means as these:

- **Sight:** Officer sees X stab Y, or S breaking into a residence.

- **Hearing:** Officer hears a shot or a cry for help from inside an apartment.

- **Smell:** Officer smells gasoline, gunpowder, gas fumes, or marijuana.

- **Touch:** Officer examines doors or windows in the dark or touches a car muffler or engine to determine if it has just been used.

- **Taste:** Officer tastes a white substance to identify it as sugar, salt, or something else.

b. Crimes in Public Places

The police are not required to obtain an arrest warrant before arresting a person in a public place, even if there was time and opportunity to do so, as long as the police are duly authorized to do so by statute (United States v. Watson, 423 U.S. 411 [1976]). In the *Watson* case, the Court noted that such authorization is given by federal law but said that such authorization is also given "in almost all of the States in the form of express statutory authorization." The warrantless arrest is valid because a public place has minimum protection under the Fourth Amendment or under the right to privacy.

c. Crimes in Private Residences

By contrast, the police may not enter a private home to make a routine warrantless arrest unless there is consent (Payton v. New York, 445 U.S. 573 [1980]). In this case, after two days of intensive investigation, detectives assembled evidence sufficient to establish probable cause to believe that Payton had murdered the manager of a gas station. They went to Payton's apartment to arrest him without a warrant. The warrantless entry and arrest was authorized by New York law. They knocked on the metal door, and when there was no response, they summoned emergency assistance and then used crowbars to open the door and enter the apartment. No one was there, but in plain view was a .30-caliber shell casing that was seized and later admitted into evidence at Payton's murder trial. Payton was convicted; he appealed, alleging that the Fourth Amendment requires police officers to obtain a warrant if making a felony arrest in a private residence when there is time to obtain a warrant. The Supreme Court agreed, saying that a warrant is needed in these types of cases (routine arrests in the absence of consent) and that state laws, such as that of New York, authorizing warrantless arrests in routine felony cases, are unconstitutional. (Read the Payton v. New York case brief at the end of this chapter.)

In a subsequent case, the Court held that a violation of the Fourth Amendment rule forbidding police from a warrantless and nonconsensual entry into a suspect's residence so as to make a routine felony arrest does not require the exclusion of a statement made by the suspect after his or her removal from that residence, as long as the arrest was supported by probable cause (New York v. Harris, 495 U.S. 14 [1990]). Despite the fruit of the poisonous tree doctrine, the Court admitted the evidence (the statement), saying that the rule in *Payton* was designed to protect the physical integrity of the home, not to grant criminal suspects protection for statements made outside their premises where the police have probable cause to make an arrest.

d. Crimes Not Committed in an Officer's Presence

For example, suppose a woman comes running to an officer to report that her husband has just been shot by a neighbor. The officer can make an arrest without a warrant.

e. Exigent (Emergency) Circumstances

The term *exigent circumstances* has many meanings, as the following examples illustrate.

■ **Example 1: Possibility of disappearance.** An officer is told by a reliable informant that he has just bought cocaine from a stranger in Apartment 141 at the corner of Main and Commerce and that the seller was getting ready to leave. Given the possibility of the suspect's disappearance, the officer can make the arrest without a warrant.

■ **Example 2: Hot pursuit.** In cases of hot pursuit, when a suspect enters his or her own or another person's dwelling, an officer can make the arrest without a warrant. In one case, police officers, acting without a search or arrest warrant, entered a house to arrest an armed-robbery suspect who had been seen entering the place just minutes before. The Supreme Court upheld the warrantless entry and search as reasonable, because to delay the entry would have allowed the suspect time to escape (Warden v. Hayden, 387 U.S. 294 [1967]). The term *hot pursuit* denotes some kind of chase, but it need not be extended. The fact that the pursuit ended almost as soon as it began does not render it any less a hot pursuit sufficient to justify an entry without warrant into a suspect's house. The following factors are relevant in a fleeing-suspect case: "(1) the gravity of the offense committed, (2) the belief that the suspect was armed, and (3) the likelihood that the suspect would escape in the absence of swift police action" (United States v. Williams, 612 F.2d 735 [3rd Cir. 1979]).

f. Danger to the Arresting Officer In Warden v. Hayden, 387 U.S. 294 (1967), the Court said, "The Fourth Amendment does not require officers to delay in the course of an investigation if to do so would gravely endanger their lives or the lives of others. Speed . . . was essential." This safety consideration has been extended by lower courts to include the safety of informants and the public.

2. Arrests for Misdemeanors

A warrantless arrest for misdemeanors may be made in the following cases if probable cause is present.

a. Offenses Committed or Attempted in an Officer's Presence This refers to misdemeanors the officer observes through any of his five senses. Under common law, the police could not make an arrest if the misdemeanor was merely reported to them by a third party. This is the one big difference in an officer's power to make an arrest in felony and in misdemeanor cases, at least in states that still adhere to the common law practice. In states that still observe this rule, the officer must obtain an arrest warrant or have the complaining party file a complaint, which can lead to the issuance of a warrant or summons. (See Form 6.2.) However, this "in police presence" rule is subject to so many exceptions specified by state laws that it becomes practically meaningless in many states. These are some of the common exceptions provided for by statute in various states:

■ If the misdemeanant will flee if not immediately arrested

■ If the misdemeanant will conceal or destroy evidence if not immediately arrested

■ If the case involves a traffic accident

MISSOURI UNIFORM COMPLAINT AND SUMMONS
ABSTRACT OF COURT RECORD

ORI NO. MO0510000
JOHNSON CO. SHERIFF'S DEPT.
STATE OF MISSOURI
IN THE CIRCUIT COURT OF JOHNSON
JOHNSON COUNTY ASSOC. CIRCUIT DIV.

№ 851402263

THE UNDERSIGNED POLICE OFFICER STATES THAT:

on or about (DATE)	upon/at or near (LOCATION/LOG PT.)	at (TIME)	☐ AM ☐ PM

WITHIN COUNTY AND STATE AFORESAID

Name (LAST, FIRST, MIDDLE)

Street Address

City		State	Zip Code

Date of Birth	Age	Race	Sex	Height	Weight

Driver's License No.   ☐ OP ☐ CH State
                              ☐ MC QUAL

Dept. of Revenue use only — Do not write in this space.

Disobeyed Signal (when light turned red)	☐ Past Middle of Intersection ☐ Middle of Intersection	☐ Not Reached Intersection
Disobeyed Stop Sign	☐ Stopped Wrong Place	☐ Walk Speed ☐ Faster
Improper Turn ☐ Left ☐ Right ☐ "U"	☐ No Signal ☐ Into Wrong Lane ☐ Cut Corner	☐ From Wrong Lane ☐ Prohibited
☐ Improper Passing ☐ Improper Lane Use	☐ At Intersection ☐ Between Traf. ☐ Cut In ☐ On Right ☐ On Hill ☐ Wrong Side of Pavement	☐ Lane Straddling ☐ Wrong Lane ☐ On Curve

DID UNLAWFULLY ☐ OPERATE ☐ PARK	V E H I L I C	Year	Make	Model	Style	Color
		Number			State	Year

AND THEN AND THERE COMMITTED THE FOLLOWING OFFENSE.

Describe Violation

Driving _____ MPH when limited to _____ MPH	Detection Method ☐ STA RADAR ☐ MOV RADAR	☐ WATCH (AIR) ☐ WATCH (GRND)	☐ PACE ☐ OTHER
In violation of	☐ RSMO ☐ ORD	Missouri Charge Code	☐ IN ACCIDENT ☐ DWI/BAC

THE ABOVE COMPLAINT IS TRUE AS I VERILY BELIEVE.

Officer	Badge No.

SWORN TO BEFORE ME THIS DATE.

Name & Title	Date

I promise to dispose of the charges of which I am accused through court appearance or prepayment of fine and court costs.	Court Date	Court Time	☐ AM ☐ PM
	Street Address COUNTY COURTHOUSE		
Signature X	City WARRENSBURG, MO 64093		

ON INFORMATION UNDERSIGNED PROSECUTOR COMPLAINS AND IN-FORMS COURT THAT ABOVE FACTS ARE TRUE AS HE VERILY BELIEVES.

Prosecutor's Signature	Date

FORM 37.1162A   G. A. THOMPSON, P. O. BOX 64681, DALLAS, TEXAS 75206   FORM MO17-5R

Form 6.2 *Complaint and Summons*

- If the officer has probable cause to believe that a misdemeanor is being committed, although not in his or her presence

- If domestic violence is involved

b. Home Entry for Minor Offenses In the case of a minor offense, a warrantless entry into a home to make an arrest will rarely be justified. For example, suppose an officer suspects a person of driving while intoxicated, a nonjailable offense in the particular state. The officer goes to the suspect's home to make an arrest before the alcohol can dissipate from his or her body. The officer cannot enter the home without a warrant or consent. Given the state's relatively tolerant view of this offense, an interest in preserving the evidence cannot overcome the strong presumption against warrantless invasion of homes.[4] Thus, in determining whether there are exigent circumstances, a court must consider the seriousness of the offense (Welsh v. Wisconsin, 466 U.S. 740 [1984]). However, home entry in felony or misdemeanor cases is justified if there is valid consent or if state law or state court decisions allow it.

3. Traffic Violations or Petty Offenses

Most states classify criminal offenses into felonies and misdemeanors. Other states, however, have such other categories as traffic offenses and petty offenses. These offenses may include acts that are prohibited by city or municipal ordinances, and not just those prohibited by the state's penal code. Penalties vary, as do permissible police actions after detention. In some jurisdictions, an arrest may be required; in others, an arrest is discretionary with the officer. There are jurisdictions where an arrest is not authorized at all, the issuance of citations being the only allowable procedure.

4. Minor Offenses Not Punishable by Jail Time

The question of whether the police can arrest persons for minor offenses not punishable by jail time has not been answered by the U.S. Supreme Court. Federal courts that have addressed this issue are not unanimous in their decisions. The closest the Supreme Court came to deciding the issue was in an appeal from Federal Court of Appeals for the Seventh Circuit in 1997. In that case, the defendant was arrested and charged with telemarketing without a required business license. He charged that the police violated the Fourth Amendment prohibition against unreasonable searches and seizures when they arrested him for a violation of an ordinance that was punishable only by a fine. The Court first accepted the case but then dismissed it a year later without deciding it, saying that the writ of certiorari was "improvidently granted" (Ricci v. Arlington Heights, No. 97-501 [1997], dismissed by the Court on May 4, 1998). With no decision from the Court, the inconsistent decisions from the various federal courts of appeals remain unresolved.

5. Citizen's Arrest

States authorize **citizen's arrest**—*an arrest made by citizens without a warrant*. Such arrests are usually limited to situations in which *a felony has actually been committed and the citizen has probable cause to believe that the person arrested committed the crime.* Some states also allow private citizens to make warrantless arrests for certain types of misdemeanors—usually those involving a "breach of the peace." The problem is that the definition of "breach of the peace" varies from one state to another and is usually ambiguous. The citizen, who may not know the difference between a felony and a misdemeanor, is taking a risk. Some states provide by law that police officers, when making an arrest, may enlist the aid of citizens and that the citizens are obliged to respond. Arrests by police officers with probable cause outside their territorial jurisdiction are valid, but they are in the category of citizen's arrests and are therefore subject to corresponding limitations.

V. WHAT THE POLICE MAY DO AFTER AN ARREST

Arrest is a significant part of the criminal justice process—for both suspect and police officer. For the suspect, the arrest signifies the start of a deprivation of freedom that can last (if convicted) until the sentence term has been served. For the police, it sets in motion certain procedures that must be followed if the arrestee is to be processed properly. It is important that the officer become fully aware of what he or she can do, particularly immediately after an arrest is made, or else the whole process might be subject to legal challenge. Some of the things an officer may do after an arrest, according to court decisions, include the following.

A. Search the Arrestee

After an arrest, the police may automatically search the arrested person regardless of the offense for which the person has been placed under arrest (United States v. Robinson, 414 U.S. 218 [1973]). In *Robinson,* the Court said that a "custodial arrest of a suspect based on probable cause is a reasonable intrusion under the Fourth Amendment; that intrusion being lawful, a search incident to the arrest requires no additional justification." The "full body search" rule, therefore, applies whether the suspect is arrested for a brutal murder or for shoplifting. The rule is designed to protect the police and to prevent the destruction of evidence. Authorization to body-search, however, does not authorize strip or body cavity searches, which are more intrusive.

B. Search the Area of Immediate Control

Once a lawful arrest has been made, the police may search the area within the suspect's immediate control, meaning the area within which the suspect may grab a weapon or destroy evidence (Chimel v. California, 395 U.S. 752 [1969]). What is meant by "area within immediate control"? In *Chimel,* the Court defined the allowable area of search as follows:

When an arrest is made, it is reasonable for the arresting officer to search the person arrested in order to remove any weapons that the latter might seek to use in order to resist arrest or effect his escape. . . . In addition, it is entirely reasonable for the arresting officer to search for and seize any evidence on the arrestee's person in order to prevent its concealment or destruction. And the area into which an arrestee might reach in order to grab a weapon or evidentiary items must, of course, be governed by a like rule.

The most limited (and perhaps accurate) interpretation of that phrase is that the area is limited to the person's wingspan—the area covered by the spread of the suspect's arms and hands. Some lower courts tend to be liberal in defining the area into which there is some possibility that an arrested person might reach for a weapon. In one case, an accused was sitting on a bed at the time of her arrest; the area underneath her bed was deemed to be within her reach. In another case, the fact that the arrestee was handcuffed (and his reach thereby limited) did not mean that the officers could not go ahead and search the area of immediate control. In a third case, the search of a kitchen shelf six feet away from the arrestee was considered by the court as a search incident to an arrest, although an officer stood between the female arrestee (who was being arrested for forgery) and the shelf while the arrest was being made.[5]

The Court has held that a search incident to arrest is valid only if it is "substantially contemporaneous with the arrest and is confined to the immediate vicinity of the arrest." The Court added that "if a search of a house is to be upheld as incident to an arrest, that arrest must take place inside the house, not somewhere outside—whether two blocks away, twenty feet away, or on the sidewalk near the front steps" (Vale v. Louisiana, 399 U.S. 30 [1970]).[6] If the search goes beyond the area of immediate control, the officer must obtain a search warrant. However, some courts have permitted the police to search areas in a residence that are beyond a defendant's reach even without a warrant if (1) there is some type of emergency requiring immediate action that cannot await the preparation of a search warrant (such as possible destruction of evidence) and (2) the search is focused on a predetermined target (such as narcotics in a particular dresser drawer), rather than being a general exploratory search.

C. Search the Passenger Compartment of a Motor Vehicle

In arrests involving automobiles, the Court has held that, when the police have made a lawful custodial arrest of the occupant of a car, they may, incident to that arrest, search the car's entire passenger compartment (front and back seats) and open any containers found therein. This includes "closed or open glove compartments, consoles, or other receptacles located anywhere within the passenger compartment, as well as luggage, boxes, bags, clothing, and the like" (New York v. Belton, 453 U.S. 454 [1981]). The only limitation is that such containers must reasonably contain something that might pose a danger to the officer or hold evidence in support of the offense for which the suspect has been arrested. However, the Court has also said that "our holding encompasses only the interior of the passenger compartment and does not encompass the trunk." Neither does it authorize the opening of a locked glove compartment.

D. Use Handcuffs Subject to Department Policy

The use of handcuffs in arrests is either governed by department rules or left to the discretion of the police. The Supreme Court has not addressed the use of handcuffs by police, and there are no authoritative lower court decisions on the issue. As a general rule, however, handcuffs are required or recommended by police departments in felony offenses but not in misdemeanor cases unless there is potential personal danger to the police. If there is a stated policy (or, if not, on grounds of discretion), it is unlikely that a police officer will be held liable for using handcuffs in the process of making an arrest.

E. Monitor the Movement of the Arrestee

The police may accompany an arrested person into his or her residence after a lawful arrest, if they allow him or her to go there before transport to the police station. For example, suppose X is arrested by virtue of an arrest warrant. After arrest, X asks permission to go to his apartment to inform his wife and pick up some things he will need in jail. The officer may allow X to do that, but the movements of the arrestee can be monitored. In one case, the Supreme Court said, "It is not unreasonable under the Fourth Amendment for a police officer, as a matter of routine, to monitor the movements of an arrested person, as his judgment dictates, following an arrest. The officer's need to ensure his own safety—as well as the integrity of the arrest—is compelling" (Washington v. Chrisman, 455 U.S. 1 [1982]). The Court held that the officer is allowed to remain with the arrestee at all times after the arrest.

F. Search the Arrestee at the Place of Detention

Once brought to the place of detention (usually either a jail or a police lockup), the arrestee may be subjected to a complete search of his or her person, if this was not done during arrest. This procedure is valid even in the absence of probable cause to search. The justification for the search of an arrestee's person on arrival at the station is that it is simply an inventory incidental to being booked in jail. The inventory, which is a search under the Fourth Amendment, has these legitimate objectives: (1) to protect the arrestee's property while he or she is in jail, (2) to protect the police from groundless claims that they have not adequately safeguarded the defendant's property, (3) to safeguard the detention facility by preventing introduction of weapons or contraband, and (4) to ascertain or verify the identity of the person arrested.[7]

Such searches may include the individual's wallet or other personal property. This rule that a routine inventory search is lawful applies only when the prisoner is to be jailed. If the suspect is brought in merely to be booked and then released, some other reasons will have to be used to justify a warrantless search by the officers.

VI. WHAT THE POLICE CANNOT DO DURING AN ARREST

A. Cannot Invite the Media to "Ride Along"

In a 1999 case, the Court held that the practice of "media ride-along" violates a suspect's Fourth Amendment rights and is therefore unconstitutional (Wilson et al. v. Layne, No. 98-83 [1999]). In this case, federal marshals and local sheriff's deputies invited a newspaper reporter and a photographer to accompany them while executing a warrant to arrest the petitioners' son in their home. The early-morning entry led to a confrontation with the petitioners. A protective sweep revealed that the son was not in the house. The reporters (who did not participate in executing the warrant) photographed the incident, but their newspaper never published the photographs. The Wilsons sued, claiming a violation of their Fourth Amendment rights. The Court agreed that their constitutional rights were violated but did not award monetary damages because of the "good faith" defense, saying that the right violated at the time of the media ride-along was not yet "clearly established." Balancing the petitioners' right to privacy and the officers' objectives for a media ride-along, the Court said, "Surely the possibility of good public relations for the police is simply not enough, standing alone, to justify the ride-along into a private home. And even the need for accurate reporting on police issues in general bears no direct relation to the constitutional justification for the police intrusion into a home in order to execute a felony arrest warrant."

B. Cannot Do a Strip or Cavity Search Unless Justified by Reasonable Suspicion

Although a full body search after an arrest is allowed, a departmental policy that orders body cavity searches in all felony arrests has been declared unconstitutional by at least one federal circuit court of appeals (Kennedy v. Los Angeles Police Department, 887 F.2d 920 [9th Cir. 1989]). The policy challenged in that case required the Los Angeles police to conduct a body cavity search in all felony arrests, but limited that form of strip search in misdemeanor cases to narcotics arrests and arrestees suspected of concealing weapons. The policy was justified by the department as necessary for "safety, security, and the proper administration of the jail system." The Ninth Circuit Court of Appeals held such searches in felony and misdemeanor arrests to be unconstitutional, saying that they are allowed only if the police have "reasonable suspicion that the individual arrested may be likely to conceal a weapon, drugs, or other contraband prior to conducting a body cavity search." The reason for the "reasonable suspicion" requirement, as opposed to automatic authorization for a full body search in arrests, is that "strip searches involving the visual exploration of body cavities [are] dehumanizing and humiliating." Unlike ordinary body searches, therefore, strip and body cavity searches are not allowed after arrest unless "reasonable suspicion" justifies the search.

C. Cannot Conduct a Warrantless Protective Sweep Unless Justified

The practice of warrantless protective sweeps has been authorized by the Court in the case of Maryland v. Buie, 494 U.S. 325 (1990), as long as it is justified. In that case, police officers obtained and executed arrest warrants for Buie and an accomplice in connection with an armed robbery. On reaching Buie's house, the officers went through the first and second floors. One of the officers watched the basement so that no one would surprise the other officers. This officer shouted into the basement and ordered anyone there to come out. A voice asked who was there. The officer ordered the person to come out three more times before that person, Buie, emerged from the basement and was placed under arrest. Another officer then entered the basement to see if anyone else was there. Once in the basement, the officer noticed in plain view a red running suit similar to the one worn by one of the suspects in the robbery. The running suit was admitted into evidence at Buie's trial over his objection, and he was convicted of robbery with the use of a deadly weapon. Buie challenged the legality of the protective sweep (which led to the discovery of the evidence) on appeal. The Court rejected Buie's challenge, saying that "[t]he Fourth Amendment permits a properly limited **protective sweep** in conjunction with an in-home arrest *when the searching officer possesses a reasonable belief based on specific and articulable facts that the area to be swept harbors an individual posing a danger to those on the arrest scene*" (emphasis added). This means that protective sweeps when making arrests are not always valid; a search is valid only if the searching officer can justify it "based on specific and articulable facts that the area to be swept harbors an individual posing a danger to those on the arrest scene." In the absence of such justification, the protective sweep is invalid.

Moreover, the protective sweep allowed in *Buie* is limited in scope. A protective sweep by the police is not allowed every time an arrest is made. The Court said that the following limitations must be observed for a valid protective sweep to take place:

- ■ "There must be specific and articulable facts which . . . would warrant a reasonably prudent officer in believing that the area to be swept harbors an individual posing a danger."

- ■ "Such a protective sweep is not a full search of the premises, but may extend only to a cursory inspection of those spaces where a person may be found."

■ "The sweep lasts no longer than is necessary to dispel the reasonable suspicion of danger and in any event no longer than it takes to complete the arrest and depart the premises."

VII. DISPOSITION OF PRISONERS AFTER ARREST

For minor offenses, police usually have the discretion to arrest or not to arrest. The more serious the offense, the less discretion the officer has to release the suspect. If an arrest is made, the officer fills out an arrest report, which is then submitted to and kept on file in the department. (See Form 6.3.) After a suspect has been arrested, the police must follow constitutionally prescribed procedures (often incorporated into departmental policy) for keeping that person in detention.

An important and often-asked question is whether a person arrested is entitled to a telephone call after the arrest. Although the Supreme Court has not addressed this issue, we can safely say that an arrestee has no *constitutional* right to a telephone call. Such right, however, may be given by state law or agency policy. When the call is to be made (whether immediately after the arrest or days later, before booking or after booking) varies by jurisdiction. It must be added, however, that an arrestee is constitutionally entitled to call an attorney and that such right, if requested by the suspect, must be granted prior to questioning. Failure to allow the suspect to exercise this right results in the exclusion of whatever evidence may be obtained during questioning.

A. Booking

As discussed in chapter 2, booking involves making an entry in the police blotter or arrest book, indicating the suspect's name, the time of arrest, and the offense involved. If the offense is serious, the suspect may also be photographed and fingerprinted. If the offense is minor, the suspect may be released based on "stationhouse bail," which involves the posting of cash and the promise to appear in court for a hearing at a specified date. If the offense is serious, the arrestee will be kept in jail or a holding facility (a temporary facility usually maintained by the police department instead of by the county) until bail, as set by the magistrate, is posted. In the process of booking, the officer may, in accordance with departmental procedures, carry out (without a warrant) an inventory of the arrestee's personal property. However, such an inventory may not be used as a fishing expedition for evidence. Although containers may be opened for the purpose of listing their contents, private documents found in the course of the inventory may not be read. If the officer feels that further search is needed beyond that allowed in the booking procedure, a search warrant must be obtained.

STATE OF VERMONT
ARREST / CUSTODY REPORT

CAUTION
Y N

AGENCY COMPLAINT NO.

DATE OF ARREST
MO   DAY   YR

ARRESTING AGENCY _____

IDENTIFICATION:

LAST NAME	FIRST NAME	MIDDLE NAME	/ / DOB	AGE	SEX	RACE*	ETHNIC*

EMPLOYED	UNEMPLOYED	STUDENT	REFUSED TO ANSWER

STREET

PLACE OF BIRTH (CITY/STATE)

CITY/TOWN

EMPLOYER/SCHOOL

STATE	ZIP CODE	SOC. SEC. NO.	ID NUMBER

ADDRESS

ALIAS	LAST NAME	FIRST NAME	MIDDLE NAME

SCARS/MARKS

1 SING	2 MAR	3 SEP	4 DIV	5 WID	6 COHAB

MARITAL STATUS

' " lb.
HEIGHT   WEIGHT

1 BLA	2 BRO	3 BLD	4 RED	5 GREY	6 BALD	7 WHI

HAIR COLOR

1 BRO	2 BLU	3 HAZ	4 OTH

EYE COLOR   SPECIFY

D.M.V. INFORMATION:

D.M.V. CASE NO. _____

OPERATOR LICENSE NO.	STATE	/ / EXPIRATION DATE	INJURY	FATAL	PROP. DAMAGE	REFUSED	NO	YES	RESULT	%

ACCIDENT   TEST

REGISTRATION NO.	STATE	/ / EXPIRATION DATE	VEHICLE MAKE	TYPE	YEAR

ARREST DATA:

TIME

PLACE

V.S.A.

GRID/COUNTY-TOWN

OFFENSE GRID

OFFENSE	TITLE	SECTION	SUB-SECTION	/ / OFFENSE DATE

FINGERPRINTS
Y N

PHOTOGRAPH
Y N

RELEASED TO GUARDIAN	ARRAIGNED	CITED	LODGED	BAIL

OFFENSE CODE
ATTACH TO A/C-3

IMMEDIATE DISPOSITION

COMMENTS

COMPANION CASE NO.

ARRESTING OFFICER SIGNATURE

ID. NO.

FINGERPRINT OFFICER

PHOTOGRAPH OFFICER

APPROVING OFFICER SIGNATURE

ID. NO.

OFFENSE: (STATE'S ATTORNEY USE)

V.S.A.

DOCKET # _____

COUNT: ____ OF ____

CHARGED	TITLE	SECTION	SUB-SECTION

NO PROSECUTION	DIVERSION	FORWARDED TO COURT	RETURNED	COMMENT:

*RACE CODE: W-WHITE, B-BLACK, I-INDIAN, A-ASIAN, U-UNKNOWN

*ETHNIC CODE: 1-HISPANIC, 2-NON HISPANIC

A/C - 1 AGENCY

VT 453
7/83

Form 6.3 *Arrest Report*

B. Appearance before a Magistrate

Statutes or court rules in most states require that an arrested person be brought before a magistrate **without unnecessary delay.** What does that mean? Although there is no fixed meaning, the Court has stated that the detention of a suspect for forty-eight hours (including weekends, holidays, and other "nonjudicial" days) is presumed to be reasonable. If the time for a probable cause hearing is longer than that, the burden of proof shifts to the police to prove reasonableness. Conversely, if the time for a probable cause hearing is shorter than forty-eight hours, there may still be unreasonable delay, but the burden of proof shifts to the suspect (County of Riverside v. McLaughlin, 59 U.S. 4413 [1991]).

In *McLaughlin,* a lawsuit was brought by a suspect challenging the process of determining probable cause for warrantless arrests in Riverside County, California. The county's policy was to combine probable cause determinations with arraignment proceedings. This policy was similar to the provisions of the California Penal Code, which states that arraignments must be conducted without unnecessary delay and within two days (forty-eight hours) of arrest, excluding weekends and holidays. The U.S. District Court issued an injunction requiring the county to provide a probable cause hearing within thirty-six hours for all persons arrested without a warrant. The issue on appeal was whether the Fourth Amendment requires a judicial determination of probable cause immediately after completing the administrative steps incident to arrest within thirty-six hours after the arrest, as the lower court had ordered. The Supreme Court said no, adding that if a probable cause determination is combined with arraignment, it is presumptively reasonable for the arrest-to-hearing period to last up to forty-eight hours. If more time than that elapses, the government bears the burden of showing that the delay is reasonable. Conversely, if the release is made before forty-eight hours after arrest, the burden of showing unreasonable delay shifts to the person arrested. (Read the County of Riverside v. McLaughlin case brief at the end of this chapter.)

In a subsequent case, the Court held that *McLaughlin* does not apply retroactively, saying that "were *McLaughlin* to be applied retroactively, untold numbers of prisoners would be set free because they were not brought before a magistrate within forty-eight hours" (Powell v. Nevada, 54 CrL 2238 [1992]).

C. The Purposes of an Initial Appearance

The purposes of the initial appearance vary from place to place, but usually they are as follows:

■ To warn the suspect of his or her rights, including being given the Miranda warnings

■ To determine if there is probable cause to process the suspect further through the system or, if not, to set the suspect free

■ If the suspect is to be further processed, to set bail for release, except if the offense is nonbailable

In many locales, the magistrate before whom the arrestee is brought is required to give the Miranda warnings during the initial appearance. If the suspect is under arrest and is asked questions by the police prior to this time, however, the Miranda warnings must be given by the officer; otherwise, the confession or admission obtained is not admissible in court to prove suspect's guilt. In arrests with a warrant, the likelihood that the suspect will be asked questions by the police prior to the initial appearance is less, because the officer has only to execute the warrant and deliver the suspect to the magistrate. Questions need not be asked. In warrantless arrests, the officer is more likely to have asked questions before the arrest was made because that may be how the officer established probable cause.

D. Bail

Many cases, particularly nonserious offenses, end at the initial appearance stage through a guilty plea, a negotiated plea, or outright release without charges being filed. If the case is not disposed of at this time, however, the arrestee is either sent back to jail, allowed to post a bail bond in an amount determined by the magistrate, or released on his or her own recognizance (ROR). In some cases, bail may be denied, particularly with serious offenses when evidence of guilt is strong.

Black's Law Dictionary defines a **bail bond** as a *"written undertaking, executed by the defendant or one or more sureties, that the defendant designated in such instrument will, while at liberty as a result of an order fixing bail . . . appear in a designated criminal action or proceeding when his attendance is required and otherwise render himself amenable to the orders and processes of the court, and that in the event he fails to do so, the signers of the bond will pay to the court the amount of money specified in the order fixing bail."*[8]

There are generally two kinds of bail bond. One is the **cash bail bond,** *"a sum of money, in the amount designated in an order fixing bail, posted by a defendant or by another person on his behalf with a court or other authorized public officer upon condition that such money will be forfeited if the defendant does not comply with the directions of a court requiring his attendance at the criminal action or proceeding involved and does not otherwise render himself amenable to the orders and processes of the court."* The other is an **unsecured bail bond,** *"a bail bond for which the defendant is fully liable upon failure to appear in court when ordered to do so or upon breach of a material condition of release, but which is not secured by any deposit of or lien upon property."*[9]

In contrast to bail bonds for which some form of monetary guarantee is involved, ROR is "a pretrial release based on the person's own promise that he will show up for trial" and therefore requires no bond."[10] Since it involves no money, ROR is considered an alternative to the traditional bail bond system. If the suspect fails to appear in court as scheduled, a warrant is usually issued for his or her arrest.

When the charge is merely a misdemeanor, most courts have bail schedules. The arrestee can post bail with the police or clerk of court in an amount designated in the schedule, without having to see the magistrate. If there is enough evidence to justify charging the accused with a felony, and if the offense is bailable and no bail has been set, the magistrate will fix the amount. The amount of bail in misdemeanor or felony cases is usually determined in light of the facts then known to the magistrate. These include the nature and seriousness of the crime, the previous criminal record of the accused, and the likelihood of flight from the state. Bail is not an absolute right—it may be denied in capital punishment cases in which evidence of guilt is strong.

The setting of bail by the magistrate, if the case gets this far, usually ends police involvement in an arrest. While bail generally is set by the courts, some jurisdictions allow the police to accept bail for minor offenses, the amount of which has been pre-determined by the magistrate. From here on, the processing of the case is in the hands of the prosecutor and the judge, except that the officer will likely be called to testify during trial.

VIII. SOME CONSEQUENCES OF AN ILLEGAL ARREST

A. Lawsuits against the Police

Illegal arrests can, and do, lead to lawsuits against the police. These lawsuits may be filed under state law or under federal law (discussed further in chapter 13 on the consequences of police misconduct). State tort law provides for possible police liability under false arrest and false imprisonment. Federal law (42 U.S.C., Section 1983) also allows plaintiffs to sue officers for violations of their constitutional rights, if the officers are acting under color of law. An illegal arrest is a violation of the Fourth Amendment and so can be the basis for a federal lawsuit. In addition to illegal arrest, excessive use of force during arrest can be the basis for a state tort case and a Section 1983 lawsuit.

B. Evidence Obtained Not Admissible in Court

If the search of the arrestee is valid, then the evidence obtained from it, and from the area within the arrestee's immediate control, is admissible in court. Conversely, if the arrest is invalid, then any evidence obtained after the arrest will not be admissible under the exclusionary rule. Some examples will help illuminate this.

- **Example 1:** The police arrest X on suspicion (not amounting to probable cause) that he has cocaine in his pockets. Immediately after the arrest, they search him and find cocaine. Since the arrest is invalid, the cocaine found is fruit of the poisonous tree and therefore will not be admitted in evidence.

- **Example 2:** The police have information (not amounting to probable cause) from an unreliable informant that Y has heroin in her car. The police spot Y driving down the street. They stop her, allegedly for speeding (actually a pretext to

AT A GLANCE

Arrest

DEFINITION: The taking of a person into custody against his or her will for the purpose of criminal prosecution or interrogation.

CONSTITUTIONAL RIGHT INVOLVED: The Fourth Amendment right to protection against unreasonable searches and seizures.

NATURE: A form of seizure and therefore governed by the Fourth Amendment.

TEST TO DETERMINE IF SEIZURE OCCURRED: The reasonable person.

ELEMENTS: Seizure and detention, intention to arrest, arrest authority, and the understanding of the arrestee.

TYPES:

With warrant: A magistrate has determined probable cause.

Without warrant: An officer determines and proves probable cause.

POWER TO ARREST:

Felonies: May arrest whether the crime is committed in the presence of the officer or not, if probable cause is present.

Misdemeanors: May arrest only if committed in the presence of the officer, subject to exceptions by state law, if probable cause is present.

APPEARANCE BEFORE MAGISTRATE: Without unnecessary delay.

KNOCK AND ANNOUNCE: Constitutionally required, but exceptions are determined by the states. The blanket exception for drug-dealing cases is not allowed.

---

stop the car), look in the car, and see cocaine on the back seat. Such evidence is not admissible, because the car stop was illegal, so the evidence obtained is fruit of the poisonous tree.

The basic principle is that *an illegal act of the police is never cured by what turns up after the arrest.* The evidence obtained can be excluded because of the initial illegal act. There is a strong temptation in these cases for the police to color their story and be "creative" about the facts in an effort to "legitimize" the arrest, believing that the ends justify the means. This is a violation of police ethics that can lead, if exposed, to administrative or legal action.

C. A Trial despite the Illegal Arrest

The jurisdiction of a court to try a person for a crime is not affected by how the custody of the accused is obtained (Frisbie v. Collins, 342 U.S. 519 [1952]). In this case, Collins brought a habeas corpus case in federal court seeking release from a Michigan state prison. He alleged that, while he was living in Chicago, Michigan officers forcibly seized, handcuffed, blackjacked, and then abducted him so that he could face murder charges in Michigan. The Court said that an unlawful arrest has no impact on a subsequent criminal prosecution and that an invalid arrest does not deprive the court of jurisdiction to try a criminal case. The Court added, "There is nothing in the Constitution that requires a court to permit a guilty person rightfully convicted to escape justice because he was brought to trial against his will."

In a case that attracted national attention, the Court held that the abduction of a foreigner that is not in violation of a treaty does not deprive a U.S. court of jurisdiction in a criminal trial (United States v. Alvarez-Machain, 112 S.Ct. 2188 [1992]). In that case, a citizen and resident of Mexico was indicted in the United States for participating in the kidnapping and murder of U.S. Drug Enforcement Agency (DEA) agent Enrique Camerena-Salazar and his pilot. Alvarez-Machain was kidnapped from his medical office in Guadalajara, Mexico, by U.S. officers and flown to El Paso, Texas, where he was arrested by DEA officials. He claimed that the U.S. district court did not have jurisdiction to try him because he was abducted in violation of an extradition treaty between the United States and Mexico. On appeal, the Court said that Alvarez-Machain's abduction was not in violation of the extradition treaty and did not deprive the United States of jurisdiction in a criminal trial.

Summary

Arrest is defined as the taking of a person into custody against his or her will for the purpose of criminal prosecution or interrogation. It constitutes a "seizure" and is therefore subject to the restrictions of the Fourth Amendment. There are four elements of arrest: intention to arrest, authority to arrest, seizure and detention, and the understanding of the individual that he or she is being arrested.

Arrests may be made with or without a warrant. In arrests with a warrant, probable cause has been determined by a magistrate; all the officer does is serve the warrant and take the person to the magistrate. In arrests without a warrant, the officer makes an on-the-spot determination of probable cause. The Supreme Court has expressed preference for arrests with a warrant, but warrants are not constitutionally required except in routine home arrests for felonies. Police officers are authorized to make warrantless arrests for felonies (committed in or outside their presence) as long as there is probable cause. Such is not the case with misdemeanors; the general rule is that a police officer has the power to arrest without a warrant only if the offense is actually committed in his or her presence. Arrests may also be made by citizens, but this practice is limited to cases in which a felony has actually been committed and probable cause is present.

After an arrest, the police may search the arrestee and the area within his or her immediate control. Police officers may also conduct a warrantless protective sweep of the area in which the suspect is arrested, provided there are specific and articulable facts that would lead a prudent officer to believe that danger is present.

The arrestee is booked and brought before the magistrate "without unnecessary delay." That phrase has no fixed meaning, but the Court has stated that detention of up to forty-eight hours without a probable cause hearing is presumptively reasonable. If it is for a longer period of time, the burden of establishing reasonableness rests with the police; if the time is shorter than forty-eight hours, the burden of establishing unreasonableness shifts to the suspect.

Illegal arrests lead to several consequences, among which are lawsuits against the police and inadmissibility of the evidence in court. However, even if the arrest is illegal, the defendant can still be tried in court for the criminal offense.

Review Questions

1. When has seizure of a person occurred under the Fourth Amendment? Whose perception prevails—that of the police, the arrestee, or neither?

2. Define arrest, and discuss its four elements.

3. How long can a suspect be detained, and how intrusive must the investigation be before a stop becomes an arrest? Explain.

4. Distinguish between a capias and a bench warrant.

5. What is meant by a "neutral and detached" magistrate? Give examples of magistrates who are not neutral or detached.

6. Give four instances in which following the knock-and-announce rule prior to arrest may not be necessary.

7. Distinguish between the power of the police to arrest in felony and in misdemeanor cases.

8. "A citizen may make an arrest any time he or she sees a crime being committed." Is this statement true or false? Discuss.

9. How long can the police detain a suspect without a probable cause hearing? Explain.

10. Is an officer required to knock and announce prior to entering a dwelling to serve a warrant? Discuss.

11. Are protective sweeps authorized after an arrest? Discuss.

12. How does a release on bail bond differ from a release on own recognizance? What are the two kinds of bail bond, and how do they differ?

Key Terms and Definitions

actual seizure: A seizure accomplished by taking the person into custody with the use of hands or firearms or by merely touching the individual without the use of force.

arrest: The taking of a person into custody against his or her will for the purpose of criminal prosecution or interrogation.

arrest warrant: A "writ issued by a magistrate, justice, or other competent authority, addressed to a sheriff, constable, or other officer, requiring him or her to arrest the person it names and bring the person

before the magistrate or court to answer, or to be examined, concerning some offense that he or she is charged with having committed."

bail bond: A "written undertaking, executed by the defendant or one or more sureties, that the defendant designated in such instrument will, while at liberty as a result of an order fixing bail . . . appear in a designated criminal action or proceeding when his attendance is required and otherwise render himself amenable to the orders and processes of the court, and that in the event he fails to do

so, the signers of the bond will pay to the court the amount of money specified in the order fixing bail."

bench warrant: A writ "from the bench," used to arrest and bring nonappearing defendants before the court.

capias: Literally meaning "you take," it is a general name for several types of writ that require an officer, for various reasons, to take a defendant into custody.

cash bail bond: "A sum of money, in the amount designated in an order fixing bail, posted by a defendant or by another person on his behalf with a court or other authorized public officer upon condition that such money will be forfeited if the defendant does not comply with the directions of a court requiring his attendance at the criminal action or proceeding involved and does not otherwise render himself amenable to the orders and processes of the court."

citation: A writ from a court ordering a person to appear in court at a scheduled time. It is usually used instead of an arrest in minor offenses.

citizen's arrest: An arrest made by a citizen without a warrant; usually limited to situations in which a felony has actually been committed and the citizen has probable cause to believe that the person arrested committed the offense.

constructive seizure: A seizure accomplished without any physical touching, grabbing, holding, or use of force; occurs when the individual peacefully submits to the officer's will and control.

exigent circumstances: Emergency circumstances that justify warrantless arrests or entries into homes or premises.

"hot pursuit" exception (to the warrant rule): A policy that authorizes peace officers from one state, through a uniform act adopted by most states, to enter another state in fresh pursuit to arrest a suspect for a felony committed in the first state.

"John Doe" warrant: A warrant in which only the name "John Doe" appears, because the real name of the suspect is not known to the police. It is valid only if it contains a description of the accused by which he or she can be identified with reasonable certainty.

neutral and detached magistrate: A magistrate (issuing a warrant) who is not unalterably aligned with the police or the prosecutor's position in a case.

protective sweep: Entry made by the police into places or areas other than where an arrest or seizure is taking place, for purposes of personal protection.

unsecured bail bond: "A bail bond for which the defendant is fully liable upon failure to appear in court when ordered to do so or upon breach of a material condition of release, but which is not secured by any deposit of or lien upon property."

without unnecessary delay: When used in connection with arrests, the provision that an arrestee must be brought before a magistrate as soon as possible. However, its meaning varies from one jurisdiction to another, taking circumstances into account. Maximum limits are set by various jurisdictions.

Principles of Cases

Berkemer v. McCarty, 468 U.S. 420 (1984) A police officer's unarticulated plan has no bearing on the question of whether a suspect was "in custody" at a particular time; the only relevant inquiry is how a reasonable person in the suspect's position would have understood the situation. Also, the roadside questioning of a motorist pursuant to a routine traffic stop (not an arrest) is not custodial interrogation and therefore does not require the Miranda warnings.

Brower v. County of Inyo, 486 U.S. 593 (1989) A seizure occurs only when there is governmental termination of freedom of movement through means intentionally applied.

California v. Hodari, 111 S.Ct. 1547 (1991) To constitute a seizure of a person, there must be either the application of physical force, however slight, or else submission to the officer's show of authority to restrain the person's liberty.

Chimel v. California, 395 U.S. 752 (1969) After making an arrest, the police may search the area of the arrestee's immediate control to discover and seize any evidence in his or her possession and to prevent its concealment or destruction.

Connally v. Georgia, 429 U.S. 245 (1977) A magistrate who receives a fee when issuing a warrant but not when denying one is not neutral and detached.

Coolidge v. New Hampshire, 403 U.S. 443 (1971) The state's chief investigator and prosecutor (state attorney general) is not neutral and detached; therefore, any warrant issued by him or her is invalid.

County of Riverside v. McLaughlin, 59 U.S. 4413 (1991) If probable cause determination is combined with arraignment, it is presumptively reasonable for the arrest-to-hearing period to last up to forty-eight hours. If more time than that elapses, the government bears the burden of showing that the delay is reasonable. Conversely, if the release is made less than forty-eight hours after arrest, the burden of showing unreasonable delay shifts to arrestee.

Dunaway v. New York, 442 U.S. 200 (1979) An arrest is defined as the taking of a person into custody against his or her will for the purpose of criminal prosecution or interrogation.

Florida v. Bostick, 111 S.Ct. 2382 (1991) The appropriate test to use to determine if the act of the officers in this case was valid was whether, taking into account all of the circumstances surrounding the encounter (in a bus), a reasonable person would feel free to decline the officers' requests for consent to search the bag or otherwise terminate the encounter.

Florida v. Royer, 460 U.S. 491 (1983) The removal of a detainee without his consent from the public area in an airport to the police room in the airport converted the stop to an arrest.

Frisbie v. Collins, 342 U.S. 519 (1952) An unlawful arrest has no impact on a subsequent criminal prosecution. An invalid arrest therefore does not deprive the court of jurisdiction to try a criminal case.

Henry v. United States, 361 U.S. 98 (1959) Probable cause exists if the facts and circumstances known to the officer would lead a prudent person to believe that the offense has been committed.

Kennedy v. Los Angeles Police Department, 887 F.2d 920 [9th Cir. 1989]) A departmental policy that orders body cavity searches in all felony arrests is unconstitutional. There must be reasonable suspicion, prior to conducting a body cavity search, that the arrestee may be likely to conceal a weapon, drugs, or other contraband.

Lo-Ji Sales, Inc., v. New York, 442 U.S. 319 (1979) A magistrate who participates in a search to determine its scope lacks the requisite neutrality and detachment.

Maryland v. Buie, 494 U.S. 325 (1990) "The Fourth Amendment permits a properly limited protective sweep in conjunction with an in-home arrest when the searching officer possesses a reasonable belief based on specific and articulable facts that the area to be swept harbors an individual posing a danger to those on the arrest scene."

Michigan v. Chesternut, 486 U.S. 567 (1988) The appropriate test to determine if a seizure has occurred is "whether a reasonable man, viewing the particular police conduct as a whole and within the setting of all the surrounding circumstances, would have concluded that the police had in some way restrained his liberty so that he was not free to leave."

Minnesota v. Olson, 495 U.S. 91 (1990) A warrantless nonconsensual entry by the police into a residence to arrest an overnight guest is not justified by exigent circumstances and therefore violates the Fourth Amendment.

New York v. Belton, 453 U.S. 454 (1981) The police may examine the contents of any container found in the passenger compartment of a car, as long as it may reasonably be thought to contain something that might pose a danger to the officer or hold evidence in support of the offense for which the suspect has been arrested.

New York v. Harris, 495 U.S. 14 (1990) A violation of the Fourth Amendment rule forbidding the police from making a warrantless and nonconsensual entry of a suspect's residence so as to make a routine felony arrest does not require the exclusion of a statement made by the suspect after his or her removal from that residence as long as the arrest was supported by probable cause.

Payton v. New York, 445 U.S. 573 (1980) In the absence of exigent circumstances or consent, the police may not enter a private home to make a routine warrantless arrest.

Powell v. Nevada, 54 CrL 2238 (1992) The decision in County of Riverside v. McLaughlin, 55 U.S. 4413 (1991), saying that the detention of a suspect for forty-eight hours is presumed to be reasonable, is not retroactive.

Richards v. Wisconsin, 61 CrL 2057 (1997) The blanket exception to the knock-and-announce rule in drug-dealing cases is unconstitutional. Exceptions must be determined on a case-by-case basis.

Shadwick v. City of Tampa, 407 U.S. 345 (1972)
A municipal court clerk can issue an arrest warrant for municipal ordinance violations as long as such issuance is authorized by state law.

Steagald v. United States, 451 U.S. 204 (1981)
An arrest warrant cannot be used as a legal authority to enter the home of a person other than the person named in the arrest warrant. If the person to be arrested is in the home of another person, a search warrant must be obtained to enter the home in order to make an arrest. The only exception is that exigent circumstances justify a warrantless entry.

United States v. Alvarez-Machain, 112 S.Ct. 2188 (1992) When a Mexican citizen was abducted in Mexico and arrested by U.S. officials in Texas, this action did not violate a treaty between the United States and Mexico, and the United States did have jurisdiction in a subsequent criminal trial.

United States v. Mendenhall, 446 U.S. 544 (1980) When determining whether a person has been arrested, the court takes into account the totality of the surrounding circumstances, including such considerations as "the threatening presence of several officers, the display of a weapon by an officer, some physical touching of the person or the citizen, or the use of language or tone of voice indicating that compliance with the officer's request might be compelled."

United States v. Ramirez, 63 CrL 2108 (1998)
The knock-and-announce rule does not set a higher standard for unannounced entries even if that entry involves property damage.

United States v. Robinson, 414 U.S. 218 (1973)
After making an arrest, the police may make a warrantless search of the arrestee.

United States v. Sharpe, 470 U.S. 675 (1985) In assessing whether a detention is too long to be justified as an investigative stop, the Court considers it appropriate to examine whether the police diligently pursued a means of investigation that was likely to confirm or dispel their suspicions quickly, during which time it was necessary to detain the defendant.

United States v. Watson, 423 U.S. 411 (1976)
Law enforcement officers may find it wise to seek arrest warrants when practical to do so, and their judgments about probable cause may be more readily accepted when backed by a warrant issued by a magistrate. Also, the police are not required to obtain an arrest warrant before arresting a person in a public place, even if there was time and opportunity to do so.

Vale v. Louisiana, 399 U.S. 30 (1970) A search incidental to an arrest is valid only if it is "substantially contemporaneous with the arrest and is confined to the immediate vicinity of the arrest." Also, "if a search of a house is to be upheld as incident to an arrest, that arrest must take place inside the house, not somewhere outside—whether two blocks away, twenty feet away, or on the sidewalk near the front steps."

Warden v. Hayden, 387 U.S. 294 (1967) Warrantless entries and searches are reasonable if delaying them would allow the suspect time to escape. Also, the Fourth Amendment does not require officers to delay an arrest if to do so would endanger their lives or the lives of others.

Washington v. Chrisman, 455 U.S. 1 (1982) It is not unreasonable under the Fourth Amendment for a police officer, as a matter of routine, to monitor the movements of an arrestee, as his or her judgment dictates, following an arrest. The officer's need to ensure his or her own safety, as well as the integrity of the arrest, is compelling.

Welsh v. Wisconsin, 466 U.S. 740 (1984) In determining whether exigent circumstances exist to justify a home entry without a warrant, the seriousness of the offense must be considered. In the case of a minor offense, a warrantless entry into a home will rarely be justified.

Williams v. Ward, 845 F.2d 374 (2nd Cir. 1988)
Arrestees may be held up to seventy-two hours in New York City without arraignment; the enormous problems involved in processing more than 200,000 arrested people each year justifies the delay.

Wilson v. Arkansas, 115 S.Ct. 1914 (1995)
The knock-and-announce rule is part of the Fourth Amendment's requirement that searches and seizures be reasonable, but that rule is not rigid and is subject to exceptions based on law enforcement interests.

Wilson v. Lane, No. 98-83 (1999) The practice of "media ride-along" violates a suspect's Fourth Amendment rights and is therefore unconstitutional.

Winston v. Lee, 470 U.S. 753 (1985) Certain types of seizures (in this case the removal of a bullet lodged in the breast of the suspect) are so intrusive that they are prohibited by the Fourth Amendment even with probable cause and prior judicial authorization, unless justified by compelling reasons.

Case Briefs

The Leading Case on Home Arrest

Payton v. New York, 445 U.S. 573 (1980)

Facts: After two days of intensive investigation, New York detectives had assembled evidence sufficient to establish probable cause to believe that Payton had murdered the manager of a gas station. Early the following day, six officers went to Payton's apartment in the Bronx, intending to arrest him. They had not obtained a warrant. Although light and music emanated from the apartment, there was no response to their knock on the metal door. They summoned emergency assistance and, about thirty minutes later, used crowbars to break open the door and enter the apartment. No one was there. In plain view was a .30-caliber shell casing that was seized and later admitted into evidence at Payton's murder trial. Payton was convicted, and he appealed.

Issue: *Does the Fourth Amendment prohibit the police from making a nonconsensual entry into a suspect's home in order to make a routine felony arrest without a warrant? Yes.*

Supreme Court Decision: In the absence of consent, the police may not enter a suspect's home in order to make a routine felony arrest without a warrant.

Case Significance: The *Payton* case settled the issue of whether the police can enter a suspect's home and make a warrantless arrest in a routine felony case, meaning cases in which there is time to obtain a warrant. The practice was authorized by the state of New York and twenty-three other states at the time *Payton* was decided. These authorizations are now unconstitutional, and officers must obtain a warrant before entering a suspect's home to make a routine felony arrest.

Excerpts from the Decision: "A long-standing, widespread practice is not immune from constitutional scrutiny. But neither is it to be lightly brushed aside. This is particularly so when the constitutional standard is as amorphous as the word 'reasonable,' and when custom and contemporary norms necessarily play such a large role in the constitutional analysis. In this case, although the weight of state-law authority is clear, there is by no means the kind of virtual unanimity on this question that was present in United States

v. Watson, with regard to warrantless arrests in public places. Only 24 of the 50 States currently sanction warrantless entries into the home to arrest . . . and there is an obvious declining trend. Further, the strength of the trend is greater than the numbers alone indicate. Seven state courts have recently held that warrantless home arrests violate their respective State constitutions. . . . That is significant because by invoking a state constitutional provision, a state court immunizes its decision from review by this Court. This heightened degree of immutability underscores the depth of the principle underlying the result."

The Leading Case on the Allowable Period of Detention without a Probable Cause Hearing

County of Riverside v. McLaughlin, 59 U.S. 4413 (1991)

Facts: A lawsuit was brought against Riverside County, California, challenging the County's process of determining probable cause in warrantless arrests. The county's policy was to combine probable cause determinations with arraignment proceedings. The policy was close to the provisions of the California Penal Code, which state that arraignments must be conducted without unnecessary delay and within two days (forty-eight hours) of arrest, excluding weekends and holidays. The U.S. district court issued a preliminary injunction requiring the county to provide a probable cause hearing within thirty-six hours for all persons arrested without a warrant. The Ninth Circuit Court of Appeals affirmed, saying that the county policy of providing a probable cause hearing at arraignment within forty-eight hours was not in accord with the requirement in Gerstein v. Pugh, 420 U.S. 103 (1975), of promptly providing the probable cause determination after arrest, because no more than thirty-six hours were needed to complete the administrative steps incident to arrest.

There was conflict among the circuit courts of appeals on this issue. The Ninth, Fourth, and Seventh Circuit Courts of Appeals all required a probable cause determination immediately following completion of the administrative procedures incident to arrest. The Second Circuit Court of Appeals allowed flexibility and permitted states to combine probable cause determinations with other pretrial proceedings.

Issue: *Does the Fourth Amendment require a judicial determination of probable cause (a probable cause hearing) immediately after completing the administrative steps incident to arrest within thirty-six hours after arrest? No.*

Supreme Court Decision: If a probable cause determination is combined with arraignment, it is presumptively reasonable for the arrest-to-hearing period to last up to forty-eight hours. If more time than that elapses, the government bears the burden of showing that the delay is reasonable. Conversely, if the release is made before forty-eight hours after arrest, the burden of showing unreasonable delay shifts to the person arrested.

Excerpts from the Decision: "Our task in this case is to articulate more clearly the boundaries of what is permissible under the Fourth Amendment. Although we hesitate to announce that the Constitution compels a specific time limit, it is important to provide some degree of certainty so that States and counties may establish procedures with confidence that they fall within constitutional bounds. Taking into account the competing interests articulated in *Gerstein,* we believe that a jurisdiction that provides judicial determinations of probable cause within 48 hours of arrest will, as a general matter, comply with the promptness requirement of *Gerstein.* For this reason, such jurisdictions will be immune from systemic challenges."

 # Notes

1. John G. Miles, Jr., David B. Richardson, and Anthony E. Scudellari, *The Law Officer's Pocket Manual* (Washington, DC: Bureau of National Affairs, 1988–89), 6:1.

2. *Black's Law Dictionary* (St. Paul, MN: West, 1968), p. 1756.

3. Ibid., p. 261.

4. Supra note 1, 6:11–6:12.

5. Steven L. Emanuel and Steven Knowles, *Emanuel Law Outlines* (Larchmont, NY: Emanuel, 1989–90) p. 59.

6. Ibid., p. 62.

7. Wayne R. LaFave and Jerold H. Israel, *Criminal Procedure* (St. Paul, MN: West, 1985), p. 147.

8. Supra note 2, p. 128.

9. Supra note 2, p. 128.

10. Supra note 2, p. 1030.

IV. Searches and Seizures of Property

7.

Searches and Seizures of Things

What You Will Learn in This Chapter

You will know the difference between a search and a seizure and will become familiar with what items are subject to seizure by the police. You will learn that there are two kinds of searches and seizures: with a warrant and without a warrant. You will also know what the requirements of a search and seizure with a warrant are and when a warrant is valid. Finally, you will learn the details of searches and seizures without a warrant and become aware of special issues related to search and seizure cases.

Introduction

This chapter discusses searches and seizures of things—as distinguished from seizures of persons, or arrests. It does not deal with searches of motor vehicles, which is discussed in chapter 8. Both searches and seizures of things and searches and seizures of persons are governed by the Fourth Amendment provision of the U.S. Constitution, which states, "The right of the people to be secure in their persons, houses, papers, and effects, against unreasonable searches and seizures, shall not be violated, and no Warrants shall issue, but upon probable cause, supported by Oath or affirmation, and particularly describing the place to be searched, and the persons or things to be seized."

There are two types of searches and seizures: with warrant and without warrant, but both types need probable cause. The term *search and seizure* often conveys the impression that it represents a single act. Search and seizure are, in fact, two separate acts, each with its own meaning, so they are treated separately in this chapter.

I. SEARCH AND SEIZURE OF THINGS

A. Search Defined

A **search** of things is defined as *the exploration or examination of an individual's house, premises, or person, in order to discover things that may be used by the government for evidence in a criminal prosecution.* A search is not limited to homes, offices, buildings, or

What the Fourth Amendment Protects

"The Fourth Amendment protects people, not places. What a person knowingly exposes to the public, even in his own home or office, is not a subject of Fourth Amendment protection. . . . But what he seeks to preserve as private even in an area accessible to the public, may be constitutionally protected."

Katz v. United States, 389 U.S. 347 (1967).

other enclosed places. Rather, it can occur in any place where a person has a **reasonable expectation of privacy,** even if the place is in a public area, meaning a place to which anyone has access (Katz v. United States, 389 U.S. 347 [1967]). For example, in one case, police installed a peephole in the ceiling of a public restroom to allow them to observe what occurred in the stalls. Officers observed two people engaging in illegal sexual acts in one of the stalls. What the officers did without a warrant was illegal, because the two people involved had a reasonable expectation of privacy—they could reasonably expect that their acts would not be observed by others, even though the restroom was in a public place. The evidence obtained was not admissible in court.

B. Seizure Defined

A **seizure** of things or items is defined as *the exercise of dominion or control by the government over a person or thing because of a violation of law.* The distinction between a search and a seizure can be summarized as follows: *Search is looking, while seizure is taking.* In one case, the Supreme Court said that "a seizure occurs when there is some meaningful interference with an individual's possessory interests in the property seized" (Maryland v. Macon, 472 U.S. 463 [1985]).

C. The General Rule for Searches and Seizures

The general rule is that searches and seizures can be made only with a warrant. Therefore, warrantless searches and seizures are exceptions to the general rule. According to the Court, the most basic constitutional rule is that searches conducted outside the judicial process, without prior approval by judge or magistrate, are per se unreasonable under the Fourth Amendment—subject only to a few specifically established and well-delineated exceptions (Katz v. United States, 389 U.S. 347 [1967]).

In reality, most searches and seizures are made without a warrant. Nonetheless, police officers must always be aware of the general rule so that they make warrantless searches only if justified under one of the exceptions. In the words of the Court:

Search and Seizure Distinguished

Although often used as one phrase, search and seizure are two separate and different acts. Search is *looking,* while seizure is *taking.* One does not necessarily lead to the other. While "looking" may or may not need probable cause (depending upon its intrusiveness and where it takes place), "taking" always requires probable cause or consent to be valid.

The point of the Fourth Amendment, which often is not grasped by zealous officers, is not that it denies law enforcement the support of the usual inferences which reasonable men draw from evidence. Its protection consists in requiring that those inferences be drawn by a neutral and detached magistrate instead of being judged by the officer engaged in the often competitive enterprise of ferreting out crime. (Johnson v. United States, 333 U.S. 10 [1948])

D.   Items Subject to Search and Seizure

Generally, four types of items can be searched and seized:

1. *Contraband,* such as drugs, counterfeit money, and gambling paraphernalia. With limited exceptions, these items are illegal for anybody to possess.

2. *Fruits of the crime,* such as stolen goods and forged checks.

3. *Instrumentalities of the crime,* such as weapons and burglary tools.

4. *"Mere evidence" of the crime,* such as a suspect's clothing containing bloodstains of the victim or a suspect's mask, shoes, or wig—provided there is probable cause to believe that the item is related to criminal activity.

These are merely general categories of things officers may search and seize. In many states, the law (usually the code of criminal procedure or the penal code) enumerates in detail the items subject to search and seizure. (See Figure 7.1.) Whatever the listing, the likelihood is that an item listed by state law will fall into one of the four categories listed here.

II.   SEARCH AND SEIZURE WITH A WARRANT

A **search warrant** is *a written order, issued by a magistrate, directing a peace officer to search for property connected with a crime and bring it before the court.* In nearly all

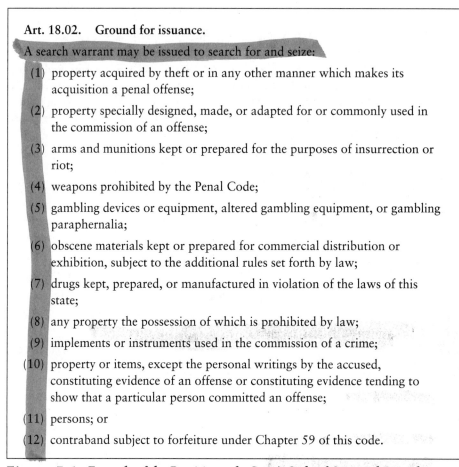

Art. 18.02. Ground for issuance.

A search warrant may be issued to search for and seize:

(1) property acquired by theft or in any other manner which makes its acquisition a penal offense;

(2) property specially designed, made, or adapted for or commonly used in the commission of an offense;

(3) arms and munitions kept or prepared for the purposes of insurrection or riot;

(4) weapons prohibited by the Penal Code;

(5) gambling devices or equipment, altered gambling equipment, or gambling paraphernalia;

(6) obscene materials kept or prepared for commercial distribution or exhibition, subject to the additional rules set forth by law;

(7) drugs kept, prepared, or manufactured in violation of the laws of this state;

(8) any property the possession of which is prohibited by law;

(9) implements or instruments used in the commission of a crime;

(10) property or items, except the personal writings by the accused, constituting evidence of an offense or constituting evidence tending to show that a particular person committed an offense;

(11) persons; or

(12) contraband subject to forfeiture under Chapter 59 of this code.

Figure 7.1 *Example of the Provisions of a State's Code of Criminal Procedure Enumerating the Items to Be Seized by the Police*

SOURCE: *Texas Code of Criminal Procedure,* 1998.

states, the police officer seeking a search warrant must state the facts that establish probable cause in a written and signed affidavit. The general rule is that a search or seizure is valid under the Fourth Amendment only if made with a warrant. Searches without a warrant may be valid, but they are the exception rather than the rule.

A. Requirements

There are four basic requirements for the valid issuance of a search warrant: (1) a statement of probable cause, (2) a supporting oath or affirmation, (3) a description of the place to be searched and the things to be seized, and (4) the signature of a magistrate.

1. Probable Cause

The conditions required to establish probable cause are discussed more extensively in chapter 3. For our purposes here, it is sufficient to restate the definition of probable cause used in chapter 3. **Probable cause** is *more than bare suspicion; it exists when the facts and circumstances within the officers' knowledge and of which they have reasonably trustworthy information are sufficient in themselves to warrant a person of reasonable caution in the belief that an offense has been or is being committed*. This is the same definition as for arrests. The difference is that in arrests the focus is on (1) whether a crime has been committed and (2) whether the person to be arrested committed the crime. By contrast, in searches and seizures of things and items, the issue of probable cause focuses on (1) whether the property to be seized is connected with criminal activity and (2) whether it can be found in the place to be searched.

2. A Supporting Oath or Affirmation

A search warrant is issued based on a sworn affidavit presented to the magistrate and establishing grounds for the warrant. The magistrate issues the warrant only if he or she is satisfied based on the affidavit that probable cause for a warrant exists. The contents of the affidavit must be sufficient to allow an independent evaluation of probable cause by the magistrate. To enable the magistrate to make an independent evaluation, the affidavit must contain more than mere conclusions by the police officer. It must allege facts showing that seizable evidence will be found in the place to be searched. The affidavit may be filed by the police officer or the offended or injured party. A warrant may be issued on the basis of affidavits containing only hearsay, as long as there is probable cause. (See Form 7.1.)

a. Oral Warrant There is no constitutional requirement for a warrant application to be in writing. In many jurisdictions, a warrant may be issued based on an oral statement, either in person or by telephone. The oral statement is usually recorded and becomes the basis for a probable cause determination.

b. Anticipatory Search Warrant An **anticipatory search warrant** is *a warrant obtained based on probable cause and on an expectation that seizable items will be found at a certain place at a certain time*. An article in the *FBI Law Enforcement Bulletin* characterizes the warrant in this manner:

> Where officers have probable cause to believe that evidence or contraband will arrive at a certain location within a reasonable period of time, they need not wait until delivery before requesting a warrant. Instead, officers may present this probable cause to a magistrate before the arrival of that evidence, and the magistrate can issue an anticipatory search warrant based on probable cause that the evidence will be found at the location to be searched at the time the warrant is executed.[1]

The same article maintains that, although the Supreme Court has not resolved the constitutionality of anticipatory warrants, "the vast majority of State and Federal courts that have considered this question have concluded that anticipatory warrants are constitutional and consistent with the long-standing preference that whenever possible,

---

THE STATE OF TEXAS
COUNTY OF _____

THE UNDERSIGNED AFFIANT, BEING A PEACE OFFICER UNDER THE LAWS OF TEXAS AND BEING DULY SWORN, ON OATH MAKES THE FOLLOWING STATEMENTS AND ACCUSATIONS.

1. THERE IS IN _____ COUNTY, TEXAS A SUSPECTED PLACE DESCRIBED AND LOCATED AS FOLLOWS:

2. SAID SUSPECTED PLACE IS IN CHARGE OF AND CONTROLLED BY EACH OF THE FOLLOWING NAMED PARTIES (HEREAFTER CALLED "SUSPECTED PARTY" WHETHER ONE OR MORE) TO WIT:

3. IT IS THE BELIEF OF AFFIANT, AND AFFIANT HEREBY CHARGES AND ACCUSES THAT SAID SUSPECTED PARTY HAS POSSESSION OF AND IS CONCEALING AT SAID SUSPECTED PLACE IN VIOLATION OF THE LAWS OF TEXAS THE FOLLOWING DESCRIBED PERSONAL PROPERTY, TO WIT:

4. AFFIANT HAS PROBABLE CAUSE FOR THE SAID BELIEF BY REASON OF THE FOLLOWING FACTS, TO WIT:

WHEREFORE, AFFIANT ASKS FOR ISSUANCE OF A WARRANT THAT WILL AUTHORIZE THE SEARCH OF SAID SUSPECTED PLACE FOR SAID PERSONAL PROPERTY AND SEIZE THE SAME AND TO ARREST EACH SAID SUSPECTED PARTY, AND TO TAKE CUSTODY OF ALL SEIZED PROPERTY AND SAFEKEEP SUCH PROPERTY AS PROVIDED BY STATUTE.

_____
AFFIANT

SUBSCRIBED AND SWORN TO BEFORE ME BY SAID AFFIANT ON THIS THE _____ DAY OF
_____, A.D., 19_____.

_____
MAGISTRATE

Form 7.1 *Affidavit for Search Warrant*

police obtain judicial approval before searching."[2] However, a magistrate is not required to issue an anticipatory warrant, so it is a matter of a magistrate's discretion. But should the magistrate decide to issue it, such a warrant would most likely be valid.

    c. Must Be Based on Fresh Information To be valid, the warrant must be based on fresh information. If the information is "stale," the warrant lacks probable cause and is invalid (United States v. Leon, 468 U.S. 897 [1984]). In the *Leon* case, the information contained in the affidavit was given by the police officer to the magistrate in September 1981. It was based partially on information the officer obtained from a confidential informant in August 1981. The Court ruled that "to the extent that the affidavit set forth facts demonstrating the basis of the informant's knowledge of criminal activity, the information included was fatally stale." The reason for the "fresh information" rule is that conditions change fast, and an item found in one place at one time may not be there when the warrant is issued and executed. The Court has not specified exactly how much time must elapse before an information becomes stale. It is safe to say, however, that "the longer the delay, the greater the chance that the information will be 'stale.'"[3]

3. A Description of the Place to Be Searched and Persons or Things to Be Seized

a. The Place to Be Searched The warrant must remove any doubt or uncertainty about which premises are to be searched. For example, if the premises are an apartment in a multiple-dwelling building, the warrant must specify which apartment is to be searched. The address of the apartment building is not sufficient. An exact address prevents confusion and avoids intrusions on the privacy of innocent persons.

In one case, however, the Court held that the validity of a warrant must be judged in light of the "information available to the officers at the time they obtained the warrant" (Maryland v. Garrison, 480 U.S. 79 [1987]). In this case, police officers obtained a warrant to search "the premises known as 2036 Park Avenue, third floor apartment" for drugs and drug paraphernalia that supposedly belonged to a person named McWebb. The police reasonably believed there was only one apartment at that location. In fact, there were two apartments on the third floor, one belonging to McWebb and the other belonging to Garrison. Before the officers became aware that they were in Garrison's apartment instead of McWebb's, they searched the apartment and discovered drugs that provided the basis for Garrison's subsequent conviction. Garrison sought exclusion of the evidence, saying that the search warrant was so unnecessarily broad as to allow the search of the wrong apartment. The Supreme Court admitted the evidence, saying that the validity of a warrant must be judged in light of the information available to the officers when the warrant is sought:

> There was reasonable effort on the part of the officers to ascertain and identify the place that was the target of the search; nonetheless, a mistake took place. This case should not be interpreted as validating all search warrants where there is a mistake made in the description of the place to be searched. The test as to the validity of search warrants that are "ambiguous in scope" appears to be "whether the officers' failure to realize the overbreadth of the warrant was objectively understandable and reasonable."

Therefore, a warrant that is overly broad in describing the place to be searched is not in violation of the Fourth Amendment *if it was based on a reasonable but mistaken belief* at the time the warrant was issued. (Read the Maryland v. Garrison case brief at the end of this chapter.)

Relying on Maryland v. Garrison, the Fourth Circuit Court of Appeals has said that the execution of a warrant for a different apartment than that named in the warrant was valid because there were only two apartments on the floor, one of which was vacant. Moreover, the correct apartment was readily ascertainable and the mistake (which in this case was a reliance on utility company information) was reasonable and made in good faith (United States v. Owens, 848 F.2d 462 [4th Cir. 1988]).

b. Things to Be Seized Things to be seized must also be described in sufficient detail that the officer will have to exercise little discretion over what may be seized. For example, the warrant cannot simply provide for the seizure of "stolen goods," since this language is too general and can lead to a fishing expedition. An acceptable identification would be "a 25-inch Zenith television set." Contraband, however, does not have to be described with as much particularity, because it is in itself seizable. So the words *cocaine* or *heroin* would suffice, as would *gambling paraphernalia*.

5. The Signature of a Magistrate

As in the cases of arrest warrants, search warrants must be issued only by a "neutral and detached" magistrate. The Court has said, "Inferences must be drawn by a neutral and detached magistrate instead of being judged by the officer engaged in the often competitive enterprise of ferreting out crime" (Johnson v. United States, 333 U.S. 10 [1948]). Several examples should help illuminate this requirement.

- **Example 1:** A magistrate who receives a fee when issuing a warrant but not when denying one is not neutral and detached (Connally v. Georgia, 429 U.S. 245 [1977]).

- **Example 2:** A magistrate who participates in the search to determine its scope lacks the requisite neutrality and detachment (Lo-Ji Sales, Inc., v. New York, 442 U.S. 319 [1979]).

- **Example 3:** The state's chief investigator and prosecutor (state attorney general) is not neutral and detached, so any warrant issued by him or her is invalid (Coolidge v. New Hampshire, 403 U.S. 443 [1971]). (See Form 7.2.)

B. The Procedure for Service of a Warrant

The search warrant is directed to a law enforcement officer and must state the grounds for issuance and the names of those who gave affidavits in support of it. The execution of a warrant is specified in detail by state law, usually in the state's code of criminal procedure. Failure to execute the warrant in accordance with state or local law generally results in exclusion of the evidence during trial.

The warrant usually directs that it be served in the daytime, but if the affidavits are positive that the property is on the person or in the place to be searched, the warrant may direct that it be served at any time. Some states, by law, authorize night searches. The warrant must designate the judge or magistrate to whom the warrant is to be returned. It also must be executed and delivered within a specified number of days from the date of issuance. Some states specify ten days; others allow less time. If the warrant is not served during that time, it expires and can no longer be served. Note that search warrants differ in this respect from arrest warrants, which are usually valid until served. The officer executing the search warrant must either (1) give a copy of the warrant and a receipt for any seized property to the person from whom it is taken or (2) leave a copy and receipt on the premises. A written inventory must be made, and the officer's report, accompanied by the inventory, must be submitted promptly. The Court recently

SEARCH WARRANT

SEARCH WARRANT FOR

DRUGS

THE STATE OF TEXAS

To the Sheriff or Any Peace Officer of _____

COUNTY OF _____ | County, Texas, GREETINGS:

Whereas, complaint in writing, under oath has been made before me by _____

which complaint is hereto attached and expressly made a part hereof alleging that on or about the _____ day of

_____ , A.D. 19 _____ in the _____ County, Texas,

one _____

_____

did then and there unlawfully possess and does at this time unlawfully possess a controlled substance, to-wit: _____

_____

and further that he has cause to believe that the said controlled substance are now concealed by _____

_____

_____

_____

_____

situated in _____ County, Texas, located _____

_____

_____

which said _____

_____

now possess, occupies, controls and has charge of.

And after examining the said complaint in writing and under oath, I have determined that the said complaint does state facts and information sufficient to establish probable cause for the issuance of this warrant to search for and seize the said controlled substance in accordance with the law in such cases provided.

YOU ARE THEREFORE COMMANDED TO FORTHWITH SEARCH THE PLACE ABOVE NAMED AND DESCRIBED WHERE THE SAID CONTROLLED SUBSTANCE, TO-WIT: _____

are alleged to be concealed, and if you find such controlled substance or any portion thereof, you will seize the same and bring it before me at my office, situated at_____ County, Texas, on the _____ day of _____ A.D.19 _____.

AND, you are commanded to arrest and bring before me, at said place and time, the said: _____

_____

accused of the possession of the said controlled substance.

HEREIN FAIL NOT, AND DUE RETURN MAKE HEREOF TO ME AT THE TIME AND PLACE ABOVE NAMED.

Form 7.2 *Search Warrant*

decided, however, that the police do not have to provide the owner of the property seized with notice of remedies specified by state law for the property's return and the information necessary to use those procedures (City of West Covina v. Perkins, No. 97-1230 [1999]).

C. The Announcement Requirement

The rule about announcements in searches and seizures is the same as the rule for arrests, discussed in chapter 6. Federal and many state statutes require that an officer making an arrest or executing a search warrant announce his or her purpose and authority before breaking into a dwelling. The goal is to allow voluntary compliance and avoid violence. Breaking into the premises without first complying with the announcement requirement may or may not invalidate the entry and any resulting search, depending on the law or court decisions in that state. Some states invalidate the entry and resulting search; others do not.

As discussed in chapter 6 for arrests, the Court recently ruled that the "knock and announce common law principle is part of the Fourth Amendment's requirement that searches and seizures be reasonable." It added, however, that this did not mean that every entry should be preceded by an announcement. The current rule is that, although knock and announce is part of the requirement of reasonableness in searches and seizures, it is not a rigid rule and is subject to exceptions based on law enforcement interests (Wilson v. Arkansas, 115 S.Ct. 1914 [1995]). **No-knock searches** may be authorized by state statute, particularly for drug cases.

In general, the announcement requirement is not needed in cases involving exigent (emergency) circumstances, such as the following:

- When an announcement would present a strong threat of violence or danger to the officer
- When there is danger that contraband or other property might be destroyed
- When officers reasonably believe that the persons within the premises are in imminent peril of bodily harm
- When persons within the premises are reasonably believed to be engaged in the process of destroying evidence or escaping because they are aware of the presence of the police
- When the person to be arrested is in the process of committing the crime

Exceptions to the announcement requirement are usually determined by state law, state court decisions, and agency regulations. They therefore vary from state to state. The Court has ruled, however, that a blanket exception (issued by a judge) to the Fourth Amendment's knock-and-announce rule in felony drug-dealing cases is not allowed (Richards v. Wisconsin, 520 U.S. 385 [1997]). This means that exceptions to the announcement requirement must be determined on a case-by-case basis. And in a 1998 case, the Court held that the knock-and-announce rule does not set a higher stan-

AT A GLANCE

Scope of the Search

A wise legal maxim for officers to remember is this: *It is unreasonable for a police officer to look for an elephant in a matchbox.* This defines the reasonableness of the scope of the search. It follows from this maxim that the smaller the item to be searched, the greater is the scope of the authority to search—and vice versa.

---

dard for unannounced entries even if that entry involves property damage (United States v. Ramirez, 62 CrL 2108 [1998]).

The knock-and-announce rule gives notice to occupants of the place that an officer is at the door, with a warrant, and wants admission or entry. After the announcement, the occupants must be given a reasonable time to respond. However, the precise duration of this "reasonable time" is an issue the Court has not categorically addressed. One publication says that the time is "generally not less than 30 seconds."[4] The meaning of the phrase "reasonable time" depends on circumstances. The same publication states that "if there is no response or there is an unreasonable delay, the officer may enter forcibly, using only such force as is reasonably necessary."[5]

D. The Scope of Search and Seizure

[handwritten: what you include on the affidavit]

The scope and manner of the search must be reasonable based on the object of the search. A wise legal maxim for officers to remember is this: *It is unreasonable for a police officer to look for an elephant in a matchbox.* For example, suppose a search warrant is issued for the recovery of a stolen "25-inch Zenith TV set." In looking for the TV set, the officer cannot open lockers and drawers—unless, of course, the locker or drawer is big enough to contain the TV set. But, if the search warrant is for the confiscation of heroin, then the officer is justified in opening lockers and drawers in the course of the search. It therefore follows that the smaller the item sought, the more extensive the scope of allowable search.

While the search is being conducted, the police may detain persons who are in the premises to be searched (Michigan v. Summers, 452 U.S. 692 [1981]). Although the police may detain persons in the premises to be searched, they cannot search persons found on the premises who are not named in the warrant. For example, a search warrant for a bar and the bartender does not authorize body searches of all bar patrons (Ybarra v. Illinois, 444 U.S. 85 [1979]). Searches of property belonging to persons not suspected of crime are permissible as long as probable cause exists to suspect that evidence of someone's guilt or other items subject to seizure will be found. For example, in one case, several police officers were hurt at a political demonstration. The police could not identify their attackers, but they knew that a newspaper staff photographer had taken photographs of the demonstration. The police were able to obtain a warrant to search the newspaper's offices, because probable cause existed that evidence of someone's guilt would be found (Zurcher v. Stanford Daily, 436 U.S. 547 [1978]).

AT A GLANCE

Time Allowed for the Search

The search cannot last indefinitely, whether it be done with or without a warrant. Once the item mentioned in the warrant is recovered, the search must cease. Continued search without justification becomes a fishing expedition for evidence and is illegal. As in most search and seizure cases, reasonableness is the standard used. This is determined by a judge or jury on a case-by-case basis.

E. The Time Allowed for a Search

The search cannot last indefinitely, whether it be done with or without a warrant. Once the item mentioned in the warrant is recovered, the search must cease. Continued search without justification becomes a fishing expedition for evidence and is illegal. An illegal search is never made legal by what is subsequently found. For example, suppose the police go to an apartment to execute a search for a shotgun allegedly used in a murder. After the shotgun is recovered, the police continue to search for other evidence in connection with the murder. They open a bedroom closet and find a pair of bloodied jeans worn by the suspect during the murder. The bloodied jeans, if seized and used in evidence, will not be admissible, because they were illegally obtained. Note, however, that items in plain view in the course of executing the warrant can be seized by the police because plain view items are not protected by the Fourth Amendment.

F. The Procedure after the Search

After the search, the usual police practice is to give the occupant a list of the things or items that have been seized. If nobody is in the premises, the list must be left "at the scene in a prominent place."[6] In a recent case, the Court held that the police are not required by the Constitution to provide the owner of the property seized with a notice of remedies specified by state law for the property's return and the information necessary to use those procedures (West Covina v. Perkins et al., No. 97-1230 [1999]). The Court stressed the need for some type of notice, saying that "individualized notice that officers have taken property is necessary in a case such as this one because the owner has no other reasonable means of ascertaining who is responsible for his loss." But the Court concluded that the other requirements specified by state law (such as detailed notice of the state procedures for the return of the seized property and the information necessary to use those procedures), required by California state law, are not required by the due process clause of the Constitution.

III. SEARCH AND SEIZURE WITHOUT A WARRANT

In searches and seizures without a warrant, the burden is on the police to prove in court that probable cause existed at the time of the warrantless search or seizure. It is therefore essential for law enforcement officers to be thoroughly familiar with the law on warrantless searches and seizures. Generally, there are seven exceptions to the rule that searches and seizures must be made with a warrant and with probable cause:

1. The "searches incident to lawful arrest" exception
2. The "searches with consent" exception
3. The "exigent circumstances" exception
4. The "special needs beyond law enforcement" exception
5. The "administrative searches and inspections" exception
6. The "stop and frisk" exception
7. The "motor vehicles" exception

The first five exceptions are discussed in this chapter. The "stop and frisk" exception is discussed in chapter 5, and the "motor vehicle" exception is discussed in chapter 6.

A. The "Searches Incident to Lawful Arrest" Exception

The "search incident to lawful arrest" exception is widely used in policing. It is invoked almost every time an officer makes an arrest, with or without a warrant. There are three justifications for warrantless searches incident to arrest: (1) to ensure officer safety, (2) to prevent escape, and (3) to prevent concealment or destruction of evidence. The authorization to search incident to arrest is automatic in that it is always available to the officer after an arrest, even if there is no probable cause to believe that it is necessary to ensure officer safety, to prevent escape, or to prevent concealment or destruction of evidence. These searches take two forms: body search and search of the area within the person's immediate control.

1. The Body Search of an Arrested Person

As discussed in chapter 6 on arrest, a body search is valid in any situation in which a full-custody arrest of a person occurs. There is no requirement that the officers fear for their safety or believe that they will find evidence of a crime before the body search can be made (United States v. Robinson, 414 U.S. 218 [1973]). But while a full body search is allowed, anal or cavity searches are prohibited unless justified by circumstances surrounding the search. For example, a police department policy that authorizes automatic anal and cavity searches after every arrest will likely be declared unconstitutional. This issue has not been decided by the U.S. Supreme Court, but lower courts have held that such searches, in the absence of compelling reason to support them, are too intrusive. Conversely, however, a policy that allows anal and cavity searches if there is reasonable suspicion—for example, if an officer has information from a reliable informant that the arrestee may be hiding contraband in these places—will likely be upheld. Even in a jail or prison setting, anal and cavity searches are not allowed unless justified—for example, after home furlough or a contact visit.

In addition to a body search after a lawful arrest, other types of body searches may be conducted by police officers. The general rule is that exterior intrusions on a person's body (such as swabbing, hand inspections, the taking of hair samples, and retrieval of evidence from the mouth) do not normally require a search warrant. In one case, a court held that the clipping by an officer of a few strands of hair from the appellant's head was so minor an imposition that the appellant suffered no true humiliation or affront to his dignity, so no search warrant was required to justify the officer's act (United States v. D'Amico, 408 F.2d 331 [2d Cir. 1969]).

Interior intrusions on a person's body (such as blood tests, stomach pumping, and surgery) are permitted by the Fourth Amendment only if they are conducted pursuant to a warrant or if exigent circumstances exist and there is a clear indication that the desired evidence will be found.[7] For example, in one case, the Court ruled that a blood test performed by a skilled technician is not conduct that shocks the conscience, nor is this method of obtaining evidence offensive to a sense of justice (Breithaupt v. Abram, 352 U.S. 432 [1957]). However, in another case, the Court held that the police restraining a suspect while a heroin capsule was removed from his stomach by a stomach pump shocks the conscience and therefore violates the suspect's right to due process (Rochin v. California, 342 U.S. 165 [1952]).

2. The Area within a Person's Immediate Control: Chimel v. California

In addition to performing a body search, the officer may also search the area within the person's immediate control. The leading case on this issue is Chimel v. California, 395 U.S. 752 (1969), also discussed in chapter 6 on arrests. In *Chimel,* the Court said:

> When an arrest is made, it is reasonable for the arresting officer to search the person arrested in order to remove any weapons that the latter might seek to use in order to resist arrest or effect his escape. . . . In addition, it is entirely reasonable for the arresting officer to search for and seize any evidence on the arrestee's person in order to prevent its concealment or destruction.

The Chimel rule holds that a warrantless search incident to arrest is valid if limited to the **area of immediate control,** meaning *the area from which the person might be able to obtain a weapon or destroy evidence.* The most limited, and arguably the most accurate, interpretation of that phrase is that the area is limited to the arrested person's *wingspan*—the area covered by the spread of the person's arms and hands. Officer protection and prevention of the destruction of evidence are the justifications for the rule. Nonetheless, courts allow officers to search the area of immediate control even after the arrested person has been handcuffed and therefore no longer poses a threat to the safety of the officer or the preservation of the evidence. (Read the Chimel v. California case brief at the end of this chapter.)

In motor vehicle searches, the Court has held that, when the police have made a lawful custodial arrest of the occupant of a car, they may search not only his or her wingspan but also the car's entire passenger compartment (front and back seats), and they may open any containers found in the compartment (New York v. Belton, 453 U.S. 454 [1981]).

3. The Requirement That the Warrantless Search Be Contemporaneous

To be **contemporaneous,** *the search must occur at the same time as, or very close in time and place to, the arrest.* A search conducted long after the arrest is illegal. In one case, the police arrested several smugglers and seized the footlocker in which they believed marijuana was being transported. One hour after the arrest, after the suspects were in jail, the officers opened and searched the footlocker without a warrant. The Court invalidated the search, saying that it was "remote in time and place from the arrest" (United States v. Chadwick, 433 U.S. 1 [1977]).

However, the custodial search may be deemed "incident to arrest" even when carried out later than the time of arrest, if there was valid reason for the delay. For example, in one case, a suspect was arrested and jailed late at night, but a clothing search for evidence was not conducted until the following morning. The Court said that the delayed search was justified, because substitute clothing was not available for the suspect's use at the time of the booking (United States v. Edwards, 415 U.S. 800 [1974]).

B. The "Searches with Consent" Exception

This is perhaps the most common exception to the warrant requirement rule. It basically states that if the object of the request gives proper consent, the consent is valid and anything illegal found and confiscated during the search may be introduced as evidence in court. There are limits to that search, however, the most important of which are discussed here.

1. Consent Must Be Voluntary

Warrantless searches with consent are valid, but the consent must be *voluntary,* meaning it was not obtained by the use of force, duress, or coercion. This is determined by looking at the *totality of circumstances.* For example, consent given only after the officer demands entry cannot be deemed to be free and voluntary. "Open the door" will most likely be interpreted by the courts as giving the occupant no choice and therefore making the consent involuntary. The better practice is for the officer to "request" rather than "demand." Requests such as "Would you mind if I come in and look around?" are more likely to result in voluntary consent.

Mere silence or failure to object to a search does not necessarily mean consent is given. The consent must be clear. For example, a shrug of the shoulder may signify indifference or resignation rather than consent. In one case, the Ninth Circuit Court of Appeals said that there was no valid consent where the resident opened his door, stepped into the hallway, listened to the officers identify themselves and explain the purpose of their visit, and then retreated wordlessly back into the apartment without closing the door (United States v. Shaibu, 920 F.2d 1423 [9th Cir. 1990]). The government in this case failed to meet its heavy burden of proving consent merely by showing that the defendant left his door open.

There is also no valid consent if permission is given as a result of police misrepresentation or deception, such as saying, "We have a warrant," when, in fact, none exists (Bumper v. North Carolina, 391 U.S. 543 [1968]). Lower courts are divided on the issue of whether consent is valid if the officer does not have a warrant but threatens to obtain one.[8] The issue has not been resolved by the Supreme Court.

2. Consent to Enter Does Not Necessarily Mean Consent to Search

For example, consent to enter for the purpose of asking questions does not mean consent to search. However, any seizable item in plain view after valid entry may be properly seized because items in plain view are not protected by the Fourth Amendment.

3. Consent to Search Need Not Be in Writing

To be valid, the consent to search does not have to be in writing. Oral consent is sufficient. Many police departments, however, suggest or require that the officer obtain such consent in writing. This is good policy because the voluntariness of the consent often becomes an issue of whose word the judge or jury believes. A written consent tilts the scale of voluntariness in favor of the officer, particularly if the consent is signed by witnesses. There are instances, however, when a written consent may be impractical or difficult to obtain. The evidence obtained will nonetheless be admissible as long as voluntariness is established by the police.

4. Knowledge of the Right to Refuse Consent Is Not Required

There is no need for the police to prove in court that the person giving consent knew that he or she actually had a right to refuse consent. The Court has held that ignorance of such a right is only one of the factors to be considered in determining whether the consent given was voluntary (Schneckloth v. Bustamonte, 412 U.S. 218 [1973]).[9]

5. The Scope of Allowable Search Depends on the Type of Consent Given

For example, the statement "You may look around" does not authorize the opening of closets, drawers, trunks, and boxes. And the consent to search a garage does not imply consent to search an adjoining house, or vice versa.

Conversely, consent for police to search a vehicle extends to closed containers found inside the vehicle, as long as it is objectively reasonable for the police to believe that the scope of the suspect's consent permitted them to open that container (Florida v. Jimeno, 111 S.Ct. 1801 [1991]). However, at least one state supreme court has held that consent to search a car does not authorize police officers to pry open a locked briefcase found in the car's trunk (State v. Wells, 539 So.2d 464 [Sup. Ct. Fla. 1989]). In general, consent to search does not include consent to open a locked (as opposed to closed) container unless the key is voluntarily given to the police.

6. Consent Given May Be Revoked at Any Time

This may be done even in the course of a search, by the person who gave the consent or by anybody else who possesses authority to do so. However, any evidence obtained before revocation is admissible.

7. Who May Give Consent to Search?

Following is a summary of who can and cannot give valid consent to a search.

a. Wife or Husband? A wife or a husband can give effective consent to search the family home. A possible exception is an area or item to which only the wife or husband has access, so that she or he has a reasonable expectation of privacy. An example would be a jewelry box owned by the wife, to which only she has a key and access.

b. Parent of a Child? There is no clear rule as to whether parents can give consent to search the room of a child who lives with them. Lower courts tend to rule that parents may give consent to search the rooms of their minor children, but not if the minor child is paying room and board to the parents.

c. Child of a Parent? In most states, a child cannot validly give consent to a search of his or her parents' home. This is because consent given by a child is not likely to be considered intelligent or voluntary. For example, suppose the police knock at an apartment door, a ten-year-old boy opens the door, and the officers ask if his parents are in. When told that the parents are out, the officers ask if they can "look around"—to which the boy willingly consents—and they find drugs on the kitchen table. The consent is invalid, the search illegal, and the evidence not admissible in court. Whether adult offspring who live with their parents can give consent to search their parents' home has not been clearly addressed by the courts.

d. Former Girlfriend? The Supreme Court has held that the warrantless entry of private premises by police officers is valid if based on the **"apparent authority" principle**. This applies *when police obtained the consent of a third party whom they, at the time of entry, reasonably believed to possess common authority over the premise but who, in fact, did not have such authority* (Illinois v. Rodriguez, 497 U.S. 117 [1990]). In that case, Rodriguez was arrested in his apartment and charged with possession of illegal drugs that the police said were in plain view on entry. The police gained entry to Rodriguez's apartment with the assistance of a certain Fischer, who represented that the apartment was "ours" and that she had clothes and furniture there. She unlocked the door with her key and gave the officers permission to enter. In reality, Fischer had moved out of the apartment and therefore no longer had any common authority over the apartment. The Court nonetheless held the consent given by Fischer to be valid because the police reasonably believed, given the circumstances, that she had the authority to give consent.

e. Roommate? A roommate may give valid consent to search the room. However, that consent cannot extend to areas in which another roommate has a reasonable expectation of privacy, because only he or she uses it. For example, suppose X gives consent for the police to search the studio apartment X and Y occupy. That consent is valid with respect to all areas that both X and Y use, such as the bathroom or study table. The consent is not valid for the search of Y's closet, to which only Y has access. If Y lives in another room (as in a multiroom apartment), X cannot give consent to search the room used only by Y.

f. Landlord? A landlord cannot give valid consent to search property that he or she has rented to another person (Stoner v. California, 376 U.S. 483 [1964]).

g. Lessor? Generally, a lessor (the person who leased out the property) cannot give valid consent to search the premises of a property leased to another person (United States v. Impink, 728 F.2d 1228 [9th Cir. 1985]).

h. Apartment Manager? The consent of an apartment manager to the warrantless search of apartment building common areas (such as public hallways and lobbies) is valid as long as the landlord has joint access to or control over those areas (United States v. Kelly, 1551 F.2d 760 [8th Cir. 1977]).

i. Driver of a Vehicle? The consent given by the driver of a vehicle for the search of the vehicle, including the trunk, glove compartment, and other areas, is valid even if the driver is not the owner of the vehicle (United States v. Morales, 861 F.2d 396 [3rd Cir. 1988]).

j. Hotel Clerk? A hotel clerk cannot give consent to the search of a guest's room (Stoner v. California, 376 U.S. 483 [1964]).

k. College and University Administrators? Most lower courts hold that college administrators (such as dormitory managers) cannot give consent for the police to search a student's dormitory room. The fact that some resident or dormitory managers may enter a student's room for certain purposes (such as health and safety issues) does not mean that they can give consent for the police to enter a student's room for purposes related to criminal prosecution (Piazzola v. Watkins, 442 F.2d 284 [5th Cir. 1971]). This issue, however, has not been authoritatively settled by the Supreme Court.

l. High School Administrators? Most lower courts hold that high school administrators, under proper circumstances, may give consent for the police to search a student's locker. This is because high school students are considered wards of the school. Therefore, the authority given to high school administrators is greater than that afforded to their college counterparts.

m. Business Employer? If the property is under the exclusive use and control of the employee, the employer cannot give valid consent to search (United States v. Block, 188 F.2d 1019 [D.C. Cir. 1951]). For example, a department store supervisor cannot give consent to search an employee's desk if only the employee is using it; similarly, a college dean or department head cannot give consent for the police to search a desk assigned to a faculty member for his or her exclusive use.

n. Business Employee? Unless specifically authorized, a business employee cannot consent to the search of his or her employer's business premises. Although the employee may have access to the property, he or she does not own it.

C. The "Special Needs beyond Law Enforcement" Exception

The Supreme Court has carved out, comparatively recently, a series of exceptions to the warrant requirement, collectively known as the **"special needs beyond law enforcement" exception.** What these situations have in common is that they are *not purely police searches but instead involve searches conducted by other public agencies that perform tasks related to law enforcement.* Examples are school searches, searches of probationers and parolees, and airport searches. The Court has repeatedly held that these types of searches may be made *without a warrant* and on *less than probable cause.*

1. Public School Searches

In 1983, the Court resolved an issue that had long bothered public school students, teachers, and administrators. Voting 6 to 3, the Court said that public school teachers and administrators *do not need a warrant or probable cause* to search a student whom they believe is violating the law or school rules. What is needed is *"reasonable grounds"* (lower than probable cause) for suspecting that the search will turn up evidence that the student has violated or is violating either the law or the rules of the school (New Jersey v. T.L.O., 469 U.S. 325 [1985]).

In this case, a teacher at a New Jersey high school discovered a student and her companion smoking cigarettes in a school lavatory, in violation of the school rule. She took them to the principal's office, where they met with the assistant vice principal. When the student denied that she had been smoking, the assistant vice principal demanded to see her purse. On opening the purse, he found a pack of cigarettes and also noticed a package of cigarette-rolling papers, which are commonly associated with the use of marijuana. He then proceeded to search the purse thoroughly and found marijuana, a pipe, plastic bags, a fairly substantial amount of money, and other items that implicated her in marijuana dealing. She moved to suppress the evidence in juvenile court, alleging that the search was illegal for lack of probable cause and a warrant. The Supreme Court rejected her allegation, saying that the Fourth Amendment prohibition against unreasonable searches and seizures applies to searches conducted by public school officials, but the school's legitimate need to maintain a positive learning environment requires some easing of the Fourth Amendment restrictions. Therefore, public school officials do not need a warrant or probable cause to conduct a search. All they need is *reasonable grounds* to suspect that the search will turn up evidence that the student has violated or is violating either the law or the rules of the school.

The *T.L.O.* ruling applies only to public school teachers and administrators. It does not apply to police officers, who are bound by the probable cause and warrant requirements even in school searches. The only possible exception is if the officers are to perform the search at the request of school authorities. The *T.L.O.* ruling does not apply to college or university students, either. Unlike high school or elementary school students, for whom teachers and administrators serve in loco parentis (in place of parents), college students are considered adults and therefore entitled to undiminished constitutional rights.

2. Searches of Probationers' and Parolees' Homes

In probation cases, the Court has held that a state law or agency rule permitting probation officers to search probationers' homes without a warrant and based on reasonable grounds (lower than probable cause) is a reasonable response to the "special needs" of the probation system and is therefore constitutional (Griffin v. Wisconsin, 483 U.S. 868 [1987]). The Court added that the supervision of probationers is a "special need" of the state that justifies a departure from the usual warrant and probable cause requirements. Although the *Griffin* case involved probationers, there is little doubt that the same principle applies to warrantless searches of parolees' homes. The Court has also ruled that evidence obtained by parole officers during an illegal search and seizure need not be excluded in a parole revocation proceeding (Pennsylvania Board of Probation and Parole v. Scott, 118 S.Ct. 2014 [1998]).

Some states allow warrantless searches of probationers' homes based on *suspicion,* a lower degree of certainty than reasonable grounds. Although the Supreme Court has not ruled on this issue, lower courts have upheld the practice based on the twin concepts of *diminished constitutional rights* and *special needs.*

3. Airport Searches

A limited search of air travelers is permissible for the purpose of discovering weapons and preventing hijacking. There is no need for probable cause, reasonable suspicion, or even mere suspicion. The search is an administrative measure based on safety needs. In one case, a court said, "The need to prevent airline hijacking is unquestionably grave and urgent. . . . A pre-boarding screening of all passengers and carry-on articles sufficient in scope to detect the presence of weapons or explosives is reasonably necessary to meet the need" (United States v. Davis, 482 F.2d 893 [9th Cir. 1973]). If an electronic search, using a magnetometer, is used and the reading indicates the possible presence of a weapon, a frisk or pat-down of the traveler's clothing is then justified. Evidence discovered is admissible in court. A person who refuses to submit to the limited search may be excluded from entry to the boarding area.

One court of appeals judge justified airport searches in this way:

> When the risk is the jeopardy to hundreds of human lives and millions of dollars of property inherent in the pirating or blowing up of a large airplane, that danger alone meets the test of reasonableness, so long as the search is conducted in good faith for the purpose of preventing hijacking or like damage and with reasonable scope and the passenger has been given advance notice of his liability to such a search so that he can avoid it by choosing not to travel by air. (United States v. Bell, 464 F.2d 667 [1972])

The use of police dogs to sniff containers and luggage to detect contraband at airports does not constitute a search. No warrant or probable cause is needed as long as the container or luggage is located in a public place. One court has said, "It cannot be considered a search within the protection of the Fourth Amendment for a dog to sniff bags handled by an airline. There can be no reasonable expectation of privacy when any passenger's bags may be subjected to close scrutiny for the protection of public safety" (United States v. Sullivan, 625 F.2d 9 [4th Cir. 1980]).[10]

D. The "Exigent (Emergency) Circumstances" Exception

The **exigent circumstances** exception is a general catchall category that encompasses a number of diverse situations. What they have in common is some kind of *an emergency that makes obtaining a search warrant impractical, useless, dangerous, or unnecessary.* Among these situations are danger of physical harm to the officer or destruction of evidence, searches in hot pursuit, danger to a third person, and driving while intoxicated.

1. Danger of Physical Harm to the Officer or Destruction of Evidence

The Court has implied that a warrantless search may be justified if there is reasonable grounds to believe that delaying the search until the warrant is obtained would endanger the physical safety of the officer or would allow the destruction or removal of the evidence (Vale v. Louisiana, 399 U.S. 30 [1970]). However, in *Vale*, the Supreme Court did not allow a warrantless search when there was *merely a possibility* that the evidence would be destroyed. Thus, *Vale* has a narrow interpretation: The threat of danger or destruction must be real or imminent. Three years later, the Court held that the taking of fingernail scrapings without consent or formal arrest does not violate the Fourth Amendment protection against unreasonable search and seizure if the evidence is likely to disappear before a warrant can be obtained (Cupp v. Murphy, 412 U.S. 291 [1973]).

The Court has ruled, however, that the fact that the place searched was the scene of a serious crime (in this case the murder of an undercover officer) did not in itself justify a warrantless search in the absence of any "indication that the evidence would be lost, destroyed, or removed during the time required to obtain a search warrant and there is no suggestion that a warrant could not easily and conveniently have been obtained" (Mincey v. Arizona, 437 U.S. 385 [1978]). In *Mincey*, an undercover police officer was shot and killed in the process of a narcotics raid on Mincey's apartment. Shortly thereafter, homicide detectives arrived at the scene of the crime and proceeded to conduct "an exhaustive four-day warrantless search of the apartment which included the opening of dresser drawers, the ripping up of carpets, and the seizure of 200 to 300 objects." At trial, Mincey sought to suppress the evidence obtained, saying that the warrantless search was invalid. The government justified the warrantless search based on the "murder scene" exception to the warrant requirement created by the Arizona Supreme Court in previous cases. The Court disagreed, saying that the warrantless search in this case could not be justified based on "the ground that a possible homicide inevitably presents an emergency situation, especially since there was no emergency threatening life or limb." The "seriousness of the offense . . . did not itself create exigent circumstances of the kind that under the Fourth Amendment justify a warrantless search, where there is no indication that evidence would be lost, destroyed, or removed during the time required to obtain a search warrant and there is no suggestion that a warrant could not easily and conveniently have been obtained." In sum, the Court said that a warrant must be obtained in crime scene investigations, regardless of the seriousness of the offense. The only exception to this rule is if obtaining a warrant would mean that the evidence would be lost, destroyed, or removed during the time required to obtain a warrant.

In a 1999 case, the Court reaffirmed its decision in *Mincey* when it said that there is no crime scene exception to the search warrant requirement, adding that "a warrantless search by the police is invalid unless it falls within one of the narrow and well-delineated exceptions to the warrant requirement" (Flippo v. West Virginia, No. 98-8770 [1999]). In this case, Flippo's conviction was influenced by photographs removed by the police from a briefcase they found at the scene and opened without a warrant. The photographs, admitted at trial, suggested that Flippo was having a homosexual affair with a member of his church and this provided a motive for him to kill his wife. The Court rejected this "murder scene" exception to the warrant requirement used by the prosecution, saying that this exception was squarely in conflict with *Mincey*.

2. Searches in "Hot Pursuit" (or "Fresh Pursuit") of Dangerous Suspects

The police may enter a house without a warrant to search for a dangerous suspect who is being pursued and whom they have reason to believe is on the premises. For example, in one case, the police pursued a robbery suspect to a house (which later turned out to be his own). The suspect's wife opened the door to the police, who asked and received permission to search for a "burglar." The police looked for weapons that might have been concealed and found incriminating clothing in a washing machine. The clothing was confiscated and introduced as evidence during the trial. The Court held that the warrantless search was justified by "hot pursuit" (regardless of the validity of the suspect's wife's consent). Because the police were informed that an armed robbery had taken place and that the suspect had entered a certain house less than five minutes before they got there, they acted reasonably when they entered the house and began to search for a man of the description they had obtained and for weapons that he had allegedly used in the robbery (Warden v. Hayden, 387 U.S. 294 [1967]).

3. Danger to a Third Person

An officer may enter a dwelling without a warrant in response to screams for help. In one case, the Court said, "The Fourth Amendment does not require police officers to delay in the course of an investigation if to do so would gravely endanger their lives or the lives of others" (Warden v. Hayden, 387 U.S. 294 [1967]).

4. Driving While Intoxicated (DWI)

The police may, without a search warrant and by force, if necessary, take a blood sample from a person arrested for drunk driving, as long as the setting and procedures are reasonable (as when the blood is drawn by a doctor in a hospital). Exigent circumstances exist because alcohol in the suspect's bloodstream might disappear in the time required to obtain a warrant (Schmerber v. California, 384 U.S. 757 [1966]).

However, a case decided by the U.S. Supreme Court has placed limits on what the police can do in simple DWI cases. The Court held that the Fourth Amendment prohibits the police from making a warrantless nighttime entry into a suspect's house in order to arrest him or her for drunk driving if the offense is a misdemeanor for which state law does not allow any jail sentence. The fact that the police had an interest in preserving the evidence (because the suspect's blood-alcohol level might diminish while the police procured a warrant) was ruled to be insufficient to create the required exigent circumstance (Welsh v. Wisconsin, 466 U.S. 740 [1984]).

In *Welsh,* the defendant had run his car off the road and abandoned it. By the time police officers arrived at the scene and learned from a witness that the defendant was either inebriated or very ill, the defendant had gone home and fallen asleep. The officers checked the vehicle's registration and learned that the defendant lived close by. Without obtaining a warrant, they went to the suspect's home and arrested him. The Wisconsin Supreme Court held that the officers' actions were justified by exigent circumstances. The U.S. Supreme Court reversed that decision, saying that "an important factor to be considered when determining whether any exigency exists is the gravity of the underlying offense for which the arrest is being made. . . . Application of the exigent circumstances exception in the context of a home entry should rarely be sanctioned when there is probable cause to believe that only a minor offense has been committed." The Court concluded that in this case there was no immediate pursuit of the defendant from the scene; nor was there any need to protect either the public or the defendant, inasmuch as he had abandoned the vehicle and was at home sleeping. Only the need to preserve the evidence remained, and that was not enough, given the type of offense involved and the state's treatment of it as a civil matter, to justify the warrantless intrusion.

The Court's decision states that "an important factor to be considered when determining whether any emergency exists is the gravity of the underlying offense for which the arrest is being made." Implicit in this is the assumption that had the offense been serious (such as if the driver had seriously injured somebody before running off the road and abandoning his car), the warrantless search of his home would have been allowed.

E. The "Administrative Searches and Inspections" Exception

Administrative searches are *searches conducted by government investigators to determine if there are violations of government rules and regulations.* These searches are usually authorized by local ordinances or regulations of administrative agencies and are generally conducted by agents or investigators of these agencies rather than by the police. In some jurisdictions, the warrant issued is known as an *administrative* instead of a *judicial* warrant. Court decisions have identified three types of administrative searches and inspections. The rules governing them differ as to the warrant and probable cause requirements.

1. Entering a Private Residence for Code Violations

The Court has held that health, safety, or other types of inspectors cannot enter private premises without the owner's consent or a search warrant (Camara v. Municipal Court 387 U.S. 523 [1967]). In this case, defendant Camara was charged with violating the San Francisco Housing Code for refusing building inspectors a warrantless inspection of a building he leased and used as a residence, allegedly in violation of the city's occupancy rules. Subsequently charged in a criminal case with refusal to permit a warrantless inspection of his residence, Camara claimed that the city ordinance authorizing such warrantless inspections was unconstitutional and a violation of the Fourth Amendment. On appeal, the Court agreed, saying, "It is surely anomalous to say that the individual and his private property are fully protected by the Fourth Amendment only when the individual is suspected of criminal behavior." But note that, although a warrant is required, as one source states:

> [T]he inspector does not have to demonstrate probable cause to believe that a violation of an ordinance within his domain will be discovered in the premises to be searched. Instead, the inspector must simply demonstrate that "reasonable legislative or administrative standards for conducting an area inspection are satisfied with respect to a particular dwelling." Thus the inspector does not have to show that the dwelling probably contains code violations, but simply that it belongs to a class of structures (e.g., multifamily apartment buildings, or commercial buildings not inspected in the previous year, etc.) the inspection of which has been administratively or legislatively provided for.[11]

2. Entering Commercial Buildings for Inspection Purposes

The rule just discussed also applies to commercial structures that are not used as private residences (See v. City of Seattle, 387 U.S. 541 [1967]). In this case, defendant See was convicted for refusing to permit an agent of the Seattle Fire Department to enter and inspect his locked commercial warehouse without a warrant and without probable cause to believe that a violation of any municipal ordinance had taken place. Such inspection was conducted routinely as part of a periodic citywide canvass to ensure compliance with Seattle's Fire Code. On appeal, the Court held that "administrative entry, without consent, upon the portions of commercial premises which are not open to the public may only be compelled through prosecution or physical force within the framework of a warrant procedure." It added that "the basic component of a reasonable search under the Fourth Amendment—that it not be enforced without a suitable warrant procedure—is applicable in this context, as in others, to business as well as to residential premises." As in the case of entries into a private residence for code violations, probable cause is not required. All that is needed is for the inspector to show that the place being inspected belongs to a class of structures that is mandated by administrative rules or ordinances to be inspected.

3. Searches of Closely Regulated Businesses

In contrast to the two situations just discussed, the Court has decided in a number of cases that searches of highly regulated businesses or industries do not need a warrant or probable cause. The justification for this "no need for warrant or probable cause" rule is the urgent public interest involved in the search. Another justification is the implied consent given for the government to search without a warrant when these businesses applied for a government license to get into this type of highly regulated business. The Court has held that the warrantless inspection of a weapons dealer by a federal agent was valid, saying that the dealer had chosen to engage in a business that was inherently subject to heavy federal licensing regulation and that such regulation could only be enforced by the government's making unannounced and frequent visits (United States v. Biswell, 406 U.S. 311 [1972]). In another case, the Court upheld the warrantless inspection of an automobile junkyard, saying that the warrantless inspection was valid because the business was "closely regulated" by the government and there was substantial government interest involved in preventing car theft (New York v. Burger, 482 U.S. 691 [1987]). The same holds true for liquor businesses (Colonade Catering Corporation v. United States, 397 U.S. 72 [1970]) and strip-mining (Donovan v. Dewey, 452 U.S. 594 [1981]).

Administrative searches differ from police searches in a number of ways. Among them are the following:

- They are usually conducted by administrative agents rather than by the police.

- Their purpose is enforcement of administrative regulations or local ordinances rather than penal code enforcement.

- A warrant is needed for searches of private residences for code violations and when entering commercial buildings for inspection purposes, but not for searches of highly regulated businesses; by contrast, police searches generally need a warrant.

- There is no need for probable cause for administrative warrants; all that is needed is a showing that the place being inspected belongs to a class of structures that is mandated by administrative rules or ordinances to be inspected (such as that it is an apartment building or commercial building); police searches always need probable cause, unless they fall under one of the many exceptions.

IV. SPECIFIC SEARCH AND SEIZURE ISSUES

A. Surgery to Remove a Bullet from a Suspect

In one case, the Court held that a proposed surgery to remove a bullet from a suspect's chest for use as evidence would involve such severe intrusion on his interest in privacy and security that it would violate the Fourth Amendment and could not be allowed unless the government demonstrated a compelling need for it. The surgery could not be constitutionally undertaken even though probable cause existed and the suspect was provided with all relevant procedural safeguards because the government failed to establish the compelling need for such surgery (Winston v. Lee, 470 U.S. 753 [1985]). This decision is significant, because in an earlier case (Schmerber v. California, 384 U.S. 757 [1966]) the Court held that a state may, over the suspect's objections, have a physician extract blood if he or she is suspected of drunken driving without violating his or her Fourth Amendment right not to be subjected to unreasonable searches and seizures. However, according to the *Schmerber* decision, the holding that the Constitution does not forbid a state's minor intrusions into an individual's body under stringently limited conditions in no way indicates that it permits more substantial intrusions or intrusions under other conditions.

In the *Lee* case, the state of Virginia sought to compel Lee, a suspect in an attempted armed robbery who had allegedly been wounded by gunfire in that attempt, to undergo a surgical procedure under a general anesthetic for removal of the bullet lodged in his chest. Prosecutors alleged that the bullet would provide evidence of the suspect's guilt or innocence. The suspect opposed the surgery. The Court concluded that the procedure was an example of the "more substantial intrusion" cautioned against in the *Schmerber* case and held that to permit the procedure to take place would violate the suspect's right to be secure in his person, as guaranteed by the Fourth Amendment. The Court did not say that evidence retrievals of this nature could never be undertaken simply because they were per se intrusive. Instead, it used a balancing test, stating that "the medical risks of the operation, although apparently not extremely severe, are a subject of considerable dispute." But the Court also said that, "although the bullet may turn out to be useful . . . in prosecuting respondent, the Commonwealth [of Virginia] failed to demonstrate a compelling need for it." The Court did not say that intrusions of this nature can never be allowed; what the Court instead said was that, on balance, the removal of the evidence in this case would have been unreasonable because the state failed to prove a compelling need.

B. Mail Searches

First-class letters and sealed packages are fully protected by the Fourth Amendment and therefore cannot be searched by the police or postal authorities without a search warrant. However, if postal authorities have probable cause to believe that such mail contains contraband or other seizable evidence, they have the right to detain the mail for a reasonable time—long enough to enable them, acting diligently, to obtain a search warrant. After the warrant has been obtained, the mail may be opened, but it cannot be read (United States v. Van Leeuwen, 397 U.S. 249 [1970]).

C. Searches and Seizures by Private Persons

Searches and seizures by private persons do not come under Fourth Amendment protection, because the constitutional amendments apply only to acts of government agencies and officers. This is true even if the act by private persons is illegal.

Evidence obtained by private persons is admissible in court as long as they acted purely on their own and the police did not encourage or participate in the private search and seizure. For example, suppose X breaks into his neighbor's house because he suspects the neighbor of having stolen his TV set. X recovers the set and now brings a case of robbery against his neighbor. The TV set is admissible in evidence, because the Fourth Amendment guarantee of protection against unreasonable searches and seizures applies only to acts of government officers. However, X may be liable for breaking into and entering his neighbor's house in a separate criminal case. Note also that the evidence is not admissible if a police officer participated in, ordered, or encouraged X to effect the search.

If a government official helps in a search or seizure by a private citizen, then the Fourth Amendment protections apply.[12] It is immaterial whether a government officer proposed the idea or merely joined in while the search was in progress. As long as he or she was involved before the object of the search was completely accomplished, the officer must be considered to have participated in it; the evidence secured is therefore inadmissible.

D. Searches by Government Agents of the Same Material Searched by Private Parties

The U.S. Supreme Court has held that, if government agents perform a search or seizure of the same material that has already been subjected to a private search or seizure, then the government search will be considered to have intruded into the owner's privacy interests *only to the extent that the government search or seizure exceeded the scope of the private search.* Moreover, it is valid for government agents to conduct a warrantless "chemical field test" of suspected controlled substances (United States v. Jacobsen, 466 U.S. 109 [1984]).

E. Searches by Off-Duty Officers

Search by an officer who is off duty is usually considered to be a government search. Many jurisdictions consider police officers to be law enforcement officers twenty-four hours a day, seven days a week. If this were not the rule, it would be easy for police officers to conduct searches while off duty and therefore subvert the provisions of the Fourth Amendment. Although this has not been litigated in court, the rule would likely be the same even in jurisdictions where a police officer is not expected to be on duty at all times.

F. Squeezing Luggage

In October 1999, the Court agreed to decide a case that raises the following issue: Can the police, when looking for illegal drugs, squeeze a person's luggage in the absence of valid consent or reasonable suspicion that a crime has been committed by the owner? In this case, Border Patrol Agent Cantu stopped a Greyhound bus in west Texas to conduct a routine immigration check. He worked his way from the front of the bus to the back but found no illegal immigrants. On his way from the back of the bus, he squeezed the luggage of some passengers to determine if they contained illegal drugs. When he squeezed the bag of passenger Bond and felt a hard object, Cantu then asked for and received Bond's consent to open the bag. He found methamphetamines tightly wrapped in tape. During trial, the judge rejected Bond's motion to suppress the evidence, saying that Cantu violated his constitutional right when he squeezed the bag prior to Bond's consent and without any suspicion of illegal activity. Bond maintained that he had a reasonable expectation of privacy regarding the contents of his bag. The Federal Court of Appeals for the Fifth Circuit upheld the admission of the evidence, saying that merely squeezing the bag, which Bond left out in the open for anyone to touch, did not constitute a search under the Constitution; therefore, the officer's action was valid despite the absence of consent or suspicion. The case will likely be decided by the Court before July 2000.[15] Stay tuned.

G. The Use of Police Dogs for Detection of Drugs

There is no "search" within the meaning of the Fourth Amendment if the police use narcotics detection dogs to smell closed containers for drugs, as long as the police are legally on the premises. There is therefore no need for a search warrant or for probable cause to conduct dog sniffs (United States v. Place, 462 U.S. 696 [1983]). Justifications for this judicial rule include the following: (1) The use of dogs does not involve any physical intrusion, (2) the intrusion upon an individual's privacy is inoffensive, (3) the intrusion is restricted because the dog is discriminate, (4) the intrusion is not aimed at persons but rather at an inanimate object, and (5) the use of dogs is not the same as using a sophisticated electronic device.[13]

H. Searches of Nonresident Aliens in a Foreign Country

The Court has held that a nonresident alien may not invoke the protections of the Fourth Amendment to challenge the warrantless seizure of items from a residence located in a foreign country (United States v. Verdugo-Urquidez, 494 U.S. 259 [1990]). In this case, Verdugo-Urquidez, a citizen and resident of Mexico, was arrested by the Mexican police in Mexico in accordance with a warrant issued in the United States. He was turned over to U.S. officials at the border and placed in a detention center in San Diego, California. Believing that Verdugo-Urquidez was involved not only in drug smuggling but also in the torture and murder of DEA Special Agent Enrique Camarena, U.S. agents decided to search two of the suspect's residences in Mexico. They obtained the cooperation of Mexican officials and, working with them, executed warrantless searches. Verdugo-Urquidez was later tried and convicted in California. On appeal, the Court ruled that the evidence was admissible, saying that the Fourth Amendment has

AT A GLANCE

Searches and Seizures of Things

DEFINITIONS: *Search* is the exploration or examination of an individual's house, premises, or person, in order to discover things that may be used by the government for evidence in a criminal prosecution. *Seizure* is the exercise of dominion or control by the government over a person or thing because of a violation of law.

TYPES: With a warrant or without a warrant.

RULE: All searches and seizures must be made with a warrant.

EXCEPTIONS TO WARRANT RULE: (1) Searches incident to lawful arrest, (2) searches with consent, (3) special needs beyond law enforcement, (4) exigent circumstances, (5) administrative searches and seizures, (6) stop and frisk, and (7) motor vehicle searches.

SCOPE OF SEARCH: The reasonableness rule applies: Do not look for an elephant in a matchbox.

SPECIFIC SEARCHES AND SEIZURES:

- Searches after arrest—may conduct a body search.
- Searches after arrest—may search the area of immediate control.
- Surgery to remove a bullet from a suspect is allowed only if justified by compelling need.
- Mail searches—warrant is generally needed.
- Searches and seizures by private persons—no warrant is needed.
- Searches by off-duty officer—warrant is needed.
- The use of police dogs for detection of drugs—no warrant is needed.
- Searches of a nonresident alien in a foreign country—Fourth Amendment does not apply.
- Searches in cyberspace—no leading cases.

"no application" to a search of an alien's residence located in a foreign country, even if that resident is later tried here and the evidence seized is used in a U.S. court.

I.   Searches and Seizures in Cyberspace

Sooner or later, law enforcement will faced problems related to searches and seizures involving cyberspace. Thus far, the use of computers, the Internet, and other forms of electronic media has raised a host of legal questions related to First Amendment rights but not to the Fourth Amendment. Cases have been decided by trial courts and courts of appeal on issues of censorship in cyberspace, the constitutionality of legislation penalizing the possession and transmission of materials through computers, jurisdiction and venue in cases involving perpetrators using computers in various states, and other akin issues.

In February 1996, Congress passed the Communications Decency Act, which was signed by the president into law. This law, part of the massive telecommunications reform bill, makes it a "crime to transmit indecent speech and images across computer and phone networks, including the Internet, in such a way that children might have access to it." Three courts have declared the act unconstitutional because it violates the First Amendment. Eleven other states have passed laws attempting to regulate communication on the Internet, and six more states are considering similar legislation.[14] There are other interesting legal issues involving cyberspace related to the use of restricted or copyrighted materials and to unauthorized entries into restricted terminals.

As of the end of 1999, there were no cases on the Fourth Amendment peculiar to cyberspace. The reason could be that computers, CD-ROMs, disks, software, and cyberspace hardware are like any other personal possessions for purposes of the Fourth Amendment; hence, rules governing their searches and seizures are similar to those discussed in this chapter. One source, however, summarizes the rule as follows:[15]

> A warrant to search computer files must satisfy the requirement of specificity by stating clearly the files to be searched and the information to be "seized"—i.e., the material being sought. The officer executing the warrant may review files to determine whether they are covered by the warrant, but once that determination has been made, material that is not covered may not be examined further.

The difficult question involving cyberspace in future cases is refining the concept of "reasonable expectation of privacy" in the face of new technology. This is the test courts use when deciding whether a search or seizure comes under the umbrella of the Fourth Amendment. Under current tests, there is no reasonable expectation of privacy for anything that is in cyberspace and is available for anybody to read, print, or download. Given the public nature of cyberspace, it will not be surprising if courts are forced to redefine the meaning of "reasonable expectation of privacy" to fit a more advanced technological age. Seizures of computers themselves come under the rules of seizures of things. Seizure of computer entries and information that are protected by privacy codes might, however, raise legal problems. For now, however, there are no legal guidelines or precedents that define the scope and role of law enforcement in cyberspace; neither have the courts been faced with issues involving searches and seizures in this emerging realm.

Summary

Although often used as one, the terms *search* and *seizure* represent two separate acts. A search is any government intrusion into a person's reasonable and justifiable expectation of privacy, whereas a seizure is the exercise of dominion or control by the government over a person or thing because of a violation of law. Searches are generally classified by the presence or absence of a warrant. The general rule is that searches

Six Rules for Analyzing Search and Seizure Cases in Law Enforcement

The following questions will help you analyze cases involving searches and seizures of things (as distinguished from arrest) and determine their legality. Ask the questions and analyze your response in the following sequence:

1. Is the police activity at issue a search and seizure case, or is it something else? If it is not a search and seizure case (such as plain view, abandonment, or open field), then the warrant and probable cause requirements of the Fourth Amendment do not apply.

2. If the police activity in question constitutes search and seizure of things, was there a search warrant? If there was a search warrant, then the search is presumably valid (although the validity may be challenged later in court).

3. If there was no search warrant, does the search and seizure come under any of the many exceptions discussed in this and other chapters? If it comes under one of the exceptions, then the warrantless search and seizure is valid, and the evidence is admissible in court, as long as the requirements for that type of search are present.

4. If the search is valid, was the scope of the police search within allowable limits? (Remember the "elephant in a matchbox" and Chimel limitations.) If within allowable limits, then the search is valid.

5. Are there limitations imposed by state law? Even if what the police did is allowed by the Constitution under the rules discussed in this chapter, state law may impose limitations that make the evidence obtained inadmissible in state courts. State law on searches and seizures, if more limiting, prevails over what the Constitution allows.

6. Is evidence obtained after an illegal act admissible in court? Nothing that turns up later in the course of the search will cure the initial illegality, so the evidence must be excluded.

---

must be made with a warrant. Searches without a warrant are therefore the exception rather than the rule.

There are various conditions under which searches can be made without a warrant, five of which are discussed in this chapter. The first exception is a search incident to a lawful arrest. The rule is that, once a lawful arrest is made, the police may conduct a body search and also search any area within the suspect's "immediate control," meaning the area into which the suspect may reach to grab a weapon or destroy evidence. The second exception is a search with consent. The third exception involves special needs beyond law enforcement. These are cases in which public officials other than police officers are involved in searches and seizures. The fourth exception is the presence of exigent circumstances, such as a threat to the officer's physical safety, the risk of destruction of evidence, danger to a third person, driving while intoxicated, or hot pursuit. The fifth exception involves administrative searches and inspections, which are governed by different rules.

Courts have addressed other specific issues related to searches and seizures of things. For example, surgery to remove a bullet from a suspect is not allowed unless justified by a compelling need. A warrant is generally needed in mail searches, but searches and seizures by private persons do not need a warrant. Searches by an off-duty police officer are considered government searches, but the use of police dogs to detect drugs is not considered a search. The Court has held that, in a search of a non-resident alien in a foreign country, the person is not protected by the Fourth Amendment even if he or she is later turned over to and tried in the United States. Searches and seizures in cyberspace will assume greater importance in the coming years. For now, however, courts have not adequately addressed this issue.

Review Questions

1. Distinguish between a search and a seizure.

2. What are the four requirements for the valid issuance of a search warrant? Discuss each.

3. What four categories of items are subject to search and seizure?

4. Discuss the current rule on "knock and announce," as decided by the Court in a number of cases.

5. Discuss the extent and scope of the "search incident to arrest" exception.

6. What does the phrase "area of immediate control" mean?

7. What is the "special needs beyond law enforcement" exception to the warrant and probable cause requirements? Give two examples.

8. What is the "exigent circumstances" exception to the warrant requirement? Give two examples.

9. What is the rule concerning searches of students by public school teachers and administrators? Does the same rule apply to school searches by police? Explain.

10. "The scope and manner of a search must be reasonable." Explain what that means, and give examples.

11. What is an administrative seizure? How does it differ from a police seizure?

Key Terms and Definitions

administrative searches: Searches conducted by government inspectors to determine if there are violations of government rules and regulations.

anticipatory search warrant: A warrant obtained based on probable cause and an expectation that seizable items will be found at a certain place at a certain time.

apparent authority principle: The principle that a search is valid if consent was given by a person whom the police reasonably believed to have authority to give such consent, even if that person turns out not to have such authority.

area of immediate control: The area from which an arrested person might be able to obtain a weapon or destroy evidence.

Chimel rule: The rule that after an arrest the police may search the areas within a suspect's immediate control, meaning the area from which the suspect might be able to obtain a weapon or destroy evidence.

contemporaneous search: A search made at the same time

as, or very close in time and place to, the arrest.

exigent circumstances: Emergency circumstances that make obtaining a warrant impractical, useless, dangerous, or unnecessary.

no-knock searches: Searches without announcement, authorized by state statutes, particularly in drug cases.

probable cause: More than bare suspicion; it exists when the facts and circumstances within the officers' knowledge and of which they have reasonably trustworthy information are sufficient in themselves to warrant a person of reasonable caution in the belief that an offense has been or is being committed. In searches and seizures (as contrasted with arrests), the issue of probable cause focuses on whether the property to be seized is connected with criminal activity and whether it can be found in the place to be searched.

reasonable expectation of privacy: The degree of privacy that entitles a person's constitutional rights to be protected from government intrusion in private or public places.

search: The exploration or examination of an individual's home, premises, or person in order to discover things or items that may be used by the government as evidence in a criminal prosecution.

search warrant: A written order issued by a magistrate, directing a peace officer to search for property connected with a crime and bring it before the court.

seizure: The exercise of dominion or control by the government over a person or thing because of a violation of law.

"special needs beyond law enforcement" exception: An exception to the requirements of a warrant and probable cause under the Fourth Amendment; it allows warrantless searches and searches on less-than-probable cause in cases where there are needs to be met other than those of law enforcement, such as the supervision of high school students, probationers, and parolees.

 Principles of Cases

Breithaupt v. Abram, 352 U.S. 432 (1957) A blood test performed by a skilled technician is not conduct that shocks the conscience, nor does this method of obtaining evidence offend a sense of justice.

Bumper v. North Carolina, 391 U.S. 543 (1968) There is no valid consent to a search if permission is given as a result of police misrepresentation or deception.

Camara v. Municipal Court, 387 U.S. 523 (1967) Health, safety, or other types of inspectors cannot enter private premises without the owner's consent or a search warrant.

Chimel v. California, 395 U.S. 752 (1969) Once a lawful arrest has been made, the police may search any area within the suspect's "immediate control," meaning the area from which the suspect may grab a weapon or destroy evidence.

City of West Covina v. Perkins, No. 97-1230 (1999) The police do not have to provide the owner of the property seized with notice of remedies specified by state law for the property's return and the information necessary to use those procedures.

Connally v. Georgia, 429 U.S. 245 (1977) A magistrate who receives a fee when issuing a warrant but not when denying one is not neutral and detached.

Coolidge v. New Hampshire, 403 U.S. 443 (1971) A state's chief investigator and prosecutor (state attorney general) is not neutral and detached, so any warrant issued by him or her is invalid.

Cupp v. Murphy, 412 U.S. 291 (1973) Without a warrant, the police may make a seizure of evidence that is likely to disappear before a warrant can be obtained.

Flippo v. West Virginia, No. 98-8770 (1999) There is no crime scene exception to the search warrant requirement.

Florida v. Jimeno, 111 S.Ct. 1801 (1991) Consent for police to search a vehicle extends to closed containers found inside the vehicle, as long as it is objectively reasonable for the police to believe that the scope of the suspect's consent permitted them to open that container.

Griffin v. Wisconsin, 483 U.S. 868 (1987) A state law or agency rule permitting probation officers to search probationers' homes without a warrant and based on reasonable grounds instead of probable cause is a reasonable response to the special needs of the probation system and is therefore constitutional.

Illinois v. Rodriguez, 497 U.S. 117 (1990) The warrantless entry into private premises by police officers is valid if based on the consent of a third party whom the police, at the time of entry, reasonably believed to possess common authority over the premises, but who in fact did not have such authority.

Johnson v. United States, 333 U.S. 10 (1948) Inferences leading to the issuance of a search warrant must be drawn by a neutral and detached magistrate, not by the officer engaged in the often competitive enterprise of ferreting out crime.

Katz v. United States, 389 U.S. 347 (1967) The prohibition against unreasonable search and seizure is not limited to homes, offices, buildings, or other enclosed places. It applies even in public places where a person has a "reasonable and justifiable expectation of privacy." The Fourth Amendment protects people, not places.

Lo-Ji Sales, Inc., v. New York, 442 U.S. 319 (1979) A magistrate who participates in a search to determine its scope lacks the requisite neutrality and detachment.

Lustig v. United States, 338 U.S. 74 (1949) If a government official aids in a search or seizure by a private citizen, the Fourth Amendment applies. It is immaterial whether a government official proposed the idea or merely joined in the search while it was in progress. As long as the officer was involved before the object of the search was completely accomplished, he or she must be considered to have participated in it.

Marshall v. Barlow's, Inc., 436 U.S. 307 (1978) What is required for the issuance of an administrative inspection warrant is merely a showing of a general enforcement plan. Probable cause may be based on such factors as the passage of time, the nature of the building, and conditions elsewhere in the same geographic area.

Maryland v. Garrison, 480 U.S. 79 (1987) The validity of a warrant must be judged in light of the information available to the officers at the time they obtained the warrant. A warrant that is overbroad in describing the place to be searched is valid if based on a reasonable but mistaken belief at the time the warrant was issued.

Maryland v. Macon, 472 U.S. 463 (1985) Seizure occurs when there is some meaningful interference with an individual's possessory interest in the property seized.

Michigan v. Summers, 452 U.S. 692 (1981) While a search is being conducted, the police may detain persons found in the premises that are to be searched.

Mincey v. Arizona, 437 U.S. 385 (1978) The fact that a place searched was the scene of a serious crime did not in itself justify a warrantless search in the absence of any "indication that the evidence would be lost, destroyed, or removed during the time required to obtain a search warrant and there is no suggestion that a warrant could not easily and conveniently have been obtained."

Piazzola v. Watkins, 442 F.2d 284 (5th Cir. 1971) A university regulation allowing inspection of rooms does not authorize university authorities to give consent to police officers to enter dormitory rooms to search for evidence.

New Jersey v. T.L.O., 469 U.S. 325 (1985) Public school teachers and administrators do not need a warrant or probable cause before searching a student. What is needed is merely reasonable grounds for suspecting that the search will turn up evidence that the student has violated or is violating either the law or the rules of the school.

New York v. Belton, 453 U.S. 454 (1981) When the police have made a lawful custodial arrest of the occupant of a car, they may, incident to that arrest, search the car's entire passenger compartment (front and back seats) and open any containers found in the compartment.

New York v. Burger, 482 U.S. 691 (1987) The warrantless inspection of an automobile junkyard is valid because the business is "closely regulated" by the government, and there is substantial government interest involved in preventing car theft.

Pennsylvania Board of Probation and Parole v. Scott, 118 S.Ct. 2014 (1998) Evidence illegally obtained in violation of parolees' Fourth Amendment rights does not have to be excluded from a parole revocation hearing.

Richards v. Wisconsin, 520 U.S. 385 (1997) A blanket exception (issued by a judge) to the knock-and-announce rule in felony drug-dealing cases is not allowed.

Rochin v. California, 342 U.S. 165 (1952) Police restraining a suspect while a heroin capsule was removed from his stomach by a stomach pump shocks the conscience and therefore violates the suspect's right to due process.

Schneckloth v. Bustamonte, 412 U.S. 218 (1973) There is no need for an officer to prove in court that the person giving consent knew, when the consent was given, that he or she had a right to refuse consent.

See v. City of Seattle, 387 U.S. 541 (1967) Administrative entry, without consent, into the portions of commercial premises that are not open to the public may be compelled through prosecution or physical force only within the framework of a warrant procedure.

Schmerber v. California, 384 U.S. 757 (1966) The police may, without a search warrant and by force, if necessary, take a blood sample from a person arrested for drunk driving, as long as the setting and procedures are reasonable (as when the blood is drawn by a doctor in a hospital). Exigent circumstances exist because alcohol in the suspect's bloodstream might disappear in the time required to obtain a warrant.

Smith v. Maryland, 442 U.S. 735 (1979) The use of pen registers to record the numbers dialed from a telephone does not constitute search or seizure and therefore does not require prior judicial authorization.

Stoner v. California, 376 U.S. 483 (1964) A landlord cannot give valid consent to search property that he or she has rented to another person, nor can a hotel clerk give valid consent to the search of a guest's room.

United States v. Biswell, 406 U.S. 311 (1972) The warrantless inspection of a weapons dealer by a federal agent is valid, because the dealer had chosen to engage in a business that is inherently subject to heavy federal licensing regulation, and such regulation could only be enforced by the government's making unannounced and frequent visits.

United States v. Block, 188 F.2d 1019 (D.C. Cir. 1951) An employer cannot give valid consent to a search if the property is under the exclusive use and control of the employee.

United States v. Chadwick, 433 U.S. 1 (1977) A search that is remote in time and place from the arrest is not contemporaneous and is therefore invalid. In this case, the officers opened and searched a footlocker without a warrant one hour after the arrest.

United States v. D'Amico, 408 F.2d 331 (2d Cir. 1969) The clipping by an officer of a few strands of hair from a suspect's head is so minor an imposition that the suspect suffered no true humiliation or affront to his dignity, so a search warrant was not required to justify the officer's act.

United States v. Davis, 482 F.2d 893 (9th Cir. 1973) A preboarding screening of all passengers and carry-on articles, sufficient in scope to detect the presence of weapons or explosives, is reasonable to meet the administrative needs (of discovering weapons and preventing hijacking) that justify it.

United States v. Edwards, 415 U.S. 800 (1974) A clothing search of a suspect arrested and jailed late at night that was not conducted until the following morning was justified because substitute clothing was not available for the suspect's use at the time of booking.

United States v. Impink, 728 F.2d 1228 (9th Cir. 1984) In general, a lessor cannot validly consent to the search of leased premises.

United States v. Jacobsen, 466 U.S. 109 (1984) If government agents perform a search or seizure of the same material that has already been subjected to a private search or seizure, that government search will be considered to have intruded into the owner's privacy only to the extent that the government search or seizure exceeded the scope of the private search.

United States v. Kelly, 551 F.2d 760 (8th Cir. 1977) Consent of an apartment manager to the warrantless search of an apartment building's common areas, over which the landlord has joint access or control, is valid.

United States v. Leon, 468 U.S. 897 (1984) Evidence obtained by the police based on a search warrant that is later found to be without probable cause (stale information and failure to establish credibility of an informant) is admissible in court because the mistake was committed by a magistrate, not by the police.

United States v. Matlock, 415 U.S. 164 (1974)
When a woman consents to the search of a defendant's room, which she said she shared as the defendant's mistress, the search is valid.

United States v. Morales, 861 F.2d 396 (3rd Cir. 1988) The driver of a vehicle has authority to consent to the search of a vehicle, including the trunk, glove compartment, and other areas.

United States v. Owens, 848 F.2d 462 (4th Cir. 1988) The execution of a warrant for a different apartment than the one named in the warrant was valid, because there were only two apartments on the floor, one of which was vacant. Moreover, the correct apartment was not readily ascertainable, and the mistake was made in good faith.

United States v. Place, 462 U.S. 696 (1983)
There is no search within the meaning of the Fourth Amendment if the police use narcotics detection dogs to smell closed containers for drugs, as long as the police are legally on the premises. There is no need for a search warrant or for probable cause to conduct dog sniffs.

United States v. Ramirez, 62 CrL 2108 (1998)
The knock-and-announce rule does not set a higher standard for unannounced entries even if that entry involves property damage.

United States v. Robinson, 414 U.S. 218 (1973)
The police may conduct a body search of the arrestee after a full custodial arrest even if the officers do not fear for their safety or believe that they will find evidence of the crime.

United States v. Shaibu, 920 F.2d 1423 (9th Cir. 1990) There is no valid consent where a resident opens his door, steps into the hallway, listens to the officers identify themselves and explain the purpose of their visit, and then retreats wordlessly back into the apartment without closing the door. The government in this case failed to meet its heavy burden of proving consent by merely showing that the defendant left his door open.

United States v. Sullivan, 625 F.2d 9 (4th Cir. 1980) It is not a search within the protection of the Fourth Amendment for a dog to sniff bags handled by an airline. There can be no reasonable expectation of privacy when any passenger's bags may be subjected to close scrutiny for the protection of public safety.

United States v. Verdugo-Urquidez, 494 U.S. 259 (1990) Nonresident aliens may not invoke the protections of the Fourth Amendment to challenge the warrantless seizure of items from a residence located in a foreign country.

Vale v. Louisiana, 399 U.S. 30 (1970) A warrantless search may be justified if there are reasonable grounds to believe that delaying the search until the warrant is obtained would endanger the physical safety of the officer or would allow the destruction or removal of the evidence.

Warden v. Hayden, 387 U.S. 294 (1967) The police may make a warrantless search and seizure when they are in "hot pursuit" of a dangerous suspect. The scope of such a search may be as extensive as is reasonably necessary to prevent the suspect from resisting or escaping.

Welsh v. Wisconsin, 466 U.S. 740 (1984) The Fourth Amendment prohibits the police from making a warrantless nighttime entry into a suspect's house in order to arrest him or her for drunken driving if the offense is a misdemeanor for which state law does not allow any jail sentence.

Winston v. Lee, 470 U.S. 753 (1985) Surgery to remove a bullet from a suspect for use as evidence would involve such severe intrusion into the suspect's privacy and security that it would violate the Fourth Amendment; it can be allowed only if the state establishes a compelling need.

Ybarra v. Illinois, 444 U.S. 85 (1979) A search warrant for a bar and its bartender does not authorize body searches of all bar patrons.

Zurcher v. Stanford Daily, 436 U.S. 547 (1978) Searches of property belonging to persons not suspected of a crime are permissible as long as probable cause exists to believe that evidence of someone's guilt or other items subject to seizure will be found.

Case Briefs

The Leading Case on a Search Incident to an Arrest

Chimel v. California, 395 U.S. 752 (1969)

Facts: Chimel was suspected of having robbed a coin shop. Armed with an arrest warrant (but not a search warrant), police officers went to Chimel's house and were admitted by his wife. Chimel was not at home but was immediately arrested when he arrived. The police asked Chimel if they could "look around." Chimel denied the request, but the officers searched the entire house anyway and discovered some stolen coins. At the trial, the coins were introduced as evidence over Chimel's objection. Chimel was convicted of robbery.

Issue: In the course of making a lawful arrest, may officers search the immediate area where the person was arrested without a search warrant? Yes.

Supreme Court Decision: After making an arrest, the police may search the area within the person's immediate control. The purpose of such a search is to discover and remove weapons and to prevent the destruction of evidence.

Case Significance: Chimel categorically states that the police may search the area in the arrestee's "immediate control" when making a valid arrest, whether the arrest takes place with or without a warrant. That area of "immediate control" is defined by the Court as "the area from within which he might gain possession of a weapon or destructible evidence." *Chimel* therefore authoritatively settled an issue over which lower courts had given inconsistent and diverse rulings. The current rule is that the police may search without a warrant after a lawful arrest, but the extent of that search is limited to the area of the arrestee's "immediate control." The safest, and most limited, interpretation of the term "area of immediate control" is a person's wingspan, within which it might be possible to grab a weapon or destroy evidence. Some lower courts have given a more liberal interpretation to include such areas as the whole room in which the person is arrested. This interpretation appears to go beyond what the Court had in mind in *Chimel.*

Excerpts from the Decision: "When an arrest is made, it is reasonable for the arresting officer to search the person arrested in order to remove any weapons that the latter might seek to use in order to resist arrest or effect his escape. Otherwise, the officer's safety might well be endangered, and the arrest itself frustrated. In addition, it is entirely reasonable for the arresting officer to search for and seize any evidence on the arrestee's person in order to prevent its concealment or destruction. And the area into which an arrestee might reach in order to grab a weapon or evidentiary items must, of course, be governed by a like rule. . . . There is ample justification, therefore, for a search of the arrestee's person and the area within his immediate control."

The Leading Case on a Particular Description of Place to Be Searched

Maryland v. Garrison, 480 U.S. 79 (1987)

Facts: Police officers obtained a warrant to search "the premises known as 2036 Park Avenue, third-floor apartment," for drugs and drug paraphernalia that supposedly belonged to a certain McWebb. The police reasonably believed that there was only one apartment at the location, but in fact there were actually two apartments on the third floor, one belonging to McWebb and one belonging to Garrison. Before the officers became aware that they were in Garrison's apartment instead of McWebb's, they discovered contraband that provided the basis for Garrison's conviction for violating Maryland's Controlled Substance Act.

Issue: Is a search valid if conducted in the wrong apartment, pursuant to a search warrant in which the officers had a reasonable but mistaken belief that the address was correct? Yes.

Supreme Court Decision: The validity of a warrant must be judged in light of the information available to officers when the warrant is sought. Thus, a warrant that is overbroad in describing the place to be searched, based on a reasonable but mistaken belief of the officer, is not in violation of the Fourth Amendment. In this case, the search warrant was valid even though the warrant proved to be too broad to authorize the search of both apartments. Evidence obtained from the search may be used in a criminal trial.

Case Significance: One of the elements of a valid search is that the warrant must contain a "particular description of the place to be searched." This means that the warrant must remove any doubt or uncertainty about which premises are to be searched. The *Garrison* case appears to soften the demands of that requirement. Here was a case of mistaken place description, leading to a mistake in the execution of the warrant. Despite this mistake, which stemmed from a warrant that was characterized as "ambiguous in scope," the Court said that the "validity of the warrant must be judged in light of the information available to the officers at the time they obtained the warrant." The fact that later discovery found the warrant to be unnecessarily broad did not invalidate the warrant, nor did it affect the admissibility of evidence obtained. It is important to note here that the Court found the warrant to be valid on its face although its broad scope led to an error in the place of execution. There was reasonable effort on the part of the officers to ascertain and identify the place that was the target of the search; nonetheless, a mistake was made. This case should not be interpreted as validating all search warrants where there is a mistake made in the description of the place to be searched. The test as to the validity of search warrants that are "ambiguous in scope" appears to be "whether the officers' failure to realize the overbreadth of the warrant was objectively understandable and reasonable."

Excerpts from the Decision: "Plainly, if the officers had known, or even if they should have known, that there were two separate dwelling units on the third floor of 2036 Park Avenue, they would have been obligated to exclude respondent's apartment from the scope of the requested warrant. But we must judge the constitutionality of their conduct in light of the information available to them at the time they acted. Those items of evidence that emerge after the warrant is issued have no bearing on whether or not a warrant was validly issued. Just as the discovery of contraband cannot validate a warrant invalid when issued, so it is equally clear that the discovery of facts demonstrating that a valid warrant was unnecessarily broad does not retroactively invalidate the warrant. The validity of the warrant must be assessed on the basis of the information that the officers disclosed, or had a duty to discover and to disclose, to the issuing magistrate. On the basis of that information, we agree with the conclusion of all three Maryland courts that the warrant, insofar as it authorized a search that turned out to be ambiguous in scope, was valid when it was issued."

 # Notes

1. A. L. Dipietro, "Anticipatory Search Warrants," *FBI Law Enforcement Bulletin,* July 1990, p. 27.

2. Ibid., p. 28.

3. John G. Miles, Jr., David B. Richardson, and Anthony E. Scudellari, *The Law Officer's Pocket Manual* (Washington, DC: Bureau of National Affairs, 1988–89), 9:27.

4. Lloyd L. Weinreb and James D. Whaley, *The Field Guide to Law Enforcement,* 1999 ed. (New York: Foundation Press), p. 24.

5. Ibid.

6. Ibid., p. 29.

7. M. Hermann, *Search and Seizure Checklists,* 3rd ed. (New York: Clark Boardman, 1983), pp. 192–193.

8. Steven L. Emanuel and Steven Knowles, *Emanuel Law Outlines: Criminal Procedure* (Larchmont, NY: Emanuel, 1995), p. 95.

9. Steven L. Emanuel and Steven Knowles, *Emanuel Law Outlines: Criminal Procedure* (Larchmont, NY: Emanuel, 1998–99), p. 101.

10. Supra note 7, p. 166.

11. Supra note 9, p. 137.

12. Supra note 9, p. 204.

13. "Constitutional Limitations on the Use of Canines to Detect Evidence of Crime," *Fordham Law Review* 973 (1976), p. 44.

14. *Houston Chronicle,* September 22, 1996, p. A15.

15. *Houston Chronicle,* October 13, 1999, p. A2.

16. Supra note 4, p. 56.

8.

Vehicle Stops, Searches, and Inventories

What You Will Learn in This Chapter

You will discover that vehicle stops and searches are different from home or residence searches because a motor vehicle is mobile; therefore, the warrant and probable cause requirements are relaxed. A warrant to stop and search a vehicle is never needed. While probable cause is needed in vehicle searches, reasonable suspicion suffices in vehicle stops. You will become familiar with what police officers can and cannot do after a vehicle stop, and you will learn about the limits and scope of a vehicle search. You will also learn it is valid to conduct a warrantless inventory search after a vehicle has been impounded, but only when department policy is followed.

Introduction

Stops and searches of motor vehicles are an important and highly visible part of routine police patrol work. They will continue to require the attention of the courts in the coming years, as the number of motor vehicles on the road grows and vehicle gadgets become more sophisticated. The Court first addressed the issue of motor vehicles and the Fourth Amendment several decades ago in the case of Carroll v. United States, arguably the most important case involving motor vehicles. Nonetheless, questions about what the police can and cannot do in motor vehicle cases are addressed by the Court each year, and this trend will continue as the case law on motor vehicles becomes more extensive and refined. It is important that the police be familiar with the laws on motor vehicle stops and searches, because a large percentage of arrests and searches are either made in or related to motor vehicles and a lot of day-to-day police work involves motor vehicles. The law on vehicle stops and searches is best understood if discussed under three general headings: vehicle stops, vehicle searches, and vehicle inventories. The Fourth Amendment rules vary for each, so they should be discussed separately.

It is best to start this chapter with a chart that summarizes the rules for vehicle stops, searches, and inventories—the three types of vehicle searches and seizures discussed in this chapter. The rest of the chapter basically expands on this chart.

	NEED FOR A WARRANT?	NEED FOR PROBABLE CAUSE?
I. To stop a vehicle	No	No, but need reasonable or articulable suspicion of involvement in criminal activity

II. To search a vehicle	No	Yes
III. To inventory a vehicle	No	No, but must be guided by department policy

I. VEHICLE STOPS

A form of seizure occurs every time a motor vehicle is stopped, so the Fourth Amendment prohibition against unreasonable searches and seizures applies. In one case, the Court said, "The Fourth and Fourteenth Amendments are implicated in this case because stopping an automobile and detaining its occupants constitute a 'seizure' within the meaning of those Amendments, even though the purpose of the stop is limited and the resulting detention quite brief" (Delaware v. Prouse, 440 U.S. 648 [1979]). The courts have long held that motor vehicles, because of their mobility, should be governed by a different set of Fourth Amendment rules.

A. The Rules Governing Vehicle Stops

1. The General Rule: The Need for Reasonable Suspicion of Involvement in Criminal Activity

Although a vehicle stop is a form of seizure, the motorist is not fully protected by the Fourth Amendment. Because the vehicle stop is less intrusive, neither a warrant nor probable cause is required. Nonetheless, some type of justification is necessary for a valid stop; a stop by a police officer for no reason or without any justification is illegal. In one case, the Court ruled that there must be at least a reasonable suspicion to justify an investigatory stop of a motor vehicle in connection with possible involvement in criminal activity (United States v. Cortez, 449 U.S. 411 [1981]). In that case, the Court stated:

> Based upon that whole picture, the detaining officers must have a particularized and objective basis for suspecting the particular person stopped of criminal activity. . . . First, the assessment must be based upon all of the circumstances. The analysis proceeds with various objective observations, information from police reports, if such are available, and consideration of the modes or patterns of operation and certain kinds of lawbreakers. . . . The second element contained in the idea that an assessment of the whole picture must yield a particularized suspicion is the concept that the process just described must raise a suspicion that the particular individual being stopped is engaged in wrongdoing.

A lower court has also said, "The police do not have an unrestricted right to stop people, either pedestrians or drivers. The 'good faith' of the police is not enough, nor is an inarticulate hunch. They must have an articulable suspicion of wrongdoing, done or in prospect" (United States v. Montgomery, 561 F.2d 875 [1977]).[1]

These cases hold that the warrantless exception in motor vehicle stop cases does not give the police unlimited authority to stop vehicles. Some justification is necessary, but it does not have to be probable cause. Some courts say *reasonable suspicion* is needed; other courts use the term *articulable suspicion*. Whatever term a jurisdiction uses, the level of certainty necessary for the police to be able to stop a car is about the same—lower than probable cause but higher than mere suspicion.

2. Roadblocks: The Exception to the "Reasonable Suspicion" Rule

Roadblocks are the exception to the rule that vehicle stops must be justified based on suspicion of involvement in criminal activity by the individual being stopped. Roadblocks are used by police for a variety of purposes, so there is always some kind of justification for the action. The difference is that the justification is generic rather than specific to the individual being stopped. Three types of roadblocks are discussed here, each having been upheld as valid by the courts even without individualized suspicion of criminal activity. These are roadblocks to combat drunk driving, roadblocks to control the flow of illegal aliens, and roadblocks for general law enforcement purposes.

a. Roadblocks to Control Drunk Driving In a 1990 case, the Court held that **sobriety checkpoints,** a form of roadblock in which *the police stop every vehicle for the purpose of controlling drunk driving,* do not violate the Fourth Amendment protection against unreasonable searches and seizures and are therefore constitutional (Michigan Department of State Police v. Sitz, 496 U.S. 444 [1990]).

In the *Sitz* case, the Michigan State Police Department established a highway checkpoint program. Pursuant to established guidelines, checkpoints were to be set up at selected sites along state roads, with all vehicles passing through the checkpoint to be stopped and their drivers checked for signs of intoxication. If intoxication was suspected, the vehicle was to be pulled to the side of the road for further tests; all other drivers would be permitted to resume their journey. During the only operation of the checkpoint, which lasted about an hour and fifteen minutes, 126 vehicles were checked, with an average delay of twenty-five seconds. Two individuals were arrested for DWI. These guidelines and the Michigan sobriety checkpoint practice were challenged in courts as violating the Fourth Amendment. The Supreme Court rejected the challenge, saying that sobriety checkpoints are a form of seizure, but one that is reasonable, because the "measure of intrusion on motorists stopped briefly at sobriety checkpoints is slight."

The *Sitz* case is significant, because for a long time lower courts had given conflicting decisions about the constitutionality of sobriety checkpoints. Courts in twenty-one states had upheld them, while courts in twelve states had declared them unconstitutional. However, by a 6 to 3 vote, the Supreme Court has ruled that the police may establish highway checkpoints in an effort to catch drunk drivers.

It is important to note that the *Sitz* case does not allow the police to make random stops; what it does authorize are well-conceived and carefully structured sobriety checkpoints, such as that of Michigan, that leave virtually no discretion to the officers operating the checkpoint. This eliminates the danger of arbitrariness. In *Sitz*, the Court adopted the balancing test applied in an earlier case (Delaware v. Prouse, 440 U.S. 647 [1979]), which focused on three factors to determine the constitutionality of what the police do in these cases: (1) the gravity of the public concerns served by the seizure, (2) the degree to which the seizure advances the public interest, and (3) the severity of the interference with individual liberty. Although sobriety checkpoints are constitutional, they may be prohibited by departmental policy or state law.

b. Roadblocks to Control the Flow of Illegal Aliens Stops in the form of roadblocks for brief questioning, routinely conducted at permanent checkpoints, are consistent with the Fourth Amendment, so it is not necessary to obtain a warrant before setting up a checkpoint (United States v. Martinez-Fuerte, 428 U.S. 543 [1976]). This case involved a "fixed checkpoint" set up not at the border, but in the interior, where all cars were stopped. After the stop, certain motorists were referred to a "secondary inspection area" where they could be questioned and their cars searched if it seemed justified. The Court permitted such "suspicionless" stops in the interest of controlling the flow of illegal aliens.

c. Stops to Check a Driver's License and Vehicle Registration Establishing a roadblock to check drivers' licenses and car registrations is legitimate. In the process, if the officers see evidence of other crimes, they have the right to take reasonable investigative steps; they are not required to close their eyes (United States v. Prichard, 645 F.2d 854 [1981]). However, police officers may not stop a single vehicle for the sole purpose of checking the driver's license and vehicle registration. To do that, the officers must reasonably believe that the motorist has violated a traffic law. Mere suspicion is not enough (Delaware v. Prouse, 440 U.S. 648 [1979]).

B. What an Officer May Do after a Vehicle Stop

What an officer may or may not do after stopping a vehicle has been addressed in a number of cases. Stopping the vehicle is not an end in itself; it is only a means to determine whether a criminal activity has occurred or is about to occur. What follows after a stop is important for both officer protection and the admissibility of any seized evidence. There are many things an officer may do after a valid stop; the most significant of these, based on decided cases, are discussed here.

1. Order the Driver to Get Out of the Vehicle

Once a vehicle is lawfully stopped for a traffic violation, the officer may order the driver to get out, even without suspecting criminal activity. If the officer then reasonably believes that the driver may be armed and dangerous, he or she may conduct a limited protective frisk for a weapon that might endanger his or her personal safety (Pennsylvania v. Mimms, 434 U.S. 106 [1977]). For example, suppose X is stopped by the police for running a red light. X may be asked to get out of the car. If, after X complies, the officer reasonably believes that X may be armed and dangerous, then X may be frisked. If during the frisk an illegal weapon is found, then X may be arrested. Conversely, if the officer does not believe that the driver may be armed and dangerous, all the officer can do is ask him or her to get out of the car. If there is no belief that the driver is armed and dangerous, a subsequent frisk is illegal even if the initial traffic stop was legal.

HIGHLIGHT

Asking the Driver to Get Out of the Car

"We think this additional intrusion [referring to the officer's order for the driver to get out of the car] can only be described as de minimis. The driver is being asked to expose to view very little more of his person than is already exposed. The police have already lawfully decided that the driver shall be briefly detained; the only question is whether he shall spend that period sitting in the driver's seat of his car or standing alongside of it. Not only is the insistence of the police on the latter choice not a 'serious intrusion upon the sanctity of the person,' but it hardly rises to the level of 'petty indignity.' . . . What is at most a mere inconvenience cannot prevail when balanced against legitimate concerns for the officer's safety."

Pennsylvania v. Mimms, 434 U.S. 106 (1977).

2. Order Passengers to Get Out of the Vehicle

The Court has long held that the driver of a car may automatically be required to get out of a car after a valid stop—whether the officer is concerned about personal safety or not. What was uncertain was whether that rule extended to vehicle passengers. But in a recent case, the Court ruled that police officers may order passengers to get out of a motor vehicle during traffic stops (Maryland v. Wilson, 60 CrL 2077 [1997]). In *Wilson*, a state trooper stopped a motor vehicle clocked at 65 miles per hour where the posted limit was 55 miles per hour. During the pursuit, the trooper noticed three occupants in the car. As the trooper approached what turned out to be a rented car, the driver got out and met him halfway. He produced a valid driver's license but was trembling and appeared extremely nervous. The trooper also noticed that one of the passengers, Wilson, was sweating and appeared extremely nervous. The trooper ordered Wilson out of the car. As Wilson got out, crack cocaine fell to the ground. Arrested and charged with possession of cocaine, Wilson argued during his trial that ordering him out of the car constituted an unreasonable seizure. The trial court and the state court of appeals agreed, but the Supreme Court reversed the decision, holding that the "danger to an officer from a traffic stop is likely to be greater when there are passengers in addition to the driver in the stopped car." It added that the government's "legitimate and weighty interest in protecting officers prevail against the minimal infringement on the liberties of both the car driver and the passengers." This decision provides a bright-line rule saying that an officer making a traffic stop may also order passengers to get out of the car pending completion of the stop.

3. Ask the Driver to Produce a Driver's License and Other Documents Required by State Law

An officer has the authority, after a valid stop, to ask the driver to show a driver's license and other documents that state laws require. A number of states require that the driver produce the vehicle registration and proof of insurance in addition to a driver's license. The justification for this authorization is that operating a motor vehicle on public highways is a privilege rather than a right. Practically all states consider the refusal to produce the required documents a criminal offense, and the driver can be punished accordingly.[2]

4. Ask Questions of the Driver and Passengers

Once a valid stop has been made, the officer may ask questions of the passengers without giving the Miranda warnings. The Court has said that the roadside questioning of a motorist pursuant to a routine traffic stop (provided it is not an arrest) does not constitute custodial interrogation and therefore does not require the Miranda warnings (Berkemer v. McCarty, 468 U.S. 420 [1984]). But while the officer may ask questions, the driver and passengers have a constitutional right not to respond. Such a refusal to respond, however, may be taken into consideration by the officer in determining whether there is probable cause to arrest or search.[3]

5. Search Passengers' Belongings

Another important issue concerning what an officer can do after a vehicle stop was recently resolved. In 1999, the Court ruled that police officers who have probable cause to search a car may inspect passengers' belongings found in the car that are capable of concealing the object of the search (Wyoming v. Houghton, No. 98-184 [1999]). In that case, a Wyoming Highway Patrol officer stopped a motor vehicle in which Houghton was riding. While questioning the driver for a traffic violation, the officer noticed a hypodermic needle in the driver's shirt pocket. When the driver admitted using the needle to inject drugs, the passengers were ordered out of the car. The officer then searched the passenger compartment of the vehicle. On the back seat, he found a purse that Houghton claimed was hers. After methamphetamines and drug paraphernalia were found in the purse, Houghton was arrested. She appealed her felony conviction for possession of drugs, claiming that the search of a passenger's personal belongings inside an automobile is a violation of Fourth Amendment rights. The Court disagreed, saying that police officers who have probable cause to search a car may also inspect the belongings of passengers found in the car that are capable of concealing the object of the search. The Court cited two justifications for the search: (1) the passenger's reduced expectation of privacy and (2) "the governmental interest in effective law enforcement [which] would be appreciably impaired without the ability to search the passenger's belongings, since an automobile's ready mobility creates the risk that evidence or contraband will be permanently lost while a warrant is obtained." But while passengers' belongings may now be searched, officers may not conduct body searches of passengers (United States v. Di Re, 332 U.S. 581 [1948]). The only time a body search is allowed is if the passenger has been arrested.

6. Require Drunk Driving Suspects to Take a Breathalyzer Test

All fifty states require drivers suspected of drunk driving to take a Breathalyzer test. Refusal to take the test, or test failure because the alcohol level is beyond that allowed by law, leads to suspension of one's driver's license. An interesting issue is whether a driver who fails a Breathalyzer test may also be criminally charged with drunk driving. Some argue that this constitutes two prosecutions for the same offense; others maintain that there is no double jeopardy because license suspensions are administrative, not criminal, proceedings. Lower courts are divided. Trial courts in eighteen states have ruled that these two proceedings arising from the same act constitute double jeopardy;

the highest courts of five states (New Mexico, Maine, Hawaii, Vermont, and Louisiana) have held otherwise. But the U.S. Supreme Court has not ruled on the issue, so uncertainty remains.[4]

7. Locate and Examine the Vehicle Identification Number

Federal rules require that vehicles sold in the United States have a vehicle identification number (VIN). The VIN must be displayed on the dashboard of recently manufactured cars, so that it can be read from outside the car through the windshield.[5] The Court has decided that motorists have no reasonable expectation of privacy with respect to the VIN located on the vehicle's dashboard, even if objects on the dashboard prevent the VIN from being observed from outside the car (New York v. Class, 475 U.S. 106 [1986]).

8. Search a Vehicle If Probable Cause Develops

As long as the vehicle stop is based on reasonable suspicion, what officers observe may quickly evolve into probable cause to believe that the car contains the fruits and instrumentalities of crime or contraband, thereby establishing a justification for a full warrantless search of the vehicle. In Colorado v. Bannister, 449 U.S. 1 (1980), the police stopped Bannister's automobile to issue him a speeding ticket. While writing out the citation, the officer made two observations: (1) Bannister and his companion fit a broadcast description of persons involved in the theft of auto parts, and (2) there were wrenches and other materials in the back seat that could have been used for that crime. The Court held that what the officer observed established probable cause to justify a warrantless search, because if a magistrate had been present while Bannister's car was stopped, the police could have obtained a warrant on the information the officer possessed. The warrantless search was therefore proper under the automobile exception.

9. Search a Vehicle Even without Probable Cause If Consent Is Given

Even if there is no probable cause or reasonable suspicion, the officer may search the car if valid consent is given. The Court has said that an officer, after validly stopping a car, may ask the person in control of the vehicle for permission to search (Schneckloth v. Bustamonte, 412 U.S. 218 [1973]). Such consent must be intelligent and voluntary, although it does not have to be in writing. The burden is on the officer to prove, if challenged, that the consent was, in fact, valid. (See Form 8.1.)

10. Search the Passenger Compartment for Weapons If There Is Reasonable Suspicion of a Threat to Officer Safety

If the officer has reasonable suspicion that the motorist who has been stopped is dangerous and may be able to gain control of a weapon in the car, the officer may conduct a brief search of the passenger compartment even if the motorist is no longer inside the car (Michigan v. Long, 463 U.S. 1032 [1983]). This search should be limited to areas in the passenger compartment where a weapon might be found or hidden. The authorization for a brief search for a weapon is an extension of stop and frisk rather than of an arrest. In contrast, a routine stop to issue a traffic ticket (not a stop and frisk situation) does not authorize the police to search the vehicle's passenger compartment.[6]

DATE: _____

I, _____ , having been informed of my constitutional right not to have a search made of the automobile hereinafter mentioned without a search warrant and of my right to refuse such a search, hereby authorize _____ and _____ , police officers of the Houston Police Department, to conduct a complete search of my automobile, which is a _____ _____ located at _____ .

These officers are authorized by me to take from my automobile any letters, papers, materials, or any other property which they may desire. This permission is being given by me to the above named officers voluntarily without threats or promises of any kind and is given with my full and free consent.

SIGNED: _____

WITNESSES:

_____

_____

Form 8.1 *Voluntary Consent for Search and Seizure of Automobile*

11. Seize Items in Plain View

After a valid stop, the officer may seize illegal items *in plain view.* The seizure then establishes probable cause, which justifies an arrest. For example, suppose officers lawfully stop a car to issue the driver a citation for running a red light. While writing out the citation, the officers see contraband in the passenger compartment. The officers may then seize the contraband and place the driver under arrest. The driver and the vehicle may then be searched.

12. Arrest If Probable Cause Develops

A stop may immediately turn into an arrest *if probable cause is established.* For example, suppose a driver is stopped by an officer for speeding and is ordered to get out of the car. The officer senses danger to himself, frisks the driver, and finds an illegal weapon. The officer may then arrest the driver and search the whole car. He may also conduct a full body search of the arrested driver.

C. Traffic Stops as a Pretext for Vehicle Searches

The Court has held that the temporary detention of a motorist based on probable cause to believe that the motorist has violated traffic laws is valid even if a reasonable officer would not have stopped the motorist if the officer did not have some other law enforcement objective—in this case determining whether the occupants of the vehicle had drugs (Whren v. United States, 59 CrL 2121 [1996]). In *Whren,* plainclothes vice officers were patrolling a high-drug area in an unmarked car when they saw a vehicle with youthful occupants waiting at an intersection. The vehicle remained at the intersection for what appeared to be an unusually long time. The officers made a U-turn and headed toward the vehicle, whereupon it suddenly made a right turn without signaling and took off at an unreasonable speed. The officers overtook the vehicle when it stopped at a red light. One of the officers approached the vehicle and observed two large plastic bags of what appeared to be crack cocaine in Whren's hands. At trial, the defendant sought to suppress the evidence, saying that, based on department policy, the plainclothes officers would not normally have dealt with this type of civil traffic violation; therefore, it was merely a **pretextual stop,** or *a stop used as a pretext to search the vehicle*—in this case to determine if the occupants had drugs.

A majority of the Court ruled that the temporary detention of the vehicle based on probable cause to believe that traffic laws had been broken did not violate the Fourth Amendment even if the officers would not have stopped the motorist if they had not had some additional law enforcement objective. The Court in effect ruled that whether ordinarily the police officers "would have" (subjective test) made the stop is not the test for validity; instead, the test is whether the officers "could have" made the stop. The fact that they "could have" made a valid stop because there was a traffic violation made the stop valid even if the actual purpose of the stop was to look for drugs. In sum, the real purpose of the stop of a motor vehicle does not make the subsequent search invalid if there was, in fact, a valid reason for the stop.

An added factor made the traffic stop in *Whren* highly questionable. Police regulations in that jurisdiction permitted plainclothes officers (who made the arrest in this case) in unmarked cars to stop vehicles and enforce traffic laws "only in the case of a violation that is so grave as to pose an immediate threat to the safety of others." Such was not the case, and so the plainclothes officers did not follow department policy. This did not make any difference to the Court, however. The Court noted, "We cannot accept that the search and seizure protections of the Fourth Amendment are so variable . . . and can be made to turn upon such trivialities." The Court concluded that the fact that local law enforcement practices did not allow such stops was not significant because, if Fourth Amendment issues were decided based on what department policy allows, it would make the Fourth Amendment protections vary from place to place.

Note, however, that although pretextual stops have now been declared constitutional by the Court, they may be invalidated by state courts based on state law or the state constitution. For example, in a case decided three years after *Whren,* the Supreme Court of the state of Washington held that there is no pretextual stop exception to the warrant requirement under the state's constitution. Therefore, pretextual stops in the state of Washington are not valid (State v. Ladson, Washington, No. 65801-3 [1999]).

D. Vehicle Stops Based on Racial Profiles

A highly controversial issue in law enforcement is the practice in some agencies of stopping motorists, particularly in so-called drug-corridor highways and streets, based on **racial profile.** In many places and groups, the perception is that law enforcement departments disproportionately stop drivers belonging to minority groups, usually blacks and Hispanics. Media reports of this practice have increased dramatically in the last few years. As one newspaper puts it: "The practice has become so common that black Americans have coined a name for it: Driving while black (DWB)." The same source states that, "by some estimates, about 72 percent of people pulled over in traffic stops are black, even though they represent only 15 percent of the population, according to the NAACP."[7]

Although the Court has not directly addressed this issue, it is safe to say, based on previous Court decisions involving race, that stopping a motorist based on race alone is clearly unconstitutional as a violation of the Equal Protection Clause. The more difficult question, however, is whether race can legally be taken into consideration at all when looking at the "totality of circumstances," a phrase the Court often uses in reasonable suspicion or probable cause cases. In United States v. Sokolow (490 U.S. 1 [1989]), the Court said that stops cannot be based on drug courier profile alone; what is needed is that the facts, taken in totality, amount to reasonable suspicion that can justify a stop. Although *Sokolow* did not involve race, it would apply even more strongly if the stop is made solely on the basis of race. Court decisions allowing certain types of discrimination have always prohibited discrimination based on race because race is a highly protected category both under the Constitution and in various federal and state laws.

In the *Whren* case, discussed previously, the Court said that, although pretextual vehicular stops are constitutional, racially motivated law enforcement could be challenged under the Equal Protection Clause of the Fourteenth Amendment, but not under the Due Process Clause. How this issue will be resolved if it reaches the Court, particularly in the context of the totality of circumstances, remains unanswered. A 1999 case related to this issue is a reported decision of a panel (in a 2-to-1 vote) in the U.S. Court of Appeals for the Ninth Circuit stating that "border patrol agents can consider ethnicity when making traffic stops."[8] That case involved "two Hispanic men who allegedly turned their cars around to avoid a checkpoint" fifty miles inside the United States and was a border patrol rather than a "DWB" case. Immigration and territorial border cases have traditionally been treated less strictly by the courts—with more authority given to government officers who deal with border patrol and immigration cases.

Various laws have been passed and others are currently pending in the U.S. Congress, state legislatures, and local legislative agencies seeking authorization to gather data that would prove racial profiling in law enforcement.[9] Lawsuits have been filed seeking damage awards for violations of constitutional rights and a discontinuance of the practice. Knowledge abounds among certain racial groups that the practice exists; the question is how pervasive the practice is and how an offended person can prove it in court in the absence of systemic data. One report states that racial minorities, "particularly African Americans, long have complained that they are routinely detained, frisked and even handcuffed by police for no apparent cause." The same report notes, however, that "police chiefs across the country have countered that racial profiling is essentially a myth, and they bridle at the suggestion that cops are motivated by racism."[10]

Given the controversy the issue has generated, legal challenges to racial profiling will doubtless escalate in criminal prosecutions and legal liability cases. It will not be surprising if the Court chooses to decide the issue squarely within the next few years or if more legislatures and police agencies flatly prohibit the practice as legally and morally wrong. For now, however, and from a purely legal perspective, stops based on racial profile cry out for a more definitive ruling from the courts.

E. Consensual Searches and the Freedom to Leave

In a case decided six months after *Whren,* the Court held that a police officer need not inform the defendant first that he or she is free to go in order for a consent to search to be valid (Ohio v. Robinette, 60 CrL 2002 [1996]). In *Robinette,* an Ohio deputy sheriff stopped the defendant for speeding, gave him a verbal warning, returned his driver's license, and then asked whether he was carrying contraband, drugs, or weapons in his car. The defendant replied "no" but consented to a search of the car. The search revealed a small amount of marijuana and a controlled substance. At trial, Robinette argued that the consent given was invalid because, even in cases of lawful detention, the suspect must first be informed by the officer that he or she is "legally free to go" before consent to search can validly be given. The Court disagreed, saying that "the Fourth Amendment does not require that a lawfully seized defendant be advised that he is 'free to go' before his consent to search will be recognized as voluntary." Again, however, the evidence obtained may not be admissible if state law requires that such information be given before consent to search is sought.

II. VEHICLE SEARCHES

A valid stop does not automatically give officers the authority to search the vehicle. As in stop and frisk, a vehicle stop is different from a vehicle search; both are governed by different rules. As discussed previously, a stop does not need a warrant, but there must be reasonable suspicion that the vehicle is involved in some criminal activity for the stop to be valid. The rule for searches is different, as discussed here.

A. Vehicle Searches and Warrants: Carroll v. United States

The rule is that *the search of an automobile does not need a warrant.* A vehicle search is therefore an exception to the warrant requirement of the Fourth Amendment. However,

AT A GLANCE

The Law on Vehicle Stops

With vehicle stops, there is no need for a warrant or probable cause, but there must be reasonable suspicion of involvement in criminal activity. Roadblocks are an exception to the "reasonable suspicion" requirement. After an officer stops a vehicle, he or she may do the following:

1. Order the driver to get out of the vehicle.
2. Order passengers to get out of the vehicle.
3. Ask the driver to produce a driver's license and other documents required by state law.
4. Ask questions of the driver and passengers.
5. Search passengers' belongings.
6. Require drunk driving suspects to take a Breathalyzer test.
7. Locate and examine the vehicle identification number.
8. Search the vehicle if probable cause develops.
9. Search the vehicle even without probable cause if consent is given.
10. Search the passenger compartment for weapons if there is reasonable suspicion of a threat to officer safety.
11. Seize items in plain view.
12. Arrest if probable cause develops.

In addition, traffic stops used as a pretext for motor vehicle search are valid. Also, vehicle stops based on racial profile are unconstitutional, although some issues are unresolved. Finally, a person stopped need not be informed first that he or she is free to leave for the consent search to be valid.

---

there are two requirements for warrantless vehicle searches: (1) There must be probable cause, and (2) the vehicle must be mobile—that is, capable of being driven away at any time. A vehicle that is up on blocks, or is missing an essential part, or is being repaired and cannot be driven away, is not mobile.[11] A warrant is needed if these immobilized vehicles are to be searched.

The seminal case on automobile stops and searches is Carroll v. United States, 267 U.S. 132 (1925). In that case, decided decades ago, Carroll and a certain Kiro were indicted and convicted for transporting "intoxicating spirituous liquor" (sixty-eight quarts of bonded whiskey and gin, in violation of the National Prohibition Act). They appealed their conviction, saying that it was wrong for the trial court to admit two of the sixty-eight bottles because they were seized by law enforcement officers without a warrant. The officers countered that they had probable cause to believe that the automobile contained bootleg liquor. They said that if they had taken the time to obtain a warrant, the car, which they had stopped on a highway, would have disappeared. The Court agreed that the warrantless search of the automobile was reasonable, because it would

The Need for a Clear-Cut Rule in Closed Container Cases

"We conclude that it is better to adopt one clear-cut rule to govern automobile searches and eliminate the warrant requirement for closed containers set forth in *Sanders*.

"We therefore interpret *Carroll* as providing one rule to govern all automobile searches. The police may search an automobile and the containers within it where

they have probable cause to believe contraband or evidence is contained."

California v. Acevedo, 111 S.Ct. 1982 (1991).

have been gone if the officers had tried to obtain a warrant. After a discussion of various laws, the Court said:

> We have made a somewhat extended reference to these statutes to show that the guaranty of freedom from unreasonable searches and seizures by the Fourth Amendment has been construed, practically since the beginning of the government, as recognizing a necessary difference between a search of a store, dwelling house, or other structure in respect of which a proper official warrant readily may be obtained and a search of a ship, motor boat, wagon, or automobile for contraband goods, *where it is not practicable to secure a warrant, because the vehicle can be quickly moved out of the locality or jurisdiction in which the warrant must be sought* [emphasis added].

Although in *Carroll* the Court ruled that there is no need for a warrant to search vehicles "where it is not practicable to secure a warrant," subsequent court decisions have held that warrantless vehicle searches are constitutional even if there is time to obtain one. (Read the Carroll v. United States case brief at the end of this chapter.)

The "automobile exception" to the warrant requirement is justified by the following considerations (Robbins v. California, 453 U.S. 420 [1981]):

- The mobility of motor vehicles often "makes obtaining a judicial warrant impractical."[12]
- A diminished expectation of privacy surrounds the automobile.
- A car is used for transportation, not as a residence or a repository of personal effects.
- The car's occupants and contents travel in plain view.
- Automobiles are necessarily highly regulated by the government.

Note that, although *Carroll* is acknowledged as the "mother" of all motor vehicle cases, it is primarily a vehicle *search* case, not a vehicle *stop* case.

B. Warrantless Vehicle Searches

As stated previously, warrantless searches of automobiles have been upheld as reasonable and therefore valid. However, the warrantless search *must be based on probable cause that seizable items are contained in the vehicle.* The absence of probable cause makes the search invalid; reasonable suspicion (such as what is required in stops) is not enough. Probable cause should focus on whether the item to be searched for is subject to seizure and whether it may be found in the place where the search is being conducted. As in all other types of searches, reasonableness governs the scope of the search; a fishing expedition for evidence is not allowed.

C. Searches Incident to the Issuance of a Traffic Citation

In a 1998 case, the Court held that a state law authorizing a search incident to the issuance of a traffic citation violates the Fourth Amendment unless there is consent or probable cause (Knowles v. Iowa, No. 97-7597 [1998]). In that case, Knowles was stopped for speeding and issued a citation. The officer then conducted a full search of Knowles's car, where he found marijuana and drug paraphernalia. The state of Iowa had a law providing that the issuance of a citation instead of an arrest "does not affect the officer's authority to conduct an otherwise lawful search." This was interpreted by the Iowa Supreme Court to mean that officers could "conduct a full-blown search of an automobile and driver in those cases where police elect not to make a custodial arrest and instead issue a citation—that is, a search incident to citation." Convicted of possession of drug paraphernalia, Knowles appealed, claiming that the search was unconstitutional. The Court agreed, saying that such searches, even if authorized by state law, violate the Fourth Amendment. They can only be done if there is valid consent or probable cause, neither of which was present in this case. The mere issuance of a citation does not justify a full-blown search. It must be stressed, however, that this decision does not include items in plain view, because such items are not protected by the Fourth Amendment. For example, suppose Officer X stops a pickup truck and issues a citation. Officer X cannot automatically conduct a full-blown search of the car, as she could if there was probable cause to arrest the driver or to search the car. But nothing prevents Officer X from looking in the car to see if there are seizable items. If there are, these can validly be seized under the plain view doctrine.

D. Searches of Passengers' Belongings

In a 1999 case, the Court held that police officers with probable cause to search a car may inspect any passengers' belongings that are capable of concealing the object of the search (Wyoming v. Houghton, No. 98-184 [1999]). In that case, officers in Wyoming stopped an automobile in which Houghton was a passenger. While questioning the driver, an officer noticed a hypodermic needle in the driver's shirt pocket. When the driver admitted to using the needle to inject drugs, the passengers were ordered out of the car. With the driver's permission, the officers then searched the passenger compartment of the car. On the back seat, they found a purse which Houghton claimed was hers. When methamphetamines and drug paraphernalia were found in the purse,

Houghton was arrested. Convicted of felony possession of drugs, Houghton appealed, claiming that the search of her belongings was invalid because she was merely a passenger. The Court rejected her argument, saying that police officers with probable cause to search a car are authorized to inspect the belongings of passengers if those belongings are capable of concealing the object of the search.

E.   Searches of the Passenger Compartment: New York v. Belton

Once a driver has been arrested, the police may conduct a warrantless search of the passenger compartment of the car. This means they may examine the contents of any container found within the passenger compartment, as long as it may reasonably be thought to contain something that might pose a danger to officers or to hold evidence related to the offense for which the suspect has been arrested.

In New York v. Belton (453 U.S. 454 [1981]), a New York state officer noticed an automobile traveling at an excessive rate of speed. The officer gave chase and ordered the car to pull over to the side of the road. The officer asked to see the driver's license and in the process smelled burnt marijuana and saw on the floor of the car an envelope marked "Supergold." He placed the four occupants under arrest, picked up the envelope, and found marijuana. He then searched the passenger compartment and, on the back seat, found a black leather jacket belonging to Belton; in one of the pockets of the jacket, he discovered cocaine. During the trial, Belton moved to suppress the cocaine, claiming it was not within the area of his immediate control, so its seizure was illegal. The Supreme Court rejected this contention, saying that the police may conduct a warrantless search of the passenger compartment of a car incident to a lawful arrest.

Belton is significant because it defines the extent of allowable search inside an automobile after a lawful arrest. Prior to *Belton,* there was confusion as to whether the police could search parts of the automobile outside the driver's "wingspan." The Court expanded the area of allowable search to the whole compartment, including the back seat; it also authorized the opening of containers found in the passenger compartment that might contain the object sought. However, *Belton* did not authorize the search of the trunk or the hood of the car.

F.   Searches of Trunks and Closed Packages Found in Trunks

If the police legitimately stop a car and have probable cause to believe that it contains contraband, they may conduct a warrantless search of the car. This search can be as thorough as a search authorized by a warrant issued by a magistrate. Therefore, every part of the vehicle in which the contraband might be stored may be inspected, including the trunk and all receptacles and packages (United States v. Ross, 456 U.S. 790 [1982]). (Read the United States v. Ross case brief at the end of this chapter.)

The Scope of Warrantless Car Searches

"We hold that the scope of the warrantless search authorized by that [automobile] exception is no broader and no narrower than a magistrate could legitimately authorize by warrant. If probable cause justifies the search of a lawfully stopped vehicle, it justifies the search of every part of the vehicle and its contents that may conceal the object of the search." United States v. Ross, 456 U.S. 798 (1982).

In the *Ross* case, after effecting a valid stop and arrest for a narcotics sale, one of the officers opened the car's trunk and found a closed brown paper bag. Inside the bag were glassine bags containing white powder, which was later determined to be heroin. The officer then drove the car to police headquarters, where another warrantless search of the trunk revealed a zippered leather pouch containing cash. During trial, the suspect argued that the police officers should not have opened either the paper bag or the leather pouch found in the trunk without first obtaining a warrant. The Supreme Court disagreed and allowed the evidence to be admitted.

The *Ross* case is important because it further defines the scope of police authority in searches of vehicles. In *Belton,* the Court specifically refused to address the issue of whether the police may open the trunk of a car in connection with a warrantless search incident to a valid arrest. Although based on slightly different facts, as it involved a warrantless search based on probable cause, *Ross* addressed that issue and authorized such action. But it went further, holding that any packages or luggage found in the trunk that could reasonably be thought to contain the items for which the officers have probable cause to search may also be opened without a warrant. *Ross* has therefore greatly expanded the scope of allowable warrantless car searches, focusing the search on the whole automobile as the possible source of evidence. Opening the brown paper bag and the pouch were legitimate by extension of police authority to conduct a warrantless search of the car.

G. Searches of Locked Trunks or Glove Compartments

Whether the police may open a *locked* (as opposed to a closed) glove compartment or trunk was not addressed by the Court in New York v. Belton, 453 U.S. 454 (1981), or in any other case involving a warrantless arrest situation. In a footnote to *Belton,* the Court stated:

> "Container" here denotes any object capable of holding another object. It thus includes closed or open glove compartments, consoles, or other receptacles located anywhere within the passenger compartment, as well as luggage, boxes, bags, clothing, and the like. Our holding encompasses only the interior of the passenger compartment of an automobile and does not encompass the trunk.

At least one state supreme court has held, however, that consent to search a car does not authorize police officers to pry open a locked briefcase found in the car's trunk (State v. Wells, 539 So.2d 464 [Sup. Ct. Fla. 1989]). In general, consent to search does not mean consent to open a locked container unless the key is voluntarily given to the police or the police lawfully obtain possession of the key. The search will most likely be valid, however, if the trunk is opened by pressing a release button inside the car. What is highly questionable is the forcible opening of locked glove compartments or car trunks. Such intrusions, if necessary, are best done with a warrant.

H.   Contemporaneousness

The cases discussed previously involved car searches conducted *contemporaneously,* meaning at the time of or immediately after the arrest. Sometimes, however, the officer may not be able to conduct a search contemporaneously. In these cases, the rule is that, if the police have probable cause to stop and search an automobile on the highway, they may take the automobile to the police station and search it there without warrant. The ruling in the *Ross* case was later used to justify the warrantless search of a container even though there was a significant delay between the time the police stopped the vehicle and the time they performed the search of the container. In a 1985 case, customs officers stopped two trucks suspected of carrying marijuana. Officers removed several sealed packages believed to contain marijuana and placed them in a government warehouse. Three days later, officers opened them without a warrant and found marijuana. The Court said that neither *Ross* nor any other case establishes a requirement that a vehicle search occur immediately as part of the vehicle inspection or soon thereafter; a three-day delay before making the search is permissible (United States v. Johns, 469 U.S. 478 [1985]). The search still must be done within a reasonable time, but the burden of proving unreasonableness is on the defendant, not the police.

I.   Warrantless Searches When There Is Time to Obtain a Warrant

Closely related to the issue of contemporaneous searches is whether the police may conduct a warrantless search even if there is time to obtain a warrant. The answer is yes. This is different from a contemporaneous search (where a warrant could not have been obtained) in that this type of search assumes that the police could have obtained a warrant because they had time to do so, but did not. For example, suppose the police, having probable cause, stopped W's car on the highway and arrested her for robbery. There was probable cause to search the car, but the police instead towed the car to the police station and searched it there. During her trial, W objected to the introduction of seized evidence, saying that the search was illegal because the police had had time to obtain a warrant. The police already had the car at the police station, so no exigent circumstances existed. The Court said that the warrantless search was proper, because the *police had probable cause to search when the vehicle was first stopped on the highway,* and that probable cause justified a later search without a warrant (Chambers v. Maroney, 399 U.S. 42 [1970]).

A subsequent case reiterated this principle; that is, a vehicle may be searched under the automobile exception to the Fourth Amendment even if it has been immobilized and released to the custody of the police (Florida v. Meyers, 466 U.S. 380 [1984]). And in a 1999 case, the Court reiterated the rule that, if the police have probable cause to search a car, they do not need a warrant even if there was ample opportunity to obtain one (Maryland v. Dyson, 65 CrL 2070 [1999]).

J. The Extent of Car Searches and the Objective Reasonableness Rule

The Court has decided that valid consent justifies a warrantless search of a container in a car if it is objectively reasonable for the police to believe that the scope of the suspect's consent permitted them to open that container (Florida v. Jimeno, 111 S.Ct. 1801 [1991]). In this case, a Dade County police officer overheard Jimeno arranging what appeared to be a drug transaction over a public telephone. The officer followed Jimeno's car, observed him make an illegal right turn at a red light, and stopped him to issue a traffic citation. After informing Jimeno why he had been stopped, the officer told Jimeno he had reason to believe Jimeno was carrying narcotics in his car and asked permission to search. The officer explained that Jimeno did not have to grant permission, but Jimeno said he had nothing to hide and gave consent to the search, whereupon the officer found a kilogram of cocaine in a brown paper bag on the floor of the passenger compartment. Jimeno appealed his conviction, saying that his consent to search the vehicle did not extend to closed containers found inside the vehicle. The Court disagreed, stating that a search is valid if it is objectively reasonable for the police to believe that the scope of the suspect's consent permits them to open a container. This case differs from *Ross,* in which the police had probable cause to search the car. Here, there was no probable cause, but there was consent to search. This ruling defines what officers can do in car searches where there may not be probable cause but where consent to search is given.

K. Warrantless Searches of Containers

The Court has held that the police may search a *container* located in a car without a search warrant even though they lack probable cause to search the *car* as a whole and have probable cause to believe only that the container itself contains contraband or evidence (California v. Acevedo, 111 S.Ct. 1982 [1991]). In this case, the police in Santa Ana, California, observed Acevedo leaving an apartment, known to contain marijuana, with a brown paper bag the size of marijuana packages the police had seen earlier. The police had probable cause to search the brown paper bag, because a federal drug agent in Hawaii had phoned earlier, saying that the bag contained marijuana. Acevedo placed the bag in his car's trunk and then drove away. The police stopped the car, opened the trunk and the bag, and found marijuana. Acevedo pleaded guilty to possession of marijuana for sale but later appealed his conviction, saying that the marijuana should have been suppressed as evidence. He claimed that, even if the police had probable cause to believe the container itself contained contraband, they did not have probable cause to search the car. The Supreme Court agreed to review the case to "reexamine the law applicable to a closed container in an automobile, a subject that has troubled courts and law enforcement officers since it was first considered in *Chadwick*."

The Court ultimately disagreed with the defendant, saying that probable cause to believe that a container in a car holds contraband or seizable evidence justifies a warrantless search of that container even in the absence of probable cause to search the car. Said the Court, "We therefore interpret *Carroll* as providing one rule to govern all automobile searches. The police may search an automobile and the containers within it where they have probable cause to believe contraband or evidence is contained."

Acevedo is significant because it reverses two earlier Court rulings on essentially the same issue. In a 1977 case, the Court held that the police could seize movable luggage or other closed containers from a car but could not open them without a warrant, because a person has a heightened privacy expectation for such containers even if they are in a car (United States v. Chadwick, 433 U.S. 1 [1977]). That case involved the seizure by government agents in Boston of a 200-pound padlocked footlocker that contained marijuana. Upon arrival by train from San Diego, the footlocker was placed in the trunk of Chadwick's car, whereupon it was seized by the agents and opened without a warrant. The Court declared the warrantless search of the footlocker unjustified. Two years later, the Court ruled unconstitutional the warrantless search of a suitcase located in a vehicle when there was probable cause to search only the suitcase but not the vehicle (Arkansas v. Sanders, 442 U.S. 753 [1979]). In this case, the police had probable cause to believe that the suitcase contained marijuana. The police watched as the suspect placed the suitcase in the trunk of a taxi, which was then driven away. The police pursued the taxi for several blocks and then stopped it. They found the suitcase in the trunk, searched it, and found marijuana. Again, however, the Court refused to extend the warrantless search doctrine enunciated in *Carroll* to searches of personal luggage if the only justification for the search was that the luggage was located in an automobile that was lawfully stopped by the police.

The Court in *Acevedo* rejected *Chadwick* and *Sanders* and reiterated instead its ruling in the *Carroll* and *Ross* cases. In *Carroll*, the Court held that a warrantless search of an automobile based on probable cause to believe that the vehicle contained evidence of crime, and in light of the vehicle's likely disappearance, was valid. In *Ross*, the Court allowed the warrantless search of a container found in a car where there was probable cause to search the car and as long as the opening of the container was reasonable—given the object of the search. *Acevedo* extends the *Carroll-Ross* line of cases in that it allows the warrantless search of a container as long as there is probable cause to believe that the container holds contraband, even if there is no probable cause to search the car itself. In essence, *Acevedo* (probable cause for the *container* but not for the car) is the opposite of *Ross* (probable cause for the *car* but not for the

HIGHLIGHT

Justification for Warrantless Searches of Motor Homes

"[There is] . . . a necessary difference between a search of a store, dwelling house or other structure in respect of which a proper official warrant readily may be obtained, and a search of a ship, motor boat, wagon or automobile, for contraband goods, where it is not practicable to secure a warrant because the vehicle can quickly be moved out of the locality or jurisdiction in which the warrant must be sought."

Carroll v. United States, 267 U.S. 132 (1925).

container), but the effect is the same—it expands the power of the police to conduct warrantless car searches.

L. Seizure of Vehicles from Public Places

In a 1999 case, the Court held that "the Fourth Amendment does not require the police to obtain a warrant before seizing an automobile from a public place if they have probable cause to believe it is forfeitable contraband" (Florida v. White, No. 98-223 [1999]). In that case, officers had previously observed White using his car to deliver cocaine, but White was not arrested at that time. However, he was arrested several months later at his workplace on unrelated charges. During the arrest, the officers seized White's car without a warrant, claiming they were authorized to do so because the car was subject to forfeiture under the Florida Contraband Forfeiture Act. The car was searched, and two pieces of crack cocaine were found in the ashtray. Convicted of a state drug violation, White moved to suppress the evidence seized during that search, saying his Fourth Amendment rights had been violated. On appeal, the Court disagreed, holding that the search and seizure was valid because the car itself constituted forfeitable contraband under state law and probable cause was present. The Court added that, "because the police seized respondent's vehicle from a public area—respondent's employer's parking lot—the warrantless seizure also did not involve any invasion of respondent's privacy."

M. Searches of Motor Homes without a Warrant

The Court has held that motor homes are automobiles for purposes of the Fourth Amendment and are therefore subject to the automobile exception: They can be searched without a warrant. However, the application of this decision is limited to a motor home capable of being driven on the road and located in a place not regularly used for residential purposes. The Court decision specifically stated that the case does not resolve whether the automobile exception applies to a motor home "situated in a way or place that objectively indicates that it is being used as a residence" (California v. Carney, 471 U.S. 386 [1985]).

In the *Carney* case, federal narcotics agents had reason to believe that the defendant was exchanging marijuana for sex with a boy in a motor home parked on a public lot in downtown San Diego. The vehicle was outfitted to serve as a residence. The agents waited until the youth emerged and convinced him to return and ask the defendant to come out. When the defendant came out, an agent entered the motor home without a warrant and found marijuana lying on a table. During the trial, the defendant sought to suppress the evidence, saying that it was excludable because it was obtained without a warrant. The Court disagreed, saying that the evidence was admissible. The Court added that the vehicle in question was readily mobile, that there was a reduced expectation of privacy stemming from its use as a licensed motor vehicle, and that it was so situated as to suggest that it was being used as a vehicle, not a residence. The Court refused to distinguish motor homes from ordinary automobiles simply because motor homes are capable of functioning as dwellings, saying that motor homes lend themselves easily to use as instruments of illicit drug traffic and other illegal activity.

N. Beepers to Detect Cars

A person traveling in a car on a public road has *no reasonable expectation of privacy,* so visual surveillance by the police does not constitute a search. Moreover, the Fourth Amendment does not prohibit the police from supplementing their sensory faculties with technological aids to help the police identify the car's location (United States v. Knotts, 459 U.S. 276 [1983]). The facts in *Knotts* are as follows: With the cooperation of a chemical supply company, state narcotics agents installed an electronic **beeper** in a container of chloroform. When a man the agents suspected of manufacturing controlled substances turned up at the chemical company to purchase chloroform, the bugged can was sold to him. The agents used both the beeper signal and visual means to follow the suspect to a house, where the container was placed in another car. The second car then proceeded into another state, where the agents lost both visual and beeper contact. However, the beeper signal was picked up again by a monitoring device aboard a helicopter. By this means, the agents learned that the container was located in or near a secluded cabin owned by Knotts. Armed with this and other information, the agents obtained a search warrant and discovered a secret drug laboratory. The Court held the police act to be valid and the evidence admissible, saying that by using the public roadways the driver of the car voluntarily conveyed to anyone that he was traveling over particular roads and in a particular direction. Moreover, no expectation of privacy extended to the visual observation of the automobile arriving on private premises after leaving the public highway, nor to movements of objects such as the drum of chloroform outside the cabin in the "open fields."

But the *Knotts* case did not address the question of monitoring in private places, nor did it examine the legality of the original installation and transfer of the beeper. That issue was addressed in United States v. Karo, 468 U.S. 705 (1984), decided a year later. In *Karo,* government agents, upon learning that the defendants had ordered some cans of ether from a government informant to use in extracting cocaine, obtained a court order authorizing the installation and monitoring of a beeper in one of the cans. The agents installed the beeper with the informant's consent, and the can was subsequently delivered to the defendants. Over a period of months, the beeper enabled the agents to monitor the can's movements to a variety of locations, including several private residences and two commercial storage facilities. The agents obtained a search warrant for one of the homes. When the evidence obtained from that warrant was introduced in court, the defendant promptly objected. The Supreme Court first explained that neither the initial installation of the beeper nor the container's subsequent transfer to defendant Karo infringed any constitutional right to privacy of the defendant, nor did they constitute a search or seizure under the Fourth Amendment. The monitoring of the beeper, however, was an entirely different matter. The Court said that the monitoring of a beeper in a private dwelling, a location not open to visual surveillance, violates the rights of individuals to privacy in their own homes. Although the monitoring here was less intrusive than a full search, it revealed facts that the government was interested in knowing and that it could not otherwise have obtained legally without a warrant. The Court considered the use of the beeper to have violated Karo's Fourth Amendment right. Nevertheless, the evidence obtained was not suppressed, because there was ample evidence other than that obtained through use of the beeper to establish probable cause for the issuance of the warrant.

Karo is different from *Knotts*. In *Knotts,* the agents learned nothing from the beeper that they could not have visually observed, so there was no Fourth Amendment intrusion. Moreover, the monitoring in *Knotts* occurred in a public place, whereas the beeper in *Karo* intruded on the privacy of a home.

O. Other Car Searches

Other circumstances that may justify warrantless car searches include the following:

- **Accident cases.** Sometimes, because of an accident or other circumstances, a car must remain in a location where it is vulnerable to intrusion by vandals. If the police have probable cause to believe that the vehicle contains a weapon or a similar device that would constitute a danger if it fell into the wrong hands, they may make a warrantless search for the particular item (Cady v. Dombrowski, 413 U.S. 433 [1973]).

- **Cases in which the vehicle itself has been the subject of crime.** An officer who has probable cause to believe that a car has been the subject of burglary, tampering, or theft may make a limited warrantless entry and investigation of those areas that are reasonably believed to contain evidence of ownership.

- **Cases in which the vehicle is believed abandoned.** A limited search of an automobile in an effort to ascertain ownership is allowable when the car has apparently been abandoned or when the arrested driver is possibly not the owner and does not otherwise resolve the matter of ownership.

The Law on Vehicle Searches

1. Vehicle searches do not need a warrant.
2. Warrantless vehicle searches are valid, but probable cause is required.
3. Searches of passengers' belongings are valid.
4. Searches of passenger compartments are valid.
5. Searches of trunks and closed packages found in trunk are valid.
6. No authoritative decision has been handed down regarding searches of locked trunks or glove compartments.
7. Searches of vehicles need not be made immediately after an arrest.
8. Warrantless vehicle searches are valid even if there was time to obtain a warrant.
9. The extent of car searches is governed by the objective reasonableness rule.
10. Warrantless searches of containers found inside the car, when the police have probable cause to search the container but not the car, are valid.
11. There is no need for a warrant before seizing a vehicle from a public place if there is probable cause to believe that the car itself is forfeitable contraband.
12. Searches of motor homes without a warrant are valid.
13. A warrant is sometimes needed to use beepers to locate cars.

III. VEHICLE INVENTORY SEARCHES

A. Warrantless Vehicle Inventory Searches Immediately after an Arrest

The Court has decided two cases addressing the validity and scope of **vehicle inventory** searches without a warrant immediately after an arrest. In the first case, the Court held that warrantless inventory searches of the person and possessions of arrested individuals are permissible under the Fourth Amendment (Colorado v. Bertine, 479 U.S. 367 [1987]). Bertine was arrested for driving under the influence of alcohol. After he was taken into custody and before the arrival of a tow truck to impound his van, an officer inventoried the van in accordance with departmental procedures. During the inventory search, the officer opened a backpack and found controlled substances, drug paraphernalia, and money. Bertine challenged the admissibility of the evidence, saying that a warrant was needed to open the closed backpack. The Court rejected his challenge, saying that the police must be allowed to conduct warrantless inventory searches to secure an arrestee's property from loss or damage and to protect the police from false claims. Since closed containers may hold items that need to be secured, the police must be allowed to open them without a warrant. The *Bertine* case specified two prerequisites for the valid inventory search of a motor vehicle: (1) The police must follow standardized procedures so as to eliminate uncontrolled discretion to determine the scope of the search, and (2) there must be no bad faith on the part of the police (the inventory search must not be used as an excuse for a warrantless search).

In a subsequent case reiterating *Bertine,* the Court ruled that a police department's "utter lack of any standard policy regarding the opening of closed containers encountered during inventory searches requires the suppression of contraband found in a locked suitcase removed from the trunk of an impounded vehicle and pried open by police after the driver's arrest on drunken driving charges" (Florida v. Wells, 495 U.S. 1 [1990]). In this case, Wells gave the Florida Highway Patrol permission to open the trunk of his car following his arrest for DWI. An inventory search turned up two marijuana cigarette butts in an ashtray and a locked suitcase in the trunk. The suitcase was opened, and marijuana was found. Wells sought to reverse his conviction for drug possession on appeal, saying that the marijuana found in his locked suitcase should not have been admitted as evidence. The Court agreed to suppress the evidence, saying that, "absent any Highway Patrol policy with the opening of closed containers . . . the instant search was insufficiently regulated to satisfy the Fourth Amendment."

The message for the police from the *Bertine* and *Wells* cases is clear: A standardized policy is a must in cases where the police list the personal effects and properties found in the vehicle after impoundment. Such a policy, said the Court, "prevents individual police officers from having so much latitude that inventory searches are turned into a ruse for a general rummaging in order to discover incriminating evidence." It is also clear from the preceding cases that opening a closed container or a locked suitcase is allowed in a vehicle inventory search, but only if specifically authorized by departmental policy. The absence of a departmental policy authorizing the opening of closed or locked containers means that such opening is prohibited. But if such a departmental policy is in place, officers may inspect the outside and inside of a vehicle in the process of taking an inventory, including the passenger compartment, the trunk, and any containers found in the vehicle —as long as such search is conducted for legitimate reasons, not as a fishing expedition.

B. Warrantless Inventory Searches of Vehicles Impounded by Police

The police have authority for **vehicle impoundment** for various reasons, such as when the vehicle has been used for the commission of an offense or when it should be removed from the streets because it impedes traffic or threatens public safety. This type of search is distinguished from searches immediately after an arrest, where the vehicle is not necessarily impounded. When the police lawfully impound a vehicle, they may conduct a routine inventory search without warrant or probable cause to believe that the car contains seizable evidence. The leading case on impoundment searches is South Dakota v. Opperman, 428 U.S. 364 (1976). In that case, the defendant's illegally parked

HIGHLIGHT

Why the Court Requires Standardized Criteria for an Inventory Search

"Our view that standardized criteria or established routine must regulate the opening of containers found during inventory searches is based on the principle that an inventory search must not be a ruse for a general rummaging in order to discover incriminating evidence. The policy or practice governing inventory searches should be designed to produce an inventory. The individual officer must not be allowed so much latitude that inventory searches are turned into a 'purposeful and general means of discovering evidence of crime.'"

Florida v. Wells, 495 U.S. 1 (1990).

car was taken to the city impound lot, where an officer, observing articles of personal property in the car, proceeded to inventory it. In the process, he found a bag of marijuana in the unlocked glove compartment. The Court concluded that, "in following standard police procedures, prevailing throughout the country and approved by the overwhelming majority of courts, the conduct of the police was not 'unreasonable' under the Fourth Amendment." The ruling legitimizes car inventories, but the Court has also made it clear in *Opperman* and other cases that inventory searches must be guided by departmental policy, so that the inventory becomes merely an administrative function by the police. Inventory searches conducted solely for the purposes of discovering evidence are illegal regardless of what is discovered in the course of the inventory. In the words of the Court, "Our view that standardized criteria or established routine must regulate the opening of containers is based on the principle that an inventory search must not be a ruse for a general rummaging in order to discover incriminating evidence" (Florida v. Wells, 495 U.S. 7 [1990]).

It is true that, when vehicles are abandoned or illegally parked or when the owner is arrested, the courts permit them to be impounded and inventoried. But that rule should not apply when the driver has been arrested for a minor traffic violation, primarily because the police are expected to give the suspect a reasonable opportunity to post bail and obtain his or her prompt release. In Dyke v. Taylor Implement Manufacturing Company, 391 U.S. 216 (1968), a driver who had been arrested for reckless driving was at the courthouse to make bail when his vehicle was searched. The Court concluded that the search of the vehicle could not be deemed incident to impoundment, because the police seemed to have parked the car near the courthouse merely as a convenience to the owner, who, if he were soon to be released from custody, could then have driven it away.

Another issue in car impoundment is whether other alternatives to impoundment should be explored before placing the vehicle under police control (at least in cases in which the vehicle itself has not been involved in the crime). One writer notes:

> There is a growing body of authority that when the arrestee specifically requests that his car be lawfully parked in the vicinity of the arrest or that it be turned over

to a friend, the police must honor his request. Indeed more and more courts are moving to the sound conclusion that the police must take the initiative with respect to apparent alternatives, such as permitting a licensed passenger to take custody of the car.[12]

IV. A WORD OF CAUTION

The rules discussed in this chapter on motor vehicle searches are based primarily on U.S. Supreme Court decisions. They do not reflect state law or regulations in specific police departments, both of which may vary greatly. State law and department policies may limit what the police can do. Where state law or department policy is more limiting than Court decisions, an officer must follow state law and department policy. They are binding on the police officer, regardless of what the Court held in the cases discussed in this chapter. For example, the Court has decided that, if the police have probable cause to stop and search an automobile on the highway, they may take it to the police station and search it there without a warrant—thus doing away with the contemporaneous requirement. Assume, however, that, according to state law and department policy, once the car is brought to the police station and the driver incarcerated, the police must obtain a warrant before conducting a search of the car. In this case, a warrant must be obtained; otherwise, the search is illegal and the evidence obtained inadmissible.

Summary

A seizure occurs every time a motor vehicle is stopped. However, searches and seizures of motor vehicles generally do not need a warrant; they constitute an exception to the warrant requirement of the Fourth Amendment. There are various types of vehicle stops: stops for suspicion of involvement in criminal activity, roadblocks, sobriety checkpoints, stops for brief questioning, and stops to check driver's licenses and registrations. All these vehicular stops may be made without a warrant and on less than probable cause.

After the vehicle is validly stopped, the officer can do a number of things. These include asking the driver to get out of the vehicle, asking the driver to produce a driver's license and other documents required by state law, asking questions of the driver and passengers, locating and examining the vehicle identification number, searching the vehicle, seizing items in plain view, and making an arrest if probable cause is established.

Vehicle searches must be based on probable cause. The officer may search the passenger compartment, search the trunk and closed packages found in the trunk, conduct a vehicle inventory search immediately after an arrest, and search motor homes.

Case law on motor vehicle searches is complex and is made more difficult by the fact that constitutional rules are often superseded by state law or agency rules. For example, what the Constitution allows in vehicle stops may be prohibited by state law or agency policy. In addition to knowing the constitutional rules discussed in this chapter, police officers must know their own state laws and agency rules on vehicle searches.

Review Questions

1. What is meant by the "automobile exception" to the search and seizure rule? Give reasons for this exception.

2. What rules govern motor vehicle stops? Is either a warrant or probable cause needed? Discuss.

3. Identify and discuss three constitutional uses of vehicle roadblocks.

4. "Under certain circumstances, a stop for a traffic violation may eventually lead to a search of the entire vehicle." Is this statement true or false? Defend your answer.

5. Assume that a police officer has made a valid arrest of a driver for possession of drugs. To what extent may the police search the vehicle incident to that arrest?

6. Taking into consideration the Supreme Court cases on car searches presented in this chapter, discuss what an officer can do and cannot do in car searches.

7. What are pretextual stops? Discuss whether they are valid or invalid.

8. What are stops based on racial profile? Discuss whether they are valid or invalid.

9. Taken together, what do the *Bertine* and *Wells* cases say about vehicle inventory searches after an arrest?

10. Give the rule concerning searches of motor homes.

Key Terms and Definitions

beeper: An electronic device sometimes used by the police to monitor the movement and location of a motor vehicle.

pretextual stops: Stops used as a pretext for motor vehicle searches.

racial profile stops: Stops of motor vehicles based on the driver's race.

roadblock: A law enforcement practice for halting traffic. It is not strictly a form of detention,

but it limits a person's freedom of movement by blocking vehicular movement. It is used by the police for a variety of purposes, including spot checks of drivers' licenses, car registrations, and violations of motor vehicle laws and apprehension of fleeing criminals and suspects.

sobriety checkpoint: A checkpoint set up by the police at a selected site along a public road; all vehicles passing through the

checkpoint are stopped and the drivers checked for signs of intoxication.

vehicle impoundment: The act of taking a vehicle into custody for such reasons as use in a crime, impeding of traffic, and a threat to public safety.

vehicle inventory: The listing by the police of personal effects and properties found in the vehicle after impoundment.

Principles of Cases

Arkansas v. Sanders, 442 U.S. 753 (1979) The Carroll doctrine allowing warrantless searches of automobiles does not extend to warrantless searches of personal luggage merely because it was located in an automobile lawfully stopped by the police.

Berkemer v. McCarty, 468 U.S. 420 (1984) The roadside questioning of a motorist pursuant to a routine traffic stop is not custodial interrogation and therefore does not require the Miranda warnings.

Brower v. County of Inyo, 489 U.S. 593 (1989) Roadblocks are a form of seizure under the Fourth Amendment.

Cady v. Dombrowski, 413 U.S. 433 (1973) If, because of an accident or other circumstances, a car must remain in a location where it is vulnerable to intrusion by vandals, the police, if they have probable cause to believe that the vehicle contains a weapon or a similar device that would constitute a danger if it fell into the wrong hands, may make a warrantless search for the particular item.

California v. Acevedo, 111 S.Ct. 1982 (1991) Probable cause to believe that a container in a car holds contraband or seizable evidence justifies a warrantless search of that container even if there is no probable cause to search the car.

California v. Carney, 471 U.S. 386 (1985) Motor homes are automobiles for purposes of the Fourth Amendment and are therefore subject to the automobile exception—meaning that they can be searched without a warrant.

Carroll v. United States, 267 U.S. 132 (1925) The search of an automobile does not require a warrant, where it is not practicable to obtain one, because the vehicle can be quickly moved out of the locality or jurisdiction in which the warrant must be sought.

Chambers v. Maroney, 399 U.S. 42 (1970) For constitutional purposes, there is no difference between seizing and holding a car before presenting the probable cause issue to a magistrate and carrying out an immediate search without a warrant. Given probable cause to search, either course is reasonable under the Fourth Amendment.

Colorado v. Bannister, 449 U.S. 1 (1980) As long as the stopping of the vehicle was lawful, what officers observe can evolve into probable cause to believe that the car contains the fruits and instrumentalities of crime or contraband, thereby establishing a justification for a full warrantless search of the vehicle.

Colorado v. Bertine, 479 U.S. 367 (1987) Inventory searches without a warrant to search the person and possessions of arrested individuals are permissible under the Fourth Amendment.

Delaware v. Prouse, 440 U.S. 648 (1979) Stopping an automobile and detaining its occupants constitute a "seizure" within the meaning of the Fourth and Fourteenth Amendments, even if the purpose of the stop is limited and the resulting detention is quite brief. Roadblocks may be set up for inspection purposes, provided the officer stops every car passing the checkpoint or has an articulable, neutral principle (such as stopping every fifth car) for justifying the stop.

Dyke v. Taylor Implement Manufacturing Co., 391 U.S. 216 (1968) The search of the vehicle in this case could not be deemed incident to impoundment, because the police seemed to have parked the car near the courthouse merely as a convenience to the owner, who, if he were soon to be released from custody, could then have driven it away.

Florida v. Jimeno, 111 S.Ct. 1801 (1991) Valid consent justifies a warrantless search of a container in a car if it is objectively reasonable for the police to believe that the scope of the suspect's consent permitted them to open that container.

Florida v. Meyers, 466 U.S. 380 (1984) A vehicle may be searched under the automobile exception to the Fourth Amendment even if it has been immobilized and released to the custody of the police.

Florida v. Wells, 495 U.S. 7 (1990) A police department's utter lack of any standard policy regarding the opening of closed containers encountered during inventory searches requires the suppression of contraband found in a locked suitcase removed from the trunk of an impounded vehicle and pried open by the police after the driver's arrest for drunk driving.

Florida v. White, No. 98-223 (1999) The Fourth Amendment does not require the police to obtain a warrant before seizing an automobile from a public place if they have probable cause to believe it is forfeitable contraband.

Knowles v. Iowa, No. 97-7597 (1998) State law that authorizes a search incident to the issuance of a traffic citation violates the Fourth Amendment unless there is consent or probable cause.

Maryland v. Dyson, 65 CrL 2070 (1999) If the police have probable cause to search a car, they do not need a warrant even if there was ample opportunity to obtain one.

Maryland v. Wilson, 60 CrL 2077 (1997) Police officers may order passengers to get out of a motor vehicle during traffic stops.

Michigan Department of State Police v. Sitz, 496 U.S. 444 (1990) Sobriety checkpoints in which the police stop every vehicle do not violate the Fourth Amendment protections against unreasonable searches and seizures and are therefore constitutional.

Michigan v. Long, 463 U.S. 1032 (1983) If the officer has reasonable suspicion that the motorist who has been stopped is dangerous and may be able to gain control of a weapon in the car, the officer may conduct a brief search of the passenger compartment even if the motorist is no longer inside the car. Such a search should be limited to areas in the passenger compartment where a weapon might be found or hidden.

New York v. Belton, 453 U.S. 454 (1981) Once a driver has been arrested, the police may conduct a warrantless search of the passenger compartment of the automobile. The police may examine the contents of any container found within the passenger compartment, as long as it may reasonably be thought to contain something that might pose a danger to the officer or hold evidence of the offense for which the suspect has been arrested.

New York v. Class, 475 U.S. 106 (1986) Motorists have no reasonable expectation of privacy with respect to the vehicle identification number (VIN) located on the car's dashboard, even if objects on the dashboard prevent the VIN from being observed from outside the car.

Pennsylvania v. Labron, 59 CrL 3090 (1996) A warrantless search of a vehicle is valid if the vehicle is readily mobile.

Pennsylvania v. Mimms, 434 U.S. 106 (1977) Once a vehicle has been lawfully stopped for a traffic violation, the officer may order the driver to get out even without suspecting criminal activity. If the officer then reasonably believes that the driver may be armed and dangerous, the officer may conduct a limited protective frisk for a weapon that might endanger his or her personal safety.

Ohio v. Robinette, 60 CrL 2002 (1996) The Court reiterated its ruling in Whren v. United States, saying that the subjective motivation of a law enforcement officer in asking a lawfully stopped motorist to exit his or her vehicle does not affect the lawfulness of the detention. The Court also held that the officer need not inform the defendant first that he or she is free to go in order for a consent to search to be valid.

Robbins v. California, 453 U.S. 420 (1981) The automobile exception to the warrant requirement is justified by the following considerations: (1) the mobility of motor vehicles, (2) the diminished expectation of privacy, (3) the fact that the car is used for transportation, not as a residence or a repository of personal effects, (4) the fact that the car's occupants and contents travel in plain view, and (5) the necessarily high degree of regulation of automobiles by the government.

Schneckloth v. Bustamonte, 412 U.S. 218 (1973) After validly stopping a car, an officer may ask the person in control of the car for permission to search.

South Dakota v. Opperman, 428 U.S. 364 (1976) When the police lawfully impound a vehicle, they may conduct a routine inventory search without a warrant or probable cause to believe that the car contains seizable evidence. This procedure is reasonable to protect the owner's property, to protect the police against a claim that the owner's property was stolen while the car was impounded, and to protect the police from potential danger.

State of Washington v. Ladson, No. 65801-3 (1999) The Supreme Court of the state of Washington held that there is no pretextual stop exception to the warrant requirement under the state's constitution, so pretextual stops in that state are not valid.

United States v. Chadwick, 433 U.S. 1 (1977) The warrantless search of a footlocker that has been loaded into an automobile is invalid, because the container does not come under the automobile exception even if it happens to have been removed from a car.

United States v. Cortez, 449 U.S. 411 (1981) There must be at least a reasonable suspicion to justify an investigatory stop of a motor vehicle.

United States v. Di Re, 332 581 (1948) An officer may not conduct a body search of a passenger in a car.

United States v. Johns, 469 U.S. 478 (1985) The warrantless search of containers found in a car is valid even if there is a significant delay (three days in this case) between the time the police stop the vehicle and the time they perform the search.

United States v. Karo, 468 U.S. 705 (1984) The monitoring by a beeper in a private dwelling, a location not open to visual surveillance, violates the rights of individuals to privacy in their own homes. It therefore cannot be conducted without a warrant.

United States v. Knotts, 460 U.S. 276 (1983) The use by the police of a beeper to locate a car on a public road does not constitute a search, because there is no reasonable expectation of privacy. Moreover, the Fourth Amendment does not prohibit the police from supplementing their sensory faculties with technological aids to help them pinpoint a car's location.

United States v. Martinez-Fuerte, 428 U.S. 543 (1976) Stops for brief questioning that are routinely conducted at permanent checkpoints are consistent with the Fourth Amendment, so it is not necessary to obtain a warrant before setting up a checkpoint.

United States v. Prichard, 645 F.2d 854 (1981) Establishing a roadblock to check drivers' licenses and car registrations is legitimate. If in the process of doing so, the officers see evidence of other crimes, they have the right to take reasonable investigative steps and are not required to close their eyes.

United States v. Ross, 456 U.S. 798 (1982) If the police legitimately stop a car and have probable cause to believe that it contains contraband, they can conduct a warrantless search of the car. The search can be as thorough as a search authorized by a warrant issued by a magistrate. Therefore, every part of the vehicle in which the contraband might be stored may be inspected, including the trunk and all receptacles and packages that could possibly contain the object of the search.

Whren v. United States, 59 CrL 2121 (1996) The temporary detention of a motorist that is supported by probable cause to believe that the motorist has committed a traffic violation is valid even if the actual motivation of the law enforcement officer is to determine if the motorist has drugs.

Wyoming v. Houghton, No. 98-184 (1999) Police officers with probable cause to search a car may inspect passengers' belongings found in the car that are capable of concealing the object of the search.

 ## Case Briefs

Leading Case on Warrantless Car Searches

Carroll v. United States, 267 U.S. 132 (1925)

Facts: Officers observed the automobile of Carroll while on regular patrol between Detroit and Grand Rapids. The same officers had been in contact with Carroll twice in the four months prior to this sighting. In September, the officers had attempted to buy illegal liquor from Carroll, but he was alerted to their true identity and did not produce the contraband. In October, the officers had recognized Carroll's automobile returning to Grand Rapids from Detroit. They gave chase but failed to catch the car. Carroll was later apprehended, and he and his companion were ordered out of the car. No liquor was visible in the front seat of the car. One of the officers struck the "lazyback" of the seat, tore open the seat cushion, and discovered sixty-eight bottles of gin and whiskey. Carroll was arrested and convicted of transporting intoxicating liquor.

Issue: *May officers search an automobile without a search warrant but with probable cause to believe that it contains contraband? Yes.*

Supreme Court Decision: The risk of the vehicle being moved from the jurisdiction, or the evidence being destroyed or carried off, justifies a warrantless search as long as such search is conducted with probable cause to believe that the vehicle that is subject to seizure contains contraband.

Case Significance: Carroll v. United States is the "mother" of all automobile exception cases; most other cases involving automobiles that have been decided since then have referred to what is now known as the Carroll doctrine. This doctrine states that warrantless searches of automobiles are valid as long as there is probable cause to search. The main justification for this exception is the mobile nature of the automobile. Although a search warrant is not required in car searches, probable cause is necessary.

Excerpts from the Decision: "[T]he guarantee of freedom from unreasonable searches and seizures by the Fourth Amendment has been construed, practically since the beginning of government, as recognizing a necessary difference between a search of a store, dwelling house, or other structure in respect of which a proper official warrant readily may be obtained and a search of a ship, motor boat, wagon, or automobile for contraband goods, where it is not practicable to secure a warrant, because the vehicle can be quickly moved out of the locality or jurisdiction in which the warrant must be sought."

Leading Case on the Search of Car Trunks and Closed Packages in Trunks

United States v. Ross, 456 U.S. 798 (1982)

Facts: Police in Washington, DC, received information from an informant that Ross was selling narcotics kept in the trunk of his car, which was parked at a specified location. The police drove to the location, spotted the person and car that matched the description given by the informant, and made a warrantless arrest. The officers opened the car's trunk and found a closed brown paper bag containing glassine bags of a substance that turned out to be heroin. The officers then drove the car to police headquarters, where another warrantless search of the trunk revealed a zippered leather pouch containing cash. Ross was charged with possession of heroin with intent to distribute. He sought to suppress the heroin and cash as evidence, alleging that both were obtained in violation of his constitutional rights, because there were no exigent circumstances that would justify a warrantless search.

Issue: After a valid arrest, may the police open the trunk of the car and containers found therein without a warrant and in the absence of exigent circumstances? Yes.

Supreme Court Decision: When the police have probable cause to justify a warrantless search of a car, they may search the entire car and open the trunk and any packages or luggage found therein that could reasonably be thought to contain the items for which they have probable cause to search.

Case Significance: The Ross case is important in that it further defines the scope of police authority in vehicle searches. The Court's Belton decision had specifically refused to address the issue of whether the police could open the trunk of a car in connection with a search incident to a valid arrest. Ross addressed that issue and authorized such action. But it went beyond that: Any packages or luggage found in the car that could reasonably be thought to contain the items for which there was probable cause to search could also be opened without a warrant. Ross has therefore greatly expanded the scope of allowable warrantless search, limited only by what is reasonable.

Excerpts from the Decision: "A lawful search of fixed premises generally extends to the entire area in which the object of the search may be found and is not limited by the possibility that separate acts of entry or opening may be required to complete the search. Thus, a warrant that authorizes an officer to search a home for illegal weapons also provides authority to open closets, chests, drawers, and containers in which the weapon might be found. A warrant to open a footlocker to search for marijuana would also authorize the opening of packages found inside. A warrant to search a vehicle would support a search of every part of the vehicle that might contain the object of the search. When a legitimate search is under way, and when its purpose and its limits have been precisely defined, nice distinctions between closets, drawers, and containers, in the case of a home, or between glove compartments, upholstered seats, trunks, and wrapped packages, in the case of a vehicle, must give way to the interest in the prompt and efficient completion of the task at hand."

Notes

1. Michele G. Herman, *Search and Seizure Checklists,* 3rd ed. (New York: Clark Boardman, 1983), p. 78.

2. J. Gales Sauls, "Traffic Stops: Police Powers under the Fourth Amendment," *FBI Law Enforcement Bulletin,* September 1989, p. 29.

3. Ibid.

4. Tommy Sangchommpuphen, "Drunk Drivers Claim They Are Punished Twice," *The Wall Street Journal,* June 21, 1995, p. B1.

5. Steven L. Emanuel and Steven Knowles, *Emanuel Law Outlines: Criminal Procedure* (Larchmont, NY: Emanuel, 1998–99), p. 100.

6. *Houston Chronicle,* May 2, 1999, p. A10.

7. *Houston Chronicle,* May 16, 1999, p. A17.

8. Supra note 2, p. 30.

9. *Washington Post,* August 11, 1999, p. A13.

10. Lloyd L. Weinreb and James D. Whaley, *The Field Guide to Law Enforcement* (Westbury, NY: Foundation Press, 1999), p. 49.

11. Supra note 1, p. 78.

12. Steven L. Emanuel and Steven Knowles, *Emanuel Law Outlines* (Larchmont, NY: Emanuel, 1995–96), p. 86.

9. Plain View, Open Fields, Abandonment, and Electronic Surveillance

Chapter Outline

I. THE "PLAIN VIEW" DOCTRINE
   A. Plain View Defined
   B. Requirements of the Plain View Doctrine
   C. The Application of the Plain View Doctrine to a Variety of Situations
   D. Plain View As But One of Many Justifications for Admission of Evidence
   E. Issues Raised by the Plain View Doctrine

II. THE OPEN FIELDS DOCTRINE
   A. Open Fields Defined
   B. Areas Not Included in Open Fields
   C. The Test to Determine Curtilage: United States v. Dunn
   D. Aerial Surveillance of Curtilage: California v. Ciraolo
   E. Open Fields despite a Locked Gate and a "No Trespassing" Sign: Oliver v. United States
   F. Open Fields versus Plain View

III. ABANDONMENT
   A. Abandonment Defined
   B. Factors Determining When Items Are Considered Abandoned
   C. Abandonment of Motor Vehicles
   D. The Legality of Police Actions
   E. Abandonment versus Plain View

IV. ELECTRONIC SURVEILLANCE
   A. The Old Concept—Constitutional If There Is No Trespass: Olmstead v. United States
   B. The New Concept—Unconstitutional If It Violates a Reasonable Expectation of Privacy: Katz v. United States
   C. Federal Law: Title III of the Omnibus Crime Control and Safe Streets Act of 1968
   D. Federal Law: The Electronic Communications and Privacy Act of 1986 (ECPA)
   E. Federal Law: The Communications Assistance for Law Enforcement Act of 1994
   F. Electronic Devices That Do Not Intercept Communication
   G. Recording Devices in Prisons and Jails

Case Briefs

Oliver v. United States
Katz v. United States

What You Will Learn in This Chapter

You will be introduced to three concepts in police work (plain view, open fields, and abandonment) that do not come under the Fourth Amendment prohibition against unreasonable searches and seizures and one concept (electronic surveillance) that is governed by provisions of federal law, state law, and the Constitution. You will also learn the differences between these four concepts in law enforcement, as well as their limitations. Finally, you will become familiar with three federal laws, applicable to the states, that govern electronic surveillance by law enforcement agents.

Introduction

This chapter discusses four concepts related to searches and seizures, each of which deserves separate consideration because of its importance in law enforcement work. These are "plain view," "open fields," abandonment, and electronic surveillance. What these concepts have in common is some form of "taking" by the government of something that belongs to or used to belong to somebody. But they do differ enough in legal rules and requirements to justify separate discussion. Plain view, open fields, and abandonment do not require any warrant or probable cause, because they do not come under the Fourth Amendment; by contrast, electronic surveillance is governed strictly by the Fourth Amendment and by federal and state laws.

I. THE PLAIN VIEW DOCTRINE
A. Plain View Defined

The **"plain view" doctrine** states that *items that are within the sight of an officer who is legally in a place from which the view is made may properly be seized without a warrant— as long as such items are immediately recognizable as subject to seizure.* In the words of the Court, "It has long been settled that objects falling in the plain view of an officer who has a right to be in a position to have that view are subject to seizure and may be introduced in evidence" (Harris v. United States, 390 U.S. 234 [1968]). In that case, a police

HIGHLIGHT

The Plain View Doctrine versus Privacy Interests

"The plain view doctrine authorizes seizure of illegal or evidentiary items visible to a police officer whose access to the object has some prior Fourth Amendment justification and who has probable cause to suspect that the item is connected with criminal activity. The plain view doctrine is grounded on the proposition that once police are lawfully in a position to observe an item firsthand, its owner's privacy interest in that item is lost; the owner may retain the incidents of title and possession but not privacy."

Illinois v. Andreas, 463 U.S. 765 (1983).

officer searched an impounded automobile in connection with a robbery. When opening the door, the officer saw, in plain view, the automobile registration card belonging to the victim of the robbery. Harris was charged with robbery. At trial, he moved to suppress the automobile registration card, claiming that it was obtained illegally because the officer had no warrant although he had time to obtain one. On appeal, the Court admitted the evidence, saying that the automobile registration card was in plain view and therefore did not need a warrant to be seized.

Although generally considered to be an exception to the search warrant requirement, plain view is really not a search within the terms of the Fourth Amendment, because no search for that specific item has been or is being undertaken. No warrant or probable cause is necessary; the officer simply seizes what is seen, not something that has been searched. Seeing the item is usually accidental and unexpected.

B. Requirements of the Plain View Doctrine

There are three basic requirements of the plain view doctrine, all of which must be met for the evidence to be seized legally by the police.

1. Awareness of Item Through Use of Sight

Awareness of the items must be gained solely through the officer's sight, not through the other senses—hearing, smelling, tasting, or touching. This means that the item must be *plainly visible* to the officer for plain view to apply. For example, suppose that, while executing a search warrant for a stolen typewriter, an officer sees marijuana on the suspect's nightstand. Seizure may be made, because he knows through the sense of sight that the items are contraband and therefore seizable. But if he merely suspects that there is marijuana in the apartment because of the smell, as might occur if it were hidden in a closet or drawer, its seizure in the course of a search cannot be justified under the plain view doctrine. Of course, it may be validly seized without a warrant if the officer can establish probable cause and the presence of exigent circumstances.

2. The Officer Must Be Legally in the Place from Which the Item Is Seen

The officer must not have done anything illegal to get to the spot from which he or she sees the items in question. An officer comes to be in a place properly in a number of ways: (1) when serving a search warrant, (2) while in hot pursuit of a suspect, (3) having made entry through valid consent, and (4) when making a valid arrest with or without a warrant. For example, suppose that, while executing a search warrant for a stolen TV set, an officer sees gambling slips on a table. She may properly seize them even though they were not included in the warrant, as long as her presence on the premises is legal. By contrast, a police officer who forces his way into a house and then sees drugs on the table cannot validly seize the drugs because he entered the house illegally. What the officer sees subsequent to entry can never cure the initial illegality.

3. It Must Be "Immediately Apparent" That the Item Is Subject to Seizure

Recognition of the items in plain view must be immediate and not the result of further prying or examination. In other words, the items must be out in the open, and it must be immediately apparent that they are seizable. For example, suppose an officer sees something that she immediately recognizes as gambling paraphernalia. She may seize it under plain view. By contrast, suppose that after a valid entry the officer sees a typewriter she suspects is stolen. She calls the police station to ask for the serial number of a typewriter earlier reported stolen and, after verification of the number, seizes the typewriter. This seizure cannot be justified under the plain view doctrine, because the item was not immediately recognizable as subject to seizure. The evidence may be seized, but the seizure will have to be justified based on other legal grounds, such as consent or exigent circumstance.

The "immediately apparent" requirement must be based on *probable cause,* not on any lesser degree of certainty, such as reasonable suspicion (Arizona v. Hicks, 480 U.S. 321 [1987]). In this case, a bullet fired through the floor of Hicks's apartment injured a man below, prompting the police to enter Hicks's apartment to search for the suspect, weapons, and other potential victims. An officer discovered three weapons and a stocking cap mask. He also noticed several pieces of stereo equipment, which seemed out of place in the ill-appointed apartment. The officer therefore read and recorded the serial numbers of the equipment, moving some of the pieces in the process. A call to police headquarters confirmed that one of the pieces of equipment was stolen; a later check revealed that the other pieces were also stolen. Hicks was convicted of robbery. On appeal, he sought suppression of the evidence, saying that the plain view search was illegal. The Court agreed, noting that with plain view there must be probable cause to believe that items being searched are, in fact, contraband or evidence of criminal activity. A lesser degree of certainty, such as reasonable suspicion, as in this case, would not suffice.

On the other hand, "certain knowledge"—a higher degree of certainty than probable cause—is not necessary. For example, in one case, an officer stopped a car at night to check the driver's license. He shone his flashlight into the car's interior and saw the driver holding an opaque green party balloon, knotted about a half inch from the tip. The officer also saw white powder in the open glove compartment. In court, the officer testified that he had learned from experience that inflated, tied-off balloons often were used to transport narcotics. The Court concluded that the officer had probable cause to

Requirements of the Plain View Doctrine

All three of the following requirements must be met for the item to be seized legally; the absence of one means the plain view doctrine does not apply.

1. Awareness of item must be through use of sense of sight.

2. The officer must be legally in the place from which the item is seen.

3. It must be immediately apparent that the item is subject to seizure.

believe that the balloon contained narcotics, so the warrantless seizure was justified under plain view (Texas v. Brown, 460 U.S. 730 [1983]).

C. The Application of the Plain View Doctrine to a Variety of Situations

There are many situations in police work when the plain view doctrine applies and the items seen may be seized without a warrant. Among these are the following:

- When making an arrest with or without a warrant

- When in hot pursuit of a fleeing suspect

- When making a search incident to a valid arrest

- When out on patrol

- When making a car inventory search subsequent to impoundment

- When conducting an investigation in a residence

- When making an entry into a home after obtaining valid consent

This list is illustrative, not comprehensive. In sum, the plain view doctrine applies to every aspect of police work as long as all three of the requirements of plain view are met.

D. Plain View As But One of Many Justifications for Admission of Evidence

The plain view doctrine is only one of many possible legal justifications for admitting evidence obtained by the police. It is used as a legal justification for seizure only if all three requirements are met. The absence of one of these elements means that the evidence is not admissible under plain view, but it may still be admissible under another legal doctrine. For example, suppose an officer arrests a suspect at home by authority of an arrest warrant. While there, the officer sees in the living room several TV sets that he suspects may be stolen. He telephones the police department to give the serial numbers and is informed that those sets have been reported stolen. At this stage, the officer has probable cause to seize the items. The officer cannot seize them under plain view, because the items were not immediately recognizable as subject to seizure. Ordinarily, the officer would need a warrant to seize the sets, but warrantless seizures may be justified if the officer can establish exigent circumstances (such as that the sets would most likely be hauled away by the other occupants should the officer leave the house). The sets are then admissible in court on the basis of probable cause and exigent circumstances.

E. Issues Raised by the Plain View Doctrine

To understand the plain view doctrine better, several related issues must be addressed and clarified, including inadvertence, open spaces, motor vehicles, mechanical devices, open view, plain feel, and plain odor.

1. Inadvertence (Accidental Finding): Horton v. California

For a long time, the prevalent view was that **inadvertence** was one of the plain view requirements. Inadvertence means that *the officer must have no prior knowledge that the evidence was present in the place; the discovery must be purely accidental.* In the words of one court, "The plain view doctrine is properly applied to situations in which a police officer is not searching for evidence against the accused but nevertheless inadvertently comes across an incriminating object" (United States v. Sedillo, 496 F.2d 151 [9th Cir. 1974]). In another case, the Supreme Court said, "The . . . discovery of evidence in plain view must be inadvertent. . . . But where the discovery is anticipated, where the police know in advance the location of the evidence and intend to seize it, the situation is altogether different" (Coolidge v. New Hampshire, 403 U.S. 443 [1971]).

The inadvertence requirement has now been abandoned by the Court. In a 1990 case, the Court stated, "The Fourth Amendment does not prohibit the warrantless seizure of evidence in plain view even though the discovery of the evidence was not inadvertent. Although inadvertence is a characteristic of most legitimate plain view seizures, it is not a necessary condition" (Horton v. California, 496 U.S. 128 [1990]). In that case, a police officer determined that there was probable cause to search Horton's home for the proceeds from a robbery and for weapons used in the robbery. The affidavit filed by the officer referred to police reports that described both the weapons and the proceeds, but for some reason the warrant issued by the magistrate only authorized a search for the proceeds. When the officer went to Horton's home to execute the warrant, he did not find the stolen property (proceeds), but he did see the weapons (an Uzi machine gun, a .38-caliber revolver, and two stun guns) in plain view and seized them. At trial, the officer testified that, while he was searching Horton's home for the proceeds, he was also interested in finding "other evidence" related to the robbery. Tried and convicted, Horton argued on appeal that the weapons should have been suppressed because their discovery was not "inadvertent." The Court disagreed, saying that,

Inadvertence No Longer a Requirement under Plain View

The Fourth Amendment does not prohibit the warrantless seizure of evidence in plain view even if the police officer knew beforehand that evi- dence could be found in a particular place. In Horton v. California, 496 U.S. 128 (1990), the Court said: "We conclude that even though inadvertence is a characteris- tic of most legitimate 'plain view' seizures, it is not a nec- essary condition."

"although inadvertence is a characteristic of most legitimate plain view seizures, it is not a necessary condition." The Court expressly rejected the inadvertence requirement, noting that (1) even-handed law enforcement is best achieved by the application of objective standards of conduct, rather than by standards that depend on the officer's subjective state of mind, and (2) the suggestion that the inadvertence requirement is necessary to prevent the police from conducting a general search or from converting specific warrants into general warrants is not persuasive. In this case, "the scope of the search was not enlarged in the slightest by the omission of any reference to the weapons in the warrant." The evidence was held admissible.

The *Horton* decision means that most plain view cases will still be the result of inadvertence (meaning that the officer sees a seizable item that he or she did not expect to see); but in the process of serving a warrant, an officer may also seize an item he or she knew beforehand would be there even if the item is not listed in the warrant as one of those to be seized. One source interprets *Horton* this way:

> The "plain view" doctrine applies even where the police's discovery of a piece of evidence they want to seize is not inadvertent. Thus if the police know that they are likely to find, say, both the gun used in a robbery as well as the proceeds of the robbery, they may procure a warrant for the proceeds, and may then seize the gun if they happen upon it in plain view while they are searching for the proceeds.[1]

2. Open Spaces

Plain view usually applies when the officer is within an enclosed space (such as a house, an apartment, or an office)—hence the concept used by some courts of a "prior valid intrusion into a constitutionally protected area." It also applies when the officer is out in the open, such as out on the street on patrol. In open spaces, however, a distinction must be made between *seeing* and *seizing*. For example, suppose that, while walking around an apartment complex, an officer sees illegal weapons through a window. This, too, is plain view. The difference between this scenario and one in which the officer is within an enclosed space is that here the officer cannot make an entry to seize the items without a warrant unless he or she obtains consent or establishes exigent circum- stances. When the officer is in an enclosed space (such as a house or apartment), *seiz- ing follows seeing* as a matter of natural sequence. By contrast, when an entry is needed, seeing and seizing become two separate acts because of the need for a legal entry. In the absence of consent or exigent circumstances, a warrant is needed if some form of entry is to be made before something is seized. An exigent circumstance would exist, for example, if the officer could establish that the evidence would most likely no longer be available unless immediate action were taken. Without an exigent circumstance, a warrant must be obtained.

Plain view also applies to items seen from outside fences or enclosures. For example, suppose an officer on patrol sees pots of marijuana inside a fenced yard. This falls under plain view, but a warrant still is needed for entry.

3. Motor Vehicles

Plain view also applies to motor vehicles. For example, suppose that, while out on patrol, Officer Y observes a car parked on the street, looks at the front seat, and sees drugs and drug paraphernalia. This scenario falls under plain view. Whether Officer Y can seize these items without a warrant, however, is not clear, particularly if the vehicle is closed and locked. This is different from the usual plain view situation in which seeing immediately leads to seizing because no further entry is necessary. The Supreme Court has not addressed this issue. In view of this uncertainty, the better practice would be for Officer Y to obtain a warrant to gain entry to the vehicle, unless entry may be made without using force (as when Officer Y obtains possession of the key), consent is given, or exigent circumstances are present that would justify immediate entry.

4. The Use of Mechanical Devices

The use of mechanical devices by the police does not affect the applicability of the plain view doctrine. For example, the use of a flashlight by an officer to look into the inside of a car at night does not constitute a search under the Fourth Amendment. Evidence that would not have been discovered and seized without the use of a flashlight is nonetheless admissible in court (Texas v. Brown, 460 U.S. 730 [1983]). The same is true for the use of binoculars. In another case, the police use of a beeper to monitor the whereabouts of a person traveling in a car on public highways did not turn the surveillance into a search. Such monitoring on a public highway was considered by the Court to fall under the plain view doctrine (United States v. Knotts, 460 U.S. 276 [1983]).

The officer need not be standing upright for plain view to apply. For example, in the *Brown* case, the police officer who legally stopped the automobile bent down so that he could see what was inside the car. The Court said that the fact that the officer got into an unusual position in order to see the contents of the vehicle did not prevent the plain view doctrine from applying.

5. Plain View versus Open View

Some lower courts distinguish between plain view and open view. They apply plain view to cases in which the officer has made a "prior valid intrusion into a constitutionally protected area" (meaning when the officer is inside an enclosed space, such as a house or an apartment) and apply the term **"open view"** to instances when *the officer is out in open space (such as the street) but sees an item within an enclosed area* (State v. Stachler, 570 P.2d 1323 [1977]). The Supreme Court, however, has not made this distinction, so the discussion of plain view in this text includes the concept of open view.

6. Plain View versus Plain Feel

As discussed in chapter 3, probable cause is usually established through the use of the officer's five senses—sight, touch, smell, hearing, and taste. Plain view refers to the

AT A GLANCE

Plain View

DEFINITION: Items that are within the sight of an officer who is legally in a place from which the view is made, and who had no prior knowledge that the items were present, may properly be seized without a warrant—as long as the items are immediately recognizable as subject to seizure.

THREE REQUIREMENTS: (1) Awareness of the item through use of sense of sight, (2) the officer must be legally in the place from which the item is seen, and (3) it must be immediately apparent that the item is subject to seizure.

OTHER CONSIDERATIONS: An item that does not come under plain view may nonetheless be seized. Seizure may be justified under other legal justifications, such as probable cause and exigent circumstances.

ISSUES RAISED BY PLAIN VIEW:

- Inadvertence is no longer a plain view requirement.
- Plain view applies to open spaces.
- Plain view applies to motor vehicles.
- Plain view applies even if mechanical devices are used.
- There is no authoritative answer as to whether plain view differs from open view.
- Plain view and plain feel are different concepts.
- Plain view and plain odor are different concepts.

---

sense of sight, which is the most common way probable cause is established. Does a similar doctrine apply to the sense of touch?

Although not as well known or as extensively developed in case law as plain view, recent Court decisions have reaffirmed the existence of the **"plain feel"** (or *"plain touch"*) **doctrine.** It holds that *if an officer touches or feels something that is immediately identifiable as seizable, the object can be seized as long as such knowledge amounts to probable cause.* The most recent Court case on plain touch is Minnesota v. Dickerson, 53 CrL 2186 (1993), discussed in chapter 5 in the context of stop and frisk. The Court in *Dickerson* excluded the evidence obtained because the officer went beyond what is allowable in a pat-down frisk when he proceeded to "squeeze, slide, and manipulate" the item he felt in the suspect's jacket and which he admitted was not a dangerous weapon.

The Court, however, refused to go along with the Minnesota Supreme Court's rejection of an analogy between plain view and plain touch, saying that "the very premise of *Terry* [Terry v. Ohio, 392 U.S. 1 (1968)], after all, is that officers will be able to detect the presence of weapons through the sense of touch." The Court added, "If a police officer lawfully pats down a suspect's outer clothing and feels an object whose contour or mass makes its identity immediately apparent, there has been no invasion of the suspect's privacy beyond that already authorized by the officer's search for weapons; if the object is contraband, its warrantless seizure would be justified by the same practical considerations that inhere in the plain-view context."

The Court in *Dickerson* would likely have held the evidence admissible had the officer testified that during the pat-down he felt something that, although not a weapon, he knew from his background and experience and the totality of circumstances was contraband. That would have been a clear case of plain feel leading to probable cause.

7. Plain View versus Plain Odor

Some writers maintain that the plain view doctrine also applies to plain odor. In the **plain odor doctrine,** *if an officer smells something that is immediately recognizable as seizable, that object can be seized as long as that knowledge amounts to probable cause.* These writers cite the case of United States v. Johns, 469 U.S. 478 (1985), in which the Court said that "whether defendant ever had a privacy interest in the packages reeking of marijuana is debatable."[2] This issue has not been directly addressed by the Court; most plain view cases involve the sense of sight and, more recently, the sense of touch. In the absence of any definitive pronouncement from the Court, it is better to limit the "plain" doctrine, for now, to the twin senses of sight and touch.

II. THE OPEN FIELDS DOCTRINE

A. Open Fields Defined

The **"open fields" doctrine** holds that *items in open fields are not protected by the Fourth Amendment's guarantee against unreasonable searches and seizures, so they can properly be taken by an officer without a warrant or probable cause.* The Fourth Amendment protects only "houses, papers, and effects" against unreasonable searches and seizures. Open fields do not come under "houses, papers, and effects," so the constitutional protection does not apply. In the words of Justice Oliver Wendell Holmes, "The special protection accorded by the Fourth Amendment to the people in their persons, houses, papers, and effects is not extended to the open fields" (Hester v. United States, 265 U.S. 57 [1924]).

B. Areas Not Included in Open Fields

Certain areas come under the protection of the Fourth Amendment and therefore cannot be classified as open fields.

1. Houses

Courts have interpreted the term *houses* under the Fourth Amendment broadly, applying it to homes (owned, rented, or leased), apartments, hotel or motel rooms, hospital rooms, and even sections not generally open to the public in places of business. *Black's Law Dictionary* defines a "house" as a "structure that serves as living quarters for one or more persons or families."[3] Under this definition, a homeless person can have a "house" that is protected against unreasonable searches and seizures as long as whatever shelter there is has a reasonable expectation of privacy.

2. Curtilage

Curtilage means *"the area to which extends the intimate activity associated with the 'sanctity of a man's home, and the privacies of life'"* (Boyd v. United States, 116 U.S. 616 [1886]). In general, "curtilage has been held to include all buildings in close proximity to a dwelling, which are continually used for carrying on domestic employment; or such place as is necessary and convenient to a dwelling and is habitually used for family purposes" (United States v. Potts, 297 F.2d 68 [6th Cir. 1961]). Curtilage is considered a part of the building and is therefore protected against unreasonable searches and seizures. Items seized in the curtilage need a warrant and probable cause. Curtilage may encompass a variety of places, including the following:

- **Residential yards.** Courts disagree on whether yards are part of the curtilage. If members of the public have access to the yard at any time, it is probably not curtilage. But if only members of the family have access to it, it may be part of the curtilage.

- **Fenced areas.** A fence around a house makes the immediate environs within that fence a part of the curtilage, because the owner clearly intended for that area to be private and not open to the general public.

- **Apartment houses.** Areas of an apartment building that are used in common by all tenants are not considered part of any tenant's curtilage. However, if the apartment building is of limited size (such as a four-unit building) and each apartment has its own backyard or front yard that is not accessible to the general public, such areas would be part of the curtilage.

- **Barns and other outbuildings.** Outbuildings are usually considered part of the curtilage if they are used extensively by the family, are enclosed by a fence, or are close to the house. The farther such buildings are from the house, the less likely it is that they will be considered part of the curtilage.

- **Garages.** Garages are usually considered part of the curtilage, unless they are far from the house and seldom used.

C. The Test to Determine Curtilage: United States v. Dunn

How is curtilage to be determined? The Court has ruled that determining whether an area is considered a part of the curtilage and therefore covered by Fourth Amendment protections rests on four factors:

1. The proximity of the area to the home

2. Whether the area is in an enclosure surrounding the home

3. The nature and uses of the area

4. The steps taken to conceal the area from public view

The Court quickly added this caution, however:

> We do not suggest that combining these factors produces a finely tuned formula that, when mechanically applied, yields a "correct" answer to all extent-of-curtilage questions. Rather, these factors are useful analytical tools only to the degree that, in any given case, they bear upon the centrally relevant consideration— whether the area in question is so intimately tied to the home itself that it should be placed under the "umbrella" of Fourth Amendment protection.

Applying these factors in United States v. Dunn, 480 U.S. 294 (1987), the Court concluded that the barn in this case could not be considered part of the curtilage. In *Dunn,* after learning that a codefendant had purchased large quantities of chemicals and equipment used in the manufacture of controlled substances, drug agents obtained a warrant to place an electronic tracking beeper in some of the equipment. The beeper ultimately led agents to Dunn's farm. The farm was encircled by a perimeter fence with several interior fences of the type used to hold livestock. Without a warrant, officers entered the premises over the perimeter fence, interior fences, and a wooden fence that encircled a barn, approximately fifty yards from the respondent's home. En route to the barn, the officers crossed two barbwire fences and one wooden fence. Without entering the barn, the officers stood at a locked gate and shone a flashlight into the barn, where they observed what appeared to be a drug laboratory. Officers returned twice the following day to confirm the presence of the laboratory, each time without entering the barn. Based on information gained from these observations, officers obtained a search warrant and seized incriminating evidence from the barn.

Dunn was convicted of conspiracy to manufacture controlled substances. On appeal, he sought exclusion of the evidence, saying that (1) a barn located sixty yards from a house and fifty yards from a second fence surrounding the house is part of the curtilage and therefore could not be searched without a warrant, and (2) the officers committed trespass en route to the barn. The Court disagreed, saying that, judged in terms of the four tests (enumerated previously), this particular barn could not be considered a part of the curtilage, despite the presence of three fences. The Court added that the concept of *physical trespass is no longer the test* that determines whether the Fourth Amendment applies. Instead, the test is *whether there exists a reasonable expectation of privacy* that deserves protection. In this case, despite the presence of fences, there was none. But the Court added that, while the barn itself was part of the open field, the inside of the barn was protected by the Fourth Amendment, and so a warrant was needed for a lawful entry.[4]

The good news about the *Dunn* case is that for the first time the Court has laid out the tests lower courts should use to determine whether a barn, building, garage, or the like is part of the curtilage. The bad news is that these factors are difficult to apply with precision by trial courts. Given the existing tests, what is curtilage to one court may not be curtilage to another. Nonetheless, they are an improvement over the complete absence of a standard under which the lower courts decided cases prior to *Dunn.*

D. Aerial Surveillance of Curtilage: California v. Ciraolo

The fact that a space is part of a home curtilage does not mean it is automatically entitled to constitutional protection against any and all intrusions. In a 1986 case, the Court decided that the constitutional protection against unreasonable search and seizure is not violated by the naked-eye aerial observation by the police of a suspect's backyard, which admittedly is a part of the curtilage (California v. Ciraolo, 476 U.S. 207 [1986]). In this case, police in Santa Clara, California, received an anonymous phone tip that marijuana was being grown in Ciraolo's backyard. The backyard was shielded from public view by a six-foot outer fence and a ten-foot inner fence completely enclosing the yard. On the basis of the tip, officers trained in marijuana identification obtained a private airplane and flew over the suspect's house at an altitude of 1,000 feet. They readily identified the plants growing in the yard as marijuana. A search warrant was obtained on the basis of the naked-eye observation of one of the officers, supported by a photograph of the surrounding area taken from the airplane. The warrant was executed, and the marijuana plants were seized. In a motion to suppress the evidence, the defendant alleged that the warrantless aerial observation of the yard violated the Fourth Amendment.

The Court rejected Ciraolo's contention, saying that no Fourth Amendment right was violated. The Court admitted that he "took normal precautions to maintain his privacy" by erecting the fence, but added:

> The area is within the curtilage and does not itself bar all police observation. The Fourth Amendment protection of the home has never been extended to require law enforcement officers to shield their eyes when passing by a home on public thoroughfares. Nor does the mere fact that an individual has taken measures to restrict some views of his activities preclude an officer's observations from a public vantage point where he has a right to be and which renders the activities clearly visible. . . . The observations by Officers Shutz and Rodriguez in this case took place within public navigable airspace, in a physically nonintrusive manner; from this point they were able to observe plants readily discernible to the naked eye as marijuana. . . . On this record, we readily conclude that respondent's expectation that his garden was protected from such observation is unreasonable and is not an expectation that society is prepared to honor.

In the *Ciraolo case,* the private airplane flew over the suspect's house at an altitude of 1,000 feet to make the observations. Suppose the flight had been made by the police in a helicopter at a height of 400 feet. Would the evidence still have been admissible? The Court answered yes, saying that, as long as the police are flying at an altitude at which Federal Aviation Administration (FAA) regulations allow members of the public to fly (the FAA sets no minimum for helicopters), such aerial observation is valid because, in the absence of FAA prohibitions, the homeowner would have no reasonable expectation of privacy from such flights (Florida v. Riley, 488 U.S. 445 [1989]). Note, however, that these cases involved mere "looking" or "peering," but not entering, so the degree of intrusion is minimal.

E. Open Fields despite a Locked Gate and a "No Trespassing" Sign: Oliver v. United States

In a 1984 decision, the Supreme Court gave the open fields doctrine a broader meaning. In that case, the Court said that it is legal for the police to enter and search unoccupied or underdeveloped areas outside the curtilage without either a warrant or probable cause, as long as the place comes under the category of "fields," even if the police had to pass a locked gate and a "no trespassing" sign. The field in this case was secluded and not visible from any point of public access. The Court defined the term *open fields* to include "any unoccupied or underdeveloped area outside the curtilage"—a definition sufficiently broad to include the heavily wooded area where the defendant's marijuana crop was discovered by the police (Oliver v. United States, 466 U.S. 170 [1984]). (Read the Oliver v. United States case brief at the end of this chapter.)

The significance of *Oliver* is that it reiterates the doctrine that the "reasonable expectation of privacy" standard does not apply when the property involved is an open field. The Court stressed that steps taken to protect privacy—such as planting the marijuana on secluded land, erecting a locked gate (but with a footpath along one side), and posting "no trespassing" signs around the property—do not necessarily establish any reasonable expectation of privacy. The test, according to the Court, is not whether the individual chooses to conceal assertedly "private activity, but whether the government's intrusion infringes upon the personal and societal values protected by the Fourth Amendment." The fact that the government's intrusion upon an open field (as in this case) is a trespass according to common law does not make it a "search" in the constitutional sense, so the Fourth Amendment does not apply.

The *Oliver* case involved a warrantless observation of a marijuana patch located more than a mile from Oliver's house. The *Dunn* case, also discussed previously, involved the warrantless observation of a barn located just sixty yards from a house and fifty yards from a wooden fence that, in turn, was within a bigger perimeter fence. In both cases, the Court concluded that neither property could be considered a part of the curtilage and therefore became open field.

The *Dunn, Ciraolo,* and *Oliver* cases indicate that the concept of curtilage has become severely restricted and that of open field has been significantly expanded by the Court, giving law enforcement officials much greater leeway in search and seizure cases. The relationship among houses and buildings, curtilage, and open fields may generally be stated as follows: First comes houses and buildings, then comes curtilage, then comes open fields. Houses, buildings, and curtilage are protected by the Fourth Amendment; open fields are not.

F. Open Fields versus Plain View

1. Similarities

In each case, there is no need for a search warrant or probable cause to seize items because neither is considered a search or a seizure under the Fourth Amendment.

Open Fields

DEFINITION: Items in open fields are not protected by the Fourth Amendment guarantee against unreasonable searches and seizures, so they can be seized by an officer without a warrant or probable cause.

CURTILAGE: "The area to which extends the intimate activity associated with the sanctity of a man's home, and the privacies of life."

TEST TO DETERMINE CURTILAGE: If a person has a reasonable expectation of privacy in a place, it is part of the curtilage and is protected by the Fourth Amendment.

APPLICATIONS: Aerial surveillance of curtilage is valid. Also, an area may be open field despite a locked gate and a "no trespassing" sign.

2. Differences

Open fields and plain view differ in two basic ways: (1) Under the open fields doctrine, the seizable property is not in a house or other place to which that term applies (apartments, hotel or motel rooms, hospital rooms, places of business not open to the public, or curtilage), whereas items under plain view are found in those places; and (2) under the open fields doctrine, items hidden from view may be seized—something not permitted under plain view, which limits seizure to items within sight of the police officer.

III. ABANDONMENT
A. Abandonment Defined

Abandonment is defined as *the giving up of a thing or item absolutely, without limitation as to any particular person or purpose.* Abandonment implies the giving up of possession or ownership or of any reasonable expectation of privacy. Abandoned property is not protected by the Fourth Amendment guarantee against unreasonable searches and seizures, so it may be seized without warrant or probable cause. For example, if a car is left in a public parking lot for so long that it is reasonable to assume that the car has been abandoned, the police may seize the car without a warrant.

Abandoned property does not belong to anyone, because the owner has given it up—in some cases involuntarily (such as when items are thrown out of a house or car for fear of discovery by the police). Persons who find such property, including the police, may therefore keep it and introduce it as evidence in a criminal proceeding. For example, suppose the police approach a group of juveniles in an apartment complex parking lot to quiet them down because of complaints from nearby residents. One of the juveniles throws away an envelope, which is retrieved by the police and later ascertained to contain drugs. The recovery is legal, and the evidence is usable in court.

B. Factors Determining When Items Are Considered Abandoned

Abandonment is frequently difficult to determine, but the two basic guidelines are (1) where the property is left and (2) what the intent is.

1. Where the Property Is Left

a. Property Left in an Open Field or Public Place Property discarded or thrown away in an open field or public place is considered abandoned. For example, drugs discarded by a suspect at an airport restroom when she realizes she is under surveillance or drugs thrown by the suspect from a speeding car when he realizes that the police are closing in would be considered abandoned.

b. Property Left on Private Premises Property may sometimes be considered abandoned on private premises if circumstances indicate that the occupant has left the premises. For example, if a suspect pays his bill and checks out of a hotel room, items left behind that are of no apparent value but that the police can use as evidence—such as photographs or clippings—are considered abandoned property and may be seized by the police.

If the occupant has not left the premises, there is no abandonment. For example, suppose that, while "looking around" the house after receiving valid consent, the police see the occupant grab a package containing marijuana from the kitchen table and throw it into the bedroom. That package might be seized by the police, but not under the abandonment doctrine, because the property is still in the house and the occupant has not left the premises. The seizure might still be justified under probable cause and exigent circumstance.

c. Trash or Garbage The Court has decided that garbage left outside the curtilage of a home for regular collection is considered abandoned and therefore may be seized by the police without a warrant (California v. Greenwood, 486 U.S. 35 [1988]). In this case, the Court said that "having deposited their garbage in an area particularly suited for public inspection . . . [owners] could have no reasonable expectation of privacy in the inculpatory items that they discarded" (here, items indicating narcotics use). There is no Fourth Amendment protection if trash is left in an area accessible to the public, so no warrant or probable cause is needed. By contrast, leaving trash in the curtilage of a home (not accessible to the public but where trash collectors are allowed to enter) or on one's own property would not be considered an abandonment, so Fourth Amendment protections would apply. This means that the police would need a warrant to enter the premises and retrieve that trash.

May trash obtained by trash collectors be legally turned over to the police? Once trash is gathered by trash collectors, it loses its reasonable expectation of privacy even if

HIGHLIGHT

Trash Collection and Privacy

. . . a person does not retain a reasonable expectation of privacy in trash once it leaves the curtilage. A trash collector who enters the curtilage to collect trash subsequently turned over to police is considered a private actor for Fourth Amendment purposes when acting in the scope of a routine trash collection.

Law enforcement officers who request assistance from trash collectors should ensure that they do nothing that exceeds the routine performance of their duties.

Source: Thomas V. Kukura, "Trash, Inspections, and the Fourth Amendment," *FBI Law Enforcement Bulletin*, February 1991, p. 32.

obtained inside a curtilage. It may therefore be voluntarily turned over by trash collectors to the police. Problems may arise, however, if this is done on request by the police. In these cases, trash collectors may be considered as having acted as agents of the police and doing something the police themselves cannot legally do. Court decisions have not addressed this issue authoritatively, so police officers are cautioned to seek advice from legal counsel before resorting to this course of action.

2. What the Intent Is

The intent to abandon is generally determined objectively—by what a person does. Throwing items away in a public place shows an intent to abandon; denial of ownership when questioned also constitutes abandonment. For example, suppose that, when questioned by the police, a suspect denies that the confiscated wallet belongs to him. If, in fact, the suspect owns that wallet, it may now be considered abandoned. Failure to claim something over a long period of time also indicates abandonment—and the longer the period, the clearer the intent. But the prosecution must prove that there was, in fact, an intent to abandon the item.

C.   Abandonment of Motor Vehicles

An article in the *FBI Law Enforcement Bulletin* sheds light on the issue of motor vehicle abandonment. The writer states that courts consider "somewhat different" factors in determining whether a vehicle has been abandoned or not. He identifies four key factors:[5]

- **"Flight from the vehicle by the person in an apparent effort to avoid apprehension by law enforcement."** Quoting a lower court decision, the writer says, "When Tate fled the scene of the murder, leaving the van unoccupied and unlocked, he abandoned his expectation of privacy in the van and its contents."

- **"Where, and for how long, a vehicle is left unattended."** Saying that "a person who leaves a car in a traveled lane of a busy highway should expect the police to remove the car with some promptness," the author adds, "the more difficult abandonment question is presented when a person parks a vehicle lawfully. Unless other factors are present, such as flight, abandonment is only found in such cases where the vehicle is parked on someone else's property either without authorization or for a period of time that exceeds the permission granted."

- **"The condition in which the vehicle is left unattended."** Quoting a lower court decision, the writer says, "One who chooses to leave luggage in an unlocked burned-out automobile at the side of a highway in the country can fairly be thought to have a much lower expectation of privacy."

- **"Denial, by a person who is present, of possession or ownership of the vehicle."** The example used is the case of three men who, when approached by customs agents after the three had loaded the contents of two boxes into the rear of a Chevrolet station wagon, denied any knowledge of the station wagon or its cargo (understandably, because the agents discovered thirty milligrams of cocaine in the car). The writer quotes the Court of Appeals for the Eleventh Circuit, which concluded that the defendants "effectively abandoned any fourth amendment rights he possessed in the station wagon and its contents."

D. The Legality of Police Actions

The activities of the police that led to the abandonment must be legal, or else the evidence obtained is not admissible in court. For example, suppose the police, for no justifiable reason, decide to search a pedestrian one evening. Terrified, the pedestrian throws away what turns out to be a bag of cocaine. The cocaine cannot be used in evidence because the abandonment was caused by illegal police conduct. Or suppose police officers stop a motor vehicle on the highway for no justifiable reason. Just before the vehicle stops, the driver throws away a pistol that is later ascertained to have been a weapon used in a robbery. The pistol is not admissible in evidence because the abandonment was triggered by illegal police conduct.

E. Abandonment versus Plain View

1. Similarities

In both cases, there is no need for a search warrant or probable cause, because both are outside the protection of the Fourth Amendment.

2. Differences

Abandonment means that the owner or possessor of the item has given up ownership prior to its being seized by the police. The giving up of ownership or possession may have taken place earlier (as in the case of abandoned barns) or just seconds before the evidence is obtained by the police (as when contraband is thrown out of a car during a chase). By contrast, under plain view, ownership or possession has not been given up; it

Abandonment

DEFINITION: The giving up of a thing or item absolutely, without limitation as to any particular person or purpose.

FACTORS DETERMINING WHEN ITEMS ARE CONSIDERED ABANDONED: (1) Property left in an open field or public place is abandoned; (2) for property left on private premises, it depends on whether the occupant has left the premises; (3) for trash or garbage, it depends on where it is left; and (4) intent to abandon is determined by what a person does.

MOTOR VEHICLES: Abandonment of motor vehicles is determined by four key factors: (1) flight from the vehicle, (2) where and for how long a vehicle is left unattended, (3) the condition in which the vehicle is left unattended, and (4) denial of possession or ownership of the vehicle.

POLICE ACTIONS: Police actions must be legal; otherwise, evidence is not admissible.

---

simply has no Fourth Amendment protection, unless ownership or possession has been established. The item is seized by the police without any form of abandonment by the owner or possessor.

IV. ELECTRONIC SURVEILLANCE

Electronic surveillance is *the use of electronic devices to monitor a person's activities or whereabouts.* It is a type of search and seizure and can take various forms, such as wiretapping or bugging. This form of surveillance is regulated strictly by the U.S. Constitution, federal law, and state statutes. The Fourth Amendment prohibition against unreasonable searches and seizures protects a person's conversation from unreasonable intrusion. Federal and state laws further limit what the police can do.

A. The Old Concept—Constitutional If There Is No Trespass: Olmstead v. United States

The first major case in electronic surveillance was Olmstead v. United States, 277 U.S. 438 (1928). *Olmstead* involved a bootlegging operation against which evidence was gathered through the use of wiretaps on telephone conversations. The Court held that wiretapping did not violate the Fourth Amendment unless there was "some trespass into a constitutionally protected area." Under this concept, evidence obtained through a bugging device placed against a wall to overhear conversation in an adjoining office was admissible, because there was no actual trespass. Said the Court, "The Amendment does not forbid what was done here. There was no searching. There was no seizure. The evidence was secured by the use of the sense of hearing and that only. There was no entry of the houses or offices of the defendants." This **old concept of electronic surveillance** prevailed from 1928 to 1967.

In 1934, Congress passed the Federal Communications Act, which provided that "no person not being authorized by the sender shall intercept any communication and divulge or publish the existence, contents, substance, purport, effect or meaning of such intercepted communication to any person." In 1937, the Court interpreted this provision as forbidding federal agents, as well as other persons, from intercepting and disclosing telephone messages by the use of wiretaps (Nardone v. United States, 302 U.S. 379 [1937]). In 1942, the Court held that wiretap evidence could be used against persons other than those whose conversations had been overheard and whose Fourth Amendment rights were therefore violated (Goldstein v. United States, 316 U.S. 114 [1942]). That same year, the Court also held that the use of a "bug" (an electronic listening device but not a wiretap on telephone lines) was not in violation of the Federal Communications Act, because the act applied only to actual interference with communication wires and telephone lines.

In 1961, the Court took a tougher view on electronic surveillance in the case of Silverman v. United States, 365 U.S. 505 (1961). In *Silverman,* the Court held that the Fourth Amendment was violated by the use of a "spike-mike" driven into a building wall without a warrant to allow police to overhear conversations within the building. The fact that the device, although tiny, actually penetrated the building wall was held by the Court to be sufficient to constitute physical intrusion in violation of the Fourth Amendment. In 1964, the Court further decided that evidence obtained by the police using an electronic device attached to the exterior wall of a building was illegally obtained (Clinton v. Virginia, 377 U.S. 158 [1964]). These decisions eroded the impact of the *Olmstead* decision.

B. The New Concept—Unconstitutional If It Violates a Reasonable Expectation of Privacy: Katz v. United States

The old concept of "some trespass into a constitutionally protected area" was abandoned by the Court in 1967 in Katz v. United States, 389 U.S. 347 (1967). (Read the Katz v. United States brief at the end of this chapter.)

Under the **new concept of electronic surveillance** enunciated in *Katz, a search occurs whenever there is police activity that violates a "reasonable expectation of privacy."* Such activity includes any form of electronic surveillance, with or without actual physical trespass or wiretap. In the *Katz* case, the police attached an electronic listening device to the outside of a public telephone booth that the defendant was using. Although there was no tapping of the line, the Court held that the listening device violated the defendant's reasonable expectation that his conversations, held in a public telephone booth, were private. The Court said that what Katz "sought to exclude when he entered the booth was not the intruding eye—it was the uninvited

The Significance of <u>Katz</u>

The *Katz* case is significant because it makes the Fourth Amendment "portable": It follows the individual wherever he or she goes. In the words of the Court, the Fourth Amendment "protects people, not places." Knowing this is fundamental to understanding the extent of the protection afforded by the Fourth Amendment prohibition against unreasonable searches and seizures. A person enjoys the protection of the Fourth Amendment not only at home, but also in a public place if there is a reasonable expectation of privacy which is acceptable to the public.

ear." He did not shed his right to do so simply because he made his calls from a place where he might be seen. Thus, the key phrase in determining intrusion is "reasonable expectation of privacy."

In a concurring opinion in *Katz,* which lower courts used and the Supreme Court itself later adopted, Justice John Harland specified two requirements for a "reasonable expectation of privacy" to exist: (1) The person must have exhibited an *actual expectation of privacy,* and (2) The expectation must be *one that society is prepared to recognize as "reasonable."* An example of the first requirement is somebody who cups the mouthpiece with her hand and talks in a subdued voice while using a telephone in a public place. By contrast, somebody using a public telephone in an airport who talks loudly and does not care who hears what he is saying does not exhibit any actual expectation of privacy. What society is prepared to recognize as reasonable evolves over time, particularly as technology and concepts of privacy change. But this will always be a question of fact that will ultimately be determined by a judge or a jury.

Aside from popularizing and giving substance to the phrase "reasonable expectation of privacy," (the current standard used in Fourth Amendment cases), the *Katz* case is also significant because it makes the Fourth Amendment protection "portable," meaning that its protections accompany the individual wherever he or she goes. In the words of the Court, the Fourth Amendment "protects people, not places." This concept is key to understanding the full extent of the protection afforded by the Fourth Amendment against any and all unreasonable searches and seizures, not just in electronic surveillance cases. The question always asked in Fourth Amendment cases is: Was there a violation of a person's reasonable expectation of privacy? If there was, then the Fourth Amendment applies; conversely, if there was no such violation, the actions of the law enforcement agents are deemed valid and constitutional.

C. Federal Law: Title III of the Omnibus Crime Control and Safe Streets Act of 1968

1. The Main Provision

The use of wiretaps, electronic surveillance, and bugging devices is largely governed by the provisions of **Title III of the Omnibus Crime Control and Safe Streets Act of**

The Justification for a Reasonable Expectation of Privacy

". . . what he [Katz] sought to exclude when he entered the booth was not the intruding eye—it was the uninvited ear. He did not shed his right to do so simply because he made his calls from a place where he might be seen. No less than an individual in a business office, in a friend's apartment, or in a taxicab, a person in a telephone booth may rely upon the protection of the Fourth Amendment. One who occupies it, shuts the door behind him, and pays the toll that permits him to place a call is surely entitled to assume that the words he utters into the mouthpiece will not be broadcast to the world. To read the Constitution more narrowly is to ignore the vital role that the public telephone has come to play in private communication."

Katz v. United States, 389 U.S. 347 (1967).

1968. That law is long and complicated, but its main provision may be summarized as follows: Law enforcement officers nationwide, federal and state, cannot tap or intercept wire communications or use electronic devices to intercept private conversations, except in one of two situations:

- **If there is a court order authorizing the wiretap.** The state, however, must have passed a law authorizing the issuance of a court order; without such a law, courts are not authorized to issue a judicial order.

- **If consent is given by one of the parties.** The exception is if such recording is prohibited by state law even with the consent given by one of the parties.

a. Court Orders If the legislature, federal or state, has passed a law authorizing the issuance of a court order, a judge may then issue such an order as long as the following four conditions are present:

1. There is probable cause to believe that a specific individual has committed one of the crimes enumerated under the act.

2. There is probable cause to believe that the interception will furnish evidence about the crime.

3. Normal investigative procedures have been tried and have failed or reasonably appear likely to fail or to be dangerous.

4. There is probable cause to believe that the facilities or the place from which or where the interception is to be made are used in connection with the offense or are linked to the individual under suspicion.

Once law enforcement officials have obtained judicial authorization to intercept wire or oral communications, they do not have to obtain another judicial authorization to enable them to enter the premises to install the listening device. Such authorization comes with the court order.

b. Consent by One of the Parties Consent is one of the exceptions to the court order requirements under Title III and has also been exempted from the warrant requirement by several court decisions. However, some states, by law, expressly prohibit, on pain of civil consequences or criminal prosecution, electronic eavesdropping or wiretapping even if consent is given by one of the parties.[6] Such statutes take precedence over any consent given by one of the parties and must therefore be followed. A recent example is Linda Tripp's taping of her conversations with Monica Lewinsky during the Clinton-Lewinsky affair. Tripp's recordings constituted crucial evidence in the impeachment proceedings against President Clinton in 1999. Later, however, Tripp was indicted in Maryland on charges of illegal wiretapping, based on a "rarely used Maryland law that makes it a crime to record telephone conversations without the consent of all parties."[7] Maryland law requires that the person doing the recording knew that it was illegal without the other person's consent and yet went ahead and did it anyway.

The Court has concluded that the Constitution does not prohibit a government agent from using an electronic device to record a telephone conversation between two parties with the consent of one party to the conversation (United States v. White, 401 U.S. 745 [1971]). The Court has also ruled that the Fourth Amendment does not protect persons from supposed friends who turn out to be police informants. Thus, a person assumes the risk that whatever he or she says to others may be reported by them to the police, there being no police "search" in such cases. It follows that, if the supposed friend allows the police to listen in on a telephone conversation with the suspect, there is no violation of the suspect's Fourth Amendment rights. The evidence obtained is admissible because of the consent given by one party to the conversation (On Lee v. United States, 343 U.S. 747 [1952]).

The Fourth Amendment is not violated when a police informant carries into the suspect's home an electronic device that transmits the conversation to the police outside. But the evidence obtained is not admissible if the defendant has been charged with an offense and has obtained a lawyer. In one case, the Court said that such evidence was inadmissible, not because the right to protection against unreasonable search and seizure under the Fourth Amendment was violated but because the right to counsel under the Sixth Amendment was violated (Massiah v. United States, 377 U.S. 201 [1964]). Therefore, if the suspect does not yet have a lawyer, the evidence obtained from this procedure is admissible because the right to counsel in such types of questioning applies only after a lawyer has been obtained.

2. The Constitutionality of Title III

The constitutionality of Title III has not been directly tested in the Supreme Court, but lower courts have held it to be constitutional. Also, in 1972, the Court unanimously rejected the contention of the Nixon administration that the provisions of Title III did not require judicial approval of warrants for wiretaps or surveillance in national security cases (United States v. U.S. District Court, 407 U.S. 297 [1972]). In 1974, the Court in effect nullified hundreds of criminal prosecutions based on evidence obtained by surveillance when it held that then–Attorney General John Mitchell had not himself signed the applications for the warrant authorizing the surveillance and had allowed an aide other than the designated assistant attorney general to approve the application (United States v. Giordano, 416 U.S. 505 [1974]). In 1979, the Court held that, because Congress must have recognized that most electronic bugs can be installed only by agents who secretly enter the premises, warrants authorizing such surveillance need not explicitly authorize entry.

3. State Laws and Title III

As discussed previously, under Title III of the Omnibus Crime Control and Safe Streets Act of 1968, an electronic surveillance is illegal even if authorized by state or local judge if there is no law passed by the state legislature authorizing the judge to issue the order. Such enabling legislation has not been passed in twenty-eight states, including such big states as California, Illinois, Pennsylvania, Michigan, and Ohio.[8] It is therefore important that police officers ascertain whether electronic surveillance is specifically authorized in their state and, if so, what procedures are to be followed. Without an enabling state statute, a police officer faces possible federal criminal prosecution for unauthorized electronic surveillance, punishable by a maximum of five years of imprisonment and/or a $10,000 fine. Moreover, evidence obtained in violation of this federal law is not admissible in any federal or state proceeding.

States may pass laws *further limiting, but not broadening,* the restrictions imposed by Title III. For example, although Title III allows the use of evidence obtained with the consent of one party to the conversation, a state statute may prohibit such use without the consent of both parties. In states having that prohibition, the evidence is not admissible in state court for criminal prosecution.

4. Berger v. New York and Title III

If the language of a state law authorizing eavesdropping is too broad in scope, it intrudes into a constitutionally protected area and therefore violates the Fourth Amendment. An example of such a statute was a New York law that the Supreme Court declared unconstitutional because it was too broad and did not contain sufficient safeguards against unwarranted intrusions on constitutional rights (Berger v. New York, 388 U.S. 41 [1967]). *Berger* is significant because it specifies six requirements for a warrant authorizing any form of electronic surveillance to be valid:

1. The warrant must describe with *particularity* the conversations that are to be overheard.

2. There must be a showing of *probable cause* to believe that a specific crime has been or is being committed.

3. The wiretap must be for a *limited period,* although extensions may be obtained upon adequate showing.

4. The *suspects* whose conversations are to be overheard *must be named* in the judicial order.

5. A *return must be made to the court,* showing what conversations were intercepted.

6. *The wiretapping must terminate when the desired information has been obtained.*

The *Berger* case was decided in 1967, one year before the enactment of Title III of the Omnibus Crime Control and Safe Streets Act. Since then, these six requirements have been enacted into law by Title III, along with the other provisions discussed here. *Berger* is important because it tells us that overly broad eavesdropping statutes are unconstitutional and also lays out what state statutes need to include if they are to be declared valid.

D. Federal Law: The Electronic Communications and Privacy Act of 1986 (ECPA)

Title III of the Omnibus Crime Control and Safe Streets Act of 1968 continues to be the main federal law on electronic surveillance. In 1986, however, the U.S. Congress passed the **Electronic Communications and Privacy Act (ECPA),** which *amends and supplements the provisions of Title III.* A series of law-oriented articles in the *FBI Law Enforcement Bulletin* discusses the main provisions of that law.[9] According to this author, ECPA contains three provisions that relate to federal, state, and local law enforcement work:

1. "It amends the law of nonconsensual interception of wire communications [wiretaps] and oral communications by a concealed microphone or electronic device [bugs]."

2. "It sets forth specific procedures for obtaining authorization to use pen registers [telephone decoders], which record the numbers dialed from a telephone, and trap and trace devices, which ascertain the origin of a telephone call."

3. "It prescribes the procedure law enforcement officers must follow to obtain stored communications and records relating to communications services, such as telephone toll records and unlisted telephone subscriber information."[10]

E. Federal Law: The Communications Assistance for Law Enforcement Act of 1994

Do users of cellular telephones have a "reasonable expectation of privacy," thereby enjoying protection under the Fourth Amendment? Although the Supreme Court has not resolved this issue, lower courts have said no. The rationale is that cell phones—"unlike standard wire phones and sophisticated cellular devices—transmit radio signals between a handset and a base unit that occasionally can be intercepted by other cordless telephones or even by short-wave radio sets."[11] In the words of one observer,

Cellular Telephones

Conversations on cordless telephones are not considered private. Conversations on cordless telephones can be monitored by others. Hence, an individual does not have a reasonable expectation of privacy when using a cordless telephone. The only possible exception is if monitoring by others is specifically prohibited by law.

"Those who seek privacy protection for their conversations on cordless telephones should remember that the airwaves are public."[12] Despite the public nature of cell phone conversations, federal and local agents at present can monitor those calls only with a warrant.

Recognizing the importance of and growing concern over cell phones, the U.S. Congress passed the Communications Assistance for Law Enforcement Act of 1994. Its stated purpose is "to make clear a telecommunications carrier's duty to cooperate in the interception of communications for law enforcement purposes, and for other purposes." Its provisions require the cell phone industry to design its systems to comply with new standards that would make it easier for the FBI to monitor calls. The act also left it to the Federal Communications Commission (FCC) to determine specific standards related to the FBI's authority to monitor more than just cell phone conversations. After years of negotiations, the FCC, in August 1999, announced rules that expanded the power of law enforcement agents to keep track of conversations and locate suspects. Among other things, the 1999 regulations authorize government agents to (1) determine the general location of a cell phone user by identifying which cellular antenna was used by the phone company to transmit the beginning and end of any call under surveillance, (2) identify all callers on a conference call and monitor such conversations even after the target of the inquiry is no longer part of the conversation, and (3) determine if suspects are making use of such cell phone features as call forwarding and call waiting.[13]

These regulations go further than simply monitoring the content of the call. Law enforcement agencies say that this added authorization is necessary for them to be able to keep up with the increased popularity of cell phones. The number of intercepted communications approved by federal and state courts over the last decade has nearly doubled, reaching 1,329 in 1998, mostly involving drug and terrorism cases.[14] While these new regulations are applauded by law enforcement agencies, they have been greeted with dismay by various sectors that feel they unduly intrude into an individual's right to privacy.

F. Electronic Devices That Do Not Intercept Communication

Some electronic devices gather information (such as a suspect's location) but do not necessarily intercept communication. These devices do not come under Title III coverage, nor are they governed strictly by the concept of a reasonable expectation of privacy under the Fourth Amendment. Pen registers and beepers are two examples.

AT A GLANCE

Electronic Surveillance

DEFINITION: The use of electronic devices to monitor a person's activities or whereabouts.

OLD CONCEPT: Constitutional if there was no trespass into a constitutionally protected area (Olmstead v. United States).

NEW CONCEPT: Unconstitutional if the police activity violates a reasonable expectation of privacy, even if there is no trespass into a constitutionally protected area (Katz v. United States).

THREE FEDERAL LAWS ON ELECTRONIC SURVEILLANCE:

- Title III of the Omnibus Crime Control and Safe Streets Act of 1968—forbids law enforcement officers from tapping or intercepting wire communications or using electronic devices to intercept private conversations, except if (1) there is a court order authorizing the wiretap and (2) consent is given by one of the parties.

- The Electronic Communications and Privacy Act of 1986 (ECPA)—(1) amends the law of nonconsensual interception of wire communications and oral communications by a concealed microphone or electronic device, (2) specifies procedures for obtaining authorization to use pen registers, and (3) prescribes the procedure law enforcement officers must follow to obtain stored communications and records relating to communications services, such as telephone toll records and unlisted telephone subscriber information.

- The Communications Assistance for Law Enforcement Act of 1994—governs the use of cellular telephones through regulations passed by the Federal Communications Commission. New 1999 regulations allow government agents to (1) determine the general location of a cell phone user by identifying which cellular antenna was used by the phone company to transmit the beginning and end of any call under surveillance, (2) identify all callers on a conference call and monitor such conversations even after the target of the inquiry is no longer part of the conversation; and (3) determine if suspects are making use of such cell phone features as call forwarding and call waiting.

EXCEPTION: Monitoring telephone conversations of inmates in prisons and jails is allowed.

1. Pen Registers

The Fourth Amendment does not require that the police obtain judicial authorization before using **pen registers,** which *record the numbers dialed from a particular telephone.* In Smith v. Maryland, 442 U.S. 735 (1979), the Court held that not every use of an electronic device to gather information is governed by the Constitution. Pen registers gather information but do not necessarily intercept communication, so they do not come under Fourth Amendment protection. The Court gave two reasons for this decision. First, it is doubtful that telephone users in general have any expectation of privacy regarding the numbers they dial, since they typically know that the telephone company has facilities for recording all phone numbers dialed and in fact records them routinely for various legitimate business and billing purposes. Second, even if the petitioner did harbor some subjective expectation of privacy, this expectation is not one that society is prepared to recognize as reasonable. When the petitioner voluntarily conveyed numerical information to the phone company and "exposed" that information to its equipment in the normal course of business, he assumed the risk that the company would reveal the information to the police.

The Court has held that the police may obtain a court order to require the telephone company to assist in installing the pen register (United States v. New York Telephone Company, 434 U.S. 159 [1977]). Note, however, that ECPA, discussed previously, requires law enforcement agencies to obtain a court order (instead of a wiretap order) and specifies the procedure to be followed for obtaining that order. In sum, the Fourth Amendment does not require the police to obtain judicial authorization before using pen registers, but federal law requires it and sets the procedure for obtaining it.

2. Electronic Beepers

The use of a beeper to keep track of a person traveling on public roads does not constitute a search, because a person has no reasonable expectation of privacy when traveling on a public thoroughfare (United States v. Knotts, 460 U.S. 276 [1983]). In a subsequent case that same year, the Court said that the warrantless monitoring of a beeper (which was installed by the police in an ether can and later delivered to the defendants), after the device had been unwittingly taken into a private residence, violated the Fourth Amendment rights of the residents and others. Nonetheless, the Court concluded that the evidence obtained could not be excluded, because there was ample probable cause, aside from the information that had been obtained as a result of the beeper, to justify the issuance of a warrant. In sum, beepers can be used legally to monitor the movements of a suspect in a public place but not in a private residence (United States v. Karo, 468 U.S. 1705 [1984]).

G. Recording Devices in Prisons and Jails

Monitoring telephone conversations of inmates in prisons or jails, without a court order, is allowed as long as its purpose is the preservation of institutional order and the maintenance of security. Such monitoring cannot be carried out, however, "for the specific purpose of listening for evidence of a crime."[15] Although the issue has not been decided by the Supreme Court, monitoring is allowed for two compelling reasons: (1) the diminished constitutional rights, including the right to privacy, of inmates in prisons and jails, and (2) institutional safety and security. Fishing for evidence of crime, however, goes beyond institutional needs and is therefore disallowed.

Summary

The "plain view" doctrine, the "open fields" doctrine, abandonment, and electronic surveillance have in common some form of "taking" by the government of something that belongs to, or used to belong to, somebody. They differ in concept, legal rules, and practice.

The plain view doctrine states that items within the sight of an officer, who is legally in a place from which the view is made, may properly be seized without a warrant—as long as such items are immediately recognizable as subject to seizure. The requirements for the plain view doctrine are that (1) the item must be within the officer's line of sight, (2) the officer must be legally in the place from which the item is seen, and (3) the item must be immediately recognizable as subject to seizure. Inadvertence, once considered a requirement for plain view, has recently been rejected by the Court. Court decisions have also recognized the plain feel doctrine, but whether there is a plain odor doctrine is still an open question.

The open fields doctrine holds that items in open fields may be legally taken by an officer without a warrant or probable cause, because they are not protected by the Fourth Amendment. A curtilage is considered part of a house and is therefore protected by the constitutional requirements of a warrant and probable cause. However, the Court has recently restricted the concept of curtilage and expanded the extent of open fields.

Abandonment means the giving up of a thing or item absolutely. Abandoned property may be seized without a warrant, because it no longer belongs to anyone and therefore does not enjoy a reasonable expectation of privacy.

Electronic surveillance is governed by the Constitution, federal law, and state statutes. The Fourth Amendment protects communication if the person has a reasonable expectation of privacy. Three federal laws govern the use by federal, state, or local law enforcement agencies of electronic surveillance: Title III of the Omnibus Crime Control and Safe Streets Act of 1968, the Electronic Communications and Privacy Act of 1986 (ECPA), and the Communications Assistance for Law Enforcement Act of 1994.

Review Questions

1. What is the plain view doctrine? Discuss its three basic requirements.

2. Explain what is meant by the "immediately apparent" requirement of the plain view doctrine.

3. What is inadvertence? Is it currently a plain view requirement?

4. Distinguish between plain view and open view.

5. In what ways are plain view and plain touch similar? In what ways are they dissimilar?

6. What is the open fields doctrine?

7. What is a curtilage? How is curtilage determined?

8. Is trash or garbage considered abandoned? Discuss.

9. Distinguish between the old and the new concepts of electronic surveillance.

10. What did the U.S. Supreme Court say in the *Katz* case? Why is *Katz* important to our understanding of when a warrant is needed in search and seizure cases?

11. Discuss the extent and scope of the current law on bugging and wiretapping.

12. "Electronic surveillance by law enforcement officers is always valid if there is a court order authorizing it." Is that statement true or false? Justify your answer.

Key Terms and Definitions

abandonment: The giving up of a thing or item absolutely, without limitation as to any particular person or purpose. It implies the giving up of possession or ownership or of any reasonable expectation of privacy.

curtilage: "The area to which extends the intimate activity associated with the 'sanctity of a man's home and the privacies of life.'"

Electronic Communications and Privacy Act of 1986 (ECPA): An act passed by Congress modifying and supplementing Title III of the Omnibus Crime Control and Safe Streets Act of 1968.

electronic surveillance: The use of electronic devices to monitor a person's activities or whereabouts.

inadvertence: The concept that, to come under the plain view doctrine, the evidence must be discovered by the officer accidentally; the officer must have had no prior knowledge that the evidence was present in the place. Inadvertence is no longer required by the plain view doctrine.

new concept of electronic surveillance: The idea that electronic surveillance constitutes a search under the Fourth Amendment if the police activity violates a person's "reasonable expectation of privacy."

old concept of electronic surveillance: The idea that electronic surveillance does not violate the Fourth Amendment unless there was "some trespass into a constitutionally protected area."

open fields doctrine: The doctrine that items in open fields are not protected by the Fourth Amendment guarantee against unreasonable searches and seizures, so they can properly be seized by an officer without a warrant or probable cause.

open view: The phrase used to describe the circumstances of an officer who is out in open space (such as out on the streets) but sees an item within an enclosed area.

pen register: An electronic device that records the numbers dialed from a particular telephone; installed on the property of the telephone company rather than at the place where a suspect has access to the telephone.

plain feel doctrine: The doctrine that if an officer touches or feels something that is immediately recognizable as seizable, the object can be seized as long as such knowledge amounts to probable cause.

plain odor doctrine: The doctrine that if an officer smells something that is immediately recognizable as seizable, that object can be seized as long as such knowledge amounts to probable cause.

plain view doctrine: The doctrine that items that are within the sight of an officer who is legally in the place from which the view is made, and who had no prior knowledge that the items were present, may properly be seized without a warrant —as long as the items are immediately recognizable as subject to seizure.

Title III of the Omnibus Crime Control and Safe Streets Act of 1968: The federal law that law enforcement officers nationwide, federal and state, cannot tap or intercept wire communications or use electronic devices to intercept private conversations, except if (1) there is a court order authorizing the wiretap or (2) consent is given by one of the parties.

Principles of Cases

Arizona v. Hicks, 480 U.S. 321 (1987) The "immediately apparent" requirement of the plain view doctrine must be based on probable cause, not on any lesser degree of certainty such as reasonable suspicion.

Atwell v. United States, 414 F.2d 136 (1969) Inasmuch as the protection of the Fourth Amendment against unreasonable searches and seizures does not extend to open fields, there is no unreasonable search. Moreover, even if the officers were trespassing on private property, a trespass does not itself constitute an illegal search.

Berger v. New York, 388 U.S. 41 (1967) A valid warrant authorizing any form of electronic surveillance, including wiretapping, must satisfy certain stringent requirements.

Boyd v. United States, 116 U.S. 616 (1986) Curtilage is the area to which extends the intimate activity associated with the sanctity of a man's home and the privacies of life.

California v. Ciraolo, 476 U.S. 207 (1986) The constitutional protection against unreasonable search and seizure is not violated by the naked-eye aerial observation by the police of a suspect's backyard, which is admittedly a part of the curtilage.

California v. Greenwood, 486 U.S. 35 (1988) Garbage left outside the curtilage of a home for regular collection is considered abandoned and therefore may be seized by the police without a warrant.

Clinton v. Virginia, 377 U.S. 158 (1964) Evidence obtained by the police using an electronic device attached to the exterior wall of a building is inadmissible.

Florida v. Riley, 488 U.S. 445 (1989) Evidence obtained by the police in a helicopter flight at a 400-feet altitude is admissible, because such flights are allowed by FAA regulations, so the homeowner would have no reasonable expectation of privacy from such flights.

Goldstein v. United States, 316 U.S. 114 (1942) Wiretap evidence can be used against persons other than those whose conversations were overheard and whose Fourth Amendment rights were therefore violated.

Harris v. United States, 390 U.S. 234 (1968) Objects falling within the plain view of an officer who has a right to be in a position to have that view are subject to seizure and may be introduced in evidence.

Hester v. United States, 265 U.S. 57 (1924) The special protection accorded by the Fourth Amendment to people in their persons, houses, papers, and effects is not extended to open fields.

Horton v. California, 496 U.S. 128 (1990) The Fourth Amendment does not prohibit the warrantless seizure of evidence in plain view, even though the discovery of the evidence was not inadvertent.

Illinois v. Andreas, 463 U.S. 765 (1983) The plain view doctrine is grounded on the proposition that, once police are lawfully in a position to observe an item firsthand, its owner's privacy interest in that item is lost; the owner may retain the incidents of title and possession but not privacy.

Katz v. United States, 389 U.S. 347 (1967) Any form of electronic surveillance, including wiretapping, that violates a reasonable expectation of privacy constitutes a search. No actual physical trespass is required.

Massiah v. United States, 377 U.S. 201 (1964) When a police informer carries into the suspect's home an electronic device that transmits the conversation to the police outside, the evidence obtained is not admissible if the defendant was questioned without his or her lawyer by police after the defendant has been charged and has obtained a lawyer.

Minnesota v. Dickerson, 53 CrL 2186 (1993) Although the evidence in this case was not admissible because the officer went beyond what is allowable in frisk cases, the Court said that officers may detect the presence of contraband through the sense of touch and confiscate it if probable cause exists.

Nardone v. United States, 302 U.S. 379 (1937) The Court interpreted the 1934 Federal Communications Act as forbidding federal agents, as well as other persons, from intercepting and disclosing telephone messages by the use of wiretaps.

Oliver v. United States, 466 U.S. 170 (1984) A place that is posted with a "no trespassing" sign, has a locked gate (with a footpath around it), and is located more than a mile from the owner's house has no reasonable expectation of privacy and is considered an open field, unprotected by the Fourth Amendment.

Olmstead v. United States, 277 U.S. 438 (1928)
Wiretapping does not violate the Fourth Amendment unless there is some trespass into a "constitutionally protected area." Under this concept, evidence obtained through a bugging device placed against a wall to overhear conversation in an adjoining office is admissible, because there is no actual trespass. (*Note:* This doctrine was expressly overruled by the Court in the *Katz* case.)

On Lee v. United States, 343 U.S. 747 (1952)
There is no violation of a suspect's Fourth Amendment rights if his or her supposed friend allows the police to listen in on a telephone conversation; the evidence thereby obtained is admissible in court.

Silverman v. United States, 365 U.S. 505 (1961)
The Court held that the Fourth Amendment was violated by the use of a "spike-mike" driven into a building wall without a warrant to allow police to overhear conversations within the building. This was physical intrusion in violation of the Fourth Amendment.

Smith v. Maryland, 442 U.S. 735 (1979) Pen registers (devices that record the number dialed from a particular telephone and installed on the property of the telephone company) do not come under the Fourth Amendment, so the police do not have to obtain judicial authorization before using them.

State v. Stachler, 570 P.2d 1323 (1977) The plain view doctrine can be applied to cases in which the officer has made "a prior valid intrusion into a constitutionally protected area" (meaning when the officer is inside an enclosed space, such as a house or an apartment); the term *open view* applies to instances when the officer is out in open space (such as on the streets) but sees an item within an enclosed area.

Texas v. Brown, 460 U.S. 730 (1983) Although items must be immediately recognizable as subject to seizure if they are to fall under the plain view doctrine, it is not necessary that there be certain knowledge that incriminating evidence is involved. Probable cause is sufficient to justify seizure. Also, the use of a flashlight by an officer to look into the inside of a car at night does not constitute a search under the Fourth Amendment. The items discovered still fall under plain view.

United States v. Dunn, 480 U.S. 294 (1987)
Whether an area is considered a part of the curtilage and therefore covered by the Fourth Amendment rests on four factors: (1) the proximity of the area to the home, (2) whether the area is in an enclosure surrounding the home, (3) the nature and uses of the area, and (4) the steps taken to conceal the area from public view.

United States v. Giordano, 416 U.S. 505 (1974)
The Court nullified hundreds of criminal prosecutions based on evidence obtained by surveillance when it held that then–Attorney General John Mitchell had not himself signed the applications for the warrant authorizing the surveillance and had allowed an aide other than the designated assistant attorney general to approve the applications.

United States v. Jackson, 544 F.2d 407 (9th Cir. 1976) The term *abandonment* should not be interpreted in the strict property right sense. The critical factor is whether the person so relinquishes his or her interest in the property that he or she no longer retains a reasonable expectation of privacy in it at the time of a search.

United States v. Johns, 469 U.S. 478 (1985) The plain view doctrine might not be limited to plain sight, but might also include plain odor ("Whether defendant ever had a privacy interest in packages reeking of marijuana is debatable").

United States v. Karo, 468 U.S. 705 (1984) The warrantless monitoring of a beeper after the device has been unwittingly taken into a private residence violates the Fourth Amendment rights of the residents and others.

United States v. Knotts, 459 U.S. 276 (1983)
The use of a beeper to monitor the whereabouts of a person traveling in a car on public highways does not turn the surveillance into a search. Such monitoring falls under the plain view doctrine and therefore does not require a warrant.

United States v. New York Telephone Company, 434 U.S. 159 (1977) The police may obtain a court order to require the telephone company to assist in installing a pen register device.

United States v. Potts, 297 F.2d 68 (6th Cir. 1961) In general, the term *curtilage* has been held to include all buildings that are in close proximity to a dwelling and are continually used for carrying on domestic employment, or places that are necessary and convenient to a dwelling and habitually used for family purposes.

United States v. Sedillo, 496 F.2d 151 (9th Cir. 1974) The plain view doctrine is properly applied to situations in which the police officer is not searching for evidence against the accused but nevertheless inadvertently comes across an incriminating object.

United States v. U.S. District Court, 407 U.S. 297 (1972) The Court rejected the contention of the Nixon administration that the provisions of Title III of the Omnibus Crime Control and Safe Streets Act did not require judicial approval of warrants for wiretaps or surveillance in national security cases.

United States v. White, 401 U.S. 745 (1971) The Constitution does not prohibit a government agent from using an electronic device to record a telephone conversation between two parties with the consent of one party to the conversation.

 **Case Briefs**

Leading Case on "Open Fields"

Oliver v. United States, 466 U.S. 170 (1984)

Facts: Acting on reports that marijuana was being grown on the petitioner's farm, but without a search warrant, probable cause, or exigent circumstances, police officers went to a farm to investigate. They drove past Oliver's house to a locked gate with a "no trespassing" sign but with a footpath around one side. Officers followed the footpath around the gate and found a field of marijuana more than a mile from Oliver's house. He was charged with and convicted of manufacturing a controlled substance.

Issue: *Is a place that is posted with a "no trespassing" sign, has a locked gate (with footpath around it), and is located more than a mile from the owner's house considered an open field? Yes.*

Supreme Court Decision: A place where the property owner posts a "no trespassing" sign and has a locked gate but with a footpath around it, located more than a mile from the house, has no reasonable expectation of privacy and is considered an open field. Therefore, it is legal for the police to enter that area without a warrant or probable cause, because it is unprotected by the Fourth Amendment.

Case Significance: This case makes clear that the "reasonable expectation of privacy" doctrine does not apply when the property involved is an open field. The Court defines what areas enjoy the protection extended by reasonable expectation of privacy. The Court stressed that steps taken to protect privacy, such as planting marijuana on secluded land, erecting a locked gate (but with a footpath along one side), and posting "no trespassing" signs around the property, do not establish any reasonable expectation of privacy, so the property comes under open fields. Therefore, the police could enter the property without a warrant or probable cause. The test to determine whether the property comes under a reasonable expectation of privacy or is considered open fields is not whether the individual chooses to conceal assertedly "private activity," but whether the government's intrusion infringes upon the personal and societal values protected by the Fourth Amendment."

Excerpts from the Decision: "No single factor determines whether an individual legitimately may claim under the Fourth Amendment that a place should be free of government intrusion not authorized by warrant. . . . In assessing the degree to which a search infringes upon individual privacy, the Court has given weight to such factors as the intention of the Framers of the Fourth Amendment . . . the uses to which the individual has put a location . . . and our societal understanding that certain areas deserve the most scrupulous protection from government invasion.

"The [Fourth] Amendment reflects the recognition of the Founders that certain enclaves should be free from arbitrary government interference. For example, the Court since the enactment of the Fourth Amendment has stressed 'the overriding respect for the sanctity of the home that has been embedded in our traditions since the origins of the republic.'

"We conclude, from the text of the Fourth Amendment and from the historical and contemporary understanding of its purposes, that an individual has no legitimate expectation that open fields will remain free from warrantless intrusion by government officers."

Leading Case on the Right to Privacy

Katz v. United States, 389 U.S. 347 (1967)

Facts: Katz was convicted in federal court of transmitting wagering information by telephone across state lines. Evidence of Katz's end of the conversation, overheard by FBI agents who had attached an electronic listening and recording device to the outside of the telephone booth from which the calls were made, was introduced at the trial. Katz sought to suppress the evidence, but the trial court admitted it. The court of appeals affirmed the conviction, finding that there was no Fourth Amendment violation, since there was "no physical entrance into the area occupied" by Katz.

Issue: Is a public telephone booth a constitutionally protected area such that obtaining evidence by attaching an electronic listening/recording device to the top of it violates the user's right to privacy? Yes.

Supreme Court Decision: Any form of electronic surveillance, including wiretapping, that violates a reasonable expectation of privacy constitutes a search. No actual physical trespass is required.

Case Significance: The *Katz* decision expressly overruled the decision thirty-nine years earlier in *Olmstead v. United States,* 277 U.S. 438 (1928), whereby wiretapping did not violate the Fourth Amendment unless there was some trespass into a "constitutionally protected area." In *Katz,* the Court said that the coverage of the Fourth Amendment does not depend on the presence or absence of a physical intrusion into a given enclosure. The current test is that a search exists and therefore comes under the Fourth Amendment protection whenever there is a "reasonable expectation of privacy." The concept that the Constitution "protects people rather than places" is significant, because it makes the protection of the Fourth Amendment "portable"—carried by persons wherever they go, as long as their behavior and circumstances are such that they are entitled to a reasonable expectation of privacy.

Excerpts from the Decision: "We conclude that the underpinnings of *Olmstead* and *Goldman* have been so eroded by our subsequent decisions that the 'trespass' doctrine there enunciated can no longer be regarded as controlling. The Government's activities in electronically listening to and recording the petitioner's words violated the privacy upon which he justifiably relied while using the telephone booth and thus constituted a 'search and seizure' within the meaning of the Fourth Amendment. The fact that the electronic device employed to achieve that end did not happen to penetrate the wall of the booth can have no constitutional significance.

"The question remaining for decision, then, is whether the search and seizure conducted in this case complied with constitutional standards. In that regard, the Government's position is that its agents acted in an entirely defensible manner: They did not begin their electronic surveillance until investigation of the petitioner's activities had established a strong probability that he was using the telephone in question to transmit gambling information to persons in other States, in violation of federal law. Moreover, the surveillance was limited, both in scope and in duration, to the specific purposes of establishing the contents of the petitioner's unlawful telephonic communications. The agents confined their surveillance to the brief periods during which he used the telephone booth, and they took great care to overhear only the conversations of the petitioner himself."

Notes

1. Steven L. Emanuel and Steven Knowles, *Emanuel Law Outlines: Criminal Procedure* (Larchmont, NY: Emanuel, 1998–99), p. 91.

2. Ibid., p. 23.

3. *Black's Law Dictionary,* 5th Ed. (St. Paul, MN: West, 1979), p. 665.

4. Edward M. Hendrie, "Curtilage: The Expectation of Privacy in the Yard," *FBI Law Enforcement Bulletin,* April 1998, p. 25.

5. John Gales Sauls, "Search of Abandoned Property: Fourth Amendment Considerations," *FBI Law Enforcement Bulletin,* May 1994, pp. 29–31.

6. John G. Miles, Jr., David B. Richardson, and Anthony E. Scudellari, *The Law Officer's Pocket Manual* (Washington, DC: Bureau of National Affairs, 1988–89), 10:4–10:6.

7. *Houston Chronicle,* July 31, 1999, p. A6.

8. Supra note 1, p. 172.

9. Robert A. Fiatal, "The Electronic Communications [and] Privacy Act: Addressing Today's Technology" (Part I), *FBI Law Enforcement Bulletin,* February 1988, pp. 25–30; Robert A. Fiatal, "The Electronic Communications [and] Privacy Act: Addressing Today's Technology" (Part II), *FBI Law Enforcement Bulletin,* March 1988, pp. 26–30; Robert A. Fiatal, "The Electronic Communications [and] Privacy Act: Addressing Today's Technology" (Part III), *FBI Law Enforcement Bulletin,* April 1988, pp. 24–30.

10. Ibid., Part I, p. 25.

11. *Time Magazine,* January 1, 1990, p. 55.

12. *Time Magazine,* February 12, 1990, p. 8.

13. Ibid.

14. Ibid.

15. Lloyd L.Weinreb and James D. Whaley, *The Field Guide to Law Enforcement* (Westbury, NY: Foundation Press, 1999), p. 57.

V. Identifications, Confessions, and Admissions

10. Lineups and Other Pretrial Identification Procedures

Chapter Outline

I. LINEUPS
   A. The Right to Counsel
   B. The Right to Due Process
   C. The Right to Protection against Unreasonable Searches and Seizures
   D. The Right to Protection against Self-Incrimination

II. SHOWUPS
   A. The Right to Counsel
   B. The Right to Due Process
   C. The Right to Protection against Unreasonable Searches and Seizures
   D. The Right to Protection against Self-Incrimination

III. PHOTOGRAPHIC IDENTIFICATIONS
   A. The Right to Counsel
   B. The Right to Due Process
   C. The Right to Protection against Unreasonable Search and Seizure
   D. The Right to Protection against Self-Incrimination

IV. OTHER MEANS OF PRETRIAL IDENTIFICATION
   A. DNA Testing
   B. Polygraph Examinations
   C. Hypnotically Induced Testimony

Case Briefs

Kirby v. Illinois
United States v. Wade

What You Will Learn in This Chapter

You will learn that the police are likely to use three procedures when making pretrial identification: lineups, showups, and photographic identification. You will learn as well that suspects usually invoke four constitutional rights during these proceedings: the right to counsel, the right to due process, the right to protection against unreasonable searches and seizures, and the right to protection against self-incrimination. You will discover that the rights to counsel and to due process apply in lineups, showups, and photographic identification, but that the rights involving unreasonable searches and seizures and self-incrimination do not apply. Finally, you will be introduced to three other means of pretrial identification—DNA testing, polygraph examinations, and hypnosis—and learn about the admissibility in court of the results of these procedures.

Introduction

The police use a variety of procedures to verify whether a suspect who has been taken into custody is, in fact, guilty of an offense. These identification procedures serve the dual function of solving crimes and providing evidence at trial. The police are likely to use three procedures to identify suspects who have been taken into custody: (1) a lineup, at which a victim of or witness to a crime is shown several possible suspects at the police station for identification, (2) a showup, at which only one suspect is shown to the witness or victim, usually at the scene of the crime and immediately following a quick arrest of the suspect, and (3) photographic identification, at which photographs of possible suspects are shown to the victim or witness. Four constitutional rights are often invoked by suspects during the pretrial identification stage: (1) the right to counsel, (2) the right to due process, (3) the right to protection against unreasonable searches and seizures, and (4) the right to protection against self-incrimination. The applicability of these four rights to the three pretrial identification procedures discussed in this chapter may be summarized and charted as follows:

	LINEUPS	SHOWUPS	PHOTOGRAPHIC IDENTIFICATION
1. Counsel	Yes, after formal charge No, before formal charge	Yes, after formal charge No, before formal charge	No

2. Due process	Yes	Yes	Yes
3. Searches and seizures	No	No	No
4. Self-incrimination	No	No	No

I. LINEUPS

Black's Law Dictionary defines a **lineup** as *"a police identification procedure by which the suspect in a crime is exhibited, along with others with similar physical characteristics, before the victim or witness to determine if he can be identified as having committed the offense."*[1] The same source says, "Lineup involves and requires lining up of a number of individuals from which one of those lined up may or may not be identified as committer of a crime and there cannot be a one-man lineup."

A. The Right to Counsel

The right to counsel in lineups must be considered in terms of two stages: prior to the filing of a formal charge and after the filing of a formal charge.

1. Prior to the Filing of a Formal Charge: Kirby v. Illinois

A suspect in a lineup has no right to a lawyer if he or she has not been **formally charged with an offense,** meaning *before an indictment, information, preliminary hearing, or arraignment* (Kirby v. Illinois, 406 U.S. 682 [1972]). In the *Kirby* case, a robbery suspect was identified by the victim in a pretrial procedure at the police station. No lawyer was present in the room during the identification, nor was Kirby advised by the police of any right to the presence of counsel. Kirby later was convicted of robbery and appealed his conviction. The Court held that Kirby was *not entitled to the presence and advice of a lawyer in a lineup or other face-to-face confrontation, because he had not been formally charged with an offense;* this is now known as the **Kirby rule.** The identification process in which he participated was a matter of routine police investigation and thus was not considered a "critical stage of the prosecution." Only when the proceeding is considered a "critical stage of the prosecution" is a suspect entitled to the presence and advice of counsel. (Read the Kirby v. Illinois case brief at the end of this chapter.)

Most lower courts have held that taking the accused into custody under an arrest warrant is equivalent to filing a formal charge. But if the lineup is conducted after a warrantless arrest, formal charges have not yet been filed; the suspect therefore has no right to the presence of counsel. In these cases, though, officers must be careful not to violate the suspect's right to due process (discussed shortly). Some states require the presence of counsel for the suspect at all lineups, whether before or after formal charges are filed. State law or local policy prevails. The stage at which formal charges are consid-

HIGHLIGHT

The Right to Counsel and Formal Charges

"The initiation of judicial proceedings is far from mere formalism. It is the starting point of our whole system of adversary criminal justice. For it is only then that the government has committed itself to prosecute, and only then that the adverse positions of government and defendant have solidified. It is then that a defendant finds himself faced with the prosecutorial forces of organized society and immersed in the intricacies of substantive and procedural criminal law. It is this point, therefore, that marks the commencement of the 'criminal prosecutions' to which alone the explicit guarantees of the Sixth Amendment [right to counsel] are applicable."

Kirby v. Illinois, 406 U.S. 682 (1972).

ered to have been filed varies from state to state, or even from one court to another, so it is best to know the law in a particular jurisdiction.

2. After the Filing of a Formal Charge: United States v. Wade

In contrast, a lineup or other face-to-face confrontation after the accused has been formally charged with an offense is considered a "critical stage of the proceedings." Therefore, the accused has a right to have counsel present (United States v. Wade, 388 U.S. 218 [1967]). As with other rights, however, the right to counsel at this stage may be waived by the suspect. (Read the United States v. Wade case brief at the end of this chapter.)

In the *Wade* case, the suspect was arrested for bank robbery and later indicted. He was subsequently assigned a lawyer to represent him. Fifteen days after the lawyer was assigned, an FBI agent, without notice to Wade's lawyer, arranged to have two bank employees observe a lineup of Wade and five or six other prisoners in a courtroom of the local county courthouse. Each person in the lineup wore strips of tape like those allegedly worn by the robber during the bank robbery. On request, each said something like, "Put the money in the bag," the words allegedly uttered by the robber. Wade was tried for the offense and convicted. He appealed, claiming that the bank employees' courtroom identifications were unconstitutional because the lineup violated his rights to protection against self-incrimination and to the assistance of counsel. The Court rejected the first claim but upheld the second. The Court noted that there is grave potential for prejudice, intentional or not, in the pretrial lineup, which might do damage at trial. Since the presence of counsel itself can often avert prejudice and assure a meaningful confrontation at trial, the lineup is a "critical stage of the prosecution" at which the accused is as much entitled to the aid of counsel as at the trial itself.

Is the filing of a formal charge a logical dividing line by which to determine whether an accused should have a right to counsel in cases involving pretrial identification? The Supreme Court certainly believes so. In the *Kirby* case, the Court said that "the initiation of judicial criminal proceedings is far from a mere formalism," adding that "it is . . . only then that the adverse positions of government and defendant have solidified. . . . [A] defendant finds himself faced with the prosecutorial forces of organized society and immersed in the intricacies of substantive and procedural criminal law."

Critics of the Court maintain that the boundary between "prior to" and "after" filing is artificial; any identification made against the suspect at any stage is important in establishing guilt or innocence.

In a companion case to *Wade,* the Court held that requiring a suspect to give a handwriting sample without a lawyer present does not violate the suspect's right to avoid compulsory self-incrimination or the right to counsel (Gilbert v. California, 388 U.S. 263 [1967]). In the *Gilbert* case, the lineup was conducted in an auditorium in which were gathered about a hundred witnesses to alleged offenses by the suspect. They made wholesale identification of the suspect in one another's presence. Aside from the procedure's being legally deficient because of absence of counsel, the Court also said that this procedure was "fraught with dangers of suggestion." Taken together, the decisions in United States v. Wade and Gilbert v. California are known in legal circles as the **Wade-Gilbert rule,** as distinguished from the Kirby rule (taken from Kirby v. Illinois) discussed earlier. According to Wade-Gilbert, *a suspect in a lineup or other confrontation after being formally charged with a crime is entitled to have a lawyer present.*

Failure to provide a lawyer at a lineup after a formal charge has been filed against the suspect makes the evidence inadmissible. However, it does not automatically exclude the testimony of the witness if the witness can identify the accused in court without having to rely on the earlier lineup identification (Gilbert v. California, 388 U.S. 263 [1967]). To determine if this in-court testimony is admissible, the judge must conclude that the testimony is "purged of the primary taint" caused at the lineup. For example, suppose the police require X, a suspect, to appear in a lineup without a lawyer after he has been indicted by a grand jury. The witness identifies X as the person who raped her. This identification is invalid, because X was not assigned a lawyer. However, if it can be established in court that the victim would have identified X in court anyway without the lineup (if, for instance, it is established that she, in fact, saw X a couple of times before the lineup or had a good view of the suspect at the time of the crime), then the identification may be admissible, because it may be considered to have been purged of the illegality associated with the lineup.

Although a suspect is entitled to a lawyer during a lineup after formal charges are filed, the suspect cannot refuse to participate in the lineup, even if the lawyer advises against appearing. The lawyer is present primarily to observe the proceedings. If the suspect cannot afford a lawyer, one must be appointed by the state. A lawyer may be appointed temporarily just for the lineup.

a. The Right to Counsel versus the Miranda Warnings

Why is a suspect not entitled to a lawyer during a lineup prior to the filing of formal charges and yet is entitled to the Miranda warnings (which state that the suspect has a right to a lawyer and that, if the suspect cannot afford a lawyer, the state will provide one) immediately upon arrest even if he or she is still out in the streets? The answer is that the Miranda warnings must be given any time a police officer interrogates a suspect who is in custody. This rule protects the suspect's right not to incriminate him- or herself. By contrast, lineups do not involve any form of interrogation, and the danger of self-incrimination is merely physical, not testimonial or communicative.

b. The Role of the Lawyer during the Lineup

The main role of a lawyer is to *make sure the procedure is fair.* The lawyer's function is that of a "watchman," who makes sure that things are done right so as not to violate the suspect's due process rights. One source puts it this way: "The role of the attorney at a lineup is that of a nonparticipant observer."[2] The Supreme Court, however, has not given any authoritative guidelines on the role of a lawyer during lineups. Most commentators believe the lawyer should, at the very least, observe the proceedings—including taking notes or making a recording—and be able to state any objection to the proceedings. Others have suggested that the lineup procedure should be treated as an adversarial proceeding in which the lawyer may question the witnesses, make objections, and have any reasonable recommendations respected by the police. Since no guidelines have been set by the Supreme Court, the officer should follow the practice in the local jurisdiction. Most jurisdictions follow the "observe the proceeding" rule for the lawyer and nothing beyond that.

Lawyers should be accorded all professional courtesies but *must not be allowed to control the proceedings;* nor should an attorney's disruptive presence be tolerated. If the lawyer acts improperly, it is best to invite the judge or the district attorney to witness the proceedings. Counsel should not be allowed to question the witness before, during, or after the lineup, although if an attorney asks to speak to his or her client prior to or after the lineup, he or she should be allowed to do so. If the suspect has an attorney (that is, after the suspect has been formally charged with the offense), the attorney must be notified of the lineup in advance. If the main role of a lawyer during the lineup is as an observer (unless local practice provides otherwise), how does the suspect benefit from the lawyer's presence? One justice of the Court has answered thus: "Attuned to the possibilities of suggestive influences, a lawyer could see any unfairness at a lineup, question the witnesses about it at trial, and effectively reconstruct what had gone on for the benefit of the jury or trial judge" (United States v. Ash, 413 U.S. 300 [1973]).

c. Nonappearance of the Lawyer The officer has a number of options if the lawyer, after having been duly informed of the lineup, fails to show up:

1. Ask the suspect if he or she is willing to waive the right to counsel; such a waiver is valid as long as it is voluntary and intelligent. The waiver is best obtained in writing.

2. Postpone the lineup to another time when counsel can be present.

3. Get a substitute counsel only for the lineup.

4. If the preceding options are not feasible, conduct a "photo lineup": Those appearing are photographed or videotaped in one room, and the witness is kept isolated in a different room. The photograph or tape is then shown to the witness. The theory is that "because there is no constitutional right to have counsel present when a suspect's photograph is shown to witnesses for identification, the Sixth Amendment is not implicated."[3]

B. The Right to Due Process

1. An Impermissibly Suggestive Identification Procedure

A suspect has a right to due process of law in a lineup. This means that the lineup must not be unfair. In the words of the Court: "The influence of improper suggestion upon identifying witnesses probably accounts for more miscarriages of justice than any other single factor—perhaps it is responsible for more such errors than all other factors combined" (United States v. Wade, 388 U.S. 218 [1967]).[4] In determining what is fair or unfair in identification procedures, courts generally consider all the circumstances leading up to the identification. Unfairness will be found only when, in light of all such circumstances ("totality of circumstances"), the identification procedure is so *impermissibly suggestive* as to give rise to a real and substantial likelihood of irreparable misidentification (Neil v. Biggers, 409 U.S. 188 [1972]). When that point is reached is determined by the trial court, with some guidelines provided by the Supreme Court, as the cases discussed in this chapter show.

Recall that in Gilbert v. California, 388 U.S. 363 (1967), the Court held that a lineup conducted in an auditorium where the defendant was identified by about a hundred witnesses violated the suspect's due process rights, because the procedure was "fraught with dangers of suggestion." Similarly, the use of force to compel the suspect to appear in a lineup may also make the proceeding so suggestive as to violate the suspect's due process rights. In Foster v. California, 394 U.S. 440 (1969), the Court found that a pretrial identification by a certain David, the only witness to the crime, violated due process. In the *Foster* case, the suspect was lined up with two other men several inches shorter. The suspect was close to six feet tall while the two other men were short—"five feet, five or six inches." Only the suspect wore a jacket similar to that of the robber. When the lineup produced no positive identification, the police used a one-man showup of the suspect. Because even the showup was inconclusive, the police later used a second lineup in which only the suspect was a repeater from the earlier lineup. The Court said that the suspect's due process rights were violated, because under those conditions the identification of the suspect was inevitable. Said the Court: "The suggestive elements in this identification procedure made it all but inevitable that David would identify petitioner whether or not he was in fact 'the man.' In effect, the police repeatedly said to the witness, 'This is the man.'"

2. Factors in Determining Violations of Due Process

The courts are likely to take five factors into account when determining whether, in the totality of circumstances, the suspect's due process rights have been violated during a lineup (Neil v. Biggers. 409 U.S. 188 [1973]):

1. The witness's opportunity to view the criminal at the time of the crime

2. The witness's degree of attention at that time

3. The accuracy of any prior description given by the witness

4. The level of certainty demonstrated by the witness at the identification

5. The length of time between the crime and the identification

3. Lineup Composition and Procedure

To ensure that due process rights are observed, the International Association of Chiefs of Police (IACP) Legal Center recommends the following guidelines for every lineup:[5]

- All lineups should consist of at least five, and preferably six, people, including the suspect. (See Form 10.1.)

- All prisoners and suspects placed in the lineup must execute the lineup waiver form, unless an attorney is present. (See Form 10.2.)

- All persons in the lineup must be of the same sex and race and nearly the same age. The participants should also be of about the same height, weight, coloring of skin and hair, and physical build as the accused. If this cannot be done with reasonable proximity, the lineup should be postponed.

- All participants should wear the same type of clothing; for example, the suspect must not appear in prison garb if others are clothed in civilian attire. Detectives dressed in suits should not appear with a suspect who is clothed in slacks and a wrinkled shirt.

- The accused should be placed in the lineup at random, so as not to suggest identity by position.

- Persons who may be known to the witness must not be placed in the lineup with the suspect.

- If private citizens are recruited to participate in a lineup due to a lack of sufficient prisoners in custody matching a suspect's general appearance, they should execute a written consent form indicating that they are aware that there are no charges against them and that they have not been arrested, are under no compulsion to participate, are legally free to leave at any time, and, if minors, have consulted with and received permission from a parent or guardian to participate in the lineup.

In addition to these guidelines, the IACP Legal Center recommends that the following practices be observed every time a lineup is conducted:[6]

- Each witness should view the lineup separately, so as to avoid the situation in which one witness identifies the suspect out loud. If multiple lineups cannot be held, the witnesses should be separated in the room.

- Each participant in the lineup must be given the same instructions. For example, if the suspect is told to repeat the phrase "This is a stickup," each participant from left to right should repeat the phrase. Similarly, if the suspect has to try on a mask, each participant should put it on, in the order of position in the lineup.

- During the lineup, witnesses should be instructed not to make any statement or comment pertaining to an identification. Each witness should be given a sheet of paper and pen and told to write down the position number of any person he or she recognizes.

- Two photographs should be taken of the lineup—one a frontal view, the other a profile. All persons in the lineup should be included in the two photographs. Whenever possible, color film should be used. Such photographs are admissible in court, if it is later claimed that the lineup was visually suggestive.

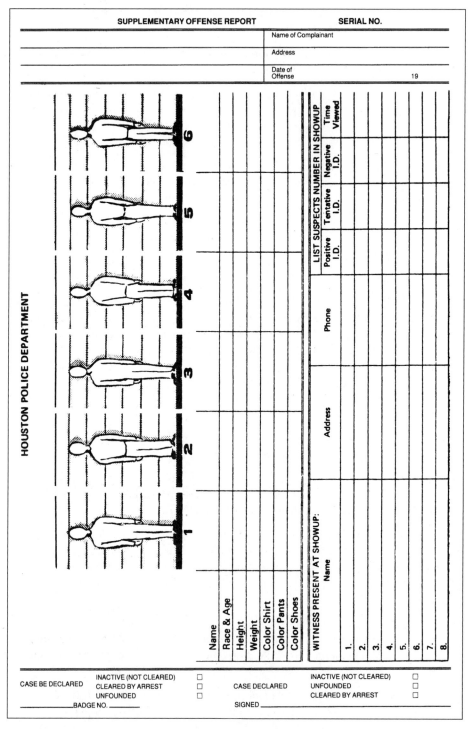

Form 10.1 *Lineup Form*

HOUSTON POLICE DEPARTMENT — OFFENSE REPORT SUPPLEMENT INCIDENT NO._____

OFFENSE... LOCATION..

COMPLAINANT(S).. DATE OF OFFENSE............................

.... DATE SUPPLEMENT MADE................................

	SHORT FORM SUPPLEMENT INFORMATION	
☐ CONTACTED COMPLAINANT NO ADDITIONAL INFORMATION	☐ CONTACTED WITNESS/S LISTED NO ADDITIONAL INFORMATION	☐ UNABLE TO CONTACT COMPLAINANT AND/OR WITNESS/S LISTED
DATE & TIME:	DATE & TIME	DATE & TIME

RECOVERED STOLEN VEHICLE: YEAR......... MAKE.................. MODEL.................. LIC.YR.STATE&NO. ....

CONDITION OF VEHICLE: ☐ DAMAGED ☐ WRECKED ☐ BURNED AMOUNT OF DAMAGE $_____

☐ STRIPPED (LIST ITEMS STRIPPED AND THEIR VALUE AT START OF NARRATIVE BELOW)

VEH. RELEASED TO: TOWED TO: BY:

PROGRESS OF INVESTIGATION, ADDITIONAL INFORMATION, ETC.: ....

I, _____ , have been notified

that I will be placed in a lineup (showup) at _____

                                            (time)   (Date)

_____ , in Harris County, Texas.

        (Building)

The purpose of this showup is to let witnesses view me to see whether or not
they can identify me as a person who has committed crime or crimes. I have
been informed that I have a right to have my lawyer present at said showup
and to have a lawyer appointed free of charge for such purpose if I cannot afford
to hire one, and I here and now state that I do not now have a lawyer and I do not
want one for this showup. No threats or promises have been made to me in
connection with this waiver which I now sign of my own free will.

                        _____

WITNESSES:

_____

_____

☐ SUPPLEMENT COMPLETE   ☐ CONTINUED

OFFICER(S) MAKING REPORT: STATUS: ☐ OPEN ☐ CLEARED ☐ INACTIVE ☐ UNFOUNDED

.... EMP. NO. .... UCR DISPOSITION: ....

.... EMP. NO. .... S.R.OFFICER .... EMP. NO. ....

Form No. ROB-0005

Form 10.2 *Offense Report Supplement with a Waiver Form*

■ A single officer, usually the detective assigned to the case, should (1) advise the participants of their rights and obtain the waivers, (2) conduct the actual lineup, (3) take the photographs, and (4) question the witnesses afterward. This is important because it will reduce the number of officers who may have to appear in court, as well as preserve the chain of evidence.

■ If a suspect waives his or her right to have an attorney present, it is best to obtain the waiver in writing.

C. The Right to Protection against Unreasonable Searches and Seizures

In Schmerber v. California, 384 U.S. 757 (1966), the defendant claimed a violation of the guarantee against unreasonable search and seizure during pretrial identification. A sample of Schmerber's blood was taken by a doctor in a hospital, upon request of a police officer, for use as evidence in a drunk-driving case. The defendant raised the issue on appeal, claiming that the police should have obtained a warrant before extracting blood from him. The Court rejected this claim, saying that the officer might reasonably have believed that he was confronted with an emergency in which the delay necessary to obtain a warrant, under the circumstances, would have led to the destruction of the evidence. The Court added, "Particularly in a case such as this, where time had to be taken to bring the accused to a hospital and to investigate the scene of the accident, there was no time to seek out a magistrate and secure a warrant. Given these special facts, we conclude that the attempt to secure evidence of blood-alcohol content in this case was an appropriate incident to petitioner's arrest."

Claims of unreasonable search and seizure in pretrial identification procedures are few and, when raised, do not succeed. They fail because they basically allege, as in *Schmerber,* that the police should have obtained a warrant before conducting the identification procedure. Compelling a suspect to appear in a lineup or showup is a form of seizure, but it is usually easily justified under the numerous exceptions to the warrant rule, such as the "exigent circumstances" justification invoked by the police in *Schmerber.* Moreover, many lineups occur after a warrant has been issued or the suspect has been brought before a magistrate. In these cases, the search and seizure challenge becomes moot because of the issuance of a warrant.

D. The Right to Protection against Self-Incrimination

5th Amendment

Suspects sometimes claim that they cannot be required to appear in a lineup or showup because it forces them to incriminate themselves. That claim appears logical—indeed, it is incriminating to be fingered as the culprit in a lineup or to be identified in a showup. However, the Supreme Court has repeatedly rejected this claim. The rule is that a suspect may be required to appear in a police lineup before or after being charged with an offense. The reason is that the right to protection against compulsory self-incrimination applies only to evidence that is **testimonial or communicative,** or *that is communicated orally.* It does not extend to **real or physical self-incrimination,** which *involves the physical body or objects.* Courts have decided that the government can force a suspect to do the following because they involve only the giving of physical, not testimonial, evidence:

1. Appear in a police lineup, before or after formal charge.

2. Give a blood sample, even unwillingly, as long as proper conditions are present; even if state law allows a suspect to refuse to take a blood-alcohol test, a refusal may be constitutionally introduced as evidence of guilt in court.

3. Submit to a photograph.

4. Give handwriting samples.

5. Submit to fingerprinting.

6. Repeat certain words or gestures or give voice exemplars (the voice here is used as an identifying physical characteristic, not to give oral testimony).

The rule that the Fifth Amendment right not to incriminate oneself protects only against self-incrimination that is testimonial or communicative rather than real or physical was reiterated in Schmerber v. California, 384 U.S. 757 (1966). Recall that in that case Schmerber was arrested for drunk driving, and a blood sample was extracted from him, over his objection, by a medical doctor acting under police direction. Schmerber objected to the use of the incriminating evidence during his trial, claiming that it was obtained in violation of his right to protection against self-incrimination. The Court disagreed, saying that the seizure of real or physical evidence does not involve Fifth Amendment guarantees. That amendment applies only to testimonial or communicative, rather than real or physical, evidence. Testimonial or communicative self-incrimination occurs *when a suspect is required to "speak his guilt."*

Following the *Schmerber* decision, the Court ruled that appearance in a police lineup is a form of physical, not testimonial, self-incrimination and therefore is not protected by the Fifth Amendment. There is no self-incrimination even if the suspect is required to "speak up" for identification by repeating phrases such as "Put the money in the bag." This is because the purpose of having the suspect speak up is not to evaluate what is said, which would be testimonial, but to measure the level, tone, and quality of voice, which are physical properties (United States v. Wade, 388 U.S. 218 [1967]).

It follows from the *Schmerber* ruling that a suspect does not have a constitutional right to refuse to appear or participate in a lineup. A suspect who is in custody of the police may be required to appear in a lineup. The use of force, however, to compel a suspect's appearance is inadvisable because it might constitute a violation of the suspect's right to due process. If the suspect is not in custody, appearance in a lineup may be compelled only by court order.[7] If a suspect refuses to appear despite a court order, he or she may be held in contempt of court and kept in jail. A suspect's refusal to cooperate in the identification procedure may also be commented on by the prosecution during the trial. Alternatively, if a suspect refuses to participate in a lineup, the police might be justified in arranging a showup in which the suspect alone is viewed by a witness.[8]

II. SHOWUPS

A **showup** is defined as a *"one-to-one confrontation between a suspect and a witness to crime."* It usually "occurs within a short time after the crime or under circumstances

AT A GLANCE

Lineups and Constitutional Rights

DEFINITION: "A police identification procedure by which the suspect in a crime is exhibited, along with others with similar physical characteristics, before the victim or witness to determine if he or she can be identified as having committed the offense."

RIGHT TO COUNSEL: Applies after a formal charge has been filed, but not before.

ROLE OF LAWYER DURING LINEUP: Make sure the procedure is fair. But the lawyer must not be allowed to control the proceedings.

RIGHT TO DUE PROCESS: Applies and is violated if the identification procedure is impermissibly suggestive.

RIGHT TO PROTECTION AGAINST UNREASONABLE SEARCHES AND SEIZURES: Does not apply.

RIGHT TO PROTECTION AGAINST SELF-INCRIMINATION: Does not apply because the type of self-incrimination involved is physical, not testimonial.

---

which would make a lineup impractical or impossible."[9] As in the case of lineups, the rights to counsel and to due process apply; the rights to protection against unreasonable searches and seizures and against self-incrimination do not.

No - if they have not been charged
yes - if they have been changed

A. The Right to Counsel

1. Prior to the Filing of a Formal Charge

In most cases, the police bring a suspect to the scene immediately after the commission of a crime to be identified by the victim or other eyewitnesses. Since the suspect has not been charged with a crime, there is no right to counsel (Kirby v. Illinois, 406 U.S. 682 [1972]). For example, suppose that, minutes after a purse is snatched, a suspect fitting the description given by the victim is apprehended several blocks away and is brought back to the scene of the crime for identification by the victim. The suspect has no right to counsel even if he or she requests it. If the police question the suspect, however, they must give the Miranda warnings because the situation has escalated beyond a police lineup, where no questions are asked, to a custodial interrogation, which then triggers Miranda.

2. After the Filing of a Formal Charge

The rule is different once the adversarial judicial criminal proceedings are initiated. In one case, for example, a rape suspect appeared with a police officer in the courtroom for a preliminary hearing to determine whether his case should be sent to the grand jury and to set bail. After the suspect's appearance before the judge, the rape victim was asked by the prosecutor if she saw the perpetrator in the courtroom. She then pointed to the suspect. During trial, this identification was admitted in court, over the defendant's objections. But on appeal, the Supreme Court held that this violated the defendant's right to counsel; since the adversary criminal proceedings had been initiated at that time, the defendant was entitled to a lawyer at that form of showup (Moore v. Illinois, 434 U.S. 220 [1977]).

The Right to Due Process

The leading case on the right to due process in showups is Neil v. Biggers, 409 U.S. 188 (1972). In this case, the rape victim could give no description of her attacker other than that he was a black man wearing an orange-colored shirt and that he had a high-pitched voice. The victim was assaulted in her dimly lighted kitchen, and then forcibly taken out of the house and raped under a full, bright moon. The victim went through a number of photographs and was shown several lineups but could not make a positive identification. The police arrested the defendant seven months later on information supplied by an informant. The defendant was brought before the victim alone. The police showed the victim the defendant's orange-colored shirt and asked her if she could identify the defendant's voice (from an adjoining room). No other voices were provided for comparison. The Court held that, though the confrontation procedure itself was suggestive, the totality of circumstances made the identification reliable. Among the factors considered by the Court was "the opportunity of the witness to view the criminal at the time of the crime, the witness's degree of attention, the accuracy of the witness's prior description of the criminal, the level of certainty demonstrated by the witness at the confrontation, and the length of time between the crime and the confrontation." Applying these factors, the Court concluded that the totality of circumstances showed that the identification was reliable, saying:

> The victim spent a considerable period of time with her assailant, up to half an hour. She was with him under adequate artificial light in her house and under a full moon outdoors, and at least twice, once in the house and later in the woods, faced him directly and intimately. She was no casual observer, but rather the victim of one of the most personally humiliating of all crimes. Her description to the police, which included the assailant's approximate age, height, weight, complexion, skin texture, build, and voice, might not have satisfied Proust, but was more than ordinarily thorough. She had "no doubt" that respondent was the person who raped her.

In another case, the Court ruled a showup in a hospital valid because the possible unfairness of the showup was justified by the urgent need to confront the suspect since the only living eyewitness, who was hospitalized, was in danger of dying (Stovall v. Denno, 388 U.S. 293 [1967]). In this case, defendant Stovall was convicted and sentenced to die for murdering a certain Dr. Behrendt. Stovall was arrested the day after the murder and, without having been given time to obtain a lawyer, was taken by police officers to the hospital to be viewed by Mrs. Behrendt, who was seriously wounded by her husband's assailant. After observing Stovall and hearing him speak, when told to do so by an officer, Mrs. Behrendt identified him as the murderer of her husband. On

HIGHLIGHT

Due Process and the Showup

"Though the practice of showing suspects singly for purposes of identification has been widely condemned, a violation of due process of law in the conduct of a confrontation depends on the totality of the surrounding circumstances. There was no due process denial in the confrontation here since Mrs. Behrendt was the only person who could exonerate the suspect; she could not go to the police station for the usual lineup; and there was no way of knowing how long she would live."

Stovall v. Denno, 388 U.S. 293 (1967).

appeal, Stovall claimed a violation of his right to due process. The Court rejected his claim, quoting with approval the findings of the State Court of Appeals, which said:

> Here was the only person in the world who could possibly exonerate Stovall. Her words, and only her words, "He is not the man" could have resulted in freedom for Stovall. The hospital was not far distant from the courthouse and jail. No one knew how long Mrs. Behrendt might live. Faced with the responsibility of identifying the attacker, with the need for immediate action and with the knowledge that Mrs. Behrendt could not visit the jail, the police followed the only feasible procedure and took Stovall to the hospital room. Under these circumstances, the usual police station line-up, which Stovall now argues he should have had, was out of the question.

C. The Right to Protection against Unreasonable Searches and Seizures

As in the case of lineups, showups are not considered to be unreasonable searches and seizures because the circumstances usually warrant them. They are usually conducted at the scene of the crime (as when the victim is taken to the scene to identify an alleged purse snatcher) and immediately following the quick arrest of the suspect. Showups are a form of intrusion, but they are usually justified under the exigent circumstances exception because of the absence of an opportunity to obtain a warrant. Moreover, the degree of intrusion is usually minimal and necessary under the circumstances.

D. The Right to Protection against Self Incrimination

As in the case of lineups, showups do not violate the prohibition against self-incrimination because, although self-incriminatory, the self-incrimination involved is real or physical, not testimonial or communicative.

Showups and Constitutional Rights

DEFINITION: A "one-to-one confrontation between a suspect and a witness to a crime." It usually "occurs within a short time after the crime or under circumstances which would make a lineup impractical or impossible."

RIGHT TO COUNSEL: Applies after a formal charge has been filed, but not before.

RIGHT TO DUE PROCESS: Applies and is violated if the identification procedure is impermissibly suggestive.

RIGHT TO PROTECTION AGAINST UNREASONABLE SEARCHES AND SEIZURES: Does not apply.

RIGHT TO PROTECTION AGAINST SELF-INCRIMINATION: Does not apply because the type of self-incrimination involved is physical, not testimonial.

III. PHOTOGRAPHIC IDENTIFICATIONS

Photographic identification (rogue's gallery) is a process whereby *a victim or witness is shown photographs of possible suspects in a one-on-one situation.* Only the right to due process applies in this form of pretrial identification.

A. The Right to Counsel

There is no right to counsel when the prosecution seeks to identify the accused by displaying photographs to witnesses prior to trial (a process otherwise known as *mug shot identification*) (United States v. Ash, 413 U.S. 300 [1973]). This is true even if the suspect has already been formally charged with the crime. In the *Ash* case, the defendant was charged with five counts of bank robbery. In preparing for trial, the prosecutor decided to use a photographic display to determine whether the witnesses he planned to call would be able to make in-court identifications of the accused. Shortly before the trial, an FBI agent and the prosecutor showed five color photographs to the four witnesses who had tentatively identified the black-and-white photograph of Ash. Three of the witnesses selected the picture of Ash, but one was unable to make any selection. The post-indictment identification provided the basis for Ash's claim on appeal that he was denied the right to counsel at a "critical stage" of the prosecution. The Court disagreed, holding that photographic identification is not like a lineup because the suspect is not present when the witnesses view the photographs. Since the main reason for lawyers' presence at lineups is to prevent suspects from being disadvantaged by their ignorance and failure to ascertain and object to biased conditions, there is no need for lawyers when the suspects themselves are absent.

HIGHLIGHT

Due Process and Photographic Identification

"We hold that each case must be considered on its own facts, and that convictions based on eyewitness identification at trial following a pretrial identification by photograph will be set aside on that ground only if the photo-graphic identification procedure was so impermissibly suggestive as to give rise to a very substantial likelihood of irreparable misidentification. This standard accords with our resolution of a similar issue in Stovall v. Denno, 388 U.S. 293 (1967), and with decisions of other courts on the question of identification by photograph."

Simmons v. United States, 390 U.S. 377 (1968).

B. The Right to Due Process

As in the case of lineups and showups, the right to due process applies, meaning that the photographic identification must not be unduly suggestive. In photographic identifi-cations, a number of photographs must be shown so as to avoid charges of impermissi-ble suggestion. In addition, there should be nothing in the photographs that focuses attention on a single person. For example, if the suspect is Hispanic, the photographs should feature several Hispanic-looking individuals. To do otherwise would be funda-mentally unfair to the suspect and would violate due process.

In one case, witnesses identified a bank robbery suspect from six photos that were obtained from a relative a day after the crime. This was followed by an in-court identifi-cation of the suspect by the same five witnesses. The Court held that the photographic identification was not unnecessarily suggestive, so as to create a "very substantial likeli-hood of irreparable misidentification" (Simmons v. United States, 390 U.S. 377 [1968]). Among the factors the Court took into account were the seriousness of the crime, the need for immediate apprehension, and the fact that the risk of misidentification was small.

In another case, the Court held that the showing to a witness of a single photo-graph was unnecessary and suggestive, but the Court nonetheless admitted the identi-fication based on the totality of circumstances (Manson v. Brathwaite, 432 U.S. 98 [1977]). In this case, Glover, an undercover state police officer, purchased heroin from a seller through the open doorway of an apartment while standing for two or three min-utes within two feet of the seller in the hallway, which was illuminated by natural light. A few minutes later, Glover described the seller to another police officer as "a colored man, approximately five feet eleven inches tall, dark complexioned, black hair, short Afro style, and having high cheekbones, and of heavy build." The other officer, suspect-ing that the defendant was the seller, left a police photograph of the suspect in the office of Glover, who viewed it two days later and identified the individual in the photo-graph as the seller. The photograph was introduced during trial as the picture of the suspect, and an in-court identification was made. On appeal the Court agreed with the trial court that the examination of the single photograph was unnecessary and sugges-tive but ruled that the identification in court did not have to be excluded. The Court

Photographic Identifications and Constitutional Rights

DEFINITION: A process whereby a victim or witness is shown photographs of possible suspects in a one-on-one situation.

RIGHT TO COUNSEL: Does not apply.

RIGHT TO DUE PROCESS: Applies and is violated if the identification procedure is impermissibly suggestive.

RIGHT TO PROTECTION AGAINST UNREASONABLE SEARCH AND SEIZURE: Does not apply.

RIGHT TO PROTECTION AGAINST SELF-INCRIMINATION: Does not apply because the type of self-incrimination involved is physical, not testimonial.

---

noted that "Glover, no casual observer but a trained police officer, had a sufficient opportunity to view the suspect, accurately described him, positively identified respondent's photograph as that of the suspect, and made the photograph identification only two days after the crime." The photograph identification alone would have violated defendant's due process right, but the totality of circumstances justified admission of the court identification.

This case reiterates previous Court decisions holding that the suggestiveness of the identification procedure is but one of the factors courts should take into account to determine whether a suspect's due process rights were violated. Much more important than a single factor is the totality of circumstances. The Court in Brathwaite also restated the main concern of the Court in identification cases, saying, "Reliability is the linchpin in determining the admissibility of identification testimony for confrontations."

C. The Right to Protection against Unreasonable Searches and Seizures

Photographic identification does not involve any unreasonable search and seizure because no search or seizure takes place, as long as the photographs are obtained legally. Showing photographs does not come under the Fourth Amendment, nor is it unduly intrusive.

D. The Right to Protection against Self-Incrimination

There is no self-incrimination when photographs are shown because, as in the case of lineups and showups, the self-incrimination involved is real or physical, not testimonial or communicative.

IV. OTHER MEANS OF PRETRIAL IDENTIFICATION

In addition to lineups, showups, and photographic arrays, the police sometimes use indirect forms of identification such as DNA testing, polygraph examinations, and hypnosis. These are forms of scientific evidence whose admissibility in court varies. Constitutional rights may also be involved in each procedure.

A. DNA Testing

1. Background

Law enforcement agencies use **DNA testing** (which used to be called DNA "fingerprinting") to screen out or identify possible suspects. DNA testing *matches the suspect's DNA with DNA (such as that found in the semen or blood) recovered from the scene of the crime.* DNA may now be recovered from a variety of sources including semen, blood, hair, skin, sweat, and saliva. The October 1999 issue of the *National Institute of Justice Journal* says, "Today's investigators can solve crimes using the DNA collected from the perspiration on a rapist's discarded baseball cap, the saliva on a stamp of a stalker's threatening letter, and the skin cells shed on a ligature of a strangled victim."[10]

If performed properly, the chances of the method producing a false match are reportedly several hundred thousand to one and sometimes several million to one.[11] DNA has become an important and effective tool in law enforcement. From 1992 through 1998, the FBI reportedly made DNA matches in more than 425 crimes.[12]

DNA testing first gained prominence in England in the mid-1980s and quickly caught the fancy of the law enforcement community and prosecutors as an infallible means of suspect identification.[13] When first introduced in a U.S. court in 1987, DNA typing was billed as the "greatest advance in forensics since the discovery of fingerprints."[14] A federal court of appeals has ruled that "the district court properly exercised its discretion in admitting the DNA profiling evidence proffered by the government in this case; we also conclude that courts facing a similar issue in the future can take judicial notice of the general theories and specific techniques involved in DNA profiling" (United States v. Jakobetz, 955 F.2d 786 [1992]). In addition to affirming the trial court's admission of the evidence, *Jakobetz* features a lengthy discussion of the science and technology of DNA testing and the reasons it is reliable.

2. Results and Some Doubts

While DNA testing has been useful for the police, it has also led to the exoneration of some defendants. The National Institute of Justice, upon orders of the attorney general, conducted a study to determine how often DNA had exonerated wrongfully convicted defendants. The report, released in 1996, stated that it identified "28 inmates for whom DNA analysis was exculpatory."[15] As of September 1999, DNA testing had overturned the conviction of sixty-five prisoners, eight of whom were on death row.[16] Recent newspaper headlines have featured the following:

HIGHLIGHT

DNA Testing and Wrongfully Convicted Defendants

As of September 1999, DNA testing had overturned the conviction of sixty-five prisoners, eight of whom were released from death row. More inmates are establishing innocence through DNA tests. "In rape cases semen is generally recovered, and in murder cases there is often hair or skin evidence." The DNA has become a potent tool for establishing innocence.

Source: *Time Magazine*, September 13, 1999, p. 26.

- "After 12 years, DNA clears inmate in rape case"[17]

- "DNA tests free two men convicted of rape in '83"[18]

- "DNA tests are freeing scores of prison inmates"[19]

- "DNA testing leads to freedom for 2 jailed 12 years in murder"[20]

- "Bias, witness accuracy questioned as DNA tests clear more prisoners"[21]

Although DNA testing has become an effective law enforcement tool, headlines like the preceding have led some prosecutors to question its reliability. In some cases, rather than freeing convicts whose innocence has been established by DNA testing, prosecutors have argued that "cases should be retried so that DNA could be weighed alongside other evidence."[22]

Although the admissibility of DNA testing results in evidence is settled, other legal questions persist. For example, in early 1998, a judge in Massachusetts "halted the gathering of blood samples for DNA profiling from thousands of prison inmates, probationers and parolees after several sued the state, arguing that it was an illegal search and seizure performed without proper safeguards."[23] DNA samples that have been left behind by a suspect obviously raise no search and seizure issues because of abandonment. Legal experts say that the abandonment justification for seizure will likely apply to DNA abandoned in a public place, such as "saliva left on a glass in a restaurant . . . or a cigarette butt thrown on a sidewalk."[24]

3. Unassailable Scientific Reliability

The consensus is that the scientific foundation for DNA testing is solid and unassailable. If competently interpreted, the test is reliable and the results are admissible in court. It is generally accepted that each person's DNA is unique, except for the DNA of identical twins, and that the chances of similarity in DNA are infinitesimally small. The controversy centers around the skill of technicians who conduct the tests and the validity of their interpretations. In April 1992, the chairman of a National Academy of Sciences panel looking into DNA testing recommended that laboratories analyzing DNA should be held to higher standards in the way the tests are performed and interpreted. Admitting that, when performed properly, DNA testing can be invaluable in solving crimes, the panel also called for adherence to very strict standards to assure that the "technique is performed properly in crime laboratories and that its results are accurate."

It further urged that scientists set the standards for admissibility. Judges and jurors should not be put in a position where, based on complex data, they have to decide whether a laboratory test result is reliable.[25]

Problems concerning the admissibility of DNA evidence continue to bother some courts. It came under heavy scrutiny and challenge during the celebrated O. J. Simpson criminal trial, a trial that did little to increase public confidence in the reliability of DNA testing and the way it is administered in some government laboratories. Despite that, DNA testing methods over the past decade have improved tremendously, prompting one former DNA testing opponent to admit that the remaining scientific debate is purely academic and that the "DNA wars are over."[26] DNA technology has made giant strides over the years. Some years ago, a DNA test required a sizable sample (such as a blood stain or semen) with high-quality DNA, and the test took several weeks. Today, as the *FBI Law Enforcement Bulletin* states, "FBI scientists can type DNA from the back of a postage stamp, the shaft of a hair, and the end of a cigarette in a matter of days."[27] DNA testing results constitute convincing evidence, but jurors are nonetheless free to disregard it, as they are with any type of evidence. What DNA does is establish that the odds of a false match are astronomically high; what it cannot do, however, is "positively link a specific person with a particular evidence stain."[28]

4. Toward a National DNA Database

In 1998, the federal government opened a national DNA database aimed at significantly reducing the number of rapes and other crimes by identifying and catching repeat offenders earlier. The database contains genetic profiles of 250,000 state-level felons and DNA information taken from the scenes of 4,600 unsolved crimes.[29] Some states have intensified the effort to expand their state DNA database. Under a new law passed in the state of New York, starting December 1, 1999, "Anyone convicted of a long list of felonies will have a DNA profile entered into a state database for use in solving crimes and aiding prosecutions. The law permits DNA to be collected either from a blood sample or by taking cells from the inside of the mouth with a cotton swab." New York already "collects fingerprints, and has begun taking blood samples from people convicted of sex crimes and a few other violent offenses."[30] Other states obtain DNA database of prisoners serving time for felonies. Virginia now requires all felons to submit their DNA to a databank.[31] As of 1999, forty-three states and the federal government had DNA databases.[32]

A national commission to explore the future of DNA testing has formed a working group to deal with such legal issues associated with DNA testing as privacy, storage of DNA samples, investigation of crimes whose statute of limitations has expired, and possible legal remedies for defendants who were wrongly convicted and have now been exonerated but whose appellate process for the original case has expired.[33] Moreover, the commission will address specific DNA issues in five areas: "(1) the use of DNA in post-conviction relief cases, (2) legal concerns including Daubert challenges and the scope of discovery in DNA cases, (3) criteria for training and technical assistance for criminal justice professionals involved in the identification, collection and preservation of DNA evidence at the crime scene, (4) essential laboratory capabilities in the face of emerging technologies, and (5) the impact of future technological developments on the use of DNA in the criminal justice system." Each topic will be analyzed in depth by a working group of prominent professionals who will report back to the commission.[34]

The Future of DNA Testing

"The day is coming when, conceivably, a criminal would have to wrap himself in a plastic body bag to avoid leaving some trace of his DNA at a scene. When you realize that it took more than 20 years for fingerprints to become an accepted form of identification, it shows how rapidly DNA technology has advanced."

Source: Walter F. Rowe, George Washington University, as quoted in the *Houston Chronicle*, September 12, 1999, p. 1.

In sum, admissibility of DNA test results has largely been settled, but other legal issues, focusing mainly on the right to privacy, have arisen. The National Commission on the Future of DNA Evidence, created in 1998 by Attorney General Janet Reno, is looking into the various facets of DNA testing. The results of that study will go a long way toward resolving the more pressing issues associated with this potent law enforcement tool. Once those issues are resolved, the use of DNA testing as a tool in the war on crime will likely become even more popular and pervasive. Once costing several thousand dollars, the average cost has dropped to $1,500 per DNA test.[35] DNA testing has become an effective instrument in the search for justice, both for the state and for the wrongfully accused or convicted. Its potential is impressive. As one expert notes, "The day is coming when, conceivably, a criminal would have to wrap himself in a plastic body bag to avoid leaving some trace of his DNA at a scene."[36]

B.   Polygraph Examinations

Most courts refuse to admit the results of polygraph (lie detector) tests in either civil or criminal proceedings unless admissibility is agreed to by both parties. The reliability of polygraphs is questionable, particularly when the test is administered by unqualified operators. In the words of one observer, "Polygraphy is very different from other scientific evidence. It is in essence the opinion of the polygrapher. The underlying scientific basis for polygraphy has always been the subject of extreme controversy."[37] Despite progress in technology, most courts still consider it "junk science."[38] Aside from the problem of unqualified operators, many scholars feel that people who are adept at deception or who have convinced themselves that they are telling the truth can beat the polygraph.

Use of polygraph results fails to conform to the **Frye doctrine.** This doctrine, enunciated in Frye v. United States, 293 F. 1013 (D.C. Cir. 1923), states that, before the results of scientific tests will be admissible as evidence in a trial, *the procedures used must be sufficiently established to have gained general acceptance in the particular field to which they belong.*[39] Although some states, by case law or statute, have abandoned the Frye doctrine in favor of more liberal rules, it is still the test used in most states. By contrast, the Court has held that in federal cases the Frye doctrine has been discarded by the adoption of the federal rules of evidence. These rules, constituting the Daubert doctrine, have a more liberal admissibility standard, permitting the admission of expert testimony pertaining to "scientific, technical, or other specialized knowledge" that will "assist the trier of fact to understand the evidence or to determine a fact in issue" (Daubert v. Merrell Dow Pharmaceuticals Inc., 53 CrL 2313 [1993]). Thus, in federal courts, the admissibility of polygraph results is now left to the discretion of the trial court judge. This is not true in most state courts, where strict rules prohibit the admission into evidence of polygraph results. Moreover, some states, by law, prohibit the polygraph examination by the police of a complainant for any offense.[40]

In a recent case, the Court held that a prohibition against the admissibility in court of polygraph evidence in favor of a defendant does not violate his or her constitutional right to present a defense (United States v. Scheffer, 63 CrL 28 [1998]). In that case, the results of a polygraph examination of an airman indicated that there was no deception in his denial that he used drugs. He sought to introduce that evidence to help exonerate him, but military rules of evidence prohibit the admission of polygraph evidence in court martial proceedings. Convicted of using drugs, the airman appealed, claiming that excluding the exonerating polygraph evidence violated his constitutional right to present a defense. The Court disagreed, holding that there was no violation of Scheffer's constitutional right. Significantly, the Court assessed the state of polygraph evidence reliability as follows:

> To this day, the scientific community remains extremely polarized about the reliability of polygraph techniques. Some studies have concluded that polygraph tests overall are accurate and reliable. Others have found that polygraph tests assess truthfulness significantly less accurately—that scientific field studies suggest the accuracy rate of the "control question technique" polygraph is "little better than could be obtained by the toss of a coin," that is, 50%. This lack of scientific consensus is reflected in the disagreement among state and federal courts concerning both the admissibility and reliability of polygraph evidence.

The Office of Technology Assessment has stated that "there is at present only limited scientific evidence for establishing the validity of polygraph testing." It also stated that its review of twenty-four relevant studies meeting minimal acceptable scientific criteria found that correct detections ranged from about 35 to 100 percent.[41] The mathematical chance of misidentification is highest when the polygraph is used for screening purposes. In the words of one writer:[42]

> Departmental policy should recognize that polygraph is not a perfect investigative process and that polygraph results, both examiner opinions following chart evaluation and (even) confessions and admissions obtained from examinees, are subject to error. Therefore, results should be considered in the context of a complete investigation. They should not be relied upon to the exclusion of other evidence or used as the sole means of resolving questions of verity.

Even if reliability were to be greatly enhanced in the near future, polygraphs might still find limited use in criminal proceedings, because of objections based on self-incrimination. It can be argued, with a great deal of justification, that forcing a person to take a polygraph examination and using the results against the person would violate the right to protection against compulsory self-incrimination, because the nature of the examination is testimonial or communicative instead of real or physical. Issues pertain-

HIGHLIGHT

Admissibility of Scientific Evidence— The Frye Doctrine versus the Daubert Doctrine

The Frye doctrine holds that the "procedures used must be sufficiently established to have gained general acceptance in the particular field to which they belong." By contrast, the Daubert doctrine holds that admissibility is determined by whether the expert testimony will "assist the trier of fact to understand the evidence or to determine a fact in issue." The Daubert doctrine, used in federal courts, has a more liberal admissibility standard than the Frye doctrine, which is used in most state courts.

ing to the right to counsel and due process might also arise, but chances of their being upheld in court will likely be minimal.

C. Hypnotically Induced Testimony

In hypnosis, a witness may be able to give a physical description of a suspect that can then be sketched by an artist and used as the basis for a search or investigation. Some states allow the use of hypnosis-induced identification and testimony in court, subject to carefully drawn trustworthiness standards, but most states exclude it because of its unreliability. There is disagreement about who should perform the hypnosis and whether the testimony of a witness whose memory has been hypnotically enhanced helps or harms a case when it gets to court. Some courts admit it for limited purposes, such as "helping a witness recall details that may bolster other witnesses' accounts of an incident."[43]

Although the procedure does not trigger any challenges relating to self-incrimination or right to counsel (primarily because the suspect is not present during the hypnotic session), questions about due process might arise, particularly if suggestions by the person conducting it were injected into the procedure. There has been no Supreme Court decision on the admissibility of this type of testimony. The Court has decided, however, that a rule adopted by a trial court that automatically bars hypnotically refreshed favorable testimony from criminal defendants violates the constitutional right to testify in one's own behalf (Rock v. Arkansas, 483 U.S. 44 [1987]). The *Rock* case involved a defendant who wanted to take the witness stand to present hypnotically induced testimony favorable to her defense in a manslaughter case but was barred from doing so by the trial judge. It was not a case in which a witness produced incriminating testimony against a suspect while under hypnosis.

A federal appeals court ruled in 1995 that "hypnotically refreshed memories can be the basis for a lawsuit even if the plaintiff wasn't aware of the allegations before being hypnotized for psychotherapy." The case involved child abuse memories suppressed for thirty years until the plaintiff underwent hypnosis. In admitting the evidence, the Second Circuit Court of Appeals said that under the **Daubert doctrine,** which is now *the test for admissibility of scientific evidence in federal courts,* "it no longer

HIGHLIGHT

The Polygraph

Departmental policy should recognize that polygraph is not a perfect investigative process and that polygraph results, both examiner opinions following chart evaluation and (even) confessions and admissions obtained from examinees, are subject to error. Therefore, results should be considered in the context of a complete investigation. They should not be relied upon to the exclusion of other evidence or used as the sole means of resolving questions of verity.

Source: R. Ferguson, "Polygraph Policy Model for Law Enforcement," *FBI Law Enforcement Bulletin,* June 1987, p. 7.

is required that such evidence be based on 'generally accepted' science or technology. Instead, it's left to trial judges to decide whether the science involved is legitimate and the results are significant to a case."[44] It is likely that other federal trial and appellate courts will adopt the same approach to hypnosis evidence and that the admission of such evidence in federal courts might influence state courts, particularly those that do not use the Frye doctrine, to do the same.

The current status of the admissibility of hypnotically enhanced testimony was summarized by an appellate court in Maryland, in a 1999 decision, as involving four differing scenarios:

> (1) that the fact that a witness's memory was hypnotically enhanced goes only to the weight or credibility of the testimony based on that enhancement, not to its admissibility; (2) that because hypnosis has not been generally accepted within the relevant scientific community as producing a reliably accurate recollection and, indeed, may serve to distort one's memory, a witness who has undergone hypnosis may not testify with respect to any matter discussed during hypnosis; (3) that testimony based on hypnotically enhanced recollections is admissible if certain specified safeguards were employed to assure that the testimony was not improperly influenced by the hypnosis; and (4) that, because hypnosis as a memory-enhancing technique is not generally accepted within the scientific community, testimony based on hypnotically enhanced memory is inadmissible, but that does not preclude the admission of testimony based on and consistent with the witness's recollections recorded prior to the hypnosis. (Burral v. State, 352 Md. 707 [1999])

Scenario 4 is what is currently used in most courts.

Summary

There are three types of pretrial identification proceedings: lineups, showups, and photographic identification. A lineup is a procedure in which a victim or witness to a crime is shown several possible suspects at the police station for identification; a showup is a procedure in which only one suspect is shown to the witness or victim, usually at the scene of the crime and immediately following a quick arrest of the suspect; a photographic identification involves photographs of possible suspects being shown to the victim or witness.

Pretrial identification raises issues of possible violations of four constitutional rights: the right to counsel, the right to due process, the right to protection against unreasonable searches and seizures, and the right to protection against self-incrimination. The right to counsel applies in lineups and showups after a suspect has been charged, but not before; the right to due process applies in all three identification procedures. But the rights to protection against unreasonable searches and seizures and against self-incrimination do not apply in any of the three procedures.

There are other means of pretrial identification, including DNA testing, polygraph examinations, and hypnosis. The results of DNA testing are admissible in court, although some doubts remain. The results of polygraph examinations are not admissible in most courts because their scientific reliability has not been fully established. The results of testimony or identification obtained under hypnosis are not admissible in most courts, also because their scientific reliability has not been established.

Review Questions

1. What four constitutional rights are likely to be invoked by suspects during the pretrial identification stage? Briefly discuss how each applies to lineups, showups, and photographic displays.

2. Discuss the constitutional issues that might arise if a suspect is compelled by force to appear in a police lineup.

3. "A suspect's right to protection against self-incrimination is violated in a police lineup." Is that statement true or false? Support your answer.

4. What can the police do if a suspect refuses to appear in a lineup?

5. "A suspect is entitled to counsel during a lineup." Is that statement true or false? Discuss your answer.

6. Discuss the role of a lawyer during a lineup.

7. Give an example of a lineup in which a suspect's right to due process is violated.

8. What are showups? Does a suspect have any constitutional rights in a showup?

9. What is DNA testing? What is its likely future in law enforcement?

10. What is the Frye doctrine? Is it universally used in American courts?

11. Distinguish between the Frye doctrine and the Daubert doctrine as test for the admissibility of scientific evidence in court.

12. Hypnotically induced evidence is generally not admissible in court. Why?

Key Terms and Definitions

Daubert doctrine: The doctrine that expert testimony pertaining to scientific, technical, or other specialized knowledge that will assist the trier of fact to understand the evidence or to determine whether a fact in issue is admissible in evidence. Used in federal courts, the Daubert doctrine replaces the more strict Frye doctrine, which requires that, for scientific evidence to be admissible, the procedures used must be sufficiently established to have gained general acceptance in the particular scientific field to which they belong.

DNA testing: A procedure that matches the suspect's DNA with the DNA found in semen or blood recovered from the scene of the crime.

formally charged with an offense: Indictment, information, preliminary hearing, or arraignment of the suspect.

Frye doctrine: The doctrine that, before the results of scientific tests will be admissible as evidence in a trial, the procedures used must be sufficiently established to have gained general acceptance in the particular field to which they belong.

Kirby rule: The rule that a suspect in a lineup or other face-to-face confrontation before being formally charged with a crime is not entitled to have a lawyer present.

lineup: "A police identification procedure by which the suspect in a crime is exhibited, along with others with similar physical characteristics, before the victim or witness to determine if he or she can be identified as having committed the offense."

photographic identification (rogue's gallery): A procedure in which photographs of possible suspects are shown to the victim or witness.

real or physical self-incrimination: Incrimination that involves the physical body or objects; not protected by the Fifth Amendment.

showup: A "one-to-one confrontation between a suspect and a witness to a crime."

testimonial or communicative self-incrimination: Self-incrimination through oral testimony or communication; prohibited by the Fifth Amendment. It occurs when the suspect is required to "speak his guilt."

Wade-Gilbert rule: The rule that a suspect in a lineup or other face-to-face confrontation after being formally charged with a crime is entitled to have a lawyer present.

Principles of Cases

Daubert v. Merrell Dow Pharmaceuticals Inc., 53 CrL 2313 (1993) The Frye doctrine has been superseded in federal cases by the adoption of the federal rules of evidence. In particular, those rules have a more liberal admissibility standard, permitting the admission of expert testimony pertaining to scientific, technical, or other specialized knowledge that will assist the trier of fact to understand the evidence or to determine a fact in issue.

Foster v. California, 394 U.S. 440 (1969) The suspect's right to due process is violated during a lineup in which the circumstances are such that identification of the suspect by the witness is inevitable.

Frye v. United States, 293 F. 1013 (D.C. Cir. 1923) Before the results of scientific tests will be admissible as evidence in a trial, the procedures used must be sufficiently established to have gained general acceptance in the particular field to which they belong.

Gilbert v. California, 388 U.S. 263 (1967) Police identification procedures that are "fraught with dangers of suggestion" are invalid because they violate the accused's right to due process.

Kirby v. Illinois, 406 U.S. 682 (1972) There is no right to counsel at police lineups or identification procedures prior to the time the suspect is formally charged with a crime.

Manson v. Brathwaite, 432 U.S. 98 (1977) The suggestiveness of the identification procedure is but one factor courts will take into account to determine whether there was a violation of suspect's due process right.

Moore v. Illinois, 434 U.S. 220 (1977) A defendant is entitled to a lawyer at a showup during the preliminary hearing, because at that time the criminal proceedings are considered to have been initiated.

Neil v. Biggers, 409 U.S. 188 (1972) Identification procedures must not be unfair. To determine that, courts consider all the circumstances leading up to the identification. Unfairness will be found only when, in the light of all such circumstances, the identification procedure is so suggestive as to give rise to a real and substantial likelihood of irreparable misidentification. The courts will most likely take the following factors into account: (1) the witness's opportunity to view the criminal at the time of the crime, (2) the witness's degree of attention at that time, (3) the accuracy of any prior description given by the witness, (4) the level of certainty demonstrated by the witness at the identification, and (5) the length of time between the crime and the identification.

Rock v. Arkansas, 483 U.S. 44 (1987) A rule adopted by the trial court that automatically bars hypnotically refreshed favorable testimony from criminal defendants violates the constitutional right to testify in one's own behalf.

Schmerber v. California, 384 U.S. 757 (1966) The removal of blood from a suspect without his or her consent to obtain evidence is not a violation of any constitutional rights, as long as the removal is done by medical personnel using accepted medical methods.

Stovall v. Denno, 388 U.S. 293 (1967) Holding the showup of a suspect in a hospital is valid when the only living eyewitness is in danger of dying.

United States v. Ash, 413 U.S. 300 (1973) There is no right to counsel when the prosecution seeks to identify the accused by displaying photographs to witnesses prior to trial.

United States v. Jakobetz, 955 F.2d 786 (1992) Held that the trial court properly exercised its discretion in admitting the DNA profiling evidence and that trial courts facing a similar issue in the future can take judicial notice of the general theories and specific techniques involved in DNA profiling.

United States v. Wade, 388 U.S. 218 (1967) A police lineup or other face-to-face confrontation after the accused has been formally charged with a crime is considered a "critical stage of the proceedings," so the accused has a right to have counsel present. The absence of counsel during such proceeding renders the evidence obtained inadmissible. Also, requiring the suspect to "speak up" for identification is not a violation of the safeguard against self-incrimination, because it is physical instead of testimonial self-incrimination.

 ## Case Briefs

Leading Case on the Right to Counsel during a Lineup before Formal Charges Are Filed

Kirby v. Illinois, 406 U.S. 682 (1972)

Facts: A man named Willie Shard reported to the Chicago police that the previous day on a Chicago street, two men had robbed him of a wallet containing traveler's checks and a Social Security card. The following day, two police officers stopped Kirby and a companion named Bean. When asked for identification, Kirby produced a wallet that contained three traveler's checks and a Social Security card, all bearing the name of Willie Shard. Papers with Shard's name on them were also found in Bean's possession. The officers took Kirby and his companion to a police station. Only after arriving at the police station and checking the records there did the arresting officers learn of the Shard robbery. A patrol car was dispatched to Shard's place of employment and brought him to the police station. Immediately upon entering the room in the police station where Kirby and his companion were seated at a table, Shard positively identified them as the men who had robbed him two days earlier. No lawyer was present in the room, and neither Kirby nor his companion had asked for legal assistance or been advised by the police of any right to the presence of counsel. Kirby was convicted of robbery and appealed his conviction, alleging that his identification should have been excluded because it was extracted unconstitutionally.

Issue: *Was Kirby entitled to the presence and advice of a lawyer during this pretrial identification stage? No.*

Supreme Court Decision: There is no right to counsel at police lineups or identification procedures prior to the time the suspect is formally charged with the crime.

Case Significance: *Kirby* was decided five years after United States v. Wade. It clarified an issue that was not directly resolved in *Wade:* whether the ruling in *Wade* applies to cases in which the lineup or pretrial identification takes place prior to the filing of a formal charge. The Court answered this question in the negative, saying that what happened in *Kirby* was a matter of routine police investigation, hence not considered a "critical stage of the prosecution." The Court reasoned that a postindictment lineup is a "critical stage," whereas a preindictment lineup is not. Some justices disagreed with this distinction, but the majority of the Court apparently felt that it was a good standard to use in determining when a suspect's right to counsel applies in pretrial identification procedure.

Excerpts from the Decision: "The initiation of judicial criminal proceedings is far from a mere formalism. It is the starting point of our whole system of adversary criminal justice. For it is only then that the government has committed itself to prosecute, and only then that the adverse positions of government and defendant have solidified. It is then that a defendant finds himself faced with the prosecutorial forces of organized society, and immersed in the intricacies of substantive and procedural criminal law. It is this point, therefore, that marks the commencement of the 'criminal prosecutions' to which alone the explicit guarantees of the Sixth Amendment are applicable.

"In this case we are asked to import into a routine police investigation an absolute constitutional guarantee historically and rationally applicable only after the onset of formal prosecutorial proceedings. We decline to do so. Less than a year after *Wade* and *Gilbert* were decided, the Court explained the rule of those decisions as follows: 'The rationale of those cases was that an accused is entitled to counsel at any "critical stage of the prosecution," and that a postindictment lineup is such a "critical stage."' We decline to depart from that rationale today by imposing a per se exclusionary rule upon testimony concerning an identification that took place long before the commencement of any prosecution whatever."

Leading Case on the Right to Counsel during a Lineup after Formal Charges Are Filed

United States v. Wade, 388 U.S. 218 (1967)

Facts: A federally insured bank in Eustace, Texas, was robbed on September 21, 1964. A man with a small strip of tape on each side of his face entered the bank, pointed a pistol at the female cashier and the vice president, the only persons in the bank at the time, and forced them to fill a pillowcase with money. The man then drove away with an accomplice, who had been waiting in a stolen car outside the bank. On March 23, 1965, an indictment was returned against Wade and two others for conspiring to rob the bank, and against Wade and the accomplice for the robbery itself. Wade was arrested on April 2, and counsel was appointed to represent him on April 26. Fifteen days later, an FBI agent, without giving notice to Wade's lawyer, arranged to have the two bank employees observe a lineup consisting of Wade and five or six other prisoners, conducted in a courtroom of the local county courthouse. Each person in the line wore strips of tape such as those allegedly worn by the robber. Each was ordered to say something like "Put the money in the bag," the words allegedly uttered by the robber. Both bank employees identified Wade in the lineup as the bank robber.

At trial, the two employees, when asked on direct examination if the robber was in the courtroom, pointed to Wade. The prior lineup identification was then elicited from both employees on cross-examination. At the close of testimony, Wade's counsel moved for a judgment of acquittal or, alternatively, to strike the bank employees' courtroom identifications on the grounds that the conduct of the lineup, without notice to and in the absence of appointed counsel, violated Wade's Fifth Amendment right not to incriminate himself and his Sixth Amendment right to the assistance of counsel. The motion was denied, and Wade was convicted.

Issue: *Should the courtroom identification of an accused at trial be excluded as evidence because the accused was exhibited to the witnesses before trial at a postindictment lineup, conducted for identification purposes, without notice to and in the absence of accused's appointed lawyer? Yes.*

Supreme Court Decision: A police lineup or other face-to-face confrontation after the accused has been formally charged with a crime is considered a "critical stage of the proceedings," so the accused has a right to have counsel present. The absence of counsel during such a proceeding renders the evidence obtained inadmissible.

Case Significance: The *Wade* case settled the issue of whether an accused has a right to counsel after the filing of a formal charge. The standard used by the Court was whether the identification was part of the "critical stage of the proceedings." However, the Court did not clarify exactly what this phrase meant, so lower courts did not know where to draw the line. In a subsequent case, Kirby v. Illinois, the Court said that any pretrial identification prior to the filing of a formal charge was not a "critical stage of the proceeding," so no counsel was required. Also, the *Wade* case did not authoritatively state what is meant by "formal charge," so that phrase has been subject to varying interpretations, depending upon state law or practice.

Excerpts from the Decision: "We have no doubt that compelling the accused merely to exhibit his person for observation by a prosecution witness prior to trial involves no compulsion of the accused to give evidence having testimonial significance. It is compulsion of the accused to exhibit his physical characteristics, not compulsion to disclose any knowledge he might have. It is no different from compelling Schmerber to provide a blood sample or Holt to wear the blouse, and as in those instances, is not within the cover of the privilege. Similarly, compelling Wade to speak within hearing distance of the witnesses, even to utter words purportedly uttered by the robber, was not compulsion to utter statements of a 'testimonial' nature; he was required to use his voice as an identifying physical characteristic, not to speak his guilt. . . .

"The Government characterizes the lineup as a mere preparatory step in the gathering of the prosecution's evidence, not different—for Sixth Amendment purposes—from various other preparatory steps, such as systematized or scientific analyzing of the accused's fingerprints, blood sample, clothing, hair, and the like. We think there are differences which preclude such stages being characterized as critical stages at which the accused has the right to the presence of his counsel. Knowledge of the techniques of science and technology is sufficiently available, and the variables in techniques few enough, that the accused has the opportunity for a meaningful confrontation of the Government's case at trial through the ordinary processes of cross-examination of the Government's expert witnesses and the presentation of the evidence of his own experts. The denial of a right to have his counsel present at such analyses does not therefore violate the Sixth Amendment; they are not critical stages since there is minimal risk that his counsel's absence at such stages might derogate from his right to a fair trial."

Notes

1. *Black's Law Dictionary* (St. Paul, MN: West, 1991), p. 641.

2. Lloyd L. Weinreb and James D. Whaley, *The Field Guide to Law Enforcement* (Westbury, NY: Foundation Press, 1999), p. 67.

3. L. Rissler, "The Role of Defense Counsel at Lineups," *FBI Law Enforcement Bulletin,* February 1980, p. 24.

4. Ibid., p. 23.

5. "Eyewitness Identification," *Legal Points* (Gaithersburg, MD: IACP Legal Center, 1975), p. 1. This material is adapted with the permission of the International Association of Chiefs of Police, 13 Firstfield Road, P.O. Box 6010, Gaithersburg, MD 20878.

6. Ibid., pp. 1–2.

7. Supra note 2, p. 64.

8. W. LaFave and J. Israel, *Criminal Procedure* (St. Paul, MN: West, 1985), p. 325.

9. Supra note 1, p. 962.

10. "DNA Commission Continues to Hear Testimony," *National Institute of Justice Journal,* October 1999, p. 32.

11. *Houston Chronicle,* August 8, 1992, p. A3.

12. *USA Today,* August 6, 1999, p. 1.

13. "A Trial of High-Tech Detectives," *Time Magazine,* June 5, 1989, p. 63.

14. "Courtroom Genetics," *U.S. News & World Report,* January 27, 1992, pp. 60–61.

15. Christopher H. Asplen, "Forensic DNA Evidence: National Commission Explores Its Future," *National Institute of Justice Journal,* January 1999, p. 18.

16. *Time Magazine,* September 28, 1999, p. 26.

17. *Houston Chronicle,* September 28, 1997, p. 1.

18. *New York Times,* December 4, 1997, p. 1.

19. *New York Times,* April 19, 1999, p. 1.

20. *Chicago Tribune,* April 16, 1999, p. 1.

21. *Houston Chronicle,* June 16, 1999, p. A7.

22. *USA Today,* August 28, 1997, p. 1.

23. *New York Times,* February 19, 1998, p. 1.

24. David Rohde, "Quietly, Tests of DNA Transform Sleuth's Job," *New York Times,* March 9, 1999, p. 1.

25. *New York Times,* April 15, 1992, p. 1.

26. *U.S. News & World Report,* November 7, 1994, p. 14.

27. *FBI Law Enforcement Bulletin,* February 1998, p. 24.

28. Ibid.

29. *New York Times,* October 12, 1998, p. 1.

30. *New York Times,* August 16, 1999, p. 1.

31. *Time Magazine,* September 28, 1999, p. 28.

32. Ibid.

33. Supra note 12, p. 1.

34. Supra note 12, p. 1.

35. *Houston Chronicle,* September 12, 1999, p. A19.

36. Professor Walter F. Rowe, George Washington University, as quoted in the *Houston Chronicle,* September 12, 1999, p. 1.

37. U.S. Deputy Solicitor General Michael Dreeben, as quoted in the *Houston Chronicle,* November 4, 1997, p. A9.

38. *USA Today,* April 6, 1999, p. A11.

39. P. Lewis and K. Peoples, *The Supreme Court and the Criminal Process—Cases and Comments* (Philadelphia: Saunders, 1978), p. 496.

40. See, for example, *Texas Code of Criminal Procedure,* Article 15.051.

41. *Houston Chronicle,* November 23, 1985, Sec. 3, p. 1.

42. R. Ferguson, "Polygraph Policy Model for Law Enforcement," *FBI Law Enforcement Bulletin,* July 1987, p. 7.

43. *The Wall Street Journal,* November 9, 1995, p. 12.

44. Ibid.

11.

Confessions and Admissions: Miranda v. Arizona

Chapter Outline

(*continued*)

Chapter Outline (continued)

Case Briefs

Berkemer v. McCarty

Arizona v. Fulminante

What You Will Learn in This Chapter

You will develop a good working knowledge of the most widely known case ever to be decided by the U.S. Supreme Court—Miranda v. Arizona. You will be introduced to the standard used by the courts for admissibility of admissions and confessions before *Miranda* and after *Miranda*. You will also learn when, in police work, the Miranda warnings must be given and when they need not be given. You will become familiar as well with the cases decided since 1966 affirming the Miranda rule and cases eroding it. Finally, you will learn about the latest assault on *Miranda*, based on an old federal law.

Introduction

The terms *confession* and *admission* are often used as though they are interchangeable, but they are not. In criminal justice, a **confession** means that *a person says he or she committed the act;* an **admission** means that *the person owns up to something related to the act but may not have committed it.* A confession is therefore more incriminating than an admission. Here are examples:

- **Confession:** "Yes, I shot him."

- **Admission:** "Yes, I was there, but I did not shoot him. Somebody else did."

The Fifth Amendment to the U.S. Constitution provides that "No person shall . . . be compelled in any criminal case to be a witness against himself, nor be deprived of life, liberty, or property, without due process of law." This right has been a source of controversy and has generated a host of litigated issues, some of which are still unresolved. The main question is, When are confessions and admissions admissible as evidence in a criminal trial and when are they excludable? The answers are not simple, but this chapter's discussion should provide some insights. One case stands out over all other cases on the admissibility of confessions and admissions—Miranda v. Arizona. By the **Miranda rule,** *evidence obtained by the police during custodial interrogations of a suspect cannot be used in court during trial, unless the suspect was first informed of the right not to incriminate him- or herself and of the right to counsel,* and unless these rights are waived intelligently and voluntarily.

I. PRIOR TO <u>MIRANDA</u>: VOLUNTARINESS WAS THE TEST FOR ADMISSIBILITY

Before the *Miranda* decision, the Supreme Court decided the admissibility of confessions and admissions on a case-by-case basis, with voluntariness the key criteria. This meant that cases were decided by the courts based on whether the suspect's will was "broken" or "overborne" by the police during interrogation in such a way that it made the confession involuntary and violated the suspect's due process rights. The method was confusing to the lower courts, because the Supreme Court had failed to set any definitive standard by which the admissibility of confessions could be judged. In general, the Court held that confessions obtained by force or coercion could not be used in court; conversely, confessions were admissible if they were voluntary. Voluntariness was the standard used; but the meaning of that term was imprecise and changed over the years.

Originally, only confessions or statements obtained by physical force (such as beating, whipping, or maiming) were considered inadmissible. Later, it was recognized that coercion could be mental as well as physical. Even then, the hard question remained, At what point did physical or mental (psychological) coercion become so excessive as to render the confession involuntary? Clearly, physical torture was prohibited, but what about a push, a shove, a slap, or a mere threat? As for mental coercion, suppose the police did not physically abuse the suspect but simply detained him "until he talks"? Was this coercion? If so, how long must the detention last before the confession could be considered coerced? A few hours? A day? A week?

The following cases, all decided prior to *Miranda,* give a glimpse into the evolution of the Court's rulings and illustrate the difficulty the Court faced in prescribing a viable criterion for the admissibility of confessions or statements before the *Miranda* decision. Each case was decided on the old voluntariness standard and under circumstances that could hardly be replicated in other cases. This led to confusing and conflicting decisions in the lower courts, a confusion that has largely been cleared by the *Miranda* decision.

①Brown v. Mississippi, 297 U.S. 278 (1936)— Confession Not Valid because of Coercion and Brutality

A deputy sheriff, accompanied by other persons, took one of the suspects to a murder scene, where he was questioned about the crime. Brown denied his guilt and was hanged by a rope from the limb of a tree for a period of time. He was then let down, after which he again denied his guilt. He was next tied to the tree and whipped, but he still refused to confess and was allowed to go home. Later Brown was seized again and whipped until he confessed. The Court reversed the conviction and held that the confession was a product of utter coercion and brutality and thus violated the Fourteenth Amendment right to due process. (At that time, the Fifth Amendment protection against compulsory self-incrimination had not been applied to state prosecutions, so the Court had to use the Due Process Clause of the Fourteenth Amendment to reverse the conviction.)

2. Chambers v. Florida, 309 U.S. 227 (1940)—
Confession Not Valid because of Coercion

Four youths were convicted of murder, primarily on the basis of their confessions. No physical coercion was used by the police, but pressure was exerted through prolonged questioning while the defendants were held in jail without contact with the outside world. The Court reversed the convictions on the grounds that the confessions had been coerced and that the defendants had therefore been deprived of their Fourteenth Amendment right to due process.

3. Spano v. New York, 360 U.S. 315 (1959)—
Confession Not Valid because of Deception

The defendant was suspected of murder in New York. About ten days after the murder, Spano telephoned a close friend who was a rookie police officer in the New York police. Spano told his friend that he (Spano) had taken a terrific beating from the murder victim, and since he was dazed he did not know what he was doing when he shot the victim. The officer relayed this information to his superiors. Spano was brought in for questioning, but his attorney advised him not to answer any questions. Spano's rookie friend was called and told to inform Spano that the telephone call from Spano had caused the officer a lot of trouble. The officer was instructed to win sympathy from Spano for the sake of his wife and children. Spano refused to cooperate, but after his friend's fourth try, Spano finally agreed to tell the police about the shooting. Spano was convicted and appealed. The Court said that the use of deception as a means of psychological pressure to induce a confession was a violation of the defendant's constitutional rights and therefore excluded the evidence.

4. Rogers v. Richmond, 365 U.S. 534 (1961)—
Confession Not Valid because of Involuntariness

The defendant was charged with murder and found guilty by a jury. While in jail pending trial, Rogers was questioned about the killing. The interrogation started in the afternoon of the day of his arrest and continued through the evening. During the interrogation, Rogers was allowed to smoke and was given a sandwich and some coffee. At no time was he ever subjected to violence or threat of violence by the police. Six hours after the start of the interview, Rogers still refused to give any information. The police then indicated that they were about to have Rogers's wife taken into custody, whereupon Rogers indicated his willingness to confess. The confession was introduced as evidence during the trial, and Rogers was convicted. The Court held that the confession by Rogers was involuntary and therefore not admissible, on the grounds that the accused did not have complete freedom of mind when making his confession.

5. Escobedo v. Illinois, 378 U.S. 748 (1964)—
Confession Not Valid because the Suspect
Was Denied Counsel at the Police Station

Escobedo was arrested for murder and interrogated for several hours at the police station, during which time he was persuaded to confess. During the interrogation,

Escobedo repeatedly asked to see his lawyer, who was also at the police station at that time and who demanded to see him. The police refused both requests and proceeded to interrogate Escobedo. He eventually confessed, was tried, and was convicted. On appeal, the Court held that Escobedo was denied his right to counsel, so no statement taken during the interrogation could be admitted against him at the trial. The Court said that "where, as here, the investigation is no longer a general inquiry into the unsolved crime but has begun to focus on a particular suspect . . . no statement elicited by the police during the investigation may be used against him at a criminal trial."

This was an easy case for the Court to decide, because the police had indeed grossly violated Escobedo's right to counsel. However, the *Escobedo* case left two issues unsettled: (1) Did the right to counsel apply only when the facts were similar to those in *Escobedo* (the suspect was accused of a serious offense, was being questioned at the police station, and had asked to see his lawyer, and the lawyer was present and demanded to confer with his client)? and (2) What did the Court mean when it said that the right to counsel could be invoked when the investigation had begun to "focus" on a particular suspect? Did it refer to when a suspect was under investigation, had been arrested, had been charged with an offense, or had been arraigned?

Because of its unique facts, the *Escobedo* case raised more questions than it answered. Trial courts disagreed on the meaning of *Escobedo*, particularly the interpretation of the term *focus*, leading to conflicting decisions. Further guidance from the Court became necessary. *Escobedo* therefore set the stage for *Miranda* and, in fact, made *Miranda* necessary because the confusion had to be cleared up.

II. MIRANDA REJECTS THE VOLUNTARINESS TEST IN FAVOR OF A "THREE QUESTIONS" TEST

In *Miranda,* the Court rejected "voluntariness" as the sole test to determine whether statements from suspects are admissible in court. Voluntariness is still required today, but it is assumed from a "yes" answer to three questions the trial court must ask:

1. Were the Miranda *warnings given?*

2. If they were given, was there a *waiver?*

3. If there was a waiver, was it *intelligent and voluntary?*

Miranda, in effect, establishes a three-question test for admissibility. For question 1, if the statement is voluntary but the Miranda warnings were not given when they should have been (because there was custodial interrogation), the evidence cannot be admitted in court. For question 2, even if the statement is voluntary and the Miranda warnings were given, the statement is not admissible if the government cannot establish that there was a waiver. For question 3, if the statement is voluntary, the Miranda warnings were given, and there was a waiver but the waiver was not intelligent and voluntary, the evidence obtained is not admissible in court. These three scenarios may be illustrated as follows:

- **Question 1: Were the Miranda warnings given?** After arrest and in response to questions without the Miranda warnings, Y gives the police a confession that is clearly voluntary. The evidence cannot be used in court, except for impeachment should Y take the witness stand, because Y was not given her Miranda warnings. (Note, however, that the court's decision in Minnesota v. Dickerson discussed at the end of this chapter may change this rule.)

- **Question 2: If they were given, was there a waiver?** The prosecutor cannot prove in court that D in fact waived his rights prior to giving a confession, so the evidence is not admissible.

- **Question 3: If there was a waiver, was it intelligent and voluntary?** M gives a voluntary statement to the police after having been given the Miranda warnings. During the trial, however, the prosecutor cannot prove that M's waiver was intelligent and voluntary, so the evidence is not admissible.

For trial court judges, the importance of Miranda lies in the shift from the old "voluntariness" test to a new, mechanical standard that is easier to apply: Can the police answer "yes" to all three questions? Voluntariness is still a requirement for admissibility, but it is no longer the immediate focus of the trial court's initial inquiry. Involuntary confessions are not admissible under Miranda, but voluntariness is assumed if the answers to the three questions are all affirmative. Trial courts no longer need to investigate specific facts in each case to determine if the statement was, in fact, voluntary. Now, they can now simply ask three questions and, depending on the answers, admit or disallow the statement to establish a defendant's guilt.

III. THE BASICS OF MIRANDA V. ARIZONA

A. The Case Itself

Miranda v. Arizona, 384 U.S. 436 (1966), decided in a 5-to-4 vote, is undoubtedly the best-known and arguably the most significant law enforcement case ever to be decided by the U.S. Supreme Court. Because of its importance, the case deserves detailed discussion.

1. The Facts

Ernesto Miranda was arrested at his home in Phoenix, Arizona, and taken to a police station for questioning in connection with a rape and kidnapping. Miranda was then twenty-three years old, was poor, and was a ninth-grade dropout. The officers interrogated him for two hours, after which they emerged from the interrogation room with a written confession signed by Miranda. The confession was admitted as evidence during the trial. Miranda was convicted of rape and kidnapping and sentenced to twenty to thirty years' imprisonment on each count. The Arizona Supreme Court affirmed the conviction; Miranda appealed to the U.S. Supreme Court.

2. The Legal Issue

Must the police inform a suspect, who is subject to a custodial interrogation, of his or her constitutional rights involving self-incrimination and counsel prior to questioning in order for the evidence to be admissible in court during the trial?

3. The Court's Decision

Evidence obtained by the police during custodial interrogation of a suspect cannot be used in court during the trial unless the suspect was first informed of the right not to incriminate him- or herself and of the right to counsel. The Court said:

> We hold that when an individual is taken into custody or otherwise deprived of his freedom by the authorities and is subject to questioning, the privilege against self-incrimination is jeopardized. Procedural safeguards must be employed. . . . He must be warned prior to any questioning that he has a right to remain silent, that anything he says can be used against him in a court of law, that he has a right to the presence of an attorney, and that if he cannot afford an attorney one will be appointed for him prior to any questioning if he so desires. Opportunity to exercise these rights must be afforded to him throughout the interrogation.

4. The Case's Significance

Miranda v. Arizona has had a huge impact on day-to-day crime investigation. It has drawn a *"bright-line" rule for admissibility* of confessions and admissions and has led to changes that have since become an accepted part of routine police work. No other law enforcement case has generated more controversy within and outside police circles. Supporters of the *Miranda* decision hail it as properly protective of individual rights, whereas critics have accused the Court of being soft on crime and of coddling criminals. The 5-to-4 split among the justices served to fan the flames of the controversy in its early stages, with opponents of the ruling hoping that a change in Court composition would hasten its demise. But that has not happened, nor is it likely to happen in the near future.

   Miranda is unusual, because the Court seldom tells the police, in a Court decision, exactly what the police should do. In *Miranda,* the Court did not simply say that a constitutional right was violated; it went further and prescribed in no uncertain terms what the police should do. In clear language, the Court mandated that a suspect "must be warned prior to any questioning that he has a right to remain silent, that anything he says can be used against him in a court of law, that he has a right to the presence of an attorney, and that if he cannot afford an attorney one will be appointed for him prior to any questioning if he so desires." Seldom is the Court as explicit in its instructions.

   Miranda also clarified some of the ambiguous terms used in *Escobedo.* "By custodial interrogation," said the Court, "we mean questioning initiated by law enforcement officers after a person has been taken into custody or otherwise deprived of his freedom of action in any significant way." It then added this footnote, "This is what we meant in *Escobedo* when we spoke of an investigation which had focused on an accused." Yet the "focus" test used in *Escobedo* was abandoned by the Court in later cases; in its place, the "custodial interrogation" test was used to determine if the Miranda warnings needed to be given. The *Escobedo* case brought the right to counsel to the police station prior to trial; the *Miranda* case went beyond the police station and brought the right to counsel out into the street if custodial interrogation was to take place.

B. The Miranda Warnings

Miranda mandates that the following warnings must be given to a suspect or accused prior to custodial interrogation:

1. You have a right to remain silent.

2. Anything you say can be used against you in a court of law.

3. You have a right to the presence of an attorney.

4. If you cannot afford an attorney, one will be appointed for you prior to questioning.

Practically all jurisdictions add a fifth warning, saying, "You have the right to terminate this interview at any time." (See Form 11.1.) This additional statement, however, is not constitutionally required under the *Miranda* decision. Most police departments direct officers to issue the warnings as given here (taken directly from the *Miranda* decision). However, in some cases, warnings that are not worded exactly as given here may still comply with *Miranda,* provided the defendant is given adequate information concerning the right to remain silent and to have an attorney present. In one case, the police gave the following warnings:

> "You have a right to talk to a lawyer for advice before we ask you any questions, and to have him with you during questioning.
>
> "You have the right to the advice and presence of a lawyer even if you cannot afford to hire one.
>
> "We have no way of giving you a lawyer, but one will be appointed for you, if you wish, if and when you go to court."

The last part of that warning—"if you wish, if and when you go to court"—was challenged as ambiguous and therefore inadequate. In a 5-to-4 vote, the Court disagreed, saying that the warning, although ambiguous, was sufficient to inform the suspect of his rights (Duckworth v. Eagan, 492 U.S. 195 [1989]). The Court further said that *Miranda* does not require that lawyers be producible on call. It is enough that the suspect be informed of his or her right to an attorney and to appointed counsel, and that, if the police cannot provide appointed counsel, they will not question the suspect until and unless there is a valid waiver.

The Court also stated, "If the individual indicates in any manner any time prior to or during questioning that he wishes to remain silent, the interrogation must cease." If it does not cease, any information obtained by the police is not admissible as evidence in court, unless the government can prove that the defendant knowingly and intelligently waived that right. As for access to a lawyer, the Court said:

> If the individual states that he wants an attorney, the interrogation must cease until an attorney is present. At that time, the individual must have an opportunity

Statement of Miranda Rights

1. You have the right to remain silent.

2. Anything you say can and will be used against you in a court of law.

3. You have the right to talk to a lawyer and have him present with you while you are being questioned.

4. If you cannot afford to hire a lawyer, one will be appointed to represent you before any questioning, if you wish.

5. You can decide at any time to use these rights and not answer questions or make a statement.

Waiver of Rights

I have read the above statement of my rights and I understand each of those rights, and having these rights in mind I waive them and willingly make a statement.

SIGNED _____ Age _____

Address _____

Date _____ Time _____ Location _____

Witnessed by _____ Department _____

Witnessed by _____ Department _____

Witnessed by _____ Department _____

Remarks:

GO-WRITE FORM: 710/75/MF

Form 11.1 *Miranda Warnings*

to confer with the attorney and to have him present during any subsequent questioning. If the individual cannot obtain an attorney and he indicates that he wants one, before speaking to the police, they must respect his decision to remain silent.

C. The Miranda Warnings Must Be Given for All Offenses except Routine Traffic Stops

Should the Miranda warnings be given for all or only for some offenses? The Court answered this important question in Berkemer v. McCarty, 468 U.S. 420 (1984). The Court's answer may be summarized as follows:

- **The rule:** A person subjected to custodial interrogation must be given the Miranda warnings regardless of the nature or severity of the offense and whether the person goes to jail or not. This includes felonies, misdemeanors, and petty and traffic offenses.

- **The only exception:** The roadside questioning of a motorist detained pursuant to a routine traffic stop does not require the Miranda warnings.

In *McCarty*, an officer of the Ohio State Highway Patrol observed a driver weaving in and out of a highway lane. The officer stopped the car and forced McCarty to get out. Noticing that he had difficulty standing, the officer asked McCarty to perform a field sobriety test and asked him if he had been using intoxicants. McCarty replied that he had consumed two beers and had smoked marijuana a short time before. The officer then arrested him and drove him to the county jail, where a blood test was performed. Questioning was resumed, and McCarty again gave incriminating statements. Convicted of driving while under the influence of alcohol and/or drugs, he sought exclusion of his incriminating statements, saying that at no point in the whole proceeding was he given the Miranda warnings. The state of Ohio countered that the warnings were unnecessary because McCarty was charged with a misdemeanor traffic offense. The Court agreed with McCarty, saying, "We therefore hold that a person subjected to custodial interrogation is entitled to the benefit of the procedural safeguards enunciated in Miranda, regardless of the nature or severity of the offense of which he is suspected or for which he was arrested."

The Court went on to say that the only exception is routine questioning of a motorist detained pursuant to a routine traffic stop. This is because a routine traffic stop is usually brief, and the motorist expects that, although he or she may be given a citation, in the end he or she most likely will be allowed to continue. Contrary to McCarty's allegations, there is no deprivation of freedom in a significant way in a routine traffic stop. The Court said that there is no custodial interrogation in these cases because the typical traffic stop is public; such exposure to public view reduces the opportunity for unscrupulous police officers to use illegitimate means to solicit self-incriminating statements and diminishes the motorist's fear of being subjected to abuse unless he or she cooperates. The Court further noted, "A motorist's expectations, when he sees a policeman's light flashing behind him, are that he will be obliged to spend a short period of time answering questions and waiting while the officer checks his license and registration, that he may then be given a citation, but that in the end he most likely will be allowed to continue his way."

Four years later, the Court reiterated this principle, saying that the curbside stop of a motorist for a traffic violation, although representing a Fourth Amendment seizure of the person, is not sufficiently custodial as to require the Miranda warnings (Pennsylvania v. Bruder, 488 U.S. 9 [1988]). However, traffic offenses that involve more than roadside questioning pursuant to a routine traffic stop need the Miranda warnings. In general, the arrest of a driver in connection with a traffic offense triggers the Miranda warnings because this is no longer a case of roadside questioning pursuant to a routine traffic stop.

These rules may be illustrated as follows:

- **Example 1:** Y is stopped by an officer for driving while intoxicated. State law or local ordinance allows the officer to arrest the driver for this traffic offense, so he arrests Y and takes her to the police station for booking. If the officer asks questions other than preliminary questions (such as name and address), Y must be given the Miranda warnings. Otherwise, statements made by Y will not be admissible in court.

- **Example 2:** Z is stopped by an officer for failure to stop at a stop sign. The officer asks Z questions and then issues a citation or releases Z. The officer does not have to give Z the Miranda warnings even if she asks Z questions.

In sum, the Miranda warnings must be given when the suspect is interrogated for any type of offense—whether it be a felony, misdemeanor, or petty traffic offense. The only exception is roadside questioning of a motorist detained pursuant to a routine traffic stop. (Read the Berkemer v. McCarty case brief at the end of this chapter.)

D. Miranda Is a "Protection against Self-Incrimination," Not a "Right to Counsel," Case

Miranda is primarily a case relating to the Fifth Amendment protection against self-incrimination. Miranda warnings 1 and 2, as listed previously, protect the right not to incriminate oneself. Warnings 3 and 4 are right-to-counsel warnings, but they are there primarily to protect suspects against compulsory self-incrimination. In other words, a suspect is entitled to a lawyer during interrogation so that his or her right to avoid self-incrimination may be protected properly. Even if the proper Miranda warnings are given, however, the evidence is not admissible if the right to counsel under the Sixth Amendment has been violated. Clearly, therefore, in cases involving confessions and admissions, the Fifth Amendment protection against compulsory self-incrimination and the Sixth Amendment right to counsel are closely intertwined. Moreover, it is not enough that the accused be afforded an opportunity to consult a lawyer prior to questioning. *Miranda* includes the right to have a lawyer present while the suspect is being questioned.

E. Miranda Rights May Be Waived

In *Miranda,* the Court said, "After . . . warnings have been given, and such opportunity [to exercise these rights] afforded him, the individual may knowingly and intelligently waive these rights and agree to answer questions or make a statement." A **waiver** is *an intentional relinquishment of a known right or remedy.* The rights under *Miranda* may be waived, expressly or implicitly, but the Court said that "a heavy burden rests on the government to demonstrate that the defendant knowingly and intelligently waived his privilege against self-incrimination and his right to retained or appointed counsel." Certain aspects of a valid waiver warrant further discussion.

1. The Waiver Must Be Intelligent and Voluntary

The *Miranda* decision specifically states that the prosecution must prove that the defendant intelligently and voluntarily waived his or her right to silence and to retained or court-appointed counsel. An **intelligent waiver** means one given *by a suspect who knows what he or she is doing and is sufficiently competent to waive his or her rights.* In cases involving a suspect who is drunk, under the influence of drugs, or in a state of trauma or shock, or who has been seriously injured, is senile, or is too young, intelligent waiver is difficult for the prosecution to prove. There is no definite guidance from the courts in these cases; the best policy is for the police either to wait until the suspect's competency is restored (even if temporarily) or to be certain that the suspect understands the warnings sufficiently.

A **voluntary waiver** is one that *is not the result of any threat, force, or coercion and is made of the suspect's own free will.* It is determined based on a totality of circumstances. In one case, a suspect in the killing of an undercover officer, who was in the intensive care unit of the hospital and under heavy sedation, was asked by the police if he had shot anyone. The suspect replied, "I can't say, I have to see a lawyer." The Court said that the statements obtained by the police were not "the product of his free and rational choice" and could not be used even for impeachment purposes (Mincey v. Arizona, 437 U.S. 385 [1978]). The Court added:

> It is hard to imagine a situation less conducive to the exercise of a "rational intellect and a free will" than Mincey's. He had been seriously wounded just a few hours earlier, and had arrived at the hospital "depressed almost to the point of coma," according to his attending physician. Although he had received some treatment, his condition at the time of . . . interrogation was still sufficiently serious that he was in the intensive care unit. He complained to [the detective] that the pain in his leg was "unbearable." He was evidently confused and unable to think clearly about the events of that afternoon or the circumstances of his interrogation, since some of his written answers were on their face not entirely coherent.

Moreover, the waiver must be shown on the record. Quoting from an earlier case, the Court in *Miranda* said, "Presuming waiver from a silent record is impermissible. The record must show, or there must be an allegation and evidence which shows that an accused was offered counsel but intelligently and understandingly rejected the offer. Anything less is not a waiver."

2. A Waiver "Following the Advice of God" May Be Valid

The admissibility of statements made when the mental state of the suspect interferes with his or her "rational intellect" and "free will" is governed by state rules of evidence rather than by Supreme Court decisions on coerced confessions. Such statements are therefore not automatically excluded; admissibility instead depends on state rules (Colorado v. Connelly, 479 U.S. 157 [1986]). In that case, Connelly approached a uniformed Denver police officer and confessed that he had murdered someone in Denver in 1982 and wanted to talk to the officer about it. The officer advised Connelly of his Miranda rights. Connelly indicated that he understood his rights and wanted to talk about the murder. After a homicide detective arrived, Connelly was again advised of his Miranda rights and again indicated that he wanted to speak with the police. Connelly was then taken to the police station, where he told officers that he had come from Boston to confess to the murder. When he became visibly disoriented, he was sent to a state hospital. In an interview with a psychiatrist, Connelly revealed that he was "following the advice of God" in confessing to the murder. He sought exclusion of the evidence during trial, saying that the confession was, in effect, coerced. The Court rejected the challenge, saying that confessions and admissions are involuntary and invalid under the Constitution *only if the coercion is exerted by the police*, not if exerted by somebody else—in this case, allegedly, by God. The police did not act improperly or illegally, so the confession is constitutionally admissible. It may, however, be excluded by state law.

3. There Is No Presumption of a Waiver from Silence after the Warnings

The Court in Miranda said that a waiver cannot be presumed from silence after the defendant has been warned of his or her rights. The trial court cannot presume waiver from the failure of the accused to complain after the giving of warning or from the fact that the accused spoke with the police after the warnings were given (Teague v. Louisiana, 444 U.S. 469 [1980]). The Court has not decided authoritatively whether a nod or a shrug constitutes a valid waiver.

4. An Express Waiver Is Not Required

An express waiver is not required. The failure to make an explicit statement regarding the waiver does not determine whether the evidence is admissible. Instead, the trial court must look at all the circumstances to determine whether a valid waiver has, in fact, been made. An express waiver, although easier to establish in court, is not required (North Carolina v. Butler, 441 U.S. 369 [1979]). The court will most likely take into account a variety of considerations, such as the age of the suspect, whether the suspect was alone with the officers at the time of interrogation or was in the presence of other people, the time of day, and the suspect's mental condition at the time of questioning.

5. A Signed Waiver Is Not Required

A signed waiver is not required. Refusal by the suspect to sign the waiver form (used by most police departments) does not necessarily mean that there is no valid waiver. The

Court has said that "the question is not one of form, but rather whether the defendant in fact knowingly and voluntarily waived the rights delineated in *Miranda*." A written waiver, however, makes it easier to prove a valid waiver in court.

6. The Warnings Must Be Repeated after a Prolonged Interruption

In *Miranda,* the Court hinted that, even if there is a waiver, if there is a prolonged interruption before an interrogation is resumed, it is best to give the Miranda warnings again. Although no time has been specified, "prolonged interruption" should be taken to mean an interruption of several hours. The longer the time lapse, the greater is the need to give the warnings again. For example, suppose a suspect is given the Miranda warnings and waives his rights. The police interrogate him but then go on a lunch break. Fours hours later, when the officers resume their interrogation, he should be given the Miranda warnings again.[1]

7. A Request for Someone Other Than a Lawyer Is a Waiver

The request by the suspect for somebody other than a lawyer constitutes a valid waiver of the right to counsel. For example, the request of a juvenile on probation to see his probation officer instead of a lawyer (after having been given the Miranda warnings by the police and asked if he wanted to see a lawyer) was considered by the Court to be a waiver of the juvenile's right to a lawyer, because a probation officer and a lawyer perform two different functions (Fare v. Michael C., 442 U.S. 707 [1979]).

8. A Waiver May Be Valid Even If a Lawyer Has Been Retained

A suspect who already has a lawyer may waive the right to a lawyer in the absence of that lawyer, as long as the waiver is intelligent and voluntary. If the retained lawyer, however, wishes to see the client, even though the client has not requested to see the lawyer, the police are best advised at least to tell the defendant that his or her lawyer wants to speak to him or her.

9. A Waiver May Be Withdrawn at Any Time

A suspect may withdraw a waiver once given. If the waiver is withdrawn, the interrogation must stop immediately. However, evidence obtained before the waiver is withdrawn is admissible in court. For example, suppose a suspect waives her rights and agrees to talk to the police. She gives incriminating information but changes her mind after fifteen minutes of questioning. The interrogation must cease immediately, but any statements she made prior to changing her mind are admissible.

F. The Prosecution Must Prove Intelligent and Voluntary Waiver

The Court in *Miranda* held that the prosecution has a "heavy burden . . . to demonstrate that the defendant knowingly and intelligently waived his privilege against self-incrimination and his right to a retained or appointed counsel." If that burden is not met, the evidence obtained is inadmissible even if it is voluntary.

AT A GLANCE

Waiver of Miranda Warnings

1. The waiver must be intelligent and voluntary.
2. A waiver "following the advice of God" may be valid, depending on state rules of evidence.
3. There is no presumption of a waiver from silence after the warnings.
4. An express waiver is not required.
5. A signed waiver is not required.
6. The warnings must be repeated after a prolonged interruption.
7. A request for someone other than a lawyer is a waiver.
8. A waiver may be valid even if a lawyer has been retained.
9. A waiver may be withdrawn at any time.

Although a written waiver is not constitutionally required, most police departments have a written waiver form that suspects are asked to sign. The written waiver may be a part of the written confession, either before or after the statement by the accused, or be attached to it. If witnesses to the waiver are available (such as police officers, other police personnel, or private persons), they should be asked to sign the waiver to strengthen the showing of voluntariness. If the confession is typewritten, it is good practice to have the defendant read it and correct any errors in his or her own handwriting. This procedure reinforces the claim of a valid waiver. In the absence of a written waiver, the issue boils down to the testimony of the suspect against the testimony of the police officer that the waiver was, in fact, voluntary. A written waiver makes the claim of voluntariness by the police more credible.

In juvenile cases, the waiver of rights is usually governed by state law. In many states, there is a minimum age below which a juvenile cannot waive his or her rights. In other states, the waiver is valid only if signed by a parent or guardian and/or signed in the presence of a lawyer.

IV. THE MIRANDA WARNINGS MUST BE GIVEN WHENEVER THERE IS "CUSTODIAL INTERROGATION"

When must the Miranda warnings be given? The simple but sometimes difficult-to-determine answer is, *Whenever there is custodial interrogation.* The next question is, When is there custodial interrogation? In Escobedo v. Illinois, discussed previously, the Court stated that the warnings must be given when the investigation has "focused" on the individual as a suspect. In *Miranda,* the Court abandoned the "focus of the investigation" test and replaced it with the "custodial interrogation" standard. In other words, a person who is the focus of an investigation is not entitled to the Miranda warnings unless that person is under **custodial interrogation,** which means *the suspect is (1) in custody and (2) under interrogation.* Although one phrase, these are two distinct terms; in the absence of either one, there is no custodial interrogation. For example, when a suspect is in custody but no questions are being asked, there is obviously no need for the Miranda warnings. Conversely, if an individual is being interrogated but he or she is not in custody, there is no need to give the Miranda warnings. It is therefore important that the terms *custodial* and *interrogation* be discussed separately.

A. When Is a Suspect in Custody?

A suspect is in custody in two general situations: (1) when the suspect is *under arrest* or (2) when the suspect is not under arrest but is *"deprived of freedom in a significant way."* According to the Court, the test that determines whether a person is in custody for Miranda purposes is "whether the suspect has been subjected to a formal arrest or to equivalent restraints on his freedom of movement" (California v. Beheler, 463 U.S. 1121 [1983]). Whether a person is in custody is determined by the totality of circumstances. Each of these situations deserves an extended discussion.

Situation 1: When the Suspect Is under Arrest

The rule is clear that, when a person is under arrest, the Miranda warnings must be given prior to interrogation. It makes no difference whatsoever whether the arrest be for a felony or a misdemeanor. When, then, is a suspect under arrest? The answer is, whenever the four elements of arrest are present: intent, authority, custody, and understanding (as discussed in chapter 6).

- **Example 1:** A suspect is arrested by virtue of a warrant. En route to the police station, the officer questions the suspect about the crime. The suspect must first be given the Miranda warnings.

- **Example 2:** A suspect is arrested without a warrant, because the police have probable cause to make a warrantless arrest (as when a crime is committed in the presence of the police). If the suspect is questioned at any time by the police, the suspect must first be given the Miranda warnings.

Note that brief questioning of a person by the police is not an arrest if the police officer intends to let the person go after the brief detention. Also, stopping a motor vehicle for the purpose of issuing the driver a ticket or citation is not an arrest, so the Miranda warnings are not needed even if the police ask questions.

Situation 2: When the Suspect Is Not under Arrest but Is Deprived of Freedom in a Significant Way

This is the more difficult situation. The question is, When is a person **deprived of freedom in a significant way,** so as to be considered in custody for purposes of Miranda? The answer is, *when the person's freedom of movement has been limited by the* *police.* Therefore, even if the investigation has focused on a person, the Miranda warnings need not be given unless the defendant will not be allowed to leave after the questioning. "Focus of the investigation" is no longer the test (as it was under Escobedo v. Illinois in 1964) to determine if the Miranda warnings must be given; "custodial interrogation" is now the test.

Whose perception determines whether a suspect has been deprived of freedom—that of the police or of the suspect? The Court has said that a "policeman's unarticulated plan has no bearing on the question whether a suspect was 'in custody' at a particular time; the only relevant inquiry is how a reasonable man in the suspect's position would have understood his position" (Berkemer v. McCarty, 468 U.S. 420 [1984]). In the words of one writer, "To trigger the *Miranda* safeguards, it is not sufficient that the suspect have a subjective belief that he is not free to go, nor that unknown to him, the officers intend to restrain him if he tries to leave. The test is whether a reasonable person in the suspect's position would conclude that he is not free to go."[2] This is based on the totality of the circumstances and is therefore determined on a case-by-case basis. Some factors to be considered are the location of the encounter and the nature and tone of the officer's questions.[3]

A more recent case clarifies what the Court means by "in custody." In Stansbury v. California, 55 CrL 2016 (1994), the Court rejected the "subjective test" by the officer and adopted instead the "objective test" in determining whether a person is in custody. The Court said that "an officer's subjective and undisclosed view concerning whether the person being interrogated is a suspect is irrelevant to the assessment whether the person is in custody," adding that "in determining whether an individual was in custody, a court must examine all of the circumstances surrounding the interrogation, but the ultimate inquiry is simply whether there [was] a 'formal arrest or restraint on freedom of movement' of the degree associated with a formal arrest." The fact that the police denied that the suspect was "in custody" at the time some of the incriminating statements were made did not determine whether the suspect was, in fact, in custody. Therefore, the Court remanded the case for further proceedings. The Court admitted, however, that "an officer's knowledge or beliefs may bear upon the custody issue if they are conveyed, by word or deed, to the individual being questioned. Those beliefs are relevant only to the extent that they would affect how a reasonable person in the position of the individual being questioned would gauge the breadth of his or her 'freedom of action.'"

In sum, police intent is less important than the circumstances surrounding the interrogation when determining whether a person was in custody. A person may be in custody even if he or she is at home, in the office, or on the street. The objective test (meaning whether a reasonable person under the same circumstances would conclude that he or she was not free to go) determines whether a person actually is in custody.

Here are some specific issues related to situation 2.

a. Questioning at the Police Station

Questioning at the police station generally requires that the Miranda warnings be given. For example, suppose the police invite a suspect to come to the police station "to answer a few questions." This type of interrogation requires the Miranda warnings, because a police station lends a "coercive atmosphere" to the interrogation. The exceptions to this general rule are (1) if the suspect on his or her own goes to the police station and knows that he or she is free to leave at any time and (2) if the suspect goes to the police station upon invitation of the police but is told that he or she is not under arrest and is free to leave at any time.

In one case, the police suspected a parolee of involvement in a burglary. The suspect came to the police station in response to an officer's message that the officer would "like to discuss something with you." It was made clear to the suspect that he was not under arrest but that the police believed he was involved in the burglary. The suspect confessed, but he later sought to exclude the evidence. The Court said that the Miranda warnings are necessary only if the suspect is in custody "or otherwise deprived of freedom in a significant way." Since those things had not occurred, the confession was admissible (Oregon v. Mathiason, 429 U.S. 492 [1977]).

b. Questioning in a Police Car Questioning in police cars generally requires the Miranda warnings because of its custodial nature. The warnings must be given even if the suspect has not been placed under arrest. The reason is that questionings in police cars tend to be inherently coercive—the suspect is being deprived of freedom in a significant way.

c. Questioning When the Suspect Is Not Free to Leave When the police will not allow the suspect to leave their presence, or will not leave the suspect alone, or will not leave if asked to do so by the suspect, then the Miranda warnings *must be given.* If the police consider the suspect's attempt to leave or his or her refusal to answer questions as reason enough to stop the suspect from leaving or to arrest him or her formally, then the Miranda warnings must be given. Clearly, under these conditions, the suspect is being deprived of freedom in a significant way.

d. Questioning in the Home Whether the Miranda warnings must precede questioning in a suspect's home depends upon the circumstances of the case. The Court has held that the questioning of a suspect in his bedroom by four police officers at four o'clock in the morning required the Miranda warnings (Orozco v. Texas, 394 U.S. 324 [1969]). In a later case, however, the Court held that statements obtained by Internal Revenue Service agents during a noncustodial, noncoercive interview with a taxpayer under criminal tax investigation, conducted in a private home where the taxpayer occasionally stayed, did not require the Miranda warnings, as long as the taxpayer had been told that he was free to leave (Beckwith v. United States, 425 U.S. 341 [1976]).

Note that, in both the *Orozco* and *Beckwith* cases, the investigation had already focused on the suspect. Under the old *Escobedo* standard, therefore, the warnings ought to have been given in both cases. The key consideration under *Miranda,* however, is whether the suspect's freedom of movement has been limited in a significant way— whether the suspect is truly free to leave after the questioning. In *Orozco,* aside from the coercive nature of the questioning, the suspect was not free to leave after the questioning, whereas in *Beckwith* the suspect was free to go. The current test to determine whether the Miranda warnings need to be given is not whether the investigation has focused on the individual but whether the suspect is under arrest or has been deprived of freedom in a significant way, such that there is custodial interrogation.

e. Questioning a Person Who Is in Custody for Another Offense Any time the suspect being questioned for another offense is in jail or prison, the Miranda warnings must be given, because the suspect is in custody. For example, suppose a prison inmate serving a state sentence is questioned by federal agents regarding a completely separate offense. The suspect is entitled to the Miranda warnings even though no federal criminal charges are contemplated at the time of questioning. Failure to give the Miranda warnings when the suspect is in jail or prison means that the evidence obtained cannot be used in a criminal trial. However, there is no need for jail or prison officials to give the Miranda warnings in prison disciplinary cases, since these are administrative proceedings. A defendant who is in custody for another offense is not under arrest, at least for this second offense, but is certainly being deprived of freedom in a significant way. A safe policy in situations involving the issue of "deprived of freedom in a significant way" is, when in doubt, give the Miranda warnings so as not to jeopardize the admissibility of any evidence obtained.

B. When Is a Suspect under Interrogation?

There are two situations when a suspect is under **interrogation:** *(1) when the police are asking questions that tend to incriminate, and (2) when the police ask no questions but, through their actions, create the "functional equivalent" of an interrogation.*

1. When the Police Ask Questions That Tend to Incriminate

Most interrogations fall into this category. These questions are aimed at obtaining what may be an admission or confession from the suspect: "Did you kill her?" "Where is the gun?" "Why did you do it?" Note, however, that there is no need to give the Miranda warnings when asking identification or routine booking questions: "What is your name?" "Where do you live?" "Do you have a driver's license?" "What is your Social Security number?" Such questions are not self-incriminatory, so no warning is necessary.

2. When No Questions Are Asked but the Police Create the "Functional Equivalent" of an Interrogation

There are instances when *no questions are actually being asked by the police, but the circumstances are so conducive to making a statement or giving a confession* that the courts consider them to be the **"functional equivalent" of an interrogation.** In one case, the Court said:

> A practice that the police should know is reasonably likely to evoke an incriminating response from a suspect thus amounts to interrogation. But since the police surely cannot be held accountable for the unforeseeable results of their words or actions, the definition of interrogation can extend only to words or actions on the part of the police officers that they would have known were reasonably likely to elicit an incriminating response. (Rhode Island v. Innis, 446 U.S. 291 [1980])

In specific cases, the Court has made clarifications related to the following scenarios.

a. When Police Appeal to the Defendant's Religious Interests
In one case, the suspect in a murder case turned himself in to the police. His lawyer told him he would not be interrogated or mistreated. On the drive from Davenport, Iowa (where he had turned himself in), to Des Moines, Iowa (where he was facing the charge), the officer gave the suspect the now-famous "Christian burial" speech. The officer called the suspect "Reverend" and indicated that the parents of the missing girl should be entitled to give a Christian burial to the poor child who had been snatched away from them on Christmas Eve. The defendant then showed the officers where the body was to be found. The Court said that the evidence obtained was not admissible because of a violation of the suspect's right to counsel. The defendant had clearly asserted this right, and there was no evidence of knowing and voluntary waiver. Moreover, although there was no actual interrogation, the Court held that interrogation nonetheless occurs when the police, knowing of the defendant's religious interests, make remarks designed to appeal to those interests and thus induce the defendant to confess (Brewer v. Williams, 430 U.S. 387 [1977]).

b. When Two Officers Converse between Themselves
Compare the *Brewer* case with Rhode Island v. Innis. In *Innis,* the officers were conversing between themselves while they had the suspect in the back of the car. The suspect had been arrested in connection with the shotgun robbery of a taxicab driver. The officers talked about the fact that it would be a terrible thing if one of the handicapped students from the school near the crime scene were to find a loaded shotgun and get hurt. The conversation, although held by fellow officers, was within the hearing of the suspect. The suspect then interrupted the police and told them the location of the shotgun. The Court held that this did not constitute interrogation, so the volunteered evidence was admissible (Rhode Island v. Innis, 446 U.S. 291 [1980]). What the police did was not the functional equivalent of an interrogation.

c. When a Conversation between a Suspect and His Wife Is Recorded by an Officer
In one case, the police received a call that a man had just entered a store claiming that he had killed his son. When officers reached the store, the man admitted to committing the act and directed officers to the body. He was then arrested and advised of his Miranda rights. He was taken to the police station where he was again given the Miranda warnings. The suspect then told the officers that he did not wish to make any more statements until a lawyer was present. At that time, the police stopped questioning him. The suspect's wife was in another room, and when the police questioned her, she insisted on speaking with the suspect. The police allowed the meeting on the condition that an officer be present to tape the conversation. The tape was later used to impeach the suspect's contention that he was insane at the time of the murder. During trial, the suspect sought the exclusion of the recording, saying that he should have been given the Miranda warnings prior to the recording. The Court disagreed, saying that a conversation between a suspect and his or her spouse that is recorded by and in the presence of an officer does not constitute the functional equivalent of an interrogation under *Miranda,* so the evidence was admissible (Arizona v. Mauro, 481 U.S. 520 [1987]). The Court added that what the police did was merely to "arrange a situation" in which there was a likelihood that the suspect would say something incriminating.

TABLE 11.1 *Cases Affirming* Miranda

Case	Evidence Obtained How?	Evidence Admissible?
1. United States v. Henry (1980)	Questioning after indictment	No
2. Edwards v. Arizona (1981)	No valid waiver of right to counsel	No
3. Smith v. Illinois (1984)	Interrogation after invocation of right to counsel during questioning	No
4. Arizona v. Roberson (1988)	Interrogation about second offense after invoking Miranda for first offense	No
5. Minnick v. Mississippi (1991)	Questioning after request for lawyer	No

V. OTHER CASES AFFIRMING MIRANDA

Leading decisions after *Miranda* (other than those already discussed) may be classified under two general categories: (1) those affirming *Miranda* and (2) those rejecting *Miranda* or not applying *Miranda* in full. The cases discussed here hold that the evidence obtained was not admissible, thus affirming *Miranda*. (See Table 11.1.)

A. Further Questioning about the Same Offense after a Suspect Asks for a Lawyer

A suspect was charged with robbery, burglary, and murder. At his first interrogation, he asked for a lawyer. Interrogation was stopped. The next day, the suspect still had not seen a lawyer, but he talked to two detectives and implicated himself in the crimes. The confession, admittedly voluntary, was ruled inadmissible in court, because it had not been established that the suspect waived his right to counsel "intelligently and knowingly." The Court said that, *once a suspect invokes his right to remain silent until he consults a lawyer, he cannot be questioned again for the same offense unless he himself initiates further communication, exchanges, or conversations with the police.* This is known as the **Edwards rule.** In this case, the suspect did not initiate further communication. Instead, the police came back the next morning and gave the suspect his Miranda warnings a second time. Since Edwards had learned by that time that another suspect had already implicated him in the crime, he gave an incriminating statement. The Court held the evidence obtained to be inadmissible (Edwards v. Arizona, 451 U.S. 477 [1981]).

In a subsequent case, the Court held that, once the suspect requests a lawyer, the interrogation must stop—whether the defendant confers with the lawyer or not. The Fifth Amendment is violated when the suspect requests a lawyer, is given an opportunity to confer with the lawyer, and then is forced to talk to the police without the lawyer being present. Prior consultation with the lawyer is not enough. The lawyer must be present at all subsequent questionings; otherwise, the evidence obtained is not admissible (Minnick v. Mississippi, 111 S.Ct. 486 [1991]).

B. Further Questioning about an Unrelated Offense after a Suspect Asks for a Lawyer

Following the Edwards rule, Court has said that invoking the Miranda rights in one offense also invokes the Miranda rights for an unrelated offense (Arizona v. Roberson, 480 U.S. 675 [1988]). In that case, Roberson, after having been given his Miranda warnings, advised the police that he wanted an attorney. The police stopped questioning him. Three days later, however, while Roberson was still in custody, another police officer, who did not know that Roberson had previously invoked his right to an attorney, again advised him of his Miranda rights and then interrogated him about an unrelated burglary. Roberson incriminated himself. During trial, he sought exclusion of the evidence, relying on the Edwards rule. The Court agreed, saying that this case came under the "bright-line rule" enunciated in *Edwards,* so the evidence could not be admitted. The rule is now clear: Once the Miranda rights are invoked by a suspect in one offense, that suspect cannot be interrogated further for that or for an unrelated offense.

C. Questioning a Defendant without a Lawyer after an Indictment

When a defendant is questioned without a lawyer present by police agents after an adversarial judicial proceeding (such as an indictment) has been started, the evidence is not admissible. The Court has ruled that incriminating statements made to a government informant sharing a suspect's jail cell were not admissible in evidence because they violated the suspect's right to a lawyer (United States v. Henry, 447 U.S. 264 [1980]). In *Henry,* the defendant was indicted for armed robbery of a bank. While the defendant was in jail pending trial, government agents contacted an informant who was confined in the same cell block as Henry. An FBI agent instructed the informant to be alert to any statements Henry made but not to initiate conversations with Henry or question him regarding the charges against him. After the informant was released from jail, he reported to the FBI agent that he and Henry had engaged in conversation and that Henry had made incriminating statements about the robbery. The informant was paid for giving the information. The Court excluded the evidence, saying that the government had violated Henry's Sixth Amendment right to a lawyer by intentionally creating a situation likely to induce the accused to make incriminating statements in the absence of a lawyer. The right was violated even if the defendant was not explicitly questioned because the incriminating information was secured in the absence of a lawyer and after the defendant had been indicted.

D. Asking for a Lawyer during the Giving of Miranda Warnings

Once a suspect has clearly invoked his or her right to counsel, nothing the suspect says in response to further interrogation may be used to cast doubt on that invocation. An invocation of rights may be made very early in the process, such as *during* the interrogator's reading of the suspect's Miranda rights. Therefore, the questioning of an in-custody suspect may have to end even before it starts (Smith v. Illinois, 469 U.S. 91 [1984]). In the *Smith* case, the defendant was interrogated by the police. They informed him that they wanted to talk about a particular robbery and then began to advise him of his rights. As they read the suspect each right, they asked if he understood. Warnings on the right to silence and on the state's right to use what the suspect might say were given. Then the right-to-counsel warning was given as follows: "You have a right to consult a lawyer and to have a lawyer present with you when you're being questioned. Do you understand that?" The suspect responded, saying, "Uh, yeah. I'd like to do that." The officer continued with the rest of the Miranda warnings. When the suspect was asked whether he wanted to talk without a lawyer, he replied, "Yeah and no, uh. I don't know what's that, really." The officer replied, "Well, you either have to talk to me this time without a lawyer being present and if you do agree to talk with me without a lawyer being present you can stop at any time you want to." The suspect agreed to talk and made some incriminating statements before cutting off the questioning with a request for counsel. The Court held that the evidence obtained could not be admitted in court because the suspect had invoked the right to counsel even before the giving of the Miranda warnings was completed.

VI. OTHER CASES EITHER REJECTING MIRANDA OR NOT APPLYING MIRANDA IN FULL

In the cases discussed here, the Court held that the evidence obtained was admissible despite the absence of the Miranda warnings, thus rejecting *Miranda* or not applying it in full.

A. Police May Question a Suspect on an Unrelated Offense after the Suspect Indicates a Wish to Remain Silent

Suppose a suspect indicates a desire to remain silent (as opposed to asking for a lawyer) after being given the Miranda warnings; may that suspect be interrogated again? The answer is yes as long as five conditions are present: (1) The suspect is given the Miranda warnings prior to the first interrogation; (2) the first interrogation stops right after the defendant indicates a desire to remain silent; (3) the questioning is resumed only after a significant period of time has lapsed (although the Court has not specified how long); (4) the suspect must again be given the Miranda warnings; and (5) the second questioning must be about crimes not covered in the first interrogation (Michigan v. Mosley, 423 U.S. 96 [1975]).

In this case, Mosley was arrested in connection with certain robberies and was given the Miranda warnings. He declined to discuss the robberies but did not indicate any desire to consult with a lawyer. More than two hours later, another detective, after again giving the Miranda warnings, questioned Mosley about an unrelated offense—a murder. Mosley gave an incriminating statement, which was used in his murder trial. Convicted, he appealed, saying that he should not have been asked any questions after he exercised his right to remain silent. The Court disagreed, admitting the evidence and saying that Mosley's second interrogation about another offense took place only after a significant time lapse and after a fresh set of warnings was given.

This scenario, in which a suspect indicates a *desire to remain silent,* should be distinguished from one in which the suspect indicates a *desire to see a lawyer*—as was the case in Edwards v. Arizona, discussed earlier. In *Edwards,* decided six years after *Mosley,* the Court held that, once a suspect indicates a desire for a lawyer, law enforcement agents must not question the suspect again—unless the suspect initiates the conversation. The Court apparently does not consider the desire to remain silent as highly protected as the desire to see a lawyer, and therefore the evidence is admissible as long as the five conditions listed previously are present. *Mosley* is a Miranda warning case, whereas *Edwards* is considered by the Court to be a right-to-counsel case; hence, the rules are different.

B. After a Knowing and Voluntary Waiver, Officers May Continue Questioning until the Suspect Clearly Requests a Lawyer

The Court has held that the statement "I think I want a lawyer before I say anything else" by a suspect, after a knowing and voluntary waiver of his or her Miranda rights, does not constitute an invocation of the right to counsel because it is merely an ambiguous request for a lawyer (Davis v. United States, 55 CrL 2206 [1994]). In *Davis,* a navy sailor who was charged with the murder of another sailor had earlier waived his rights to remain silent and to counsel, both orally and in writing. Ninety minutes into the interrogation, however, Davis said, "Maybe I should talk to a lawyer." When agents inquired if he was asking for an attorney, Davis replied that he was not. The interrogation continued, and Davis's statements were used to convict him of murder. At his court martial hearing, Davis moved to suppress the statements obtained after he suggested that he might need a lawyer. The Court admitted the evidence, saying that, unless a suspect makes a statement that a reasonable interrogator under the circumstances would interpret as an unambiguous request for counsel, the right to counsel under Miranda is not considered invoked.

Davis was decided on a 5-to-4 split. The justices who dissented did not think the preceding phrase, "I think," made that much of a difference in the tone of the request. It was clear to them that the suspect wanted a lawyer. The majority disagreed, holding that the request for counsel must be clear and unambiguous, judged from the perspective of a reasonable interrogator, before the Edwards rule applies. The Court said:

> To recapitulate: We held in *Miranda* that a suspect is entitled to the assistance of counsel during custodial interrogation even though the Constitution does not provide for such assistance. We held in *Edwards* that if the suspect invokes the right to counsel at any time, the police must immediately cease questioning him until an attorney is present. But we are unwilling to create a third layer of prophylaxis to prevent police questioning when the suspect *might* want a lawyer. Unless the suspect actually requests an attorney, questioning may continue.

The Court added that, in cases in which suspect's statement is unclear, it is entirely proper for law enforcement officers to clarify whether the suspect, in fact, wants to see a lawyer. Seeking clarification from the suspect does not violate *Miranda*.

C. An Inadmissible Statement May Be Used to Impeach a Defendant's Credibility As Long As It Is Voluntary

Trustworthy statements taken in violation of *Miranda* may be used to impeach the credibility of a defendant who takes the witness stand. The jury is to be instructed that the confession may not be considered as evidence of guilt, but only as a factor in determining whether the defendant is telling the truth (Harris v. New York, 401 U.S. 222 [1971]).

Note, however, that the admission or confession cannot be used in court for any purpose whatsoever if it was obtained involuntarily. For example, suppose a suspect confesses to the police even though she was not given the full Miranda warnings (she may have been warned that she has a right to remain silent but not of her right to a lawyer). The evidence is not admissible in court to prove her guilt. But suppose further that she takes the witness stand during the trial and testifies that she knew nothing at all about the crime. The confession may be used by the prosecutor to challenge her credibility as a witness. In this case, the confession is voluntary. But if the confession is involuntary (obtained, for example, through threats by the police), it cannot be used for any purpose, not even for impeachment.

D. A Suspect's Statement May Be Used to Obtain Collateral Derivative Evidence

Trustworthy statements obtained in violation of *Miranda* may be used to obtain collateral derivative evidence (referring to evidence of a secondary nature that is related to the cases but not directly a part of it). In Michigan v. Tucker, 417 U.S. 433 (1974), the police interrogated a suspect without giving the Miranda warnings (the interrogation had actually taken place before *Miranda* was decided in 1966, but the trial was conducted after the *Miranda* decision came out). In the process, they obtained from the suspect the name of a person who eventually became a prosecution witness. The Court held that, although the defendant's own statements could not be used against him because they were obtained in violation of *Miranda*, the prosecution witness's testimony had been purged of its original taint and was therefore admissible.

E. An Undercover Officer Posing as a Fellow Inmate Need Not Give Miranda Warnings

The Court has decided that an undercover law enforcement officer posing as a fellow inmate need not give the Miranda warnings to a suspect in jail before asking questions that may produce an incriminating response (Illinois v. Perkins, 495 U.S. 292 [1990]). In this case, the police placed undercover agent Parisi in a jail cell block with suspect Perkins, who had been detained on charges unrelated to the murder that Parisi was investigating. When Parisi asked Perkins if he had ever killed anybody, Perkins made statements incriminating himself in the murder. He was subsequently charged, tried, and convicted. On appeal, he sought to exclude the evidence, claiming that he should have been given the Miranda warnings before being asked the incriminating question by the agent. The Court disagreed, saying that the doctrine must be enforced strictly, but only in situations in which the concerns underlying that decision are present. These concerns were not present here, because the essential ingredients of a police-dominated atmosphere and compulsion were absent. The Court said that a coercive atmosphere is "not present when an incarcerated person speaks freely to someone whom he believes to be a fellow inmate and whom he assumes is not an officer having official power over him." The Court then added that in such circumstances *Miranda* does not forbid mere strategic deception by taking advantage of a suspect's misplaced trust.

In an earlier case, the Court also held that the right to counsel is not violated if an informant is merely placed in a suspect's cell and therefore held the evidence obtained admissible. The informant must take some action, beyond mere listening, that is designed deliberately to obtain incriminating remarks before the right to counsel is violated (Kuhlmann v. Wilson, 477 U.S. 436 [1986]).

The *Perkins* case must be distinguished from another case, United States v. Henry, 447 U.S. 264 (1980), in which the evidence obtained by a cell mate informant was excluded. In that case, Henry was indicted for armed robbery. While Henry was in jail, government agents contacted an informant who was a cell mate of Henry and instructed him to be alert to any statements made by Henry, but not to initiate any conversations regarding the robbery. After the informant was released, he was contacted by the agents and paid for the information he provided concerning Henry's incriminating statements about the robbery. Convicted, Henry appealed, saying that the testimony of the informant should have been excluded. The Court agreed, holding the informant's testimony to be inadmissible. The Court believed it probable that the informant used his position to secure incriminating information and therefore likely acted beyond "mere listening" for information. The Court added that, although the government agent told the informant not to initiate any questioning of Henry, the agent must have known that the informant was likely to do that anyway. More importantly, in *Henry,* the basis for the claim was a violation of the right to counsel, not the right to protection against self-incrimination—as was the case in *Miranda.*

In sum, the Miranda warnings and the right to counsel are not one and the same right. Some cases, like *Perkins,* primarily involve the Miranda warnings and are self-incrimination cases; others, like *Henry,* involve the right to counsel before or after indictment. The rule is that, after a suspect has obtained counsel and is in custody, interrogation about any offense that is likely to elicit incriminating answers (as in this case)—in the absence of a lawyer—violates the suspect's right to counsel.

F. A Suspect Need Not Be Informed of All Crimes before Interrogation

A suspect's waiver of Miranda rights is valid even if he or she believes the interrogation will focus merely on minor crimes but the police bring up a different and more serious crime (Colorado v. Spring, 479 U.S. 564 [1987]). In that case, Spring and a companion shot a man during a hunting trip in Colorado. An informant told federal agents that Spring was engaged in interstate trafficking in stolen firearms and that he had participated in the murder. Spring was arrested in Kansas City and advised of his Miranda rights. He signed a statement that he understood and waived his rights. He was asked about the firearms transaction (which had led to his arrest) and also whether he had ever shot a man. Spring answered yes but denied the shooting in question. He confessed to the murder later, however, after having been given the Miranda warnings. Tried and convicted, he appealed, saying that he needed to be informed of all crimes about which he was to be questioned before there could be a valid waiver of his Miranda rights. The Court rejected his challenge, saying that the Constitution does not require that a suspect know and understand every possible consequence of a waiver of a Fifth Amendment privilege. There was no allegation here that Spring failed to understand that privilege or that he did not understand the consequences of speaking freely.

G. A Statement Need Not Be Written

An oral confession is admissible even if the suspect tells the police he will talk with them but will not make a written statement without a lawyer present (Connecticut v. Barrett, 479 U.S. 523 [1987]). In that case, Barrett was arrested in connection with a sexual assault. Upon arrival at the police station, he was advised of his Miranda rights and signed a statement saying he understood his rights. Barrett then said that he would not give a written statement in the absence of counsel but would talk to the police about the incident. In two subsequent interrogations, Barrett was again advised of his rights and signed a statement of understanding. On both occasions, he gave an oral statement admitting his involvement in the sexual assault but refused to make or sign a written statement. After being convicted of sexual assault, he appealed, alleging that his oral statements should not be admissible in court. The Court rejected his challenge, saying that refusal by a suspect to put his or her statement in writing does not make an admission or confession inadmissible, as long as the police can establish that the Miranda warnings were given and the waiver was intelligent and voluntary. Note, however, that the admissibility of oral statements may be the subject of limiting rules in some states. For example, state law might provide that oral confessions are admissible only if corroborated by other evidence indicating guilt, such as a weapon or eyewitnesses.

H. A Confession Is Admissible despite the Failure of Police to Inform a Suspect of a Retained Attorney

The Court has held that a suspect's waiver of the Fifth Amendment right to remain silent and to have counsel present during custodial interrogation is not nullified either by the failure of police officers to inform the suspect that the attorney retained on his or her behalf by a third party is attempting to reach the suspect or by misleading information given to the attorney by the police regarding their intention to interrogate the suspect at that time (Moran v. Burbine, 475 U.S. 412 [1986]). In that case, the failure of police officers to inform a suspect that the attorney retained for him by his sister was attempting to reach him did not make the evidence obtained inadmissible. If the officer knows, however, that the defendant has retained a lawyer and the lawyer wants to be present during interrogation, that wish must be respected.

VII. WHEN THE MIRANDA WARNINGS ARE NOT REQUIRED

The easy and quick answer to the question "When are the Miranda warnings not required?" is, *whenever there is no custodial interrogation*. The *Miranda* case itself and subsequent Court decisions have identified a number of situations in which there is no need to give the Miranda warnings. (See Table 11.2).

A. When No Questions Are Asked by the Officer

The Miranda warnings are unnecessary when the police do not ask questions of the suspect. *Miranda* applies only if the police interrogate the suspect; if they do not ask questions, no warnings need be given. For example, suppose X is arrested by the police by

TABLE 11.2 *Other Cases Either Rejecting* Miranda *or Not Applying* Miranda *in Full*

Case	Evidence Obtained How?	Evidence Admissible?
1. Harris v. New York (1971)	Impeachment of credibility	Yes
2. Michigan v. Tucker (1974)	Collateral derivative evidence	Yes
3. Michigan v. Mosley (1975)	Questioning on an unrelated offense	Yes
4. New York v. Quarles (1984)	Threat to public safety	Yes
5. Berkemer v. McCarty (1984)	Roadside questioning of motorist pursuant to routine traffic stop	Yes
6. Oregon v. Elstad (1985)	Confession obtained after warnings given following earlier voluntary but unwarned admission	Yes
7. Moran v. Burbine (1986)	Failure of police to inform suspect of attorney retained for him	Yes
8. Kuhlman v. Wilson (1986)	Informant in same cell	Yes
9. Colorado v. Connelly (1986)	Confession following advice of God	Yes
10. Connecticut v. Barrett (1987)	Oral confession	Yes
11. Colorado v. Spring (1987)	Shift to another crime	Yes
12. Arizona v. Mauro (1987)	Conversation with defendant's wife recorded	Yes
13. Pennsylvania v. Bruder (1988)	Curbside stop for traffic violation	Yes
14. Duckworth v. Eagan (1989)	Variation in warning	Yes
15. Michigan v. Harvey (1990)	Impeachment of testimony	Yes
16. Illinois v. Perkins (1990)	Officer posing as inmate	Yes
17. Pennsylvania v. Muniz (1990)	Routine questions and videotaping for DWI	Yes
18. Arizona v. Fulminante (1991)	Harmless involuntary confessions	Yes
19. Davis v. United States (1994)	No clear request to see attorney	Yes

virtue of an arrest warrant. If the police do not question X during the time he is in police custody, the Miranda warnings need not be given. In many states, the magistrate gives the Miranda warnings when the arrested person is brought before him or her for initial appearance or presentment.

B. During General On-the-Scene Questioning

Miranda warnings do not have to be given prior to **general on-the-scene questioning,** *at the scene of the crime for the purpose of gathering information about the people involved.* In the words of the Court in *Miranda:*

> General on-the-scene questioning as to facts surrounding a crime is not affected by our holding. It is an act of responsible citizenship for individuals to give what-

ever information they may have to aid in law enforcement. In such situations the compelling atmosphere inherent in the process of in-custody interrogation is not necessarily present.

A distinction must be made, however, between general on-the-scene questioning and questioning at the scene of the crime after the police have focused on an individual, which requires the Miranda warnings. Consider these two examples:

- **Example 1:** Z has been stabbed fatally in a crowded bar. A police officer arrives and questions people at the scene of the crime to determine if anyone saw the actual stabbing. This is considered general on-the-scene questioning, for which there is no need to give the Miranda warnings.

- **Example 2:** Assume instead that upon arrival at the bar the officer sees X with a bloody knife in his hands. The suspicion of the officer will doubtless be focused on X. Therefore, any questioning of X requires the Miranda warnings even though such questioning is at the scene of the crime.

C. When the Statement Is Volunteered

A person who volunteers a statement does not have to receive Miranda warnings before speaking. A **volunteered statement** is *made by a suspect without interrogation.* For example, suppose X enters the police station and announces, "I just killed my wife." The statement is admissible in court because it was volunteered. A volunteered statement is different from a **voluntary statement,** which *is given without coercion and of the suspect's own free will.* A volunteered statement is one given to the police apart from and not in response to any interrogation.

D. When Questioning a Suspect about Identification

When asking questions about a suspect's identification—"What is your name?" "Where do you live?" "How long have you lived here?"—the Miranda warnings are not required (Pennsylvania v. Muniz, 496 U.S. 582 [1990]). In this case, Muniz was arrested for driving while under the influence of alcohol. He was taken to a booking center and was told that his actions and voice would be videotaped. He was asked seven questions regarding his name, address, height, weight, eye color, date of birth, and current age, which he answered. He later sought exclusion of his answers, saying he was not given the Miranda warnings before those questions were asked. The Court disagreed, saying that Muniz's answers were admissible because these questions fall within a "routine booking question" exception to the Miranda rule. The Court agreed with the state court that "the first seven questions were requested for record-keeping purposes only." No possible self-incrimination was involved; hence, the Miranda warnings were not needed.

HIGHLIGHT

Police Acceptance of <u>Miranda</u>

Despite their initial reaction of dismay, the police seem to have adjusted to *Miranda* fairly well. Under these circumstances, the Court is probably willing to "live with" a case that has become part of American culture, especially if it continues to view it as a serious effort to strike a proper balance between the need for police questioning and the need to protect a suspect against impermissible police pressure.

Source: Yale Kamisar, in *The Oxford Companion to the Supreme Court of the United States,* ed. Kermit L. Hall (New York: Oxford University Press, 1992), p. 555.

E. When Questioning Witnesses

When the person being interrogated is merely a witness to a crime, not a suspect, the Miranda warnings are not needed. However, if the officer suspects in the course of the questioning that the witness might be involved in the offense, then the warnings must be given.

F. In Stop and Frisk Cases

There is no need to give the Miranda warnings if a person is stopped by the police and asked questions to determine if criminal activity is about to take place. In this brief encounter, which is preceded by a casual type of questioning, the suspect is not deprived of freedom in a significant way. The purpose of a stop is to determine whether criminal activity is about to take place, and the purpose of a frisk is to protect the officer. In neither case is custodial interrogation involved. Note, however, that once a stop and frisk situation turns into an arrest, the Miranda warnings must be given.

G. When Asking Routine Questions of Drunk-Driving Suspects and Videotaping the Proceedings

The Court has said that the police may ask people suspected of driving while intoxicated routine questions and videotape their responses without giving the Miranda warnings (Pennsylvania v. Muniz, 496 U.S. 582 [1990]). In this case, an officer stopped Muniz's vehicle and directed him to perform three standard field sobriety tests. Muniz performed poorly and informed the officer that he failed the tests because he had been drinking. The officer then arrested Muniz and took him into custody. After being informed that his actions and voice would be videotaped, but without being given his Miranda warnings, Muniz was asked seven questions regarding his name, address, height, weight, eye color, date of birth, and age. He was also asked but was unable to give the exact date of his sixth birthday. The videotape of his performance during booking was submitted into evidence over his objections. Muniz was convicted of DWI and appealed, alleging that the evidence should have been excluded because he was not given the Miranda warnings.

The Court disagreed, saying that the Miranda warnings were not needed because the police were merely asking routine questions and videotaping the proceedings. The seven questions asked were not intended to obtain information for investigatory purposes. As for the self-incrimination aspect of Muniz's responses, the Court said that videotaping the suspect and taking his slurred responses into consideration when determining his guilt constituted physical, not mental or testimonial, self-incrimination and therefore did not come under the Fifth Amendment umbrella. Significantly, however, the Court held that Muniz's answer to the question about the exact date of his sixth birthday was not admissible because "the content of his answer supported the inference that his mental state was confused," meaning that such evidence was *mental* instead of *physical*.

H. During Lineups, Showups, or Photographic Identifications

There is no need to give the Miranda warnings in lineups, showups, or photographic pretrial identifications, because they are not protected by the Fifth Amendment guarantee against self-incrimination. The evidence obtained is physical in nature and does not constitute oral or testimonial self-incrimination.

I. When the Statement Is Made to a Private Person

Miranda does not apply to statements or confessions made to private persons. Protection against compulsory self-incrimination applies only to interrogations initiated by law enforcement officers. Therefore, incriminating statements made by the accused to friends or cell mates while in custody are admissible even if made without the Miranda warnings, unless government agents arranged the situation. This is because the Bill of Rights does not apply to the actions of private persons. Private persons include "bounty hunters," who are paid or commissioned by bail companies to go after defendants who jump bail. State constitution or legislation, however, may prohibit the admission of a confession made to a private person.

J. When a Suspect Appears before a Grand Jury

In an interrogation of a potential criminal defendant before a grand jury, the Miranda warnings are not required, even if the prosecutor intends to charge the witness with an offense. This is because grand jury questioning does not constitute custodial interrogation. The theory is that such interrogation does not present the same opportunities for abuse as custodial interrogation by the police. Questioning in a grand jury room is different from custodial police interrogation (United States v. Mandujano, 425 U.S. 564 [1976]). The evidence obtained may be held inadmissible, however, if state law requires the giving of the Miranda warnings even in grand jury proceedings. State laws that give more rights to suspects than the Constitution does are binding on government agencies in that state.

K. When There Is a Threat to Public Safety

The Court has carved out a **"public safety" exception** to the Miranda rule, saying that, *when questions asked by police officers are reasonably prompted by concern for public safety, the responses are admissible in court even though the suspect was in police custody and not given the Miranda warnings* (New York v. Quarles, 467 U.S. 649 [1984]). In the *Quarles* case, a woman approached two police officers who were on patrol, told them that she had just been raped, described her assailant, and said that the man had just entered a nearby supermarket and was carrying a gun. One officer entered the store and spotted Quarles, who matched the description given by the woman. Quarles ran toward the rear of the store but was finally subdued. The officer noticed that Quarles was wearing an empty shoulder holster. After handcuffing the suspect, the police asked where the gun was; Quarles nodded toward some empty cartons, where the gun was found. The suspect was given the Miranda warnings only after the gun was recovered. The Court said that the gun was admissible as evidence under the public safety exception.

The public safety exception is best limited to cases in which there is immediate danger to the public; otherwise, it might be abused. It must be limited to danger arising from a criminal act that has just been committed, as in this situation involving a firearm. It should not apply to cases in which the danger to public safety is not immediate or serious.

VIII. THE "HARMLESS ERROR" RULE AND MIRANDA CASES ON APPEAL: ARIZONA V. FULMINANTE

The **"harmless error" rule** provides that *an error made by the trial court in admitting illegally obtained evidence does not require a reversal of the conviction if the error is deter-*

AT A GLANCE

When the Miranda Warnings Are Not Required

1. When no questions are asked by the officer
2. During general on-the-scene questioning
3. When the statement is volunteered
4. When questioning a suspect about identification
5. When questioning witnesses
6. In stop and frisk cases
7. When asking routine questions of drunk-driving suspects and videotaping the proceedings
8. During lineups, showups, or photographic identifications
9. When the statement is made to a private person
10. When the suspect appears before a grand jury
11. When there is a threat to public safety

---

mined to be harmless. Conversely, if the error was *harmful,* the conviction must be reversed. The Court has ruled that the harmless error rule is applicable to cases involving involuntary confessions (Arizona v. Fulminante, 111 S.Ct. 1246 [1991]). But the burden of proving harmless error rests with the prosecution and must be established "beyond a reasonable doubt." This is significant because prior to *Fulminante* the rule was that the erroneous admission into evidence by the trial court of an involuntary confession led to an automatic reversal of the conviction on appeal, regardless of whether the admission was harmless or harmful. That has now changed.

The facts of the case are sad, and the Court decision was complex, with three issues decided by the Court on close votes. Fulminante was suspected by police of having murdered his stepdaughter, but no charges were filed against him. He left Arizona for New Jersey, where he was later convicted on an unrelated charge of firearms possession. While incarcerated in a federal prison in New York on that charge, Fulminante was befriended by a fellow inmate, a certain Sarivola, who was serving a sixty-day sentence for extortion. Sarivola later become an informant for the FBI. Sarivola offered Fulminante protection from the other inmates (because of the rumor that he was a child murderer) in exchange for the truth. Fulminante admitted to Sarivola that he had driven his stepdaughter to the desert on his motorcycle, choked and sexually assaulted her, and made her beg for her life before shooting her twice in the head. After his release from prison, Fulminante also confessed to Sarivola's wife about the same crime. Indicted for first-degree murder, Fulminante sought exclusion of his confessions to Sarivola and Sarivola's wife. The trial court admitted the confession; Fulminante was convicted and sentenced to death. On appeal, the Court addressed three issues raised by Fulminante:

1. Should the harmless error rule apply to *Miranda* confessions on appeal? Yes.

2. Was Fulminante's confession voluntary? No, it was coerced.

3. Was the admission of Fulminante's confession by the trial court a harmless error in his conviction? No, because the government failed to establish beyond a reasonable doubt that the admission was a harmless error.

The result of the Court decision was that Fulminante was to be given a new trial, but the involuntary confession was not to be admitted. Under the Fulminante rule, the reversal of a conviction on appeal in *Miranda*-type cases involves two steps. The first step is determining whether the confession is voluntary or involuntary. If the confession is voluntary, then the admission by the trial court of the evidence is proper. If it is involuntary, the second step becomes necessary—determining whether the admission of such evidence by the trial court was a harmless error. The burden of proof rests with the prosecution. If the admission constitutes a harmless error (as determined by the appellate court), the conviction is affirmed. Conversely, the conviction is reversed (1) if the error is deemed harmful by the appellate court or (2) if the prosecution fails to establish beyond a reasonable doubt that the error is harmless (as was the situation in *Fulminante*). (Read the Arizona v. Fulminante case brief at the end of this chapter.)

IX. THE LATEST THREAT TO <u>MIRANDA</u>: UNITED STATES V. DICKERSON

In what has been described as the most serious challenge to the Miranda rule since the decision came out in 1966, a three-judge panel in the Federal Court of Appeals for the Fourth Circuit held, by a 2-to-1 vote, in February 1999, that voluntary confessions given without the Miranda warnings do not have to be excluded in federal court prosecutions and that congressional law overrules *Miranda* in federal courts (<u>United States v. Dickerson, No. 97-4750</u> (4th Cir. 1999). The ruling is a virtual legal bombshell and has the effect of overturning the Miranda rule in federal prosecutions. The case was promptly appealed to the full thirteen-member court, but in July 1999, the full court, in an 8-to-5 vote, decided not to rehear the case. Therefore, the panel ruling stands and, as of this writing, governs federal prosecutions in the Federal Court of Appeals for the Fourth Circuit. Unless reversed by the Supreme Court, it is law for the prosecution of federal offenses in the states of Maryland, North Carolina, South Carolina, Virginia, and West Virginia.

The media coverage of the *Dickerson* decision has been massive. No other case in recent years has generated so much controversy and debate. In December 1999, the Court agreed to review the *Dickerson* case. Unless postponed for another term, the case will likely be decided before July 2000, when the Court's 1999–2000 term ends. Hopefully, this important legal issue will be decided soon.

A. The Facts in <u>Dickerson</u>

In United States v. Dickerson, defendant Dickerson confessed to robbing a series of banks in Maryland and Virginia. He was indicted by a federal grand jury on various counts of bank robbery and three counts of using a firearm while committing a crime. During trial, Dickerson moved to suppress his confession. The court agreed, saying that,

AT A GLANCE

The Miranda Warnings

1. You have a right to remain silent.
2. Anything you say can be used against you in a court of law.
3. You have a right to the presence of an attorney.
4. If you cannot afford an attorney, one will be appointed for you prior to questioning.

IMPORTANCE: *Miranda* sets the standard for admissibility of admissions or confessions.

STANDARD FOR ADMISSIBILITY BEFORE *MIRANDA:* Voluntariness.

STANDARD FOR ADMISSIBILITY AFTER *MIRANDA:* Were the Miranda warnings given, and if so was there an intelligent and voluntary waiver? The answer to both questions must be yes.

WHEN MUST THE MIRANDA WARNINGS BE GIVEN? Whenever there is custodial interrogation.

WHEN IS A PERSON IN CUSTODY? When under arrest or deprived of freedom in a significant way.

WHEN IS A PERSON UNDER INTERROGATION? When being asked questions or when the police create a situation that is likely to elicit a confession or admission.

FOR WHAT OFFENSES MUST THE MIRANDA WARNINGS BE GIVEN? All offenses, felonies, or misdemeanors, except routine traffic stops.

CAN THE MIRANDA RIGHTS BE WAIVED? Yes, but the government must prove that the waiver was intelligent and voluntary.

RULE FOR *MIRANDA* **CASES ON APPEAL:** Conviction is reversed if the admission of excludable evidence by the trial court is harmful; conviction is not reversed if the admission of excludable evidence is harmless.

---

although admittedly voluntary, the confession had to be suppressed because no Miranda warnings were given. The prosecution appealed the ruling to the Fourth Circuit. The appeal was based on an obscure federal law, passed by Congress as part of the Omnibus Crime Control and Safe Streets Act of 1968, two years after *Miranda* was decided. That law, 18 U.S.C. Section 3501(a), provides:

> In any criminal prosecution brought by the United States or by the District of Columbia, a confession, as defined in subsection (e) hereof, shall be admissible in evidence if it is voluntarily given. Before such confession is received in evidence, the trial judge shall, out of the presence of the jury, determine any issue as to voluntariness. If the trial judge determines that the confession was voluntarily made it shall be admitted in evidence and the trial judge shall permit the jury to hear relevant evidence on the issue of voluntariness and shall instruct the jury to give weight to the confession as the jury feels it deserves under all the circumstances.

B. The Issue in Dickerson

The issue before the Fourth Circuit three-judge panel was whether this law is constitutional, which, in turn, hinged on the issue of whether Congress had the authority to pass the law. The panel said, "We have little difficulty concluding . . . that Section 3501, enacted at the invitation of the Supreme Court and pursuant to Congress's unquestioned power to establish the rules of procedure and evidence in the federal courts, is constitutional."

Section 3501 was enacted by Congress for the express purpose of overturning the *Miranda* decision in federal courts. Some lower courts have found that Section 3501, not *Miranda*, governs the admissibility of confessions in federal courts. But the Clinton administration, like previous administrations, refused to invoke the law. In fact, Attorney General Janet Reno sent a letter to Congress in 1997 saying that the law was unconstitutional. That letter, however, was dismissed by the three-judge panel as politically motivated. The panel noted, "Fortunately, we are a court of law and not politics," and went on to say that the U.S. Department of Justice could not prevent the court from deciding the case even if the Department of Justice refused to argue it.

Dickerson has understandably generated intense debate and media attention. It has elicited heated reactions from law scholars and criminal justice practitioners on both sides of the *Miranda* issue.

C. The Implications of Dickerson

Should the Court affirm *Dickerson* on appeal, the 1966 *Miranda* ruling requiring that the Miranda warnings be given will be overturned in all federal prosecutions through the congressional legislation. States can then pass similar legislation applicable to their own criminal prosecutions. At the core of the controversy is a crucial issue that was not decided clearly by the Court in *Miranda* and that was the focus in *Dickerson*. That issue is whether the Miranda rule is required by the Constitution or whether it is a judge-made rule. Some scholars say it is constitutionally required; others say it is judge-made. If it is constitutionally required, then Congress (and state legislatures) cannot overrule it by legislation, as Congress did when it enacted Section 3501. In *Dickerson,* the Fourth Circuit held that the Miranda rule is not required by the Constitution, so Congress can undo it by legislation. This is contrary to the currently accepted concept in federal and state courts and made a part of day-to-day police practice over the past three-plus decades.

For police officers, the meaningful question in *Dickerson* is whether purely voluntary admissions or confessions that are given by a suspect without the Miranda warnings are nonetheless admissible as evidence in court. Although no figures are readily available, the likelihood is that this will affect only a few cases where such warnings were not given and the admission or confession was voluntary. Under the Court's current interpretation of *Miranda,* an admission or confession that is 100 percent voluntary must be suppressed if it was made without the Miranda warnings. An affirmance by the Court of the *Dickerson* decision will not mean that officers can do away with the Miranda warnings. If affirmed, it will mean that voluntary confessions given without

Contrasting Views on the <u>Dickerson</u> Decision

"I'm really going to be surprised if any reputable group of prosecutors or police take a stand in favor of that decision." —Donald E. Wilkes, Jr., University of Georgia law professor, who has been studying *Miranda* issues for twenty-eight years

"I've become convinced that Miranda is the most damaging thing that was done to law enforcement in the last half-century." —Paul G. Cassell, University of Utah law professor, who helped lead the drive to overturn *Miranda*

Source: *Dallas Morning News*, April 18, 1999, p. J1.

the Miranda warnings will then be admissible, but only if states enact a law similar to Section 3501(a) of the previously quoted federal law and as long as the confession is voluntary. Involuntary confessions will still remain excludible even if *Dickerson* is affirmed.

If the *Dickerson* decision is upheld, can the federal government and the states then do away completely with the Miranda warnings by enacting legislation abolishing it? The answer will likely depend on whether the Court considers the Miranda warnings as constitutionally required or as judge-made. If constitutionally required, then the legislature cannot do away with the warnings and the controversy ends. If the Court says the warnings are judge-made, then another issue arises: whether the legislature can undo what the judicial department has done—an interesting legal issue over which the judicial department has the final say.

A decision by a three-judge panel, on a split vote, has forced an intense reexamination of an accepted practice in law enforcement. More than three decades after it became an integral part of policing, the fate of the Miranda rule once again rests with the U.S. Supreme Court. How will the *Dickerson* saga end? Stay tuned.

X. THE FUTURE OF <u>MIRANDA</u>

Quite apart from and in spite of *Dickerson, Miranda* has thus far withstood the test of time and will most likely survive the latest controversy. The panel decision in *Dickerson* hinted that Justice Antonin Scalia has expressed concern with the Department of Justice's failure to enforce Section 3501. Justice Clarence Thomas is also reported to be sympathetic to the Dickerson ruling. Nonetheless, scholars believe that the overruling of *Miranda,* even by a conservative Court, appears unlikely. As one noted scholar says, "It would be an interesting battle, but I think Miranda would win out."[5] But, then, legal scholars have been known to be wrong before.

When first announced, the Miranda rule was seen by some critics as the precursor of doom for law enforcement, shackling the police and making it difficult for prosecutors to convict. In his dissent in *Miranda,* Justice Byron White warned: "The rule announced today will measurably weaken the ability of the criminal law to perform these [law enforcement] tasks. It is a deliberate calculus to prevent interrogations, to reduce the incidence of confessions and pleas of guilty and to increase the number of trials." This dire prediction has not materialized. In the words of one chief prosecutor of a major city, "I don't think it is the terrible thing we thought it was. We still get as many confessions as we ever did, and we still get as much evidence."[6] However, *Miranda* and the exclusionary rule "are widely credited with improving professionalism among policemen—and as a result the reforms enjoy growing support among even the most hard-bitten cops."[7] Studies show that the warnings rarely stop people from confessing and that less than 1 percent of cases are thrown out because of illegally obtained confessions.[8]

Nonetheless, the clamor for a reversal of *Miranda* has not completely faded away, as the Dickerson case shows. In the words of one former attorney general, "The interesting question is not whether *Miranda* should go, but how we should facilitate its demise, and what we should replace it with. We regard a challenge to *Miranda* as essential."[9] Another writer proposes scrapping the Miranda rules, suggesting instead that the police "be required to videotape all custodial interrogations while observing the Fifth Amendment's prohibition against coercion."[10] The same writer makes this interesting observation:

> To my knowledge, no one has attempted to quantify the number of criminal cases that are lost each year because of Miranda. Yet it is possible tentatively to calculate such a cost using the available information. Multiplying the 17-percentage-point reduction in the confession rate after Miranda by the 24% need for confessions suggests that 4.1% of all criminal cases will be "lost"—that is, cannot be successfully prosecuted—because of the Miranda requirements. (By way of comparison, the exclusionary rule results in the loss of somewhere between 0.6% and 2.4% of all cases.)[11]

However, such concerns are more the exception than the rule. It is generally recognized that *Miranda* has hastened reforms rather than impeded law enforcement. It has made the police more aware of their responsibilities as agents of the state in a "free society." In the words of a former police director, "Officers want respect. We have gotten away from force and coercion. Nor do we want to be accused of that."[12] More than three decades after the decision, it can be said that, on balance, *Miranda* has done more good than harm to U.S. society and that it has led to better law enforcement. There will always be some who wish its demise. But despite critics and the *Dickerson* decision, chances are that *Miranda,* in its present form, will continue to be a part of law enforcement for years to come. If this prediction is wrong, it will not be the first time nor the last time that this writer will have made a bad prediction.

Summary

The Fifth Amendment to the U.S. Constitution prohibits forcible self-incrimination. This means that involuntary admissions or confessions cannot be admitted as evidence in a criminal prosecution. Originally, "involuntariness" referred only to the use of physical force or coercion. This interpretation was later extended to include mental coercion. However, voluntariness was difficult for the courts to determine, so decisions were made on a case-by-case basis and became subjective.

Miranda changed the rules on admissibility of confessions and admissions from voluntariness to a mechanical test consisting of three questions. Voluntariness is assumed if the answer to all three questions is yes. The Miranda warnings must be given for any offense, regardless of severity; the only exception is the roadside questioning of a motorist pursuant to a routine traffic stop. The *Miranda* decision now governs the admissibility of confessions and incriminating statements. *Miranda* requires that specific warnings be given in cases of custodial interrogation—that is, when a suspect is questioned while under arrest or deprived of freedom in a significant way. If the warnings are not given, the evidence will not be admitted in court, even if it was voluntary. In addition to voluntariness and the giving of the Miranda warnings, courts require that there be an intelligent and voluntary waiver if a suspect's statement is to be admissible.

The Miranda rule exceptions are of two kinds: when the questioning is not custodial and where there is no interrogation. The most important of these exceptions are the roadside questioning of a motorist detained pursuant to a routine traffic stop and cases in which there is a threat to public safety.

Miranda has been refined by the Court in subsequent decisions. Refinement cases can generally be classified into those affirming *Miranda* and those rejecting *Miranda* or not applying it in full.

The "harmless error" rule has been extended to confessions, meaning that the trial court's erroneous admission of a confession will no longer lead to an automatic reversal of the conviction if the error was harmless. The most recent controversy over *Miranda* involves whether voluntary statements should be held admissible despite the fact that a suspect was not given the Miranda warnings. The Federal Court of Appeals for the Fourth Circuit says yes; the U.S. Supreme Court has agreed to resolve the issue. Chances are that, despite a current conservative Court, the Miranda rule will survive this latest challenge and continue to be a controlling force in law enforcement.

Review Questions

1. Distinguish between a confession and an admission. As a police officer, which would you rather have, and why?

2. What was the old standard for the admissibility of confessions and admissions? Discuss what that standard meant and why it was difficult to apply.

3. What is the new standard for admissibility as enunciated in Miranda v. Arizona?

4. In general, when must the Miranda warnings be given? Explain.

5. A police officer stops a motorist for a traffic violation. Must the motorist be given the Miranda warnings if he or she is to be interrogated?

6. What is the "functional equivalent" concept in interrogation? Give an example.

7. Which Court decisions have affirmed the Miranda rule?

8. Which Court decisions have eroded the Miranda rule or did not apply the rule in full?

9. What is the "public safety" exception to the Miranda rule?

10. "If the Miranda warnings are not given by the officer, the confession or admission might as well be thrown away because it is useless." Is that statement true or false? Defend your answer.

11. What did the Court say in Arizona v. Fulminante? How does that case apply to *Miranda*-type cases?

12. What is the latest controversy over the Miranda rule, which was generated by a decision of the Federal Court of Appeals for the Fourth Circuit? Will Miranda survive?

Key Terms and Definitions

admission: Refers to when a person owns up to something related to the act but may not have committed it.

confession: Refers to when a person says that he or she committed the act.

custodial interrogation: Interrogation that takes place (1) when the suspect is under arrest or (2) when the suspect is not under arrest but is deprived of his or her freedom in a significant way.

deprived of freedom in a significant way: Phrase that describes a person whose freedom of movement has been limited by the police.

Edwards rule: The rule that a suspect who invokes the right to consult a lawyer cannot be questioned again for the same offense unless the suspect initiates further communication, exchanges, or conversations with the police.

functional equivalent of interrogation: Instances in which no questions are actually asked by the police, but the circumstances are so conducive to making a statement or confession that the courts consider them to be the equivalent of interrogation.

general on-the-scene questioning: Questioning at the scene of the crime for the purpose of gathering information that might enable the police to identify the criminal. Miranda warnings are not needed.

harmless error rule: The rule that an error made by the trial court in admitting illegally obtained evidence does not lead to a reversal of the conviction if the error is determined to be harmless. The prosecution has the burden of proving that the error is, in fact, harmless.

intelligent waiver: A waiver by a suspect who knows what he or she is doing and is sufficiently competent to waive his or her rights.

interrogation: The asking of questions by the police. For purposes of the Miranda rule, however, "interrogation" means not only express questioning but also words or actions (other than those attendant to arrest and custody) on the part of the police that the police should have known are reasonably likely to elicit an incriminating response from the suspect.

Miranda rule: The rule that evidence obtained by the police during custodial interrogation of a suspect cannot be used in court during the trial, unless the suspect was first informed of the right not to incriminate him- or herself and of the right to counsel.

public safety exception: The concept that responses to questions asked by police officers, if reasonably prompted by concern for public safety, are admissible in court even though the suspect was in police custody and not given the Miranda warnings.

voluntary statement: A statement given without threat, force, or coercion and of the suspect's own free will.

voluntary waiver: A waiver that is not the result of any threat, force, or coercion and is of the suspect's own free will.

volunteered statement: A statement made by a suspect without interrogation. Miranda warnings are not needed.

waiver: The intentional relinquishment of a known right or remedy. The waiver of Miranda rights must be intelligent and voluntary.

Principles of Cases

Arizona v. Fulminante, 111 S.Ct. 1246 (1991)
The harmless error rule is applicable to cases involving confessions. Fulminante's confession was not admissible because it was involuntary and the prosecution failed to establish beyond a reasonable doubt that its admission during the trial was harmless error.

Arizona v. Mauro, 481 U.S. 520 (1987) A conversation between a suspect and his or her spouse that is recorded by and in the presence of an officer does not constitute the functional equivalent of an interrogation under *Miranda,* so the evidence obtained is admissible.

Arizona v. Roberson, 486 U.S. 675 (1988) Invoking the Miranda rights to one offense also invokes the Miranda rights to an unrelated offense.

Beckwith v. United States, 425 U.S. 341 (1976)
Statements obtained by Internal Revenue Service agents during a noncustodial, noncoercive interview with a taxpayer under criminal tax investigation, conducted in a private home where the taxpayer occasionally stayed, did not require the Miranda warnings as long as the taxpayer had been told he was free to leave at any time.

Berkemer v. McCarty, 468 U.S. 420 (1984) The Court decided that (1) a person subjected to custodial interrogation must be given the Miranda warnings regardless of the nature or severity of the offense of which the person is suspected or for which he or she was arrested; but (2) the roadside questioning of a motorist detained pursuant to a routine traffic stop does not constitute custodial interrogation, so there is no need to give the Miranda warnings.

Brewer v. Williams, 430 U.S. 387 (1977) Interrogation takes place when the police officers, knowing of the defendant's religious interest, make remarks designed to appeal to that interest and thus induce a confession. Moreover, the courts must look carefully at confessions obtained from defendants who have retained lawyers when the police do not allow the lawyer to assist in interrogation. When the police have promised the attorney that no questioning will take place, any confession obtained after questioning, without clear waiver of the right to counsel, is inadmissible.

Brown v. Mississippi, 297 U.S. 278 (1936) Confessions obtained as a result of utter coercion and brutality by law enforcement officers violate the Due Process Clause of the Fourteenth Amendment and therefore are inadmissible.

California v. Beheler, 463 U.S. 1121 (1983) The ultimate determinant of whether a person is "in custody" for *Miranda* purposes is whether the suspect has been subjected to a formal arrest or to equivalent restraints on freedom of movement.

Chambers v. Florida, 309 U.S. 227 (1940) Protracted questioning of defendants held in jail without contact with the outside world violates the defendants' right to due process of law under the Fourteenth Amendment, so the evidence thereby obtained is inadmissible.

Colorado v. Connelly, 479 U.S. 157 (1986) The admissibility of statements made when the mental state of the suspect interferes with his or her rational intellect and free will is governed by state rules of evidence rather than by Supreme Court decisions on coerced confessions. Confessions and admissions are involuntary and invalid under the Constitution only if the coercion is exerted by the police, not if the suspect was "following the advice of God."

Colorado v. Spring, 479 U.S. 564 (1987) A suspect's waiver of Miranda rights is valid even if the suspect believes the interrogation will merely focus on minor crimes, but the police actually cover a different and more serious crime.

Connecticut v. Barrett, 479 U.S. 523 (1987) An oral confession is admissible even if the suspect tells the police he or she will talk with them but will not make a written statement without a lawyer present.

Davis v. United States, 55 CrL 2206 (1994)
After a knowing and voluntary waiver of the Miranda rights, law enforcement officers may continue questioning until and unless the suspect clearly requests an attorney.

Duckworth v. Eagan, 492 U.S. 195 (1989) The Miranda warnings need not be given exactly as worded in the *Miranda* case. What is required is that the wording reasonably convey to a suspect his or her rights. Informing a suspect that an attorney will be appointed "if and when you go to court" does not render the Miranda warnings inadequate. *Miranda* does not require that lawyers be producible on call. It is enough that the suspect be informed of his or her right to an attorney and to appointed counsel and that, if the police cannot provide appointed counsel, the police will not question the suspect until and unless there is valid waiver.

Edwards v. Arizona, 451 U.S. 477 (1981) Once the suspect has invoked the right to remain silent until he or she consults a lawyer, the suspect cannot be questioned again for the same offense unless the suspect him- or herself initiates further communication, exchanges, or conversations with the police.

Escobedo v. Illinois, 378 U.S. 748 (1964) A confession obtained from a defendant is inadmissible, even though an adversarial judicial proceeding has not yet been started, when he or she requested and was denied an opportunity to consult with his or her lawyer even though the lawyer was present and available to consult with him or her.

Fare v. Michael C., 442 U.S. 707 (1979) The request of a juvenile on probation to see his probation officer instead of a lawyer is considered to be a waiver of the juvenile's right to a lawyer, because a probation officer and a lawyer perform two different functions.

Harris v. New York, 401 U.S. 222 (1971) Trustworthy statements taken in violation of *Miranda* may be used to impeach the credibility of a defendant who takes the witness stand, as long as the statements are voluntary.

Illinois v. Perkins, 496 U.S. 292 (1990) An undercover law enforcement officer posing as a fellow inmate need not give the Miranda warnings to a suspect in jail before asking questions that may produce an incriminating response.

Kuhlmann v. Wilson, 477 U.S. 436 (1986) Asking an informer who is in the same cell as a suspect to "keep his ears open" for information does not violate the suspect's right to counsel, and therefore evidence obtained is admissible.

Malloy v. Hogan, 378 U.S. 1 (1964) The Fifth Amendment protection against compulsory self-incrimination was incorporated under the Fourteenth Amendment of the Constitution and is applicable to state criminal proceedings.

Michigan v. Tucker, 417 U.S. 433 (1974) Trustworthy statements obtained in violation of *Miranda* may be used to obtain collateral derivative evidence.

Mincey v. Arizona, 437 U.S. 385 (1978) Statements given by a suspect to the police that are not the product of free and rational choice are not admissible.

Minnesota v. Murphy, 465 U.S. 420 (1984) The Miranda warnings need not be given in cases of noncustodial interrogation of a probationer by a probation officer.

Minnick v. Mississippi, 111 S.Ct. 486 (1991) Once a suspect asks for a lawyer, interrogation must stop—whether the defendant confers with the lawyer or not.

Miranda v. Arizona, 384 U.S. 436 (1966) Evidence obtained by the police during custodial interrogation of a suspect cannot be used in court unless the suspect is first informed of the right not to incriminate him- or herself and of the right to counsel. The following warnings must be given prior to interrogation (wording may vary):

1. You have a right to remain silent.

2. Anything you say can be used against you in a court of law.

3. You have a right to the presence of an attorney.

4. If you cannot afford an attorney, one will be appointed for you prior to questioning.

5. You may terminate this interview at any time.

Moran v. Burbine, 475 U.S. 412 (1986) A suspect's waiver of the Fifth Amendment right to remain silent and to have counsel present during custodial interrogation is not nullified either by the failure of police officers to inform the suspect that the attorney retained on his or her behalf by a third party is attempting to reach the suspect or by misleading information given to the attorney by the police regarding their intention to interrogate the suspect at that time.

New York v. Quarles, 467 U.S. 649 (1984) When questions asked by police officers are reasonably prompted by concern for public safety, the responses are admissible in court even though the suspect was in police custody and was not given the Miranda warnings.

North Carolina v. Butler, 441 U.S. 369 (1979) Failure to make an explicit statement regarding the waiver does not determine whether the evidence is admissible. Instead, the trial court must look at all the circumstances to determine if a valid waiver has, in fact, been made. Although an express waiver is easier to establish in court, it is not required.

Oregon v. Elstad, 470 U.S. 298 (1985) If a confession is made after proper Miranda warnings and a waiver of rights, the self-incrimination clause of the Fifth Amendment does not require it to be suppressed solely because the police have obtained an earlier voluntary but unwarned admission from the suspect.

Oregon v. Mathiason, 429 U.S. 492 (1977) The Miranda warnings are necessary only if the suspect is interrogated while in custody or otherwise deprived of freedom in a significant way. In this case, the suspect came to the police station in response to an officer's message that the officer would "like to discuss something with you." It was made clear to the suspect that he was not under arrest. The confession made without the Miranda warnings was admissible.

Orozco v. Texas, 394 U.S. 324 (1969) The questioning of a suspect in his or her home by police officers at four o'clock in the morning requires the Miranda warnings.

Pennsylvania v. Bruder, 488 U.S. 9 (1988) The curbside stop of a motorist for a traffic violation, although representing a Fourth Amendment seizure of the person, is not sufficiently custodial as to require the Miranda warnings.

Pennsylvania v. Muniz, 496 U.S. 582 (1990) The police may ask routine questions of people suspected of driving while intoxicated (DWI) and may videotape their responses without giving the Miranda warnings.

Rhode Island v. Innis, 446 U.S. 291 (1980) Conversation between police officers while in a police car about the danger that one of the handicapped children from a school near the scene of the crime might find a loaded shotgun did not constitute interrogation, even though it was within hearing of the suspect. The information given by the suspect, who interrupted the conversation, was not given in response to an interrogation and was therefore admissible in court. However, a practice that the police should know is likely to evoke an incriminating response from the suspect amounts to interrogation. Such was not the case here.

Rogers v. Richmond, 365 U.S. 534 (1961) A confession obtained as a result of interrogation that continues for more than a day, accompanied by a threat that the suspect's spouse will be taken into custody if the suspect does not confess, is involuntary and therefore not admissible in court.

Smith v. Illinois, 469 U.S. 91 (1984) Once a suspect has clearly invoked his or her right to counsel during questioning, nothing the suspect says in response to further interrogation may be used to cast doubt on that invocation. Moreover, an invocation of rights may be made very early in the process—even during the interrogator's recitation of the suspect's rights. Therefore, the questioning of an in-custody suspect may have to end even before it starts.

Spano v. New York, 360 U.S. 315 (1959) The use of deception as a means of psychological pressure to induce a confession violates a defendant's constitutional rights, so the evidence obtained is not admissible in court. The trial court's mistaken admission of a confession leads to an automatic reversal of the conviction.

Stansbury v. California, 55 CrL 2016 (1994) A police officer's subjective and undisclosed view whether the person being interrogated is a suspect does not determine whether the person is, in fact, in custody for purposes of the Miranda warnings.

Teague v. Louisiana, 444 U.S. 469 (1980) The trial court cannot presume a waiver from the failure of the accused to complain after the giving of the Miranda warnings or from the fact that the accused spoke with the police after the warnings were given.

United States v. Dickerson, No. 97-4750 (4th Cir. 1999) Voluntary confessions given without the Miranda warnings do not have to be excluded in federal court prosecutions; congressional law overrules *Miranda* in federal courts.

United States v. Henry, 447 U.S. 264 (1980) The government violates a defendant's Sixth Amendment right to counsel by intentionally creating a situation likely to induce the accused to make incriminating statements without the presence of a lawyer.

United States v. Mandujano, 425 U.S. 564 (1976) Grand jury investigations do not require the Miranda warnings, because the answers given are not statements in response to custodial interrogation.

Case Briefs

Leading Case on the Types of Offenses That Require Miranda Warnings

Berkemer v. McCarty, 468 U.S. 420 (1984)

Facts: After observing McCarty's car weaving in and out of a highway lane, Officer Williams of the Ohio State Highway Patrol forced McCarty to stop and get out of the car. Upon noticing that McCarty was having difficulty standing, the officer concluded that he would be charged with a traffic offense and would not be allowed to leave the scene, but McCarty was not told that he would be taken into custody. When McCarty could not perform a field sobriety test without falling, Officer Williams asked if he had been using intoxicants, whereupon McCarty replied that he had consumed two beers and had smoked marijuana a short time before. The officer then formally arrested McCarty and drove him to a county jail, where a blood test failed to detect any alcohol in his blood. Questioning was resumed, and McCarty again made incriminating statements, including an admission that he was "barely" under the influence of alcohol. At no point during this sequence was McCarty given the Miranda warnings. He was subsequently charged with operating a motor vehicle under the influence of alcohol and drugs, a misdemeanor under Ohio law. He pleaded "no contest" but later filed a writ of habeas corpus, alleging that the evidence obtained should not have been admitted in court.

Issue: *Was evidence obtained by the police without giving the suspect the Miranda warnings admissible in a prosecution for a misdemeanor offense? No.*

Supreme Court Decision: The Court decided that (1) a person subjected to custodial interrogation must be given the Miranda warnings, regardless of the nature or severity of the offense of which the person is suspected or for which he or she was arrested, but that (2) the roadside questioning of a motorist detained pursuant to a routine traffic stop does not constitute "custodial interrogation," so there is no need to give the Miranda warnings.

Case Significance: This case settled two legal issues that had long divided lower courts. It is clear now that, once a suspect has been placed under arrest for any offense, be it a felony or a misdemeanor, the Miranda warnings must be given before interrogation. This rule is easier for the police to follow than the requirement of determining if the arrest was for a felony or a misdemeanor before giving the warning. The Court said that the purpose of the Miranda warnings, which is to ensure that the police do not coerce or trick captive suspects into confessing, is applicable equally to misdemeanor and felony cases. The second part of the decision is equally important, in that it identifies a particular instance when the warnings need not be given. There is no custodial interrogation in a traffic stop, because it is usually brief and the motorist expects that, although a citation may be forthcoming, in the end he or she will most likely be allowed to continue on his or her way. However, if a motorist who has been detained is thereafter subjected to treatment that renders him or her "in custody" for practical purposes, then he or she is entitled to be given the Miranda warnings.

Excerpts from the Decision: "Two features of an ordinary traffic stop mitigate the danger that a person questioned will be induced 'to speak where he would not otherwise do so freely,' Miranda v. Arizona, 384 U.S., at 467. First, detention of a motorist pursuant to a traffic stop is presumptively temporary and brief. The vast majority of roadside detentions last only a few minutes. A motorist's expectations, when he sees a policeman's light flashing behind him, are that he will be obliged to spend a short period of time answering questions and waiting while the officer checks his license and registration, that he may then be given a citation, but that in the end he most likely will be allowed to continue on his way.

"Second, circumstances associated with the typical traffic stop are not such that the motorist feels completely at the mercy of the police. To be sure, the aura of authority surrounding an armed, uniformed officer and the knowledge that the officer has some discretion in deciding whether to issue a citation, in combination, exert some pressure on the detainee to respond to questions. But other aspects of the situation substantially offset these forces. Perhaps most importantly, the typical traffic stop is public, at least to some degree. Passersby, on foot or in other cars, witness the interaction of officer and motorist. This exposure to public view both reduces the ability of an unscrupulous policeman to use illegitimate means to elicit self-incriminating statements and diminishes the motorist's fear that, if he does not cooperate, he will be subjected to abuse. The fact that the detained motorist typically is confronted by only one or at most two policemen further mutes his sense of vulnerability. In short, the atmosphere surrounding an ordinary traffic stop is substantially less 'police dominated' than that surrounding the kinds of interrogation at issue in *Miranda* itself, and in the subsequent cases in which we have applied *Miranda*."

Leading Case on the Harmless Error Doctrine on Appeal

Arizona v. Fulminante, 111 S.Ct. 1246 (1991)

Facts: Fulminante was suspected of having murdered his stepdaughter. His statements to the police concerning her disappearance were inconsistent, but no charges were filed against him. Fulminante left Arizona for New Jersey, where he was later convicted on an unrelated federal charge of possession of a firearm. While incarcerated in a federal prison in New York, Fulminante was befriended by a fellow inmate, Anthony Sarivola, who was serving a sixty-day sentence for extortion. Sarivola later became a paid informant for the FBI. Sarivola told Fulminante that he knew Fulminante was getting tough treatment from the other inmates because of a rumor that he was a child murderer. Sarivola offered Fulminante protection in exchange for the truth. Fulminante admitted to Sarivola that he had driven his stepdaughter "to the desert on his motorcycle, where he choked her, sexually assaulted her, and made her beg for her life, before shooting her twice in the head."

After Fulminante's release from prison, he also confessed the same crime to Sarivola's wife. Fulminante was indicted in Arizona for first-degree murder. He sought to exclude the confession to Sarivola, alleging that it was coerced and thus barred by the Fifth and Fourteenth Amendments. He also challenged his confession to Sarivola's wife as "fruit" of the first confession. Both confessions were admitted by the trial court. Fulminante was convicted and sentenced to death.

Issue: This case raises a number of issues:

(1) *Should the harmless error rule be applied to Miranda confessions? Yes.*

(2) *Was Fulminante's confession coerced? Yes.*

(3) *Was the admission of Fulminante's confession by the trial court a harmless error in his conviction? No.*

Supreme Court Decision: The harmless error rule is applicable in cases involving involuntary confessions. Fulminante's confession was involuntary because it was motivated by a fear of physical violence if he were not to be protected by Sarivola. The government failed to prove beyond a reasonable doubt that the admission of Fulminante's confession was harmless error by the trial court, so his conviction was reversed.

Case Significance: This case raised a number of issues on which the justices were sharply divided. The issues are best discussed separately.

1. On the issue of whether the harmless error doctrine should be applied to cases of involuntary confession, the Court answered yes. The harmless error doctrine, enunciated by the Court in Chapman v. California, 386 U.S. 18 (1967), holds that an error by a trial court need not lead to the reversal of a conviction, as long as the error is harmless. The burden of proving harmless error lies with the prosecution, and harmlessness must be established beyond a reasonable doubt. To establish harmless error, it is not enough for the prosecution to show that there was other evidence sufficient to support the verdict. Rather, it must show that there was no reasonable possibility that a different result would have been reached without the tainted evidence. Under *Fulminante,* a trial judge's admission of an involuntary confession that ought to have been excluded no longer automatically leads to reversal of defendant's conviction. Lower courts had previously applied the automatic reversal rule to confessions, believing that the harmless error doctrine did not apply to erroneous admission of confessions, since confessions were presumed to be inherently harmful to the defendant. This case applies that doctrine to all errors made by the judge, including the erroneous admission of confessions.

2. On the issue of whether Fulminante's confession was voluntary, the Court answered no, agreeing with the finding of the Arizona courts that "Sarivola's promise was extremely coercive" and that "the confession was obtained as a direct result of extreme coercion and was

tendered in the belief that the defendant's life was in jeopardy if he did not confess." Since the confession was coerced, it could not be admissible in a court of law.

3. On the issue of whether the trial court's admission of Fulminante's coerced confession was a harmless error, the Court said it was not. A majority of the Court opined that the prosecution in this case failed to establish that the error committed by the trial court in admitting the evidence was harmless beyond a reasonable doubt. Fulminante was to be given a new trial, but the coerced confession was not to be admitted.

Fulminante is a convoluted case settled in a 5-to-4 split. Its importance centers on the first issue—whether the harmless error doctrine applies to trial court errors involving the admission of involuntary confessions. Many appellate courts had been automatically reversing any conviction involving the erroneous admission of a confession, regardless of the confession's significance. This practice has now been replaced by the harmless error doctrine. Under this rule, reversal of a conviction on appeal now involves two steps. The first step is determining whether the confession is voluntary. If it is involuntary, the second step is determining whether the admission of such evidence by the trial court was harmless error. If the admission constitutes harmless error (as determined

by the appellate court), the conviction is affirmed. Conversely, if the error is harmful or if the prosecution fails to establish beyond a reasonable doubt that the error is harmless (as in the *Fulminante* case), the conviction is reversed.

Excerpts from the Decision: "Since five Justices have determined that harmless error analysis applies to coerced confessions, it becomes necessary to evaluate under that ruling the admissibility of Fulminante's confession to Sarivola. Chapman v. California (386 U.S., at 24) made clear that 'before a federal constitutional error can be held harmless, the court must be able to declare a belief that it was harmless beyond a reasonable doubt.' The Court has the power to review the record *de novo* in order to determine any error's harmlessness. In so doing, it must be determined whether the State has met its burden to Fulminante's conviction. Five of us are of the view that the State has not carried its burden and accordingly affirm the judgment of the court below reversing petitioner's conviction.

"Because a majority of the Court has determined that Fulminante's confession to Anthony Sarivola was coerced and because a majority has determined that admitting this confession was not harmless beyond a reasonable doubt, we agree with the Arizona Supreme Court's conclusion that Fulminante is entitled to a new trial at which the confession is not admitted."

Notes

1. Lloyd L. Weinreb and James D. Whaley, *The Field Guide to Law Enforcement* (Westbury, NY: Foundation Press, 1999), p. 79.

2. G. M. Caplan, *Modern Procedures for Police Interrogation* (Washington, DC: Police Executive Research Forum, n.d.), p. 2.

3. Ibid.

4. *Boston Globe,* July 25, 1999, p. A31.

5. Yale Kamisar, professor of law, Michigan State University, as quoted in the *Houston Chronicle,* February 12, 1999, p. A15.

6. *Houston Chronicle,* January 23, 1987, p. 23.

7. *Newsweek,* July 18, 1988, at p. 53.

8. Ibid.

9. Ibid.

10. Paul G. Cassell, "How Many Criminals Has Miranda Set Free?" *Wall Street Journal,* March 1, 1995, p. A17.

11. Ibid.

12. Ibid.

VI.
Constitutional Rights and the Consequences of Police Misconduct

12. Constitutional Rights of the Accused during Trial

Chapter Outline

Chapter Outline *(continued)*

Case Briefs

J.E.B. v. Alabama
Gideon v. Wainwright
Powell v. Alabama

What You Will Learn in This Chapter

In this chapter, you will learn about the basic constitutional rights of an accused during trial. You will get an overview of the rights to trial by jury, counsel, protection against self-incrimination and against double jeopardy, confrontation of witnesses, the presence of witnesses, a speedy and public trial, a fair and impartial trial, and a finding of guilt beyond a reasonable doubt. You will also learn the scope and limitations of these rights and the stages at which these rights apply.

Introduction

The individual rights guaranteed in the Bill of Rights are most carefully protected during the trial stage of a criminal proceeding. This is when the adversarial proceeding is at its peak. The government is represented by the prosecutor, and the accused's rights are championed by the defense counsel, either retained by the accused or appointed by the state. The judge, a neutral party, presides over the trial, setting the rules for the lawyers to follow. In bench trials, the judge also determines the facts; in jury trials, that function is performed by the jury.

The Constitution guarantees an accused important rights during trial, the most basic of which are discussed in this chapter. These are the rights to (1) a trial by jury, (2) counsel, (3) due process, (4) protection against self-incrimination, (5) protection against double jeopardy, the (6) confrontation of witnesses, a (7) compulsory process to obtain witnesses, a (8) speedy and public trial, a (9) fair and impartial trial, and (10) proof of guilt beyond a reasonable doubt. All of these rights apply to both federal and state criminal prosecutions. These rights are of constitutional origin and therefore cannot be diminished in any way or abrogated by federal or state legislation. However, the federal government or state governments may, by statute or court decisions, grant *more* rights than those given by the Constitution. In short, states cannot diminish the rights given in the Constitution because those are guaranteed rights, but states and the federal government can add more rights. Two examples will help illuminate this.

- **Example 1:** There is no constitutional right to a twelve-member jury trial, but the federal government and most states provide for twelve-member juries by statute or by provision in the state constitution.

- **Example 2:** The Constitution does not guarantee a defendant the right to appeal from a criminal conviction, but the federal government and all states provide for the right to appeal, either by state law or a provision of the state constitution.

I. THE RIGHT TO A TRIAL BY JURY

Article III, Section 2, Clause 3, of the Constitution provides that "[t]he Trial of all Crimes, except in cases of Impeachment, shall be by Jury." The Sixth Amendment also provides that "In all criminal prosecutions, the accused shall enjoy the right to a speedy and public trial, by an impartial jury of the State and district wherein the crime shall have been committed."

A. Jury Size

In all criminal trials, a jury of twelve is required by federal statute, but not by the Sixth Amendment. Thus, the Supreme Court has upheld a Florida law providing for a six-member jury in all state criminal cases except those involving capital offenses (Williams v. Florida, 399 U.S. 78 [1970]). The minimum number of jurors is six. Juries fewer than six members are unconstitutional because the membership would be too small to provide for effective group discussion and also because it would diminish the chances of drawing from a fair, representative cross-section of the community, thus impairing the accuracy of fact finding (Ballew v. Georgia, 435 U.S. 223 [1978]). Although most juries are composed of either twelve or six members, any number between six and twelve is constitutional. Whether death penalty cases can be decided by juries of fewer than twelve is an issue the Court has not addressed. Chances are that the Court, given the severity of the punishment involved, would not approve a jury of fewer than twelve people in capital cases.

B. Unanimous versus Nonunanimous Verdicts

In federal criminal cases, a unanimous jury verdict is required, but a **nonunanimous verdict** is sometimes adequate in state trials. For example, in Johnson v. Louisiana, 406 U.S. 356 (1972), a 9-to-3 vote for conviction was upheld as constitutional. But the Court has not decided whether an 8-to-4 or a 7-to-5 vote for conviction would be constitutional. What this means is that a state can provide for a less-than-unanimous verdict for conviction (usually by law) and that such a procedure is constitutional. The Court has rejected the argument that permitting a nonunanimous verdict violates the "reasonable doubt" standard for conviction in criminal cases, saying that disagreement among jurors would not in itself establish that there was a reasonable doubt as to the defendant's guilt. Reasonable doubt refers to the thinking of an individual juror, not to a split vote among the jurors. A **hung jury** is *a jury that cannot come to a unanimous agreement (in jurisdictions where unanimity is required) to convict or to acquit.* When this happens, the defendant can be tried again at the discretion of the prosecutor. There is no constitutional limit on how many times an accused can be tried again after a hung jury. This decision is left to the discretion of the prosecutor.

Currently, forty-five states require unanimity in criminal cases, but twenty-nine states do not require unanimity in civil trials. The vote needed to convict varies among jurisdictions that do not require unanimity, ranging from two-thirds in Montana to five-sixths in Oregon. All states require a unanimous verdict in capital cases. The Court prohibits a finding of guilty by less than a six-person majority; therefore, in a six-person criminal trial, the jury must always be unanimous in finding guilt.[1]

C. Serious versus Petty Offenses

Despite the wording of Article III, Section 2, Clause 3, of the Constitution, which states that "the Trial of all Crimes . . . shall be by Jury," the Court has stated that the Constitution guarantees a jury trial only when a *serious offense* is charged. Such offenses must be distinguished from mere "petty" offenses. For purposes of the constitutional right to a trial by jury, a serious offense is one for which more than six months' imprisonment is authorized (Baldwin v. New York, 399 U.S. 66 [1970]). Courts look at the maximum possible sentence that may be imposed in making this determination. An offense is considered serious if the maximum punishment authorized by statute is imprisonment for more than six months, regardless of the penalty actually imposed; therefore, the accused is entitled to jury trial. For example, suppose X is tried for theft, the maximum penalty for which is one year in jail. If X is denied a jury trial, convicted, and sentenced to five months in jail, the conviction must be reversed because it violates X's right to a trial by jury, even though the actual penalty imposed was less than six months.

By contrast, an offense whose maximum penalty is six months or less is "petty" for purposes of the right to trial by jury (regardless of how that offense is classified by state law). Therefore, no right to a jury trial exists. The Court has ruled that, when a state treats drunk driving as a petty offense, no jury trial is needed even if other peripheral sanctions (such as a fine and automatic loss of one's driver's license) may also be imposed (Blanton v. North Las Vegas, 489 U.S. 538 [1989]). Some states classify drunk driving as a serious offense for which the maximum penalty is more than six months of confinement. In those states, a jury trial is constitutionally required.

In a recent case, the Court held that a defendant who is prosecuted in a single case for more than one petty offense does not have a constitutional right to a trial by jury even if the total penalty exceeds six months (Lewis v. United States, 59 CrL 2206 [1996]). In *Lewis,* the defendant was charged in a single proceeding with two counts of mail obstruction. Each charge carried a penalty of six months' imprisonment. The defendant argued that he was entitled to a jury trial because he faced a total imprisonment of up to one year for the two petty offenses. On appeal, the Court disagreed, saying that the "scope of the Sixth Amendment does not change just because a defendant faces multiple charges" and that "the maximum penalty is an objective criterion that reveals the legislature's judgment about the offense's severity." The Court added, "Where we have a judgment by the legislature that an offense is petty, we do not look to the potential prison term faced by a particular defendant who is charged with more than one such petty offense." In sum, the maximum authorized penalty for one offense determines whether a defendant is entitled to a jury trial, not the total penalty the defendant faces in cases of multiple charges.

In general, if no punishment is prescribed by statute, the offense is considered petty when the actual sentence imposed is six months or less. Juvenile offenders have no constitutional right to a trial by jury, regardless of the length of confinement. However, such right may be given by state law.

D. Waiver of a Jury Trial

The right to a trial by jury may be waived by the accused, provided the waiver is *express* and *intelligent*. In some cases, however, the prosecution has the right to demand a jury trial even if the defendant waives it. This is because criminal defendants have no constitutional right to waive a jury trial and have their cases tried before a judge alone (Singer v. United States, 380 U.S. 24 [1965]). For example, in states where the death penalty may be imposed only by a jury, the prosecutor may insist on a jury trial even if the defendant waives that right and chooses to be tried by a judge in an effort to escape the death penalty. In these cases. the prosecution may demand a jury trial. Their demand takes precedence over an accused's waiver of a jury trial.

E. The Selection of a Jury of Peers

The Supreme Court interpretation of the Sixth Amendment requires that trial juries in both federal and state criminal trials be selected from "a representative cross-section of the community." It also guarantees trial by a **jury of peers.** That phrase does not mean that, say, a student facing criminal charges must have a jury of students or that female defendants must have an all-female jury. What it does mean is that *jury service cannot be consciously restricted to a particular group.* For example, excluding women from juries or giving them automatic exemptions, with the result that jury panels are almost totally male, is invalid (Taylor v. Louisiana, 419 U.S. 522 [1975]). Likewise, the exclusion of persons because of race, creed, color, or national origin is unconstitutional.

A defendant is not entitled to have all diverse groups in the community represented in the jury. It is enough that the jurors be drawn from a group that represents a reasonable cross-section of the community. For example, it is unconstitutional to exclude for cause potential jurors who merely have reservations about the death penalty. This would result in "stacking the deck" in favor of the death penalty, thus violating the defendant's right to due process (Witherspoon v. Illinois, 391 U.S. 510 [1968]). However, persons who are unwilling to impose the death penalty under any circumstances, regardless of the offense, may be disqualified from a capital offense jury (Lockhart v. McCree, 476 U.S. 162 [1986]).

F. Disqualification of Jurors Based on Race

A prosecutor's use of **peremptory challenges**—challenges *for which no reason is stated,* as opposed to challenges for cause, for which legal reasons for the challenge must be stated—to exclude from a jury members of the defendant's race solely on racial grounds violates the equal protection rights of both the defendant and the excluded jurors (Batson v. Kentucky, 476 U.S. 79 [1986]). In that case, a trial judge in Kentucky conducted the examination of the jury and excused certain jurors for cause. After that, the prosecutor used his peremptory challenges to strike all four black persons from the jury pool, resulting in an all-white jury. On appeal, the Court reaffirmed the principle announced in an 1880 case (Strauder v. West Virginia, 100 U.S. 303 [1880]), saying that "the State denies a black defendant equal protection of the laws when it puts him on trial before a jury from which members of his race have been purposefully excluded." Interestingly, however, the prosecution's racially motivated use of peremptory challenges to exclude people from the trial jury does not violate the defendant's Sixth Amendment right to a trial by an impartial jury (Holland v. Illinois, 493 U.S. 474 [1990]). But the Court did hint that such a challenge could have been raised as a violation of the constitutional right to equal protection under the Fourteenth Amendment. Since that challenge was not raised in this case, the result was different from *Batson.*

In *Batson,* the Court outlined the three steps courts must follow in resolving cases of peremptory jury disqualification based on race:

- **Step 1:** The side making the allegation must establish a prima facie (at first sight) case of discrimination based on race or other forbidden grounds.

- **Step 2:** If step 1 is established, then the burden shifts to the side that made the peremptory strike to come up with a race-neutral explanation for the strike.

- **Step 3:** The trial court is then required to decide whether the side opposing the peremptory challenges has proved purposeful discrimination.

To illustrate the three-step process, suppose defendant X is tried and convicted by an all-white jury. X alleges that potential African American jurors were scratched from the jury pool by the prosecutor because of race. If X establishes a prima facie case that race was, in fact, the reason for the disqualification (admittedly difficult to do in peremptory challenges because no reason is given), then the burden shifts to the prosecutor to establish that race was not the basis for the disqualification. The trial court then must decide whether X has, in fact, proved discrimination based on race.

In a subsequent case, the Court held that the reasons offered by the side using the peremptory strike do not have to be "persuasive or even plausible" to comply with *Batson*'s step-2 requirement (Purkett v. Elem, 57 CrL 3044 [1995]). In *Purkett,* the defendant challenged a prosecutor's exercise of peremptory challenges against two potential black male jurors, saying that the prosecutor did not establish step 2 and alleging that the prosecutor failed to come up with a race-neutral explanation for the strike. As an explanation for his strike, the prosecutor later said that he struck one potential juror because of "unkempt" hair and that the mustaches and beards the two potential jurors had were "suspicious." The defendant claimed that this explanation was unacceptable and not race neutral. The Court disagreed, saying that the explanation need not be persuasive or even plausible for the trial court to be able to go on to step 3, which involves determining whether the party opposing the peremptory challenge has proved purposeful discrimination. The trial court concluded that the prosecutor had satisfied step 2, but that defendant had not established step 3—purposeful discrimination—so the defendant's claim lacked validity.

The Court has also held that the Constitution prohibits a criminal defendant, as well as the prosecution, from engaging in purposeful discrimination on the grounds of race in the exercise of peremptory challenges (Georgia v. McCullum, 60 L.W. 4574 [1992]). In that case, several white defendants were charged with assaulting two African Americans. Before the jury selection process began, the trial judge denied the prosecution's motion to prohibit defendants from exercising their peremptory challenges in a racially discriminatory manner, as the prosecution expected the defendants would do. On appeal, the Court said that in previous cases it had held that the exercise of racially discriminatory peremptory challenges violates the Equal Protection Clause of the Fourteenth Amendment when the offending challenges are made by the state and, in civil cases, when they are made by private litigants. Using a four-factor analysis, the Court held that the prohibition should also be extended to discriminatory challenges made by criminal defendants.

May a white defendant object to the exclusion of black jurors from the jury through the use of a peremptory challenge, and vice versa? The answer is yes: The defendant need not be a member of the group excluded to successfully invoke the Equal Protection Clause (Powers v. Ohio, 111 S.Ct. 1364 [1991]). In that case, Powers, a white man, objected to the prosecution's use of peremptory challenges to remove seven African Americans from the jury. The Court upheld his challenge on appeal, saying that under the Equal Protection Clause a defendant may object to the race-based exclusion of jurors through peremptory challenges even though the defendant and the excluded jurors are not of the same race. And, in a 1998 case, the Court extended that decision, ruling that a white defendant had reason to complain of discrimination against blacks in the selection not of a trial jury but the grand jury (Campbell v. Louisiana, 63 CrL 94 [1998]).

G. Disqualification of Jurors Based on Gender

In a significant case decided in 1994, the Court held that the Constitution forbids discrimination in the selection of jurors based on "gender" or "on the assumption that an individual will be biased on a particular case solely because the person happens to be a woman or a man" (J.E.B. v. Alabama, 114 S.Ct. 1419 [1994]). (Read the J.E.B. v. Alabama case brief at the end of this chapter.)

AT A GLANCE

The Right to a Trial by Jury

SOURCE OF THE RIGHT: The Sixth Amendment.

SIZE OF JURY: May vary from six to twelve.

UNANIMITY VERDICT: Not required by the Constitution. Most states require a unanimous jury in criminal cases but not in civil cases. Jury of six members, however, must hand down unanimous verdicts.

WHEN IS A JURY TRIAL REQUIRED? When more than six months' imprisonment is authorized for the offense.

TWO TYPES OF JURY CHALLENGES: Challenge for cause and peremptory challenge.

WHAT IS A JURY OF PEERS? A jury whose membership is not consciously restricted to a particular group. It does not mean a jury of the same race, gender, financial status, educational status, or other attributes or characteristics of the defendant.

WHAT IS UNCONSTITUTIONAL IN JURY SELECTION? Disqualification of jurors based on race, gender, creed, color, national origin, and other prohibited categories.

This case involved a paternity and child support trial in which the state used nine of its ten peremptory challenges to remove male jurors, resulting in an all-female civil jury. The state assumed that male jurors would be biased in favor of a man in a child support–paternity lawsuit. In holding that the disqualifications violated the Equal Protection Clause, the Court said that "the conclusion that litigants may not strike potential jurors solely on the basis of gender does not imply the elimination of all peremptory challenges," as some had feared, adding that "so long as gender does not serve as a proxy for bias, unacceptable jurors may still be removed, including those who are members of a group or class that is normally subject to 'rational basis' review and those who exhibit characteristics that are disproportionately associated with one gender." Although this case involved peremptory challenges in a civil case, there is every reason to believe that it also applies to criminal cases, in terms of both peremptory challenges and challenges for cause.

The principles and cases involving challenges based on race and gender represent an attempt by the Court to ensure that all juries are selected in a nondiscriminatory manner and that race and gender are not factors, whether in challenges for cause or in peremptory challenges. However, since peremptory challenges are made without reasons given, it is difficult to determine whether a peremptory challenge is based on race— unless the results are clear, obvious, and can be proved, or one party admits to such bias.

The controversy over peremptory challenges based on race and gender may extend to similar challenges based on other grounds. Although discrimination based on race and gender has generated the most heat and attention in recent years, factors such as lifestyle, mental disability, religion, class, ethnicity, national origin, occupation, economics, and physical status may gain prominence in an era of inclusion and increasing diversity. Although some of these issues have been raised in lower courts, the U.S. Supreme Court has thus far not addressed them, continuing instead to focus on race and gender.

II. THE RIGHT TO COUNSEL

The Sixth Amendment to the Constitution provides that, "in all criminal prosecutions, the accused shall enjoy the right . . . to have the Assistance of Counsel for his defence." This right has been held applicable to the states since 1963 (Gideon v. Wainwright, 372 U.S. 335 [1963]). A defendant has the right to be represented by counsel at "every critical stage" of the criminal proceeding. The meaning of the term *critical stage* has been determined by the Court on a case-by-case basis.

A. Why Is Counsel Needed?

In a celebrated case of long ago, the Court stated the justification for the right to counsel in criminal proceedings in the case of Powell v. Alabama (287 U.S. 45 [1932]). The *Powell* case was one of the two famous "Scottsboro cases" (the other was Norris v. Alabama, 294 U.S. 587 [1935]), in which nine black youths were charged with the rape of two white girls. Justice George Sutherland wrote the following often-quoted statement on why an accused needs counsel during the trial:

> Even the intelligent and educated layman has small and sometimes no skill in the science of the law. Left without aid of counsel, he may be put on trial without a proper charge, and convicted upon incompetent evidence irrelevant to the issue or otherwise inadmissible against him. Without counsel, though he may not be guilty, he faces the danger of conviction because he does not know how to establish his innocence.

(Read the Powell v. Alabama case brief at the end of this chapter.)

B. How Is Counsel Obtained?

The term *right to counsel* refers to either retained counsel or court-appointed counsel. The discussion here is limited to the right to court-appointed counsel, because most criminal cases deal only with that issue.

1. Retained Counsel

Retained counsel is *an attorney chosen and paid by the accused.* According to two noted legal authorities, "the state has no Sixth Amendment obligation to allow representation by retained counsel in a proceeding as to which it has no Sixth Amendment obligation to appoint counsel for the indigent." The same authors add, however, that jurisdictions usually allow retained counsel to be present even in proceedings involving misdemeanors punishable only by a fine—offenses for which the Constitution does not require states to provide counsel to indigents.[2]

HIGHLIGHT

Indigent Defense

- States and localities use several methods for delivering indigent defense services: public defender programs, assigned counsel, and contract attorney systems.

- Twenty-eight percent of state court prosecutors reported that their jurisdictions used public defender programs exclusively to provide indigent counsel.

- In 1990 state and local governments spent approximately $1.3 billion on public defenders' services. In 1979 this figure was about $300 million.

- About three-fourths of the inmates in state prisons and about half of those in federal prisons received publicly provided legal counsel for the offense for which they were serving time.

- In 1992 about 80 percent of defendants charged with felonies in the nation's 75 largest counties relied on a public defender or on assigned counsel for legal representation.

- Little current information is available regarding the workload, staffing, procedures, and policies for indigent defense services across the nation.

Source: *Indigent Defense Highlights, Bureau of Justice Statistics: Selected Findings,* U.S. Department of Justice, Office of Justice Programs, February 1996, p. 1.

A defendant's right to hire an attorney of his or her own choosing (as opposed to an attorney provided by the state for an indigent) may be limited by the trial court to avoid a possible conflict of interest (Wheat v. United States, 486 U.S. 153 [1988]). In that case, the defendant and others were charged with conspiracy to distribute drugs. Two days before trial, one of the defendants asked to replace his counsel with an attorney who represented two of the other alleged coconspirators. These two coconspirators had either already pleaded guilty to the charges or were getting ready to do so. The prosecution objected to the change of counsel, alleging conflict of interest if the same defense lawyer represented all three defendants because, for some reason, that would have limited cross-examination by the prosecutor. The trial court refused to allow the change of counsel by the defendant, saying that it would indeed create a conflict of interest, a decision upheld by the Court on appeal. In sum, a defendant's right to hire his or her own lawyer may be limited by the trial court if there is compelling justification for it, such as a conflict of interest.

2. Court-Appointed Counsel

Court-appointed counsel is an attorney appointed by the judge and paid by the county or state to represent an "indigent" accused at a "critical stage" in the criminal proceedings. There is no uniform rule to determine indigency. Standards used by judges include being unemployed, not having a car, not having posted bail, and not having a house. The judge enjoys wide discretion in making this determination, and his or her decision is rarely reversed on appeal. The standards for indigency therefore vary from one jurisdiction or judge to another. Nevertheless, more than half of all defendants charged with felonies are classified as indigents.

The method of appointing counsel for an **indigent defendant,** meaning *defendants who are too poor to hire their own lawyers,* also varies. In some jurisdictions, judges

HIGHLIGHT

Are Assigned Lawyers Well Paid? You Be the Judge

- Virginia: Assigned lawyers are paid a maximum of $845 for serious felony cases with sentences of 20 years to life and are reimbursed only minimally for expenses.

- Illinois: Hourly rates of $30 out of court, $40 in court are unchanged since 1975.

- Texas: In many of the 254 counties, judges set rates. Lawyers in Bexar County (San Antonio) make $25 an hour in major criminal cases.

Source: *Time Magazine*, July 5, 1999, p. 38.

use a list containing the names of available and willing attorneys, who are then assigned to cases on a rotation basis. In others, judges make assignments at random, assigning any lawyer who may be available in the courtroom at the time the appointment is to be made. Still other jurisdictions employ full-time public defenders to handle indigent cases. The decision to create a public defender's office is usually driven by considerations of cost-effectiveness. From an economic perspective, the bigger the city or county, the more attractive the public defender model becomes.

An indigent defendant has no right to designate an attorney of his or her choice. The selection of a defense lawyer is made purely at the discretion of the court, although the judge may allow the accused some input in the process. Some states provide counsel to defendants but specify as a condition of probation or parole that the defendant reimburse the state or county for the fees of the appointed lawyer. Such laws are valid as long as they exempt indigents who cannot afford to pay (Fuller v. Oregon, 417 U.S. 40 [1974]).

C. Pretrial Proceedings to Which the Right to Counsel Applies

To get a full grasp of the extent of the right to counsel, it's important to know the types of proceedings prior to trial to which the right to counsel applies. Generally, the Court has held that a suspect or defendant has a right to counsel only in pretrial proceedings that are considered "critical stages" in the criminal process. By implication, a lawyer is not required when the proceeding is not deemed to be a "critical stage," as determined by the Court in a series of cases. The following are considered to be critical pretrial stages, and therefore the right to counsel applies:

- **Custodial interrogations before or after charges have been filed** (Miranda v. Arizona, 384 U.S. 436 [1966]).

- **Noncustodial interrogations after the accused has been formally charged with an offense and has a lawyer.** For example, in one case, a defendant made incriminating statements to a codefendant whom federal agents had "wired for sound." Wiring the codefendant was held to violate the defendant's Sixth Amendment right to counsel, because the defendant at that time was out on bail after having been formally charged with the crime (Massiah v. United States, 377 U.S. 201 [1964]).

■ **Postindictment lineups in which witnesses seek to identify the accused** (United States v. Wade, 388 U.S. 218 [1967]).

■ **Preliminary hearings to determine whether there is sufficient evidence against the accused to go to a grand jury** (Coleman v. Alabama, 399 U.S. 1 [1970]).

D. Pretrial Proceedings to Which the Right to Counsel Does Not Apply

The following proceedings prior to trial are not considered by the Court to be in the "critical stage," so the right to counsel does not apply:

■ **Grand jury proceedings.** A witness, including one who faces possible indictment, called to appear before a grand jury is not entitled to have either retained or court-appointed counsel present. The theory is that such proceedings are only investigative in nature. However, to protect a witness's self-incrimination rights, the witness who is in doubt about whether his or her answer may be self-incriminating generally may consult his or her attorney outside the jury room to obtain advice.

■ **Purely investigative proceedings.** There is no constitutional right to either retained or court-appointed counsel at purely investigative hearings. For example, counsel is not required at a hearing by the state fire marshal to determine if a particular fire was the result of arson. Likewise, there is no right to counsel if a police officer is under administrative investigation, except if counsel is otherwise allowed or provided under administrative or departmental policy.

■ **Police lineups prior to the filing of charges.** There is generally no constitutional right to retained or court-appointed counsel before criminal charges are filed against a suspect. After charges are filed, the suspect has a constitutional right to counsel.

E. The Right to Court-Appointed Counsel during Trial

1. The Extent of a Defendant's Right to Court-Appointed Counsel in All Criminal Proceedings

Although the Sixth Amendment extends to "all criminal prosecutions," the Court has held that the right to court-appointed counsel applies only in the following instances:

■ The crime charged is a serious offense (Gideon v. Wainwright, 372 U.S. 335 [1963]). (Read the Gideon v. Wainwright case brief at the end of this chapter.)

■ The crime charged is a misdemeanor for which the defendant faces a possible jail sentence (Argersinger v. Hamlin, 407 U.S. 25 [1972]).

To illustrate these two decisions, suppose Y is charged with robbery, a serious offense in that jurisdiction. Y, if indigent, is entitled to court-appointed counsel during the trial. Y would also be entitled to a lawyer if indigent and charged with a misdemeanor for which he faced a possible jail sentence. However, if Y is charged with a traffic violation for which no jail sentence is attached, Y is not entitled to a lawyer.

Despite *Gideon* and *Argersinger,* the Court, in a 5-to-4 decision, later held that the state is not required to appoint counsel for an indigent defendant charged with a non-petty offense that is punishable by imprisonment if the defendant is not, in fact, sentenced to prison (Scott v. Illinois, 440 U.S. 367 [1979]). In *Scott,* the defendant was tried without a lawyer for the crime of theft (shoplifting). The maximum penalty prescribed by state law for the offense was a fine of $500 or a year in prison, or both. Scott was convicted and sentenced to pay a fine of $50. On appeal, the Court affirmed the conviction, saying that the "federal Constitution does not require a state trial court to appoint counsel for a criminal defendant such as petitioner." Under *Scott,* the state is arguably not required to provide counsel, whether an indigent defendant be charged with a serious offense or a misdemeanor, if the defendant is not sentenced to prison (such as if the judge assigns the defendant to community service or imposes a fine). Some observers note, however, that "states have the option of providing appointed counsel for all misdemeanor defendants and many states follow that policy—at least where the misdemeanors are not punishable only by fine."[3]

2. The Extent of a Defendant's Right to Confer with Counsel

During the trial itself, a judge may not prevent the defendant from talking with counsel during an overnight recess, because otherwise his or her right to counsel is violated (Geders v. United States, 425 U.S. 80 [1976]). In that case, the trial judge directed the defendant not to talk with his attorney during an overnight recess, because the defendant was going to continue his testimony the following day. However, in a subsequent case, the Court ruled that a defendant who takes the witness stand has no Sixth Amendment right to consult with his lawyer during a brief recess while testifying (Perry v. Leeke, 488 U.S. 272 [1989]). In that case, the trial judge declared a fifteen-minute recess and ordered the witness-defendant not to talk to anyone, including counsel. The different Court rulings are explained by the fact that the *Geders* case involved an overnight recess, where it would be natural for defendant to confer with counsel about the whole case, whereas *Perry* involved a fifteen-minute recess, where "it is appropriate to presume that nothing but the defendant's testimony will be discussed."

Although juvenile proceedings are not criminal in nature, a juvenile is nonetheless entitled to court-appointed counsel if the proceeding can lead to commitment in an institution in which the juvenile's freedom is restricted (In re Gault, 387 U.S. 1 [1967]).

F. The Right to Effective Assistance of Counsel

A defendant may challenge his or her conviction on the grounds that the lawyer at trial was so incompetent as to deprive the defendant of effective assistance of counsel.

Although this claim is frequently raised, it is difficult to prove and therefore seldom succeeds.

The meaning of "effective assistance of counsel" bothered lower courts for years because of the absence of a clear standard. In two 1984 cases, the Court clarified the issue by specifying the following criteria:

- A claim of ineffective assistance of counsel can be made only by pointing out specific errors of trial counsel. It cannot be based on an inference drawn from the defense counsel's inexperience or lack of time to prepare, the gravity of the charges, the complexity of defense, or the accessibility of witnesses to counsel (United States v. Cronic, 466 U.S. 648 [1984]).

- The Court assumes that effective assistance of counsel is present unless the adversarial process is so undermined by counsel's conduct that the trial cannot be relied upon to have produced a just result. An accused who claims ineffective counsel must show the following: (1) deficient performance by counsel and (2) a reasonable probability that but for such deficiency the result of the proceeding would have been different (Strickland v. Washington, 466 U.S. 668 [1984]). In a 1993 case, however, the Court made the standard for reversal of conviction even more difficult: "To show prejudice under *Strickland,* a defendant must demonstrate that counsel's errors are so serious as to deprive him of a trial whose result is fair or reliable, not merely that the outcome would have been different" (Lockhart v. Fretwell, 52 CrL 2107 [1993]).

Under these standards, mere generalizations about the quality of the lawyer or the inadequacy of his or her efforts will not suffice. Specificity is required, and the burden is on the defendant to show a reasonable probability that if the lawyer's performance had not been deficient, the results would have been different. This is difficult to establish, and in most cases, the accused needs another lawyer who knows enough law to be able to prove this. For example, suppose that, after conviction, defendant X alleges that he had ineffective counsel because the lawyer assigned by the court to defend him (as an indigent) had limited experience handling criminal cases and finished last in his law school class. This will not suffice to establish ineffective counsel. Instead, X must specify the errors the defense lawyer committed that contributed to his conviction. Likewise, a mere error of law in advising a defendant to enter a guilty plea does not in itself constitute the denial of effective counsel. The test is whether the mistake was "within the range of competency" of most criminal defense lawyers. However, if the lawyer fails to follow state procedural rules, resulting in the dismissal of the appeal, this represents ineffective assistance of counsel.

A guilty plea waives all defenses and most objections. Therefore, counsel's advice to enter such a plea may be more carefully examined. Lower courts have held that if counsel falsely represents that the state has accepted a plea bargain, and the defendant relied on counsel's misrepresentation in entering his or her guilty plea, the defendant has been denied the effective assistance of counsel, so the plea should be set aside.

G. The Right to Act as One's Own Counsel

Under certain conditions, an accused has a constitutional right to waive counsel and represent him- or herself in a criminal proceeding (Faretta v. California, 422 U.S. 806 [1975]). In *Faretta,* the defendant had a high school education, had represented himself before, and had not wanted a public defender to represent him because of the public defender's heavy caseload. The right to self-representation does not require legal skills, but in cases in which the defendant is ignorant or too inexperienced, the request to act as his or her own counsel will probably be denied by the court. Before an accused can be permitted to waive counsel and represent him- or herself, the following constitutional requirements must be met:

- **Awareness of the right to counsel.** The court must fully advise the accused of his or her right to be represented by counsel.

- **Express waiver.** The accused's waiver of counsel cannot be inferred from his or her silence or from his or her failure to request the appointment of counsel.

- **Competency of the accused.** The trial judge must determine whether the accused (1) is competent to waive the right to counsel and (2) is competent to make an intelligent choice in the case. In determining the defendant's competency to make an intelligent choice, the court must make the defendant aware of the dangers and disadvantages of self-representation. An accused who elects to represent him- or herself cannot later claim ineffective counsel.

III. THE RIGHT TO DUE PROCESS

There are two due process clauses in the U.S. Constitution. The Fifth Amendment (applicable to federal prosecutions) provides that "No person shall be held to answer for a capital, or otherwise infamous crime, . . . nor be deprived of life, liberty, or property, without due process of law; nor shall private property be taken for public use, without just compensation." A second due process clause is found in Section 1 of the Fourteenth Amendment (applicable to state prosecutions), which provides that "No state shall make or enforce any law which shall abridge the privileges or immunities of citizens of the United States; nor shall any state deprive any person of life, liberty, or property, without due process of law; nor deny to any person within its jurisdiction the equal protection of the laws."

Due process means "fundamental fairness," but it has no fixed meaning. What process is due varies from one proceeding to another, depending upon what type of proceeding it is and what is at stake. For example, due process during a criminal trial is different from due process in probation or parole revocation proceedings or in prison disciplinary proceedings. What rights are due in a particular proceeding is ultimately

AT A GLANCE
The Right to Counsel

SOURCE OF THE RIGHT: The Sixth Amendment.

WHY COUNSEL IS NEEDED: The accused's lack of skill in law might result in a wrongful conviction.

TWO TYPES OF COUNSEL: Retained by defendant and court-appointed (if indigent).

PRETRIAL PROCEEDINGS TO WHICH THE RIGHT APPLIES:

- Custodial interrogations before or after charges have been filed.
- Noncustodial interrogations after the accused has been formally charged with an offense and has a lawyer.
- Postindictment lineups.
- Preliminary hearings.

PRETRIAL PROCEEDINGS TO WHICH THE RIGHT DOES NOT APPLY:

- Grand jury proceedings.
- Purely investigative proceedings.
- Police lineups prior to the filing of charges.

PROCEEDINGS TO WHICH THE RIGHT TO COUNSEL APPLIES: All serious offenses, as well as misdemeanors for which the defendant faces a possible jail sentence.

RIGHT TO EFFECTIVE ASSISTANCE OF COUNSEL: Guaranteed, but difficult to establish ineffective counsel on appeal.

RIGHT TO ACT AS ONE'S OWN COUNSEL: Allowed but only if the accused is aware of his or her right to counsel, there is an express waiver, and the accused is competent.

---

decided by the courts. Any time fundamental fairness is an issue, due process can likely be raised in a criminal case. This is illustrated by the Brady rule.

A. The Brady Rule on Disclosure of Evidence to the Accused

Due process is protected to the utmost during criminal trials. In a criminal proceeding, the prosecutor has a duty to disclose evidence favorable to a defendant; failure to disclose violates a defendant's constitutional right to due process. This obligation was first declared in Mooney v. Holohan, 294 U.S. 103 (1935), when the Court said that the "due process requirement is not satisfied by mere notice and hearing if the state, through prosecuting officers acting on state's behalf, has contrived conviction through pretense of trial which in truth is used as a means of depriving defendant of liberty through deliberate deception of court and jury by presentation of testimony known to be perjured."

The *Holohan principle* was reiterated almost three decades later in Brady v. Maryland, 373 U.S. 83 (1963), when the Court said that "suppression by the prosecution of evidence favorable to an accused who has requested it violates due process where the evidence is material either to guilt or to punishment, irrespective of the good faith or bad faith of the prosecution." *Brady* involved a case in which the defendant admitted participating in the crime but claimed that his companion did the actual killing. Prior to the trial, Brady's lawyer requested that the prosecutor allow him to examine the companion's extrajudicial statements. The prosecutor showed these to Brady's lawyer but withheld the statement in which the companion admitted doing the actual killing. The defense did not know about that statement until after Brady had been tried, convicted, and sentenced. On appeal, the Court reversed Brady's conviction, saying that *"the suppression by the prosecution of evidence favorable to an accused upon request violates due process where the evidence is material either to guilt or to punishment, irrespective of the good faith or bad faith of the prosecution."* This holding, better known as the **Brady rule,** has been interpreted and refined by the Court in subsequent cases.

B. Cases after <u>Brady</u>

One of the cases interpreting *Brady* is United States v. Agurs, 427 U.S. 97 (1976). In *Agurs,* the Court said that the defendant's failure to request that favorable evidence be shown to the defense did not free the government of all obligation, but that the prosecutor's failure in this particular case did not violate the defendant's right to due process. In *Agurs,* the Court distinguished three situations that can give rise to a Brady claim. These are (1) "where previously undisclosed evidence revealed that the prosecution introduced trial testimony that it knew or should have known was perjured," (2) "where the Government failed to accede to a defense request for disclosure of some specific kind of exculpatory evidence," and (3) "where the Government failed to volunteer exculpatory evidence never requested, or requested only in a general way." In this case, however, the Court stated:

> [the] prosecutor's failure to tender [defendant's] criminal record to the defense did not deprive respondent of a fair trial . . . where it appears that the record was not requested by defense counsel and gave rise to no inference of perjury, that the trial judge remained convinced of respondent's guilt beyond a reasonable doubt after considering the criminal record in the contest of the entire record, and that the judge's firsthand appraisal of the entire record was thorough and entirely reasonable.

In essence, the Court in *Agurs* limited the defendant's right to discovery procedure under the circumstances described here. Then, in United States v. Bagley, 473 U.S. 667 (1985), the Court held that, "regardless of request, favorable evidence is material, and constitutional error results from its suppression by the government, if there is reasonable probability that, had the evidence been disclosed to the defense, the result of the proceeding would have been different."

Another case on disclosure of evidence and the right of an accused to due process is Kyles v. Whitley, 57 CrL 2003 (1995). In *Kyles,* the Court held that, because the effect of the state-suppressed evidence favorable to the defendant raised a reasonable probability that its disclosure would have produced a different result at trial, the conviction had to be reversed. In that case, Kyles was convicted of first-degree murder in Louisiana and sentenced to death. Later, it was revealed that the state had failed to disclose certain evidence favorable to the accused, including the following: (1) contemporaneous eyewitness statements taken by the police following the murder, (2) various statements made to the police by an informant who was never called to testify, and (3) a computer printout of license plate numbers of cars parked at the crime scene on the night of the murder, which did not contain the number of Kyles's car. The Court held that this evidence, taken together, raised a reasonable probability that its disclosure would have produced a different result at trial; hence, the conviction was reversed.

In a 1999 case, the Court held that the prosecution's failure to disclose evidence, in the form of interview notes from a detective, that seriously undermined the truthfulness of the only eyewitness's testimony in a murder case, did not violate the Brady rule because the evidence was not material to the issue of guilt or innocence (Strickler v. Greene, 119 S.Ct. 1936 [1999]). In this case, the only eyewitness to the crime testified at trial that she had an exceptionally good memory and that she had absolutely no doubt that she had identified the defendant correctly. But it was later learned that the notes of her interview with a detective showed that she could not identify the defendant during that first interview. On appeal, the Court held that the failure by the prosecution to disclose the detective's notes did not require a reversal of the conviction because the defendant had not shown by reasonable probability that disclosure of the notes would have changed the results of the trial.

In sum, the rule concerning an accused's right to disclosure of evidence by the prosecution has undergone refinement since the Court first held in *Holohan* that the presentation by prosecutors in court of testimony known to be perjured violated a defendant's right to due process. The latest rule states that, if the circumstances surrounding the nondisclosure raise a "reasonable probability" that the disclosure would have made a difference in the trial's result, the defendant's due process right has been violated and the conviction must be reversed. But undisclosed favorable evidence that is not material to the issue of guilt or innocence does not lead to a reversal of the conviction.

 IV. THE RIGHT TO PROTECTION AGAINST SELF-INCRIMINATION

The prohibition against compulsory self-incrimination springs from the Fifth Amendment provision that "no person . . . shall be compelled in any criminal case to be a witness against himself." This guarantee is designed to restrain the government from using force, coercion, or other such methods to obtain any statement, admission, or confession.

A. The Scope of the Provision

The prohibition against self-incrimination extends only to testimonial (or communicative) self-incrimination; it does not prohibit **physical self-incrimination,** *which stems from real or physical evidence.* For example, the accused can be forced to submit to reasonable physical or psychiatric examinations, and the prosecution may introduce evidence obtained thereby—such as fingerprints, footprints, blood or urine samples, or voice identifications. Also, a defendant can be forced to stand up for identification in the courtroom, to put on certain items of clothing, or to give a handwriting sample (Gilbert v. California, 388 U.S. 263 [1967]). **Testimonial or communicative self-incrimination** is *that which in itself explicitly or implicitly relates a factual assertion or discloses information.* It is in the form of verbal or oral communication. For example, a question that asks whether the defendant killed the deceased is testimonially self-incriminatory, because it relates a factual assertion or discloses information of a non-physical nature.

The Fifth Amendment's protection extends only to natural persons, meaning human beings. Corporations or partnerships (which are considered persons by law) cannot claim the privilege, so the records of such entities cannot be withheld on these grounds. For example, suppose a corporation faces charges of violating labor and anti-monopoly laws. The corporation may be required to produce its official books and records even if they contain incriminating evidence.

The search and seizure of a person's private papers in accordance with legal process, with or without a warrant, does not violate the right to protection against self-incrimination—at least if the information on the papers was written voluntarily, not obtained by testimonial compulsion. This is because the protection given to books and papers under the Fifth Amendment is very limited. Although they are perhaps the products of a mental process (such as a diary), the books or documents themselves constitute physical evidence.

Another aspect of the right to protection against self-incrimination is discussed in South Dakota v. Neville, 459 U.S. 553 (1983). That case involved a South Dakota law that permitted a person suspected of driving while intoxicated to refuse to submit to a blood-alcohol test but also authorized revocation of the driver's license of anyone who refused to take the test. Moreover, the statute permitted such a refusal to be used against the driver as evidence of guilt during the trial. The Supreme Court held that the admission into evidence of a defendant's refusal to submit to a blood-alcohol test does not violate the defendant's Fifth Amendment right to protection against compulsory self-incrimination. A refusal to take the test, after a police officer has lawfully requested it, is not an act coerced by the officer and therefore is not protected by the Fifth Amendment. This case legalized the practice used in some states of giving DWI suspects a choice to take or refuse a blood-alcohol test and then using a refusal as evidence of guilt later in court. The Court said that any self-incrimination resulting from a blood-alcohol test is physical in nature, not testimonial or communicative, so it is not protected by the Fifth Amendment.

May a parent, as the custodian of a child pursuant to a court order, invoke the right to protection against self-incrimination to resist an order of a juvenile court to produce the child? The Court has answered in the negative, saying that, even though producing the child could be self-incriminating, a parent who agreed to certain conditions in assuming custody of a child may be required to produce that child (Baltimore City Department of Social Services v. Bouknight, 493 U.S. 549 [1990]). In that case, the child was originally taken from the mother because of suspected child abuse. The mother regained custody of the child after agreeing to submit to various conditions. Several months later, the social service agency (suspecting further child abuse or even murder) obtained a court order for the mother to produce the child, with which the mother refused to comply. The Court said that the mother could be cited for contempt and rejected her claim of noncompliance based on self-incrimination.

B. Two Separate Privileges during Trial

The privilege against compulsory self-incrimination during trial guarantees two separate privileges: the privilege of the accused and the privilege of a witness.

1. The Privilege of the Accused

The defendant in a criminal case has a **privilege of the accused** *not to take the stand and not to testify.* The Court has ruled that the accused "may stand mute, clothed in the presumption of innocence." Moreover, prosecutors cannot comment on a defendant's assertion of the right not to testify. No conclusion of guilt may be drawn from the failure of the accused to testify during the trial. Therefore, the prosecutor is not permitted to make any comment or argument to the jury suggesting that the defendant is guilty because he or she refused to testify (Griffin v. California, 380 U.S. 609 [1965]). However, this rule has been modified by the concept of **fair response,** which provides that *a prosecutor's statement to the jury, during closing arguments, that the defendant could have taken the witness stand but refused to do so is proper as long as it is in response to defense counsel's argument that the government did not allow the defendant to explain his or her side of the story* (United States v. Robinson, 485 U.S. 25 [1988]). Unless it is in the context of a fair response, the comments of a prosecutor suggesting that the defendant must be guilty because he or she refused to take the stand will lead to a reversal of the conviction.

The privilege to remain silent and not to take the stand applies in all stages of a criminal proceeding, starting with when the suspect is first taken into custody. It applies in criminal prosecutions or contempt proceedings, but not in situations in which there is no prosecution and no accused, as in grand jury investigations or legislative or administrative hearings.

Once an accused takes the witness stand in his or her own defense, he or she waives the privilege not to testify. Therefore, the accused must answer all relevant inquiries about the crime for which he or she is on trial. This is one reason defense lawyers may not want the accused to take the witness stand, particularly if the accused has a bad record or a background that is better kept undisclosed.

2. The Privilege of a Witness

Any witness, other than an accused on the witness stand, has the **privilege of the witness** *to refuse to disclose any information that may "tend to incriminate" him or her.* The reason for this is that the witness is not on trial; he or she is in court merely to provide information about what happened. A question tends to incriminate a witness if the answer would directly or indirectly implicate that witness in the commission of a crime. The privilege does not apply if the answer might expose the witness to civil liability; but if the facts involved would make the witness subject to both civil and criminal liability, the privilege can be claimed. However, the privilege cannot be claimed merely because the answer would hold the witness up to shame, disgrace, or embarrassment. The answer to the question need not prove guilt in order to give rise to the privilege. All that is needed is a reasonable possibility that the answer would "furnish a link in the chain of evidence needed to prosecute." In a recent case, the Court held that a witness, an immigrant from Lithuania, could be forced to testify in a case in the United States even if the testimony given might subject that witness to prosecution (for Nazi war crimes) in a foreign country—Lithuania (United States v. Balsys, 63 CrL 425 [1998]).

The witness's privilege protects only against the possibility of prosecution, so if a witness could not be or can no longer be prosecuted, he or she can be compelled to testify. Several examples will help illuminate this provision.

- **Example 1:** If the **statute of limitations**—*a law providing that a crime must be prosecuted within a certain period of time*—has run out on the crime, the witness can be forced to answer the question.

- **Example 2:** If the witness has been acquitted and therefore cannot be reprosecuted, he or she can be forced to answer the question.

- **Example 3:** If the witness is assured of immunity, he or she may not be forced to answer the question.

The decision as to whether a witness's answer tends to incriminate him or her is usually made by the hearing officer or judge immediately after the question is asked and the opposing lawyer objects on the grounds that the question is self-incriminatory. The decision is appealable only after the trial, so the witness must testify, if so ordered, or face contempt proceedings.

The following chart summarizes the two privileges.

ACCUSED	WITNESS
1. An accused cannot be forced to testify. Refusal cannot be commented on by the prosecution.	1. A witness can be forced to testify if ordered by the court. Refusal can result in a contempt citation.
2. An accused who testifies cannot refuse to answer incriminating questions because the privilege is considered waived.	2. A witness who testifies can refuse to answer questions that might result in criminal prosecution.

C. The Grant of Immunity

There are many situations in which the government grants immunity to a witness or a codefendant in return for his or her testimony. **Immunity** in criminal cases means that *the person granted immunity will not be prosecuted in a criminal case, either fully or partially*—depending upon the type of immunity granted—for testimony given before a grand jury, in court, or in some other proceeding from which prosecution could otherwise have resulted.

Immunity is usually given when the testimony of the witness is crucial to proving the government's case or when the government needs further information for investigative purposes, particularly in cases involving organized crime. A witness who is granted immunity from prosecution may be forced to testify because the reason for the privilege (protection from self-incrimination) no longer exists. Once immunity is granted, a witness who still refuses to testify can be held in contempt of court.

Immunity is granted by law (which usually lists a category of witnesses who may be granted immunity), by judges, or by prosecutors. In a growing number of cases, such as gambling or drug possession, the same act may constitute a crime under both federal and state laws. The question then arises whether a grant of immunity from prosecution in one jurisdiction, state or federal, disqualifies the witness from claiming the privilege in another jurisdiction. The rules governing the grant of immunity are as follows:

- If a state has granted the witness valid immunity, the federal government is not permitted to make use of the testimony (or any of its "fruits") in a federal prosecution against the witness (Murphy v. Waterfront Commission, 378 U.S. 52 [1964]). Therefore, the witness may be forced to testify in the state proceedings.

- The Supreme Court has not decided whether a state should be allowed to use compelled testimony given in federal court under a grant of federal immunity. However, its use would probably be prohibited under the reasoning of the *Murphy* case.

- Similarly, testimony given under a grant of immunity in a state court could not be used as evidence against the witness in the court of another state.

D. Transactional versus "Use and Derivative Use" Immunity

Does the grant of immunity to a witness automatically exempt the witness from any further criminal prosecution? Not necessarily. There are two types of immunity: transactional and "use and derivative use." With **transactional immunity,** *the witness can no longer be prosecuted for any offense whatsoever arising out of that act or transaction.* In contrast, **"use and derivative use" immunity** means that *the witness is assured only that his or her testimony and evidence derived from it will not be used against him or her in a subsequent prosecution.* But the witness can be prosecuted on the basis of evidence

AT A GLANCE

The Right to Protection against Self-Incrimination

SOURCE OF THE RIGHT: The Fifth Amendment.

SCOPE OF THE RIGHT: Applies only to testimonial, and not physical, self-incrimination.

TWO SEPARATE PRIVILEGES DURING TRIAL: The privilege of an accused and the privilege of a witness.

HOW DO PRIVILEGES OF AN ACCUSED AND A WITNESS DIFFER? (1) An accused cannot be forced to answer questions or testify, while a witness can be forced to testify; (2) an accused who testifies cannot refuse to answer incriminating questions, while a witness who testifies can refuse to answer incriminating questions.

WHO MAY GRANT IMMUNITY? The legislature, judge, or prosecutor.

EFFECT OF A GRANT OF IMMUNITY: The person can be forced to testify.

TYPES OF IMMUNITY: Transactional (cannot be prosecuted for any offense related to the transaction) and use-and-derivative-use (can be prosecuted if there is evidence other than the testimony).

WHEN IS THE RIGHT WAIVED? When there is failure to assert or partial disclosure, and when the accused takes the witness stand.

---

other than his or her testimony, if the prosecutor has such independent evidence. The type of immunity given to Oliver North by Congress in the Iran-Contra hearings was use-and-derivative-use immunity.

The Court has decided that prosecutors need only grant use-and-derivative-use immunity to compel an unwilling witness to testify. The witness is not constitutionally entitled to transactional immunity before he or she can be compelled to testify (Kastigar v. United States, 406 U.S. 441 [1972]). In the *Kastigar* case, the witness refused to testify under a grant of use-and-derivative-use immunity, claiming that the Fifth Amendment guarantee against compulsory self-incrimination requires that transactional immunity be given before a witness can be forced to testify. The Court disagreed, saying that use-and-derivative-use immunity is sufficient for purposes of Fifth Amendment protection; the granting of transactional immunity is not required.

E. When the Right Is Waived

A witness's right to protection against self-incrimination may be waived through the following actions:

- **Failure to assert.** The witness is the holder of the privilege, and only the witness (or his or her lawyer) can assert it. If the witness fails to assert the privilege at the time an incriminating question is asked, the privilege is waived.

- **Partial disclosure.** When the witness discloses a fact that he or she knows to be self-incriminating, the witness also waives his or her privilege with respect to all further facts related to the same transaction.

- **Taking the witness stand.** When the witness is also the accused and voluntarily takes the stand, he or she must answer all relevant inquiries about the charge for which he or she is on trial. The accused is therefore "fair game" on all such matters during the cross-examination.

V. THE RIGHT TO PROTECTION AGAINST DOUBLE JEOPARDY

The Fifth Amendment to the U.S. Constitution provides that "no person shall be . . . subject for the same offense to be twice put in jeopardy of life or limb." **Double jeopardy** is defined as *the successive prosecution of a defendant for the same offense by the same jurisdiction.* In the words of the Court, "It protects against a second prosecution for the same offense after acquittal. It protects against a second prosecution for the same offense after conviction. And it protects against multiple punishments for the same offense" (North Carolina v. Pearce, 395 U.S. 711 [1969]). Like most other constitutional rights, the prohibition against double jeopardy has been extended to state criminal proceedings.

This definition has three elements, all of which must be present for double jeopardy to occur:

- **Successive prosecution.** This means two criminal proceedings; if one case is criminal and the other civil, there is no double jeopardy. For example, there was no double jeopardy in the O. J. Simpson trials because the first case was criminal (for double murder) and the second case was civil (for wrongful death).

- **Same offense.** The two cases must be for the same criminal offense. If the elements of the two criminal prosecutions are different, there is no double jeopardy. Thus, if a police officer is criminally charged with abuse of authority and then with illegal detention, there is no double jeopardy if the two offenses require different elements for conviction.

- **Same jurisdiction.** There can be two criminal prosecutions essentially for the same offense, but if they take place in different jurisdictions there is no double jeopardy. For example the four police officers charged in the Rodney King beating in Los Angeles in 1991 were first tried and acquitted under California law and in state court. They were then charged with essentially the same offense under federal law and in federal court. Two were acquitted; the other two were convicted and sentenced to a federal prison. There was no double jeopardy because the two criminal proceedings were in different jurisdictions—one state and the other federal.

A. The Scope of the Provision

A person who has committed a criminal act can be subjected to only one prosecution or punishment for the same offense. Accordingly, when a defendant has been prosecuted for a criminal offense and the prosecution has resulted in either a conviction or an acquittal, or the proceeding has reached a point at which dismissal would be equivalent to an acquittal, any further prosecution or punishment for the same offense is prohibited.

The prohibition against double jeopardy applies (and the defendant cannot be retried for the same offense) when the trial has reached the following stage: (1) in a *jury trial,* when a competent jury has been sworn, or (2) in a *nonjury (bench) trial,* when the first witness has been called and sworn. If the charge is dismissed before either stage is reached, the defendant may be charged and tried again.

B. When Is Double Jeopardy Considered Waived?

Even though double jeopardy attaches under the conditions just discussed, it is considered waived in the following instances.

1. In Mistrials

When a new trial is ordered before a verdict on a motion of the defendant or otherwise with the defendant's consent, the defendant waives his or her right to protection against double jeopardy. Thus, if in the course of a trial the defendant moves for a mistrial because of what a prosecutor or a witness has done, and the motion is granted by the judge, the case can be tried again.

2. When a Verdict of Conviction Is Set Aside on a Defendant's Motion or Appeal

The general view is that a defendant asking for a new trial or appealing a guilty verdict waives his or her right to protection against double jeopardy, so the defendant can be tried again for the same offense for which he or she was convicted in the first trial. If the convicted defendant is serving time, he or she will be released from prison and freed on bail or will be detained in jail pending another trial for the same or a related offense. The prosecutor may choose not to reprosecute, but there is no double jeopardy if the same or a similar charge is again filed.

In the celebrated *Miranda* case (discussed earlier in connection with custodial interrogation of suspects), defendant Miranda appealed his original conviction for rape on the grounds that his confession was obtained in violation of the guarantee against compulsory self-incrimination. His conviction was reversed by the Court, but he was tried again (under an assumed name) for the same offense in Arizona and was reconvicted on the basis of other evidence. There was no double jeopardy because, by appealing his first conviction, he waived his right not to be retried for the same offense.

However, at a second trial for the same offense following a successful appeal, a defendant cannot be tried on or convicted of charges that are more serious than the

HIGHLIGHT

Double Jeopardy and Government Appeals

"In the course of the debates over the Bill of Rights, there was no suggestion that the Double Jeopardy Clause imposed any general ban on appeals by the prosecution. . . . Nor does the common-law background of the Clause suggest an implied prohibition against state appeals. . . . The development of the Double Jeopardy Clause from its common-law origins thus suggests that it was directed at the threat of multiple prosecutions, not at government appeals, at least where those appeals would not require a new trial."

United States v. Wilson, 420 U.S. 332 (1975).

ones for which he or she was originally tried and convicted. For example, suppose a defendant is charged with second-degree murder but is convicted of negligent homicide (a lower offense). If the defendant appeals the conviction and obtains a new trial, he or she cannot be charged with first-degree murder in the second trial (Green v. United States, 355 U.S. 184 [1957]). Also, a defendant whose conviction is reversed because the evidence is insufficient as a matter of law to sustain the conviction cannot be retried; the reversal amounts to an acquittal (Burks v. United States, 437 U.S. 1 [1978]).

If the jury cannot agree on conviction or acquittal, the judge can declare a hung jury, and the defendant may be tried again before another jury. How soon this is declared is a matter of the judge's discretion. Some courts will declare a hung jury after several days of deadlocked jury deliberations; others require a longer period of stalemate.

3. In Habeas Corpus Cases

Habeas corpus cases are filed by defendants who are serving time in prison or jail and who seek release on the grounds that their conviction is unconstitutional or invalid. They are different from appeals in that habeas corpus is filed after the appellate process has been exhausted and is a separate civil proceeding seeking the defendant's release. If a habeas corpus case succeeds, the defendant can be tried again because the filing is considered a waiver of the right to protection against double jeopardy since the defendant is essentially saying, "Give me a new trial because there was something wrong with the first one."

C. What Does "Same Offense" Mean?

Double jeopardy applies only to prosecution for the "same offense." Once double jeopardy attaches, a defendant cannot be prosecuted a second time for the same offense involved in the first trial or for any other offense included in the act charged in the first trial, nor can the defendant be punished more than once for the same offense. In a 1932 case, the Court held that a second prosecution is barred if the two prosecutions reveal that the offenses have identical statutory elements or that one is a lesser included offense of the other (Blockburger v. United States, 284 U.S. 299 [1932]). To illustrate:

- **Example 1:** In one case, the Court said that a conviction for failure to reduce speed to avoid an accident does not necessarily prohibit a second charge of involuntary manslaughter, because vehicular manslaughter does not always require proof of failure to reduce speed (Illinois v. Vitale, 447 U.S. 410 [1980]).

- **Example 2:** In contrast, a conviction for joyriding prohibits a second charge of motor vehicle theft, because no additional facts are needed for the second charge (Brown v. Ohio, 432 U.S. 161 [1977]).

The current test to determine what **"same offense"** means is the Blockburger standard: *double jeopardy applies if the two offenses for which the defendant is being punished come under the "same elements" test.* The key is whether one offense contains the same elements as the other. If it does, then double jeopardy applies; but if one offense requires an element not needed in the other offense, then double jeopardy does not apply.

D. What Does "Lesser Included Offense" Mean?

Double jeopardy attaches when the second prosecution is for a lesser included offense. **"Lesser included offense"** is defined as an *offense that is "composed of some, but not all, of the elements of the greater crime, and which does not have any element not included in the greater offense."*[4] For example, suppose X is charged with murder and is acquitted. She cannot be prosecuted again for homicide arising out of the same act because homicide is a lesser included offense in that it contains all the elements of murder and does not contain any element that is not included in murder. Note that if X is charged with murder, most states will allow her to be convicted of homicide in the same proceeding. Consequently, prosecutors usually charge an accused with the highest possible offense warranted by the facts. If the higher charge fails, the accused may still be convicted of a lesser offense. In contrast, an accused can never be convicted of an offense higher than that with which he or she was charged; that would be a violation of an accused's constitutional rights. This may be illustrated as follows:

- A person accused of murder can be convicted of homicide (a lesser included offense) in the same criminal proceeding, but a person accused of homicide cannot be convicted of murder (a higher offense) in the same criminal proceeding.

- A person accused and acquitted of murder can no longer be charged with homicide because it is a lesser included offense.

In a 1996 case, the Court unanimously held that there cannot be two punishments for two offenses if one is a lesser included offense (Rutledge v. United States, 58 CrL 2076 [1996]). In this case, Rutledge was convicted in federal court of conspiracy to distribute cocaine and of operating a continuing criminal enterprise. He received life sentences for each conviction. On appeal, he argued that the Double Jeopardy Clause prohibits him from being convicted of both offenses because conspiracy is a lesser included offense of the continuing offense of criminal enterprise. The Court reversed the conviction but not based on double jeopardy. Instead, the Court relied on the "merger rule" for lesser included offenses. According to the merger rule, a lesser offense is merged with a more serious offense, so that the offense becomes one and can be prosecuted only once. The Court added that the test to determine if a defendant is being punished twice for the same crime is the "same elements" test. In the *Rutledge* case, the "in concert" element of the continuing criminal enterprise offense was the same element that formed the basis of the conspiracy charge; hence, the "same elements" test was met and multiple punishment was disallowed.

E. Prosecution for a Higher Offense after Conviction for a Lesser Included Offense

Suppose X is tried for a lesser included offense (homicide) and is convicted, but circumstances later reveal or develop that could hold X liable for a higher offense (murder)? Can X be charged and convicted again for the higher offense? The answer is yes, if the government cannot be blamed for the inadequacy of the first charge.[5] This can happen in two ways: (1) "if the facts needed to prove the higher offense had not yet been discovered at the time of the first trial, despite the prosecution's due diligence," and (2) "if at the time the first case is tried, events have not yet occurred that are needed for the second crime."[6] These may be illustrated as follows:

- **Example 1:** Suppose that D has been convicted of kidnapping V, but at the time of conviction the prosecutor did not know whether V was still alive. While D is serving time, the prosecutor learns and obtains evidence that V was, in fact, killed in the course of the kidnapping and that the body has been found. D can now be tried again for the higher crime of kidnapping with murder. There is no double jeopardy because the murder, although it had already occurred, was undiscovered at the time of the first trial.

- **Example 2:** Suppose Z is charged with and convicted of inflicting serious bodily injury and is now in prison. Months later, the victim dies as a result of these injuries. Z can now be charged with and convicted of homicide or murder. There is no double jeopardy because death had not yet occurred at the time Z was tried for the lesser included offense. However, although constitutionally there is no double jeopardy, state law or policy may prohibit a second prosecution for a higher offense if the defendant has already been convicted of a lesser included offense.

F. Prosecution for the Same Offense by Two States

In a 1985 case, the Court decided that under the dual sovereignty doctrine successive prosecutions by two states for the same offense do not violate the Double Jeopardy

AT A GLANCE

The Right to Protection against Double Jeopardy

SOURCE OF THE RIGHT: The Sixth Amendment.

DEFINITION: Successive prosecution of a defendant for the same offense by the same jurisdiction.

WHEN DOES IT ATTACH? In a jury trial, when a competent jury has been sworn; in a trial before a judge, when the first witness has been called and sworn.

WHEN IS IT CONSIDERED WAIVED?

- In mistrials.

- When a verdict of conviction is set aside on the defendant's own motion.

- When a defendant appeals.

- In habeas corpus cases.

WHAT "SAME OFFENSE" MEANS: If two or more offenses have the same elements— for example, joyriding and theft of a vehicle.

WHAT "LESSER INCLUDED OFFENSE" MEANS: An offense that "is composed of some, but not all, of the elements of the greater crime, and which does not have any element not included in the greater offense." For example, homicide is a lesser included offense in murder. Both have the same elements, but murder also requires malice, ill will, or premeditation (depending upon how the law is worded), which is usually not required in homicide.

Clause of the Fifth Amendment (Heath v. Alabama, 474 U.S. 82 [1985]). In the *Heath* case, the defendant had hired two men to kill his wife. In accordance with the defendant's plan, the hired men kidnapped the woman from her home in Alabama. Her body was later found on the side of a road in Georgia. The defendant pleaded guilty to murder "with malice" in a Georgia court, in exchange for a sentence of life imprisonment. Subsequently, he was tried and convicted of murder during a kidnapping (arising out of the same act) by an Alabama trial court and was sentenced to death. His claim of double jeopardy was rejected by the Alabama court, so he appealed his conviction to the U.S. Supreme Court.

In rejecting the double jeopardy claim, the Court said that, according to the dual sovereignty doctrine, when a defendant in a single act violates the "peace and dignity" of two sovereigns by breaking the laws of each, the defendant has committed two distinct offenses for double jeopardy purposes. The crucial question is whether the two entities that seek to prosecute a defendant successively for the same course of conduct can be termed separate sovereigns. If they are, no double jeopardy occurs. The states of Georgia and Alabama are separate from the federal government and from each other, so there is no double jeopardy. For purposes of criminal law and criminal procedure, therefore, there are, in effect, fifty-one different sovereigns in the United States: the fifty states and the federal government.

VI. THE RIGHT TO CONFRONT WITNESSES

The Sixth Amendment provides that "in all criminal prosecutions, the accused shall enjoy the right . . . to be confronted with the witnesses against him." The right to confrontation exists in all criminal proceedings—including trials, preliminary hearings, and juvenile proceedings in which the juvenile is suspected of having committed a crime. The right does not apply to purely investigative proceedings, such as grand jury proceedings, coroner's inquests, and legislative investigations. The right to confrontation includes the following rights: to cross-examine witnesses, to be physically present, to physically face witnesses at trial, and to know the identity of prosecution witnesses.

A. The Right to Cross-Examine Opposing Witnesses

The opportunity to cross-examine all opposing witnesses is an important right of the accused and is guaranteed by the Sixth Amendment. It is through skillful cross-examination that any falsehood or inaccuracy in a witness's testimony can be detected and exposed, and it is then that a skillful lawyer may elicit testimony that can be helpful to his or her client. Probably because this right is strictly observed during trial, there are only a few cases on the scope and meaning of the right. Any limitations on the right to cross-examine a witness are imposed by the judge during trial.

B. The Right to Be Physically Present during Trial

The right to confrontation also includes the opportunity for the accused to be physically present in the courtroom at the time any testimony against him or her is offered. However, the right to be present may be waived under certain circumstances.

1. Deliberate Absence
If an accused is present at the start of the trial but later voluntarily absents him- or herself, the Court has held that the trial may continue because the accused is considered to have waived his or her right to be present (Taylor v. United States, 414 U.S. 17 [1973]). But the issue of whether a defendant can be tried in absentia if he or she was not present at the start of the trial has not been authoritatively decided by the Court. Some states allow criminal trials in absentia under certain circumstances; others provide that the accused must be present in court for the trial to be held.

2. Disruptive Conduct in the Courtroom
Likewise, an accused who persists in disorderly or disrespectful conduct in the courtroom will be held to have waived his or her right to be present and may be excluded

[handwritten margin note: If the defendant is in contempt of court.]

from his or her own trial. The Court has approved the following methods for dealing with a disruptive defendant: (1) holding the defendant in contempt of court, (2) binding and gagging the defendant in the courtroom, and (3) removing the defendant from the courtroom until he or she promises to behave properly (Illinois v. Allen, 397 U.S. 337 [1970]).

The Right to Physically Face Witnesses at Trial

The Court has decided that the right to confrontation also includes the right to physically face witnesses at trial. Therefore, a state law that allows testimony via closed-circuit television or behind a screen violates a defendant's Sixth Amendment rights (Coy v. Iowa, 487 U.S. 1012 [1988]). In Coy, the trial court allowed a semitransparent screen to be erected in court between the defendant and two youthful complainants in a child sex abuse trial, so that the children could not see the defendant when they testified. The Court rejected this method, saying that face-to-face confrontation is the "core" of the constitutional right to confrontation.

Two years later, however, the Court carved out an exception to this rule: Face-to-face confrontation may be dispensed with "when preventing such confrontation is necessary to further important public policy and the reliability of the testimony is otherwise assured" (Maryland v. Craig, 497 U.S. 836 [1990]). In that case, Craig was tried in a Maryland court for sexual abuse of a six-year-old child. In accordance with Maryland law, the judge permitted the child to testify in a different room, saying that courtroom testimony would result in the child's suffering such serious emotional distress that she could not reasonably communicate. This procedure allows the child, prosecutor, and defense counsel to withdraw from the courtroom to another room, where the child is examined and cross-examined. The judge, jury, and defendant remain in the courtroom, where the testimony is seen and heard via one-way closed-circuit television. Craig claimed that the Maryland law violated his right to confrontation. The Court rejected the challenge, saying that although face-to-face confrontation forms the "core" of this constitutional right, it is not an indispensable element thereof.

D. The Right to Know the Identity of Prosecution Witnesses

Any witness who testifies against the accused must reveal his or her true name and address. Such information may be crucial to the defense in investigating and cross-examining the witness for possible impeachment. However, the Court has concluded that the admission into evidence of a prior, out-of-court identification of a witness, who is unable (due to loss of memory) to explain the basis for the identification, is not a violation of the right to confrontation (United States v. Owens, 484 U.S. 554 [1988]). The Court added that the confrontation clause is satisfied if the defendant had a full and fair opportunity to bring up the witness's lapse of memory and other facts that consequently would tend to discredit the testimony.

VII. THE RIGHT TO COMPULSORY PROCESS TO OBTAIN WITNESSES

The Sixth Amendment expressly provides that the accused in a criminal prosecution shall have the right to compulsory process for obtaining witnesses in his or her favor. The right to obtain witnesses includes (1) the power to require the appearance of witnesses and (2) the right to present a defense, which, in turn, includes the defendant's right to present his or her own witnesses and his or her own version of the facts. The essence of this principle is that the defendant is given the same right as the prosecutor to present witnesses in state and federal proceedings. Thus, if the trial judge makes threatening remarks to the only defense witness, in effect driving the witness from the stand, the accused is deprived of the right to present a defense (Webb v. Texas, 409 U.S. 95 [1972]).

If the trial court excludes evidence crucial to the defense and bearing substantial assurances of trustworthiness, this violates the right to present a defense—even when the evidence is technically not admissible under local rules of evidence. For example, in one case, a defendant offered evidence of oral confessions to the crime by another witness. The trial court excluded the evidence because it constituted inadmissible hearsay under the local rules of evidence. This ruling was held to violate the defendant's right to present a defense, since the confessions bore substantial assurances of trustworthiness (Chambers v. Mississippi, 410 U.S. 284 [1973]).

VIII. THE RIGHT TO A SPEEDY AND PUBLIC TRIAL

The Sixth Amendment provides that "in all criminal prosecutions the accused shall enjoy the right to a speedy and public trial." Two separate rights are guaranteed by this provision: a speedy trial and a public trial.

A. A Speedy Trial

A **speedy trial** is *a trial free from unnecessary and unwanted delay.* As the wording indicates, the Sixth Amendment applies only after a person becomes an "accused," meaning after the person has been formally charged with a crime or placed under arrest and detained to answer to a criminal charge. Most jurisdictions hold that, once a person is arrested, he or she is deemed an accused and is entitled to a speedy trial, even if later released on bail.

Violation of the constitutional right to a speedy trial is not established by delay alone. Instead, the determination of whether a case must be dismissed for lack of a speedy trial requires a balancing test. The conduct of both the prosecution and the defense are weighed, and the following factors are considered: (1) the length of the delay, (2) the reason for the delay, (3) the defendant's assertion or nonassertion of rights, and (4) any prejudice to the defendant. Any one factor alone is usually not sufficient either to justify or to condemn the delay in the trial (Barker v. Wingo, 407 U.S. 514 [1972]). If the delay is due to willful delay tactics by the accused, the accused will be deemed to have waived the right to a speedy trial. If the defendant's constitutional right to a speedy trial is violated, the only remedy is dismissal of charges. Dismissal prevents any further prosecution of the accused for the same offense.

In another case, a defendant was indicted on federal drug charges in 1980 but left the country before the Drug Enforcement Agency (DEA) could arrest him. The DEA knew the defendant was later imprisoned in Panama, but after requesting that he be returned to the United States, the DEA never followed up on the case. The DEA knew that the defendant had left Panama for Colombia, but it made no further attempt to locate him. The DEA was not aware that the defendant had reentered the United States in 1982 and that he had "subsequently married, earned a college degree, found steady employment, lived openly under his own name, and stayed within the law." He was eventually located during a simple credit check on individuals with outstanding warrants and was arrested in September 1988, eight and a half years after his original indictment. He objected to his prosecution, saying that it violated his Sixth Amendment right to a speedy trial. On appeal, the Court held that the extraordinary lag of eight and a half years between his indictment and arrest violated the defendant's right to a speedy trial (Doggett v. United States, 505 U.S. 647 [1992]). The Court concluded that the defendant could have faced trial six years earlier (when he reentered the United States) "but for the Government's inexcusable oversights."

In addition to the constitutional provision for a speedy trial, some statutes also provide for dismissal of an action when there have been unjustified delays in filing charges or bringing the defendant to trial. An example is the **Federal Speedy Trial Act of 1974,** whose goal is to bring all federal criminal cases to trial within one hundred days following arrest. *The act requires that an information or indictment be filed within thirty days after arrest, that arraignment follow within ten days thereafter, and that the trial commence within sixty days after arraignment.* Similarly, many states require a trial within a given number of days after the filing of charges against the accused; otherwise, the charges are dismissed. Whether the charges can later be filed again in court depends upon the provisions of the state statute. Many statutes require, however, that the time limitation apply only after a request for a trial is initiated by the defendant.

B. A Public Trial

The accused has a right to a **public trial**—one that can be *seen and heard by persons interested in ensuring that the proceedings are fair and just.* The right, however, is not

The Right to a Speedy and Public Trial

SOURCE OF THE RIGHT: The Sixth Amendment.

SPEEDY TRIAL: A trial free from unnecessary and unwanted delay. If the delay is due to willful delay tactics by the accused, the accused will be deemed to have waived the right.

SPEEDY TRIAL LEGISLATION: The federal government and some states have speedy trial acts that require trial within a certain number of days after the filing of charges; otherwise, the charges are dismissed. Whether the charges can be refiled depends upon provisions of the law, but there is no constitutional prohibition against refiling.

PUBLIC TRIAL: A trial that can be seen and heard by persons interested in ensuring that the proceedings are fair and just. The right is not absolute. The trial judge may excuse some or all spectators during particular parts of the proceedings, but under no circumstances may the friends and relatives of the accused be excluded from the trial. Juveniles have no constitutional right to a public trial.

absolute. The trial judge, at his or her discretion, may exclude some or all spectators during particular parts of the proceedings for good cause, but under almost no circumstances may the friends and relatives of the accused be excluded from the trial. Spectators are frequently excluded if necessary to spare a victim extreme public embarrassment or humiliation, as in certain rape cases. Likewise, a judge may properly exclude certain persons if it can be shown that they are likely to threaten witnesses. Criminal defendants also have a constitutional right to have their pretrial hearings conducted in public. However, the Court has not decided whether the public and the press have a right to attend pretrial hearings when the defendant wants them conducted in secret.

There is a split of authority on the issue of who may object to exclusions. Some courts hold that only the accused has the right to object. Others have indicated that the right also belongs to the public and that members of the public, such as the press, may therefore properly object to being excluded.

Juveniles have no constitutional right to a public trial. Many states still provide for closed juvenile adjudication proceedings and either limit or prohibit press reports. These practices are justified by the concept of *parens patriae* (a doctrine by which the government supervises children or other persons who suffer from legal disability), which diminishes the constitutional rights of juveniles and protects them from unnecessary public exposure.

IX. THE RIGHT TO A FAIR AND IMPARTIAL TRIAL

The due process clauses of the Fifth and Fourteenth Amendments guarantee the accused a fair trial by an impartial jury. What this guarantee basically means is that the circumstances surrounding the trial must not be such that they unduly influence the jury. Undue influence usually takes the form of publicity so massive that it becomes prejudicial to the accused.

A. The Prohibition against Prejudicial Publicity

Two basic principles of the U.S. system of criminal justice are that (1) a person must be convicted by an impartial tribunal and (2) a person must be convicted solely on the basis of evidence admitted at the trial. The publicity given to a notorious case before or during trial may bias a jury or create a significant risk that the jury will consider information other than the evidence produced in court. Here are two examples:

- **Example 1:** Headlines announced that D had confessed to six murders and twenty-four burglaries, and reports were widely circulated that D had offered to plead guilty. Ninety percent of the prospective jurors interviewed expressed an opinion that D was guilty, and eight out of twelve jurors finally seated, familiar with the material facts, held such a belief. The Court held that D had been denied due process, stressing that this was a capital case (Irvin v. Dowd, 366 U.S. 717 [1961]).

- **Example 2:** Police arranged to have B's prior confession shown several times on local television. The Court held that B had, in effect, been "tried" thereby— and that no actual prejudice need be shown to establish a denial of due process under such circumstances (Rideau v. Louisiana, 373 U.S. 723 [1963]).

B. Controlling Prejudicial Publicity

In an effort to control prejudicial publicity, the judge has power to order the following steps.

1. Change of Venue
A defendant claiming undue pretrial publicity or other circumstances that would endanger his or her right to a fair and impartial trial locally can move to have the *venue* (place) of the trial changed to another county, from which more impartial jurors can be drawn. This is allowable in both felony and misdemeanor cases.

2. Sequestration
If there is danger that jurors will be exposed to prejudicial publicity during the trial, some states permit **sequestration**—*keeping jurors together during trial and strictly controlling contact with the outside world*—at the judge's discretion, immediately following jury selection and continuing for the duration of the trial. A few states automatically sequester the jury throughout the trial, but most states sequester jurors only for serious cases and then only after the case is given to the jury for deliberation.

3. Continuance

If the prejudice is severe, a *continuance* (postponement) may be granted to allow the threat to an impartial trial to subside.

4. Issuance of a "Gag Rule"

The judge may impose a gag rule, prohibiting the various parties in the trial from releasing information to the press or saying anything in public about the trial. Gag orders usually include the participating attorneys, witnesses, the police, and members of the jury. These orders are valid for the duration of the trial. However, the validity of a gag order beyond the duration of the trial is suspect, because it may run afoul of constitutional rights.

5. Control of the Press

This is a very difficult problem for the judge because of the First Amendment guarantee of freedom of the press. The press has a right to attend a criminal trial, but the media may be excluded if specific findings indicate that closure is necessary for a fair trial. The media do not have a Sixth Amendment right to attend a pretrial hearing in a criminal case. Generally, it is difficult to justify attempts to control the kinds of news items the news media can report in connection with a criminal case—even where such items may create a "clear and present danger" of an unfair trial for the accused. Courts usually prohibit the taking of photographs or the televising of courtroom proceedings. In a number of states, however, the televising of courtroom proceedings is left to the discretion of the trial judge. In the celebrated O. J. Simpson case, Judge Lance Ito allowed the camera in the courtroom, and so the whole criminal trial was on television. By contrast, in the civil case that followed after O. J. Simpson's acquittal, Judge Hiroshi Fujisaki banned all television cameras, news photographers, and radio microphones from the courtroom, and he also imposed a gag order on all participants.

If the judge allows the televising of court proceedings, care must be taken not to create a "carnival atmosphere" inside the courtroom. The Supreme Court has reversed a conviction because press coverage was too intrusive. The Court found the coverage so distracting to the judge, jurors, witnesses, and counsel that it created a "carnival atmosphere" and denied the defendant a fair trial (Sheppard v. Maxwell, 384 U.S. 333 [1966]).

X. THE RIGHT TO PROOF OF GUILT BEYOND A REASONABLE DOUBT

The requirement that guilt be proved beyond a reasonable doubt derives from the Due Process Clause of the Constitution. The Bill of Rights contains no specific provisions on the degree of certainty needed for conviction, but the assumption is that it would be

AT A GLANCE

The Right to a Fair and Impartial Trial

SOURCE OF THE RIGHT: The due process clauses of the Fifth and Fourteenth Amendments.

WHAT IT MEANS: The circumstances surrounding the trial must not be such that they unduly influence the judge or jury.

WAYS A JUDGE MAY CONTROL PREJUDICIAL PUBLICITY:

- Change of venue.
- Sequestration.
- Continuance.
- Issuance of a gag rule.
- Control of the press.

---

fundamentally unfair to convict anyone if there was any reasonable doubt that he or she had committed the crime.

A. What Must Be Proved?

In every criminal case, the prosecution must prove the following beyond a reasonable doubt: (1) the question of guilt and (2) every element of the crime. Failure to prove both results in an acquittal of the accused.

For example, in a crime of theft, the element of intent and the fact that the property belongs to another person must be proved beyond a reasonable doubt. However, only elements of the crime that have to do with the defendant's guilt must be established beyond a reasonable doubt. Other issues are decided at a lower level of proof. Questions relating to the admissibility of evidence, such as whether the evidence was obtained by lawful search or whether the defendant's confession was voluntary, need only be proved by a preponderance of the evidence.

B. What Constitutes Reasonable Doubt?

Reasonable doubt is difficult to define. One court has defined it as follows:

It is such a doubt as would cause a juror, after careful and candid and impartial consideration of all the evidence, to be so undecided that he cannot say that he has an abiding conviction of the defendant's guilt. It is such a doubt as would

AT A GLANCE

The Right to Proof of Guilt beyond a Reasonable Doubt

SOURCE OF THE RIGHT: No specific constitutional provision, but inferred from the due process clauses of the Fifth and Fourteenth Amendments.

DEFINITION: Difficult to define with precision. The definition varies from one state to another and even from court to court within a state. No specific definition is constitutionally required as long as, "taken as a whole, the instructions correctly convey the concept of reasonable doubt" (whatever that means).

WHAT MUST BE PROVED BEYOND A REASONABLE DOUBT? The question of guilt and every element of the crime charged.

---

cause a reasonable person to hesitate or pause in the graver or more important transactions of life. However, it is not a fanciful doubt nor a whimsical doubt, nor a doubt based on conjecture. (Moore v. United States, 345 F.2d 97 [DC Cir. 1965])

In the O. J. Simpson criminal case, Judge Lance Ito gave the following definition to the jury, as prescribed by California law:

Reasonable doubt is defined as follows. It is not a mere possible doubt, because everything relating to human affairs is open to some possible or imaginary doubt. It is that state of the case which, after the entire comparison and consideration of all the evidence, leaves the minds of the jurors in that condition that they cannot say they feel an abiding conviction of the truth of the charge.

These and other definitions used in various jurisdictions are unclear and do not provide a bright-line rule to guide jurors in their deliberations. In some states, reasonable doubt is defined by law; in other states, the term is defined by case law; and in a few states, there is no definition at all—leaving each court in the state to come up with its own definition. Federal courts do not prescribe a single definition.

In reality, despite instructions from the judge (couched in terms similar to those in the definition), an individual juror really determines for him- or herself what is meant by reasonable doubt. Definitions such as those given here are too legalistic and difficult to apply. In most cases, they merely provide a general framework for decision making. Ultimately, jurors define the term subjectively. Quantifying the term (such as defining reasonable doubt as comparable to 95 percent certainty of guilt) removes a lot of confusion, but such quantification is frowned upon by the legal community.

In a 1990 case, the Supreme Court invalidated a conviction where the instructions of the trial court defined reasonable doubt as "such doubt as would give rise to grave uncertainty" and contrasted it with "a moral certainty" rather than "an absolute or mathematical certainty." These terms require a higher degree of doubt than reasonable doubt (Cage v. Louisiana, 111 S.Ct. 328 [1990]). Despite the absence of a clear and workable definition, the Court in 1993 said that a constitutionally deficient reasonable-doubt instruction by a judge to a jury can never be harmless error (that is, be automatically harmful) and therefore leads to a reversal of the conviction on appeal (Sullivan v. Louisiana, 61 L.W. 4518 [1993]). In a case decided in 1994, the Court held that references to "moral evidence," "moral certainty," and "substantial doubt" in the jury instructions given by a Nebraska trial court did not violate the due process requirement of the Fourteenth Amendment (Victor v. Nebraska, 54 CrL 2225 [1994]). The Court added that the Constitution does not prescribe any particular phrasing to be used when giving the jury instructions, so long as, "taken as a whole, the instructions correctly convey the concept of reasonable doubt." The Court refrained, however, from saying what *reasonable doubt* really means.

 # Summary

Defendants enjoy basic constitutional rights during trial. These are the rights to trial by jury, to counsel, to due process, to protection against self-incrimination, to protection against double jeopardy, to confrontation of witnesses, to compulsory process to obtain witnesses, to a speedy and public trial, to a fair and impartial trial, and to proof of guilty beyond a reasonable doubt.

Trial by jury is required in all serious criminal cases, referring to cases in which the possible penalty is imprisonment for more than six months. Federal cases require twelve-member juries and a unanimous conviction, but the Court has decided that states are not constitutionally required to have a jury of twelve members, even in felony cases, or a unanimous verdict for conviction. Moreover, disqualification based on race or gender is unconstitutional because it violates an accused's right to trial by a jury of peers.

An accused is entitled to a lawyer, retained or appointed by the state, if indigent. Moreover, the accused has the right to effective assistance of counsel, although a violation of this right is difficult to prove. An accused has the right to act as his or her own lawyer, provided there is competent waiver and the accused is capable of making an intelligent choice. An accused has a right to due process, including the right to know any evidence the prosecutor might have that may be favorable to the accused.

The prohibition against self-incrimination protects an accused from being forced to testify in court or to answer questions asked by the government. It also protects a witness who is not an accused from being compelled to answer a question that tends to incriminate. The privilege applies only to testimonial evidence, not physical evidence. The right to protection against double jeopardy ensures that a person who has been tried once for an offense cannot be tried again for the same offense unless he or she appeals the conviction—in which case the accused is considered to have waived this right.

The right to a fair and impartial trial means that circumstances surrounding the trial must not be such that they unduly influence the jury. Prejudicial publicity is prohibited and is avoided through such controls as sequestration, change of venue, the issuance of a gag rule, and control of the press. In all proceedings, the accused is convicted only upon proof of guilt beyond a reasonable doubt. Although difficult to define, this requirement ensures that flimsy evidence against the accused cannot be the basis for conviction.

Review Questions

1. Suppose California passes a law providing that all crimes are to be tried by six-member juries. Will such a law be constitutional? Assume that the same law also provides that a 5-to-1 vote for conviction results in conviction. Will the law be valid? Explain your answer.

2. Assume that X, a man accused of rape, was tried and convicted by a jury made up of all women. Were his constitutional rights violated?

3. Is a defendant entitled to a lawyer in all judicial trials, regardless of the offense charged? Justify your answer.

4. Compare and contrast the protection against compulsory self-incrimination of an accused and that of a witness.

5. Distinguish between transactional immunity and use-and-derivative-use immunity. If given a choice, which would you rather have, and why?

6. Suppose a witness is given immunity to testify in a state court proceeding. May that witness be compelled to testify in a subsequent federal criminal trial arising out of the same act? Justify your answer.

7. Suppose P is convicted five years after he was charged with robbery. Was P denied his right to a speedy trial? Justify your answer.

8. Suppose W, a prisoner, alleges that he had "ineffective assistance of counsel." What must W prove if he is to get a new trial based on that allegation?

9. Define double jeopardy and discuss its three basic elements. Are there instances when an accused may be tried twice for the same offense? Explain.

10. What is meant by a lesser included offense? Can a defendant be prosecuted for a lesser included offense after acquittal?

11. List four ways a trial judge can control the impact of prejudicial trial publicity. Briefly discuss each.

12. What is meant by guilt beyond a reasonable doubt? Is that concept easy or hard to apply? Justify your answer.

Key Terms and Definitions

Brady rule: The rule that "the suppression by the prosecution of evidence favorable to an accused upon request violates due process where the evidence is material either to the guilt or punishment, irrespective of the good faith or bad faith of the prosecution."

double jeopardy: The successive prosecution of a defendant for the same offense by the same jurisdiction.

fair response: A prosecutor's statement to the jury during closing arguments that the defendant could have taken the witness stand but refused to do so is proper as long as it is in response to defense counsel's argument that the government did not allow the defendant to explain his or her side of the story.

Federal Speedy Trial Act of 1974: A law that specifies time standards for each stage in the federal court process. Thirty days are allowed from arrest to the filing of an indictment or an information; seventy days are allowed between information or indictment and trial.

hung jury: A jury that cannot agree unanimously (in jurisdictions where unanimity is required) to convict or acquit the defendant.

immunity: Exemption from prosecution, granted to a witness in exchange for testimony against a suspect or an accused.

indigent defendant: A defendant who is too poor to hire his or her own lawyer.

jury of peers: A jury that is not consciously restricted to a particular group.

lesser included offense: An offense that is "composed of some, but not all, of the elements of the greater crime and which does not have any element not included in the greater offense."

nonunanimous verdict: A verdict for conviction that is not the product of a unanimous vote by jury members. A 9-to-3 vote for conviction in a state court has been declared constitutional by the Court.

peremptory challenge: Disqualification of a juror, by the defense or the prosecution, for which no reason is given.

physical self-incrimination: A form of self-incrimination, not protected under the Fifth Amendment, that stems from real or physical evidence. Examples are footprints, fingerprints, blood, and urine samples.

privilege of the accused: The Fifth Amendment right not to answer incriminating questions or to take the witness stand. If the accused takes the witness stand, he or she must answer incriminating questions.

privilege of a witness: The Fifth Amendment right not to

be forced to answer incriminating questions while on the witness stand.

public trial: A trial open to all persons interested in ensuring that the proceedings are fair and just.

reasonable doubt: "Such a doubt as would cause a juror, after careful and candid and impartial consideration of all the evidence, to be so undecided that he or she cannot say that he or she has an abiding conviction of the defendant's guilt."

retained counsel: A lawyer paid by the defendant, not by the state.

same offense: Two offenses that have the same elements.

sequestration: The practice of keeping jurors together during the trial and strictly controlling their contact with the outside world.

speedy trial: A trial that is free from unnecessary and unwanted delay.

statute of limitations: A law providing that a crime must

be prosecuted within a certain period of time or else it lapses and can no longer be prosecuted.

testimonial (or communicative) self-incrimination: A form of self-incrimination, protected under the Fifth Amendment, that in itself explicitly or implicitly relates a factual assertion or discloses information. It is in the form of verbal or oral communication.

transactional immunity: A type of immunity that exempts the witness from prosecution for any offense arising out of an act or transaction.

"use and derivative use" immunity: A type of immunity that assures the witness only that his or her testimony and evidence derived from it will not be used against him or her in a subsequent prosecution. However, the witness can be prosecuted on the basis of evidence other than his or her own testimony, if the prosecutor has such independent evidence.

Principles of Cases

Argersinger v. Hamlin, 407 U.S. 25 (1972) The right to counsel applies even in misdemeanor cases if the accused faces the possibility of imprisonment, however short.

Baldwin v. New York, 399 U.S. 66 (1970) An offense is considered serious if the maximum punishment authorized by statute is imprisonment for more than six months, regardless of the actual penalty

imposed. Therefore, the accused is entitled to a jury trial.

Ballew v. Georgia, 435 U.S. 223 (1978) The minimum number of jurors is six. Juries of five or fewer members are unconstitutional because the membership is too small to provide for effective group discussion. Juries of less than six members would also diminish the chances of drawing from a fair, representative cross-section of the community, thus impairing the accuracy of fact finding.

Baltimore City Department of Social Services v. Bouknight, 493 U.S. 549 (1990) Even though requiring the custodial parent to present his or her child to the authorities could be self-incriminating, a parent who agreed to extensive conditions in assuming custody of such a child may be required to produce the child in court or otherwise face contempt citation.

Barker v. Wingo, 407 U.S. 514 (1972) Violation of the right to a speedy trial is not established by delay alone. Rather, the determination requires a balancing test. The conduct of both the prosecution and the defense are weighed, and the following factors are considered: (1) the length of the delay, (2) the reason for the delay, (3) the defendant's assertion or nonassertion of rights, and (4) any prejudice to the defendant. Usually, any one factor alone is not sufficient either to justify or to condemn the delay in the trial.

Batson v. Kentucky, 476 U.S. 79 (1986) A prosecutor's use of peremptory challenges to exclude from a jury members of the defendant's race solely on racial grounds violates the equal protection rights of both the defendant and the excluded jurors.

Blanton v. North Las Vegas, 489 U.S. 538 (1989) When a state treats drunk driving as a petty offense, no jury trial is needed, even if other peripheral sanctions (such as a fine and automatic loss of a driver's license) may also be imposed.

Blockburger v. United States, 284 U.S. 299 (1932) A second prosecution is barred if the two prosecutions are for offenses that have identical statutory elements or if one is a lesser included offense of the other.

Brady v. Maryland, 373 U.S. 83 (1963) Due process is violated when the prosecution suppresses evidence favorable to an accused upon request where the evidence is material either to guilt or to punishment. This applies whether the prosecution acted in bad faith or in good faith in suppressing the evidence.

Brown v. Ohio, 432 U.S. 161 (1977) Prosecution for joyriding prohibits a second trial for theft of a vehicle, because no additional facts are needed for the second charge.

Burks v. United States, 437 U.S. 1 (1978) A defendant whose conviction is reversed because the evidence is insufficient as a matter of law to sustain the conviction cannot be retried; such a reversal amounts to an acquittal.

Cage v. Louisiana, 111 S.Ct. 328 (1990) A trial court's jury instructions on reasonable doubt that equates it with "grave uncertainty" and "actual substantive doubt" is invalid, because these terms require a higher standard of doubt than reasonable doubt.

Campbell v. Louisiana, 63 CrL 94 (1998) A white defendant has standing to complain of discrimination against blacks in the selection, not of a trial jury, but of a grand jury.

Chambers v. Mississippi, 410 U.S. 284 (1973) The defendant offered evidence of an oral confession to the crime by another witness. The trial court excluded the evidence because it constituted inadmissible hearsay under the local rules of evidence. This ruling was held to violate the defendant's right to present a defense, since the confessions bore substantial assurances of trustworthiness.

Coleman v. Alabama, 399 U.S. 1 (1970) In a preliminary hearing to determine whether there is sufficient evidence against the accused to go to a grand jury, the accused has the right to an attorney.

Cooper v. Oklahoma, 59 CrL 2012 (1996) Criminal defendants should not be required to prove their incompetence to stand trial by the heightened standard of "clear and convincing evidence"; instead, the lower standard of "preponderance of the evidence" is sufficient.

Coy v. Iowa, 487 U.S. 1012 (1988) The right to confrontation includes the right to physically face witnesses at trial. Hence, a state law that allows testimony via closed-circuit television or behind a screen violates a defendant's Sixth Amendment rights.

Doggett v. United States, 505 U.S. 647 (1992) The delay of eight and a half years between a defendant's indictment and arrest, caused by government negligence, can violate the Sixth Amendment even if no actual prejudice to the defendant is shown.

Faretta v. California, 422 U.S. 806 (1975) An accused has a constitutional right to waive counsel and represent him- or herself in a criminal proceeding.

Fuller v. Oregon, 417 U.S. 40 (1974) A system that provides counsel to defendants but specifies as a condition of probation or parole that the defendant reimburse the state or county for the fees of the appointed lawyer is valid as long as it exempts indigents who cannot afford to pay.

In re Gault, 387 U.S. 1 (1967) Although juvenile proceedings are not criminal in nature, a juvenile is nonetheless entitled to appointed counsel if the proceeding can lead to commitment in an institution where the juvenile's freedom would be restricted.

Geders v. United States, 425 U.S. 80 (1976) During the trial itself, a judge may not prevent the defendant from talking with counsel during an overnight recess. That would violate his or her right to counsel.

Georgia v. McCullum, 60 L.W. 4563 (1992) The Constitution prohibits a criminal defendant from engaging in purposeful discrimination based on race in the exercise of peremptory challenges.

Gideon v. Wainwright, 372 U.S. 335 (1963) The Sixth Amendment right to counsel is applicable to state proceedings via the Due Process Clause of the Fourteenth Amendment. The right to counsel applies every time an accused is charged with a felony offense.

Gilbert v. California, 388 U.S. 263 (1967) A defendant can be forced to stand up for identification in the courtroom, to put on certain items of clothing, or to give a handwriting sample.

Grady v. Corbin, 495 U.S. 508 (1990) The Double Jeopardy Clause bars a subsequent prosecution if, to establish an essential element of an offense charged in that prosecution, the government will have to prove conduct that constitutes an offense for which the defendant has already been prosecuted.

Green v. United States, 355 U.S. 184 (1957) A defendant who appeals a conviction and obtains a new trial cannot be charged with an offense that is higher than that for which he or she was originally convicted.

Griffin v. California, 380 U.S. 609 (1965) The prosecutor is not permitted to make any comment or argument to the jury suggesting that the defendant is guilty because he or she refused to testify; making such comments will lead to a reversal of the conviction on appeal.

Heath v. Alabama, 474 U.S. 82 (1985) Under the dual sovereignty doctrine, successive prosecutions by two states for the same conduct do not violate the Double Jeopardy Clause of the Fifth Amendment.

Holland v. Illinois, 493 U.S. 474 (1990) The prosecution's racially motivated use of peremptory challenges to exclude people from the trial jury does not violate the defendant's Sixth Amendment right to trial by an impartial jury. However, the Court hinted that the prosecution's actions could have been challenged as a violation of the constitutional right to equal protection.

Illinois v. Allen, 397 U.S. 337 (1970) The following methods for dealing with a disruptive defendant are approved: (1) holding the defendant in contempt of court, (2) binding and gagging the defendant in the courtroom, and (3) removing the defendant from the courtroom until he or she promises to behave properly.

Illinois v. Vitale, 447 U.S. 410 (1980) A conviction for failure to reduce speed to avoid an accident does not necessarily prohibit a second charge for involuntary manslaughter, because vehicular manslaughter does not always require proof of failure to reduce speed.

Irvin v. Dowd, 366 U.S. 717 (1961) Headlines announced that the defendant had confessed to six murders and twenty-four burglaries, and reports were widely circulated that the defendant had offered to plead guilty. Ninety percent of the prospective jurors interviewed expressed an opinion that the defendant was guilty, and eight out of twelve jurors finally seated held such a belief. All these circumstances denied the defendant his due process right, particularly because this was a capital punishment case.

J.E.B. v. Alabama, 114 S.Ct. 1419 (1994) The Equal Protection Clause prohibits discrimination in the selection of jurors based on gender.

Johnson v. Louisiana, 406 U.S. 356 (1972) A 9-to-3 jury verdict for conviction is constitutional.

Kastigar v. United States, 406 U.S. 441 (1972) Prosecutors need only grant "use and derivative use" immunity to compel an unwilling witness to testify. The witness is not constitutionally entitled to transactional immunity before he or she can be compelled to testify.

Kyles v. Whitley, 57 CrL 2003 (1995) Because the effect of the state-suppressed evidence favorable to the defendant raised a reasonable probability that its disclosure would have produced a different result at trial, the conviction had to be reversed.

Lewis v. United States, 59 CrL 2206 (1996) A defendant who is prosecuted in a single case for more than one petty offense does not have a constitutional right to trial by jury even if the total penalty exceeds six months.

Lockhart v. Fretwell, 52 CrL 2107 (1993) To show prejudice in appeals based on ineffective counsel, the defendant must demonstrate that counsel's errors were so serious as to result in a trial whose result was unfair or unreliable—not merely that the outcome would have been different.

Lockhart v. McCree, 476 U.S. 162 (1986) Persons who are unwilling to vote for the death penalty under any circumstances may be disqualified from a capital offense jury.

Maryland v. Craig, 497 U.S. 836 (1990) Despite defendants' Sixth Amendment rights, face-to-face confrontation may be dispensed with when preventing such confrontation is necessary to further important public policy and the reliability of the testimony is otherwise assured.

Massiah v. United States, 377 U.S. 201 (1964) Noncustodial interrogations made after the accused has been formally charged are not admissible in evidence if the interrogation is conducted without a lawyer present and using a federal agent who has been "wired for sound."

Medina v. California, 112 S.Ct. 2572 (1992) Procedural due process is not violated by a state law requiring that the party claiming incompetency of the defendant to stand trial must bear the burden of proving such status. Neither is due process violated by a law providing that defendants are presumed to be competent.

Moore v. United States, 345 F.2d 97 (DC Cir. 1965) Reasonable doubt is defined as follows: "It is such a doubt as would cause a juror, after careful and candid and impartial consideration of all the evidence, to be so undecided that he cannot say that he has an abiding conviction of the defendant's guilt."

Murphy v. Waterfront Commission, 378 U.S. 52 (1964) If a state has granted a witness valid immunity from prosecution, the federal government is not permitted to make use of the testimony (or any of its "fruits") in a federal prosecution against the witness.

Perry v. Leeke, 488 U.S. 272 (1989) A defendant who takes the witness stand has no Sixth Amendment right to consult with his or her lawyer during a brief fifteen-minute recess while testifying.

Powell v. Alabama, 287 U.S. 45 (1932) The trial in state court of nine youths for a capital offense without a defense lawyer violated their right to due process.

Powers v. Ohio, 111 S.Ct. 1364 (1991) A criminal defendant may object to a race-based exclusion of jurors through peremptory challenges even though the defendant and the excluded jurors are not of the same race.

Purkett v. Elem, 57 CrL 3044 (1995) The reasons offered by the side using the peremptory strike do not have to be "persuasive or even plausible" to comply with Batson's step-2 requirement.

Rideau v. Louisiana, 373 U.S. 723 (1963) Police arranged to have the defendant's prior confession shown several times on local television. The Court held that the defendant had, in effect, been "tried" thereby and that no actual prejudice need be shown to establish a denial of due process under such circumstances.

Rutledge v. United States, 58 CrL 2076 (1996) There cannot be two punishments for two offenses if one is a lesser included offense.

Scott v. Illinois, 440 U.S. 367 (1979) The state is not required to appoint counsel for an indigent defendant charged with a nonpetty offense that is punishable by imprisonment if the defendant is not, in fact, sentenced to imprisonment.

Sheppard v. Maxwell, 384 U.S. 333 (1966) A courtroom television process that is so distracting to the judge, jurors, witnesses, and counsel that it creates a "carnival atmosphere" denies the defendant a fair trial.

Singer v. United States, 380 U.S. 24 (1965) The prosecution has the right to demand a trial by jury even if the defendant waives it. Criminal defendants have no constitutional right to have their cases tried before a judge alone.

South Dakota v. Neville, 459 U.S. 553 (1983) A law that allows the accused to refuse to take a blood-alcohol test and provides that such refusal may be admitted in evidence against him or her is constitutional.

Strickland v. Washington, 466 U.S. 668 (1984) The Court assumes that effective assistance of counsel is present unless the adversarial process is so undermined by counsel's conduct that the trial cannot be relied upon to have produced a just result. An accused who claims ineffective counsel must show the following: (1) deficient performance by counsel and (2) a reasonable probability that, but for such deficiency, the result of the proceedings would have been different.

Strickler v. Greene, 119 S.Ct. 1936 (1999) The prosecution's failure to disclose evidence in the form of interview notes from a detective that seriously undermined the truthfulness of the only eyewitness's testimony in a murder trial did not violate the Brady rule because such evidence was not material to the issue of guilt or innocence.

Sullivan v. Louisiana, 61 L.W. 4518 (1993) A constitutionally deficient reasonable-doubt instruction cannot be harmless error and therefore requires a reversal of a conviction.

Taylor v. Louisiana, 419 U.S. 522 (1975) Excluding women from juries, or giving them automatic exemptions with the result that jury panels are almost totally male, is invalid.

Taylor v. United States, 414 U.S. 17 (1973) If an accused is present at the start of the trial but later voluntarily absents him- or herself, the trial may continue in the absence of the accused; the accused is considered to have waived his or her right to be present.

United States v. Agurs, 427 U.S. 97 (1976) A defendant's failure to request that favorable evidence be shown to the defense does not leave the government free of all obligation, but the prosecutor's failure in this particular case to show the favorable evidence did not violate the defendant's right to due process.

United States v. Balsys, 63 CrL 425 (1998) A witness's fear that the testimony he is ordered to give in a proceeding in the United States will subject him to prosecution in another country is not a valid basis for asserting his Fifth Amendment right to protection against self-incrimination.

United States v. Cronic, 466 U.S. 648 (1984) A claim of ineffective assistance of counsel can be made only by pointing out specific errors of trial counsel. It cannot be based on an inference drawn from defense counsel's inexperience or lack of time to prepare, the gravity of the charges, the complexity of the defense, or the accessibility of witnesses to counsel.

United States v. Dixon, 53 CrL 2291 (1993) Double jeopardy applies if the two offenses for which the defendant is being punished have "the same elements."

United States v. Owens, 484 U.S. 554 (1988) It does not violate a defendant's right to confrontation if the court admits into evidence a prior out-of-court identification of the accused by a witness who is unable, due to loss of memory, to explain the basis for the identification.

United States v. Robinson, 485 U.S. 25 (1988) A prosecutor's statement to the jury during closing arguments that the defendant could have taken the witness stand but refused to do so is proper as long as it is in response to defense counsel's argument that the government had not allowed the defendant to explain his or her side of the story.

United States v. Wade, 388 U.S. 218 (1967) A postindictment lineup in which witnesses seek to identify the accused requires the presence of a lawyer.

Victor v. Nebraska, 54 CrL 2225 (1994) References to "moral evidence," "moral certainty," and "substantial doubt" in the jury instructions do not violate the Due Process Clause.

Webb v. Texas, 409 U.S. 95 (1972) If the trial judge makes threatening remarks to the only defense witness, in effect driving the witness from the stand, the accused is deprived of the right to present a defense.

Wheat v. United States, 486 U.S. 153 (1988) A defendant's right to hire an attorney of his or her own choosing may be limited by the trial court to avoid a conflict of interest.

Williams v. Florida, 399 U.S. 78 (1970) A Florida law providing for a six-member jury in all criminal cases except those involving capital offenses is constitutional.

Witherspoon v. Illinois, 391 U.S. 510 (1968) It is unconstitutional to exclude for cause potential jurors who have reservations about the death penalty.

Case Briefs

Leading Case on Gender Discrimination

J.E.B. v. Alabama, 114 S.Ct. 1419 (1994)

Facts: The state of Alabama filed a complaint for paternity and child support against J.E.B., on behalf of the mother of a minor child. The trial court assembled a panel of 36 potential jurors—12 males and 24 females. Three jurors were excused for cause, leaving 10 males and 23 females in the jury pool. The state of Alabama used nine out of its ten peremptory challenges to remove male jurors; the petitioner used nine strikes to remove female jurors. The result was an all-female jury. Even before the jury was impaneled, the petitioner objected to the peremptory challenges by the state, saying that they were exercised against male jurors solely on the basis of gender. Trial was held, and the jury found the petitioner to be the father of the child; he was ordered to pay child support. He appealed.

Issue: *Does the Constitution prohibit discrimination in jury selection based on gender? Yes.*

Supreme Court Decision: "The Equal Protection Clause of the Constitution prohibits discrimination in jury selection on the basis of gender, or on the assumption that an individual will be biased in a particular case solely because that person happens to be a woman or a man."

Case Significance: This case extends the *Batson* ruling, which prohibits discrimination based on race on jury peremptory challenges, to discrimination based on gender, hence proscribing both types of discrimination. The petitioner in this case was a man who alleged that his equal protection rights were violated because the state of Alabama used its peremptory challenges to strike males from the jury, the result being an all-female jury that found him to be the father of the child and required him to pay child support. The Court upheld the challenge, saying that gender discrimination in jury selection is unconstitutional. The Court added, however, that "[t]he conclusion that litigants may not strike potential jurors solely on the basis of gender does not imply the elimination of all peremptory challenges. So long as gender does not serve as a proxy for bias, unacceptable jurors may still be removed, including those who are members of a group or class that is normally subject to 'rational basis' review and those who exhibit characteristics that are disproportionately associated with one gender." What is prohibited are challenges based on bias simply because a potential juror is a male or a female and is therefore expected to vote in a certain way. Peremptory challenges based in gender bias are usually difficult to prove because they are made without reasons given. There are cases, however, such as this one, in which the obvious reason for the strikes was gender bias. In these types of cases, the constitutional prohibition applies.

Excerpts from the Decision: "Equal opportunity to participate in the fair administration of justice is fundamental to our democratic system. It not only furthers the goals of the jury system. It reaffirms the promise of equality under the law—that all citizens, regardless of race, ethnicity, or gender, have the chance to take part directly in our democracy. When persons are excluded from participation in our democratic processes solely because of race or gender, this promise of equality dims, and the integrity of our judicial system is jeopardized.

"In view of these concerns, the Equal Protection Clause prohibits discrimination in jury selection on the basis of gender, or on the assumption that an individual will be biased in a particular case for no reason other than the fact that the person happens to be a woman or happens to be a man. As with race, the core guarantee of equal protection, ensuring citizens that their State will not discriminate . . . would be meaningless were we to approve the exclusion of jurors on the basis of such assumptions, which arise solely from the jurors' [gender]."

Leading Case on the Right to Counsel

Gideon v. Wainwright, 372 U.S. 335 (1963)

Facts: Gideon was charged in a Florida state court with breaking and entering a poolroom with intent to commit a misdemeanor, an act classified as a felony under Florida law. Appearing in court without funds and without a lawyer, Gideon asked the court to appoint a lawyer for him. The court refused, saying that under Florida law the only time the court could appoint a lawyer to represent an accused was when the crime charged was a capital offense. Gideon conducted his own defense and was convicted. He appealed.

Issue: *Does the Constitution require the appointment of a lawyer for an indigent who is charged with a felony in state court? Yes.*

Supreme Court Decision: The Sixth Amendment requires that a person charged with a felony in state court be given appointed counsel if he or she is indigent.

Case Significance: This case mandates that, when an indigent is charged with a felony in state court, counsel must be provided by the state. This settled a controversy among lower courts, which had given inconsistent rulings on the types of offenses an indigent had to be charged with in order to be entitled to a lawyer. An earlier case (Betts v. Brady, 316 U.S. 455 [1942]) held that the requirement that counsel be provided to all indigent defendants in federal felony trials did not extend to the states, so the states were free to provide or not to provide counsel. This was overruled in *Gideon* when the Court held that the rule applied to criminal proceedings in state courts as well. Since 1963, both federal and state felony defendants have been legally entitled to a court-appointed attorney if indigent.

The *Gideon* ruling required the appointment of counsel for indigents only in felony cases. This was later extended to misdemeanor cases in Argersinger v. Hamlin, 407 U.S. 25 (1972).

Excerpts from the Decision: "The fact is that in deciding as it did—that 'appointment of counsel is not a fundamental right, essential to a fair trial'—the Court in Betts v. Brady made an abrupt break with its own well-considered precedents. In returning to these old precedents, sounder we believe than the new, we but restore constitutional principles established to achieve a fair system of justice. Not only these precedents but also reason and reflection require us to recognize that in our adversary system of criminal justice, any person haled into court, who is too poor to hire a lawyer, cannot be assured a fair trial unless counsel is provided for him. This seems to us to be an obvious truth. Governments, both state and federal, quite properly spend vast sums of money to establish machinery to try defendants accused of crime. Lawyers to prosecute are everywhere deemed essential to protect the public's interest in an orderly society. Similarly, there are few defendants charged with crime, few indeed, who fail to hire the best lawyers

they can get to prepare and present their defenses. That government hires lawyers to prosecute and defendants who have the money hire lawyers to defend are the strongest indications of the widespread belief that lawyers in criminal courts are necessities, not luxuries."

Leading Case on the Right to Counsel

Powell v. Alabama, 287 U.S. 45 (1932)

Facts: Nine black youths were charged, in 1932, with the rape of two white girls while on a train in Alabama. All were illiterate. The atmosphere in the town was such that the boys had to be held in a different town under military guard during the proceedings. The judge appointed "all members of the bar" to assist the boys during the proceedings, but they were not represented by any attorney by name until the day of the trial. Each of the trials lasted only a day and resulted in convictions. The youths were given the death penalty.

Issue: *Were the accused denied their constitutional right to counsel and due process? Yes.*

Supreme Court Decision: "In a capital case, where the defendant is unable to employ counsel, and is incapable adequately of making his own defense because of ignorance, feeblemindedness, illiteracy, or the like, it is the duty of the court, whether requested or not, to assign counsel for him as a necessary requisite of due process of law, and that duty is not discharged by an assignment at such a time and under such circumstances as to preclude the giving of effective aid in the preparation and trial of the case."

Case Significance: The Sixth Amendment to the Constitution provides that "in all criminal prosecutions, the accused shall enjoy the right . . . to have the assistance of counsel for his defense." This case provides the often-quoted reason (penned by Justice George Sutherland) for this constitutional provision. Without a lawyer, an accused may be convicted, not because he or she is guilty, but because the accused does not know how to establish innocence. The right to counsel is a basic and fundamental right under the Constitution and must be respected by the police and the courts. Note that this case used the Due Process Clause of the Fourteenth Amendment instead of the Sixth Amendment right to counsel to overturn the conviction. This is because in 1932, when the case was decided, the provisions of the Bill of Rights had not yet been extended to state proceedings. Were this case to be decided today, the Sixth Amendment right to counsel would doubtless have been the constitutional right used.

Excerpts from the Decision: "Even the intelligent and educated layman has small and sometimes no skill in the science of the law. Left without aid of counsel, he may be put on trial without proper charge, and convicted upon incompetent evidence irrelevant to the issue or otherwise against him. Without counsel, though he may not be guilty, he faces the danger of conviction because he does not know how to establish his innocence."

 ## Notes

1. Bureau of Justice Statistics, *Report to the Nation on Crime and Justice,* 2nd ed. (Washington, DC: U.S. Government Printing Office, 1988), p. 84.

2. W. LaFave and J. Israel, *Criminal Procedure,* 2nd ed. (St. Paul, MN: West, 1992), p. 523.

3. Ibid., p. 535.

4. *Black's Law Dictionary,* 6th ed. (St. Paul, MN: West, 1991), p. 812.

5. Steven L. Emanuel and Steven Knowles, *Emanuel Law Outlines: Criminal Procedure* (Larchmont, NY: Emanuel, 1998–99), p. 365.

6. Ibid.

13.

Civil Lawsuits against the Police

Chapter Outline

Case Briefs

What You Will Learn in This Chapter

In this chapter, you will discover why knowledge about civil lawsuits against the police is important. You will become familiar with civil liability lawsuits and learn that police officers may be held liable under federal and state laws for violations of citizens' civil rights. You will also find out who is likely be sued and why, who represents an officer who is sued, and what defenses are available to the officer and the other defendants in civil lawsuits. Finally, you will learn what measures officers can take to minimize their risk of exposure to civil liability.

Introduction

One of the realities of modern-day policing is the threat of a civil lawsuit. American society is litigation prone, and the police are a popular target because they exercise immense authority and are involved in highly charged and often emotional confrontations with the public. The police are generally loved and respected because they provide a needed service to the community, but they are also sometimes reviled because some officers behave in a manner that reflects poorly on the department and the other officers. Lawsuits have become so pervasive that it is safe to say there is no major police department in the country that has not had its officers sued in state or federal court for damages or injunctive relief.

I. LAWSUITS AGAINST THE POLICE: AN OCCUPATIONAL HAZARD

The *Liability Reporter*, published by the police-oriented Americans for Effective Law Enforcement, Inc., an organization that monitors lawsuits against the police, featured the following headlines in 1999:

- "City reaches $11 million settlement with man paralyzed after being struck by police vehicle at crosswalk"[1]

- "Federal appeals court upholds $2 million award against city and officers for releasing tapes of informant's calls to police to suspect; release of tapes allegedly led to informant's murder"[2]

- "City liable for $8.2 million to man struck by police vehicle not engaged in emergency assignment."[3]

- "Jury awards $12.6 million for death of man shot with submachine gun in his home by officer who was executing warrant."[4]

- "$5 million jury award to woman strip searched after arrest on minor charges."[5]

- "City liable for $1.575 million for off-duty officer's 'negligent storage' of his weapon at home and subsequent shooting of minor at a party by his 14-year-old son"[6]

- "$1 million settlement in suit over man's shooting in the back by officer."[7]

The most widely publicized police liability case is the Rodney King case in Los Angeles. The beating of King took place in Los Angeles in the early morning hours of March 3, 1991. King, who was on parole for robbery, had been drinking with two friends and was speeding. When asked to stop by two California Highway Patrol officers, King led the officers on a high-speed chase involving several police cars. When King finally stopped, he refused to leave his vehicle but was forced out by the police. Once outside the vehicle, the police allegedly struck a total of fifty-six blows, resulting in severe injuries to King. The incident would likely have been forgotten were it not for a video-tape of the beating by an amateur cameraman who recorded the incident from his balcony. He sold the eighty-one-second videotape to a television station, and it was later shown on various television outlets throughout the country and the world.

The first criminal case against the officers was tried in state court in Simi Valley, California, and ended in acquittals. A second criminal case, filed in federal court and tried in Los Angeles, resulted in the conviction of two of the four officers, each of whom was given a thirty-month prison sentence. In 1994, a Los Angeles jury awarded King $3.8 million in compensatory damages. All in all, the Rodney King beating resulted in two criminal trials, a civil liability case against the officers and the county, suspension and then dismissal of the four officers involved, the resignation of Chief Daryl Gates, and the investigation of the Los Angeles Police Department by two different commissions. The Rodney King incident illustrates what can happen when police actions get out of control. Everyone involved in the incident paid a high personal and professional price.

Most officers will not be sued in the course of their careers. However, although the fear of a lawsuit is more often exaggerated than warranted, the effect on police officers can be real. One study of police trainees at a regional law enforcement academy concludes that law enforcement candidates have real concerns about work-related lawsuits, fostering an "us versus them" attitude among officers.[8] Others believe that the courts have handcuffed law enforcement officers and made police work unattractive and dangerous. According to one publication, "70 percent of officers involved in a shooting leave police work within five years due to the emotional strain and lack of

HIGHLIGHT

Police Accountability

The truth is, police brutality has been with us forever. So has corruption. The two feed on each other. We don't recruit from the Planet Perfect. We recruit from society. But things are vastly better than they were. . . . Police departments must map brutality and corruption complaints the same way we mapped murders and shootings. Then commanders must be held accountable to prevent their recurrence. Stings of every kind must be run for theft, brutality and discourtesy. Once caught, serious offenders should be interrogated like any criminal so we can make more cases on other bad cops.

Source: Jack Maple (former New York Police Department deputy commissioner), "Police Must Be Held Accountable," *Newsweek,* June 21, 1999, p. 67.

departmental support."[9] Whatever the reaction, liability lawsuits are a presence in police work that is difficult to ignore.

Available cost estimates on police civil liability vary. It is reported that in 1990 alone the city of Los Angeles paid $11 million in damage awards for police misconduct,[10] and another $13 million in 1991.[11] Miami Beach, Florida, a medium-sized city, paid out a total of $3.5 million for claims against its police department from 1986 to 1992, an average of $11,254 for each of its 311 police officers.[12] The city of Detroit reportedly paid $20 million in judgments and verdicts in 1990 alone.[13] Between 1987 and 1991, the city of New York reportedly paid $44 million to settle cases involving police misconduct.[14]

The *New York Times* reported that in 1998 New York City paid $40 million to settle legal claims and lawsuits that accused its police officers of brutality.[15] This was an increase of 40 percent from 1997. In 1999, New York City paid $2.55 million to the family of a certain Anthony Baez, who had been choked to death by a Bronx police officer years before. In another case, the "city agreed to pay $2.75 million to an electrician who said that, while walking to work in Greenwich Village on his birthday in 1996, he was beaten by police officers because he fit the profile of a black suspect they were seeking."[16]

A recent case involving a New York City police officer shows how brutal some police cases can be and why huge damage awards are sometimes imposed. In what was perhaps the most highly publicized police brutality case in 1999, one newspaper ran this headline: "I sodomized . . . Abner Louima."[17] In that case, officer Justin Volpe, along with "a ring of white cops," was charged with beating and brutalizing Abner Louima, a Haitian immigrant, after a fight outside a Brooklyn nightclub in August 1997. They were tried in federal court in May 1999. At first, Volpe denied all charges. During trial, however, he changed his mind and decided to plead guilty to ramming a stick into Louima's rectum, causing severe internal injuries and violating his civil rights. In a hushed voice, Volpe told the federal judge that, "in the bathroom of the precinct house, I sodomized Mr. Abner Louima and threatened to kill him if he told anybody." Despite his guilty plea, Volpe was sentenced by a federal judge to thirty years in prison. Observers believe that the Louima case represents one of those uncommon instances when fellow police officers break the "blue wall of silence" in police brutality and corruption cases and inform on one another. A civil lawsuit arising from this incident will surely follow.

II. AN OVERVIEW OF POLICE LEGAL LIABILITIES

Police legal liabilities come from varied sources, but the whole arena of legal liabilities may be classified as follows:

	State Law	**Federal Law**
A. Civil liabilities	State tort law	1. Title 42 of U.S. Code, Section 1983—Civil Action for Deprivation of Civil Rights 2. Title 42 of U.S. Code, Section 1985—Conspiracy to Interfere with Civil Rights 3. Title 42 of U.S. Code, Section 1981—Equal Rights under the Law
B. Criminal liabilities	1. State penal code provisions specifically aimed at public officers for crimes like these: a. Official oppresion b. Official misconduct c. Violation of the civil rights of prisoners 2. Regular penal code provisions punishing such criminal acts as assault, battery, false arrrest, serious bodily injury, and homicide	1. Title 18 of U.S. Code, Section 242—Criminal Liability for Deprivation of Civil Rights 2. Title 18 of U.S. Code, Section 241—Criminal Liability for Conspiracy to Deprive a Person of Rights 3. Title 18 of U.S. Code, Section 245—Violations of Federally Protected Activities
C. Administrative liabilities	Agency rules or guidelines on the state or local level—vary from one agency to another	Federal agency rules or guidelines—vary from one agency to another

As this chart shows, police legal liability cases may be classified into liabilities under state law and liabilities under federal law. Each of these two categories is also subclassified into civil liability, criminal liability, and administrative liability. *Civil liability* results in monetary awards for damages; *criminal liability* leads to imprisonment, fines, or other forms of criminal sanction; and *administrative liability* results in dismissal, demotion, transfer, reprimand, or other forms of sanction authorized by agency rules or guidelines.

Although various legal remedies are available, plaintiffs are likely to use two remedies against police officers and agencies. The discussion in this chapter focuses on those two sources of liability to the exclusion of others: (1) civil liability under federal law (under 42 U.S. Code, Section 1983—also known as civil rights cases) and (2) civil liability under state tort law.

III. CIVIL LIABILITY UNDER FEDERAL LAW— SECTION 1983 CASES

For purposes of police liability, a **Section 1983 case** (also referred to as a civil rights case) may be defined as *a lawsuit, filed under federal law, seeking damages from a police officer, supervisor, and/or department, on the ground that these defendants, acting under color of law, violated the plaintiff's constitutional rights or rights given by federal law.* Section 1983 and state tort cases (discussed later in this chapter) are not mutually exclusive; in fact, plaintiffs are likely to sue under both laws and in the same lawsuit. For example, suppose Officer P tries to arrest a suspect, but the suspect flees. Officer P shoots the suspect, killing him instantly. In addition to a criminal case, Officer P will also likely be charged civilly (1) under Section 1983 for violating the suspect's constitutional right to due process and (2) under state tort law for wrongful death.

A. The Federal Law

Liability under federal law is based primarily on the provisions of Title 42 of the U.S. Code, Section 1983, entitled Civil Action for Deprivation of Rights. That law provides as follows:

> Every person who, under color of any statute, ordinance, regulation, custom, or usage, of any State or Territory, subjects, or causes to be subjected, any citizen of the United States or other persons within the jurisdiction thereof to the deprivation of any rights, privileges, or immunities secured by the Constitution and laws, shall be liable to the party injured in an action at law, suit in equity, or other proper proceeding for redress.

This law, commonly referred to as the *civil rights law* or *Section 1983,* is the most frequently used provision among the legal liability statutes available to plaintiffs. The law, originally passed by Congress in 1871, was then known as the *Ku Klux Klan law* because it sought to control the activities of state officials who were also members of that organization. For a long time, the law was given a limited interpretation by the courts and was seldom applied. In 1961, the Court adopted a much broader interpretation, thus opening wide the door for liability action in federal courts.

Among the reasons for the popularity of Section 1983 cases are that they are usually filed in federal court, where discovery procedures are more liberal, and that the plaintiff, if successful, may recover attorney's fees in accordance with the Attorney's Fees Act of 1976. Conversely, a police officer or agency can be held liable for damages, as well as for plaintiff's attorney's fees. As noted previously, the same act by the police may be the basis of both a Section 1983 lawsuit and an action under state tort law. For example, arrest without probable cause may constitute false arrest under state tort law and a violation of the arrestee's Fourth Amendment right to protection against unreasonable search and seizure, compensable under Section 1983. In such cases, a plaintiff may combine his or her claims and sue under multiple legal theories in federal court.

B. Requirements of a Section 1983 [Civil Rights] Lawsuit

The plaintiff must prove two elements in a Section 1983 lawsuit: (1) The defendant was acting under color of law, and (2) there was a violation of a right given by the Constitution or by federal law. Unless these two elements are proved by the plaintiff, the liability lawsuit will fail.

1. Acting under Color of Law

The phrase **acting under color of law** refers to *the use of power possessed by virtue of law and made possible only because the officer is clothed with the authority of the state.* The problem is that, although it is usually easy to identify acts that are wholly within the *color of law* (as when an officer makes a search or an arrest while on duty), some acts are not as easy to categorize. For example, suppose a police officer working during off hours as a private security guard in a shopping center shoots and kills a fleeing shoplifter. Is he acting under color of law? Or suppose an officer arrests a felon during off hours when she is not in uniform. Is she acting under color of law? The answer usually depends upon job expectations. Many police departments (by state law, judicial decision, or agency regulation) require police officers to act in their official capacity twenty-four hours a day. In these jurisdictions, any arrest made, whether on or off duty, is made under color of law. In the case of police officers who "moonlight," courts have held that wearing a police uniform while acting as a private security agent, carrying a gun issued by the department, and informing department authorities of the second job combine to indicate that the officer is acting under color of law.

The courts have interpreted the term *color of law* broadly to include state laws, local ordinances, and agency regulations. It is not required that the act was, in fact, authorized by law. It suffices that the act *appeared* to be lawful even if it was not authorized. Therefore, an officer acts under color of law even if he or she exceeds lawful authority. Moreover, the concept includes clearly illegal acts committed by the officer by reason of position or opportunity. For example, suppose an officer arrests a suspect without probable cause or brutalizes a suspect in the course of an arrest. These acts are clearly illegal, but they come under *color of law.*

2. Violation of a Right Given by the U.S. Constitution or by Federal Law

The second element that a plaintiff must prove in a Section 1983 case is that the right violated is a constitutional right or a right given by federal law. Therefore, violations of rights given by state law cannot lead to liability under Section 1983. For example, the right to a lawyer during a police lineup prior to being charged with an offense is not given by the Constitution or by federal law. Therefore, if an officer forces a suspect to appear in a lineup without a lawyer (assuming that right is given by state law), the officer is not liable under Section 1983. If the right is given by state law, its violation may be actionable under state law or agency regulation, but not under Section 1983.

The constitutional rights usually used by plaintiffs in cases against police officers are as follows:

- The Fourth Amendment right to protection against unreasonable searches and seizures

- The Fifth Amendment right to protection against self-incrimination and the right to due process

- The Sixth Amendment right to assistance of counsel.

- The Eighth Amendment prohibition against cruel and unusual punishment

- The Fourteenth Amendment rights to due process and equal protection of the laws

It is not hard for a plaintiff to file a Section 1983 lawsuit based on alleged violation of a constitutional right by the police. This is because the rights in the Bill of Rights and the other constitutional amendments are "elastic" and may accommodate many alleged violations. For example, a violation of the Fourth Amendment protection against unreasonable searches and seizures can be alleged just about any time an arrest or a search or seizure of things takes place. Violation of due process can be charged any time a person feels that he or she has suffered unfairness at the hands of the police. The constitutional right to equal protection has traditionally been applied to discrimination based on race, but some courts have applied it to gender, lifestyle, and other types of discriminatory treatment. The right to privacy may include a host of violations that can form the basis for a Section 1983 lawsuit, ranging from search and seizures to interception of electronic communication. The scope of these constitutional rights makes it quite easy to file a Section 1983 lawsuit against police officers. Proving these allegations, however, is an entirely different story.

C. Defenses in Section 1983 Cases

Many defenses are available in Section 1983 cases. Two are discussed here because they are the defenses most likely to be used by defendants in police civil liability cases. These are the good faith defense and the probable cause defense.

1. The Good Faith Defense: Harlow v. Fitzgerald

The **"good faith" defense in Section 1983 cases** holds that *an officer is not civilly liable unless he or she violated a clearly established statutory or constitutional right of which a reasonable person would have known* (Harlow v. Fitzgerald, 457 U.S. 800 [1982]). The Court said:

> We therefore hold that government officials performing discretionary functions generally are shielded from liability for civil damages insofar as their conduct does not violate a clearly established statutory or constitutional right of which a reasonable person would have known. . . . The judge appropriately may determine, not only the currently applicable law, but whether that law was clearly established at the time an action occurred. If the law at that time was not clearly established, an official could not reasonably be expected to anticipate subsequent legal develop-

The Good Faith Defense in Section 1983 Cases

The good faith defense in Section 1983 cases holds that an officer is not civilly liable unless he or she violated a clearly established statutory or constitutional right of which a reasonable person would have known. This implies two requirements for liability: (1) that the right violated was clearly established at the time of the violation and (2) that a reasonable person would have known that the action taken violated that right. Both of these requirements are ultimately decided by the court on a case-by-case basis.

ments, nor could he fairly be said to "know" that the law forbade conduct not previously identified as unlawful.

As this excerpt indicates, the good faith defense has two requirements: (1) An officer violated a clearly established statutory or constitutional right, and (2) of which a reasonable person would have known. Both must be established by the plaintiff; otherwise, no liability is imposed. When is a right considered to be "clearly established"? The Federal Court of Appeals for the Fifth Circuit set this standard: "A plaintiff must show that, when the defendant acted, the law established the contours of a right so clearly that a reasonable official would have understood his acts were unlawful." The court then added that, "If reasonable public officials could differ on the lawfulness of the defendant's actions, the defendant is entitled to qualified immunity" (Fraire v. City of Arlington, 957 F.2d 1268 [5th Cir. 1992]).

The right violated must be a constitutional right or a right given by federal law. Therefore, if the right violated by the police is a right given by state law, there is no liability under Section 1983. For example, suppose that state law provides that a juvenile may be kept in custody by the police for no longer than ten hours, but Officer X takes a juvenile into custody and keeps him under detention for more than ten hours. Officer X may be held liable under department policy or state law, but not in a federal Section 1983 case, because no constitutional right was violated. Instead, the right violated by the officer was a right given by state law.

Although the *Harlow* case, discussed earlier, did not involve police officers (it involved two White House aides under former President Nixon), the Court later said that the Harlow standard applies to police officers who are performing their duties (Anderson v. Creighton, 483 U.S. 635 [1987]). In the *Anderson* case, a federal agent and other law enforcement officers made a warrantless search of a home, believing that a bank robber was hiding there. The family that occupied the home then sued for violation of the Fourth Amendment right to protection against unreasonable searches and seizures, alleging that the agents' act was unreasonable. On appeal, the Court said that the lower court should have considered not only the general rule about home entries but also the facts known to the agents at the time of entry. According to the Court, the proper inquiry was whether a law enforcement officer could reasonably have concluded that the circumstances surrounding that case added up to probable cause and exigent circumstances, which would then justify a warrantless search. If such a conclusion is possible, then the good faith defense applies.

The good faith defense in Section 1983 cases may be illustrated by the media ride-along case, a case decided by the Court in 1999. In this case, federal and local law enforcement agents invited a newspaper reporter and a photographer to accompany them while executing a warrant to arrest a suspect who was the son of the plaintiffs. The son was not in the house, but the reporters photographed the incident, although the photographs were never even published by their newspaper. The parents sued. The issue on appeal was whether the plaintiffs' constitutional rights were violated when law enforcement agents invited the reporter and photographer to ride along with them during the arrest. The Court said yes but did not impose monetary damages on the officers because the officers acted in good faith. The Court said that the right violated at the time of the incident was not yet "clearly established" since at that time it was not clear whether ride-alongs violated constitutional rights. The law enforcement officers, therefore, did not violate a "clearly established constitutional right of which a reasonable person would have known" (Wilson et al. v. Layne, No. 98-93 [1999]). Now, however, law enforcement officers who invite the media to ride along to take pictures during an arrest may be held liable because they will be violating a "clearly established constitutional right of which a reasonable person would have known."

The good faith defense has two important implications for police officers and agencies. First, officers must know the basic constitutional and federal rights of the public they serve. Although officers should be familiar with these rights from college courses and police academy training, their knowledge needs constant updating in light of new court decisions in criminal procedure and constitutional law. Second, police agencies have an obligation to constantly inform their officers of new cases that establish constitutional rights, such as the recent media ride-along case. Moreover, agencies must update their manuals or guidelines to reflect cases decided not only by the Supreme Court but also by federal courts in their jurisdiction.

2. The Probable Cause Defense in Fourth Amendment Cases

The second defense in Section 1983 discussed in this chapter is the **probable cause defense,** whereby *the officer is not liable in cases in which probable cause is present.* It is a limited type of defense because it applies only in Fourth Amendment cases in which probable cause is required for the police to be able to act legally. It cannot be used in cases alleging violations of other constitutional rights, such as the First, Fifth, Sixth, or Fourteenth Amendments.

One court has said that, for purposes of a legal defense in Section 1983 cases, probable cause simply means "a reasonable good faith belief in the legality of the action taken" (Rodriguez v. Jones, 473 F.2d 599 [5th Cir. 1973]). That expectation is lower than for the Fourth Amendment concept of probable cause, which is defined as "more than bare suspicion; it exists when the facts and circumstances within the officers' knowledge and of which they had reasonably trustworthy information are sufficient in themselves to warrant a man of reasonable caution in the belief that an offense has been or is being committed" (Brinegar v. United States, 338 U.S. 160 [1949]). For example, suppose Officer X makes an arrest that is later determined to be without probable cause. According to *Rodriguez,* Officer X may be exempt from liability if he or she reasonably and in good faith believed at the time of the arrest that the arrest was legal.

AT A GLANCE

Section 1983 (Federal) Cases

DEFINITION: A Section 1983 case is a case, usually filed in federal court, in which the plaintiff seeks monetary damages and/or an injunction from a government official who, while acting within the scope of authority, violated the plaintiff's constitutional rights or a right given by federal law.

SOURCE OF THE RIGHT: Law passed by the U.S. Congress in 1871.

TWO REQUIREMENTS FOR A LAWSUIT TO SUCCEED: (1) The defendant was acting under color of law, and (2) there was a violation of a constitutional right or a right given by federal law.

DEFENSES IN SECTION 1983 CASES: Two defenses are discussed here:

- Good faith defense—an officer is not civilly liable unless he or she violated a clearly established statutory or constitutional right of which a reasonable person would have known.

- Probable cause defense—there is no liability in Fourth Amendment cases if probable cause was present.

IV. CIVIL LIABILITY UNDER STATE TORT LAW

In addition to federal Section 1983 cases, a second type of civil liability is liability under state tort law. **Tort** is defined as *a civil wrong in which the action of one person causes injury to the person or property of another, in violation of a legal duty imposed by law.* Tort law is primarily a product of judicial decisions, so it is not as precise as criminal law, which is neatly laid out in a state's penal code. State tort actions are the second most common form of lawsuit against police (Section 1983 cases being the most common). But more plaintiffs may be using the "state tort route" in the future if the Court continues to limit the use of Section 1983 cases as a remedy for violations of rights.

A. Types of State Tort Cases

There are two types of state tort cases: intentional tort and negligence tort. Each deserves extended discussion because each is often used by plaintiffs in police liability cases.

1. Intentional Tort

An **intentional tort** occurs when *there is an intention on the part of the officer to bring some physical harm or mental coercion upon another person.* Intent is mental and thus difficult to establish. However, courts and juries are generally allowed to infer the existence of intent from the facts of the case. For example, suppose an officer takes a person to the police station in handcuffs for questioning. When charged with false arrest, the officer denies that he intended to place the person under arrest. Chances are that the judge or jury will decide that intent to arrest was, in fact, present because the person was handcuffed and obviously not free to leave. Here we discuss five of the more common kinds of intentional tort that are brought against police officers.

a. False Arrest and False Imprisonment In a tort case for **false arrest,** the plaintiff alleges that *the officer has made an illegal arrest.* A claim of false arrest also arises if the officer fails to arrest the person named in the warrant. An officer who makes a warrantless arrest bears the burden of proving that the arrest was, in fact, based on probable cause and that an arrest warrant was not necessary because the arrest came under one of the exceptions to the warrant rule. If the arrest is made with a warrant, the presumption is that probable cause exists, unless the officer obtained the warrant with malice, knowing that there was no probable cause (Malley v. Briggs, 475 U.S. 335 [1986]). An arrest with warrant is therefore unlikely to result in civil liability for false arrest unless the officer serves a warrant that he or she knows to be illegal or unconstitutional. For example, if Officer M serves an unsigned warrant or one that is issued for the wrong person, M will be liable for false arrest despite the issuance of a warrant.

False arrest is a different tort from **false imprisonment,** but in police tort cases the two are virtually identical. This is because arrest necessarily means confinement, which is in itself an element of imprisonment.[18] In both cases, the individual is restrained or deprived of freedom without legal justification. The cases do differ, however, in that a false arrest leads to false imprisonment, but false imprisonment is not necessarily the result of a false arrest. For example, a suspect may be arrested with probable cause (a valid arrest) but be illegally detained in jail for several days without the filing of charges (false imprisonment). If an officer makes an arrest based on probable cause but later finds out that the person is innocent, continuing to hold the person constitutes false imprisonment even though the arrest was valid.

b. Assault and Battery Although sometimes used as one term, assault and battery represent two separate acts. **Assault** is *the intentional causing of an apprehension of harmful or offensive conduct;* it is the attempt or threat (accompanied by the ability) to inflict bodily harm on another person. An assault is committed if the officer causes another person to think that he or she will be subjected to harmful or offensive contact. **Battery** is *the intentional infliction of harmful or offensive body contact.* Given this broad definition, the potential for battery exists every time an officer uses force on a suspect or arrestee. The main difference between assault and battery is that assault is generally menacing conduct that results in a person's fear of imminently receiving battery, whereas battery involves unlawful, unwarranted, or hostile touching—however slight. In some jurisdictions, assault is attempted battery.

c. Excessive Use of Nondeadly Force Any discussion of the use of force by police must be separated into use of nondeadly force and use of deadly force. Lumping the two together confuses the issue because different rules govern them.

Excessive use of force, nondeadly or deadly, leads to liability under state tort law and also under Section 1983.

The police are often charged with "brutality" or use of "excessive force." The general rule is that nondeadly force may be used by police in various situations as long as such force is reasonable. **Reasonable force** is *force that a prudent and cautious person would use if exposed to similar circumstances;* it is limited to the amount of force necessary to achieve legitimate results. In one case, a court found that the police used excessive force on a family when responding to a call to settle a neighborhood dispute. The father was not physically strong and was already being subdued by his brother when the police kicked him in the groin and struck him on the head with a nightstick. The officers also allegedly kicked the mother in the back and buttocks after she was handcuffed and lying face down in the mud. The son was injured as well during the arrest process (Lewis v. Downs, 774 F.2d 711 [6th Cir. 1985]). The police were ordered to pay $10,000 because the court said they used excessive force.

For the purpose of day-to-day policing, it is best to think of nondeadly force as either reasonable or punitive, rather than as reasonable or unreasonable. This is because it is often hard for an officer to distinguish between what is reasonable force and what is unreasonable force, particularly when making split-second decisions when emotions are running high and personal safety (the officer's and other people's) is at risk. In contrast, an officer is more likely to know when he or she is using **punitive force,** which is *force that is meant to punish rather than merely to bring the situation under control.* In police work, the use of reasonable force is always legal, whereas the use of punitive force is always illegal and exposes the officer, his or her supervisors, and the city to lawsuits.

d. Excessive Use of Deadly Force **Deadly force** is defined as *force that, when used, would lead a reasonable officer objectively to conclude that it poses a high risk of death or serious injury to its target.* The general rules on the use of deadly force may be summarized as follows: In misdemeanor cases, the safest practice is for officers to refrain from using deadly force, except for self-defense or the defense of the life of a third person. The use of deadly force in misdemeanor cases to prevent an escape raises questions of disproportionality, because the designation of the offense as a misdemeanor denotes that that state does not consider that offense serious. Hence, using deadly force to prevent the escape of a misdemeanant may be a disproportionate sanction.

In felony cases, the safest rule is to use deadly force only when the life of the officer or another person is in danger and the use of such force is immediately necessary to preserve that life. The use of deadly force is usually governed by specific departmental rules that must be followed strictly. If there are no departmental rules, state law must be followed. One writer summarizes the current case law on the use of deadly force to prevent the commission of a felony as follows: "There is no dispute that such force may be used to prevent the commission of a felony which threatens the life or safety of a human being, including the burglary of a dwelling house. . . . As to felonies which involve no such danger, the tendency in the modern cases is to say that the use of deadly force is unreasonable in proportion to the offense."[19]

e. Wrongful Death **Wrongful death** arises whenever death occurs as a result of an officer's action or inaction. An officer has a duty to use not merely ordinary care but a high degree of care in handling a weapon, or else he or she can become liable for wrongful death.[20] Sometimes an officer is held liable because of failure to follow good police procedure. In one case, a police officer was held liable for $202,295.80 in a wrongful death action for shooting and killing a man suspected of buying marijuana, though he thought he was shooting in self-defense. The district judge, relying on the testimony of an expert witness on police procedures, found that the police officer had acted negligently and contrary to sound police procedure in the following respects:

- Failing to utilize a backup unit

- Placing his patrol car in a dangerous cutoff position

- Ordering the two men to exit their car rather than issuing an immobilization command to remain in the car with their hands in plain view

- Increasing the risk of an incident by having the two suspects get out of a car

- Abandoning a covered position and advancing into the open, where the odds of overreacting would be greater

The judge concluded that the officer's fault in not following sound police procedure not only placed the officer in a position of greater danger but also imperiled the deceased suspect by creating a situation in which a fatal error was more likely (Young v. City of Killeen, 775 F.2d 1349 [5th Cir. 1985]).

f. Infliction of Mental or Emotional Distress Tort liability for **infliction of mental or emotional distress** arises when *an officer inflicts severe emotional distress on a person through intentional or reckless extreme and outrageous conduct.* Physical harm need not follow. For example, suppose a plaintiff who is illegally arrested suffers psychological dysfunction and trauma because the officer pointed a loaded gun at her during the arrest. This tort may be alleged any time an officer's conduct is so extreme and outrageous as to cause severe emotional distress. However, what is extreme and outrageous is difficult to determine, and the effect of an act may vary according to the plaintiff's disposition or state of mind. The plaintiff must allege and prove some kind of pattern of behavior or practice by the officer over a period of time, rather than merely isolated incidents.

2. Negligence Tort

The second type of tort in state tort cases is **negligence tort,** which may be defined as *the breach of a common law or statutory duty to act reasonably toward those who may foreseeably be harmed by one's conduct.* This general definition may be modified or superseded by specific state law providing for a different type of conduct, usually making it more restrictive than this definition. Negligence tort applies in many aspects of police work, five of which will be briefly discussed here:[21]

- Liability for failing to protect a member of the public

- Liability for negligent use by police of motor vehicles

- Liability for injury caused by a fleeing motorist-suspect

The General Rule in Negligence Tort

The general rule is that there is no liability on the part of police officers for failing to protect a member of the public. This is because of the public duty doctrine, which holds that government functions are owed to the general public, but not to specific individuals. Therefore, police officers who fail to prevent crime while acting within the scope of their official capacity are not liable to specific individuals for injury or harm that may have been caused by a third party.

- Liability for failure to respond to calls
- Liability for failure to arrest drunk drivers

a. Liability for Failing to Protect a Member of the Public The general rule is that there is no liability on the part of police officers for failing to protect a member of the public. This is because of the **"public duty" doctrine,** which holds that *government functions are owed to the general public, but not to specific individuals.* Therefore, police officers who fail to prevent crime while acting within the scope of their official capacity are not liable to specific individuals for injury or harm that may have been caused by a third party. For example, the police would not liable if X was sexually assaulted, Y murdered, Z robbed, or McDonald's burglarized.

There is one major but multiphased exception to the public duty doctrine: **special relationship,** which means that, *if a duty is owed to a particular person rather than to the general public, then a police officer or agency that breaches that duty can be held liable for damages. Special relationship* has many meanings depending on state law, court decisions, and agency regulations. Liability might be imposed in the following instances based on the special relationship exception to the public duty doctrine. What these situations have in common is that the duty of the police has shifted from protecting the public in general to protecting a particular person, so a special relationship has been established.

1. **When the police deprive an individual of liberty by taking him or her into custody.** For example, in a Florida case, a person was arrested for possession of a lottery ticket. He was handcuffed by the police but then was stabbed by another person. The court ruled that, once the suspect was handcuffed and taken into custody, a special relationship was created in which the city was responsible for his safety, just as though he had been incarcerated in the city jail. In this case, however, the court did not find the officers liable, because there was no negligence in their handling of the suspect. They were just as surprised as the arrestee when a woman ran up and stabbed him (Sanders v. City of Belle Glade, 510 So. 2d 962 [Fla. App. 1987]). In a 1989 case, the Court held that a person who is not in the custody of the state has no constitutional right to protection under the Due Process Clause of the Fourteenth Amendment, but liability may nonetheless arise under state court decisions or under state tort law—if state law so provides (DeShaney v. Winnebago County Department of Social Services, 489 U.S. 189 [1989]).

2. **When the police assume an obligation that goes beyond police duty to protect the general public.** For example, a certain Schuster provided New York City police officers with information that led to the arrest of a fugitive. The incident received considerable media attention, exposing Schuster as the individual who had assisted in the fugitive's capture. When Schuster received life-threatening phone calls, he notified the police. Several weeks later, Schuster was shot and killed. Schuster's family brought suit, alleging that the city police failed to provide Schuster with adequate protection and that New York City thereby breached a special duty owed to individuals who provide the police with information about a crime. A New York court rejected a motion to dismiss, saying that "in our view the public (acting in this instance through the City of New York) owes a special duty to use reasonable care for the protection of persons who have collaborated with them in the arrest or prosecution of criminals" (Schuster v. City of New York, 154 N.E. 2d 534 [N.Y. 1958]).

3. **When protection is mandated by law.** Some states enact laws expressly protecting special groups or individuals. In other states, judicial decisions regard certain laws as protecting special groups or individuals even though they are not specifically protected by law. For example, in a case in Massachusetts, the police were found liable for failing to arrest a drunk driver who subsequently caused injury to the plaintiff. A special relationship was considered to have been created by the legislature in a state statute that prohibited drunk driving. The court reasoned that "statutes which establish police responsibility in such circumstances evidence a legislative intent to protect both the intoxicated persons and users of the highway" (Irwin v. Town of Ware, 467 N.E. 2d 1292 [Mass. 1984]). This case does not necessarily mean that an automatic special relationship exists every time there is a DWI statute. What it means is that the Massachusetts court interpreted the statute to have established a special relationship sufficient to hold the police liable.

4. **When protection is ordered by the court.** This is illustrated in Sorichetti v. City of New York, 482 N.E. 2d 70 (1985), a much-publicized case. The New York Court of Appeals upheld a judgment for $2 million against the New York police for failure to protect a child who was under an order of protection issued by the court. The mother had obtained the order, curtailing her husband's access to their child, because of his violent tendencies. One weekend, the mother agreed to permit the husband to keep the child if he met her at the police station. At the station, the husband yelled to the wife that he was going to kill her and then pointed to the daughter and said, "You better do the sign of the cross before this weekend is up." The wife immediately asked the police to arrest her husband; the police replied that there was nothing they could do. The wife went to the police the next day and again demanded that they return her daughter and arrest her husband, but the police denied her request. That same weekend, the child was attacked by the father and suffered severe wounds. The appellate court upheld the huge damages award, saying that the court-issued protective order created a special relationship that required the police to take extra steps to protect the daughter from harm from a known source.

In another case, a wife claimed that her due process rights were violated when the police failed to arrest or restrain her husband, although a protective order had been issued by the court and she had reported several violations of the order to the police department. She brought a civil rights suit, and the court held that a protective order from a court did create a constitutionally enforceable right to police protection, so liability existed (Coffman v. Wilson Police Department, 739 F. Supp. 257 [E.D. Pa. 1990]).

5. **In some domestic abuse cases.** The general rule is that the police do not have any liability in domestic abuse situations, because the duty to protect an abused spouse comes under the public duty doctrine. In some instances, however, a special relationship has been established, so failure to protect would lead to liability. For example, suppose a state passes legislation authorizing courts to issue protective orders to spouses in domestic abuse situations, an order is issued (creating a special relationship), and the police fail to enforce the order. Or suppose police behavior shows discrimination against a group in society (usually women) in protecting them against domestic abuse, thereby violating their constitutional right to equal protection. In these cases, liability might result if police actions or department policy disproportionately disadvantage that group and if intent to discriminate is proved. For example, a police department would be liable if its policy mandated no arrest in cases involving abused wives on the grounds that these cases usually do not result in charges being pressed against the offender.

b. Negligent Use of Police Vehicles As in other state tort negligence cases, the general rule is that there is no liability for police use of motor vehicles. If liability is imposed at all, it is usually based on police conduct that "shocks the conscience of the court," rather than a lower standard. Liability under state law may also arise if there are violations of state law or department policy. Police departments have rules that must be followed during vehicular chases. Failure to abide by department policy might establish a level of negligence that can lead to liability in a state tort action.

c. Injury Caused by a Fleeing Motorist-Suspect Some cases have been filed by third parties against police officers and departments, seeking damages for injuries caused by a fleeing motorist-suspect who, in the course of the pursuit, hits and injures a pedestrian. Most states hold that the police are not liable for injuries or harm caused by a fleeing violator, because the proximate cause of the injury was not the conduct of the police in making the chase, but the negligent behavior of the fleeing violator.

d. Failure to Respond to Calls Numerous cases have been filed against the police based on alleged negligent failure to respond to calls for police help, including 911 calls. Most police departments encourage the public to call 911 in cases of emergency, and some have assured the public that such calls will be given priority and responded to promptly—even stating the number of minutes it will take the police to respond. The general rule, based on court decisions, is that the police cannot be held liable for either slow or improper response to calls for police help, including 911 calls, except when a special relationship exists between the police and the caller. It is not a good policy for police departments to assure the public that they will respond within, say, five or ten or fifteen minutes after a 911 call. Such a policy exposes the department to liability in case the police are unable to live up to that promise.

   e. Failure to Arrest a Drunk Driver Most states hold that police officers are not liable for injuries inflicted on the public by drunk drivers whom the police fail to arrest. Illustrative of this rule is a Maryland Court of Appeals decision (Ashburn v. Ann Arundel County, 510 A.2d 1078 [Md. 1986]). In that case, a police officer found a certain Millham, intoxicated, sitting behind the wheel of a pickup truck in the parking lot of a 7-Eleven store. The officer told Millham to pull his truck to the side of the lot and to refrain from driving that evening, but he did not make an arrest. As soon as the officer left, Millham drove off and soon collided with the plaintiff, a pedestrian. After losing his left leg and suffering other injuries, the plaintiff brought suit. On appeal, the Maryland Court of Appeals held as follows:

- The officer was acting in a discretionary capacity and was therefore immune from liability.

- The officer was not in a special relationship with pedestrians and therefore did not have a duty to prevent a driver from injuring pedestrians.

- The law that requires officers to detain and investigate a driver does not impose any duty on the police to prevent drivers from injuring pedestrians.

   The public duty doctrine, although alive and well in cases of police failure to arrest drunk drivers, has started to erode. Some states now impose liability based on the concept of duty as a mandatory function or on the special relationship exception to the public duty rule. An example is the Massachusetts case of Irwin v. Town of Ware, 467 N.E. 2d 1292 (1984), mentioned earlier, in which the police were found liable for failing to arrest a drunk driver who subsequently caused injury to the plaintiff. The special relationship in that case was considered by the court to have been created by the legislature in a state statute that prohibited drunk driving. Although only a few states thus far have imposed liability, it is probable—given the impetus of the victims' rights movement—that other states might follow suit and create exceptions to the public duty doctrine that would make police officers liable (through the special relationship route) for failure to arrest drunk drivers.

B. Defenses in State Tort Cases

There are a number of defenses in state tort case, the most significant of which are discussed here: the good faith defense and the official immunity defense.

1. The Good Faith Defense

As discussed previously, good faith is often used as a defense in federal Section 1983 cases. In federal cases, good faith is a valid defense when the officer did not violate a clearly established constitutional or federal right of which a reasonable person would have known. The meaning of "good faith" in state tort cases is not as precise or as singu-

AT A GLANCE

Civil Liability under State Tort Law

DEFINITION: Tort is a civil wrong in which the action of one person causes injury to the person or property of another, in violation of a legal duty imposed by law.

TYPES OF STATE TORT CASES:

- Intentional tort—occurs when there is an intention on the part of the officer to bring some physical harm to or mental coercion upon another person.

- Negligence tort—occurs when there is a breach of a common law or statutory duty to act reasonably toward those who may foreseeably be harmed by one's conduct.

LIABILITY IN NEGLIGENCE TORT: Generally, there is no liability under negligence tort for failing to protect a member of the public, because the officer is protected by the public duty doctrine, which holds that government functions are owed to the general public, but not to specific individuals. However, liability might be imposed if a special relationship has been established with a particular individual.

DEFENSES IN STATE TORT CASES:

- Good faith defense—the officer is not liable if he or she acted in the honest belief that the action taken or the decision made was appropriate under the circumstances.

- Official immunity defense—the officer is not liable if he or she is performing a discretionary duty, in good faith, and is acting within the scope of his or her authority.

---

lar as it is in Section 1983 cases because its meaning can vary from one state to another. One court states that **good faith in state tort cases** means that *the officer "acted in the honest belief that the action taken or the decision was appropriate under the circumstances"* (Tamez v. City of San Marcos, No. 96-50594 [5th Cir. 1997]). In that case, four police officers responded one night to a "shots fired" call at a private house where many people were present. The officers arrived at the site and started to question people who were outside the house. One officer "leaned into the residence" and saw Tamez, sitting on a chair with his back to the door and apparently talking on the telephone. The officer did not know that Tamez was holding a revolver in his right hand that had no live bullets; nor did the officer know that Tamez was severely drunk. When asked, "Are you all right, sir?" Tamez turned around and pointed his gun at the officer. The officer immediately stepped into the house, crouched, and fired six rounds from his service revolver. Most of the shots missed, but Tamez was hit in the arm and leg. Tamez brought a Section 1983 and a state tort case (these cases can be combined in some jurisdictions) against the officer, claiming negligence. The Court of Appeals for the Fifth Circuit dismissed both charges, saying that there was no liability under Section 1983 because the officer's behavior did not violate Tamez's Fourth Amendment rights. In the state tort case, the court concluded that there was no liability because the officer acted in the honest belief that the action taken was appropriate under the circumstances.

Black's Law Dictionary defines good faith thus: "Good faith is an intangible and abstract quality with no technical or statutory definition, and it encompasses, among other things, an honest belief, the absence of malice and the absence of design to defraud or to seek an unconscionable advantage, and an individual's personal good faith is concept of his own mind and inner spirit and, therefore, may not conclusively be determined by his protestations alone."[22] This definition best captures the fluidity of good faith and explains why the term is usually ill defined. There are some states, however, in which good faith is defined either by case law or by statute. In these states, good faith becomes a clearer concept.

2. The "Official Immunity" Defense

The official immunity defense in state tort cases has no counterpart in Section 1983 cases. Its meaning, like good faith in state tort cases, varies from state to state. One state court states that government employees are entitled to **official immunity** from lawsuits arising from *the performance of their "discretionary duties, in good faith, as long as they are acting within the scope of their authority"* (City of Lancaster v. Chambers, 883 S.W. 2d [Tex. 1994]). This definition requires that, for the official immunity defense to succeed, three elements must be proved by the officer: (1) The officer must have been performing a discretionary, not a mandatory, act; (2) the officer must have acted in good faith; and (3) the officer must have acted within the scope of his or her authority. What do these terms mean?

An act is **discretionary** if it *involves personal deliberation, decision, and judgment.* Actions that require obedience to orders or performance of duties about which the officer has no choice are not discretionary; they are instead ministerial (City of Pharr v. Ruiz, 944 S.W. 2d 709 [Tex. Cr. App. 1997]). For example, the decision whether to arrest a suspect for a minor offense is usually left to the discretion of the officer. At the same time, respecting the constitutional rights of a suspect is ministerial in that these rights must be respected by the police. As noted previously, good faith means that the officer "acted in the honest belief that the action taken or the decision was appropriate under the circumstances." For example, making an arrest without a warrant on the reasonable belief that the suspect would otherwise flee would be acting in good faith. **Acting within the scope of authority** means that the officer is *discharging the duties generally assigned* (City of Lancaster v. Chambers, 883 S.W. 2d 650 [Tex. 1994]). For example, an officer serving a search warrant is acting within the scope of authority. In contrast, an officer who beats up a suspect is clearly acting outside the scope of authority.

The following chart summarizes the differences between federal (Section 1983) and state tort cases.

Federal (Section 1983) Cases	State Tort Cases
1. Based on federal law.	1. Based on state law.
2. Law passed in 1871.	2. Developed in decided cases.
3. Usually filed in federal court.	3. Usually filed in state court.
4. Only public officials can be sued.	4. Public officials and private persons can be sued.

5. Basis for liability is violation of a constitutional right or of a right given by federal law.

5. Basis for liability is injury to a person or the property of another in violation of a duty imposed by state law.

6. Good faith defense means the officer did not violate a clearly establish constitutional or federal right of which a reasonable person should have known.

6. Good faith defense usually means the officer acted in the honest belief that the action taken was appropriate under the circumstances.

V. DEFENDANTS IN CIVIL LIABILITY CASES: LEGAL REPRESENTATION AND INDEMNIFICATION

A. The Police Officer as Defendant

The officer is an obvious liability target, because he or she allegedly committed the violation. The general rule is that, if what happened can be blamed on the officer alone and on nobody else, the officer alone is liable. For example, suppose an officer, despite excellent training, brutalizes a suspect. If what happened is solely the fault of the officer, then the officer alone is liable. If sued, an officer has two immediate concerns: (1) Who will represent him or her? and (2) If the jury finds liability, who will pay damages?

1. Who Will Represent the Officer in a Lawsuit?

Most state agencies, by law or official policy, provide representation to state law enforcement officers in civil actions. Such representation is usually undertaken by the state attorney general. The situation is different in local law enforcement agencies where representation is usually decided on a case-by-case basis. This means that the local agency is under no obligation to provide a lawyer should an officer be sued, although most agencies will provide some form of representation unless what the officer did constitutes gross abuse of authority. If the agency provides a lawyer, it will probably be the district attorney, the county attorney, or another lawyer who works with the government in some capacity. In some cases, the officer is allowed to choose a lawyer, whose fees are then paid by the agency. This is ideal for the officer but unpopular with agencies because of the high cost. It is cheaper to use somebody already employed by the municipality (such as a county attorney or a district attorney) to represent an officer than to hire an outside lawyer.

2. Who Will Pay If an Officer Is Held Liable?

A majority of states provide some form of indemnification (meaning the reimbursement of any damages paid by the officer) for state employees. The amount varies considerably; some states set no limit, but most states do. If the court awards the plaintiff an amount larger than the maximum allowed by the agency, the employee pays the difference. Although most state agencies provide some form of indemnification, it does not follow that the agency will automatically indemnify every time liability is imposed. Most agencies will pay if the officer acted within the scope of employment, but the agency will not indemnify if the officer's act was gross, blatant, or outrageously violative of individual rights or of agency regulations, as determined by the court.

However, local agencies' practices vary from full indemnification to no indemnification whatsoever. Many state and local agencies will not pay for punitive damages (as opposed to token or actual damages) against a public employee, because the imposition of punitive damages indicates that the employee acted outside the scope and course of employment. Therefore, it would be against public policy for the agency to reimburse him or her.

B. The Supervisor as Defendant

Police supervisors may be held liable in three general ways. First, a supervisor is liable if he or she is personally involved in an act—either by participating in, directing, or ratifying the act. Second, a supervisor is liable if he or she was present at the time the act was committed and could have stopped it, but did not. For example, Sergeant Stacey Koon of the Los Angeles Police Department was present during the Rodney King beating. Although the court found that Koon did not participate in the beating, he could have stopped it; therefore, he was held liable. Third, a supervisor is liable if the illegal act by a subordinate comes under any of the following categories of supervisory negligence:

- Negligent failure to train

- Negligent failure to direct

- Negligent failure to supervise

- Negligent hiring

- Negligent failure to discipline

- Negligent assignment

- Negligent entrustment

Liability might arise, usually under state tort law, if the plaintiff can prove that the injury caused by a subordinate can be linked or traced to any negligence on the part of the police supervisor in any of these seven areas. The level of negligence needed for supervisory liability varies from state to state. The Court has decided, however, that in cases based on federal law (Section 1983), supervisory liability based on failure to train is based on "deliberate indifference" (City of Canton v. Harris, 4889 U.S. 378 [1989]). There is no good definition of what *deliberate indifference* means. It is, however, a higher form of negligence than "mere indifference," but it is lower than "conduct that shocks the conscience."

C. The City or County as Defendant

The inclusion of the city or county as defendant is anchored in the **deep pockets theory,** which means that, whereas *officers and supervisors may have limited financial resources to pay the plaintiff, police agencies have a broader financial base.*

States and state agencies generally cannot be sued and held liable under Section 1983 because they enjoy sovereign immunity under the Eleventh Amendment to the Constitution. This does not mean, however, that state officials are immune to liability. Sovereign immunity extends only to the state itself and its agencies; state officials may be sued and held liable just like local officials. Although states are generally immune to liability in Section 1983 cases because of the Eleventh Amendment, that protection has largely been terminated for liability purposes in state courts. Accordingly, states may generally be sued under state tort law for what their officers do. Many states, however, have waived their sovereign immunity by law or court decisions. In these states, a liability lawsuit may be brought against the state itself.

The rule is different in cases involving cities and counties. The Court held that a municipality can be held liable if an unconstitutional action taken by an employee is caused by a **municipal policy or custom** (Monell v. Department of Social Services, 436 U.S. 658 [1978]) One federal court of appeals defines *policy or custom* as follows:

a. a policy statement, ordinance, regulation, or decision that is officially adopted and promulgated by the municipality's lawmaking officers or by an official to whom the lawmakers have delegated policy-making authority; or
b. a persistent widespread practice of city officials or employees that, although not authorized by officially adopted and promulgated policy, is so common and well settled as to constitute a custom that fairly represents municipal policy. (Webster v. City of Houston, 735 F.2d 838 [5th Cir. 1984])

The distinction is that a policy is usually written, whereas a custom is unwritten. There are instances when an officer or a supervisor will not be held liable for damages but the agency or municipality may be. In Owen v. City of Independence, 445 U.S. 622 (1980), the Court said that a municipality sued under Section 1983 cannot invoke the good faith defense if its policies violate constitutional rights. In that case, a police chief was dismissed by the city manager and city council for certain misdeeds while in office. The police chief was not given any type of hearing or due process rights, because the city charter under which the city manager and city council acted did not grant him any rights prior to dismissal. The Court held that the city manager and members of the city council acted in good faith based on the provisions of the city charter but that the city itself could not invoke the good faith defense.

In a 1985 decision, the Court ruled that a monetary judgment against a public officer "in his official capacity" imposes liability upon the agency that employs him or her, regardless of whether the agency is named as a defendant in the suit (Brandon v. Holt, 469 U.S. 464 [1985]). In *Brandon,* the plaintiff alleged that, although the director of the police department had no actual notice of the police officer's violent behavior, administrative policies were such that he should have known. The Court added that, although the director could be shielded by qualified immunity, the city could be held liable.

In a 1986 case, the Court decided that municipalities can be held liable in a civil rights case for violating constitutional rights on the basis of a *single decision* (rather than a "pattern of decisions") made by an authorized municipal policy maker (Pembaur v. City of Cincinnati, 475 U.S. 469 [1986]). In *Pembaur,* the county prosecutor made official policy, and thereby exposed his municipal employer to liability, by instructing law enforcement officers to forcibly enter a doctor's office, without a search warrant, to serve certain writs on persons thought to be there. The officers were trying to arrest two of the doctor's employees, who had failed to appear before a grand jury. The Court held that this action violated the Fourth Amendment rights of the office owner and concluded that the city of Cincinnati could be held liable. In a later case, the Court ruled that a county cannot be held liable under Section 1983 for a single hiring decision made by a county official (Board of County Commissioners of Bryan County, Oklahoma v. Brown, 520 U.S. 397 [1997]).

VI.   CAN THE POLICE SUE BACK?

Can the police retaliate by suing those who sue them? The answer is yes, and some departments have, in fact, struck back. Illustrative is this newspaper headline: "Grand jurors face $1.7 million suit for criticism of police."[23] The Fifth Circuit Court of Appeals has held that a city can criminally prosecute individuals for knowingly filing false complaints against the police (Gates v. City of Dallas, 729 F.2d 343 [5th Cir. 1984]). New York City has adopted a policy of countersuing individuals who have brought civil suits accusing police officers of brutality, asserting that it was the complainant who attacked the police.[24] Nonetheless, the number of civil cases actually brought by the police against members of the public has remained comparatively small.

The reality is that, although police officers may file tort lawsuits against arrestees or suspects, there are disincentives to doing that. For example, the officer will have to hire his or her own lawyer, a financial outlay that the officer is unlikely to recover from the defendant. Even if the officer wins the case, most of those who have encounters with the police are too poor to pay damages anyway. Thus, officers may prefer to get back at the suspect in a criminal case. States have criminal laws penalizing such offenses as assaulting a peace officer, resisting arrest or a search, hindering apprehension or prosecution, refusing to obey a police order, and committing aggravated assault. These offenses can be added to the original criminal charges filed against the person, thereby increasing the total penalty that may be imposed. Some officers also feel that the antagonistic treatment they sometimes get from the public is simply part of police work, to be accepted without retaliation. In sum, alternatives to suing back plaintiffs civilly exist that police might find more effective and convenient.

VII. WAYS TO MINIMIZE CIVIL LIABILITIES

Liability lawsuits against an officer may be filed by anybody at any time. One of the fundamental rights in American society is the right of access to court. Whether the lawsuit will succeed, however, is a different matter. Figures show that most cases filed against public officers fail, for various reasons, but it is still unrealistic in modern-day policing to expect that no lawsuits will ever be filed against officers during their years of police work. However, there are ways for officers to minimize lawsuits:

1. Know and follow the department's manual or guidelines to ensure a strong claim to a good faith defense.

2. Act within the scope of professional duties.

3. Act in a professional and responsible manner at all times. When faced with a difficult situation, use reason instead of emotion.

4. Know the constitutional rights of the public and respect them.

5. Consult legal counsel or a supervisor when in doubt, and document the advice given.

6. In sensitive cases, document activities, and keep good written records.

7. Establish and maintain good relations with the community.

8. Keep well informed on current issues and trends in civil and criminal liability cases.

Departmental manuals and guidelines play an important role in police work. The advantages in having a good manual are twofold: (1) Manuals tell police officers what is expected of them and how their tasks can be performed properly, and (2) manuals constitute a good defense for police officers and the agency in liability cases. The provisions of a manual have the force and effect of law for the officers. If the provisions of the manual are illegal, the agency or supervisor may be held liable, but not the officer. For example, suppose an agency manual provides that the officer may shoot to kill a fleeing misdemeanant. If Officer Z does that and is sued, and the statute is declared unconstitutional, the department could be held liable because of the violation of a constitutional right. Chances are, however, that Z would have a good faith defense. The only possible exception would be if Z should have known that the provisions of the manual were clearly illegal.

The preceding list is not exhaustive. Nor is there any substitute for the specific advice of a competent lawyer when an officer is faced with a difficult situation that carries potential legal consequences. Sources of liability and defenses vary from state to state and even from one jurisdiction to another within a state. When a lawsuit is filed, it is important for the officer to obtain the services of a good lawyer, either on his or her own or through the department. Liability lawsuits must be taken seriously even if the allegations appear to be groundless or trivial. Otherwise, undesirable consequences can follow.

Summary

Lawsuits against officers may be filed under state and federal laws, and the sanctions can be civil or criminal. Most plaintiffs prefer to sue under the provisions of state tort laws and the Federal Civil Rights Act, otherwise referred to as Section 1983. The requirements of a Section 1983 case are that the officer must have been acting under color of law and that there must be a violation of the plaintiff's constitutional or federally guaranteed rights. In contrast, a state tort case involves a civil wrong in which the action of one person causes injury to the person or property of another, in violation of a legal duty imposed by law. Liability under state tort law may come under intentional tort or negligence tort. Section 1983 and state tort cases may be combined into one case, if allowed in a particular jurisdiction.

A number of defenses are available in civil liability cases. In Section 1983 cases, the defenses often used are the good faith defense and the probable cause defense. The good faith defense means that the officer is not liable unless he or she violated a clearly established constitutional right or a right given by federal law. The probable cause defense means that the officer is not liable in Fourth Amendment cases if probable cause was present. In state tort cases, good faith is also a defense, but it does not have as singular a meaning. One court has held that an officer acts in good faith if he or she had an honest belief that the action taken or the decision made was appropriate under the circumstances. Another defense in state tort cases is the official immunity defense. This defense requires that the officer was performing a discretionary duty, in good faith, and was acting within the scope of authority.

In addition to the police officer, plaintiffs almost always include the supervisors and the governmental agency as defendants. This approach enables the plaintiff to dip into the deep pockets of the supervisors or local agency in case the officer-defendant cannot pay. Legal representation is usually undertaken by the agency unless what the officer did was grossly outside the scope of authority. Indemnification is also usually provided by the agency under the standard of acting within the scope of authority.

Review Questions

1. Give an overview of the types of legal liabilities to which police officers may be exposed in connection with their work.

2. What are the two types of liabilities under state tort law? Give a brief description of each.

3. What standard do courts apply to determine whether the police have used excessive force?

4. What is the public duty doctrine? What is its exception?

5. "The police are never liable for failure to protect." Is this statement true or false? Discuss fully.

6. What is a Section 1983 case? Give its two basic elements.

7. What is the good faith defense in Section 1983 cases? Give two instances in which the good faith defense is likely to succeed.

8. What is the probable cause defense in Section 1983 cases? How does it differ from the concept of probable cause in search and seizure cases?

9. What is the official immunity defense in state tort cases?

10. Give four differences between a Section 1983 and a state tort case.

11. If an officer is sued, will the agency provide a lawyer to defend him or her? If the officer is held liable, will the agency pay? Discuss.

12. What are some reasons police officers do not countersue even if there are legal remedies available to them?

13. Give five ways to minimize liability lawsuits against the police.

Key Terms and Definitions

acting under color of law: The use of power possessed by virtue of law and made possible only because the officer is clothed with the authority of the state.

acting within the scope of authority: The situation in which an officer is discharging the duties generally assigned to him or her.

assault: An intentional tort wherein an officer causes apprehension of harmful or offensive conduct; it is the attempt or threat of bodily harm on another person, accompanied by the ability to inflict it.

battery: An intentional tort in which an officer causes the infliction of harmful or offensive body contact on another person. It usually involves unlawful, unwarranted, or hostile touching—however slight.

deadly force: Force that when used would lead a reasonable officer objectively to conclude that it poses a high risk of death or serious injury to its human target.

deep pockets theory: The theory that individual officers may lack resources to pay damages but the government agency has a broader financial base, so plaintiffs include government agencies in their lawsuits.

discretionary act: An act that involves personal deliberation, decision, and judgment.

false arrest: An intentional tort that results when an officer makes an illegal arrest—usually one without probable cause.

false imprisonment: A tort case that may result when one person unlawfully detains another.

good faith defense in Section 1983 cases: In civil liability cases, the concept that an officer should not be held liable if he or she did not violate a clearly established constitutional right of which a reasonable person would have known.

good faith defense in state tort cases: The situation in which an officer "acted in the honest belief that the action taken or the decision was appropriate under the circumstances."

infliction of mental or emotional distress: A form of intentional tort consisting of the infliction of severe emotional distress on a person through intentional or reckless extreme and outrageous conduct.

intentional tort: A type of tort that occurs when an officer intends to bring some physical harm or mental coercion upon another person.

municipal policy or custom: A policy statement, ordinance, regulation, or decision (usually in writing) that is officially adopted by the municipality's lawmaking officers (or those delegated by them) or a persistent practice of city employees that, although not formally authorized in writing, is so common that it is the equivalent of municipal policy.

negligence tort: A tort arising from the breach of a common law or statutory duty to act reasonably toward those who may foreseeably be harmed by one's conduct.

official immunity: The concept that officers are not liable when they perform discretionary duties, in good faith, and are acting within the scope of their authority.

probable cause defense: In Section 1983 cases, an officer's reasonable good faith belief in the legality of the action taken.

public duty doctrine: A doctrine holding that government functions are owed to the general public but not to specific individuals. Therefore, police officers who fail to prevent crime while acting within the scope of their official capacity are not liable to specific individuals for injury or harm that may have been caused by a third party.

punitive force: Force that is meant to punish rather than merely to bring the situation under control.

reasonable force: The kind of force that a prudent and cautious person would use if exposed to similar circumstances; it is limited to the amount of force that is necessary to achieve valid and proper results.

Section 1983 case (or civil rights case): A lawsuit, filed under federal law, seeking damages from a police officer, supervisor, and/or department, on the grounds that these defendants, acting under color of law, violated a plaintiff's constitutional rights or rights given by federal law.

special relationship: An exception to the public duty doctrine (which exempts the police from liability for failure to protect), by which the police will be held civilly liable if a special relationship with a particular individual has been created.

tort: A civil wrong in which the action of one person causes injury to the person or property of another in violation of a legal duty imposed by law.

wrongful death: A tort action in which the surviving family, relatives, or legal guardians of the estate of the deceased bring a lawsuit against an officer on account of death caused by the officer's conduct.

Principles of Cases

Anderson v. Creighton, 483 U.S. 635 (1987) The Harlow standard, which affords immunity from acts that the official could have reasonably believed were lawful, applies to police officers in the performance of their responsibilities.

Ashburn v. Ann Arundel County, 510 A.2d 1078 (Md. 1986) Police officers are not liable for injuries inflicted on the public by drunk drivers whom the police fail to arrest.

Board of the County Commissioners of Bryan County, Oklahoma v. Brown, 520 U.S. 397 (1997) A county cannot be held liable under Section 1983 for a single hiring decision made by a county official.

Brandon v. Holt, 469 U.S. 464 (1985) A monetary judgment against a public officer in his or her official capacity imposes liability upon the agency that employs him or her, regardless of whether the agency was named as a defendant in the suit.

Brinegar v. United States, 338 U.S. 160 (1949) Probable cause is defined as more than bare suspicion; it exists when the facts and circumstances within the officers' knowledge and of which they had reasonably trustworthy information are sufficient in themselves to warrant a man of reasonable caution in the belief that an offense has been or is being committed.

City of Canton v. Harris, 489 U.S. 378 (1989) Inadequate police training may serve as the basis for municipal liability under Section 1983 if the failure to train amounts to "deliberate indifference" to the rights of people with whom the police come into contact and the deficiency in the training program is closely related to the injury suffered.

City of Lancaster v. Chambers, 883 S.W. 2d (Tex. 1994) Government employees are entitled to official immunity from lawsuits arising from the performance of their discretionary duties, in good faith, as long as they are acting within the scope of their authority.

City of Pharr v. Ruiz, 944 S.W. 2d 709 (Tex. Cr. App. 1997) An act is discretionary if it involves personal deliberation, decision, and judgment. Actions that require obedience to orders or performance of duties about which the officer has no choice are not discretionary; they are instead ministerial.

Coffman v. Wilson Police Department, 739 F. Supp. 257 (E.D. Pa. 1990) A protective order from a court creates a constitutionally enforceable right to police protection.

Deshaney v. Winnebago County Department of Social Services, 489 U.S. 189 (1989) A person who is not under the custody of the state has no constitutional right to protection under the Due Process Clause of the Fourteenth Amendment, but there may be liability under state court decisions or state tort law.

Fraire v. City of Arlington, 957 F.2d 1268 (5th Cir. 1992) A right is "clearly established" when, at the time the defendant acted, the law established the contours of a right so clearly that a reasonable official would have understood his or her acts were unlawful.

Gates v. City of Dallas, 729 F.2d 343 (5th Cir. 1984) A city can criminally prosecute individuals for knowingly filing false complaints against the police.

Harlow v. Fitzgerald, 457 U.S. 800 (1982) Government officials performing discretionary functions are generally shielded from liability for civil damages insofar as their conduct does not violate clearly established statutory or constitutional rights of which a reasonable person would have known.

Irwin v. Town of Ware, 467 N.E. 2d 1292 (Mass. 1984) Statutes that establish police responsibility in DWI cases show a legislative intent to protect both the intoxicated person and the users of the highway and therefore create a special relationship that can lead to police liability.

Lewis v. Downs, 774 F.2d 711 (6th Cir. 1985) Police who used excessive force on a family when responding to a call to settle a neighborhood dispute were liable for damages under state tort law.

Malley v. Briggs, 475 U.S. 335 (1986) A police officer, when applying for an arrest warrant, is entitled only to qualified immunity, not absolute immunity, in Section 1983 cases. This means that even if a warrant is issued by a magistrate as a result of the officer's complaint, the officer could be held liable if it is established that the complaint was made maliciously and without probable cause.

Monell v. Department of Social Services, 436 U.S. 658 (1978) Local units of government may be held liable in a civil rights lawsuit if the allegedly unconstitutional action was taken by the officer as a part of an official policy or custom.

Owen v. City of Independence, Missouri, 445 U.S. 622 (1980) A municipality sued under Section 1983 cannot invoke the good faith defense, which is available to its officers and employees, if its policies violate constitutional rights.

Pembauer v. City of Cincinnati, 475 U.S. 469 (1986) Municipalities can held liable in a civil rights case for violating constitutional rights on the basis of a single decision (rather than a pattern of decisions) made by an authorized municipal policy maker.

Rodriguez v. Jones, 473 F.2d 599 (5th Cir. 1973) Probable cause, as a defense in civil rights cases, simply means a reasonable good faith belief in the legality of the action taken.

Sanders v. City of Belle Glade, 510 So. 2d 962 (Fla. App. 1987) Once a suspect is handcuffed and taken into custody, a special relationship is created that makes the city responsible for his or her safety as though he or she were incarcerated in the city jail.

Schuster v. City of New York, 154 N.E. 2d 534 (N.Y. 1958) The police owe a special duty to use reasonable care to protect people who have collaborated with them in the arrest or prosecution of criminals.

Sorichetti v. City of New York, 482 N.E. 2d 70 (1985) The police may be civilly liable for failure to protect if a special relationship has been created—for example, if a judicial order has been issued for the police to protect a child but they fail to do so.

Stanfield v. Laccoarce, 588 P.2d 1271 (1978) To determine whether a police officer's actions are within the scope of employment, the court considers whether the act in question is of a kind he or she was hired to perform, whether the act occurred within the authorized time and space, and whether the employee was motivated, at least in part, by the purpose of serving the employer.

Tamez v. City of San Marcos, No. 96-50594 (1997) Good faith means the officer acted in the honest belief that the action taken or the decision made was appropriate under the circumstances.

Thurman v. City of Torrington, 595 F. Supp. 1521 (D. Conn. 1984) Liability may be imposed based on a violation of the Equal Protection Clause if police policy deliberately discriminates against women or manifests a deliberate indifference to their safety.

Webster v. City of Houston, 735 F.2d 838 (5th Cir. 1984) "Official policy or custom" means "(a) a policy statement, ordinance, regulation, or decision that is officially adopted and promulgated by the municipality's lawmaking officers or by an official to whom the lawmakers have delegated policy-making authority; or (b) a persistent widespread practice of city officials or employees that, although not authorized by officially adopted and promulgated policy, is so common and well settled as to constitute a custom that fairly represents municipal policy."

Wilson et al. v. Layne, No. 98-93 (1999) The police violated the plaintiffs' constitutional rights during a police "media ride-along," but that right was not as yet "clearly established" when the violation took place, so there was no liability under Section 1983.

Young v. City of Killeen, 775 F.2d 1349 (1985) The court found a police officer liable for $202,295.80 in a wrongful death action for shooting and killing a man suspected of buying marijuana. The officer was liable even though he thought he was shooting in self-defense. The judge, relying on the testimony of an expert witness on police procedures, found that the officer had acted negligently and contrary to good police procedure. The action of the officer not only placed him in a position of greater danger but also imperiled the deceased suspect by creating a situation in which a fatal error was likely.

Case Briefs

Leading Case on the Immunity of Police Officers

Malley v. Briggs, 475 U.S. 335 (1986)

Facts: On the basis of two monitored telephone calls carried out under a court-authorized wiretap, Rhode Island state trooper Malley prepared felony complaints charging Briggs and others with possession of marijuana. The complaints were given to a state judge together with arrest warrants and supporting affidavits. The judge signed the warrants, and the defendants were arrested. The charges were subsequently dropped when the grand jury refused to return an indictment. The defendants then brought action under Section 1983, alleging that Malley, in applying for the arrest warrants, had violated their right to protection

against unreasonable search and seizure. The case was tried by a jury, and the court granted a directed verdict in favor of the officer. The trial court's decision stated that a police officer who believes that the facts stated in an affidavit are true and submits them to a neutral magistrate may be entitled to absolute immunity. The court of appeals reversed that decision.

Issue: *What type of immunity is accorded a defendant police officer in Section 1983 actions when it is alleged that the officer caused the plaintiffs to be unconstitutionally arrested by presenting a judge with a complaint and a supporting affidavit that failed to establish probable cause? Qualified immunity.*

Supreme Court Decision: A police officer is not entitled to absolute immunity—only to qualified immunity—from liability for damages in Section 1983 cases. Qualified immunity is not established simply by virtue of the fact that the officer believed the allegations in the affidavit, which the magistrate found to be sufficient.

Case Significance: Malley argued that he should be given absolute immunity, despite previous decisions to the contrary, because his function in seeking an arrest warrant was similar to that of a complaining witness. However, the Court responded that complaining witnesses were not absolutely immune according to common law. In fact, by the generally accepted rule in 1871, when the civil rights law was passed, a person who obtains an arrest warrant by submitting a complaint can be held liable if the complaint is made maliciously and without probable cause. If malice and lack of probable cause are proved, the officer enjoys no absolute immunity. The Court also refused to be swayed by the officer's argument that policy considerations require absolute immunity for the officer applying for a warrant: "As the qualified immunity defense has evolved, it provides ample protection to all but the plainly incompetent or those who knowingly violate the law." The Court considered this protection sufficient because, under current standards, the officer is not liable anyway if he or she acted in an objectively reasonable manner. The *Malley* case therefore makes clear that under no circumstance will the Court extend to police officers the absolute immunity defense that is available to judges, prosecutors, and legislators. The only exception occurs when the officer is testifying in a criminal trial. Thus, officers enjoy only qualified immunity; they will not be liable if they act in an objectively reasonable manner.

Excerpts from the Decision: "As the qualified immunity defense has evolved, it provides ample protection to all but the plainly incompetent or those who knowingly violate the law. At common law, in cases where probable cause to arrest was lacking, a complaining witness's immunity turned on the issue of malice, which was a jury question. Under the *Harlow* standard, on the other hand, an allegation of malice is not sufficient to defeat immunity if the defendant acted in an objectively reasonable manner. The *Harlow* standard is specifically designed to 'avoid excessive disruption of government and permit the resolution of many insubstantial claims on summary judgment,' and we believe it sufficiently serves this goal. Defendants will not be immune if, on an objective basis, it is obvious that no reasonably competent officer would have

concluded that a warrant should issue; but if officers of reasonable competence could disagree on this issue, immunity should be recognized."

Leading Case on Police Liability for Excessive Use of Force

Graham v. Connor, 490 U.S. 386 (1989)

Facts: Graham, a diabetic, asked a friend, Berry, to drive him to a convenience store to buy orange juice, which he needed to counteract the onset of an insulin reaction. They went to the store, but Graham saw many people ahead of him in line so he hurried out and asked Berry to drive him instead to a friend's house. Officer Connor became suspicious after he saw Graham hastily enter and leave the store. He followed Berry's car, made an investigative stop, and ordered Graham and Berry to wait while he determined what happened at the store. Other officers arrived, handcuffed Graham, and ignored Graham's attempt to explain his condition. In a subsequent struggle, Graham sustained multiple injuries. Graham was later released when Officer Connor learned that nothing had happened at the store. Graham brought a Section 1983 lawsuit against the police, alleging a violation of his Fourth Amendment rights.

Issue: *May police officers be held liable under Section 1983 for using excessive force? Yes. If so, what should be the standard for liability? Objective reasonableness.*

Supreme Court Decision: Police officers may be held liable under the Constitution for using excessive force. Such liability must be judged under the Fourth Amendment's objective reasonableness standard, rather than under a substantive due process standard.

Case Significance: This case gives police officers a break in civil liability cases involving the use of force. The old substantive due process test previously used by many lower courts turned on whether the officer acted in good faith or "maliciously and sadistically for the very purpose of causing harm." Thus, the officer's subjective motivations were of central importance in deciding whether the force used was unconstitutional. The *Graham* decision establishes a new test—that of objective reasonableness under the Fourth Amendment. In addition, the reasonableness of an officer's use of force must be judged "from the perspective of a reasonable officer on the scene, rather than with the 20/20 vision of hindsight." This makes a big difference in determining whether the use of force was reasonable. This new test recognizes that police officers often make split-second judgments in situations that involve their own lives and must, therefore, be judged in the context of the perceptions of a reasonable officer at the scene. This is a test most police officers welcome.

Excerpts from the Decision: "The 'reasonableness' of a particular use of force must be judged from the perspective of a reasonable officer on the scene, rather than with the 20/20 vision of hindsight. The Fourth Amendment is not violated by an arrest based on probable cause, even though the wrong person is arrested, nor by the mistaken execution of a valid search war-

rant on the wrong premises. With respect to a claim of excessive force, the same standard of reasonableness at the moment applies: 'Not every push or shove, even if it may later seem unnecessary in the peace of a judge's chamber,' violates the Fourth Amendment. The calculus of reasonableness must embody allowance for the fact that police officers are often forced to make split-second judgments—in circumstances that are tense, uncertain, and rapidly evolving—about the amount of force that is necessary in a particular situation."

 # Notes

1. Americans for Effective Law Enforcement, *Liability Reporter,* 1999 (315), cover page.

2. Ibid.

3. Americans for Effective Law Enforcement, *Liability Reporter,* 1999 (316), cover page.

4. Americans for Effective Law Enforcement, *Liability Reporter,* 1999 (318), cover page.

5. Americans for Effective Law Enforcement, *Liability Reporter,* 1999 (320), cover page.

6. Ibid.

7. Americans for Effective Law Enforcement, *Liability Reporter,* 1999 (321), cover page.

8. F. Scogins and S. Brodsky, "Fear of Litigation among Law Enforcement Officers," *American Journal of Police,* 10, p. 45.

9. *Training Aids Digest,* December 1992, p. 2.

10. E. Chemerinsky, "Policing the Police," *Trial Magazine,* December 1991, p. 32.

11. *Houston Chronicle,* April 6, 1992, p. A3.

12. *Miami Herald,* May 20, 1992, p. 4.

13. J. Skolnick and J. Fyfe, *Above the Law: Police and the Excessive Use of Force* (New York: Free Press, 1993), p. 202.

14. V. Kappeler, *Critical Issues in Police Civil Liability* (Prospect Heights, IL: Waveland Press, 1993), p. 7.

15. *New York Times,* October 1, 1999, p. 1.

16. Ibid.

17. *USA Today,* May 26, 1999, p. A3.

18. I. Silver, *Police Civil Liability* (New York: Matthew Bender, 1986), 4-3.

19. Ibid., 5–7.

20. Ibid.

21. This section on liability for failure to protect is taken, with modification, from R. V. del Carmen, *Civil Liabilities in American Policing* (Englewood Cliffs, NJ: Prentice-Hall, 1991), Ch. 11.

22. *Black's Law Dictionary,* 6th ed. (St. Paul, MN: West, 1991), p. 477.

23. *Houston Chronicle,* January 19, 1984 , p. 31.

24. *New York Times,* February 20, 1985, p. B1.

A. Guide to Case Briefing

Case briefs help readers understand court cases better and are used extensively as a learning tool in law schools and in the practice of law. Students read a case, break it into segments, and then reassemble it in a more concise and organized form so as to facilitate learning.

To familiarize students with the basics of case briefing, a sample case brief is presented here. There is no agreement among scholars on how a case should be briefed for instructional purposes. The elements of a brief ultimately depend on the preferences of the instructor or of the student doing the briefing. The sample brief given here is as simple as it gets. Some briefs are more complex; they include dissenting and concurring opinions (if any), comments, case significance, case excerpts, and other elements an instructor or student might deem necessary.

The basic elements of a simple case brief are:

1. Case title

2. Citation

3. Year decided

4. Facts

5. Main issue

6. Court decision

7. Holding

THE CASE OF MINNESOTA V. DICKERSON (For comparison, see the original of this case in Appendix B.)

1. **Case title:** Minnesota v. Dickerson

2. **Citation:** 508 U.S. 366

3. **Year decided:** 1993

Note: In your brief, the above elements go in this order: Minnesota v. Dickerson, 508 U.S. 366 (1993). This means that the case of Minnesota v. Dickerson is found in volume 508 of the United States Reports, *starting at page 366, and was decided in 1993.*

4. **Facts:** During routine patrol, two police officers spotted Dickerson leaving an apartment building that one of the officers knew was a "crack house." Dickerson began walking toward the police but upon making eye contact with them,

reversed direction and walked into an alley. Because of his evasive actions, the police became suspicious and decided to investigate. They pulled into the alley and ordered Dickerson to stop and submit to a pat-down search. The search revealed no weapons, but one officer found a small lump in Dickerson's pocket, which he examined with his fingers and determined, after the examination, that it felt like a lump of cocaine in cellophane. The officer then reached into Dickerson's pocket and retrieved the lump, which turned out to be a small plastic bag of crack cocaine. Dickerson was arrested and charged with possession of a controlled substance.

Note: *The facts section can be too detailed or too sketchy, both of which can be misleading. In general, be guided by this question: What minimum facts must be included in your brief so that somebody who has not read the whole case (as you have) will nonetheless understand it? That amount of detail is for you to decide—you must determine what facts are important or unimportant. Keep the important, but weed out the unimportant.*

5. **Main issue:** Was the seizure of the crack cocaine valid under stop and frisk? No.

Note: *The issue statement must always be in question form, as here. The issue statement should not too broad (so as to apply to every case even remotely similar in facts) or too narrow (as to be applicable only to the peculiar facts of that case). Here are some examples:*

> Are police seizures without probable cause valid? *(too broad)*
> Are police searches based on reasonable suspicion valid? *(too broad)*
> Is police seizure of something that feels like lump in a suspect's pocket valid? *(too narrow)*
> Was the seizure of the crack cocaine valid under stop and frisk? *(just about right)*

Some cases have more than one issue. If these issues cannot be merged, they must be stated as separate issues.

6. **Court decision:** The United States Supreme Court affirmed the decision of the Minnesota Supreme Court that held the seizure to be invalid.

Note: *The court decision answers two questions: Did the court affirm, reverse, or modify the decision of the immediate lower court (in this case the Minnesota Supreme Court) where the case came from? and What happened to the case? Sometimes students confuse this with the* holding *of the case. The difference is that the court decision is a brief statement that tells you what happened to the case on appeal and what the court said is to be done with it. In this briefed case, the case ends because the lower court decision was affirmed. It would have been different had the court ordered that the case be "reversed and remanded." The case would then have gone back to the lower courts.*

7. **Holding** (sometimes also known as the doctrine or ruling): A frisk that goes beyond that allowed in Terry v. Ohio in stop and frisk cases is not valid. In this case, the search went beyond the pat-down search allowed by *Terry* because the officer "squeezed, slid, and otherwise manipulated the packet's content" before knowing it was cocaine. The evidence obtained is not admissible in court.

Note: *State in brief, exact, clear language what the court said. In some cases, the holding may be taken verbatim from the case itself, usually toward the end. The holding is the most important element of the case because it states the rule announced by the court. The holding becomes precedent, which means the same rule is applicable to future similar cases to be decided by the courts.*

B.

The Case of Minnesota v. Dickerson—— A Full Reprint

MINNESOTA v. DICKERSON
508 U.S. 366 (1993)
CERTIORARI TO THE SUPREME COURT OF MINNESOTA
No. 91-2019. Argued March 3, 1993—Decided June 7, 1993

Based upon respondent's seemingly evasive actions when approached by police officers and the fact that he had just left a building known for cocaine traffic, the officers decided to investigate further and ordered respondent to submit to a patdown search. The search revealed no weapons, but the officer conducting it testified that he felt a small lump in respondent's jacket pocket, believed it to be a lump of crack cocaine upon examining it with his fingers, and then reached into the pocket and retrieved a small bag of cocaine. The state trial court denied respondent's motion to suppress the cocaine, and he was found guilty of possession of a controlled substance. The Minnesota Court of Appeals reversed. In affirming, the State Supreme Court held that both the stop and the frisk of respondent were valid under *Terry* v. *Ohio*, 392 U.S. 1, but found the seizure of the cocaine to be unconstitutional. Refusing to enlarge the "plain-view" exception to the Fourth Amendment's warrant requirement, the court appeared to adopt a categorical rule barring the seizure of any contraband detected by an officer through the sense of touch during a patdown search. The court further noted that, even if it recognized such a "plain-feel" exception, the search in this case would not qualify because it went far beyond what is permissible under *Terry*.

Held:

1. The police may seize nonthreatening contraband detected through the sense of touch during a protective patdown search of the sort permitted by *Terry*, so long as the search stays within the bounds marked by *Terry*. Pp. 372–377.

    (a) *Terry* permits a brief stop of a person whose suspicious conduct leads an officer to conclude in light of his experience that criminal activity may be afoot, and a patdown search of the person for weapons when the officer is justified in believing that the person may be armed and presently dangerous. This protective search—permitted without a warrant and on the basis of reasonable suspicion less than probable cause—is not meant to discover evidence of crime, but must be strictly limited to that which is necessary for the discovery of weapons which might be used to harm the officer or others: If the protective search goes beyond what is necessary to determine if the suspect is armed, it is no longer valid under *Terry* and its fruits will be suppressed. *Sibron v. New York,* 392 U.S. 40, 66–67. Pp. 372–373.

(b) In *Michigan v. Long,* 463 U.S. 1032, 1050, the seizure of contraband other than weapons during a lawful *Terry* search was justified by reference to the Court's cases under the "plain-view" doctrine. That doctrine— which permits police to seize an object without a warrant if they are law- fully in a position to view it, if its incriminating character is immediately apparent, and if they have a lawful right of access to it—has an obvious application by analogy to cases in which an officer discovers contraband through the sense of touch during an otherwise lawful search. Thus, if an officer lawfully pats down a suspect's outer clothing and feels an object whose contour or mass makes its identity immediately apparent, there has been no invasion of the suspect's privacy beyond that already authorized by the officer's search for weapons. Cf., *e.g., Illinois v. Andreas,* 463 U.S. 766, 771. If the object is contraband, its warrantless seizure would be jus- tified by the realization that resort to a neutral magistrate under such cir- cumstances would be impracticable and would do little to promote the Fourth Amendment's objectives. Cf., *e.g., Arizona v. Hicks,* 480 U.S. 321, 326–327. Pp. 374–377.

2. Application of the foregoing principles to the facts of this case demonstrates that the officer who conducted the search was not acting within the lawful bounds marked by *Terry* at the time he gained probable cause to believe that the lump in respondent's jacket was contraband. Under the State Supreme Court's interpretation of the record, the officer never thought that the lump was a weapon, but did not immediately recognize it as cocaine. Rather, he determined that it was contraband only after he squeezed, slid, and otherwise manipulated the pocket's contents. While *Terry* entitled him to place his hands on respondent's jacket and to feel the lump in the pocket, his continued exploration of the pocket after he concluded that it contained no weapon was unrelated to the sole justification for the search under *Terry.* Because this fur- ther search was constitutionally invalid, the seizure of the cocaine that fol- lowed is likewise unconstitutional. Pp. 377–379.

481 N. W 2d 840, affirmed.

WHITE, J., delivered the opinion for a unanimous Court with respect to Parts I and II, and the opinion of the Court with respect to Parts III and IV, in which STEVENS, O'CONNOR, SCALIA, KENNEDY, and SOUTER, JJ., joined. SCALIA, J., filed a concurring opinion, *post,* p. 379. REHNQUIST, C. J., filed an opinion concurring in part and dissenting in part, in which BLACKMUN and THOMAS, JJ., joined, *post,* p. 383.

Michael O. Freeman argued the cause for petitioner. With him on the briefs were *Hubert H. Humphrey III,* Attorney General of Minnesota, *Patrick C. Diamond,* and *Beverly J. Wolfe. Richard H. Seamon* argued the cause for the United States as *amicus curiae* urging reversal. With him on the brief were *Solicitor General Starr, Assistant Attorney General Mueller, Deputy Solicitor General Bryson,* and *Kathleen A. Felton.*

Peter W. Gorman argued the cause for respondent. With him on the brief were *William R. Kennedy, David H. Knutson, Warren R. Sagstuen,* and *Renée J. Bergeron.*

JUSTICE WHITE delivered the opinion of the Court.

In this case, we consider whether the Fourth Amendment permits the seizure of contraband detected through a police officer's sense of touch during a protective patdown search.

I.

On the evening of November 9, 1989, two Minneapolis police officers were patrolling an area on the city's north side in a marked squad car. At about 8:16 P.M., one of the officers observed respondent leaving a 12-unit apartment building on Morgan Avenue North. The officer, having previously responded to complaints of drug sales in the building's hallways and having executed several search warrants on the premises, considered the building to be a notorious "crack house." According to testimony credited by the trial court, respondent began walking toward the police but, upon spotting the squad car and making eye contact with one of the officers, abruptly halted and began walking in the opposite direction. His suspicion aroused, this officer watched as respondent turned and entered an alley on the other side of the apartment building. Based upon respondent's seemingly evasive actions and the fact that he had just left a building known for cocaine traffic, the officers decided to stop respondent and investigate further.

The officers pulled their squad car into the alley and ordered respondent to stop and submit to a patdown search. The search revealed no weapons, but the officer conducting the search did take an interest in a small lump in respondent's nylon jacket. The officer later testified:

> "[A]s I pat-searched the front of his body, I felt a lump, a small lump, in the front pocket. I examined it with my fingers and it slid and it felt to be a lump of crack cocaine in cellophane." Tr. 9 (Feb. 20, 1990).

The officer then reached into respondent's pocket and retrieved a small plastic bag containing one fifth of one gram of crack cocaine. Respondent was arrested and charged in Hennepin County District Court with possession of a controlled substance.

Before trial, respondent moved to suppress the cocaine. The trial court first concluded that the officers were justified under *Terry* v. *Ohio,* 392 U.S. 1 (1968), in stopping respondent to investigate whether he might be engaged in criminal activity. The court further found that the officers were justified in frisking respondent to ensure that he was not carrying a weapon. Finally, analogizing to the "plain-view" doctrine, under which officers may make a warrantless seizure of contraband found in plain view during a lawful search for other items, the trial court ruled that the officers' seizure of the cocaine did not violate the Fourth Amendment:

> "To this Court there is no distinction as to which sensory perception the officer uses to conclude that the material is contraband. An experienced officer may rely

upon his sense of smell in DWI stops or in recognizing the smell of burning marijuana in an automobile. The sound of a shotgun being racked would clearly support certain reactions by an officer. The sense of touch, grounded in experience and training, is as reliable as perceptions drawn from other senses. 'Plain feel,' therefore, is no different than plain view and will equally support the seizure here." App. to Pet. for Cert. C-5.

His suppression motion having failed, respondent proceeded to trial and was found guilty. On appeal, the Minnesota Court of Appeals reversed. The court agreed with the trial court that the investigative stop and protective patdown search of respondent were lawful under *Terry* because the officers had a reasonable belief based on specific and articulable facts that respondent was engaged in criminal behavior and that he might be armed and dangerous. The court concluded, however, that the officers had overstepped the bounds allowed by *Terry* in seizing the cocaine. In doing so, the Court of Appeals "decline[d] to adopt the plain feel exception" to the warrant requirement. 469 N.W. 2d 462, 466 (1991).

The Minnesota Supreme Court affirmed. Like the Court of Appeals, the State Supreme Court held that both the stop and the frisk of respondent were valid under *Terry,* but found the seizure of the cocaine to be unconstitutional. The court expressly refused "to extend the plain view doctrine to the sense of touch" on the grounds that "the sense of touch is inherently less immediate and less reliable than the sense of sight" and that "the sense of touch is far more intrusive into the personal privacy that is at the core of the [F]ourth [A]mendment." 481 N.W. 2d 840, 846 (1992). The court thus appeared to adopt a categorical rule barring the seizure of any contraband detected by an officer through the sense of touch during a patdown search for weapons. The court further noted that "[e]ven if we recognized a 'plain feel' exception, the search in this case would not qualify" because "[t]he pat search of the defendant went far beyond what is permissible under *Terry.*" *Id.,* at 843, 844, n. 1. As the State Supreme Court read the record, the officer conducting the search ascertained that the lump in respondent's jacket was contraband only after probing and investigating what he certainly knew was not a weapon. See *id.,* at 844.

We granted certiorari, 506 U.S. 814 (1992), to resolve a conflict among the state and federal courts over whether contraband detected through the sense of touch during a patdown search may be admitted into evidence. We now affirm.

II.

A.

The Fourth Amendment, made applicable to the States by way of the Fourteenth Amendment, *Mapp v. Ohio,* 367 U.S. 643 (1961), guarantees "[t]he right of the people to be secure in their persons, houses, papers, and effects, against unreasonable searches and seizures." Time and again, this Court has observed that searches and seizures "'conducted outside the judicial process, without prior approval by judge or magistrate, are *per se* unreasonable under the Fourth Amendment—subject only to a few specifically established and well delineated exceptions.' " *Thompson v. Louisiana,* 469 U.S. 17, 19–20 (1984) *(per curiam)* (quoting *Katz v. United States,* 389 U.S. 347, 357 (1967) (footnotes omitted)); *Mincey v. Arizona,* 437 U.S. 385, 390 (1978); see also *United States v. Place,* 462 U.S. 696, 701 (1983). One such exception was recognized in *Terry v. Ohio,* 392 U.S. 1 (1968), which held that "where a police officer observes unusual conduct which leads him reasonably to conclude in light of his experience that criminal activity may be afoot . . . ," the officer may briefly stop the suspicious person and make "reasonable inquiries" aimed at confirming or dispelling his suspicions. *Id.,* at 30; see also *Adams v. Williams,* 407 U.S. 143, 145–146 (1972).

    Terry further held that "[w]hen an officer is justified in believing that the individual whose suspicious behavior he is investigating at close range is armed and presently dangerous to the officer or to others," the officer may conduct a patdown search "to determine whether the person is in fact carrying a weapon." 392 U.S., at 24. "The purpose of this limited search is not to discover evidence of crime, but to allow the officer to pursue his investigation without fear of violence. . . ." *Adams, supra,* at 146. Rather, a protective search—permitted without a warrant and on the basis of reasonable suspicion less than probable cause—must be strictly "limited to that which is necessary for the discovery of weapons which might be used to harm the officer or others nearby." *Terry, supra,* at 26; see also *Michigan v. Long,* 463 U.S. 1032, 1049, and 1052, n. 16 (1983); *Ybarra v. Illinois,* 444 U.S. 85, 93–94 (1979). If the protective search goes beyond what is necessary to determine if the suspect is armed, it is no longer valid under *Terry* and its fruits will be suppressed. *Sibron v. New York,* 392 U.S. 40, 65–66 (1968).

    These principles were settled 25 years ago when, on the same day, the Court announced its decisions in *Terry* and *Sibron.* The question presented today is whether police officers may seize nonthreatening contraband detected during a protective patdown search of the sort permitted by *Terry.* We think the answer is clearly that they may, so long as the officers' search stays within the bounds marked by *Terry.*

B.

We have already held that police officers, at least under certain circumstances, may seize contraband detected during the lawful execution of a *Terry* search. In *Michigan v. Long, supra,* for example, police approached a man who had driven his car into a ditch and who appeared to be under the influence of some intoxicant. As the man moved to reenter the car from the roadside, police spotted a knife on the floorboard. The officers stopped the man, subjected him to a patdown search, and then inspected the interior of the vehicle for other weapons. During the search of the passenger compartment, the police discovered an open pouch containing marijuana and seized it. This Court upheld the validity of the search and seizure under *Terry.* The Court held first that, in the context of a roadside encounter, where police have reasonable suspicion based on specific and articulable facts to believe that a driver may be armed and dangerous, they may conduct a protective search for weapons not only of the driver's person but also of the passenger compartment of the automobile. 463 U.S., at 1049. Of course, the protective search of the vehicle, being justified solely by the danger that weapons stored there could be used against the officers or bystanders, must be "limited to those areas in which a weapon may be placed or hidden." *Ibid.* The Court then held: "If, while conducting a legitimate *Terry* search of the interior of the automobile, the officer should, as here, discover contraband other than weapons, he clearly cannot be required to ignore the contraband, and the Fourth Amendment does not require its suppression in such circumstances." *Id.,* at 1050; accord, *Sibron,* 392 U.S., at 69–70 (WHITE, J., concurring); *id.,* at 79 (Harlan, J., concurring in result).

The Court in *Long* justified this latter holding by reference to our cases under the "plain-view" doctrine. See *Long, supra,* at 1050; see also *United States v. Hensley,* 469 U.S. 221, 235 (1985) (upholding plain-view seizure in context of *Terry* stop). Under that doctrine, if police are lawfully in a position from which they view an object, if its incriminating character is immediately apparent, and if the officers have a lawful right of access to the object, they may seize it without a warrant. See *Horton v. California,* 496 U.S. 128, 136–137 (1990); *Texas v. Brown,* 460 U.S. 730, 739 (1983) (plurality opinion). If, however, the police lack probable cause to believe that an object in plain view is contraband without conducting some further search of the object—*i.e.,* if "its incriminating character [is not] 'immediately apparent,' " *Horton, supra,* at 136—the plain-view doctrine cannot justify its seizure. *Arizona v. Hicks,* 480 U.S. 321 (1987).

We think that this doctrine has an obvious application by analogy to cases in which an officer discovers contraband through the sense of touch during an otherwise lawful search. The rationale of the plain-view doctrine is that if contraband is left in open view and is observed by a police officer from a lawful vantage point, there has been no invasion of a legitimate expectation of privacy and thus no "search" within the meaning of the Fourth Amendment—or at least no search independent of the initial intrusion that gave the officers their vantage point. See *Illinois v. Andreas,* 463 U.S. 765, 771 (1983); *Texas v. Brown, supra,* at 740. The warrantless seizure of contraband that presents itself in this manner is deemed justified by the realization that resort to a neutral magistrate under such circumstances would often be impracticable and would do little to promote the objectives of the Fourth Amendment. See *Hicks, supra,* at 326–327; *Coolidge v. New Hampshire,* 403 U.S. 443, 467–468, 469–470 (1971) (opinion of Stewart, J.). The same can be said of tactile discoveries of contraband. If a police officer lawfully pats down a suspect's outer clothing and feels an object whose contour or mass makes its identity immediately apparent, there has been no invasion of the suspect's privacy beyond that already authorized by the officer's search for weapons; if the object is contraband, its warrantless seizure would be justified by the same practical considerations that inhere in the plain-view context.

The Minnesota Supreme Court rejected an analogy to the plain-view doctrine on two grounds: first, its belief that "the sense of touch is inherently less immediate and less reliable than the sense of sight," and second, that "the sense of touch is far more intrusive into the personal privacy that is at the core of the [F]ourth [A]mendment." 481 N.W. 2d, at 845. We have a somewhat different view. First, *Terry* itself demonstrates that the sense of touch is capable of revealing the nature of an object with sufficient reliability to support a seizure. The very premise of *Terry,* after all, is that officers will be able to detect the presence of weapons through the sense of touch and *Terry* upheld precisely such a seizure. Even if it were true that the sense of touch is generally less reliable than the sense of sight, that only suggests that officers will less often be able to justify seizures of unseen contraband. Regardless of whether the officer detects the contraband by sight or by touch, however, the Fourth Amendment's requirement that the officer have probable cause to believe that the item is contraband before seizing it ensures against excessively speculative seizures. The court's second concern—that touch is more intrusive into privacy than is sight—is inapposite in light of the fact that the intrusion the court fears has already been authorized by the lawful search for weapons. The seizure of an item whose identity is already known occasions no further invasion of privacy. See *Soldal v. Cook County,* 506 U.S. 56, 66 (1992); *Horton, supra,* at 141; *United States v. Jacobsen,* 466 U.S. 109, 120 (1984). Accordingly, the suspect's privacy interests are not advanced by a categorical rule barring the seizure of contraband plainly detected through the sense of touch.

III.

It remains to apply these principles to the facts of this case. Respondent has not challenged the finding made by the trial court and affirmed by both the Court of Appeals and the State Supreme Court that the police were justified under *Terry* in stopping him and frisking him for weapons. Thus, the dispositive question before this Court is whether the officer who conducted the search was acting within the lawful bounds marked by *Terry* at the time he gained probable cause to believe that the lump in respondent's jacket was contraband. The State District Court did not make precise findings on this point, instead finding simply that the officer, after feeling "a small, hard object wrapped in plastic" in respondent's pocket, "formed the opinion that the object . . . was crack . . . cocaine." App. to Pet. for Cert. C-2. The District Court also noted that the officer made "no claim that he suspected this object to be a weapon," *id.,* at C-5, a finding affirmed on appeal, see 469 N.W. 2d, at 464 (the officer "never thought the lump was a weapon"). The Minnesota Supreme Court, after "a close examination of the record," held that the officer's own testimony "belies any notion that he 'immediately' " recognized the lump as crack cocaine. See 481 N.W. 2d, at 844. Rather, the court concluded, the officer determined that the lump was contraband only after "squeezing, sliding and otherwise manipulating the contents of the defendant's pocket"—a pocket which the officer already knew contained no weapon. *Ibid.*

Under the State Supreme Court's interpretation of the record before it, it is clear that the court was correct in holding that the police officer in this case overstepped the bounds of the "strictly circumscribed" search for weapons allowed under *Terry.* See *Terry,* 392 U.S., at 26. Where, as here, "an officer who is executing a valid search for one item seizes a different item," this Court rightly "has been sensitive to the danger . . . that officers will enlarge a specific authorization, furnished by a warrant or an exigency, into the equivalent of a general warrant to rummage and seize at will." *Texas v. Brown,* 460 U.S., at 748 (STEVENS, J., concurring in judgment). Here, the officer's continued exploration of respondent's pocket after having concluded that it contained no weapon was unrelated to "[t]he sole justification of the search [under *Terry*:] . . . the protection of the police officer and others nearby" 392 U.S., at 29. It therefore amounted to the sort of evidentiary search that *Terry* expressly refused to authorize, see *id.*, at 26, and that we have condemned in subsequent cases. See *Michigan v. Long*, 463 U.S., at 1049, n. 14; *Sibron*, 392 U.S., at 65–66.

Once again, the analogy to the plain-view doctrine is apt. In *Arizona v. Hicks*, 480 U.S. 321 (1987), this Court held invalid the seizure of stolen stereo equipment found by police while executing a valid search for other evidence. Although the police were lawfully on the premises, they obtained probable cause to believe that the stereo equipment was contraband only after moving the equipment to permit officers to read its serial numbers. The subsequent seizure of the equipment could not be justified by the plain-view doctrine, this Court explained, because the incriminating character of the stereo equipment was not immediately apparent; rather, probable cause to believe that the equipment was stolen arose only as a result of a further search—the moving of the equipment—that was not authorized by a search warrant or by any exception to the warrant requirement. The facts of this case are very similar. Although the officer was lawfully in a position to feel the lump in respondent's pocket, because *Terry* entitled him to place his hands upon respondent's jacket, the court below determined that the incriminating character of the object was not immediately apparent to him. Rather, the officer determined that the item was contraband only after conducting a further search, one not authorized by *Terry* or by any other exception to the warrant requirement. Because this further search of respondent's pocket was constitutionally invalid, the seizure of the cocaine that followed is likewise unconstitutional. *Horton*, 496 U.S., at 140.

IV.

For these reasons, the judgment of the Minnesota Supreme Court is

Affirmed.

JUSTICE SCALIA, concurring.

I take it to be a fundamental principle of constitutional adjudication that the terms in the Constitution must be given the meaning ascribed to them at the time of their ratification. Thus, when the Fourth Amendment provides that "[t]he right of the people to be secure in their persons, houses, papers, and effects, against *unreasonable searches and seizures,* shall not be violated" [emphasis added], it "is to be construed in the light of what was deemed an unreasonable search and seizure when it was adopted," *Carroll v. United States*, 267 U.S. 132, 149 (1925); see also *California v. Acevedo*, 500 U.S. 565, 583–584 (1991) (SCALIA, J., concurring in judgment). The purpose of the provision, in other words, is to preserve that degree of respect for the privacy of persons and the inviolability of their property that existed when the provision was adopted—even if a later, less virtuous age should become accustomed to considering all sorts of intrusion "reasonable."

My problem with the present case is that I am not entirely sure that the physical search—the "frisk"—that produced the evidence at issue here complied with that constitutional standard. The decision of ours that gave approval to such searches, *Terry v. Ohio,* 392 U.S. 1 (1968), made no serious attempt to determine compliance with traditional standards, but rather, according to the style of this Court at the time, simply adjudged that such a search was "reasonable" by current estimations. *Id.,* at 22–27.

There is good evidence, I think, that the "stop" portion of the *Terry* "stop-and-frisk" holding accords with the common law—that it had long been considered reasonable to detain suspicious persons for the purpose of demanding that they give an account of themselves. This is suggested, in particular, by the so-called night-walker statutes, and their common-law antecedents. See Statute of Winchester, 13 Edw. I, Stat. 2, ch. 4 (1285); Statute of 5 Edw. III, ch. 14 (1331); 2 W. Hawkins, Pleas of the Crown, ch. 13, § 6, p. 129 (8th ed. 1824) ("It is holden that this statute was made in affirmance of the common law, and that every private person may by the common law arrest any suspicious night-walker, and detain him till he give a good account of himself"); 1 E. East, Pleas of the Crown, ch. 5, § 70, p. 303 (1803) ("It is said . . . that every private person may by the common law arrest any suspicious night-walker, and detain him till he give a good account of himself"); see also M. Dalton, The Country Justice, ch. 104, pp. 352–353 (1727); A. Costello, Our Police Protectors: History of the New York Police 25 (1885) (citing 1681 New York City regulation); 2 Perpetual Laws of Massachusetts 1788–1798, ch. 82, § 2, p. 410 (1797 Massachusetts statute).

I am unaware, however, of any precedent for a physical search of a person thus temporarily detained for questioning. Sometimes, of course, the temporary detention of a suspicious character would be elevated to a full custodial arrest on probable cause —as, for instance, when a suspect was unable to provide a sufficient accounting of himself. At *that* point, it is clear that the common law would permit not just a protective "frisk," but a full physical search incident to the arrest. When, however, the detention did not rise to the level of a full-blown arrest (and was not supported by the degree of cause needful for that purpose), there appears to be no clear support at common law for physically searching the suspect. See Warner, The Uniform Arrest Act, 28 Va. L. Rev. 315, 324 (1942) ("At common law, if a watchman came upon a suspiciously acting nightwalker, he might arrest him and then search him for weapons, but he had no right to search before arrest"); Williams, Police Detention and Arrest Privileges— England, 51 J. Crim. L., C. & P.S. 413, 418 (1960) ("Where a suspected criminal is also suspected of being offensively armed, can the police search him for arms, by tapping his pockets, before making up their minds whether to arrest him? There is no English authority . . .").

I frankly doubt, moreover, whether the fiercely proud men who adopted our Fourth Amendment would have allowed themselves to be subjected, on mere *suspicion* of being armed and dangerous, to such indignity—which is described as follows in a police manual:

> "Check the subject's neck and collar. A check should be made under the subject's arm. Next a check should be made of the upper back. The lower back should also be checked.
>
> "A check should be made of the upper part of the man's chest and the lower region around the stomach. The belt, a favorite concealment spot, should

be checked. The inside thigh and crotch area also should be searched. The legs should be checked for possible weapons. The last items to be checked are the shoes and cuffs of the subject." J. Moynahan, Police Searching Procedures 7 (1963) [citations omitted].

On the other hand, even if a "frisk" prior to arrest would have been considered impermissible in 1791, perhaps it was considered permissible by 1868, when the Fourteenth Amendment (the basis for applying the Fourth Amendment to the States) was adopted. Or perhaps it is only since that time that concealed weapons capable of harming the interrogator quickly and from beyond arm's reach have become common —which might alter the judgment of what is "reasonable" under the original standard. But technological changes were no more discussed in *Terry* than was the original state of the law.

If I were of the view that *Terry* was (insofar as the power to "frisk" is concerned) incorrectly decided, I might—even if I felt bound to adhere to that case—vote to exclude the evidence incidentally discovered, on the theory that half a constitutional guarantee is better than none. I might also vote to exclude it if I agreed with the original-meaning-is-irrelevant, good-policy-is-constitutional-law school of jurisprudence that the *Terry* opinion represents. As a policy matter, it may be desirable to *permit* "frisks" for weapons, but not to *encourage* "frisks" for drugs by admitting evidence other than weapons.

I adhere to original meaning, however. And though I do not favor the mode of analysis in *Terry,* I cannot say that its result was wrong. Constitutionality of the "frisk" in the present case was neither challenged nor argued. Assuming, therefore, that the search was lawful, I agree with the Court's premise that any evidence incidentally discovered in the course of it would be admissible, and join the Court's opinion in its entirety.

CHIEF JUSTICE REHNQUIST, with whom JUSTICE BLACKMUN and JUSTICE THOMAS join, concurring in part and dissenting in part.

I join Parts I and II of the Court's opinion. Unlike the Court, however, I would vacate the judgment of the Supreme Court of Minnesota and remand the case to that court for further proceedings.

The Court, correctly in my view, states that "the dispositive question before this Court is whether the officer who conducted the search was acting within the lawful bounds marked by *Terry* [v. *Ohio*, 392 U.S. 1 (1968),] at the time he gained probable cause to believe that the lump in respondent's jacket was contraband." *Ante,* at 377. The Court then goes on to point out that the state trial court did not make precise findings on this point, but accepts the appellate findings made by the Supreme Court of Minnesota. I believe that these findings, like those of the trial court, are imprecise and not directed expressly to the question of the officer's probable cause to believe that the lump was contraband. Because the Supreme Court of Minnesota employed a Fourth Amendment analysis which differs significantly from that now adopted by this Court, I would vacate its judgment and remand the case for further proceedings there in the light of this Court's opinion.

Thirty Suggestions on How to Be an Effective Witness

Note: This appendix is based on the work of John Scott Blonien, senior assistant attorney general of the state of Washington, with additions and modifications by the author.

As a witness, you have an important job to do. In order for the court to make a correct and wise decision and for justice to be served, the evidence in a case must be presented by all the parties in a truthful manner. Otherwise, the administration of justice becomes tainted and flawed.

All witnesses are required to take an oath "to tell the truth, the whole truth and nothing but the truth." There are two ways, however, to tell the truth. One is ineffectively—in a halting, stumbling, hesitant manner—which makes the court and the jury doubt your testimony. The other is effectively—in a confident, straightforward, and candid manner—which makes you a more credible and useful witness.

Here is a list of thirty suggestions to help you become a more effective witness. Go over this list before testifying.

1. **Be prompt.** Never keep the court and the jury waiting.

2. **Dress properly and be neat.** Do not wear gaudy or "loud" clothing or dark glasses. If your work requires a uniform, ask your attorney whether wearing a uniform for the occasion is appropriate.

3. **When taking the oath, stand upright, pay attention, and say "I do" clearly.**

4. **Be serious.** Avoid laughing, giggling, or talking about the case in the hallway or restrooms of the courthouse.

5. **Be sincere and candid; do not bluff.** It is better to admit a mistake than to try to bluff your way through.

6. **Testify from memory, but do not try to memorize what you are going to say.** If you do that, your testimony will sound "pat" and "rehearsed" and will not be as believable. You are allowed to consult the notes you made concerning the event about which you are testifying. Ordinarily, however, these notes are also available to the opposing attorney and will probably be referred to during cross-examination. Remember your notes well.

7. **Prior to your testimony, try to picture the scene, the objects there, the distances, and what happened.** This will make your recollection more accurate. If the question is about distances or time, and your answer is only an estimate, be sure to say so.

8. **Speak clearly and loudly.** The person farthest away in the courtroom should be able hear you. Remember to glance at the judge and the jury and to talk to them honestly and openly, as you would to a friend or neighbor. Direct your answers mostly to the jury rather than to the opposing lawyer, your own lawyer, or the judge.

9. **Listen carefully to the questions asked.** Do not appear too eager to respond. Pause briefly before answering, and then give a well-considered answer.

10. **Never try to answer a question you do not understand.** If you do not understand a question, politely ask the person posing the question to repeat it.

11. **Explain your answer, if necessary.** Do not be afraid to ask the judge to allow you to explain your answer, particularly if the question cannot be answered truthfully with a simple "yes" or "no."

12. **Answer simply and directly, and answer only the question asked.** Do not volunteer information not actually sought by the questioner.

13. **Keep your answer short and to the point.** Avoid long narration.

14. **If you feel you did not answer the question correctly, make your correction immediately.** If your answer was not clear, clarify it.

15. **If you can, give categorical, definite answers.** Avoid saying, "I think," "I believe," or "In my opinion." If you do not know, say so. If asked about details that a person is not likely to remember, it is best simply to say, "I do not remember." Do not bluff, guess, or speculate.

16. **Do not give conclusions or opinions, unless asked.** In a court of law, only expert witnesses are usually allowed to give conclusions or opinions. The court and jury are interested only in the facts, not in an opinion or conclusion. For example, "X's death was caused by stab wounds" is stating an opinion. On the other hand, saying that you saw Y stab X is stating a fact, assuming that was what you saw happen.

17. **Avoid saying, "That is all of the conversation," or "Nothing else happened."** Instead say, "That is all I recall," or "That is all I remember happening." It is possible that after some thought you might remember something else.

18. **Be polite and courteous.** This suggestion applies even if the attorney questioning you behaves otherwise. Do not be cocky or antagonistic, or else you will lose credibility with the judge and jury.

19. **Remember that you are sworn to tell the truth; tell it.** Admit every material truth even if it is not to the advantage of your side. Do not stop to figure out whether your answer will help or hurt your cause. Just answer the questions truthfully and to the best of your recollection.

20. **Be aware that you are likely to be asked about earlier statements you made, if any, related to the case.** This would include any statements you

may have made in an affidavit, deposition, or earlier testimony. Listen carefully to what is being read or repeated, and give a truthful answer.

21. **Do not be afraid to admit that you made an earlier statement.** As much as possible, your answer should be consistent with your previous statement. However, if there are discrepancies between your earlier statement and your current testimony, admit them and, if you can, explain them.

22. **Try not to appear nervous.** Avoid mannerisms (such as touching your nose or eyeglasses, wiping your eyebrow, or covering your mouth), which convey the impression that you are scared or are not telling the truth.

23. **Never lose your temper or show irritation.** The opposing attorney may try to agitate or aggravate you on cross-examination, in hopes that you will lose your temper and say things that will hurt your cause. Keep your cool at all times.

24. **If you do not want to answer a question, do not ask the court whether you must answer it.** This might make the judge or jury think you have something to hide. If the court wants you to answer the question, do so.

25. **Do not look at the attorney for your side or at the judge for help.** If the question is improper, the attorney for your side will probably object to it or have your answer stricken from the record after it is given. Give the attorney for your side an opportunity to react to or object to the question asked. Pause before giving an answer.

26. **Do not argue with the opposing attorney.** It is the job of the lawyer for your side to do that.

27. **Do not nod your head for a "yes" or "no" answer.** Speak clearly, so that the court reporter or a recording device can hear or pick up your answer.

28. **Do not be intimidated by questions about whether you have conferred with your lawyer.** The opposing attorney might ask you the following question: "Have you talked to anybody about this case?" If you say, "No," the court will know that is probably not true, because good attorneys try to talk to a witness before he or she takes the stand. If you say, "Yes," the defense lawyer might imply that you have been told what to say. Be honest and say that you have talked with whomever you have talked with—an attorney, the victim, other witnesses—and that you were simply told them what the facts were. Suppose the opposing lawyer asks, in a loud and mocking voice, "Do you mean to tell this honorable court that you discussed your testimony in this case with the district attorney?" If you did, simply answer, "Yes." Remember, there is nothing wrong with your discussing the facts of the case with your attorney; that is expected. What is wrong is your lawyer telling you what to say.

29. **Avoid any discussion of any kind with a juror or potential juror in or out of the courthouse.** Do not discuss the case with anyone at the courthouse other than your attorney, particularly if somebody is listening.

30. **When you leave the witness stand after testifying, act confident.** Do not smile, appear downcast, or exude an air of triumph.

D. The Constitution of the United States

We the People of the United States, in Order to form a more perfect Union, establish Justice, insure domestic Tranquility, provide for the common defence, promote the general Welfare, and secure the Blessings of Liberty to ourselves and our Posterity, do ordain and establish this Constitution for the United States of America.

Article I

Section 1. All legislative Powers herein granted shall be vested in a Congress of the United States, which shall consist of a Senate and House of Representatives.

Section 2. The House of Representatives shall be composed of Members chosen every second Year by the People of the several States, and the Electors in each State shall have the Qualifications requisite for Electors of the most numerous Branch of the State Legislature.

No Person shall be a Representative who shall not have attained to the Age of twenty five Years, and been seven Years a Citizen of the United States, and who shall not, when elected, be an Inhabitant of that State in which he shall be chosen.

Representatives and direct Taxes shall be apportioned among the several States which may be included within this Union, according to their respective Numbers, which shall be determined by adding to the whole Number of free Persons, including those bound to Service for a Term of Years, and excluding Indians not taxed, three fifths of all other Persons. The actual Enumeration shall be made within three Years after the first Meeting of the Congress of the United States, and within every subsequent Term of ten Years, in such Manner as they shall by Law direct. The Number of Representatives shall not exceed one for every thirty Thousand, but each State shall have at Least one Representative; and until such enumeration shall be made, the State of New Hampshire shall be entitled to chuse three, Massachusetts eight, Rhode-Island and Providence Plantations one, Connecticut five, New-York six, New Jersey four, Pennsylvania eight, Delaware one, Maryland six, Virginia ten, North Carolina five, South Carolina five, and Georgia three.

When vacancies happen in the Representation from any State, the Executive Authority thereof shall issue Writs of Election to fill such Vacancies.

The House of Representatives shall chuse their Speaker and other Officers; and shall have the sole Power of Impeachment.

Section 3. The Senate of the United States shall be composed of two Senators from each State, chosen by the Legislature thereof, for six Years; and each Senator shall have one Vote.

Immediately after they shall be assembled in Consequence of the first Election, they shall be divided as equally as may be into three Classes. The Seats of the Senators of the first Class shall be vacated at the Expiration of the second Year, of the second Class at the Expiration of the fourth Year, and of the third Class at the Expiration of the sixth Year, so that one third may be chosen every second Year; and if Vacancies happen by Resignation, or otherwise, during the Recess of the Legislature of any State, the Executive thereof may make temporary Appointments until the next Meeting of the Legislature, which shall then fill such Vacancies.

No person shall be a Senator who shall not have attained to the Age of thirty Years, and been nine Years a Citizen of the United States, and who shall not, when elected, be an Inhabitant of that State for which he shall be chosen.

The Vice President of the United States shall be President of the Senate, but shall have no Vote, unless they be equally divided.

The Senate shall chuse their other Officers, and also a President pro tempore, in the Absence of the Vice President, or when he shall exercise the Office of President of the United States.

The Senate shall have the sole Power to try all Impeachments. When sitting for that Purpose, they shall be on Oath or Affirmation. When the President of the United States is tried, the Chief Justice shall preside: And no Person shall be convicted without the Concurrence of two thirds of the Members present. Judgment in Cases of Impeachment shall not extend further than to removal from Office, and disqualification to hold and enjoy any Office of honor, Trust or Profit under the United States: but the Party convicted shall nevertheless be liable and subject to Indictment, Trial, Judgment and Punishment, according to law.

Section 4. The Times, Places and Manner of holding Elections for Senators and Representatives, shall be prescribed in each State by the Legislature thereof; but the Congress may at any time by Law make or alter such Regulations, except as to the Places of chusing Senators.

The Congress shall assemble at least once in every Year, and such Meeting shall be on the first Monday in December, unless they shall by Law appoint a different Day.

Section 5. Each House shall be the Judge of the Elections, Returns and Qualifications of its own Members, and a Majority of each shall constitute a Quorum to do Business; but a smaller Number may adjourn from day to day, and may be authorized to compel the Attendance of absent Members, in such Manner, and under such Penalties as each House may provide.

Each House may determine the Rules of its Proceedings, punish its Members for disor-

derly Behaviour, and, with the Concurrence of two thirds, expel a Member.

Each House shall keep a journal of its Proceedings, and from time to time publish the same, excepting such Parts as may in their Judgment require Secrecy; and the Yeas and Nays of the Members of either House on any question shall, at the Desire of one fifth of those Present, be entered on the Journal.

Neither House, during the Session of Congress, shall, without the Consent of the other, adjourn for more than three days, nor to any other Place than that in which the two Houses shall be sitting.

Section 6. The Senators and Representatives shall receive a Compensation for their Services, to be ascertained by Law, and paid out of the Treasury of the United States. They shall in all Cases, except Treason, Felony and Breach of the Peace, be privileged from Arrest during their Attendance at the Session of their respective Houses, and in going to and returning from the same; and for any Speech or Debate in either House, they shall not be questioned in any other Place.

No Senator or Representative shall, during the Time for which he was elected, be appointed to any civil Office under the Authority of the United States, which shall have been created, or the Emoluments whereof shall have been encreased during such time; and no Person holding any Office under the United States, shall be a Member of either House during his Continuance in Office.

Section 7. All Bills for raising Revenue shall originate in the House of Representatives; but the Senate may propose or concur with Amendments as on other Bills.

Every Bill which shall have passed the House of Representatives and the Senate, shall, before it become a Law, be presented to the President of the United States; If he approve he shall sign it, but if not he shall return it, with his Objections to that House in which it shall have originated, who shall enter the Objections at large on their Journal, and proceed to reconsider it. If after such Reconsideration two thirds of that House shall agree to pass the Bill, it shall be sent, together with the Objections, to the other House, by which it shall likewise be reconsidered, and if approved by two thirds of that House, it shall become a Law. But in all such Cases the Votes of both Houses shall be determined by yeas and Nays, and the Names of the Persons voting for and against the Bill shall be entered on the Journal of each House respectively. If any Bill shall not be returned by the President within ten Days (Sundays excepted) after it shall have been presented to him, the Same shall be a Law, in like Manner as if he had signed it, unless the Congress by their Adjournment prevent its Return, in which Case it shall not be a Law.

Every Order, Resolution, or Vote to which the Concurrence of the Senate and House of Representatives may be necessary (except on a question of Adjournment) shall be presented to the President of the United States; and before the Same shall take Effect, shall be approved by him, or being disapproved by him, shall be repassed by two thirds of the Senate and House of Representatives, according to the Rules and Limitations prescribed in the Case of a Bill.

Section 8. The Congress shall have Power To lay and collect Taxes, Duties, Imposts and Excises, to pay the Debts and provide for the common Defence and general Welfare of the United States; but all Duties, Imposts and Excises shall be uniform throughout the United States.

To borrow Money on the Credit of the United States;

To regulate Commerce with foreign Nations, and among the several States, and with the Indian Tribes;

To establish an uniform Rule of Naturalization, and uniform Laws on the subject of Bankruptcies throughout the United States;

To coin Money, regulate the Value thereof, and of foreign Coin, and fix the Standard of Weights and Measures;

To provide for the Punishment of counterfeiting the Securities and current Coin of the United States;

To establish Post Offices and post Roads;

To promote the Progress of Science and useful Arts, by securing for limited Times to Authors and Inventors the exclusive Right to their respective Writings and Discoveries;

To constitute Tribunals inferior to the supreme Court;

To define and punish Piracies and Felonies committed on the high Seas, and Offences against the Law of Nations;

To declare War, grant letters of Marque and Reprisal, and make rules concerning Captures on Land and Water;

To raise and support Armies, but no Appropriation of Money to that Use shall be for a longer Term than two Years;

To provide and maintain a Navy;

To make rules for the Government and Regulation of the land and naval Forces;

To provide for calling forth the Militia to execute the Laws of the Union, suppress Insurrections and repel Invasions;

To provide for organizing, arming, and disciplining, the Militia, and for governing such Part of them as may be employed in the Service of the United States, reserving to the States respectively, the Appointment of the Officers, and the Authority of training the Militia according to the discipline prescribed by Congress;

To exercise exclusive Legislation in all Cases whatsoever, over such District (not exceeding ten Miles square) as may, by Cession of particular States, and the Acceptance of Congress, become the Seat of the Government of the United States, and to exercise like Authority over all Places purchased by the Consent of the Legislature of the State in which the Same shall be, for the Erection of Forts, Magazines, Arsenals, dock-Yards, and other needful Buildings;—And

To make all Laws which shall be necessary and proper for carrying into Execution the foregoing Powers, and all other Powers vested by this Constitution in the Government of the United States, or in any Department or Officer thereof.

Section 9. The Migration or Importation of such Persons as any of the States now existing shall think proper to admit, shall not be prohibited by the Congress prior to the Year one thousand eight hundred and eight, but a Tax or duty may be imposed on such Importation, not exceeding ten dollars for each Person.

The Privilege of the Writ of Habeas Corpus shall not be suspended, unless when in Cases of Rebellion or Invasion the public Safety may require it.

No Bill of Attainder or ex post facto Law shall be passed.

No Capitation, or other direct, Tax shall be laid, unless in Proportion to the Census or Enumeration herein before directed to be taken.

No Tax or Duty shall be laid on Articles exported from any State.

No Preference shall be given by any Regulation of Commerce or Revenue to the Ports of one State over those of another; nor shall Vessels bound to, or from, one State, be obliged to enter, clear, or pay Duties in another.

No money shall be drawn from the Treasury, but in Consequence of Appropriations made by Law; and a regular Statement and Account of the Receipts and Expenditures of all public Money shall be published from time to time.

No Title of Nobility shall be granted by the United States: And no Person holding any Office of Profit or Trust under them, shall, without the Consent of the Congress, accept of any present, Emolument, Office, or Title, of any kind whatever, from any King, Prince, or foreign State.

Section 10. No State shall enter into any Treaty, Alliance, or Confederation; grant Letters of Marque and Reprisal; coin Money; emit Bills of Credit; make any Thing but gold and silver Coin a Tender in Payment of Debts; pass any Bill of Attainder, ex post facto Law, or Law impairing the Obligation of Contracts, or grant any Title of Nobility.

No State shall, without the Consent of the Congress, lay any Imposts or Duties on Imports or Exports, except what may be absolutely necessary for executing its inspection Laws; and the net Produce of all Duties and Imposts, laid by any State on Imports or Exports, shall be for the Use of the Treasury of the United States; and all such Laws shall be subject to the Revision and Controul of the Congress.

No State shall, without the Consent of Congress, lay any Duty of Tonnage, keep Troops, or Ships of War in time of Peace, enter into any Agreement or Compact with another State, or with a foreign Power, or engage in War, unless actually invaded, or in such imminent Danger as will not admit of delay.

Article II

Section 1. The executive Power shall be vested in a President of the United States of America. He shall hold his Office during the Term of four Years, and, together with the Vice President, chosen for the same Term, be elected, as follows

Each State shall appoint, in such Manner as the Legislature thereof may direct, a Number of Electors, equal to the whole Number of Senators and Representatives to which the State may be entitled in the Congress: but no Senator or Representative, or Person holding an Office of Trust or Profit under the United States, shall be appointed an Elector.

The Electors shall meet in their respective States, and vote by Ballot for two Persons, of whom one at least shall not be an Inhabitant of the same State with themselves. And they shall make a List of all the Persons voted for, and of the Number of Votes for each; which List they shall sign and certify, and transmit sealed to the Seat of the Government of the United States, directed to the President of the Senate. The President of the Senate shall, in the Presence of the Senate and House of Representatives, open all the Certificates, and the Votes shall then be counted. The Person having the greatest Number of Votes shall be the President, if such Number be a Majority of the whole Number of Electors appointed; and if there be more than one who have such Majority, and have an equal

Number of Votes, then the House of Representatives shall immediately chuse by Ballot one of them for President; and if no Person have a Majority, then from the five highest on the List the said House shall in like Manner chuse the President. But in chusing the President, the Votes shall be taken by States, the Representation from each State having one Vote; A quorum for this Purpose shall consist of a Member or Members from two thirds of the States, and a Majority of all the States shall be necessary to a Choice. In every Case, after the Choice of the President, the Person having the greatest Number of Votes of the Electors shall be the Vice President. But if there should remain two or more who have equal Votes, the Senate shall chuse from them by Ballot the Vice President.

The Congress may determine the Time of chusing the Electors, and the Day on which they shall give their Votes; which Day shall be the same throughout the United States.

No Person except a natural born Citizen, or a Citizen of the United States, at the time of the Adoption of this Constitution, shall be eligible to the Office of President; neither shall any Person be eligible to that Office who shall not have attained to the Age of thirty five Years, and been fourteen Years a Resident within the United States.

In Case of the Removal of the President from Office, or of his Death, Resignation, or Inability to discharge the Powers and Duties of the said Office, the Same shall devolve on the Vice President, and the Congress may by Law provide for the Case of Removal, Death, Resignation or Inability, both of the President and Vice President, declaring what Officer shall then act as President, and such Officer shall act accordingly, until the Disability be removed, or a President shall be elected.

The President shall, at stated Times, receive for his Services, a Compensation, which shall neither be increased nor diminished during the Period for which he shall have been elected, and he shall not receive within that Period any other Emolument from the United States, or any of them.

Before he enter on the Execution of his Office, he shall take the following Oath or Affirmation:—"I do solemnly swear (or affirm) that I will faithfully execute the Office of President of the United States, and will to the best of my Ability, preserve, protect and defend the Constitution of the United States."

Section 2. The President shall be Commander in Chief of the Army and Navy of the United States, and of the Militia of the several States, when called into the actual Service of the United States; he may require the Opinion, in writing, of the principal Officer in each of the executive Departments, upon any Subject relating to the Duties of their respective Offices, and he shall have Power to grant Reprieves and Pardons for Offenses against the United States, except in Cases of Impeachment.

He shall have Power, by and with the Advice and Consent of the Senate, to make Treaties, provided two thirds of the Senators present concur; and he shall nominate, and by and with the Advice and Consent of the Senate, shall appoint Ambassadors, other public Ministers and Consuls, Judges of the supreme Court, and all other Officers of the United States, whose Appointments are not herein otherwise provided for, and which shall be established by Law: but the Congress may by Law vest the Appointment of such inferior Officers, as they think proper, in the President alone, in the Courts of Law, or in the Heads of Departments.

The President shall have Power to fill up all Vacancies that may happen during the Recess of the Senate, by granting Commissions which shall expire at the End of their next Session.

Section 3. He shall from time to time give to the Congress Information of the State of the Union, and recommend to their Consideration such Measures as he shall judge necessary and expedient; he may, on extraordinary Occasions, convene both Houses, or either of them, and in Case of Disagreement between them, with Respect to the Time of Adjournment, he may adjourn them to such Time as he shall think proper; he shall receive Ambassadors and other public Ministers; he shall take Care that the Laws be faithfully executed, and shall Commission all the Officers of the United States.

Section 4. The President, Vice President and all civil Officers of the United States, shall be removed from Office on Impeachment for, and Conviction of, Treason, Bribery, or other high Crimes and Misdemeanors.

Article III

Section 1. The judicial Power of the United States shall be vested in one supreme Court, and in such inferior Courts as the Congress may from time to time ordain and establish. The Judges, both of the supreme and inferior Courts, shall hold their Offices during good Behaviour, and shall, at stated Times, receive for their Services a Compensation, which shall not be diminished during their Continuance in Office.

Section 2. The judicial Power shall extend to all Cases, in Law and Equity, arising under this Constitution, the Laws of the United States, and Treaties made, or which shall be made, under their Authority;—to all Cases affecting Ambassadors, other public Ministers and Consuls;—to all Cases of admiralty and maritime Jurisdiction;—to Controversies to which the United States shall be a Party;—to Controversies between two or more States;—between a State and Citizens of another State;—between Citizens of different States;—between Citizens of the same State claiming Lands under Grants of different States, and between a State, or the Citizens thereof, and foreign States, Citizens or Subjects.

In all Cases affecting Ambassadors, other public Ministers and Consuls, and those in which a State shall be Party, the supreme Court shall have original Jurisdiction. In all the other Cases before mentioned, the supreme Court shall have appellate Jurisdiction, both as to Law and Fact, with such Exceptions, and under such Regulations as the Congress shall make.

The Trial of all Crimes, except in Cases of Impeachment, shall be by Jury; and such Trial shall be held in the State where the said Crimes shall have been committed; but when not committed within any State, the Trial shall be at such Place or Places as the Congress may by Law have directed.

Section 3. Treason against the United States shall consist only in levying War against them, or in adhering to their Enemies, giving them Aid and Comfort. No Person shall be convicted of Treason unless on the Testimony of two Witnesses to the same overt Act, or on Confession in open Court. The Congress shall have Power to declare the Punishment of Treason, but no Attainder of Treason shall work Corruption of Blood, or Forfeiture except during the Life of the Person attainted.

Article IV

Section 1. Full Faith and Credit shall be given in each State to the public Acts, Records, and judicial Proceedings of every other State. And the Congress may by general Laws prescribe the Manner in which such Acts, Records and Proceedings shall be proved, and the Effect thereof.

Section 2. The Citizens of each State shall be entitled to all Privileges and Immunities of Citizens in the several States.

A Person charged in any State with Treason, Felony, or other Crime, who shall flee from Justice, and be found in another State, shall on Demand of the executive Authority of the State from which he fled, be delivered up, to be removed to the State having Jurisdiction of the Crime.

No person held to Service or Labour in one State, under the Laws thereof, escaping into another, shall, in Consequence of any Law or Regulation therein, be discharged from such Service or Labour, but shall be delivered up on Claim of the Party to whom such Service or Labour may be due.

Section 3. New States may be admitted by the Congress into this Union; but no new State shall be formed or erected within the Jurisdiction of any other State; nor any State be formed by the Junction of two or more States, or Parts of States, without the Consent of the Legislatures of the States concerned as well as of the Congress.

The Congress shall have Power to dispose of and make all needful Rules and Regulations respecting the Territory or other Property belonging to the United States; and nothing in this Constitution shall be so construed as to Prejudice any Claims of the United States, or of any particular State.

Section 4. The United States shall guarantee to every State in this Union a Republican Form of Government, and shall protect each of them against Invasion; and on Application of the Legislature, or of the Executive (when the Legislature cannot be convened) against domestic Violence.

Article V

The Congress, whenever two thirds of both Houses shall deem it necessary, shall propose Amendments to this Constitution, or, on the Application of the Legislatures of two thirds of the several States, shall call a Convention for proposing Amendments, which, in either Case, shall be valid to all Intents and Purposes, as Part of this Constitution, when ratified by the Legislatures of three fourths of the several States, or by Conventions in three fourths thereof, as the one or the other Mode of Ratification may be proposed by the Congress; Provided that no Amendment which may be made prior to the Year One thousand eight hundred and eight shall in any Manner affect the first and fourth Clauses in the Ninth Section of the first Article; and that no State, without its Consent, shall be deprived of its equal Suffrage in the Senate.

Article VI

All Debts contracted and Engagements entered into, before the Adoption of this Constitution, shall be as valid against the United States under this Constitution, as under the Confederation.

This Constitution, and the Laws of the United States which shall be made in Pursuance thereof; and all Treaties made, or which shall be made, under the Authority of the United States, shall be the supreme Law of the Land; and the Judges in every State shall be bound thereby, any Thing in the Constitution or Laws of any State to the Contrary notwithstanding.

The Senators and Representatives before mentioned, and the Members of the several State Legislatures, and all executive and judicial Officers, both of the United States and of the several States, shall be bound by Oath or Affirmation, to support this Constitution; but no religious Test shall ever be required as a Qualification to any Office or public Trust under the United States.

Article VII

The Ratification of the Conventions of nine States, shall be sufficient for the Establishment of this Constitution between the States so ratifying the Same.

Done in Convention by the Unanimous Consent of the States present the Seventeenth Day of September in the Year of our Lord one thousand seven hundred and Eighty seven and of the Independence of the United States of America the Twelfth *In witness whereof We have hereunto subscribed our Names,*

Amendments to the Constitution

(The first ten Amendments were ratified December 15, 1791, and form what is known as the "Bill of Rights.")

Amendment 1

Congress shall make no law respecting an establishment of religion, or prohibiting the free exercise thereof; or abridging the freedom of speech, or of the press; or the right of the people peaceably to assemble, and to petition the Government for a redress of grievances.

Amendment 2

A well-regulated Militia, being necessary to the security of a free State, the right of the people to keep and bear Arms, shall not be infringed.

Amendment 3

No Soldier shall, in time of peace be quartered in any house, without the consent of the Owner, nor in time of war, but in a manner to be prescribed by law.

Amendment 4

The right of the people to be secure in their persons, houses, papers, and effects, against unreasonable searches and seizures, shall not be violated, and no Warrants shall issue, but upon probable cause, supported by Oath or affirmation, and particularly describing the place to be searched, and the persons or things to be seized.

Amendment 5

No person shall be held to answer for a capital, or otherwise infamous crime, unless on a presentment or indictment of a Grand Jury, except in cases arising in the land or naval forces, or in the Militia, when in actual service in time of War or public danger; nor shall any person be subject for the same offence to be twice put in jeopardy of life or limb; nor shall be compelled in any criminal case to be a witness against himself, nor be deprived of life, liberty, or property, without due process of law; nor shall private property be taken for public use without just compensation.

Amendment 6

In all criminal prosecutions, the accused shall enjoy the right to a speedy and public trial, by an impartial jury of the State and district wherein the crime shall have been committed, which district shall have been previously ascertained by law, and to be informed of the nature and cause of the accusation; to be confronted with the witnesses against him; to have compulsory process for obtaining witnesses in his favor, and to have the Assistance of Counsel for his defence.

Amendment 7

In Suits at common law, where the value in controversy shall exceed twenty dollars, the right of trial by jury shall be preserved, and no fact tried by a jury, shall be otherwise re-examined in any Court of the United States, than according to the rules of the common law.

Amendment 8

Excessive bail shall not be required, nor excessive fines imposed, nor cruel and unusual punishments inflicted.

Amendment 9

The enumeration in the Constitution, of certain rights, shall not be construed to deny or disparage others retained by the people.

Amendment 10

The powers not delegated to the United States by the Constitution, nor prohibited by it to the States, are reserved to the States respectively, or to the people.

Amendment 11

(Ratified February 7, 1795)

The Judicial power of the United States shall not be construed to extend to any suit in law or equity, commenced or prosecuted against one of the United States by Citizens of another State, or by Citizens or Subjects of any Foreign State.

Amendment 12

(Ratified July 27, 1804)

The Electors shall meet in their respective states and vote by ballot for President and Vice President, one of whom, at least, shall not be an inhabitant of the same state with themselves; they shall name in their ballots the person voted for as President, and in distinct ballots the person voted for as Vice President, and they shall make distinct lists of all persons voted for as President, and of all persons voted for as Vice President, and of the number of votes for each, which lists they shall sign and certify, and transmit sealed to the seat of the Government of the United States, directed to the President of the Senate;—The President of the Senate shall, in the presence of the Senate and House of Representatives, open all the certificates and the votes shall then be counted;—The person having the greatest number of votes for President, shall be the President, if such number be a majority of the whole number of Electors appointed; and if no person have such majority, then from the persons having the highest numbers not exceeding three on the list of those voted for as President, the House of Representatives shall choose immediately, by ballot, the President. But in choosing the President, the votes shall be taken by States, the representation from each State having one vote; a quorum for this purpose shall consist of a member or members from two-thirds of the states, and a majority of all the states shall be necessary to a choice. And if the House of Representatives shall not choose a President whenever the right of choice shall devolve upon them, before the fourth day of March next following, then the Vice President shall act as President, as in case of the death or other constitutional disability of the President. —The person having the greatest number of votes as Vice President, shall be the Vice President, if such number be a majority of the whole number of Electors appointed, and if no person have a majority, then from the two highest numbers on the list, he Senate shall choose theVice President; a quorum for the purpose shall consist of two-thirds of the whole number of Senators, and a majority of the whole number shall be necessary to a choice. But no person constitutionally ineligible to the office of President shall be eligible to that of Vice President of the United States.

Amendment 13
(Ratified December 6, 1865)

Section 1. Neither slavery nor involuntary servitude, except as a punishment for crime whereof the party shall have been duly convicted, shall exist within the United States, or any place subject to their jurisdiction.

Section 2. Congress shall have power to enforce this article by appropriate legislation.

Amendment 14
(Ratified July 9, 1868)

Section 1. All persons born or naturalized in the United States, and subject to the jurisdiction thereof, are citizens of the United States and of the State wherein they reside. No State shall make or enforce any law which shall abridge the privileges or immunities of citizens of the United States; nor shall any State deprive any person of life, liberty, or property, without due process of law; nor deny any person within its jurisdiction the equal protection of the laws.

Section 2. Representatives shall be apportioned among the several States according to their respective numbers, counting the whole number of persons in each State, excluding Indians not taxed. But when the right to vote at any election for the choice of Electors for President and Vice President of the United States, Representatives in Congress, the Executive and Judicial officers of a State, or the members of the Legislature thereof, is denied to any of the male inhabitants of such State, being twenty-one years of age, and citizens of the United States, or in any way abridged, except for participation in rebellion, or other crime, the basis of representation therein shall be reduced in the proportion which the number of such male citizens shall bear to the whole number of male citizens twenty-one years of age in such State.

Section 3. No person shall be a Senator or Representative in Congress, or elector of President and Vice President, or hold any office, civil or military, under the United States, or under any State, who, having previously taken an oath, as a member of Congress, or as an officer of the United States, or as a member of any State legislature, or as an executive or judicial officer of any State, to support the Constitution of the United States, shall have engaged in insurrection or rebellion against the same, or given aid or comfort to the enemies thereof. But Congress may by a vote of two-thirds of each House, remove such disability.

Section 4. The validity of the public debt of the United States, authorized by law, including debts incurred for payment of pensions and bounties for services in suppressing insurrection or rebellion, shall not be questioned. But neither the United States nor any State shall assume or pay any debt or obligation incurred in aid of insurrection or rebellion against the United States, or any claim for the loss or emancipation of any slave; but all such debts, obligations and claims shall be held illegal and void.

Section 5. The Congress shall have power to enforce, by appropriate legislation, the provisions of this article.

Amendment 15
(Ratified February 3, 1870)

Section 1. The right of citizens of the United States to vote shall not be denied or abridged by the United States or by any State on account of race, color, or previous condition of servitude.

Section 2. The Congress shall have power to enforce this article by appropriate legislation.

Amendment 16
(Ratified February 3, 1913)

The Congress shall have power to lay and collect taxes on incomes, from whatever sources derived, without apportionment among the several States, and without regard to any census or enumeration.

Amendment 17
(Ratified April 8, 1913)

The Senate of the United States shall be composed of two Senators from each State, elected by the people thereof, for six years; and each Senator shall have one vote. The electors in each State shall have the qualifications requisite for electors of the most numerous branch of the State legislatures. When vacancies happen in the representation of any State in the Senate, the executive authority of such State shall issue writs of election to fill such vacancies: *Provided,* That the legislature of any State may empower the Executive thereof to make temporary appointments until the people fill the vacancies by election as the Legislature may direct.

This amendment shall not be so construed as to affect the election or term of any Senator chosen before it becomes valid as part of the Constitution.

Amendment 18
(Ratified January 16, 1919. Repealed December 5, 1933, by Amendment 21)

Section 1. After one year from the ratification of this article the manufacture, sale, or transportation of intoxicating liquors within, the importation thereof into, or the exportation thereof from the United States and all territory subject to the jurisdiction thereof for beverage purposes is hereby prohibited.

Section 2. The Congress and the several States shall have concurrent power to enforce this article by appropriate legislation.

Section 3. This article shall be inoperative unless it shall have been ratified as an amendment to the Constitution by the Legislatures of the several States, as provided in the Constitution, within seven years from the date of the submission hereof to the States by the Congress.

Amendment 19
(Ratified August 18, 1920)

The right of citizens of the United States to vote shall not be denied or abridged by the United States or by any State on account of sex.

Congress shall have power to enforce this article by appropriate legislation.

Amendment 20
(Ratified January 23, 1933)

Section 1. The terms of the President and the Vice President shall end at noon on the 20th day of January, and the terms of Senators and Representatives at noon on the 3d day of January, of the years in which such terms would have ended if this article had not been ratified; and the terms of their successors shall then begin.

Section 2. The Congress shall assemble at least once in every year, and such meeting shall begin at noon on the 3d day of January, unless they shall by law appoint a different day.

Section 3. If, at the time fixed for the beginning of the term of the President, the President elect shall have died, the Vice President elect shall become President. If a President shall not have been chosen before the time fixed for the beginning of his term, or if the President elect shall have failed to qualify, then the Vice President elect shall act as President until a President shall have qualified; and the Congress may by law provide for the case wherein neither a President elect nor a Vice President shall have qualified, declaring who shall then act as President, or the manner in which one who is to act shall be selected, and such person shall act accordingly until a President or Vice President shall have qualified.

Section 4. The Congress may by law provide for the case of the death of any of the persons from whom the House of Representatives may choose a President whenever the right of choice shall have devolved upon them, and for the case of the death of any of the persons from whom the Senate may choose a Vice President whenever the right of choice shall have devolved upon them.

Section 5. Sections 1 and 2 shall take effect on the 15th day of October following the ratification of this article.

Section 6. This article shall be inoperative unless it shall have been ratified as an amendment to the Constitution by the legislatures of three-fourths of the several States within seven years from the date of its submission.

Amendment 21
(Ratified December 5, 1933)

Section 1. The eighteenth article of amendment to the Constitution of the United States is hereby repealed.

Section 2. The transportation or importation into any State, Territory, or possession of the United States for delivery or use therein of intoxicating liquors, in violation of the laws thereof, is hereby prohibited.

Section 3. This article shall be inoperative unless it shall have been ratified as an amendment to the Constitution by conventions in the several States, as provided in the Constitution, within seven years from the date of the submission hereof to the States by the Congress.

Amendment 22
(Ratified February 27, 1951)

Section 1. No person shall be elected to the office of the President more than twice, and no person who has held the office of President, or acted as President, for more than two years of a term to which some other person was elected President shall be elected to the office of President more than once. But this Article shall not apply to any person holding the office of President when this Article was proposed by Congress, and shall not prevent any person who may be holding the office of President, or acting as President, during the term within which this Article becomes operative from holding the office of President or acting as President during the remainder of such term.

Section 2. This article shall be inoperative unless it shall have been ratified as an amendment to the Constitution by the Legislatures of three-fourths of the several States within seven years from the date of its submission to the States by the Congress.

Amendment 23
(Ratified March 29, 1961)

Section 1. The District constituting the seat of Government of the United States shall appoint in such manner as Congress may direct:

A number of electors of President and Vice President equal to the whole number of Senators and Representatives in Congress to which the District would be entitled if it were a State, but in no event more than the least populous State; they shall be in addition to those appointed by the States, but they shall be considered, for the purposes of the election of President and Vice President, to be electors appointed by a State; and they shall meet in the District and perform such duties as provided by the twelfth article of amendment.

Section 2. The Congress shall have power to enforce this article by appropriate legislation.

Amendment 24
(Ratified January 23, 1964)

Section 1. The right of citizens of the United States to vote in any primary or other election for President or Vice President, for electors for President or Vice President, or for Senator or Representative in Congress, shall not be denied or abridged by the United States or any State by reason of failure to pay poll tax or any other tax.

Section 2. Congress shall have power to enforce this article by appropriate legislation.

Amendment 25
(Ratified February 10, 1967)

Section 1. In case of the removal of the President from office or of his death or resignation, the Vice President shall become President.

Section 2. Whenever there is a vacancy in the office of the Vice President, the President shall nominate a Vice President who shall take office upon confirmation by a majority vote of both Houses of Congress.

Section 3. Whenever the President transmits to the President pro tempore of the Senate and the Speaker of the House of Representatives his written declaration that he is unable to discharge the powers and duties of his office, and until he transmits to them a written declaration to the contrary, such powers and duties shall be discharged by the Vice President as Acting President.

Section 4. Whenever the Vice President and a majority of either the principal officers of the executive departments or of such other body as Congress may by law provide, transmit to the President pro tempore of the Senate and the Speaker of the House of Representatives their written declaration that the President is unable to discharge the powers and duties of his office, the Vice President shall immediately assume the powers and duties of the office as Acting President.

Thereafter, when the President transmits to the President pro tempore of the Senate and the Speaker of the House of Representatives his written declaration that no inability exists, he shall resume the powers and duties of his office unless the Vice President and a majority of either the principal officers of the executive department or of such other body as Congress may by law provide, transmit within four days to the President pro tempore of the Senate and the Speaker of the House of Representatives their written declaration that the President is unable to discharge the powers and duties of his office. Thereupon Congress shall decide the issue, assembling within forty-eight hours for that purpose if not in session. If the Congress, within twenty-one days after receipt of the latter written declaration, or, if Congress is not in session within twenty-one days after Congress is required to assemble, determines by two-thirds vote of both houses that the President is unable to discharge the powers and duties of his office, the Vice President shall continue to discharge the same as Acting President; otherwise, the President shall resume the powers and duties of his office.

Amendment 26
(Ratified July 1, 1971)

Section 1. The right of citizens of the United States, who are eighteen years of age or older, to vote shall not be denied or abridged by the United States or by any state on account of age.

Section 2. The Congress shall have power to enforce this article by appropriate legislation.

Amendment 27
(Ratified May 7, 1992)

No law varying the compensation for the services of the Senators and Representatives shall take effect, until an election of Representatives shall have intervened.

Glossary

abandonment: The giving up of a thing or item absolutely, without limitation as to any particular person or purpose. It implies the giving up of possession or ownership or of any reasonable expectation of privacy.

acting under color of law: The use of power possessed by virtue of law and made possible only because the officer is clothed with the authority of the state.

acting within the scope of authority: The situation in which an officer is discharging the duties generally assigned to him or her.

actual seizure: A seizure accomplished by taking the person into custody with the use of hands or firearms or by merely touching the individual without the use of force.

administrative searches: Searches conducted by government inspectors to determine if there are violations of government rules and regulations.

admission: Refers to when a person owns up to something related to the act but may not have committed it.

affirm (a decision): The situation in which a decision of the lower court where the case came from is upheld by the appellate court.

anticipatory search warrant: A warrant obtained based on probable cause and an expectation that seizable items will be found at a certain place at a certain time.

apparent authority principle: The principle that a search is valid if consent was given by a person whom the police reasonably believed to have authority to give such consent, even if that person turns out not to have such authority.

area of immediate control: The area from which an arrested person might be able to obtain a weapon or destroy evidence.

arraignment: A procedure by which, at a scheduled time and after prior notice, the accused is called into court, informed of the charges against him or her, and asked how he or she pleads.

arrest: The taking of a person into custody against his or her will for the purpose of criminal prosecution or interrogation.

arrest warrant: A "writ issued by a magistrate, justice, or other competent authority, addressed to a sheriff, constable, or other officer, requiring him or her to arrest the person it names and bring the person before the magistrate or court to answer, or to be examined, concerning some offense that he or she is charged with having committed."

assault: An intentional tort wherein an officer causes apprehension of harmful or offensive conduct; it is the attempt or threat of bodily harm on another person, accompanied by the ability to inflict it.

bail: The security required by the court and given by the accused to ensure that the accused appears before the proper court at the scheduled time and place to answer the charges brought against him or her.

bail bond: A "written undertaking, executed by the defendant or one or more sureties, that the defendant designated in such instrument will, while at liberty as a result of an order fixing bail . . . appear in a designated criminal action or proceeding when his attendance is required and otherwise render himself amenable to the orders and processes of the court, and that in the event he fails to do so, the signers of the bond will pay to the court the amount of money specified in the order fixing bail."

battery: An intentional tort in which an officer causes the infliction of harmful or offensive body contact on another person. It usually involves unlawful, unwarranted, or hostile touching—however slight.

beeper: An electronic device sometimes used by the police to monitor the movement and location of a motor vehicle.

bench warrant: A writ "from the bench," used to arrest and bring nonappearing defendants before the court.

bifurcated procedure: A trial in which the determination of guilt or innocence and sentencing are separate.

bill of indictment: A document submitted to the grand jury by the prosecutor, accusing a person of a crime.

Bill of Rights: The first ten amendments to the U.S. Constitution.

booking: The making of an entry in the police blotter or arrest book, indicating the suspect's name, the time of arrest, and the offense involved. If the crime is serious, the suspect may also be photographed or fingerprinted.

Brady rule: The rule that "the suppression by the prosecution of evidence favorable to an accused upon request violates due process where the evidence is material either to the guilt or punishment, irrespective of the good faith or bad faith of the prosecution."

capias: Literally meaning "you take," it is a general name for several types of writ that require an officer, for various reasons, to take a defendant into custody.

case-by-case incorporation: An approach that looks at the facts of a specific case to determine whether there is an injustice so serious as to justify extending the provisions of the Bill of Rights to that state case.

case law: The law as enunciated in cases decided by the courts.

cash bail bond: "A sum of money, in the amount designated in an order fixing bail, posted by a defendant or by another person on his behalf with a court or other authorized public officer upon condition that such money will be forfeited if the defendant does not comply with the directions of a court requiring his attendance at the criminal action or proceeding involved and does not otherwise render himself amenable to the orders and processes of the court."

challenge for cause: A challenge to the fitness of a person for jury membership on the basis of causes specified by law.

Chimel rule: The rule that after an arrest the police may search the areas within a suspect's immediate control, meaning the area from which the suspect might be able to obtain a weapon or destroy evidence.

citation: An order issued by a court or law enforcement officer commanding the person to whom the citation is issued to appear in court at a specified time to answer certain charges.

citizen's arrest: An arrest made by a citizen without a warrant; usually limited to situations in which a felony has actually been committed and the citizen has probable cause to believe that the person arrested committed the offense.

common law: Law that originated from the ancient and unwritten laws of England.

complaint: A charge made before a proper officer, alleging the commission of a criminal offense.

confession: Refers to when a person says that he or she committed the act.

constructive seizure: A seizure accomplished without any physical touching, grabbing, holding, or use of force; occurs when the individual peacefully submits to the officer's will and control.

contemporaneous search: A search made at the same time as, or very close in time and place to, the arrest.

curtilage: "The area to which extends the intimate activity associated with the 'sanctity of a man's home and the privacies of life.'"

custodial interrogation: Interrogation that takes place (1) when the suspect is under arrest or (2) when the suspect is not under arrest but is deprived of his or her freedom in a significant way.

Daubert doctrine: The doctrine that expert testimony pertaining to scientific, technical, or other specialized knowledge that will assist the trier of fact to understand the evidence or to determine whether a fact in issue is admissible in evidence. Used in federal courts, the Daubert doctrine replaces the more strict Frye doctrine, which requires that, for scientific evidence to be admissible, the procedures used must be sufficiently established to have gained general acceptance in the particular scientific field to which they belong.

deadly force: Force that when used would lead a reasonable officer objectively to conclude that it poses a high risk of death or serious injury to its human target.

deep pockets theory: The theory that individual officers may lack resources to pay damages but the government agency has a broader financial base, so plaintiffs include government agencies in their lawsuits.

deprived of freedom in a significant way: Phrase that describes a person whose freedom of movement has been limited by the police.

discovery: A procedure used by either party in a case to obtain information that is in the hands of the other party and is necessary or helpful in developing the case.

discretionary act: An act that involves personal deliberation, decision, and judgment.

DNA testing: A procedure that matches the suspect's DNA with the DNA found in semen or blood recovered from the scene of the crime.

double jeopardy: The successive prosecution of a defendant for the same offense by the same jurisdiction.

drug courier profile: Identifiers developed by law enforcement agencies indicating the types of individuals who are likely to transport drugs.

dual court system: The two court systems of the United States, one for federal cases and the other for state cases.

dual sovereignty: The concept that federal and state governments are sovereign each in their own right.

Due Process Clause: A provision in the Fourteenth Amendment of the Constitution stating that no state shall deprive any person of life, liberty, or property without due process of law.

Edwards rule: The rule that a suspect who invokes the right to consult a lawyer cannot be questioned again for the same offense unless the suspect initiates further communication, exchanges, or conversations with the police.

Electronic Communications and Privacy Act of 1986 (ECPA): An act passed by Congress modifying and supplementing Title III of the Omnibus Crime Control and Safe Streets Act of 1968.

electronic surveillance: The use of electronic devices to monitor a person's activities or whereabouts.

en banc decision: A decision made by an appellate court as one body, not in divisions.

exclusionary rule: The rule of evidence providing that any evidence obtained by the government in violation of the Fourth Amendment's guarantee against unreasonable search and seizure is not admissible in a criminal prosecution to establish the defendant's guilt.

exigent circumstances: Emergency circumstances that make obtaining a warrant impractical, useless, dangerous, or unnecessary.

factory survey: A practice whereby immigration officials pay surprise visits to factories and ask employees questions to determine if they are illegal aliens.

fair response: A prosecutor's statement to the jury during closing arguments that the defendant could have taken the witness stand but refused to do so is proper as long as it is in response to defense counsel's argument that the government did not allow the defendant to explain his or her side of the story.

false arrest: An intentional tort that results when an officer makes an illegal arrest—usually one without probable cause.

false imprisonment: A tort case that may result when one person unlawfully detains another.

Federal Speedy Trial Act of 1974: A law that specifies time standards for each stage in the federal court process. Thirty days are allowed from arrest to the filing of an indictment or an information; seventy days are allowed between information or indictment and trial.

felony: A criminal offense punishable by death or imprisonment of more than one year.

fishing expedition: A search conducted by law enforcement officers with no definite seizable contraband or items in mind, in hopes of finding some usable evidence.

formally charged with an offense: Indictment, information, preliminary hearing, or arraignment of the suspect.

frisk: The pat-down of a person's outer clothing after a stop to see if he or she has a weapon or something that feels like a weapon, which can be seized by the officer; frisk is performed for the protection of the officer and of others.

"fruit of the poisonous tree" doctrine: The doctrine holding that, once the primary evidence (the "tree") is shown to have been unlawfully obtained, any secondary evidence (the "fruit") derived from it is also inadmissible.

Frye doctrine: The doctrine that, before the results of scientific tests will be admissible as evidence in a trial, the procedures used must be sufficiently established to have gained general acceptance in the particular field to which they belong.

functional equivalent of interrogation: Instances in which no questions are actually asked by the police, but the circumstances are so conducive to making a statement or confession that the courts consider them to be the equivalent of interrogation.

general on-the-scene questioning: Questioning at the scene of the crime for the purpose of gathering information that might enable the police to identify the criminal. Miranda warnings are not needed.

good faith defense in Section 1983 cases: In civil liability cases, the concept that an officer should not be held liable if he or she did not violate a clearly established constitutional right of which a reasonable person would have known.

good faith defense in state tort cases: The situation in which an officer "acted in the honest belief that the action taken or the decision was appropriate under the circumstances."

"good faith" exceptions: Exceptions to the exclusionary rule holding that evidence obtained by the police is admissible in court even if there was an error or mistake as long as such error or mistake was not committed by the police or, if committed by the police, was honest and reasonable.

grand jury: A jury, usually composed of from twelve to twenty-three members, that determines whether a suspect should be charged with an offense. A grand jury indictment is required in some states only for serious offenses.

habeas corpus: Literally, "you have the body"; it is a remedy used if a person seeks release from an allegedly illegal or unconstitutional confinement.

harmless error doctrine: The doctrine holding that, if a motion to exclude illegally seized evidence is made on time, it is an error for the court to receive the evidence. This mistake requires a reversal on appeal of any conviction, unless admission of the evidence is found to be a harmless error.

harmless error rule: The rule that an error made by the trial court in admitting illegally obtained evidence does not lead to a reversal of the conviction if the error is determined to be harmless. The prosecution has the burden of proving that the error is, in fact, harmless.

"hot pursuit" exception (to the warrant rule): A policy that authorizes peace officers from one state, through a uniform act adopted by most states, to enter another state in fresh pursuit to arrest a suspect for a felony committed in the first state.

hung jury: A jury that cannot agree unanimously (in jurisdictions where unanimity is required) to convict or acquit the defendant.

immunity: Exemption from prosecution, granted to a witness in exchange for testimony against a suspect or an accused.

inadvertence: The concept that, to come under the plain view doctrine, the evidence must be discovered by the officer accidentally; the officer must have had no prior knowledge that the evidence was present in the place. Inadvertence is no longer required by the plain view doctrine.

incorporation controversy: The issue of whether the Bill of Rights of the U.S. Constitution protects against violations of rights by the federal government only or also limits what state government officials can do.

"independent source" exception: An exception to the exclusionary rule holding that evidence obtained is admissible, despite its initial illegality, if the police can prove that it was obtained from an independent source that is not connected to the illegal search or seizure.

indictment: A written accusation filed against the defendant by a grand jury, usually signed by the jury foreperson.

indigent defendant: A defendant who is too poor to hire his or her own lawyer.

"inevitable discovery" exception: An exception to the fruit of the poisonous tree doctrine holding that the evidence is admissible, despite its initial illegality, if the police can prove that they would inevitably have discovered the evidence by lawful means, regardless of their illegal action.

infliction of mental or emotional distress: A form of intentional tort consisting of the infliction of severe emotional distress on a person through intentional or reckless extreme and outrageous conduct.

information: A written accusation of a crime, prepared by the prosecuting attorney without referring the case to a grand jury.

intelligent waiver: A waiver by a suspect who knows what he or she is doing and is sufficiently competent to waive his or her rights.

intentional tort: A type of tort that occurs when an officer intends to bring some physical harm or mental coercion upon another person.

interrogation: The asking of questions by the police. For purposes of the Miranda rule, however, "interrogation" means not only express questioning but also words or actions on the part of the police (other than those attendant to arrest and custody) that the police should have known are reasonably likely to elicit an incriminating response from the suspect.

"John Doe" warrant: A warrant in which only the name "John Doe" appears, because the real name of the suspect is not known to the police. It is valid only if it contains a description of the accused by which he or she can be identified with reasonable certainty.

judicial precedent: The concept that decisions of courts have value as precedent for future cases similarly circumstanced.

jurisdiction: The power of a court to try a case.

jury nullification: The situation in which a jury decides a case contrary to the weight of the evidence.

jury of peers: A jury that is not consciously restricted to a particular group.

Kirby rule: The rule that a suspect in a lineup or other face-to-face confrontation before being formally charged with a crime is not entitled to have a lawyer present.

lesser included offense: An offense that is "composed of some, but not all, of the elements of the greater crime and which dies not have any element not included in the greater offense."

level of proof: The degree of certainty required by law for an act or happening to be legal.

lineup: "A police identification procedure by which the suspect in a crime is exhibited, along with others with similar physical characteristics, before the victim or witness to determine if he or she can be identified as having committed the offense."

"man of reasonable caution": Not a person with training in the law, but rather an average "man on the street" who, under the same circumstances, would believe that the person being arrested had committed the offense or that items to be seized would be found in a particular place.

Miranda rule: The rule that evidence obtained by the police during custodial interrogation of a suspect cannot be used in court during the trial, unless the suspect was first informed of the right not to incriminate him- or herself and of the right to counsel.

Miranda warnings: Warnings informing suspects of their right to remain silent, the fact that anything they say can be used against them in a court of law, their right to counsel, and the fact that, if they are indigent, counsel will be provided by the state.

misdemeanor: A crime punishable by a fine or imprisonment for less than one year; not as serious as a felony.

motion for a directed verdict of acquittal: A motion by the defendant at the close of the presentation of evidence in a jury trial, asking the court for an acquittal on the grounds that the prosecution failed to introduce sufficient evidence concerning the offense charged.

motion for a mistrial: A motion filed by the defense seeking dismissal of the charges because of improper conduct on the part of the prosecution, judge, jury, or witnesses during the trial.

municipal policy or custom: A policy statement, ordinance, regulation, or decision (usually in writing) that is officially adopted by the municipality's lawmaking officers (or those delegated by them) or a persistent practice of city employees that, although not formally authorized in writing, is so common that it is the equivalent of municipal policy.

negligence tort: A tort arising from the breach of a common law or statutory duty to act reasonably toward those who may foreseeably be harmed by one's conduct.

neutral and detached magistrate: A magistrate (issuing a warrant) who is not unalterably aligned with the police or the prosecutor's position in a case.

new concept of electronic surveillance: The idea that electronic surveillance constitutes a search under the Fourth Amendment if the police activity violates a person's "reasonable expectation of privacy."

no-knock searches: Searches without announcement, authorized by state statutes, particularly in drug cases.

nolle proseque: A motion filed by the prosecutor that seeks dismissal of the charges.

nolo contendere plea: Literally, "no contest"; a plea made when the defendant does not contest the charges. The effect is the same as that of a guilty plea, except that the plea cannot be used against the defendant as an admission in any subsequent civil proceeding arising out of the same offense.

nonunanimous verdict: A verdict for conviction that is not the product of a unanimous vote by jury members. A 9-to-3 vote for conviction in a state court has been declared constitutional by the Court.

official immunity: The concept that officers are not liable when they perform discretionary duties, in good faith, and are acting within the scope of their authority.

old concept of electronic surveillance: The idea that electronic surveillance does not violate the Fourth Amendment unless there was "some trespass into a constitutionally protected area."

open fields doctrine: The doctrine that items in open fields are not protected by the Fourth Amendment guarantee against unreasonable searches and seizures, so they can properly be seized by an officer without a warrant or probable cause.

open view: The phrase used to describe the circumstances of an officer who is out in open space (such as out on the streets) but sees an item within an enclosed area.

pen register: An electronic device that records the numbers dialed from a particular telephone; installed on the property of the telephone company rather than at the place where a suspect has access to the telephone.

peremptory challenge: A challenge to a prospective juror without stating a reason; the challenge is made entirely at the discretion of the challenging party. This is the opposite of "challenge for cause," in which a reason for the challenge, usually specified by law, must be stated.

peremptory challenge: Disqualification of a juror, by the defense or the prosecution, for which no reason is given.

photographic identification (rogue's gallery): A procedure in which photographs of possible suspects are shown to the victim or witness.

physical self-incrimination: A form of self-incrimination, not protected under the Fifth Amendment, that stems from real or physical evidence. Examples are footprints, fingerprints, blood, and urine samples.

plain feel doctrine: The doctrine that if an officer touches or feels something that is immediately recognizable as seizable, the object can be seized as long as such knowledge amounts to probable cause.

plain odor doctrine: The doctrine that if an officer smells something that is immediately recognizable as seizable, that object can be seized as long as such knowledge amounts to probable cause.

plain touch doctrine: The doctrine that, "if the officer, while staying within the narrow limits of a frisk for weapons, feels what he has probable cause to believe is a weapon, contraband or evidence, the officer may expand the search or seize the object."

plain view doctrine: The doctrine that items that are within the sight of an officer who is legally in the place from which the view is made, and who had no prior knowledge that the items were present, may properly be seized without a warrant—as long as the items are immediately recognizable as subject to seizure.

plea: An accused's response in court to the indictment or information that is read to the accused in court.

plea bargaining: A process whereby a defendant is induced to plead guilty, to save the time, expense, and uncertainty of a trial, usually in exchange for a lighter sentence.

preliminary examination (or hearing): A hearing held before a magistrate to determine whether there is probable cause to support the charges against the accused. This takes place before the grand jury hearing.

pretextual stops: Stops used as a pretext for motor vehicle searches.

preventive detention: The detention of an accused person, not for purposes of ensuring his or her appearance in court, but to prevent possible harm to society by dangerous individuals.

prima facie case: A case established by sufficient evidence; it can be overthrown by contrary evidence presented by the other side.

privilege of the accused: The Fifth Amendment right not to answer incriminating questions or to take the witness stand. If the accused takes the witness stand, he or she must answer incriminating questions.

privilege of a witness: The Fifth Amendment right not to be forced to answer incriminating questions while on the witness stand.

probable cause: More than bare suspicion; it exists when the facts and circumstances within the officers' knowledge and of which they have reasonably trustworthy information are sufficient in themselves to warrant a person of reasonable caution in the belief that an offense has been or is being committed. In searches and seizures (as contrasted with arrests), the issue of probable cause focuses on whether the property to be seized is connected with criminal activity and whether it can be found in the place to be searched.

probable cause defense: In Section 1983 cases, an officer's reasonable good faith belief in the legality of the action taken.

protective sweep: Entry made by the police into places or areas other than where an arrest or seizure is taking place, for purposes of personal protection.

public duty doctrine: A doctrine holding that government functions are owed to the general public but not to specific individuals. Therefore, police officers who fail to prevent crime while acting within the scope of their official capacity are not liable to specific individuals for injury or harm that may have been caused by a third party.

public safety exception: The concept that responses to questions asked by police officers, if reasonably prompted by concern for public safety, are admissible in court even though the suspect was in police custody and not given the Miranda warnings.

public trial: A trial open to all persons interested in ensuring that the proceedings are fair and just.

punitive force: Force that is meant to punish rather than merely to bring the situation under control.

"purged taint" exception: An exception to the "fruit of the poisonous tree" doctrine, applicable when the defendant's subsequent voluntary act dissipates the taint of the initial illegality. A defendant's intervening act of free will is sufficient to break the causal chain between the tainted evidence and the illegal police conduct, so that the evidence becomes admissible.

racial profile stops: Stops of motor vehicles based on the driver's race.

real or physical self-incrimination: Incrimination that involves the physical body or objects; not protected by the Fifth Amendment.

reasonable doubt: "Such a doubt as would cause a juror, after careful and candid and impartial consideration of all the evidence, to be so undecided that he or she cannot say that he or she has an abiding conviction of the defendant's guilt."

reasonable expectation of privacy: The degree of privacy that entitles a person's constitutional rights to be protected from government intrusion in private or public places.

reasonable force: The kind of force that a prudent and cautious person would use if exposed to similar circumstances; it is limited to the amount of force that is necessary to achieve valid and proper results.

reasonable suspicion: A degree of proof that is less than probable cause, but more than suspicion. It is sufficient to enable a police officer to conduct a stop and frisk. Reasonable suspicion must be anchored in specific objective facts and logical conclusions based on officer's experience. It represents a degree of certainty (around 20 percent) that a crime has been or will be committed and that the suspect is involved in it.

rebuttal evidence: Evidence introduced by one party in the case to discredit the evidence given by the other side.

release on recognizance (ROR): An arrangement whereby the court, on the basis of the defendant's promise to appear in court as required, releases the defendant without requiring him or her to post money or securities.

retained counsel: A lawyer paid by the defendant, not by the state.

reverse (a decision): The situation in which a decision of the lower court where the case came from is overthrown, vacated, or set aside by the appellate court.

reverse and remand (a decision): The situation in which a decision by the lower court is reversed but the lower court has an opportunity to hear further arguments and give another decision in the case.

roadblock: A law enforcement practice for halting traffic. It is not strictly a form of detention, but it limits a person's freedom of movement by blocking vehicular movement. It is used by the police for a variety of purposes, including spot checks of drivers' licenses, car registrations, and violations of motor vehicle laws and apprehension of fleeing criminals and suspects.

Rule of Four: A rule providing that the Supreme Court needs the votes of at least four justices to consider a case on its merits.

same offense: Two offenses that have the same elements.

search: The exploration or examination of an individual's home, premises, or person in order to discover things or items that may be used by the government as evidence in a criminal prosecution.

search warrant: A written order issued by a magistrate, directing a peace officer to search for property connected with a crime and bring it before the court.

Section 1983 cases (or civil rights cases): A lawsuit, filed under federal law, seeking damages from a police officer, supervisor, and/or department, on the grounds that these defendants, acting under color of law, violated a plaintiff's constitutional rights or rights given by federal law.

seizure: The exercise of dominion or control by the government over a person or thing because of a violation of law.

selective incorporation: An approach holding that the Fourteenth Amendment's due process clause should be interpreted to incorporate only those rights granted in Amendments I–X of the Constitution that are considered fundamental; this is the position advocated by most Supreme Court justices.

sentencing: The formal pronouncement of judgment by the court or judge on the defendant after conviction in a criminal prosecution, imposing the punishment to be inflicted.

sequestration: The practice of keeping jurors together during the trial and strictly controlling their contact with the outside world.

sequestration: The practice of keeping members of the jury together and in isolation during a jury trial, to prevent their decision from being influenced by outside factors.

showup: A "one-to-one confrontation between a suspect and a witness to a crime."

silver platter doctrine: A doctrine applied in federal courts from 1914 to 1960, under which evidence of a federal crime that had been illegally obtained by state officers was admissible in federal courts, although it would not have been admissible if it had been obtained by federal officers.

sobriety checkpoint: A checkpoint set up by the police at a selected site along a public road; all vehicles passing through the checkpoint are stopped and the drivers checked for signs of intoxication.

"special needs beyond law enforcement" exception: An exception to the requirements of a warrant and probable cause under the Fourth Amendment; it allows warrantless searches and searches on less-than-probable cause in cases where there are needs to be met other than those of law enforcement, such as the supervision of high school students, probationers, and parolees.

special relationship: An exception to the public duty doctrine (which exempts the police from liability for failure to protect), by which the police will be held civilly liable if a special relationship with a particular individual has been created.

speedy trial: A trial that is free from unnecessary and unwanted delay.

standing: The issue of whether a party in a case is the proper party to raise a legal issue.

stare decisis: Literally, "to abide by, or adhere to, decided cases."

stationhouse detention: A form of detention, usually in a police facility, that is short of arrest but greater than the on-the-street detention of stop and frisk. It is used in many jurisdictions for obtaining fingerprints or photographs, ordering police lineups, administering polygraph examinations, or securing other identification or nontestimonial evidence.

statute of limitations: A law providing that a crime must be prosecuted within a certain period of time or else it lapses and can no longer be prosecuted.

stop: The brief detention of a person when the police officer has reasonable suspicion, in light of his or her experience, that criminal activity is about to take place.

stop and frisk: A police practice that allows an officer, based on reasonable suspicion rather than on probable cause, to stop a person in a public place and ask questions to determine if that person has committed or is about to commit an offense and to frisk the person for weapons if the officer has reasonable concern for his or her personal safety.

summons: A writ directed to the sheriff or other proper officer, requiring the officer to notify the person named that he or she is required to appear in court on a day named and answer the complaint stated in the summons.

testimonial (or communicative) self-incrimination: A form of self-incrimination, protected under the Fifth Amendment, that in itself explicitly or implicitly relates a factual assertion or discloses information. It is in the form of verbal or oral communication.

testimonial or communicative self-incrimination: Self-incrimination through oral testimony or communication; prohibited by the Fifth Amendment. It occurs when the suspect is required to "speak his guilt."

Title III of the Omnibus Crime Control and Safe Streets Act of 1968: The federal law that law enforcement officers nationwide, federal and state, cannot tap or intercept wire communications or use electronic devices to intercept private conversations, except if (1) there is a court order authorizing the wiretap or (2) consent is given by one of the parties.

tort: A civil wrong in which the action of one person causes injury to the person or property of another in violation of a legal duty imposed by law.

total incorporation: An approach holding that the Fourteenth Amendment's Due Process Clause should be interpreted to incorporate all the rights granted in Amendments I–VIII of the Constitution; this position is advocated by some Supreme Court justices.

total incorporation plus: An approach proposing that, in addition to extending all the provisions of the Bill of Rights to the states, other rights ought to be added, such as the right to clean air, clean water, and a clean environment.

"totality of circumstances" test (on information given by an informant): The test that, if a neutral and detached magistrate determines that, based on an informant's information and all other available facts, there is probable cause to believe that an arrest or a search is justified, then the warrant may be issued. This replaces the "separate and independent" two-pronged test of the *Aguilar* decision.

transactional immunity: A type of immunity that exempts the witness from prosecution for any offense arising out of an act or transaction.

unsecured bail bond: "A bail bond for which the defendant is fully liable upon failure to appear in court when ordered to do so or upon breach of a material condition of release, but which is not secured by any deposit of or lien upon property."

"use and derivative use" immunity: A type of immunity that assures the witness only that his or her testimony and evidence derived from it will not be used against him or her in a subsequent prosecution. However, the witness can be prosecuted on the basis of evidence other than his or her own testimony, if the prosecutor has such independent evidence.

vehicle impoundment: The act of taking a vehicle into custody for such reasons as use in a crime, impeding of traffic, and a threat to public safety.

vehicle inventory: The listing by the police of personal effects and properties found in the vehicle after impoundment.

venue: The place or territory in which a case is tried.

verdict: A jury or judge's pronouncement of guilt or innocence.

voir dire: Literally, "to tell the truth"; a process whereby prospective jurors may be questioned by the judge or lawyers to determine whether there are grounds for challenge.

voluntary statement: A statement given without threat, force, or coercion and of the suspect's own free will.

voluntary waiver: A waiver that is not the result of any threat, force, or coercion and is of the suspect's own free will.

volunteered statement: A statement made by a suspect without interrogation. Miranda warnings are not needed.

Wade-Gilbert rule: The rule that a suspect in a lineup or other face-to-face confrontation after being formally charged with a crime is entitled to have a lawyer present.

waiver: The intentional relinquishment of a known right or remedy. The waiver of Miranda rights must be intelligent and voluntary.

without unnecessary delay: When used in connection with arrests, the provision that an arrestee must be brought before a magistrate as soon as possible. However, its meaning varies from one jurisdiction to another, taking circumstances into account. Maximum limits are set by various jurisdictions.

wrongful death: A tort action in which the surviving family, relatives, or legal guardians of the estate of the deceased bring a lawsuit against an officer on account of death caused by the officer's conduct.

Index